Against
the Crime of Silence

*Proceedings of the Russell International
War Crimes Tribunal*

Stockholm · Copenhagen

Edited by John Duffett

Introduction by **Bertrand Russell**
Foreword by Ralph Schoenman

Bertrand Russell Peace Foundation

New York · London

O'HARE BOOKS
1968

O'Hare Books
10 Bartley Road
Flanders, New Jersey 07836

CONTENTS AND SUMMARY

PART I   THE CASE FOR LEGITIMACY

PART II: THE EVIDENCE OF STOCKHOLM

iv

PART III: THE EVIDENCE OF COPENHAGEN

PART I

The Case For Legitimacy

Introduction by Bertrand Russell

This book, which records the work and findings of the International War Crimes Tribunal, should be studied thoroughly by anyone who is still in doubt about the role in Vietnam of the United States of America. It is a role which has been disbelieved often in the West, because it is in the nature of imperialism that citizens of the imperial power are always among the last to know — or care — about circumstances in the colonies. It is my belief, therefore, that it is in the United States that this book can have its most profound effect.

In these pages, in the evidence of Tribunal members and investigators, American military personnel and Vietnamese victims, are the facts about aggression and torture, anti-personnel weapons and aerial bombardment, the systematic destruction of civilians and their agriculture, hospitals, schools and homes. From this evidence, it is clear that the United States has employed not only a huge army in Vietnam but tens of thousands of civilians at home in the harnessing of an advanced technology to the requirements of warfare in the Third World. It requires not only fiendish ingenuity but a vast industry to create and refine instruments of war to maim and terrify people, napalm which sticks more firmly to the human skin or cannisters of steel pellets which enter and circulate in the bodies of their victims. These weapons and many others are dropped from aircraft which cost millions of dollars each. The Pentagon employs thousands of highly qualified specialists who are paid handsomely to advise it on such questions as the effects of weapons on the human body or on vegetation, techniques of "pacification" of foreign populations, how to compel prisoners to reveal information, how to administer poisons or destroy crops.

Why has the United States been making these efforts at such expense and on such a scale? The answer is no different in the case of America than in that of any other imperial power. The objects are domination, markets, cheap labour, raw materials, conscript armies and strategic points from which to control or threaten. If all of these factors do not apply to Vietnam itself, there is the certain knowledge in Washington that the example of a successful Vietnamese uprising will destroy the empire by destroying the myth of American invincibility. What can happen in Vietnam can be repeated, with local variations, in Thailand, Venezuela and the Congo. The interconnection of the U.S. Government and corporations is sufficiently documented — the United Fruit Company is only a particularly blatant example — for us to know the relationship between financial greed and military adventures. The American empire is a world system of exploitation backed by the greatest military power in history. In this role, America invokes the slogans of freedom and democracy, but when the system is challenged, as it has been in Vietnam, we see the reality behind the slogans, and the reality involves war crimes. If this system is not checked, we face not only the continuing impoverishment of the Third World but also the consolidation of the American empire. Such a development would make the final confrontation with China and the Soviet Union the inevitable last step to world hegemony.

War crimes are the actions of powers whose arrogance leads them to believe that they are above the law. Might, they argue, is right. The world needs to establish and apply certain criteria in considering inhuman actions by great powers. These should not be the criteria convenient to the victor, as at Nuremburg, but those which enable private citizens to make compelling judgments on the injustices committed by any great power. It was my belief, in calling together the International War Crimes Tribunal, that we could do this, and this book is the record of the Tribunal's considerable success. It serves not only as an indictment of the United States by abundant documentation, but establishes the Tribunal as a model for future use.

4

This volume establishes beyond doubt the criminal nature of American actions in Vietnam. It is not enough, however, to identify the criminal. The United States must be isolated and rendered incapable of further crimes. I hope that America's remaining allies will be forced to desert the alliances which bind them together. I hope that the American people will repudiate resolutely the abject course on which their rulers have embarked. It is noteworthy that when there is revolt in the American ghettos, the Pentagon operations room puts away its maps of Vietnam and proves itself incapable of directing more than one struggle at once. Finally, I hope that the peoples of the Third World will take heart from the example of the Vietnamese and join further in dismantling the American empire. It is the attempt to create empires that produces war crimes because, as the Nazis also reminded us, empires are founded on a self-righteous and deep-rooted belief in racial superiority and God-given mission. Once one believes colonial peoples to be *untermenschen* — "gooks" is the American term — one has destroyed the basis of all civilized codes of conduct.

Foreword by Ralph Schoenman

The men of the American ruling class who run industry and who take their turn in administering those Governmental bureaus from which they also acquire large contracts, use propaganda techniques which are calculated to create a consciousness in the nation which serves their own ends. It has therefore been taken for granted that the United States has interests in other countries which have to be defended by arms and through the use of mercenaries.

The administrators of the vast centers of international finance manipulate the levers of public power. McNamara, Rusk, Clifford Clark and Bernard Baruch could be the "representatives" of Roosevelt, Truman, Eisenhower, Kennedy, Johnson, Goldwater, Humphrey, Nixon or McCarthy. The faces alter only for the purpose of servicing a facade behind which power, institutional and highly conscious, is concentrated. This is the power of corporate capitalism and its ruling class.

In 1961, when the Kennedy Administration spoke of counter-insurgency and dealt in napalm and poison gas, Bertrand Russell began to gather from the Western media the data, the full and proudly proclaimed record of internment camps, forced labour, chemicals, gas, bacteriological weapons and fragmentation bombs. The daily Guernica offered to the peasants of South Vietnam filled Russell with loathing and anguish. Intense anger and outrage have sustained his struggles in years past, whether in his opposition to World War I or the halving of the population in the Congo during one decade by the Christian Belgian King and his cosmopolitan financiers.

We had in our files a mass of information from the Western press. It was obvious that the U.S. was carrying out crimes on a scale which was difficult to imagine. In 1965 the Russell Foundation began to explore a method of bringing this to light dramatically. We were conscious of the problem presented by the mass media who serve the very military and industrial ruling class which wages the war.

We started with the conviction that we had as massive a case as did the anti-Nazis in relation to the occupation by Nazi Germany of Europe. The War Crimes Tribunal began after these years of collecting data on Vietnam.

So many lies and distortions have been printed about the Tribunal that even the well-intentioned have been confused. It is necessary to restate the more political distortions of our work so the methods and results of the Tribunal's activity may be more clearly understood.

The criticisms of the Tribunal included the charge that all those who were members had already made up their minds on the issues they intended to decide. It was further said that the Tribunal was a "kangaroo court" in which the evidence offered was such as could only service a pre-determined judgement. There would be, it was alleged, no right of defence; the judges would be jury, prosecution and defence all in one. The nature of the Tribunal was such, continued the critics, that it would be little more than a mock trial in which Johnson, Rusk and McNamara would be tried and found guilty *in absentia*. Also, said its detractors, the Tribunal was not interested in the crimes of the Vietcong; the Tribunal fulfilled none of the accepted canons of judicial procedure; it was self-appointed; it lacked legal standing and, most damning of all, every aspect of its work from its composition to its *modus operandi* betrayed an absence of that impartiality and objectivity on which Western jurisprudence has been founded.

The criticisms were directed as well against individuals personally. How could a man of massive intellect and unchallengable attainment such as Bertrand Russell sanction, let alone initiate, this charade? Clearly, it was because he had reached senility and, sad to say, had fallen into the hands of twisted and unscrupulous figures, who, from behind the scenes, used the prestige of Bertrand Russell to project a compulsive hatred for the much-maligned United States of America. As for Sartre and all the rest, they, too, were used and had allowed their political prejudice to cloud their judgment.

It is, in a certain sense, flattering to be the object of such angry attack on the part of one's enemies but personal indulgence can not stand in the way of correcting the passions of those who make their living by writing what the press trusts require.

When Bertrand Russell began the Committees on the Kennedy murder and supported Mark Lane, he was subjected to such attacks. None of those who touted the Warren Report now recall their praise of that fraudulent document, although they continue their abuse of Russell who exposed it.

No matter how many articles were written clearly defining the Tribunal's work, no matter how many press conferences were held and no matter how many releases were issued, the press continued to write of the Russell "mock trial," repeating all the criticism like a well-rehearsed catechism. Theologians call this invincible ignorance.

The Tribunal never pretended to be a trial. How could we have had a trial? We lack state power. We could not supoena Johnson, Rusk or McNamara. We could not force them to appear in the dock. We could not even oblige them to accept a legal representative they would regard as adequate to their defence. We never attempted an adversary proceeding. That is why we called the body a Tribunal rather than a court. The Tribunal functioned as a Commission of Inquiry. The nearest American analogy would be the Grand Jury. Like a Grand Jury we said that we had an overwhelming mass of *prima facie* data, derived largely from the Western media. On the basis of this *prima facie* evidence we brought in an indictment and we set ourselves the task of exhaustively investigating this indictment in all its aspects. This procedure is well known in every American city and county. It is never challenged by the press on formal grounds.

As to impartiality or objectivity, the press asked of us something which does not exist in the form requested. This is a philosphical point. There has never been a trial, a hearing, an investigation or a commission, the members of which did not have very well known views on public issues including those questions before them. Everyone knows what judges and Congressmen think of murder or rape or robbery. On the most elementary level, every man is shaped by his milieu and takes on the attitudes of his culture and his time. The demand for impartiality or objectivity in the sense of *tabula rasa* is dishonest. Such men do not exist. The only impartiality which has any meaning in an inquiry or a trial is to be found in the evidence: how massive it is, how verifiable and how accessible to others.

At no time did we maintain that the Tribunal consisted of men who were agnostic about the war in Vietnam. On the contrary, we proclaimed our conviction that terrible crimes were occurring and that we were in possession of evidence of such magnitude that it was essential to investigate the charges of this accusation. It is precisely the commitment of the eminent intellectuals who comprised the Tribunal which distinguished them. If a man exists who does not have strong opinions about the war in Vietnam, he is not fit for such a Tribunal. We had no desire to practice the charade of pretending that it would be interesting to learn what was happening in Vietnam. A sense of agony about what the U.S. was doing in Vietnam propelled us to put this crime on record while it was occurring.

If people think that Sartre and Russell, that Peter Weiss and Mahmud Ali Kasuri would fake or exaggerate evidence, one needs only turn to the evidence in order to test the proposition. For our part, we maintained that the *prima facie* case we investigated would traumatise those we could reach.

As for the crimes of the Vietcong, we would no more regard the Vietnamese resistance a crime than we would the rising of the Warsaw Ghetto. Far from being reluctant to examine the Vietnamese resistance, we see it as heroic. The National Liberation Front resistance was put on record in full detail. Those who wish to infer from this evidence that the partisans commit crimes may do so. The evidence, however, is the central matter and our conclusions about the peasant guerrillas and their struggle against the mechanized and devastating war of the U.S. Government relate precisely to that disparity: the David and Goliath character of the Vietnamese revolutionary war.

On the right of defence, Russell and Sartre have on three public occasions asked Johnson, Rusk and McNamara either to come before the Tribunal, to cause representatives to come before it or to send us the official papers of the United States defending its position. In the absence of their acceptance of any of these proposals we placed in evidence every official paper and statement by U.S. functionaries. This data was examined and compared with the detailed research of our historians and lawyers, with the reports of 150 investigators sent by us to Vietnam and with the evidence from witnesses and victims.

The Tribunal accused the U.S. Government of aggression, civilian bombardment, the use of experimental weapons, the torture and mutilation of prisoners and genocide involving forced labour, mass burial, concentration camps and saturation bombing of unparalleled intensity. Our evidence established that eight million people were placed in barbed wire internment camps by U.S. and South Vietnamese forces. It showed the systematic destruction of hospitals, schools, sanatoria, dams, dikes, churches and pagodas. It demonstrated that the cultural remains of a rich and complex civilization representing the legacy of generations had been smashed in a terror of five million pounds of high explosives daily. Every nine months, this destruction is roughly equivalent to the total bombardment of the Pacific theater in World War II. It is as if the Louvre and the cathedrals of Italy had been doused in napalm and pulverised by 1000 pound bombs.

The investigators were of many nationalities. They were surgeons, biochemists, radiologists, doctors, agronomists, lawyers, sociologists, physicists, chemists, writers and experts on the region. Our legal, historical and scientific Commissions brought together research and reports, collated data which filled many trunks and file cabinets. Witnesses from North and South Vietnam, hundreds of thousands of feet of film showing the bombings, the weapons, the victims and the resistance, were all placed in public evidence. The properties, precise effects and use of poison chemicals and gases hitherto unknown in war were revealed in meticulous and documented detail.

Out of this record of crime presented in public session in London, Stockholm, Copenhagen and Tokyo emerged the true account of the social dynamic of a war between a small peasant people and an industrial technology in the hands of a great imperial power. Distilled from the suffering of the Vietnamese is the inexorable nature of a war waged by a foreign occupier seeking through its ruling class to bludgeon a people into submission. U.S. Corporate capitalism would hold this people in colonial bondage and force them to yield up their nation's natural wealth and the wracked labour of their most impoverished.

It is not the evil which is new, nor is it the crisis which has changed. Imperialism, the control of peoples' resources and labour and the use of massive brutality to protect the colonial domain, now centers in Washington. The Tribunal sought to isolate, identify and expose this truth, to display the motive nestling behind the power, so that we may feel the global struggle between the powerful and the weak, the aggressor and the victim, the exploiter and the pauperised. All the contorted excuses of the apologists for cruelty will not mitigate this reality. It has been seized by millions of people — workers, students, farmers and soldiers — in Bolivia, France, Germany and the United States.

The International War Crimes Tribunal anticipates the day when similar Tribunals will be created by masses of people voicing their agony and giving expression at last to the generations wasted in despair, the opportunity lost and the potential unfulfilled. History has recorded the judgment of the privileged. Our Tribunal prepared for a day when a more excellent culture of man makes revolutionary judgment on class oppression. The nerve gas and the bio-chemical weapons used on hungry people reflect a rotten order, a civilization in its death throes. To our Tribunal the Vietnamese people are a permanent reminder of the dignity and courage of which revolutionary men and women are capable. We assert this view as a matter of honour

Editor's Preface

Though the acts and events documented in this book took place, and are taking place at this moment, in Vietnam, this is not a book about Vietnam. It is a book about the United States of America. About the United States and what it has become to the rest of the world.

Though this book documents atrocities, it is not a mere historical record of atrocities. When atrocity becomes technologized and institutionalized it is transformed into an instrument of national policy.

Above all, this book is not a plea for sympathy for the Vietnamese. It is not a plea for pacifism or compassion. The Vietnamese know how to suffer!

America is but the last in a long line of invaders. It is unfortunate for those men who manage this invading America that they cannot read history well, for if they could, names with significances like Bach Dang, Chi Lang, Dong Da, Nam Ky, Ba To, Dien Bien Phu, Tua Hai, Ap Bac, Binh Gia and now Tet, would have forecast their destiny in Vietnam.

Inexorably, patiently, courageously, and above all, determinedly, the Vietnamese have shown the way for the defeat of imperialism.

And it is for just this reason that the most powerful military and economic imperialism the world has ever known, or will know again — for imperialism is doomed by awakening revolutionary consciousness to be a relic of the past — fights on so stubbornly, why it will employ any means to win.

But, though suffering will be endured, though many will die, unless a population be exterminated to a man — and woman — and child, the ultimate invincibility of the armed struggle of the people for control of their destiny is axiomatic. Today there are but two directions to the imperial road, genocide or defeat.

So this book is not for the Vietnamese, they have shown that they do not need it. It is for the people of the world, not least Americans, who suffer oppression, injustice and servitude under an order that cannot survive without oppression, injustice and servitude.

This book is the blueprint of the men who rule present-day America for dealing with those thousands of millions of people everywhere who are bold enough to cry "Enough!"

Men of good will everywhere have as their common aspiration the thwarting of that design.

John Duffett, New York 1968

TO THE READER

A truly international group prepared the documents included in these volumes. Swedish and Danish Tribunal Support Committees, without whose selflessness the Tribunal could not have taken place, assembled the documents. Men and women whose native languages included the major tongues of the Western world and some of the Eastern, typed the testimonies, frequently from voice transcriptions. For this reason, and also because there does not as yet exist an international standard for transliteration of Vietnamese, wide diversity will be found within the individual testimonies in the rendering of Vietnamese proper names. By way of example, one Vietnamese name is found herein alternately as Phu Ly, Fu Li, and Phu Li. No attempt at standardization was made; spellings were maintained as in the original testimony. All diacritical marks were omitted from the Vietnamese names as well. If doubt arises, saying the name aloud as spelled will help toward clarification. When the transcription of testimony was ambiguous concerning a name, a question mark (?) follows. In the English, some testimonies use the British spelling, others the American, depending on how they appeared in the original translated document.

In order that all testimonies fall under the proper subject heading, it was necessary to include some evidence which was actually presented at the Copenhagen Session among the Stockholm Session material in Part II of this volume. Where such is the case an asterisk (*) appears in the heading.

Much of the material in this book is based on statistics gathered by the Commission for the Investigation of War Crimes of the Democratic Republic of Vietnam. In all cases the Tribunal's Field Investigating Teams verified such statistics by valid spot-check and sampling techniques. When this method has been used, it is so noted in the text. None of the authoritative N.L.F. or North Vietnamese testimony that was presented at the Tribunal appears in this volume. It was not necessary — there was all too much evidence of War Crimes available from Western sources.

ACKNOWLEDGEMENTS

Many people helped in making this volume possible. Translation of most French documents into English was made by Richard Miller, several were done by Judith Duffett. The manuscript could not have been completed without the work of Beverly Grant. Invaluable encouragement and guidance was given by Leonard P. Liggio; we are deeply grateful to them all.

Aims and Objectives of the International War Crimes Tribunal

The conscience of mankind is profoundly disturbed by the war being waged in Vietnam. It is a war in which the world's wealthiest and most powerful state is opposed to a nation of poor peasants, who have been fighting for their independence for a quarter of a century. It appears that this war is being waged in violation of international law and custom.

Every day, the world press and, particularly, that of the United States, publishes reports which, if proved, would represent an ever growing violation of the principles established by the Nuremberg Tribunal and rules fixed by international agreements. Moved and shocked by the suffering endured by the Vietnamese people, and convinced that humanity must know the truth in order to deliver a serious and impartial judgment on the events taking place in Vietnam and on where the responsibility for them lies, we have accepted the invitation of Bertrand Russell to meet, in order to examine these facts scrupulously and confront them with the rules of law which govern them.

It has been alleged that in the first nine months of 1966, the air force of the United States has dropped four million pounds of bombs daily in Vietnam. If it continues at this rate to the end of the year, the total will constitute a greater mass of explosives than it unloaded on the entire Pacific theatre during the whole of the Second World War. The area bombarded in this way is no bigger than the states of New York and Pennsylvania. In the south, the U.S. forces and their Saigon allies have herded eight million people, peasants and their families, into barbed wire encampments under the surveillance of the political police. Chemical poisons have been, and are being, used to defoliate and render barren tens of thousands of acres of farmland. Crops are being systematically destroyed-and this in a country where, even in normal times, the average man or woman eats less than half the food consumed by the average American, and lives to less than one half his age.

Irrigation systems are deliberately destroyed. Napalm, phosphorus bombs and a variety of other sadistically designed and hitherto unknown weapons are being used against the population of both North and South Vietnam. More than five hundred thousand Vietnamese men, woman and children have perished under this onslaught (more than the number of soldiers the United States lost in both world wars) although the population of Vietnam had already been decimated during the Japanese and French occupations and the famine which followed the Second World War.

Even though we have not been entrusted with this task by any organized authority, we have taken the responsibility in the interest of humanity and the preservation of civilization. We act on our own accord, in complete independence from any government or any official or semi-official organization, in the firm belief that we express a deep anxiety and remorse felt by many of our fellow human beings in many countries. We trust that our action will help to arouse the conscience of the world.

We, therefore, constitute ourselves a Tribunal which, even if it has not the power to impose sanctions, will have to answer, amongst others, the following questions:

1. Has the United States Government (and the Governments of Australia, New Zealand and South Korea) committed acts of aggression according to international law?

2. Has the American Army made use of or experimented with new weapons or weapons forbidden by the laws of war?

3. Has there been bombardment of targets of a purely civilian character, for example hospitals, schools, sanatoria, dams, etc., and on what scale has this occurred?

4. Have Vietnamese prisoners been subjected to inhuman treatment forbidden by the laws or war and, in particular, to torture or mutilation? Have there been unjustified reprisals against the civilian population, in particular, execution of hostages?

5. Have forced labour camps been created, has there been deportation of the population or other acts tending to the extermination of the population and which can be characterised juridically as acts of genocide?

15

If the Tribunal decides that one, or all, of these crimes have been committed, it will be up to the Tribunal to decide who bears the responsibility for them.

This Tribunal will examine all the evidence that may be placed before it by any source or party. The evidence may be oral, or in the form of documents. No evidence relevant to our purposes will be refused attention. No witness competent to testify about the events with which our enquiry is concerned will be denied a hearing. The National Liberation Front of South Vietnam and the Government of the Democratic Republic of Vietnam have assured us of their willingness to cooperate, to provide the necessary information, and to help us in checking the accuracy and reliability of the information. The Cambodian Head of State, Prince Sihanouk, has similarly offered to help by the production of evidence. We trust that they will honour this pledge and we shall gratefully accept their help, without prejudice to our own views or attitudes. We renew, as a Tribunal, the appeal which Bertrand Russell has addressed in his name to the Government of the United States. We invite the Government of the United States to present evidence or cause it to be presented, and to instruct its officials or representatives to appear and state their case. Our purpose is to establish, without fear or favour, the full truth about this war. We sincerely hope that our efforts will contribute to the world's justice, to the re-establishment of peace and the liberation of oppressed peoples.

THE INTERNATIONAL WAR CRIMES TRIBUNAL

BERTRAND RUSSELL	*Honorary President*
JEAN PAUL SARTRE	*Executive President*
VLADIMIR DEDIJER	*Chairman and President of Sessions*

TRIBUNAL MEMBERS

WOLFGANG ABENDRUTH	Doctor of Jurisprudence; Professor of Political Science at Marburg University
GUNTHER ANDERS	Writer, Philosopher
MEHMET ALI AYBAR	International Lawyer; Member Turkish Parliament; President Turkish Workers Party
JAMES BALDWIN	Afro-American Novelist and Essayist
LELIO BASSO	International Lawyer; Deputy of Italian Parliament and Member of the Commission of Foreign Affairs; Professor Rome University
SIMONE DE BEAUVOIR	Writer; Philosopher
LAZARO CARDENAS	Former President of Mexico
STOKELY CARMICHAEL	Chairman Student Non-Violent Coordinating Committee
LAWRENCE DALY	General Secretary Scottish National Union of Mineworkers
VLADIMIR DEDIJER	M.A. Oxon., Doctor of Jurisprudence; Historian
DAVE DELLINGER	American Pacifist; Editor of Liberation; Chairman Fifth Avenue Parade Committee
ISAAC DEUTSCHER	Historian
HAIKA GROSSMAN	Jurist; Liberation Fighter
AMADO HERNANDEZ	Poet Laureate of the Philippines; Chairman Democratic Labor Party; Acting President National Organization of Philippine Writers
MELBA HERNANDEZ	Chairman Cuban Committee for Solidarity with Vietnam
MAHMUD ALI KASURI	Senior Advocate Supreme Court of Pakistan
SARA LIDMAN	Author
KINJU MORIKAWA	Attorney; Vice-Chairman Japan Civil Liberties Union
CARL OGLESBY	Past President Students for a Democratic Society; Playwright; Political Essayist
SHOICHI SAKATA	Professor of Physics
LAURENT SCHWARTZ	Professor of Mathematics, Paris University
PETER WEISS	Playwright

Exchanges of Correspondence with Heads of State

25 August 1966

RUSSELL TO JOHNSON

President Lyndon B. Johnson,
The White House,
Washington, D.C., U.S.A.

Dear President Johnson,

I write in connection with the International War Crimes Tribunal which has been under preparation for a period of time. This tribunal concerns the conduct of the war in Vietnam by the United States Government. Within living memory only the Nazis could be said to have exceeded in brutality the war waged by your administration against the people of Vietnam and it is because this war is loathed and condemned by the vast majority of mankind that demands are heard throughout the world for a formal international tribunal to hear the full evidence.

Your Secretary of Defence, Mr. McNamara, has stated that the tonnages used in Vietnam exceed any used in Korea or World War II. These approach 1,500 tons daily — high explosive dropped on hospitals, schools, and sanatoria systematically. Poison gas, chemicals, napalm, phosphorus and fragmentation bombs of a particularly horrible order are freely used by your Government on your instruction against densely populated civilian areas. But no attacks have occurred on the United States. Vietnamese have not bombed one school or village or violated U.S. territory. Their troops occupy no part of the United States. The vast bombardment of their agricultural land, their villages and towns by the United States can not be resisted by a Vietnamese air force. This war is like that waged by fascist Japan and Nazi Germany in Southeast Asia and Eastern Europe, respectively.

The parallel is precise. President Eisenhower made explicit American purposes in 1953:

"Now let us assume we lost Indo-China. If Indo-China goes, the tin and tungsten we so greatly value would cease coming. We are after the cheapest way to prevent the occurrence of something terrible — the loss of our ability to get what we want from the riches of the Indo-Chinese territory and from Southeast Asia."

Here then is the reason why the peoples of the world resist as the people of Vietnam are now resisting. Here also is the reason why the torture and experimental weapons inflicted by you on Vietnam are grounds for solemn proceedings intended to examine this practice and to weigh the evidence of crimes against the peace and crimes against humanity in the precise sense laid down at Nuremburg.

"The real complaining party at the bar is civilisation. Civilisation is asking whether law is so laggard as to be utterly helpless to deal with the crimes of such magnitude as Germany's . . . Civilisation expects this Tribunal to put the forces of international law, its precepts, its prohibitions and most of its sanctions on the side of peace."

This is the indictment against your Government today. The relevance of it was also made clear by Justice Jackson:

"No future lawyer undertaking to prosecute crimes against the peace of the world will have to face the argument that the effort is unprecedented, and, therefore, by inference, improper."

I ask you to appear before this tribunal in your own defence to answer charges contained in the evidence and eye-witness testimony concerning the acts carried out on your instruction. If you are unwilling to appear personally I request you to appoint officially persons who will seek to defend the actions of your Government.

This tribunal rests for its legitimacy not only upon its public mandate, nor upon the eminence and internationally representative character of the members. The tribunal has a solemn antecedent in the Nuremburg proceedings. American Supreme Court Justice Robert Jackson summarised the issue and stated the basis of the present tribunal:

"If certain acts and violation of treaties are crimes, they are crimes whether the United States does them or whether Germany does them. We are not prepared to lay down a rule of criminal conduct against others which we would not be willing to have invoked against us."

Here, then, is the challenge before you: Will you appear before a wider justice than you recognise and risk a more profound condemnation than you may be able to understand?

Yours sincerely,

Bertrand Russell

RUSSELL CORRESPONDENCE WITH JENKINS AND WILSON

25 November, 1966

To Mr. Roy Jenkins

Dear Mr. Jenkins,

I am writing as Honorary President of the International War Crimes Tribunal to place before you a formal request in the name of its members.

We are planning to hold certain sessions of the International War Crimes Tribunal in London and will require visas for a certain number of witnesses from North and South Vietnam. I write to request these visas and to obtain your agreement, in principle, for the issuing of visas to such Vietnamese as may wish to come to Britain in order to meet the Tribunal.

I await your reply with great attention.

Yours sincerely,

Bertrand Russell

———◆———

To Bertrand Russell

5 January, 1967.

Dear Lord Russell,

In your letter of 25 November you ask for my agreement in principle to the grant of visas to certain people from North and South Vietnam.

I have carefully considered your request, in consultation with the Foreign Secretary, and I have come to the conclusion that it would not be in the national interest to grant the facilities you seek.

Yours sincerely,

Roy Jenkins

To Mr. Harold Wilson

Dear Mr. Wilson,

I have received from the Home Secretary a letter dated January 5, in which he informs me that, in consultation with the Foreign Secretary, he has considered my request for his agreement in principle to the grant of visas to people from North and South Vietnam, but has concluded that this "would not be in the national interest."

I am writing to ask you to reverse this decision.

As you know, the then Foreign Secretary, Mr. Michael Stewart, declared categorically in a 'teach-in' on Vietnam at the Oxford Union Society on June 16, 1965 that it was an "excellent thing that students should have the opportunity of having access to news, information and comment from all over the world, that they should be able, in the light of that, to form their own opinions and to express those opinions freely." This was a clear statement that your Government would welcome freedom of speech on the matter of the war in Vietnam. On that same occasion at Oxford Mr. Cabot Lodge of the United States was permitted to put forward his Government's view of the war. There has never been any explanation why your Government has permitted the public to hear American views of the war, but not those of Vietnamese citizens themselves. If you have confidence in the policies of the British and U.S. Governments on the war, what have you to lose in having those policies discussed in public by Vietnamese people?

If you do not reverse this decision by the Home Secretary, the public can only draw the following conclusions: you believe that freedom of speech is not in the national interest; you suppress freedom of speech because you fear it; and the public pronouncements of a Labour Foreign Secretary are not to be believed. Is this how you wish your Government to go down in history, or will you permit Vietnamese survivors into this country?

Yours Sincerely,

Bertrand Russell

———◆———

14 March, 1967.

To Bertrand Russell

Dear Bertrand Russell,

Thank you for your letter of February 9 in which you referred to the Home Secretary's decision that it would not be in the national interest to grant visas for your guests from North Vietnam and the Communist-controlled areas of South Vietnam.

I am not prepared to reverse this decision. You must be aware of the efforts which the Foreign Secretary and I have so recently been making to bring the fighting to an end. I do not consider that a reversal of the previous decision would contribute to these efforts; on the contrary I believe that such action would only serve to increase international tension.

The one-sided character of the International War Crimes Tribunal you are proposing to hold would make the Government's peace making efforts substantially more difficult. The basis of our approach has been to refuse to single out the suffering caused by acts of war on one side alone, but to use our influence to end the war itself. Many other Governments share the view of Her Majesty's Government about the damage your Tribunal could do to the cause of peace. Accordingly I wish to take this opportunity to inform you that Her Majesty's Government have decided in principle to deny facilities to visit Britain to all foreigners who may seek to take part in the "International War Crimes Tribunal."

Yours sincerely,

Harold Wilson

———◆———

To Harold Wilson   27 March, 1967.

Dear Mr. Wilson,

Thank you for your letter of March 14, in reply to my request that you reverse the Home Secretary's decision to withhold visas from my guests from Vietnam.

Your refusal to do this is arbitrary in the extreme: those who do not agree with your policy are to be banned. Such an illiberal action is in keeping with the record of your Administration, which has been disposed to settle many issues by peremptory fiat instead of the customary open discussion. I am still surprised, however, that you feel able to take such a retrogressive decision without even troubling to offer a plausible explanation. Such a visit as that which I propose might, you claim, "increase international tension." At the same time you continue to ignore my question about such American visits to Britain. Did Mr. Cabot Lodge's speech at Oxford "increase international tension"? If it did not, how can my attempt to redress the grossly unequal balance, between the sustained American propaganda drive in Britain and the truth as it is seen by Vietnamese people themselves, do so?

Although I should be extremely pleased to arrange for a public confrontation between Mr. Brown and my Vietnamese friends, my request for visas was in no way conditional upon the readiness of your colleagues to expose themselves to the risk of debate with my visitors.

You say that I must be aware of your efforts to bring the fighting to an end. I must tell you plainly that your repeated public apologies for the United States have ensured the failure of any such effort. In these apologies you have at times gone further than anything emanating from even Saigon or Washington. A recent example of this was your claim in the House of Commons that during the four-day Tet truce "the massive southward movement of troops and supplies in the North ... threatened to create a severe military imbalance." No other Western spokesman, however enthusiastic about the pursuit of the war, claimed that troops as well as supplies had been moved south, let alone that what did not happen could produce a severe military imbalance. You must know that what happened during the truce was exactly the reverse of what you claimed. The *Chicago Daily News* service reported from Saigon on February 10 that U.S. officials knew of no troop movements from the North into the demilitarised zone. But on the first full day of the truce "a new one-day record of 2,762 tons was set for cargo delivered by air to units in the field" by U.S. forces. The same service reported that, according to U.S. figures, "U.S. planes — not counting truck and ship movements at all — carried 7,042 tons of supplies and more than 17,000 men during the first three days of the cease-fire." Similar reports appeared in the *Washington Post* of February 12. *Le Monde* of February 12-13 reported massive U.S. reinforcements being taken during the truce to the boundaries of War Zone C. The *New York Times* of February 12 reported that during the truce "extraordinary amqunts" of supplies and ammunition were taken by U.S. forces "to forward positions." *Le Monde* of February 25 described the use of the Tet truce by U.S. forces to prepare the "Junction City" military operation. Many of these reports were summarised in a front-page dispatch from Washington in *The Guardian.*

I do not mention these reports in many Western newspapers in order to encourage you to ban their entry into Britain, but to show that what you are telling the nation about the war is quite untrue. In addition you have refused steadfastly to condemn American atrocities, in spite of the numerous appeals of your own supporters and of liberals in the United States itself. You continue to ignore the resolution of the Labour Party Conference which called for "the cessation of the bombing by the United States of North Vietnam." You have not ever intervened to prevent the issue of British medals to belligerents on the side of the aggressor. You maintain a series of military and diplomatic links with the aggressor which positively abets his aggression. You are financially indebted to the present American Administration on a large and inhibiting scale. In spite of the fact that less than three years ago you told the Trades Union Congress that if you 'got into pawn' you could not afford an independent foreign policy, you nonetheless claim continually that your attitude, which seems to nearly everybody in the world to be grotesquely subservient, is not influenced by that circumstance.

It seems to me that when you call for an end to the murderous aerial attacks on a defenceless population; when you publicly condemn the systematic use of anti-personnel weapons such as the "lazy-dog" and the "guava" against peasants and their children; when you inform President Johnson that his policies in Vietnam call forth the utmost revulsion and horror among all civilised men, then it will be possible to accept that you might begin to make a welcome, if disgracefully belated, contribution to the search for a just peace in that country.

In the context of your present almost total commitment to the American war effort, it requires no little gall on your part to claim that the International War Crimes Tribunal with which I am associated is "one-sided". The Tribunal is composed of persons whose reputation for commitment to humane values and to the pursuit of truth is unchallenged throughout the world. It might have been hoped that you would have approached such persons, all of whom have made an authentic contribution to civilisation, with a certain modesty.

After all, you did not always condemn as "one-sided" support for oppressed peoples in the world. In rightly opposing United States' policy in Vietnam, in May 1954, you quite properly said:
"Asia, like other parts of the world, is in revolution, and what we have to learn today in this country is to march on the side of the peoples in their revolution and not on the side of their oppressors."

The principal difference between yourself and the members of the War Crimes Tribunal appears to be that they are not prepared to abandon their fundamental convictions in order to secure temporary preferment. If you take stock carefully of your position, I hope that you will agree with me that you have no moral right to impede the work of the International War Crimes Tribunal, and you will quickly see that any attempt to do so can only bring down upon your head the justified contempt of civilisation.

Yours sincerely,

Bertrand Russell

To Bertrand Russell   17 April, 1967

Dear Lord Russell,

I have considered your letter of March 27 about Vietnam. I see no
value in commenting on the assertions in it. I think you would agree,
however, that the decisions to which you take exception are properly the responsibility of Her Majesty's Government. In excercise
of this responsibility I feel it right to tell you once again that I do
not intend to ask the Home Secretary to reconsider or reverse the
decisions he has already taken.

Yours sincerely,

Harold Wilson

———◆———

SARTRE TO DEAN RUSK

May 3, 1967
International War Crimes Tribunal
Folketshus
Barnhusgatan 14
Stockholm, Sweden

Hon. Dean Rusk
Secretary of State
Washington, D.C.

Dear Mr. Rusk:

The International War Crimes Tribunal is meeting in solemn session in Stockholm to investigate whether crimes against peace, crimes
against humanity and war crimes have been committed in Vietnam
by the United States and its agents. A *prima facie* case exists against
the parties based on reports and photographs appearing regularly
in American newspapers and magazines and on American television,
as well as in the world press generally. We have dispatched five
teams of investigators, comprising more than 30 qualified researchers,
to Vietnam to seek evidence on the spot. Many of these investigators,
together with other expert witnesses, are reporting to the Tribunal
at its present session.

   In addition, after our inaugural session in London, in November
1966, which established the major areas of concern and inquiry, we
invited the National Liberation Front and the governments of the

United States and the Democratic Republic of Vietnam to send witnesses or evidence which might aid the Tribunal in searching out the full truth with scientific objectivity and without fear or favor. The invitation to your government was mailed from London on November 11th, 1966. It was a follow-up of an invitation to you from Bertrand Russell which had been sent on August 25th, 1966.

Both the National Liberation Front and the Democratic Republic of Vietnam have dispatched witnesses who will be given the opportunity to testify at our present sessions and will be scrupulously examined by the members of the Tribunal and its staff. To date we have received no reply from you or any member of the government of the United States. We are anxious that the government of the United States should state its case as forcefully as possible so that we may hear and examine all data relevant to important questions which form the subject of our inquiry. As the world is well aware, the lives, liberty and welfare of the people of Vietnam are at stake in the present war. In addition the present inquiry concerns the youth of the United States, South Korea, Australia and New Zealand, many whose lives and honor are also at stake in Vietnam. Finally, a continuation of the present war threatens the peace and security of all the peoples of the world, because of the danger that the conflict may be escalated into World War.

Our present session in Stockholm opened on May 2nd and is scheduled to last through May 10th. It is concerned primarily with the following two questions:

1. Has the United States government (and have the governments of Australia, New Zealand and South Korea) committed acts of aggression according to international law?

2. Has there been bombardment of targets of purely civilian character, as for example hospitals, schools, sanitoria, dams, etc., and if so on what scale has this occurred?

We would welcome testimony by you or your designated representatives, which would present the defense of the United States government as clearly and succinctly as possible and which would help us in arriving at the truth in our deliberations. We shall make every effort to adjust our exact schedule to accommodate you or your designated representatives. We should appreciate a reply at your earliest convenience.

Yours faithfully,

Jean-Paul Sartre
Executive President

TO THE VATICAN

Copenhagen 24, November 1967.

To: Pope Paul VI
The Vatican
Rome

Deeply regretting the fact that the Pope's repeated appeals about peace in Vietnam and the diplomatic endeavors to create a basis for peace negotiations have not been successful, we now urge the Bishop of Rome, head of the Church, to implement the decision of the Council in the 80th article of the Pastoral Constitution.

"Any act of war which is meant to indiscriminately destroy cities or extensive areas together with their inhabitants, is a crime against God and humanity. It must absolutely be condemned."

Innumerable reports and bulletins have proved that American warfare in Vietnam is of such dimensions and of such a character that it comes under the conception of Total War.

The official church-authorities cannot rightly expect the World to take their decisions seriously, as long as they do not do so themselves, no matter what material loss this will cause the Church.

The above resolution has been unanimously agreed to at the ordinary general meeting of the YCW and the CW, 24th November, 1967.

Per Wedell Topp
Chairman Young Catholic Worker and Catholic Worker, Denmark

LETTER FROM DE GAULLE TO SARTRE

Paris, April 19th, 1967

My dear Master,

In your letter of April 13th, you requested me to look into the case of M. Vladimir Dedijer and, more generally, the cases of those persons appointed, in one capacity or another, to take part in the deliberations of the "Russell Tribunal".

27

The organizers of the "Russell Tribunal" are undertaking to criticize the United States policy in Vietnam. There is nothing in that which might lead the government to restrict their usual liberty of assembly and expression. After all, you are aware of what the government thinks of the war in Vietnam and of what I myself have stated, publicly and unequivocally. Aside from the fact that the pen and speech are free in our country, there can thus be no question of inhibiting private individuals whose opinons are, moreover, in line with the official position of the French Republic on this subject.

Neither is it a question of the right of assembly nor of free expression, but of duty, the more so for France, which has taken a widely known decision in the matter, and which must be on guard lest a State with which it is linked and which, despite all differences of opinion, remains its traditional friend, should on French territory become the subject of a proceedings exceeding the limits of international law and custom. Now such would seem to be the case with regard to the activity envisaged by Lord Russell and his friends, since they intend to give a juridical form to their investigations and the semblance of a verdict to their conclusions. I have no need to tell you that justice of any sort, in principle as in execution, emanates from the State. Without impugning the motives which have inspired Lord Russell and his friends, I must recognize the fact that they have no power whatsoever, nor are they the holders of any international mandate, and that therefore they are unable to carry out any legal action.

This is why the government has decided to oppose the Tribunal's meeting in our country since, through its very form, the Tribunal would be acting against that very thing which it is seeking to uphold.

Let me add that to the extent that some of these allied with Lord Russell represent a moral value outside the public legal machinery, it does not seem to me that they add to that value or to the weight of their arguments by assuming robes borrowed for the occasion.

I beg you to accept, dear Master, the assurance of my distinguished regard.

C. De Gaulle

Answer and Commentary to DeGaulle's Letter Banning the Tribunal from France, by Jean Paul Sartre

Originally published in Nouvel Observateur

I wrote to De Gaulle about Vladimir Dedijer, the Yugoslav historian, for this reason: Vladimir Dedijer is one of the members of the "tribunal" set up by Lord Bertrand Russell, and he was selected to preside over the meetings. I myself am the "executive president", but when we meet, Dedijer will preside over the working sessions and we will sit with him merely as jurors.

Vladimir Dedijer has visited London many times during the past months to meet with Bertrand Russell and other members of the tribunal. A French transit visa enabled him to stop over in Paris for twenty-four hours on each trip. During his last trip ten days ago, he made a request for a visitor's visa, rather than a transit visa, at the French Embassy in London, in order that he might attend the first meeting of the tribunal scheduled for April 26th, in Paris. Not only was his request refused, but his transit visa was cancelled. In other words, he was "undesirable" in France.

This was a serious matter, since the tribunal could not meet unless he presided and because that decision was contrary to the indirect assurances which had been given us. On four occasions, we had put out feelers to people closely connected to the government, and each time we were led to believe that we would be allowed to meet in France without any difficulty. One member of the tribunal had even received an unofficial confirmation of this approval only two days before the cancellation of Dedijer's visa.

At that time, I was requested by the tribunal to write a letter to General De Gaulle — as its representative, of course, and not in a personal capacity. This I did. In substance, I said the following: "There has been no indication up to now that the government was opposed to the tribunal's meeting in France, but the recent incident in London would seem to indicate that those in power have changed their minds; it is inconceivable to me that we should have been informed of that change through the actions of a consulate, and I would express the hope that visas will be granted not only to Dedijer, but to all those who may be invited to sit with the tribunal or to testify before it." In another connection, I stressed that Dedijer had never been involved in French affairs in any way.

Twenty-four hours later, I received the letter which you have read. De Gaulle addressed me as "my dear master". In doing this, I believe he intended to emphasize that he was addressing himself to the writer, and not to the president of a tribunal which he would prefer not to recognize. I am a "master" only to cafe waiters who are aware that I am a writer; in fact, De Gaulle is really replying to a representative of the tribunal.

Furthermore, so "private" was his letter that two days later it was followed by one from the prefect of police, which began as follows — repeating the words of De Gaulle: "As you are aware, the government has adopted the position that the convening in France of a group calling itself an 'international tribunal against Vietnam war crimes' would constitute a proceeding exceeding the limits of international law and custom . . ." The prefect of police went on to inform me that the meetings we had planned were forbidden. For that reason, I consider that De Gaulle's letter — which had since, indeed, been published by the government — is an open letter to which I must reply openly.

The letter is written, as his speeches so often are, in two parts: De Gaulle begins by saying "but of course, naturally," and then concludes by saying "no, of course not."

The "but of course, naturally," is the paragraph in which he states that "the pen and speech are both free in our country" and that "there can be no question of inhibiting private individuals whose opinions are, moreover . . . in line with the official position of the French Republic." That liberal declaration fails to impress me, particularly since recent incidents make it clear that, on the contrary, the government intends from now on to ban free and popular demonstrations against the Vietnamese war.

To give an example: the National Vietnam Committee, which is in no way connected with the tribunal, had rented the auditorium of the municipal theatre in Issy-les-Moulineaux for several meetings. The Committee then received from the Prefect of the Department of Hauts-de-Seine a letter which read as follows: "We are forced to forbid these meetings, since it would be neither customary nor legal for a political meeting to be held in a municipal theatre . . ." That reaction is particularly amusing, because many political meetings have previously been held in that theatre, and in many others. The National Vietnam Committee was finally able to hold its sessions in Paris itself, in the Salle Pleyel, but the decision of the Prefect of Hauts-de-Seine, added to the ban on the "Russell tribunal" gives evidence of an attempt to hold down as much as possible the organizing of mass movements against the Vietnam war.

This marked change in the government's attitude can, in my opinion, be explained by two facts: the first is the growing American pressure. Speaking only of the tribunal, it is very likely that Vice-President Humphrey, at his meeting with De Gaulle two weeks ago, stressed the importance the Americans put on our not being able to meet in France. And the methods for blackmail which can be employed by the United States — in spite of the policy of "independence" — are numerous. The French economy is not becoming increasingly less linked up with the American economy, as some would have us believe, but progressively more so. For example, if they wanted to disrupt our whole economy, the Americans would only have to stop renting France their enormous computers. And they have twenty other means available to them.

At present, the government is even more vulnerable to American pressure — and this is the second reason behind its change in attitude — since its set-back in the last elections, far from forcing it towards an "opening to the left" as some naive observers believed, has forced it to seek new accommodation on the right, among the "Atlantic" bloc. The banning of the tribunal is a little present for Lecanuet and Giscard, both of whom De Gaulle is going to need more and more.

INTERVIEWER: De Gaulle is defending above all a statesman's point of view. Oppose the war in Vietnam? This is the job of the government, and the government is taking care of it. Let him do it; he doesn't need your help. Moreover, the government still has commitments to its allies, and it cannot permit one of them to be found guilty through a parody of justice held on its soil.

JEAN-PAUL SARTRE: I will consider two points: "Let me do it" and the "parody of justice". The first is more important. It embodies De Gaulle's concept of political power. For him, the governmen should not find its support in the country, but should keep itself above it, without ever allowing it directly to participate in actions which it undertakes. A country, however, cannot be confined to its government. The course of action which consists of condemning United States policy in words and cautious phrases while forbidding the people from showing their opposition to the Vietnam war openly, is completely anti-democratic.

The same thing occurred at the time of the O.A.S.[1] The government fought against it alone, with its "undercover agents", but at the same time it clubbed down those who shouted "O.A.S. assassins!" It even killed eight of them at the Caronne subway stop. The whole idea behind Gaullism is revealed here: the chief has his opinions on Vietnam; he expresses them from time to time in his speeches —, always adding that he is incapable, for the time being of doing anything at all to implement them; above all, however, he does not want his own attitude to become widespread or have it supported by the majority of the population, since that would unite him with the people . . . which is, basically, the thing that most horrifies him.

Next, there is the categorical argument with which De Gaulle supports the second part of his reply: we would constitute a tribunal "outside the law". We now come up against the Gaullist concept of justice: justice, as he writes in his letter, can only be that of the "State". First the State exists, then it creates for itself institutions and picks men to make them work. The judge thus becomes a representative of State power and the State can — as the Ben Barka affair and many others made clear — exert direct pressure on him. This results in the complete subjugation of the legal machinery to the State.

Real justice must derive its strength equally from the State and from the masses. It was in this way that it was envisaged at the time of the French Revolution: the jury system was established in order that the citizen could participate in the working of justice.

But this is not even the question, since we are not proposing to set ourselves up in place of any pre-existing system of justice, as De Gaulle pretends to believe. That would be the case were we meeting to judge a private citizen we believed guilty of some crime, when courts competent to pass judgement on him already existed.

We are attempting to do something else. To begin with, we wear no robes, not even symbolic ones. Jurors — and De Gaulle should know this — don't wear them. We are simply going to hold hearings in a case which should in the ordinary way come before an international tribunal which does not exist. Over the years, the Western nations have done everything in their power to prevent the creation of such an international tribunal, and now they forbid our group the right to undertake — without passing any verdict — an investigation of the Vietnam war.

---

[1]Algerian Secret Organization which was controlled by right wing generals and which sought to maintain French rule in Algeria.

Why? Because those Western nations cannot afford, at any price, to have policy laid open to examination from the point of view of law, of criminality; that would allow the people to judge the actions of their government according to standards other than those of capability or incapability, effectiveness or ineffectiveness. There was Nuremburg, of course, but after having enforced the laws of the conqueror on the conquered — just laws, for once — the court was quickly disbanded by its creators for fear that one day they might find themselves brought before it. During the Algerian war, for example, that court would have had its work cut out for it.

Why did we appoint ourselves? For the precise reason that no one else did it. Governments or peoples could have done it. But governments want to retain the ability to commit war crimes without running the risk of being judged; they are therefore not about to set up an international body responsible for judging them. As for the people, save in time of revolution they do not appoint tribunals; therefore they could not appoint us.

Furthermore, the tribunal has never intended to pass a verdict, and it will not do so: it intends only to make public the conclusions it draws from the testimony of witnesses and the reports of expert committees, some of which have already been sent to North Vietnam. The conclusions will indicate whether or not such and such an action undertaken by the American army constitutes a war crime under existing international laws and, if so, what punishment would have been meted out to that particular crime by the Nuremburg Tribunal. The tribunal will not make its own judgment on the basis of the Nuremburg laws alone; they are not adequate for the purpose. It will also have recourse to the Kellogg-Briand pact and to the Geneva Convention which the Americans have not respected in Vietnam.

Even taken in this way, the decision will be inadequate. What should really happen is that jurors should meet and draw up a body of international law, beginning with the bases of such law, without trying to apply it to any particular war; a permanent international court should be charged with applying that law in all instances. Our conclusions will have no value if they are the conclusions of a few people: they must be ratified by the mass of the population, which we must inform with as much honesty as possible.

Let me give an example: the "guava" bombs, those little bombs containing projectiles which cannot destroy any military or industrial installation, nor any artifact and which are solely "anti-personnel". One committee appointed by the tribunal has gone to carry out on-the-spot investigations as to the use the Americans are making of them and as to their effects. The Press has spoken of them, but in a vague way. Without telling the public anything it doesn't already know, the tribunal will put before it a detailed and precise report which will be more convincing.

It is thus our intention to inform public opinion at the same time as we inform ourselves, in the hope that people will share our feelings concerning the use of napalm and anti-personnel bombs, and that they will draw the same conclusions.

Having said that, it will be necessary in order to reach the people that the reports of our committees be widely distributed, and here the Press can play a big part. I know that some newspapers, among them the *Nouvel Observateur*, will be on our side. However, I also know that the majority will devote a few lines to our reports and then quickly stop mentioning them. Thus, we will have to carry out our own publicity campaign. When we have collected all the testimony and all the experts' reports and have drawn up our conclusions, we will publish a White Paper; at the same time, we will endeavour through all the means at our disposal, to bring about demonstrations, to mobilize unions and students, and we will initiate a campaign for as many signatures as possible in the hope that our conclusions can be ratified. We will follow through on our undertaking to the very end; it is in this way that the action of the tribunal will have its true meaning.

Once again, however, we are not setting ourselves up in place of any existing tribunal, nor do we pretend to be the international tribunal which ought to exist. We are "private persons", as De Gaulle put it, who have taken an initiative and who, by informing ourselves, will inform others, in order to remind governments that the basis of all justice is in the people. Furthermore, if De Gaulle prevents us from addressing ourselves to the people, while maintaining that his position on the Vietnam war is "in line with" our own, it is because the basis of his power is not in the people, because he does not derive his authority from the masses — as the minority he received in the last elections has proved.

De Gaulle makes a pretense of believing that we can do no more than bear witness, backed up by our "moral credit". That is a joke. Unlike him, we cannot settle for a proclamation calling for the withdrawal of American troops and the setting up of talks between the two Vietnams. We must bring pressure to bear so that it is clearly stated that in this war there is only one victim of aggression, and that that victim is Ho Chi Minh.

INTERVIEWER: What kind of policy might a government unwilling to settle for words and really willing to take action formulate against the Vietnam war?

JEAN-PAUL SARTRE: First of all, it would have to take a firm stand beside Ho Chi Minh and the N.L.F. by recognizing the basic factors which form for them the basis for any negotiation and which are, simply, the Geneva Accords.

Second, that government must convince the governments of foreign countries to adopt the same position and to work with it in a common action. Considering the positions of England, Germany and Italy at the present time, I know that that would be difficult, but don't forget that a government is strong only if it is supported by the masses. If a French leftist government, supported by the people, clearly declared itself hostile to the American action in Vietnam, it is certain that the people in neighboring countries would be "contaminated" and would act upon their government in a more effectual way. At present, since there is no true democracy in Europe, governments deal with each other. In a truly democratic system, the people would serve as intermediaries between one government and another.

INTERVIEWER: But do you believe that the European masses, in particular that of France, can be mobilized against the Vietnam war today?

JEAN-PAUL SARTRE: Much more than I had thought. I have the feeling that opinion has changed. Let's admit it: the change is due in part to De Gaulle. But people believed that De Gaulle would go all the way in his condemnation, and they took him seriously, while he was merely trying to set himself up as the champion of the underdeveloped countries. In my opinion, if a leftist government wanted to mobilize the masses today, it would succeed. Look at Great Britain: even with Wilson, large demonstrations are taking place; look at Japan: in spite of the American influence, a general strike was set off. It was not one hundred per-cent successful, but it happened. Today in France, we have not yet come to that point, but people are growing restless.

I want to emphasize this point: in forbidding us to meet, De Gaulle invokes among other things the "traditional friendship" linking us to the United States. That clearly means, as I said a while ago, that as soon as it becomes a question of making a moral judgment, governments pull back. There is a widespread attempt to suppress the idea of political morality.

That is all the more striking to me because in all the socialist countries I have visited since the beginning of "de-Stalinization", the first question raised was: how can the moral element be reintegrated into Marxism — and consequently, into policy? It is very clear that this question doesn't arise anywhere in the West, and that policy there is strictly utilitarian and based on self-interest.

INTERVIEWER: Is another country already prepared to receive you?

JEAN-PAUL SARTRE: No. Several countries have already forbidden us to meet on their territory, and I am afraid that we are in for other refusals; some governments will be only too happy to point to De Gaulle's refusal in order to justify their own. We may even finally be forced to meet on a boat anchored outside territorial waters, like the pirate English radio stations. In any case, it is certain that we will meet.

It is paradoxical that the difficulties created for us make our tribunal legitimate; moreover, they prove one thing: people are *afraid* of us. Certainly they are not afraid of Bertrand Russell, who is 94 years old, nor of me at sixty-two, nor of our friends. If we were merely a dozen simple-minded intellectuals who were aspiring to set ourselves up as judges, people would let us do it in peace.

Why are people afraid of us? Because we present a problem that no Western government wants to see formulated: that of war crimes, which once again they all want to be left free to commit.

JEAN-PAUL SARTRE CONCERNING DEAN RUSK

This Tribunal invited Mr. Dean Rusk to appoint a spokesman for the American Government, to present the United States' point of view before its jury-members. It made it clear that it would agree to hear, at any time and as soon as possible, any testimony whatever, provided that the witness was appointed by the State Department. Mr. Dean Rusk has not answered us directly, but he stated to journalists that he had no intention of "playing games with a 94-year-old Briton". When that old Briton is Lord Russell the most famous living British thinker, and when the serious gentleman who refuses to waste his time with him is a mediocre American official, then the reply I have just quoted is indeed somewhat piquant. I do not know if Mr. Rusk, confronted with Lord Russell, would play games with him, or if rather it might not be Russell who would play games with the wretched arguments with which Mr.

Rusk has the habit of regaling the Press. Besides, if it is only a question of age, there are many of us here who, without wishing to compete with Lord Russell, have not yet passed the limit set by Mr. Rusk and would be happy to meet with him in public discussion. And I do not know after the reports of Dr. Behar and Professor Vigier yesterday, whether he would have had the impression yesterday that he was playing games. If I had interrogated him before witnesses about the use of pellet bombs in Vietnam. It is of little importance. I would merely like to stress the embarrassment which that off-the-cuff remark betrays. Mr. Rusk might have replied: I do not recognise the legitimacy of the Tribunal, and I will not send anyone to represent the American Government's point of view. Or else: I recognize it as legitimate, and we are so certain that we are right that I will at once send a spokesman to Stockholm. Or he might have answered: I do not recognise the legitimacy of the judges, but we possess such strong arguments and such overwhelming evidence that I am not afraid to set before them the reasons for our policies. But he said none of these things: on the contrary, he chose an ignominious way out by trying to ridicule a great old man. We consider that his embarrassment and his subterfuge ridicule nobody but himself, and do no honour to the United States. If the American Government entrusts its defence to the mediocrity of this poor fellow with his poor arguments, it thereby gives the proof that it is indeed high time to examine its policies, in all impartiality but without indulgence. That is the best way of bringing to their senses those who are still drugged by its propaganda.

Message from Bertrand Russell to the Tribunal

The International War Crimes Tribunal has been called into being because the United States is waging a war of atrocity in Vietnam. The reason for this war is that the United States controls sixty per cent of the world's natural resources, but contains only six per cent of the world's population. For the purpose of protecting this empire, the United States capitalists have had to create a great army and military machine designed to destroy popular resistance to American economic control. Several techniques have evolved in the course of the United States' efforts to eliminate social revolution in the world. The United States' rulers are in the habit of saying that the modern form of aggression is internal subversion. By this, they mean any demand for social changes on the part of the dedicated and self-sacrificing leaders of oppressed peoples. In fact, the modern form of aggression is the installation of puppet regimes which protect the interests of a foreign power. The basic characteristic of these puppet regimes is that they function as the local guarantors of foreign investment and they crush brutally all political opponents who dare to challenge the Quisling-like behaviour of these same puppets. When the forces of social revolution become too strong for the puppets to overcome, they then call on the United States, as rulers, to use the great military machines created by the United States for the very purpose of destroying social revolution. If countries succeed in overthrowing corrupt dictatorships subservient to foreign capitalists, the United States uses the Central Intelligence Agency, with vast sums of money, who buy, kill or overthrow by *coup d'etat* the popular government which defies American power.

The United States Government is aware that the cost of this brutal exploitation is mass misery, starvation and disease — the primary features of countries in Asia, Africa and Latin America. The social forces installed or protected by the United States in these countries are not only incapable of solving misery, starvation and disease, but exist to perpetuate these evils. There is only one way to remove starvation and disease in the poor countries — to overthrow the puppet regimes and create a revolution capable of withstanding American power. This is what has happened in Vietnam. This is why the United States has used every form of torture and experimental murder in its efforts to crush the Vietnamese revolution. The United States has behaved in Vietnam as Hitler behaved in Eastern Europe and essentially for the same reasons. The United States recognizes that Vietnam is not only an heroic and momentous event in the history of human affairs, but a dangerous sign for American power. It regards Vietnam in the way that Hitler regarded Spain. The Spanish revolution was capable of inspiring revolution in other European countries. The Nazis tried to crush this revolution with local fascists and also used Spain as a proving ground in which they could test inhuman weapons and experimental methods of mass murder. This is the deep significance of what the United States is doing in Vietnam.

In Vietnam, the United States is testing toxic chemicals, poison gas, nerve gas, bacteriological devices, white phosphorus, napalm and fiendish anti-people bombs, not only to destroy Vietnam but also to prepare for other struggles. The gas and napalm tested in Vietnam have already been introduced by the United States Government in several Latin American countries. In Peru, Colombia, Venezuela and

Bolivia these weapons are now being used against peasant partisans who struggle for land reform, food and an end to police torture. The great meaning of Vietnam is that the world revolution is continuous and the world counter-revolution is barbarous. This is the essential lesson and those who try to ignore it not only promote painful illusions but sacrifice whole generations of other peoples to agony and death.

It is customary to speak of aggression in terms of the violation of national frontiers by armed forces. This is aggression in the formal, conventional sense convenient for the United Nations, or the World Court, or The Hague. The world market is a major form of aggression. The world prices operate against the poor countries and are created by the rich ones for the purpose of pauperising the nations of Africa, Asia and Latin America. Ten million people suffering from famine in India experience a form of aggression. Powerful states and 'ruling groups have created institutions such as the United Nations and the World Court, but it is these same states and ruling groups which exploit cruelly the peoples of the world. This is why their institutions cannot echo the demands or the sufferings of the oppressed. This is why the only aggression recognized is the kind which is largely irrelevant to the oppressed peoples of the world. It is that the United States has committed armed aggression against Vietnam, but this is only the result of the other aggression, the more fundamental aggression, causing the Vietnamese revolution. It is because the Vietnamese revolution has challenged the aggression of the exploiting countries that the United States has moved its armed forces into Vietnam.

The International War Crimes Tribunal will, I hope, encourage people throughout the world to look on world events in the ways I have described here. I hope this Tribunal will remain in existence, so that it may meet when necessary in the future in order to expose and condemn the future war crimes which will be committed inevitably until the peoples of the world follow the example of Vietnam.

Jean Paul Sartre's Inaugural Statement to the Tribunal

Our tribunal was formed on the initiative of Bertrand Russell, with the aim of deciding whether the accusations of "war crimes" made against the government of the United States and against the governments of South Korea, of Australia and of New Zealand, in connection with the war in Vietnam, are justified. On the occasion of this inaugural session, the tribunal wishes to make known its origins, its functions, its aims and its terms of reference. It intends to make its position quite clear on the question of what has been called its "legitimacy."

In 1945, something occurred which was entirely without historical precedent: the setting up in Nuremberg of the first international tribunal called on to judge crimes committed by a belligerent power.

Up till that time, it is true, there had existed certain international agreements, such as the Briand-Kellogg pact, aimed at limiting the *jus ad bellum;* but, since no organ had been created to apply them, relations between the powers continued to be governed by the law of the jungle. It could not be otherwise: the nations which had built their wealth upon the conquest of great colonial empires would not have tolerated that their activities in Africa and in Asia should be judged according to these criteria.

After 1939, the mad rage of Nazism placed the world in such danger that the Allies, horrified, decided to sit in judgment on and to condemn, if they were victorious, wars of aggression and of conquest, cruelty to prisoners, tortures and those racist practices which can be termed "genocidal," without realizing that they were thereby condemning themselves for their conduct in the colonies.

As a consequence — that is to say, both because it condemned Nazi crimes, and because in a more universal sense it opened the way to a genuine jurisdiction permitting the denunciation and condemnation of war crimes wherever committed and whoever the authors — the Nuremberg tribunal remains the demonstration of this vitally important change: the replacement of the *jus ad bellum* by the *jus contra bellum*.

Unfortunately, as always happens when a new organism is created by the exigencies of history, that tribunal was not exempt from serious failings. It has been criticized as having been nothing but a *diktat* of the conquerors to the conquered and, which amounts to the same thing, as not having been truly international: one group of nations judging another.

Would it have been better to have chosen the judges from among the citizens of neutral countries? I do not know. What is certain is that, although its decisions were entirely just from an ethical point of view, they are far from having convinced all Germans. And that signifies that the legitimacy of the judges and of their sentences continues to be challenged; and that it has been possible to claim that, if the fortunes of war had been different, an Axis tribunal would have condemned the Allies for the bombing of Dresden or of Hiroshima.

That legitimacy, however, would not have been difficult to establish. It would have been enough if the organ created to judge the Nazis had remained in existence after having carried out that specific task, or if the organization of the United Nations had drawn all the consequences from what had just been done and had, by a vote in its General Assembly, consolidated the body's existence as a permanent tribunal empowered to take cognizance of and to judge all charges of war crimes, even if the accused should happen to be the government of one of those countries which through the agencies of their judges delivered the Nuremberg verdicts. In this way, the implicit universality of the original intention would have been made clear and explicit.

Well, what happened is well-known: hardly had the last German war criminal been judged than the tribunal disappeared into thin air, and nobody has heard anything about it since.

Are we then so innocent? Have there been no further war crimes since 1945? Since then, has nobody resorted to violence, or to aggression? Has there been no "genocide"? Has no strong country attempted to break by the use of force, the sovereignty of a small nation? Has there been no occasion to denounce, anywhere in the world, Ouradours or Auschwitzes?

You know the truth. In the last twenty years, the great historical event has been the struggle of the Third World for its liberation: colonial empires have collapsed and in their place sovereign nations have come into existence, or have recovered a lost traditional independence, destroyed by colonization.

All this has taken place in suffering, in sweat, and in blood. A tribunal such as that of Nuremberg has become a permanent necessity. Before the judgment of the Nazis, war had no laws, as I have said. The Nuremberg tribunal, an ambiguous body, was no doubt born of the right of the strongest; but at the same time it opened a perspective for the future by setting a precedent, the embryo of a tradition. None can go back on that, prevent Nuremberg from having happened, prevent people from thinking back to its sessions whenever a small, poor country is the object of aggression, prevent them from saying to themselves: "but it is *this,* precisely this, which was condemned at Nuremberg."

Thus the hurried and incomplete provisions made by the Allies in 1945 and then abandoned have created a real lacuna in international life. There is a cruel lack of that institution — which appeared, asserted its permanence and its universality, defined irreversibly certain rights and obligations, only to disappear, leaving a void which must be filled and which nobody is filling.

There are, in fact, two sources of power. The first is the state with its institutions. Well, in this time of violence, most governments would be afraid, if they took such an initiative, that it might one day turn against them, and that they might find themselves in the dock. Furthermore, for many of them the United States is a powerful ally: which of them would dare ask for the resurrection of a tribunal whose first action would obviously be to order an enquiry into the Vietnamese conflict?

The other source of power is the people, during revolutionary periods in which it changes its institutions. But, although the struggle remains an implacable one, by what means could the masses, compartmentalized by frontiers as they are, succeed in uniting and in imposing on the various governments an institution which would be a genuine Court of the People?

The Russell tribunal was born of the recognition of these two, contradictory facts: the Nuremberg verdict has made necessary the existence of an institution for the investigation and, where appropriate, the condemnation of war crimes: but neither governments nor people are, at the present time, capable of creating such an institution.

We are entirely conscious of the fact that we have received no mandate from anyone. But if we have taken the initiative of coming together, it is because we knew that nobody *could* give us a mandate. Certainly our tribunal is not an institution. But it does not claim to replace any established body; on the contrary, it emerged from a void, and in response to an appeal. We have not been recruited and invested with real powers by governments. But then we have just seen that such powers, at Nuremberg, did not suffice to endow the judges with an uncontested legitimacy. Quite the contrary: the fact that the verdicts could be carried out permitted those who had been conquered to challenge their validity; backed up by force, those verdicts appeared as the simple expression of the adage "Might is Right." The Russell tribunal considers, on the contrary, that its legitimacy derives equally from its total powerlessness, and from its universality.

We are powerless: it is the guarantee of our independence. We receive no aid — except from our supporting committees which are, like ourselves, associations of private individuals. Representing no government and no party, nobody can give us orders: we will examine the facts "in our hearts and consciences" one might say or, if you prefer, openly and independently. No one of us can say, today, how the proceedings will go, or if we will reply by a yes or a no to the accusations, or if we will not reply — considering them perhaps well-founded but not conclusively proved.

What is certain, in any case, is that our powerlessness, even if we are convinced by the evidence presented, makes it impossible for us to pass a sentence. What could a condemnation mean, even the mildest of condemnations, if we do not possess the means to see it carried out?

We will limit ourselves therefore, if that is what turns out to be necessary, to stating that such and such an act falls under the jurisdiction of Nuremberg. It is therefore, according to that jurisdiction, a war crime, and if the law was applied it would be subject to such and such a penalty. In such a case, we will, if that is possible, decide who are the authors of the crime. Thus the Russell tribunal will have no other concern, in its investigations as in its conclusions, than to bring about a general recognition of the need for an international institution for which it has neither the means nor the ambition to be a substitute, whose essential role would be the resuscitation of the *jus contra bellum* which was still-born at Nuremberg — the substitution of ethical and juridical rules for the law of the jungle.

Precisely because we are simple citizens we have been able, by recruiting our members on a wide international basis, to give our tribunal a more universal structure than that of Nuremberg. I do not mean merely that a larger number of countries are represented; from that point of view there would be many gaps to fill. But above all, whereas in 1945 the Germans were only present in the dock, or at best on the stand as witnesses for the prosecution, several of the judges here are citizens of the United States.

This means that they come from that country whose own policies are under investigation, and that they have, therefore, their own understanding of it and, whatever their opinions, an intimate relationship with it, with its institutions and its traditions — a relationship which will inevitably mark the tribunal's conclusions.

However, whatever our desire for impartiality and for universality, we are entirely conscious that this desire does not suffice to legitimize our enterprise. What we want, in fact, is that its legitimization should be retrospective or, if you prefer, *a posteriori*. For we are not working for ourselves and our own edification, neither do we have any pretensions to imposing our conclusions from on high.

What we wish is to maintain, thanks to the collaboration of the press, a constant contact between ourselves and the masses who in all parts of the world are living and suffering the tragedy of Vietnam. We hope that they will learn as we learn, that they will discover together with us the reports, the documents, the testimony, that they will evaluate them and make up their minds about them day by day, together with us. We want the conclusions, whatever they may be, to be drawn by each individual in his own mind at the same time as we draw them ourselves; even beforehand perhaps.

This session is a common enterprise whose final term must be, in the phrase of a philosopher, *une vérité devenue* [developed into truth]. Yes, if the masses ratify our judgment, then it will become truth, and we, at the very moment when we efface ourselves before those masses who will make themselves the guardians and the mighty support for that truth, we will know that we have been legitimized and that the people, by showing us its agreement, is revealing a deeper need: the need for a real "War Crimes Tribunal" to be brought into being as a permanent body — that is to say, the need that it should be possible to denounce and punish such crimes wherever and whenever they may be committed.

"What a strange tribunal: a jury and no judge"! It is true: we are only a jury, we have neither the power to condemn nor the power to acquit anybody. Therefore, no prosecution. There will not even be strictly speaking a prosecution case. Maître Matarasso, president of the legal commission is going to read you a list of charges which will take the place of a prosecution case. We, the jury, at the end of the session, will have to pronounce on these charges: are they well-founded or not? But the judges are everywhere: they are the peoples of the world, and in particular the American people. It is for them that we are working.

PART II

The Evidence Of Stockholm

The First, Second and Third Questions:

1. Has the U.S. and its co-belligerents (Australia, New Zealand and South Korea) committed aggression according to international law?

2. Has the U.S. bombarded targets of a purely civilian character?

3. Has the U.S. made use of or experimented with new and/or weapons prohibited by the Laws of War?

Opening Statement to the First Tribunal Session
by Bertrand Russell

The world is numbed by the arrogant brutality of the United States Government. We meet in this opening session of the International War Crimes Tribunal at an alarming time. The United States is beginning an enormous new onslaught against the people of Vietnam. The sordid military machine which rules Washington is readying itself for greater destruction. In a fever of frustration over the humiliating defeats inflicted on her occupying armies in South Vietnam, the United States Government in hysteria and hate boasts of its intent, and its intent is evil.

Our Tribunal is not a group of disembodied formalists, quibbling over definitions or posturing an immoral lack of decison about these events. There is one reason for this International War Crimes Tribunal: Overwhelming evidence beseiges us daily of crimes without precedent. Each moment greater horror is perpetrated against the people of Vietnam. We investigate in order to expose. We document in order to indict. We arouse consciousness in order to create mass resistance. This is our purpose and the acid test of our integrity and honour.

How frantic is the United States Government to stop us. Lies are hurled like napalm bombs. The fragments of these planned untruths find their way into the media of communication so responsible for the deception of ignorant men. The Government of France exposes itself before the world as a pathetic citadel of hypocrisy and spinelessness.

This is no token of our weakness. It is the very opposite. The feverish effort to conceal American crimes is matched by the frantic campaign against those who stand out against them. Let us take this as a tribute.

Hitler's Nazis buried the evidence of their barbarism throughout Europe. This Europe is a vast grave of interred cruelty. Auschwitz did its work for years. The evidence can not be denied.

When Nazi power was defeated belatedly, did anyone lack knowledge of the extermination and experiment, of the cold cruelty and arrogance of the Nazi war criminals? The evidence is overwhelming.

Must we contort ourselves to deny the equally compelling evidence of war crimes in Vietnam? It is unseemly for men with a particle of self respect to dissemble about what the United States Government has done to Vietnam. Auschwitz existed. It was all the more incumbent upon men to investigate why it was built, what it did and who was responsible. The vast evidence was no reason to hold back from enquiry; it was a mandate to expose, in the vain hope that men might learn the shameful lesson of their moral cowardice — for Auschwitz is our responsibility. We failed to stop it. We condemned it too late.

Crimes, barbarous crimes, are reported daily from Vietnam. They are crimes of an aggressor, an occupier, a tormentor. Our task is to display this truth to the people of the world. Our duty is to investigate every fact so that every fact will serve to arouse passionate resistance. We do this because we have knowledge which compels us to act against inhuman behavior. Those who wish to apologise for U.S. crimes and who would excuse their own failure to act against them will try to impose a distinction between moral clarity and intellectual probity. In doing so they project their own double default. We must state the evidence before our eyes. Without this overwhelming evidence there would have been no Tribunal. Where crime is known, it is cause for enquiry and judgment. The truth compels an exhaustive investigation to document and compile the full record.

The full record includes the moving and unparalleled resistance of the people of Vietnam. Those who would call the rising of the Warsaw Ghetto a crime will consider the resistance in Vietnam in the same light. Those who lack all feeling for the heroism of the partisans in Yugoslavia, Denmark and Norway will seek to equate the relentless annihilation of Vietnam by the U.S. rulers with the valiant resistance of the Vietnamese partisans. Let apologists for Nazism make this equation. There is no truth in it, less honour in its advocacy and complete moral turpitude in its imposition.

The force of our Tribunal lies in the impeccability of its procedures and the thoroughness of its investigation. The evidence we marshall will be undeniable. Let us rest confident in this mission. Let us repudiate the demand that we feign ignorance of the Lidices and Guernicas occuring daily in Vietnam.

Our enquiry is inspired by deep conviction. That is its strength. When brutal crimes are committed, conviction is a test of respect for facts and the courage to display that respect.

It is good that Sweden has received us. To our supporters we owe much gratitude. They deserve the credit for ensuring that the democratic achievements of Sweden are not submerged. This too is part of the struggle of our time. Weak men protect cruel men. Good men are the victims of both. When the Dewey Commission met in the United States no one used the absurd sanctity of a head of state to equate a brave historic enquiry by renowned men with insult. Politesse is not at issue. The right to criticise men of power should be inviolate even if governments are more culpable than any individual spokesmen for them. It is our historic duty to transform cruelty and cowardice by upholding values on which civilisation has always depended.

We do not supplicate for the right to investigate the crimes of war committed by Western Governments in Vietnam: we demand it. We do not hesitate about the connection between our knowledge of crimes and the necessity to test this knowledge in public enquiry: we proclaim it. Moral purpose can not be separated from the concern for truth. The burning children of Vietnam are martyred by the Western world. Their suffering, like that of the gassed Jews of Auschwitz, is a basic feature of the civilisation which we have built. There is, however, another part of our culture which has also been built and which has produced our own martyrs over the centuries. This Tribunal is in the tradition of that struggle and of that achievement: our art, our science, our music, our humanity.

It is our culture which is at stake. It is our barbarism which menaces it. It is not possible to organise society for plunder and mass murder without terrifying consequences. Our scientists and engineers, our chemists and researchers, our technology and economic system have been mobilised for murder. In Vietnam we have done what Hitler did in Europe. We shall suffer the degradation of Nazi Germany unless we act. *Untermensch* is a word which lives again in the vocabulary of powerful men in Washington who speak of "yellow dwarfs" and "coonskins." The pity is not in the suffering of Vietnam. Her people resist and are heroic. The pity is in the smug streets of Europe and the complacent cities of North America so debased as to be indifferent even as our own fate is enacted in Vietnam. The International War Crimes Tribunal is a revolutionary tribunal. We have no armies and no gallows. We lack power, even the power of mass communication. It is overdue that those without power sit in judgment over those who have it. This is the test we must meet, alone if need be. We are responsible before history.

Statement of the President of Sessions

The President would now like to announce that in the Aims and Objectives of this International War Crimes Tribunal, issued publicly on November 15th, 1966, it was announced that the Tribunal will examine all the evidence that may be placed before it by any source or party; that no evidence relevant to the purposes of the Tribunal will be refused attention; and that no witness competent to testify about the events with which the inquiry is concerned will be denied a hearing.

Pursuant to these aims and objectives invitations were accepted by the National Liberation Front of South Vietnam and the Government of the Democratic Republic of Vietnam as well as the Cambodian Head of State, Prince Sihanouk, who offered to help by the production of evidence. The record should also show that appeals were sent by Lord Bertrand Russell to the Government of the United States on the 25th of August inviting it to present evidence or cause it to be presented and to instruct its officials or representatives to appear and state their case. The President wishes to state that as of this moment the Government of the United States has failed to respond. So that there may be no misunderstanding of our intentions to conduct a fair and open hearing the Tribunal is this day dispatching another letter to the Hon. Dean Rusk, Secretary of State of the United States, offering to set aside time any day during this Session of the Tribunal hearing, between now and on or about May 10, 1967, to answer the charges and evidence adduced.

* Trial of Japanese War Criminals—Tokyo 1946-1948
testimony by Professor Jean Chesneaux

An Analysis of American Theories on War Crimes by the
Director of Studies at l'Ecole des Hautes Etudes, France

The International War Tribunal for the Far East took place in Tokyo from May 3, 1946 to November 12, 1948. It had to pass judgment upon the war crimes committed by Japan in the Far East during World War II, especially in the occupied zones. It terminated with the condemnation of the main accused, military leaders and politicians considered personally responsible for the crimes.

It is peculiar, however, that the work of this Far East tribunal is less known than Nuremberg. It seems as if the crimes committed in Europe by the Nazis were considered much more important than the ones executed by the Japanese even though they took place in regions populated by four times as many people, if you compare the areas occupied by, respectively: the Japanese and the Nazis. From this point of view, the historian's duty is to explain to this tribunal that there is a tendency to refer back to Nuremberg rather than to Tokyo in seeking a precedent for examining American war crimes in Vietnam.

But concerning contemporary American war crimes a reference to Tokyo seems much more germane and relevent than the reference to Nuremberg. This is for two reasons: first, American war crimes in Vietnam have been committed in the same area under the same geographical and social conditions, and second, because the USA played a far greater role in the Tokyo proceedings than in Nuremberg.

It must be stressed that the USA was very directly engaged in the Tokyo trial. This trial was in fact an American initiative, an American enterprise, with the participation of other governments who had signed the Japanese declaration of capitulation in August 1945 (Great Britain, France, Netherlands, Portugal, Nationalist China, Soviet Union) joined by India.

In contrast to Germany, which was occupied exclusively by the four victorious Western Powers, Japan was occupied — according to the Potsdam agreements — solely by American forces. McArthur was the absolute governor of Japan, although the administration which he directed bore the name of S.C.A.P. (Supreme Command of Allied Powers). The World War II Tokyo Tribunal was directly subject to McArthur's administration, the latter had chosen the judges from a list drawn up by the interested parties. He had chosen the president, the general secretary and the members of the secretariat. More importantly, he had elaborated the principles upon which the Tribunal was founded and defined the nature of "war crimes". The procedure that was followed was purely American, giving for instance, the defense extended rights to cross-examination. The defense was composed of both Americans and Japanese.

This means that the Tokyo trial engaged the USA more directly than did the Nuremberg Trials. As an aid to judge U.S. conduct in Vietnam it may be useful to examine the principles which they themselves laid down in Tokyo more than 20 years ago.

The Tokyo trial has been largely neglected at least in Europe and the USA. The more than 46,000 pages of reports from this proceeding has never been published or used by historians. Once more we have an example of the self-centeredness of the Western hemisphere. One must take cognizance of the long duration of the trial — much longer than the one in Nuremberg — and the fact that it was not terminated until other events caught the attention of the world. Events such as the cold war in Europe and the victory of the Chinese revolution, as well as armed activity in all South East Asia, not only in Vietnam. Step by step American policy towards the former enemy, Japan, changed since the time of the formation of the Tribunal. They became reconciled to the Japanese right wing and prepared to sign a separate peace treaty. All this may explain the unmerited oblivion into which the debates of the Tokyo trial had fallen.

Let us examine upon which principles the Tokyo International War Tribunal for the Far East found its action. The Tribunal's charter, signed by the American Occupation Authorities — one must again stress this point — defines its responsibilities and mandate. According to this text the Tribunal had to distinguish between three categories of crimes:

1) Crimes against Peace: To have projected, prepared, released or launched a war of aggression with or without declaration of war, or a war violating international laws, treaties, agreements or guarantees . . .

2) Crimes against Rules of War: investigations as to whether the practices and laws of war were violated.

3) Crimes against humanity: to investigate murders, extermination, degrading to slavery, deportations and other inhuman acts, committed against any civilian population before or during the war, or persecution for political or racial reasons and any other crimes subject to the Tribunal's jurisdiction, whether against the internal legislation of the country in which the crimes have been committed or not.

The indictment was signed by persons authorized by each of the countries represented by the Tribunal. It was preceded by an introduction which stressed that all the crimes blamed on the accused had as their common characteristic the fact that their consequences were "the illegal and intentional destruction of human lives". The frame of reference under which these actions were to be considered "crimes" was extremely large. Even though the term is not specifically mentioned in the documents from the Tokyo trial — they were considered genocide. The introduction also stressed that the crimes committed by the Japanese were the result of aggression and it presented a detailed study of aggression as defined by the international law of the time. It showed that in the proper sense of the term there had been conspiracy between the leaders of the country and the Japanese Army.

The indictment contained 53 Main Charges. Group I consisting ot 36 Main Charges, concerned crimes against peace. Among these were cited the fact that the Japanese had striven for domination of Southeast as well as Oriental Asia.

Group II consisting of Main Charges 37 to 52, concerned the plotting of deliberate murder: Group III, Main Charges 53, 54 and 55, concerned other crimes against the conventions of war and crimes against humanity. Main Charge number 53 especially — "to order, authorize and permit violation of treaties by means of atrocities and other crimes committed upon thousands of civilians and war prisoners" — was particularly used against the Japanese leaders. Though indirectly, among the victims of such crimes which the indictment mentioned, were the Vietnamese, who were regarded as "associates of the French Republic". In its formalism the Tribunal did not consider crimes against the population of the former colonial territories (British, French, Dutch, etc.,) but considered instead crimes against "associates" of the Western Powers which had taken part in the Japanese capitulation of 1945. Thus we see that the Tokyo tribunal considered Europeans as "aggressed" against by the Japanese in Southeast Asia and did not take into consideration the Southeast Asians themselves.

The indictment was composed of several Annexes of which Annex D deserves special mention. It concerns crimes against humanity and should be borne in mind here now because of the actions of the American forces against the Vietnamese people in the present war. Annex D cites 14 crimes against humanity which are considered crimes whether committed against prisoners of war or civilians.

1. Inhuman Treatment of Prisoners of War

2. Illegal Manpower Utilization of Prisoners of War

3. Refusal to Provision Prisoners of War

4. Excessively Severe Measures of Punishment against Prisoners of War

5. Bad Treatment of the Sick and Wounded

6. Infliction of Humiliation Upon Prisoners of War

7. Withholding of Mail To and From Prisoners of War

8. Impedimentation of Red Cross Activity

9. Use of Poisonous Products Against the Civilian Population

10. The Murder of Surrendered Enemies

11. Destruction of the Enemy's Welfare Facilities Without Justified or Necessary Military Purpose (i.e. Pillage, etc.)

12. Attacks Upon the Rights and Honor of Individuals or Families or the Life of Individuals within the Occupied Territory or Deportation of Said Persons

13. The Murder of Survivors From Sunken Ships

14. Contempt for the Safety of Army and Navy Hospitals

Besides these 14 points, the document contained very detailed references to international agreements which had been signed and broken by the Japanese, particularly the conventions of the Hague of 1907 and Geneva of 1929.

The examination of the Tokyo trial documents leads to the following conclusions: The U.S. was directly responsible in Tokyo for a solemn condemnation of war crimes committed by Japan in the Far East. They have therefore themselves created precedent binding unto themselves and which, moreover, took place in the same geographical region where you [the Russell Tribunal] are called upon to investigate these same events.

Because they were concerned about "illegal and intentional attack upon human life", the U.S. gave these war crimes an extremely broad definition. The Japanese treatment of the civilian population as well as purely military actions were brought under the heading of war crimes (see in particular Point 3 of the Far East Tribunal's charges and Points 11 and 12 in Annex D).

The American's conduct of the trial in Tokyo is not only important because of the principles which it adopted but also in its wording which contains numerous references to crimes committed by the Japanese on Vietnamese soil. The precedent here is not only in principle but also in concrete fact.

The emphasis given to Vietnam in the Tokyo trial was motivated because of the context of Japanese crimes in that country. The Tribunal members considered Vietnam under Japanese occupation only as a colony, officially called French Indochina. And only France was present to represent the government of Vietnam as a co-signatory of the Capitulation of August 1945. Therefore, the crimes committed by Japan in Vietnam were considered to be war crimes against the French Republic and its subjects. But the colonial government of French Indochina had, in fact, collaborated with Japan, with the result that the Japanese occupation in Vietnam was much less brutal than in the colonial territories of Great Britain and the Netherlands which were also occupied. This was the case, at least until the 9th of March, on which date the Japanese liquidated the French regime in Indochina and substituted for it a protectorate led by Bao-Dai. Finally, it was France and not Vietnam which was represented in Tokyo. The prosecutor for the French concerned himself only with crimes committed against the French in Vietnam rather than against the Vietnamese themselves.

Nonetheless, war crimes committed by Japan in Vietnam formed an important part of the agenda of the International Tribunal of the Far East. Particularly in question were Japanese atrocities and this matter occupied the sessions of the Tribunal on the 15th, 16th and 17th of January 1947. On these three days the French prosecutor, M. Oneto, produced numerous documents signed by witnesses to these atrocities.

The proceedings of the Tokyo War Crimes Tribunal proved clearly to its members that no matter what the political situation in the country in which they were committed such actions constituted "crimes against humanity" and were reprehensible as such.

On the 1st of January 1946, and again on the 17th, Logan and Brooks, the American lawyers for the accused Japanese, referring to the fact that the authorities of Indochina had collaborated with the Japanese and that those who had opposed them — for instance after the coup of the 9th of March — were not covered by war conventions and should be considered only as "franc-tireurs". But the president of the Tribunal remarked several times that no matter what the relations had been between Vichy, the Free French, and Japan the actions were to be regarded as crimes against humanity and were to be treated as such by the Tribunal.

This means that the Tokyo War Crimes Tribunal, which was mainly the creation of American authorities, chose to consider the matter of "crimes against humanity" as an absolute, fundamental substantive, issue which was independent of the political-military conditions that prevailed at the time.

Summary of a Historical Report
by Professor Gabriel Kolko

Historian, University of Pennsylvania

Professor Gabriel Kolko presented to the Tribunal a thoroughly researched historical report on U.S. aggression in Vietnam. The report emphasized the consistent economic-strategic basis for U.S. involvement in Vietnam since the Second World War. It also pointed out the U.S. government's absolute resistence to the struggle for national liberation by the Vietnamese which would allow Vietnam an existence independent of the Great Powers and their international machinery for hegemony. The U.S. considered Vietnam crucial to U.S. containment policy because it was believed that Vietnamese self-determination would implement the "domino theory", Dr. Kolko's report stated. The report presented the elaborations of the domino theory by major bipartisan U.S. policy makers.

In 1951 testimony on foreign aid before a Senate committee, David Bruce, then U.S. ambassador to France and now ambassador to the United Kingdom, said: "There is no question that if Indo-China went, the fall of Burma and the fall of Thailand would be absolutely inevitable. No one can convince me, for what it is worth, that Malaya wouldn't follow shortly thereafter, and India . . . the possession of Indo-China would be the most valuable and in the long run would be the most crucial one from the standpoint of the west in the east."

In 1953 Vice-president Richard Nixon asked: "Why is the United States spending hundreds of millions of dollars supporting the forces of the French Union in the fight against Communism?" "If Indo-China falls," Nixon declared, "Thailand is put in an almost impossible position. The same is true of Malaya with its rubber and tin. The same is true of Indonesia. If this whole part of Southeast Asia goes under Communist domination or Communist influence, Japan, who trades and must trade with this area in order to exist, must inevitably be oriented towards the Communist regime."

Professor Kolko stated that to prevent the fulfillment of this belief in the domino theory, in 1954 the U.S. used the Great Power conference in Geneva to retrieve through diplomacy what had been lost to the Vietnamese militarily. The Vietnamese nationalists, led by Ho Chi Minh, had liberated about three-quarters of their country and were moving to complete victory. At Geneva they were pressured by the Soviet Union and China to concede to the West on establishment of a temporary demarcation zone at the 17th parallel. The Vietnamese delegation had to place reliance on the Geneva Accords for recognition of Vietnamese national unity and its implementation by elections scheduled for July 1956.

The U.S., Professor Kolko's report indicated, had no real interest in a peaceful settlement in Vietnam because American concerns were not limited to Vietnam, but reflected a global policy that made the Vietnamese victims of an escalating U.S. intervention. Contrary to the Geneva Accords, the U.S. undertook to perpetuate the division of Vietnam by encouraging Diem's administration to reject the provision for free elections. The fight to destroy Vietnamese liberation struggles against oppressive U.S. puppet regimes became increasingly "Americanized". Defense Secretary Robert McNamara in March, 1964, justified this in global terms by emphasizing that the U.S. intervention in Vietnam was "a major test case of Communism's new strategy." Namely, that wars of national liberation against imperialism would have broad application.

A year later the "McNamara-Bundy Plan" was implemented. This plan advocated the bombing of the Democratic Republic of Vietnam in order to quickly end the struggle in the south being carried on by the National Liberation Front. In January, 1966, Under-secretary of State George Ball, refined the domino theory into a test of the capability of the U.S. to protect its self-defined economic-strategic interests against movements for national liberation. Vietnam, he said, ". . . is part of a continuing struggle to prevent the Communists from upsetting the fragile balance of power." The U.S. policy makers want this delicate hegemony of the United States over most of the world to be preserved, Professor Kolko's report concluded, even if the cost is the destruction of the entire Vietnamese people and their culture.

Recall Questioning of Professor Kolko

PETER WEISS: *We have heard about the history of the development of the American interests in Vietnam. We have heard how the United States was already involved in the beginning of the '50s in the idea of constructing a pro-Western state of Vietnam. We still need more material about the time factor in the origins of the American warfare. I would like to ask Professor*

Kolko about the situation in the beginning of 1954 when the U.S. was ready to intervene in the Indo-China conflict on the side of France. Perhaps Professor Kolko could tell us a little about the strategic plans developed by the Eisenhower Administration at that time. There are very interesting books about these questions, for example by Jules Roy, by Fleming, by David Horowitz, and even by Prime Minister Eden, where it was frequently quoted that the Eisenhower Administration — or some groups within this administration — were ready to use the atomic bomb on North Vietnam. Could you tell us something about that?

KOLKO: There has been a considerable amount of attention paid to the options which were considered by the Department of Defense in the Spring of 1954 in regard to direct military intervention in Vietnam. However, my own personal opinion in regard to this debate — which considered not only intervention in Vietnam, but the possibility of a war with China — was not the significance of the fact that they were considered, but that they were at the time rejected. That is to say, it is the function of the military to draw up plans; plans considering every possible contingency. Indeed, Gavin, in his subsequent recollections of the period, and he was involved in these considerations, did indicate that plans were developed for the possibility of war with China. The fact still remains, these options were rejected and I think that journalists have concentrated too much on the colorful options rather than the reality of what was essentially a limited response at that time.

After all, nuclear technology is not appropriate for the kind of environment one must confront in a situation such as Vietnam, where the conditions of economy and military power are highly decentralized. Nuclear technology, especially at Dien Bien Phu, would have been utterly inappropriate. In fact, it would have radioactivated the French garrison there and, of course, it would not have in any significant way, broken the military power of the Viet Minh at the time. Since there were no centralized concentrated sites, the possibility of using atomic weapons was a very small one, and I would not make too much of the colorful adventures and plans which were drawn up in Washington at this time.

WEISS: *But it seems to me that the situation at that time and the situation today is quite alike. Even today, there are groups in military forces who are very much involved with the idea of using "every means" of reaching a military victory. At the same time there was a strong opposition in the American Congress which we have today, too. But I think today the situation is more serious. The Senators who were against the war in the beginning of the '50s were stronger at that time than they are today. So the steady escalation of the war shows that the military power of the United States of America is increasing.*

KOLKO: The United States has not developed a technology appropriate for the kind of environment it confronts in South Vietnam. It hopes to try to do so. In the last analysis, wars against popular revolutionary movements can only be won on the ground by the foot soldier. Therefore, it is highly unlikely, and Washington is fully aware of this fact, that it can conceivably win such a war. Because to do so requires millions of troops and the American people and American soldiers themselves are not likely to be willing to participate in such an escapade. However, we have considered over the past week the development of modes of technology more appropriate to the kinds of conditions the United States confronts than atomic weapons. And, of course, these modes of technology are deliberately intended to reach highly decentralized economies and highly decentralized military situations in such societies. The atomic bomb is utterly useless for this purpose.

DEUTSCHER: *Is it the conclusion of your studies on the origins of the war in Vietnam that the United States government or governments blundered into this war in the same sense in which it was once said of the British empire that it was built in a "fit of absent-mindedness?" Is it your opinion that the United States blundered into it hoping that this would be a triumphal walk-over that would be quickly concluded, and then being defeated in its calculations time after time, it was driven into this escalation? Or has it moved into this war with open eyes? This is important because of the prognosis of whether the American government may be inclined, sooner or later, to muddle out of this war, whether or not such a prognostication has a basis in history. The United States did muddle out of the Korean war, for instance. The other question is whether the U.S. considers Vietnam as a bridgehead which it must have under all circumstances on the Asian Continent? I'm more inclined to the view that the United States treats Vietnam as the shooting range of the world's counter-revolutionary policemen. It employs there methods of struggle which are especially suited for the intervention against revolution. In the 1930's it was said that Hitler and Mussolini used Spain as the shooting range for the next world war. In your view, is Vietnam a shooting range for the United States for use as a proving ground in its function as gendarme of world counter-revolution?*

KOLKO: Within its own frame of reference, the State Department is composed of very able men who try to avoid blundering as much as possible. That is to say, when a basic policy decision must be made, the men in the State Department consider all of the options, all of the consequences of failure. They try to think through, like a very clever chess player, some of the possible moves and anticipate the responses on the part of the opponent. So the "teddy-bear" theory of American foreign policy decision making — of an innocent set of bunglers in Washington, bungling from one mistake to another — excludes the possibility of a firm policy which may be irrelevent to real world conditions and which may lead to failure, but which, nevertheless, is deliberately planned at each stage of the game. That is to say, if it seems as if Washington has consistently failed, it is only because it is trying to control the uncontrollable, and not because it has made mistakes of omission or ignorance. If you look at the papers which are published and available on decision-making in Vietnam, (and this point is rather important to the Tribunal Legal Commission in the definition of deliberate intent on the part of the United States to aggress in Vietnam) if you look at the papers on Vietnam, you will notice that every aspect of the possibility of failure and success in Vietnam was considered. There was full information available to the American policy decision-makers on the actual situation and conditions at any given time. So, I would reject the concept of the United States proceeding on the basis of blunders.

So far as the bridgehead concept is concerned, bases and the like: in modern warfare, one no longer needs fixed positions. One can use mobile bases which are, from a physical and material viewpoint, far more secure. For this reason, the United States developed a vast armada of Polaris armed submarines which are virtually immune from attack because they are mobile and can be shifted from place to place. So that Vietnam is not in any physical sense essential to American security interests.

The question next arises whether Vietnam is essential to the United States as a direct interest of some sort, whether economic, political or otherwise, or whether it is an experimental range for the development of weapons systems. I would reject the concept of an experimental range for weapons-systems even though, as an effect rather than a cause, Vietnam has in fact become an experimental range for various evil new types of weapons. It is clear that a modern highly industrialized society, choking in its own affluence, possessing weapons suited for conventional warfare, must develop new forms of weaponry in an experimental way; must develop them to attempt to cope with what is essentially an uncontrollable situation.

But the direct interests of the United States are more significant. I do believe that the domino theory is accepted and is the basis of American policy planning in Vietnam. The desire to control revolution everywhere in the world, the desire to stop movements of national self-determination from shaping their own fate and their course in history. This, I think, is the prime explanation of why America is willing to resort to every mode of illegal warfare in Vietnam in order to preserve its position there.

DEUTSCHER: *Wouln't you agree that the greatest miscalculation, the greatest blunder that any government can commit is when it believes that it can control the uncontrollable?...*

KOLKO: I think it is an axiomatic piece of political arithmetic that 6% of the population cannot control 100% of the globe. Therefore, the United States is simply, deliberately, and with as much reason and power as it can marshal, attempting to do the impossible. It cannot succeed.

LAWRENCE DALY: *Professor Kolko. Colonel Hau Van Lau, in his statement said that the people of Vietnam are one State and that therefore the people of the North have the right to help the people of the South in the same way as the other North American states would be entitled to help the people of Florida if they were attacked by a foreign power. There are those, however, who argue that this concedes the substance of the claim made by the American government that assistance is going to the south, that supplies are going to the south, and that this is the only reason for the bombing of the North. I would like you to give us your comments on this argument and particularly on the political morality of such argument.*

KOLKO: I'll avoid the morality, but I will try to give you some fact. The United States, as we attempted to show in my paper submitted to the Legal Commission, did not make this argument in a specific form until 1961, at the end of the year, in its first so-called White Paper. By that time there had been a very vast upheaval within the area south of the 17th parallel which had no connection whatsoever with any movement from North to South, and which was a direct consequence of the frightful oppression in South Vietnam against all forms of political dissidence, from religious to Buddhist and former Viet Minh. I think that if one examines the causal relationship between the fighting in the South and the American allegations in regard to this matter, one will see that the United States did not seriously believe this proposition. It is in the nature of successful revolutions that they are not exportable. No one can turn them on and no one can turn them off. The fight of the Vietnamese people south of the 17th parallel against the United States was in and of itself incapable of being transported by bicycles or trucks from North to South. It would be impossible. The United States government has admitted this time and time again. To stop the fighting against the regime in Saigon, even if the North Vietnamese did everything they could to participate in that end, would not be possible, and Washington understands that. Therefore, it is incorrect to accept the statement of Washington that the war was started by the North and could be stopped by the North. It is not a fact.

DELLINGER: *To continue the discussion of economic interests, many Americans point out that the United States has very little economic interest in Vietnam in terms of investment or in terms of potential resources. Therefore, it's hard to believe that this could be an economic aggression and this seems to fit in with the government's claim that it is there for higher motives. In answer to this people often quote the statement of President Eisenhower and similar statements from the Wall Street Journal and the New York Times about the "tin and tungsten and the manganese and other mineral resources in Indo-China." It seems to me that there may be another much more important element. You touched on it when you spoke of 6% of the population being unable to control 100% of the globe. Last November, when President Johnson visited the troops in Korea, he made a statement to the effect that "the trouble is that there are only 200 million of us in a world of 3 billion and we've got what they want and we're not going to give it to them." It strikes me that as in the case of Cuba, so with Vietnam, the United States can afford to lose its investment in that particular country. But what lies behind the domino theory — and I've always felt the State Department in its way was trying to speak the truth or at least come close to the truth when it refers to this domino theory — is that perhaps the United States wishes to create a lesson for the rest of the world where its investments are that these investments must not be tampered with, or else they will get the same kind of treatment we've had so graphically and horribly presented to us in these last few days. I'd like you to comment on the relationship of these forces and particularly how they've been shown historically.*

KOLKO: On page 67 of my report I quote a statement made by President Johnson in August 1965. He said, in effect, that if we are driven from the field in Vietnam then no nation can ever again have the same confidence in American promise or American protection. I think this sustains the observation you were making. The United States is fighting in Vietnam for Vietnam but also for South America.

DELLINGER: *In relation to this whole business about blundering, you referred to the debate in 1954 when the French were defeated, over whether the United States should intervene militarily or not. Where did*

*that debate take place? Did it take place in the Congress? Did it take place
among the American people or did it take place among those who have
other kinds of motive and interest.*

KOLKO: It was a running debate between the Joint Chiefs of Staff,
the Pentagon, the White House and the government of Great Britain.
And I don't believe that Congress was consulted except, perhaps,
on the level of the Senate Foreign Relations Committee; this Committee debate is colorful, but I don't think consequential.

DELLINGER: *When "Special Forces War" was launched by President
Kennedy in 1961, was that debated in Congress or resolved there or was
this an executive decision?*

KOLKO: Congress has not exercised control over American foreign
policy since the end of the First World War when it vetoed the
League of Nations. For a time in the 1930's it did so by a neutrality
legislation, although that neutrality legislation was carefully formulated to serve certain ends the White House had in mind. The
American Congress, the American public is not being consulted in
these decisions. Their opinions are not being asked and these decisions are being made unilaterally. Congress and the people, of
course, are being asked to implement them and suffer the consequences. This has been true for two or three decades.

DELLINGER: *Was there any democratic debate before the bombing in
February of 1965? I know there was a lot of protest and a lot of public
discussion but there seems to be kind of a gap between the people and
the government.*

KOLKO: Not "seems" there is. I tried to point out in my paper
that the Tonkin Bay crisis, which was artificially contrived by Washington, was an effort to discipline a Senate that was beginning to
express stirrings of unhappiness and dissent. In fact, in recent years,
escalation and the refusal to negotiate had been correlated to the
rising sentiment within the Senate in opposition to the policy in
Vietnam. Nevertheless, there is a kind of national unity called "consensus" and "bi-partisanship" which is continuously invoked by the
White House against Republicans and Democrats alike to eliminate
any kind of true debate, any kind of true polarization of options,
any kind of real way out of the morass in Vietnam. One might even
call it monolithic.

COURTLAND COX: *You stated that the only way to win the kind of war that the United States is fighting is with ground troops. It is reported that Senator Fulbright seems to feel that the United States has now settled on a military solution for Vietnam. Given your analysis of the situation in Vietnam and the kind of war that this has to be, do you think that the United States will have to ultimately invade North Vietnam with ground troops?*

KOLKO: They can barely control one-third of South Vietnam now. I don't see how an invasion of the North could conceivably increase their military security. But this is only an opinion on abstract questions of military strategy . . .

COX: *I'd like to raise a historical question in terms of the United States. I'd like to know specifically if through all the wars and conflicts the United States have gone through, has there been in your opinion, a difference in terms of strategy and techniques used when fighting in, say, World War I as opposed to, say, Cuba, World War II as opposed to their way of dealing with the Indians, the difference between the way the United States fought in Korea and so forth. Has there been a difference in the types of war fought and the mentality they fought with?*

KOLKO: You've posed a very interesting and very important question; because it must be understood that the United States is not an innocent that has blundered out on to the world arena for the first time to be confronted with difficult problems. The United States has had experience in fighting every kind of war. The most interesting kind of war in this regard is one that Amado Hernandez is probably familiar with and that was the Philippine guerilla movement. The word "guerilla" is a Filipino word. The first anti-guerilla war was fought by the United States against the Filipinos from 1899 to 1901. One hundred thousand Filipinos were killed by the United States with forms of barbarism quite akin to those presently employed against the Vietnamese. In this century the first anti-population war, the first war against a civilian population was a United States sponsored war.

MEHMET ALI AYBAR: *I would like to know if the United States is against all wars of national independence. I'd like to know if it is your opinion that the war of aggression in Vietnam is part of a whole plan for Southeast Asia and eventually of all the world.*

KOLKO: In the past it has included Guatemala, Cuba, the Dominican Republic and it is a global war on the part of the United States against the entire world now.

AYBAR: *When did the U.S. embark upon this global strategy?*

KOLKO: Having just finished a volume on the topic, I would say toward the end of the Second World War. The United States assumed at the end of the Second World War that it would be the deciding factor in determining the basic political direction of the Eastern and Western Hemispheres. It was quite willing, at the end of the Second World War, to create bases everywhere in the world, to assume responsibility for trusteeships in Indo-China, Korea and elsewhere. It was quite willing to create a United Nations organization, which would advance the assumption that China was a great power, even though China in 1945 was, on the level of international relations, hardly more than a puppet of the United States. This gave the United States a predominent position in the Security Council of the United Nations. It was globally at the end of the Second World War, 1944-45, and in Vietnam no later than 1950 at the very latest, when the United States took the basic responsibility of financing the war on the part of the French against the Vietnamese people.

MORIKAWA: *Could you give us some background on why the United States government did not ratify the poison gas article of 1925 and also the Convention on Genocide of 1946?*

KOLKO: The United States is bound by a number of treaties signed before the 1925 agreement, treaties signed with South American governments covering the use of chemical and biological agents. But in regard to the 1949 and 1955 ratifications, at the moment I'm afraid I must decline for fear of making an incorrect answer. However, I recall that in the process of preparing material for this Tribunal on the question of chemical-biological warfare, we did find an article by W. O'Brian which appeared in the *Georgetown Law Journal* of 1962 dealing exhaustively with the history of the United States obligations and ratifications under various treaties. O'Brian concluded that the United States was fully and legally bound by treaties and customary international law to the various international standards pertaining to the uses of various weapons including chemical-bacteriological weapons. I believe that Maitre Matarasso has this particular document in his possession.

COX: *You've implied that Vietnam is just one specific of a general global attitude that the United States has towards what is termed the "Third World". I'd like to ask, given the developments throughout the Third World, where do you see "special war" as conducted in Vietnam being projected next. I mean, given the political and economic implications of the situation.*

KOLKO: This is pure speculation, but for the past year-and-a-half, I've been saying Greece. The most dangerous place in the world at this time.

COX: *Why do you think that's the case?*

KOLKO: I have a very elaborate analysis on why it's the case but I wonder, Mr. Chairman, I would be happy to answer it if you think it's appropriate? ... Well, I happen to believe that virtually no one of any consequence of any important class in Greece happens to support the present regime. That includes most of the elements which are true conservatives of a nationalist character. So, therefore, the present coup is completely isolated not only from the people but from the men who own most of the economy as well. It can't succeed.

DEUTSCHER: *If this evidence and cross-examination has shown anything, it has shown that whereas the evidence about the main questions over which we deliberate is abundant, our clarity of thinking about the motives of American policy in Vietnam could be greater. One is struck by the apparent contrast in American policy. On the one hand the United States has reluctantly half-reconciled itself to the existence of a revolutionary regime established in Cuba, 90 miles away, but it cannot apparently reconcile itself to a revolutionary regime 9,000 miles away from its shores. On the face of things that is an extraordinary absurdity. If the United States government wanted to send 500,000 troops and its napalm bombs to Cuba it could wage a war that would be much cheaper, that would have much greater chances of success than the war it is waging in Vietnam. How do you account for this absurdity?*

KOLKO: I think it can be accounted for. I don't want to dodge your question, but it would take a great deal of time. I don't want to appear reluctant to answer questions, but it's not germane to the question of Vietnam. I agree entirely with you, however, on this question of the larger analysis and its critical importance to understanding what is going on in Vietnam. However, my views on the success of Cuba in surviving in the face of hostile American opposition are not directly relevant ...

DEDIJER: *As Chairman, I rule the question in order because we are discussing here the problem of aggression in Vietnam, but Vietnam is only one aspect of similar aggressions.*

KOLKO: The developments within Cuba after February 1959, were not cataclysmic or so quick moving as to assure the final outcome of the Cuban Revolution. It took the United States a while to become aware of the fact that the Cuban Revolution was a fundamentally different phenomenon. Had it been aware in February 1959, that it had in front of it a genuine revolution, a mass revolution, a mass revolution which would genuinely transform Cuban society, it would have acted then as it was quite prepared to act in Santo Domingo. I think that for this reason, the failure of the United States to respond to the developments in Cuba are really largely accidental and as much reflection of the developments within Cuba itself as United States policy.

DEDIJER: *As President of Sessions, I would like to say that Harvard University should be proud of you for your deep knowledge, for your methodological approach and your brilliance. I would also like to express in the name of the Tribunal that we have had the opportunity to hear several other American scholars. I know that in America a real revolution is occurring on American campuses. I think that all members of the Tribunal will share my admiration for your courage to stand against mighty institutions and to testify here freely.*

Resume of Testimony Concerning American Intervention in Vietnam from 1945 to 1964

by Jean Chesneux

Director of Studies at the Ecole des Hautes Etudes, Sorbonne

Roosevelt's wartime "trusteeship" plan for Indochina provided for removal of the French and for placing it under international control; the preponderant role was to have been played by the United States (cf. Cordell Hull, *Memoires).* After the English refused to accept this plan, the United States, at the Yalta Conference 1945, pressed for the adoption of a plan to divide Vietnam along the 16th parallel. It was not a question, as in Korea (divided at the 38th parallel), of separating the socialist and capitalist zones of influence, but rather of a compromise between the old colonial powers (England occupying the south for the French) and the new powers (the United States giving the North to the Kuomintang).

Kuomintang occupation lasted until February 1946, and all the evidence stresses its savagery, for which the United States was responsible. At that same time, nevertheless, the United States also made overtures to Ho Chi Minh through the O.S.S., the forerunner of the C.I.A., but soon came to realize that it had nothing to hope for on that score. When the war resumed between France and the Democratic Republic of Vietnam in 1946, America, motivated by a desire to combat communism rather than to support French colonial power, chose to back France. That decision implied the creation of a political base in Vietnam which would be directly linked with the United States. This was to be accomplished by making use of the conservative nationalists who, because of their fear of the people's movement, were prepared to work for the Americans.

That policy was launched publically by William Bullitt. In "Life" magazine, October 1947, he called on the Americans to set up their own groups in Vietnam. In November 1947, he visited the Emporer Bao Dai in Hong Kong and allayed his misgivings. The "Bao Dai solution" was American-inspired from the beginning; the fact that

Franco-American contradictions and the weakness of personnel eventually forced the United States to abandon it in favour of Diem in no way alters that fact.

The Bao Dai government was formally recognized by Dean Acheson on February 7, 1950, as soon as it was set up. Important financial aid was given to France. Very soon, however, direct aid was given to the Bao Dai by virtue of mutual security agreements between the United States and the Bao Dai government in December 1951. A plan was thus put into action which could only work to the benefit of Diem after 1954.

Thus began the procedure which was at the time called an "internationalization of the Indochinese war". In reality it was an Americanization (a United States takeover, as W. Warbey said). The Bao Dai became more and more directly dependent on Washington. After the visit of General Clark, the Commander-in-Chief for the Far East, Bao Dai called for a "general mobilization" in June 1953. In September of 1953, the Americans granted a 384 million dollar loan to France, intended for the Bao Dai army. An American general staff (M.A.A.G.) was installed at Saigon. At the time, France was committed to a war "leading to victory". The refusal to consider a pacific settlement would indelibly mark American policy in Vietnam.

In January 1954, the Assistant Secretary of State for the Far East, Robertson, made this reply to a question from an American legislator: *Question:* Basically, does this mean that the United States is undertaking to maintain American domination in the Far East for an indeterminate period of time: *Answer:* Yes.

The Crisis in the Spring and Summer of 1954

As the conflict grew and the D.R.V. grew stronger, American policy supporting a war to the finish became strengthened. Of course, economic considerations should not be ignored. In August 1953, Eisenhower declared: "If we lose Indochina, several things will immediately occur . . . The tin and tungsten we so much need will stop coming in from that region; thus, when the United States votes 400 million dollars in support of the war, we are not voting for a program of liquidation. We are voting for the least costly method of stopping something which would be disastrous for the United States, for our security, for our strength, and for our ability to draw upon the riches of Indochina for certain things we need". However, the real aim was a political victory over the communist forces, all the more desirable owing to the fact that in July 1953 the United States had been forced to accept a compromise in Korea.

In December 1953, Nixon said: "It is impossible to put down our arms before victory is complete."

The Navarre Plan in the beginning of 1954 aimed at a general French counter-offensive to be prepared in full agreement with Washington. In February 1954, the U.S. State Department stated that it was "troubled by the fact that the French are not trying to win the war, but to arrive at a negotiating position". (A. Eden, *Full Circle*, p. 100).

In the spring of 1954, when Dien Bien Phu was threatened, the United States planned to intervene directly in the war. Admiral Radford suggested an American intervention in Tonkin. Dulles still spoke of possible victory within a year. But he ran into opposition from the British. In vain, he tried to organize a "common action" by the Western Powers (France, Great Britain, Australia, New Zealand, plus the Philippines and Siam). Here we see the origins of SEATO: that military pact was drawn up before Geneva and not after; it is an essential piece of United States policy and not a compensatory measure taken after the Geneva Accords. Dulles invited neither India, Burma nor Indonesia, even though it was a question of "collective defense", since these countries were not prepared to hide American intervention.

Another element essential to the American plan was the direct collaboration of the conservative Vietnamese forces. The Emperor Bao Dai was no longer satisfactory; too weak himself, he was also too tied to France, which was itself shaky. On July 4th, in the midst of the Geneva Conference, the Americans forced Bao Dai to accept Ngo Dinh Diem as Prime Minister, in order that they might have an agent in the government. Diem had been contacted in Japan in 1950 by Wesley Fishel, a C.I.A. agent. Justice Douglas had introduced him to Mansfield and J. F. Kennedy, the leaders of a group in the Senate which was critical of French incompetence and was pushing for American intervention in the guise of "anticolonialism" (cf. R. Scheer, "How the U.S. Got involved in Vietnam").

The Geneva Conference got under way on May 8th; all the observers were impressed by the obstructive attitude of the Americans. "The Americans clearly seem to doubt the possibility of reaching an agreement, even without danger, with the Communists" (A. Eden, p. 142). On June 18th, Eisenhower telegraphed to Robertson, the acting head of the American delegation, "to do everything he could to bring an end to the Conference as soon as possible since the Communists were drawing things out for military reasons".

The American position on the Geneva Accords of July 20 is ambiguous. The United States did not sign them, insisting instead on ratification by unilateral declaration. On July 21st, Bedell Smith, the American delegate, stated that the United States "accepts the cease-fire agreement as well as the final declaration, excepting article 13, and that it would refrain from contravening them by resorting to force or threats".

The reservation on article 13 signified United States refusal to take part in further consultations among the participants at the Conference, but otherwise the Accords were formally agreed to. Nevertheless, Eisenhower stated the same day that: "The United States has not taken part in the decisions of the Conference and it is not bound by them". In other words, the United States wanted to keep a free hand without directly defying international public opinion by disavowing the Conference.

In the fall, the SEATO pact was signed as a result of the initiative taken during the spring crisis; it provided for the formation of a military bloc, that is, it turned its back on the possibility of settling problems through negotiation. It provided for intervention in case of "subversion" — a very vague notion.

Geneva to Escalation: the Bases of American Policy

We should start with the Robertson declaration of June 1, 1956, which is the best and clearest formulation of basic American policy in Vietnam.

Robertson Declaration, 1956:

Our policy in Vietnam can be simply defined as follows: to support an anti-communist Vietnamese government friendly to America and to assist it in its efforts to lessen and, if necessary, eliminate communist subversion; to assist the Vietnamese government to build up the force necessary for its internal security, and to encourage the non-communist world to support a free Vietnam; to assist in the rehabilitation and reconstruction of a ruined country, the people of which have suffered through eight disastrous years of civil and international war. Our primary efforts are aimed at assisting the government of South Vietnam to maintain a police force consisting of a regular army of 150,000 men, a mobile national guard of approximately 45,000 men, and local units to combat subversion in the villages. We are in the process of providing money and equipment to those forces and we have undertaken to train the Vietnamese army. We are also in the process of assisting the Vietnamese police forces to organize, train and equipment themselves. (Bulletin of the U.S. State Department, 11 June 1956.)

That text contains six basic ideas:

    a) to turn the South into a separate country. American documents constantly make mention of "South Vietnamese independence" That is contrary to the Geneva Accords, which made it clear that the 17th parallel was a provisional dividing line and in no way constituted a political or territorial boundary.

b) to establish itself militarily: this is a matter of turning Vietnam into a military base, "of holding onto Vietnam at any price" (Senator Jackson, 1961).

In July 1965, Cabot Lodge stated before the Senate: "We will never leave South Vietnam, even if that government requests it". The report of Mansfield in 1960 made it clear that military expenditure had priority in "aid to South Vietnam". That is a second serious violation of the Geneva Accords, even though they were overly respected for a certain time: American military personnel were called "advisors". The military pact with Diem in 1955 was called an "economic agreement". The fact that the Geneva provisions for military withdrawal from Vietnam were violated can be found clearly set forth in the reports of the International Control Commission (Poland, Canada, India): the Commission states that the Saigon authorities obstructed their investigations but that nonetheless there had been serious violations (cf. interim reports Nos. 5, 8, 10 and 11.) The special report of June, 1962 unanimously found that "the setting up of an American military command in South Vietnam, as well as the introduction of a large number of American personnel, represented a *de facto* military alliance forbidden by the Geneva Convention".

c) The United States forced South Vietnam to accept a government of U.S. choosing. Ngo Dinh Diem was brought in by the United States. In June 1956, J. F. Kennedy stated: "If we are not the parents of the young Vietnam, we are certainly its god-parents. We were present at its birth, we have helped it to live, we have assisted in pointing it towards the future."

An essential role in the setting up of Diem was played by Edward Lansdale, the C.I.A. chief in Saigon, and the man who had already implemented the Philippines "Solution" in 1950.

Of course, Diem's subordination to the Americans was only general; he was a strong personality and did not consult the Americans on every detail. Minor conflicts arose which were made much of by American journalists, but Diem was completely dependent on the Americans politically, militarily and financially, without them having to direct each of his actions.

This is the reason why it is impossible to accept the theory of a civil war in Vietnam put forth by some liberal Americans. The Vietnamese conflict is a popular movement which is opposed by a foreign power trying to hold the country through a well-chosen intermediary.

d) From 1955, there has been a refusal to negotiate and a denial to Vietnam of the benefits resulting from the lessening of international tensions; from 1954 to 1964, there was no attempt on the part of Saigon to negotiate with the North. On the contrary, as we have seen, the United States refused to accept article 13 of the Geneva Accords. In other words, the principle of consultation between the powers involved, which would have been the only solution, given the lack of control machinery. In those conditions, the recourse to armed struggle was to be expected. "When a military struggle is concluded on condition that it be transferred to the political arena, can the party who violates that condition not legitimately expect that the military struggle will recommence" (Bulletin of Atomic Scientists, June 1965, p. 31). In point of fact, the elections provided for in 1956 were prevented by the United States and Saigon.

e) Economic Infiltration.

Although it is not a fundamental motive, the Americans in Vietnam have sought profit for their industrial or commercial firms. "Business" of this sort also has its ideological side; it is a question of encouraging free enterprise and even speculation in order to demonstrate South Vietnam's dependence on the "free world" (cf. the statement made by Burrows, chief of American economic services in Saigon, to William Warbey, Labour Member of Parliament, quoted by the latter in his report on his trip to Vietnam, p. 59: "You see we are trying to build up a free society here and therefore we have to promote private enterprises".) The Americans did not undertake private, large-scale economic investment in Vietnam through a feeling of insecurity, but they nevertheless flooded the country with consumer goods and material of a military sort. Over the course of six years, they undertook to put two billion dollars into a country whose gross national product is from 200 million to 1 billion dollars. In this way, they were able to completely upset the social and economic balance of the country: the small producers were ruined, prices rose, and inflation resulted, as well as the creation of a parasitic class. This economic shock is an important part of American subversion in Vietnam.

f) attack the North.

This was also a preoccupation of the Americans well before the escalation itself. Ever since 1956, the Americans had been training special Vietnamese commandos, paratroops and saboteurs in Formosa and Guam. They have publicly admitted that part of their activities.

Intervention from Geneva to "Special War"

Beginning on August 17, 1954, Eisenhower ordered American aid to be given directly to Vietnam and no longer through the intermediary of France. Thus began the beginning of close collaboration between Diem and the United States, through the aegis of lobbies such as the "American Friends of Vietnam", the Catholic Church (Cardinal Spellman), and Michigan State University, which was charged with reorganizing and modernizing the Saigon police. An "economic" agreement in February 1955 provided for American contribution to the building of Diem's army.

The Geneva Accords, however, had provided for elections. In order to establish United States supremacy in Vietnam, this obstacle had to be removed. Diem and the Americans were opposed to elections, for they realized that elections would give a large majority to Ho Chi Minh (Eisenhower, *Mandate for Change*, p. 372; J. F. Kennedy, *Strategy of Peace*, p. 81). The pretext was put forward that the character of the government in the North would prevent free elections from being held. Ho Chi Minh, however, in *Nhan-Dan* (November 17, 1955 and February 25, 1956), proposed guarantees, such as the exchange of electoral propagandists between North and South. But elections were not held. Moreover, the closing of the American consulate in Hanoi in 1955 underlined the United States desire to break off relations systematically, in contrast to the methods of France and England.

The way was open for the consolidation of the South as an American military base. William Warbey, in 1957, pointed out the existence of 365,000 men in various categories; beginning in 1958. American schools trained 3,296 South Vietnamese army officers, whereas not even one engineering school had been set up.

Along with the army, priority was given to public works having a military interest: wide roads were constructed over ten yards in width for thirty-ton trucks, and leading to the highlands, a strategic region without any economic importance. The Saigon-Bien Hoa highway is 100 meters wide with two lateral 950-meter borders: it is a camouflaged landing field. By the end of 1960 there were 57 American military airfields in South Vietnam.

In politics, military projects were accompanied by the repression of all opposition, even though the Geneva Accords had forbidden political reprisals. The political repression antedates the reopening of armed combat (cf. Philippe Devillers, *China Quarterly*, January 1962, "Mistakes of the Diem Government"; see also Jean Lacouture, *Le Vietnam Entre Deux Paix*, pp. 83-84.)

Intervention, from "Special" War to Escalation

Armed combat recommenced in the South in 1958-59. The people were no longer able to bear the oppressive weight of the Diem regime. It was not a question of subversion from the North, as alleged by the United States. Too many observers have attested to the local origins of the N.L.F., the defensive character of the use of force, the progressive, reluctant and localized character of the recourse to armed struggle. (Cf. Devillers, *op. cit.*) The American White Paper of 1961 admitted that the Vietcong was locally recruited and that its arms were hand-made or captured from the Americans. In the course of a press conference as late as May 1963, General Harkins, the commander at Saigon, admitted that "The guerillas obviously are not being reinforced or supplied systematically from Vietnam, China or any place else. They apparently depend for weapons primarily on whatever they can capture".

It is evident that beginning in 1960 the militants from the South who had withdrawn back into the North returned. However, it was not they who impeded the elections provided for in Geneva. They had left in 1954 with the intention of returning in two years. Their return was belated, but normal.

In 1960, popular feeling stood in the way of the American plan for control of Vietnam. The United States was forced to widen its intervention: its solution was "special" war. The Saigon army furnished the large part of the troops, but American "advisors" took a direct part in the fighting. An American combat headquarters was set up at Saigon in February, 1962, and American military bases were greatly reinforced.

On the political side, a great effort was made to confine the population and to regroup it into "strategic hamlets" as recommended in the Staley-Taylor plan. However, this attempt was a complete failure. The United States thus widened the war. Between October 1961 and September 1962, the Saigon air force carried out 2,825 air-raids and 3,614 helicopter sorties. It should be noted that the transition to "special" war exactly coincided with the election of J. F. Kennedy to the presidency. One week before the opening of the International Geneva Conference on Laos (May, 1961), Lyndon Johnson arrived in Saigon to press for the build-up of the South Vietnamese army.

The "special" war was a heavy political and military set-back for the Americans. More and more military material, dollars, and men had to be sent to Diem, whose political power was dwindling: there were many deserters, a paratroop mutiny in 1961, and constant political defection. In the fall of 1963, Diem was "dropped" by the United States in highly suspicious circumstances, at the same time that De Gaulle was formulating the idea of a neutral solution leading to new contacts. Although it attempted to regain some freedom of movement *in extremis*, the Diem regime could not rid itself of its fundamental characteristic: from the beginning and in essence, it had been dependent on the United States.

What is most striking for the historian is the duration and the continuity of American intervention in Vietnam since the end of the Second World War. The role played by the United States was as important, with regard to basic decisions, during the first Vietnamese war as during the second. Their engagement in Vietnam dates from the Cold War, 1947, if not before. The myth that the United States took over from France after Geneva must be abandoned.

Furthermore, American intervention had to be supported politically. Soon disenchanted with Ho Chi Minh (1945), the United States undertook with Bao Dai a project aimed at installing itself in Vietnam. They used the same infrastructure without any basic modifications when they installed Diem.

Throughout this long period, American intervention in Vietnam has never been the result of requests from an autonomous Vietnam; it is a deliberate and systematic policy of political, military, economic and social upheaval which truly merits being called "subversion".

Historical Report on U.S. Aggression in Vietnam 1964 to 1967
testimony by Charles Fourniau

I would like to testify before the International War Crimes Tribunal concerning the question, "Has the United States Government committed aggression under international law?" This is the matter you now have under investigation.

I will testify both as an historian whose area of interest is Vietnam, and as an eye-witness. In my capacity as a correspondent for a major French newspaper, I was in the Democratic Republic of Vietnam from 1963 to 1965. I had the privilege of being the only citizen of a Western country in a position to witness at first hand one of the initial United States bombings of North Vietnam and of living through the first months of the escalation of the war.

Other reports have dealt with the period before 1964-1965. Therefore I will limit my testimony to the years 1964-1967, that is, to those events to which I was actually a witness; to the most contemporary facts, and most particularly to a consideration of what is referred to as the "escalation."

Escalation and the American Viewpoint

In the Spring of 1965, the American aggression in Vietnam entered into a new phase. The scope of the war against the Democratic Republic of Vietnam was widened in February 1965, when United States planes began bombing North Vietnam continuously.

The war in the South was intensified by massive bombing raids which were carried out by much larger forces than before, in particular with B-52's--enormous airplanes capable of carrying 27 tons of bombs, and which were soon making 7,000 kilometer round-trips from their base in Guam for the purpose of attacking certain targets in South Vietnam, and sometimes in North Vietnam (cf., the bombing raids in the Mu Gia region).

The war tended to change in kind with the arrival of American troops, no longer by the thousands, as "advisers", but by the hundreds of thousands, as combat units. this presents an historical problem; why this change in the war, this quantitative and qualitative change in United States aggression?

The United States Government undertook to give an answer to this immediately. On 27 February 1965, the State Department published a White Paper entitled: *Northern Aggression; the History of the North Vietnamese Campaign for the Conquest of South Vietnam.*

The American View

The U.S. viewpoint is very clearly set out in the first lines of the Introduction: "South Vietnam is struggling for its existence against a brutal campaign of terror and armed attack inspired, directed, supplied and controlled by the Communist regime at Hanoi. That flagrant aggression has been going on for years, but recently its tempo has been stepped up, and today the threat has become acute . . ."

Further on: "The Communist Government of Vietnam has deliberately undertaken to conquer a sovereign people in a neighboring State . . . The United States of America has answered the appeals from the South Vietnamese Government for aid in the defense of its liberty and of the independence of its territory and its people."

This thesis rests on two premises: — The United States of America answered this appeal from an ally; — The South Vietnamese have been victims of aggression from North Vietnam. The first premise is false, and the second is ridiculous.

Was the United States in the position of being legally or morally obliged to answer the appeal of an ally, the Government of South Vietnam? No. No legal obligation bound the United States Government and forced it to intervene in South Vietnam, especially not to send troops and surely not to dispatch airplanes to bomb the Democratic Republic of Vietnam.

In fact, the two texts which Secretary of State Dean Rusk attempted to invoke in support of his thesis are the Eisenhower letter to Diem of 23 October 1954 and the Special Protocol of the Manila Treaty (SEATO) which aimed at extending that treaty to South Vietnam. Now neither of those two texts implies any legal obligation to intervene militarily in South Vietnam, and certainly not in the North.

Lacking any legal obligation, was the United States Government bound by moral obligations to the Saigon Government? For this to be true, the representative nature and the legitimacy of the Government of South Vietnam must be a reality; this is not the case.

I will leave the demonstration of the illegitimacy of the Saigon Government, which is founded on the violation of the Geneva Accords, to my legal colleagues. As for that Government's representative nature, that was hardly defensible even at the time of Ngo Dinh Diem, since from the beginning more than two-thirds of the Saigon budget was supplied by credits allocated in Washington. It is also clear that Diem's numerous successors must be considered as totally void of any representative character. To imagine that the policy of the greatest imperialist power is determined by an appeal from Nguyen Khanh is ridiculous.

It is thus false to maintain that the United States, by intervening in South Vietnam, is fulfilling an obligation: it chose that policy freely, as, for that matter, a growing number of Americans have pointed out with increasing sharpness — from Schlesinger to the Republican Party, which is shaken into pre-electoral lucidity (cf., statement of 2 May 1967).

Furthermore, to maintain that South Vietnam has been the victim of North Vietnamese aggression is absurd. In fact, this thesis rests on the following notion, there are two Vietnams — since the aggression defined in the White Paper as aggression "against a sovereign people in a neighbouring State" naturally implies two national entities.

Further, Ambassador Arthur Goldberg, in a speech at the United Nations on 23 September 1966, made mention of the "two peoples of Vietnam." Now, such a statement is more than false; it is historically and socially meaningless from a logical view point.

As a matter of fact, few peoples present a unity, a national cohesion, as strong or as old as the Vietnamese people. There has been an independent Vietnamese state since the eleventh century, and the sense of belonging to a single national community is the basic characteristic of Vietnamese history. During the 1860's, when the United States was still seeking a national identity in its Civil War, the Vietnamese were fighting for their independence from French colonialism, after having repulsed Chinese invasions for eight centuries. The existence of that national Vietnamese community serves to explain how the southern limits to Chinese expansion were fixed over the course of the years, as the result of repeated attacks and defeats.

Both historians and linguists can testify to the remarkable unity of the Vietnamese language, from Saigon to Hanoi, which shows different accents but not dialectical differentiation. How can such a unified people commit aggression against itself? Is the temporary division arbitrarily prolonged by treaty violations on the part of the United States sufficient to give validity to this nonsense? No. The American thesis which serves as a basis for all Washington's justifications of policy is absurd in principle.

Furthermore, the United States cannot justify its policy by arguments based on facts and dates. When the United States leaders cite figures, they are merely empasizing the lies contained in the declarations of their State Department. For example, here are statistics taken from the White Paper:

"From 1959 to 1960, when Hanoi opened its infiltration route to the South, 1,800 men went from North to South Vietnam. This figure had reached a minimum of 3,700 by 1961 . . ."

These are American figures, for which I take no responsibility, and which do not distinguish whether those men were North Vietnamese or returning South Vietnamese who had been regrouped in the North as a result of the Geneva Accords, and thus cut off from their homes by the violation of those Accords.

Even by taking theUnited States argument in its most favourable light, does it not give rise to clear condemnation? In 1961, there were said to have been 5,5000 to 8,200 men who had infiltrated from North to South Vietnam. Now in his 1962 report, Senator Mansfield stated: "Since 1961, it has been clear that a total collapse of South Vietnam is drawing dangerously near." How could 8,200 men have led a country with a population of 14 million to the edge of "total collapse"?

I put this question to the Assistant Under-Secretary of State, Mr. Harold Kaplan, during a debate on Belgian television in January, 1967. His only reply was to say that the American statistics were inexact. That reply was not very convincing. By its own argument, the White Paper proves that it is impossible to explain the events which took place in South Vietnam in 1961 by blaming them on "Northern infiltrators".

Other official American statistics show that at no time was the thesis according to which the United States is in South Vietnam fighting against essentially North Vietnamese forces supported by facts.

In his report of 8 January 1966, Senator Mansfield evaluates the National Liberation Front forces at the end of 1965 as containing a fighting body of 73,000, 14,000 of which he considers to be North Vietnamese, or one-fifth of the fighting forces. This negates the official United States thesis.

A year later, at the beginning of 1967, the U.S. News agency A.P., on 26 January, gave the following evaluation by Secretary of Defense McNamara: "The NLF army at that time had a strength of 275,000 — 45,000, or one-sixth, of whom were North Vietnamese."

Thus, even if one accepts the figures of the American services — and in my opinion it would seem to be good historical procedure to accept them only with reservations and to suspect them of having been drawn up to support the official policy of that country — I am unable to derive from them a firm basis for official Washington policy. On the contrary, the figures bring out the inconsistency of that policy. Neither the origin of the armed struggle, nor the escalation, can be justified by the facts set forth by the United States. Those facts form the basis for all justifications put forth by the United States from time to time to quiet international public opinion, not without success.

What then are the historical facts which account for American aggression and, more specifically, the American escalation in the spring of 1965?

Escalation of the Spring of 1965

The North did not commit aggression against the South; on the contrary, there has been American aggression against the Vietnamese people as a whole. American aggression against the Democratic Republic of Vietnam did not begin on 7 February 1965, but has been, in fact, permanent.

The setting up in the South of a puppet government taking orders from a foreign power is in itself aggression against North Vietnam. That is not simply a legalistic expression of the case, but a living reality for the entire population, both on the level of national and political conscience and at the level of daily life.

The 17th parallel as an impassable frontier is a deep wound to Vietnamese patriotism. It is fiercely resented by the entire population of the North. "The South is flesh of our flesh," the slogans say. Humbly, each day, every mother translates that slogan into action; when she cooks the family rice, she takes a handful and sets it aside: that is rice for the South. Not only does the 17th parallel cross the map: it passes over broken families and consciences. Finally, by making the 17th parallel a frontier, the United States dealt a blow to the economy, that is, to the material life of all of North Vietnam. Was this not the deliberate policy of the Western powers in 1954?

Traditionally, North Vietnam lived for several months of the year on rice imported from the South. In that part of Vietnam where the area cultivated per inhabitant is barely larger than a tenth of a hectare, the cutting off of those grain shipments from Nam Bo (South Vietnam) could have given rise to famine and to other extremely serious disorders. Was this not the real aggression committed by the United States against the North? Even though an economic miracle was wrought by the socialist regime in the Democratic Republic of Vietnam which succeeded in almost trebling rice production over the ten years of that aggression; the intent of that aggression is still a fact.

This is the more true in that at the same time aggression took much more tangible forms. The "Bac-Tien" or March to the North was one of the eternal slogans used by the puppet forces in the South. I myself saw a pamphlet put out by the Diem supporters making use of that slogan as early as 1955, and it has been the *leitmotif* of Khan, Ky, and so on . . . On many occasions, long before 1965 or 1964, saboteurs were parachuted into North Vietnam; a very complete documentation containing photographs and dates, was published by the Ministry for Foreign Affairs at Hanoi in 1963, and enables us to verify the continuing nature of that aggressive policy.

Next came the so-called Tonkin Gulf affair, from 2 to 5 August 1964, and then, beginning on 7 February 1965, the continued bombing of the Democratic Republic of Vietnam. Let us dwell for a moment on each of these events.

The Tonkin Gulf Affair

On 2 August 1964, the White House announced that some American destroyers had been the victims of "unprovoked attacks" by North Vietnamese torpedo boats. Then, during the evening of the 4th, a second attack was said to have taken place. In reply to those attacks, President Johnson ordered American planes to bomb installations along the entire North Vietnamese coast: that was the first bombing of North Vietnamese territory by United States planes.

We will not linger over the facts: everyone is in agreement that on 2 August, American ships were in an area which was considered by the Democratic Republic of Viet-Nam to be within its territory. The entire world has pointed out that the information put out at the time, on 4 August, was extremely confusing and not very convincing. But even had it been convincing, nothing gave the United States the right to retaliation by a bombardment of coastal areas hundreds of miles away from where the incidents occured. Thus, on 5 August 1964 American aggression is clearly evidenced. What have to be clearly understood are the real causes for that agression; two of these causes are very clear. The bombings begun on 5 August 1964 were an operation designed to save the political situation in the South and to put an end to the growing number of attempts to open peaceful negotiations.

In 1964, Saigon was experiencing the beginning of a series of *coups d'etat;* in fact, what was beginning to flounder was the whole political and military system of "Special" War. The liquidation of Diem on 1 November 1963, had already taken place in the context of serious military setbacks, notably the Ap Bac defeat in January of 1963. At the same time one saw the liquidation of the "strategic hamlet" system — a major component of the Staley-Taylor plan designed to lead to pacification by the end of 1962 — and the rise of growing political disorder.

After three months, the military junta which had replaced Diem was in its turn replaced by Khanh. By April, however, Khanh was up against increasing difficulties; the struggle between himself and his enemies in the Dai Viet party was henceforth an open one. At the same time, the provincial administration collapsed and neutralist opinion became increasingly vociferous.

The American services then decided to act and seemed to believe that it was still possible to arrest the administrative breakdown. In order to accomplish this, however, very strong political and military measures were called for, measures which presupposed the creation of an atmosphere which would be at once dramatic and which would hold forth new prospects for victory. The attack of 5 August was ment to fulfill these requirements. In order to act in the South, a blow was struck in the North. Shortly afterwards, measures were taken in the South. On August 16, 1964, a mixed United States-Vietnamese command was set up, erasing what was left of an appearance of independence by the Saigon Government, by this General Harkins hoped to enable the decomposition of the Saigon army to be halted and to allow that army to achieve some advance on the ground. On the following day, 16 August, Nguyen Khanh had himself named President of the Republic with dictatorial powers. Less than one year after the liquidation of the Diem dictatorship, the American services felt the need to recreate another omnipotent power figure. But in fact, it was too late. From that time on, no one of the puppet leaders would be able to wield real power.

The bombing of North Vietnam in August 1964 was primarily a political and military operation undertaken on behalf of South Vietnam. But at the same time it was an operation with international significance.

Meanwhile, the summer of 1964 was marked by a series of diplomatic initiatives aimed at restoring the peace. In the course of a Press conference on 23 July, General de Gaulle took up again the idea of a conference "on the same order and having in principle the same participants as the first Geneva Conference," following a proposal put forward a few days earlier by U Thant.

On 25 July, the Soviet Union contacted the fourteen countries which had participated in the Geneva Conference on Laos (1961-62), and asked that that Conference be reconvened.

A few days later, the Democratic Republic of Vietnam also put forward the idea of a "Conference of the Geneva type," and on 4

August, Peking made it known that China was in agreement. Important steps, therefore, had been taken towards the negotiating table, aimed at ending the Vietnamese conflict. On 5 August, U.S. bombs falling on the coast of the Democratic Republic of Viet Nam put an end to that hope.

That bombing, therefore, constituted not only an aggressive act taken against the Democratic Republic of Vietnam, but at the same time a systematic sabotaging of the chances for peace: it was a crime against the Vietnamese people, a crime against peace; and a premeditated crime. In point of fact, such a large air operation could not have been gotten up on the spur of the moment, as the theory of an answering attack would have us believe. As early as 14 May, McNamara had announced in Saigon: "The United States does not exclude the possibility of carrying the war to North Vietnam." On 1 June, a military conference was held at Honolulu, and everything leads us to believe that at that time plans for the 5 August bombing were mapped out. On 23 June, Cabot Lodge was replaced as Ambassador to South Vietnam by General Maxwell Taylor. The naming of the most outstanding American military personality to that post is obviously extremely significant with regard to the bombing of 5 August.

Continuing Bombing of North Vietnam

The installation of Khanh and Taylor in Saigon was not sufficient to correct the situation, which continued to go downhill rapidly. It soon became catastrophic on at least three levels: On one hand, Khanh's dictatorial powers did not reestablish Government authority. Saigon was living through a moment of tragic buffoonery consisting of permanent *coups d'etat.* In fact, the masses in the cities went into action: at Hue, in the second half of August; at Saigon when, for example, the general strike of 2 September completely paralysed the city. Scarcely had he become dictator, when Khan was forced to withdraw into the background, reappear, face *coups d'etat,* give way to a civilian government, return...only to be fired in the end in order to bring in Nguyen Cao Ky, who was even lower on the scale of political and representative quality. For all practical purposes, beginning with that date, there was no longer any real Vietnamese power in Saigon. Here is one of the most important of the set-backs in American policy, since that policy made sense only so long as a South Vietnamese Government capable of assuming responsibility on its own could be set up with the shortest possible delay.

On the other hand, the Saigon Government was not the only thing to break up; the entire administration set up in the Diem era also went. In ninety days, from the military junta of 1 November 1963 to the end of January 1964, approximately 500 bureaucrats and superior officers — among the latter 50 officers of the highest rank — were killed, imprisoned or fired — not counting lower ranking officers and bureaucrats. In its turn, the Khanh Government fired five generals, changed three army commanders, six battalion commanders, 200 officers, 800 bureaucrats, provincial chiefs, civil service chiefs, etc., when it came to power. In addition, the entire apparatus of the Cao Lao party — the Nhu party which had held a considerable share of authority — disappeared.

Finally, in the military field, the breakdown accelerated and defeats piled up. To the firing of a large number of officers was added the wait-and-see attitude of those who had been kept in their posts and massive desertions on the part of the troops, nearly 80,000 during 1964. At the end of that year, the troops of the NLF won a big victory at Binh Gia.

Complete breakdown was imminent, and the American authorities knew it. On 27 March 1964, the U.S. news agency UPI wrote "The question is no longer one of knowing whether the war is being lost, but rather of knowing how fast the United States and South Viet Nam are losing it; and whether there is any fragile hope of saving the situation." The Mansfield report of 3 January 1966 stated: "At the beginning of 1965, the situation had become semi-desperate." Not until November 1965 did McNamara feel able to say: "We have stopped losing the war." Thus, at the end of 1966, important political decisions had to be made by the United States Government. Now, the diplomatic situation at the time did not preclude the possibility of peace initiatives; quite the contrary.

As it had repeatedly declared, the Democratic Republic of Viet Nam had decided to facilitate a peaceful settlement while at the same time firmly retaining its principles and holding to its position regarding the rights of the Vietnamese people. In a private conversation, President Pham Van Dong told me, in September 1964: "We don't have the right to lose a minute of peace, because we know what a minute of war costs our people." As a matter of fact, as we have since learned--(principally through an interview with U Thant reported by *Newsweek* in December 1966) -- Hanoi made indirect peace proposals in the fall of 1964.

At the beginning of 1965, following a proposal by Prince Norodom Sihanouk, of Cambodia the conference of the Indochinese peoples was being set up at Phnom Penh. At the same time, before going to Hanoi, Premier Kosygin was in London. Once again, without anything as yet set out in black and white, peace opportunities might have opened up. And once again, everything was wiped out by an American bombing raid, on 7 February, and by all the raids against the Democratic Republic of Viet Nam which followed.

On 7 February, while Premier Kosygin was in Hanoi, American planes bombed various locations in the Democratic Republic of Viet Nam, from Thanh Hoa to the 17th parallel. The escalation had begun. The American authorities, did not admit this immediately. That first raid was said to be in reply to the victorious attack of the NLF on Camp Holloway near Pleiku in South Viet Nam. An absurd excuse, since as a normal part of warfare a mere attack on a post could not have been justification for that outrageous reprisal, nor for the decision to move the war to above the 17th parallel to attack directly a socialist country. The reprisal was quickly abandoned, as a matter of fact, to be replaced with talk of the necessity for stopping movement of troops from North to South. The American authorities have held to that explanation, even though two years of intensive bombings have stopped nothing whatsoever. In reality, the true reasons were different, and here we touch on the causes of the escalation.

First, it was a question of escaping from the desperate situation in the South. The Americans themselves recognize this: "The increase of United States military intervention in Viet Nam", the Mansfield report of 3 January 1966 stated, "was brought about by the fact that the situation had become semi-desperate at the beginning of 1965."

General Vo Nguyen Giap expressed the same idea when he called the escalation a "life-saving plan for the United States." As the journalist Jean Lacouture noted: "Beaten in the South, the United States tried to move the war." But he added: "Strange planners are they who, in order to kill a snake whose head they are unable to crush, paint its tail red in order to cut it off...without success, as everyone knows."

At the same time, the brutality of the attack put an end to all the diplomatic approaches which had been under way to find a peaceful solution. The setback led to a new phase in the war, more horrible for the Vietnamese, more serious for world peace.

Thus, throughout the year 1964-1965, American aggression in Viet Nam, which was clear from the beginning, became overt: The United States intervened in South Viet Nam on the political and the military levels, in violation of the Geneva Accords by supporting Diem's repressive regime from 1954 to 1960; and in its special war" from 1961 to 1964. That policy failed. It failed because it was aggressive, that is, it could only give rise to continually growing resistance and opposition from the mass of the population and the vital forces in the nation. The character of American economic and military "aid" to South Viet Nam was such that, as it grew the party being assisted lost strength in an inverse ratio, tending towards zero as that aid grew to overwhelming proportions.

The setback in that policy, therefore, called for a choice to be made. At the same time, various initiatives were being taken in an attempt to create international conditions for a peaceful solution of the conflict. The alternative of peace began to appear as not only a possibility, but as an ever more desirable solution. At the same time, however, the pro-war factions in Washington and Saigon were demanding that a solution be reached through a widening of the war. It was thus that in 1960, in 1964 (and perhaps in 1967), that because of its deteriorating position the United States found itself faced with a dilemma which urgently called for solution. This dilemma could be expressed as either a peaceful solution, or the carrying forward of the war under new conditions which were more grave and more aggressive in nature.

One has to point out that on every occasion up to the present the American government has opted for widening the war. The historical analysis of the events of 1964-1965 seems to me to illustrate the permanent aggressive nature of American policy in Viet Nam.

First Bombings of North Vietnam

The aggressive nature of American policy and activity in Viet Nam can be discerned in the methods of warfare employed. This is a large field. I should like to confine myself to my own experience of the first American bombings of the Democratic Republic of Viet Nam.

My first testimony is on the bombing of Dong Hoi, capital of Quang Tri province, situated some 50 kilometers north of the 17th parallel, on 10 February, from 1 to 3 p.m. I was present during this attack. I was able to verify the results of this bombing, and of those of 7 and 8 February, that is, the first three events in the escalation of the war at Dong Hoi and Vinh Linh, near the 17th parallel.

At Dong Hoi, thirty targets were hit: a residential district built up mainly of straw huts; a secondary school on the outskirts of the city; a hospital on the outskirts, where the roof was torn off by rocket fire. During the raid, many fragmentation bombs of the "pineapple" type were found in the courtyard of the hospital. They were full of copper particles. I picked up four unexploded bombs some 100 yards from the hospital.

At Vinh Linh, which I visited during the night of 11-12 February, 50 bombs had fallen in the enclosure of and directly on the secondary school. The buildings were destroyed, four children and one teacher were killed. I interviewed the mother of two of the children.

On 20 March, I paid a visit to Thanh Dong village, in Nghe An, situated in the central region of the country on the road to Laos. Thanh Dong was bombed on 19 March. On 20 March, a Saigon communique announced that a Viet Cong supply camp on the road from Nghe An leading into Laos had been destroyed. As a matter of fact, on the 24th, I was able to verify that what had been destroyed was a group of small regional factories: a sugar refinery, a flour mill, a distillery.

At the same time, I visited Quynh Tan village in the center of the Nghe An region. Quynh Tan is a Catholic village which had been bombed a few days prior to my visit. I was taken around by the religious leader of the village: three bombs had fallen around the church, causing concussion damage to the interior of the building. Many houses had been destroyed. The leader informed me that many families had been wiped out by bombs and machine-gun fire. Finally, in May 1965, in the course of my fourth visit to the bombed regions, I was able to verify that the main force of the raids was directed against the population, but that the population was showing unparalleled courage in resisting.

International Law and the Military Draft
testimony by Stanley Faulkner

Mr. Faulkner is a Noted U.S. Civil Rights Attorney

I will try to develop the points of international law with respect to what we heard this morning and yesterday regarding the commission of atrocities by the American forces in Vietnam. The question is whether war-crimes have been committed by the United States. This Tribunal will have to arrive at a conclusion as to whether such crimes were committed in the light of international law.

The *Law of Land Warfare*, a document issued by the U.S. Department of the Army, published in July, 1956, defines war-crimes in international law and the responsibility of individuals who participate in the commission of these war-crimes. They state: "Any person, whether a member of the armed forces or a civilian, who commits an act which constitutes a crime under international law is responsible therefore and liable to punishment. Such offences in connection with war comprise a) crimes against peace, b) crimes against humanity, and c) war crimes; The term "war crime" is the technical expression for a violation of the law of war by any person or persons, military or civilian. Every violation of the law of war is a war crime. Conspiracy, direct incitement, and attempts to commit, as well as complicity in the commission of crimes against peace, crimes against humanity, and war crimes are punishable."

The Hague Convention of 1907 forbids the use of arms, projectiles or materials calculated to cause unnecessary suffering. May I emphasize the words "unnecessary suffering" . . . The use of weapons which employ fire, such as tracer ammunition, flamethrowers, napalm, and other incendiary agents, against targets requiring their use is not violative of international law. They "should not, however, be employed in such a way as to cause unnecessary suffering to individuals." While the U.S. recognizes the use of napalm it is clearly provided that where the use of such weapons of war causes "unnecessary suffering" it is a violation of the laws of warfare. The U.S. is not a party to any treaty now in force which prohibits or restricts the use in warfare of toxic or non-toxic gases, of smoke or incendiary materials or of bacteriological warfare. There was a treaty entered into by the U.S. with other countries, prohibiting the use of poisonous gases and bacteria, but the U.S. Senate never ratified this treaty. [1]

The Hague Convention of 1907 further provides that bombardment or attack on towns, villages, dwellings, or buildings which are undefended is prohibited. Even when in or near military targets — bombardments or attacks must not be out of proportion to the military advantage to be gained. The officer in command of an attacking force must, before commencing a bombardment, except in cases of assault, do all in his power to warn the authorities. There are buildings that must be spared in bombardments, such as religious institutions, historical monuments, hospitals, and places where the sick and wounded are collected.

In view of the Hague Convention of 1907 and the Geneva Conventions of 1949, which outlaws and prohibits atrocities upon others, we have experienced in the U.S. many instances where individuals who have been called into military service have said that they will not participate in the commission, either directly or indirectly, of such acts. They base the defense or position upon the fact that to do so would make them individually responsible. They say that the doctrine of individual responsibility is such that even if done on the orders of a superior officer, to commit such atrocities would make them liable for a violation of international law.

The doctrine of individual responsibility under international law dates back many, many years. Hugo Grotius, probably the founder of international law, wrote in 1645, that an individual's responsibility is always present under international law. This was affirmed very concretely during Nuremberg. There, individuals claimed that they were acting under orders of superior officers and could not therefore be held responsible. We are familiar with many of the defenses raised by the defendants in the Nuremberg Trials. Probably the one that comes closest in our period would be the trial of Adolph Eichmann. When he stood before the court in Israel, he claimed that he could not be held personally responsible because he carried out the orders of a superior. This defense was not allowed and he was found guilty. The individual U.S. soldier who will not go to Vietnam to participate in these atrocities has found himself

---

[1] According to testimony in this volume (see recall questioning by Dr. Gabriel Kolko) this is not so. The U.S. is bound by such legal treaties.

in a dilemma. I would like to read to you statements made by three soldiers who are commonly known in the United States, and probably throughout the world as the "Fort Hood Three," the name given to them because they were stationed at Ford Hood, Texas when they received orders to go to Vietnam:

"We are all of the same opinion: that should we receive orders to go to Vietnam, we would definitely take a stand and refuse to go. Our reasons were that the war was illegal and immoral. We feel this is a war of aggression, because the United States has committed troops to Vietnam without a declaration of war. It has bombed a country with which we are not at war. We could not bring ourselves to do something contrary to our beliefs and involve ourselves in something which we would consider criminal."

They were court-martialed and sentenced to 3 years in prison.

Another soldier tried on the 13th of November 1967, in California, Ronald Lockman, said the same thing. He was court-martialed and sentenced to two and one-half years in prison.

What are their defenses and to what extent are they permitted to use them in courts-martial and before the courts of the United States? The defenses in these cases are the U.S. Constitution and the fact that treaties under our Constitution are the supreme law of the land. This is set forth clearly and explicitly. The defense refers to treaties that the United States has entered into, such as the Kellogg-Briand Pact which, although we have experienced wars since 1928, is nevertheless considered in international law as still binding and existing. In the Kellogg-Briand Pact it is provided that "the high contracting parties solemnly declare in the names of the respective peoples that they condemn recourse to war for the solution of international controversies and renounce it as an instrument of national policy in relations with one another. Defenses also refer to chapters: 1 & 7, art. 2, subdiv. 4 and art. 39 respectively, of the Charter of the United Nations: "All members shall refrain in their international relations from the threat or use of force against the territorial integrity or political independence of any State or in any other manner inconsistent with the purpose of the United Nations." And further: "That the Security Council shall determine the existence of any threat to the peace, breach of the peace, or act of aggression, and shall make recommendations or shall decide what measures shall be taken to maintain or restore international peace and security."

Many interpose as a defense the Nuremberg Judgment, always referred to in law as the London Pact. This is very interesting, because in the London Pact it was provided that a soldier shall be guilty of war crimes if he is involved in crimes against peace, crimes against humanity, or war crimes. The interesting aspect is that the exact language in the London Pact has been incorporated into the U.S. military manual the *Law of Land Warfare*. I referred to what constitutes crimes under international law as contained in the *Law of Land-Warfare*, and you will recall that the exact language, "crimes against peace, crimes against humanity, and war crimes," are contained therein.

The next document used in defense of draft resisters is the Southeast Asia Treaty Organization, commonly called SEATO. This, too, provides that, where there is a conflict between the obligations of the members of the United Nations under the present charter and their obligations under any other international agreement, their obligations under the Charter of the United Nations shall prevail, and only the Security Council can first determine whether a member of the United Nations shall participate in a war. In other words, before the United States can enter into an obligation under SEATO, the Security Council must first rule that this is proper. Needless to say, none of this has been accomplished and the U.S., as a member of SEATO, carries on the war in Vietnam without the sanction of the U.N.

Under the *Law of Land Warfare* there need not be a declaration of war for its provisions to apply. As everyone knows, the U.S. has never made a declaration of war against Vietnam. Congress has never exercised that power which it, and it alone, has to declare war. I will now refer to the recent opinions of two United States Supreme Court Justices that were handed down as recently as November 6, 1967. In the context of these international treaties the individual soldier, when he raises such questions, is told that these are political issues and not juridical issues, and therefore, neither the courts-martial nor the courts are prepared to take jurisdiction. In the case of the "Fort Hood-Three", as well as in the Lockman case, we were prohibited from introducing any evidence regarding atrocities that have been committed in Vietnam. We have been prohibited from bringing forward witnesses, who could testify on their own observations, to what has been happening; both what they have seen and what they have experienced. I might add, that with the assistance of the deliberations of this Tribunal, in the most recent case, that of Ron Lockman, I was able to establish, in great detail, by mentioning names and addresses, the persons in Vietnam who were victims of atrocities. Needless to say, we were again prohibited from bringing these facts forward. The Supreme Court of the United States, in the dissenting opinion of Mr. Justice Potter Stewart in the Fort-Hood Case, stated that these questions are of the utmost importance.

94

1) Is the present United States' military activity in Vietnam a war within the meaning of Article I, sec. 8, clause 11 of the Constitution? And, if so, may the Executive, that is the President, constitutionally order the petitioners to participate in that military activity when no war has been declared by Congress?

2) Of what relevance are the present treaty obligations of the U.S.?

3) Of what relevance is the joint Congressional Tonkin-Bay Resolution of August, 10th, 1964?

4) Do the present U.S. military operations fall within the terms of the joint resolution?

5) If the joint resolution purports to give the Chief Executive authority to commit United States forces to armed conflict, limited in scope only by his own absolute discretion, is the resolution a constitutionally impermissible delegation of all or parts of Congress' power to declare war?

Justice Stewart went on to say: "These are large and deeply troubling questions. We cannot make these problems go away by simply refusing to hear the case of three obscure army Privates. I think the court should squarely face them and set this case for argument."

And Mr. Justice Douglas, in his dissent, held that Congress was intended to play a more active role in the initiation and conduct of war. The above has been espoused by Senator Fulbright, quoting Thomas Jefferson, who said, "We have already given in example one effectual check to the dog of war, by transferring the power of letting him loose from the Executive to the Legislative body, from those who are to spend to those who are to pay. We, in the United States, a constitutional form of government, feel that we are a country of laws and not of men, and when the framers of our constitution decided on a tripartite-system, we were very careful in limiting the powers of our President and also setting forth the powers of the legislature and also the judiciary. Over the course of history, we have tried to be very protective to these. We are a nation which struggled for our own independence, we knew the problems that other nations faced when the kings took nations into wars, and we did not want a similar thing to happen to a new nation that was being formed and so we were very, very careful in limiting powers, and especially of taking the country into a war."

In the trials of war criminals before the Nuremberg Military Tribunal of 1950, war was defined as implementation of political policy by means of violence. Police actions, armed reprisals, limited war and total war are nonetheless wars. They are merely different aspects of a familiar technique in inter-state relations which has never ceased to change since states first started using it.

The actions of the United States in Vietnam constitute a war within the concept defined by the authority Sir Arnold McNeil. They were first, a declaration of war by one party. And second, if there were no declaration, then a state of war would exist if the nation against which force is applied treats such acts of force as an act of war. The Geneva Conventions also applied to undeclared wars. Our own *Law of Land Warfare* indicates that treaties become applicable and operative even where there is no declared war. And when I refer to a declared war, I refer to a war declared by the only power in the United States that possesses this authority, namely, Congress. The President has indicated that authority for his action in Vietnam may be inferred or extracted from the Tonkin Bay Joint Resolution of 6th and 7th of August 1964. This resolution is of dubious constitutionality. It is at least arguable that it represents an effort by Congress to delegate to the President the power to declare war, a power which Article one I, Section 8, Clause II of the U.S. Constitution entrusts solely to Congress. I referred before to the statement of Justice Potter Stewart in which he raised the question of whether to declare war was an impermissable delegation of power by Congress to the President. The Tonkin Bay Resolution is, while broad in language, at most an ultimatum, if that. It, and I quote, "Approves and supports the determination of the President as Commander-in-Chief to take all necessary measures to repel any armed attack against the forces of the United States and prevent further aggression." It goes on to express the view that the maintenance of international peace and security in Southeast Asia is vital to the interests of the United States and declares the readiness of the United States to take all necessary steps, including the use of armed force, to assist any member or protocol SEATO State to defend its freedom. The resolution, however, provides that all such steps shall be consonant with the Constitution of the United States and the Charter of the United Nations and in accordance with its obligations under the Southeast Asian Collective Defense Treaty. I repeat: consonant with the Constitution, the Charter of the United Nations and SEATO.

I hope I have been able to convey up to this point, that our conduct in Vietnam is not consonant with the Charter of the United Nations, nor is it consonant with our Constitution nor is it consonant with SEATO. There is a firm line of court decisions in our country that subsequent acts of Congress must be construed so as to be consistent with the obligations of pre-existing treaties where-ever such prior construction is possible. Repudiation of a prior treaty can only be inferred when absolutely incompatible. This, because it must be presumed that the United States intends to abide by all its treaty obligations with good faith and fairness. The Tonkin Bay Resolution, by its very terms, states that it must be consonant with these treaties. Our constitutional system is wisely one of checks and balances. The doctrine of separation of powers is fundamental and is one of the great structural principles of the American constitutional system. Nothing in our Constitution is plainer than that a declaration of war must be entrusted to Congress. The decision to place the responsibility of declaring war exclusively in Congress was deliberated by the framers of our Constitution. It has been interpreted that their intent had as its motivation that the history of nations in which this power was vested in the ruler was not to be repeated in this new government. This power to declare war was of such concern that it was not left to the Senate alone. The framers therefore provided that the House of Representatives, larger and more representative of the people, should also decide the question. The power of the President is not an unlimited one, and in the area of war, limits of his power are clearly enunciated in the Constitution and defined by the courts. It was the opinion of Mr. Justice Jackson of the Supreme Court of the United States in 1952 who stated that "with all its defects, delays and inconveniences, men have discovered no technique for long preserving free government except that the Executive be under the law and that the law be made by parliamentary deliberations."

The events following the passage of the Tonkin Bay Resolution caused Congress to reconsider what it had done. Had Congress abdicated its sole constitutional power to declare war? Had the President, as Chief Executive, assumed by this legislation a right exclusively within the legislature? Had the United States violated international law, making its war conduct in Vietnam illegal? These very important questions of law have begun to trouble not only the U.S. Congress, but also many contemporary authorities on international law. I refer specifically to an analysis of the legality of the United States military involvement compiled by the Consultative Council of the Lawyer's Committee on American Policy in Vietnam, the chairmen of which are Richard A. Falk and Albert G. Millbank, Professor of International Law and Practice, Princeton University. In the United States Senate, hearings were held before the Committee of Foreign Relations. Senator J.W. Fulbright, Chairman, in the opening statement on 16th August 1967 said, "I am deeply concerned with the constitutional question to be considered in these hearings. The fact that the war in Vietnam is related to the constitutional problem does not mean that the latter is merely a facade for expressing opposition to the war. It means only that this war that I oppose so deeply and events connected with it, such as the adoption of the Tonkin Bay Resolution of 1964, and other events, such as the Dominican Intervention of 1965, have aroused in me an awareness of constitutional problems that I properly should have had before but in fact did not. I have another predilection that I wish to make clear at the outset. I believe that a marked constitutional imbalance between the Executive, the President and the Congress in matters of foreign policy has developed in the last 25 years as a result of which the Executive has received unrestricted power to commit the United States abroad politically and militarily". A witness before the committee was Professor Ruhl J. Bartlett, Professor of Diplomatic History, Fletcher School of Law and Diplomacy, Tufts University. It was his opinion that there was no "constitutional basis for the assumption that substantive powers were conferred on the President as the Executive, and thus the President has no authority as Commander-in-Chief to replace the authority of Congress to declare war or to determine the use of armed forces, or that he has the authority to define and execute treaties any way he desires". He testified further critically of the Secretary of State by stating as follows: "The Secretary of State has said that the U.S. is acting under the authority of the SEATO treaty in Vietnam, but the SEATO treaty under any sharp interpretation does not confer upon the President the power to use the U.S. army to implement the treaty. This is an exaggeration of the interpretation of the treaty."

The impact of the dissenting opinions of Mr. Justices Stewart and Douglas have been felt and exhibited throughout the U.S. when they raised these serious questions of whether we are violating treaties, whether we are engaged in a war which *is a war* although undeclared by Congress. This was further shown in an editorial in the *N.Y. Times* on November 14, 1967, "No one really expected that case no. 401 on the appellate docket for the July 1967 term of the U.S. Supreme Court would legally hold army draftees from going to Vietnam any more than the questions raised by the Senate Foreign Relations Committee have changed the doubtful justification contained in the 1964 Gulf of Tonkin Resolution into a formal declaration of war by Congress. Yet the purpose of the case has been served: to the legislative debate has now been added judicial questioning. Although the appeal to hear the arguments of the three soldiers was denied, the dissenting opinion of Justices Potter Stewart and William O. Douglas are significant. Their effect is to raise new constitutional questions that require steady examination and, under another set of circumstances, future justiciable findings. Justice

Potter Stewart, a stickler for constitutional tradition and court precedent reiterated Jefferson's statement about the power to declare war ... "We have already given in example one effectual check to the dog of war by transferring the power of declaring war from the Executive to the Legislative body from those who are to spend to those who are to pay." Thus he declared that questions of great magnitude exist in this case. If Vietnam is a war within the constitutional meaning, if indeed men may probably be sent there without a congressional declaration of war, if the Gulf of Tonkin Resolution is relevant, if the Chief Executive will use the armed forces at his own "absolute discretion," the court will not now decide these questions. But the country must continue to raise them if the war is not to be waged indiscriminately. That is the value of case no. 401.

As Justice Potter Stewart wrote: "We cannot make these problems go away".

The situation regarding the opposition to the war in the U.S. that interests me most, is the opposition exhibited by the young people. We heard some of this from Mr. Carl Oglesby, a member of your Tribunal. Today there are thousands of young people who are burning their registration papers, an act of dissent which Congress in hastily drawn legislation, has made a criminal offense. They are returning draft cards which by reason of nonpossession constitutes a criminal offense. These young men have refused to respond to induction; they have refused to go to Vietnam after they are already in the military — saying they will not board transportation to Vietnam. Many have deserted from the military for the same reasons. There have been numerous campus demonstrations by the young people against recruitment upon the campuses and against the Dow Chemical Company which is recruiting young people. The demonstrations against Dow Chemical are, of course, self-evident. Dow Chemical is the largest manufacturer of napalm. Reports which I have indicate that there are 8 to 10,000 American youths who have emigrated to Canada to avoid military service. There is an unknown number of others in various countries who are seeking asylum and refuge from having to engage in this unholy war. The material which I have submitted to you this morning is gathered from reliable sources. I would be glad to submit to the Tribunal the sections of the Hague Convention and the sections of the *Law of Land Warfare* which I have referred to, to justify these arguments which I have presented before many courts-martial and also before the courts.

I would like to bring to your attention one thing before closing, and that is a provision of the *Law of Land Warfare* which is directly concerned with the functions of this Tribunal and justifies its existence. Chapter 8, Section 495 states: "In the event of violation of the law of war, the injured party may legally resort to remedial action of the following types: a) publication of the facts with a view to influencing public opinion against the offending belligerent".

On Treatment of Prisoners; Defense Brief for Draft Resistors Argued in U. S. Courts

The United States' active participation in the war has made it a party to the torture of prisoners and acquiescence by others committed in the presence of United States military personnel. Professor Greenspan in his treatise *The Modern Law of Land Warfare* states the law: "In accordance with the general principles of criminal law regarding complicity, the accomplice is accountable for crimes committed in furtherance of the common purpose, even though he himself did not commit the actual crimes" (469). *The Dachau Concentration Camp Trial* (Trial of Weiss, et al.) (1945) U.S. Gen. Mil. Govmt. Ct., L.R.T. W.C., XI, 12-16 is authority for the proposition that where "a common design to violate the laws and usages of war is established, everybody taking part in the common design is guilty of war crime, though the nature and extent of the participation may vary" (469).

Under Article 17 of the Geneva Convention on Prisoners, a prisoner of war need only give his name, rank, date of birth and serial number and that "no physical or mental torture nor any other form of coercion may be inflicted on prisoners of war to secure from them information of any kind whatever."

Eyewitness reports include the following instances of torture of Viet Cong prisoners: "bamboo slivers run under their fingernails or wires from field telephone connected to arms, nipples, or testicles" (*Newsweek* correspondent William Touhy, *New York Times Magazine,* Nov. 28, 1965); dunking men head first into water tanks or slicing them up with knives" (Chief correspondent, *London Sunday Mirror,* Donald Wise, April 4, 1965); "the 'ding-a-ling' method of interrogation involves connection of electrodes from this (US field) generator to the temples of the subject *** in case of women prisoners *** to the nipples" (Malcolm Browne, Pulitzer Prize winning A.P. reporter in *The New Face of War*); "cutting off the fingers, ears, fingernails or sexual organs *** One American installation has a Viet Cong ear preserved in alcohol" (Beverly Deepe, *Herald Tribune* Saigon correspondent, April 25, 1965); "they get a Viet Cong and make him hold out his hands against his cheeks, then they take this wire and run it right through the one hand and right through his cheek and into his mouth. *** Oh you ought to see how quiet them gooks sit in a helicopter when we got them wrapped up like that", a young U.S. Marine quoted by Jimmy Breslin, *New York Herald Tribune* correspondent, September 29, 1965.

Article 12 of the Geneva Convention on Prisoners requires a country to guarantee the treatment of prisoners it turns over to others.

Even before the Geneva Convention of 1949, United States war crimes tribunals had rules that torture and killing of prisoners of war is a war crime. *Trial of Yoshio Makizawa* (1946) U.S. Mil. Commission, Shanghai, L.R.T.W.C.XV, 101; releasing prisoners to the custody of others where they are likely to be killed was held to be a crime in *The Jaluit Atol Case* (Trial of Aeuberger) (1946) Br. Mil. Ct. Germany, *ibid.*, 81.

In the case of *In re Yamishita*, 327, U.S. 1 (1946), the United States Supreme Court held that Yamishita had violated the laws of war by failing to control his troops from committing brutalities against prisoners and civilians.

Article 13 of the Geneva Convention on Prisoners of War states that "measures of reprisal against prisoners of war are prohibited."

The continued bombings of North Vietnam by the United States causing death of civilians and destruction of non-military objects are acts to destroy persons and property protected by the laws of the United States through our treaty obligations. *The Belsen Trial* (Trial of Kramer, et al.) established the rule that "a systematic course of conduct" was sufficient to prove intent.

The Charter of the United Nations makes illegal the threat or use of force contrary to the purpose of the United Nations ---however, a non-member nation or a member nation which violates these provisions of the Charter commits a further breach of international law by commencing hostilities without a declaration of war or a conditional ultimatum as required by the foregoing articles of Hague Convention No. 111. Conversely, a state which resorts to war in violation of the Charter will not render its acts of aggression or breach of the peace any the less unlawful by formally declaring war.

Summary of a Juridical Report
by Samuel Rosenwein

An Attorney, Mr. Rosenwein Practices Law in the U. S.

In his report delivered to the International War Crimes Tribunal, Mr. Rosenwein stressed that he had come to express a personal opinion. Thus he was not speaking for any person or any organization. On the other hand, he stated, the viewpoints that he expressed had also been expressed by many eminent authorities in the field of International law in the U.S. and even by some elected officials of the American Government. Mr. Rosenwein regarded it a matter of civic and professional duty to point out that the U.S. is violating international law.

The speaker described the development of international law prior to the end of the 20th Century. Up to that time international law did not prohibit war, regarding it more as a disease. Generally, it was held to be the undisputed right of rulers to decide when to wage war. During the present century, however, there has been development towards the complete outlawing of war, culminating in the punishment of individuals for crimes against peace as at Nuremberg. This development is marked by such precedents as the Hague Conference of 1899, the Briand Treaties, the agreements that initiated and followed the forming of the League of Nations, the Locarno Treaty, and finally on Aug. 27, 1928, the very important Kellogg Briand Pact. Further, Mr. Rosenwein quoted the report of Mr. Justice Jackson, Prosecutor at the Nuremberg Trial. Referring to the legal basis of the Nuremberg Trial, the Prosecutor concluded: "We therefore propose to charge that a war of aggression is a crime against the international community . . . Thus may the forces of law be mobilized on the side of peace."

Mr. Rosenwein turned then to a study of the U.N. Charter and to an interpretation of its provisions. He stressed the importance of Art. 11, Sec. 4, the essence of which is to prohibit unilateral force in international relations. He also dealt with the question of the right of self-defense in the light of Art. 51 of Chapter 7 of the Charter. After this recital of the principles of International law, to which the U.S. in one way or another is committed, the speaker examined the real actions of the American Government and described the post World War II "containment policy" and the Truman Doctrine. Although the U.S. had agreed to a rule of law for peace-keeping through the U.N., the U.S. under the Doctrine, declared that it would be its own judge of how international legal obligations should be implemented and that it would by-pass the U.N. whenever it seemed that the latter could not adequately do a given job the U.S. believed should be done.

Turning thereafter to Vietnam, the speaker traced the most salient facts previously related by one of our historians, Mr. Kolko, and made an extensive summary of the Geneva Agreements of 1954 and of the U.S. Government declaration of its position on the Geneva matter. Citing the famous passage of the memoirs of former President Eisenhower — "I have never talked or corresponded with a person knowledgeable in Indochinese affairs who would not agree that had elections been held as of the time of the fighting, possibly 80% of the population would have voted for the Communist Ho Chi Minh as their leader rather than Chief of State Bao Dai." Mr. Rosenwein said: "The U.S. policy of containment ... could not abide such results and the consequence was inevitable ... abandonment of the rule of law and resort to naked force." The conclusion is that the U.S. has violated the principles of International law embodied in the U.N. Charter and the Nuremberg Judgment. The war now waged in Vietnam is an aggressive war, forbidden by international law. The war is also a violation of the principle of the self-determination of nations.

Finally, Mr. Rosenwein went on to examine from a legal point of view some arguments made by the State Department to justify the American intervention in Vietnam. According to the legal advisors of the State Department, the U.S. together with South Vietnam has the right under international law to participate in the collective defense of South Vietnam against armed attack. Further, the U.S. has undertaken commitments to assist South Vietnam in defending itself against Communist aggression from the North. Thirdly, the legal advisers of the State Department consider American actions justified under the Geneva Accords of 1954. The fourth major point is that the President has full authority to use U.S. forces in collective defense of Vietnam.

As a reply Mr. Rosenwein cited the major objections made by the Consultative Council of the Lawyers Committee on American

Policy toward Vietnam. The basic conclusion of the Consultative Council is: (1) The U.S. claim of acting in collective self-defense is contrary to the previously discussed Art. 51 of the U.N. Charter (2) The U.S. military intervention therefore also violates the fundamental prohibition of the use of force proclaimed in Art. 2-4 of the Charter. (3) The U.S. has refused for more than a decade to seek the settlement of international disputes by peaceful means, an obligation contained in Art 33-1. (4) The U.S. has refused to make proper use of the elaborate machinery created by the Geneva Accords for the purpose of preventing any improper developments in Vietnam. (5) The State Department contention that an armed attack by North Vietnam upon South Vietnam occurred before February 7, 1965, implies that the use of force by the U.S. in Vietnam during the four year period between 1961 and early 1965 was illegal. (6) The war actions started against North Vietnam in February, 1965 and formally declared by the U.S. to be reprisals, must be regarded as illegal reprisals under the rules of international law. (7) The U.S. abetted the breach of the central provision of the Geneva Accords of 1954 by South Vietnam, namely the obligation to hold nation-wide elections under international supervision looking toward the reunification of the Southern and Northern zones of Vietnam under a single government. (8) The fostering of a military build-up in Vietnam and the bringing of South Vietnam into a military alliance also constitutes contraventions of other provisions of the Geneva Accords. (9) So does the presence of large U.S. military units in South Vietnam and the introduction of military equipment. (10) Finally, the actual war actions are not authorized by the SEATO Treaty but in fact appear to be in violation of it.

Mr. Rosenwein concluded his report to the International War Crimes Tribunal with the following words: "A world of peace is my primary desire. A peace, however which I believe can never be established by the use of unbridled power and naked force, but only by adherence to the rule of law."

Juridical Report on Aggression in Vietnam
testimony by the Japanese Legal Committee

Our testimony concerns a new form of aggressive war. Peoples of former colonies have been achieving independence one after another. There has been an increased awakening to independence and a growing demand for betterment among the oppressed peoples of the world since the end of World War II. Because of this, imperialist and colonialist powers have found themselves unable to maintain colonial rule in its old form and have begun to develop new forms of colonialism. A resolution of the Organization of Solidarity of the Peoples of Asia and Africa, held in Bandung, stated that this new colonialism aims to "deprive the new emerging nations of the essence of real independence by means of indirect and subtle forms of domination in political, economic, social, military and technical spheres while nominally recognizing their political independence, constituting by this means a threat to those countries which have newly won or are winning independence." With this new form of rule the imperialist and colonial powers attempt 1) under the cloak of economic, military and technical aid, to dominate the economic, and military structures of the newly emerging nations, 2) to dominate these nations politically by raising and manipulating puppet governments, and 3) to incorporate these countries into military blocks and to set up military bases within them. Some of the techniques used by the imperialist and colonial powers to maintain rule are 1) the abuse of procedures of "recognition" toward a state or a government according to international law, 2) to suppress the will of the people by resorting to terrorism, intimidation and deceitful means or to utilize the results of elections obtained by such means, 3) to abuse the right to collective self-defense guaranteed by international law, and 4) to exert political and armed repression by means of governments and armed forces on genuine movements for national liberation. 5) and to resort to direct military ascendancy over such movements on the alleged "request" of puppet governments. Far from being inferior to the old colonialism, the new colonialist powers utilize to the maximum the achievements of modern science.

Though such new form of rule seems to have legitimacy, it is in fact complete colonial rule and wars carried on for such purposes are truly wars of aggression. These new means of domination are nothing but formal methods for evasion of law and run completely counter to the spirit of the law.

The policies and actions of the U.S. government and its armed forces are typical of this new colonial rule. The war being carried on by them in Vietnam is nothing but a war of aggression in the true sense of the word. It is from this viewpoint that we intend to examine the juridical basis for the struggle of independence of the Vietnamese people, together with the colonial rule and aggressive actions of the United States Government and its armed forces and by the French Government and its armed forces. By closely examining historical developments we shall show that the United States Government's actions do by legal definition constitute a war of aggression.

Legitimacy of the D.R.V. as the Sole State in Vietnam

The history of the national independence movement of the Vietnamese people, who achieved independence in the nationwide general insurrection, known as the "August Revolution" in 1945, is well known. On September 2nd the same year the independence of the Democratic Republic of Vietnam was declared. The first general elections of the National Assembly were held in all parts of North and South Vietnam on January 6, 1946. On March 3, 1946, the first session of the National Assembly was held. The Assembly's composition was based on the results of the general elections. At that first session Ho Chi Minh was elected President and Premier, thus bringing into being the legal Government. On March 6, 1946, the preliminary agreement on the cease-fire and the disposition of French Indo-China was concluded between this new Government and the French Government, which stated "France recognizes the Democratic Republic of Vietnam as a free nation constituting the Indo-China Union in the French Union having its own government, assembly, armed forces, and financial control." This preliminary agreement was also confirmed in the *modus vivendi* concluded on September 14th of the same year between the two governments. In November, 1946, the first Constitution of the Democratic Republic of Vietnam was established and provided that all parts of North and South Vietnam were to be included in the sphere of sovereign territory. Article I of that 1960 Constitution stipulates: "The territory of Vietnam is a single and inseparable whole from North to South".

Beginning of United States Aggression

Through the Marshall Plan the U.S. exerted great pressure on France and for this reason it was feasible for the United States to take over from the French colonialists after their defeat. The war gradually came to assume the character of an anti-Communist aggressive war as part of U.S. plans for containment in Asia.

In March, 1949, a nominal "State of Vietnam" was established with Bao Dai, who had once abdicated the throne, as head of state. Remaining within the framework of the French Union, this state allegedly recognized the independence and unity of Vietnam. But the government had no real power and had no basis for existence in the will of the people. This notwithstanding, the U.S. and other Western countries recognized this state in 1950. Particularly after the People's Republic of China was established in October of 1949, the U.S. began to strengthen its anti-Communist military network in Southeast Asia and concluded a mutual aid and defense treaty with France. Under terms of this treaty aircraft carriers of the U.S. Seventh Fleet anchored in the port of Saigon. After the People's Republic of China, Russia and other socialist countries recognized the Democratic Republic of Vietnam, on January 18, 1950, the other Western nations led by the U.S. hastened to recognize the Bao Dai regime, even though Bao Dai had been installed in direct violation of the terms of the cease fire agreements with the DRV.

It is generally acknowledged that the Ngo Dien Diem regime which replaced Bao Dai was a puppet regime maintained by the U.S. A document entitled *An Economic Survey of the Republic of Vietnam* published in November, 1961, by the Japanese Foreign Ministry reads in part: "Economic aid from the U.S.A. occupies the greatest part of all aid to Vietnam from different countries.

At present about 90% of total imports into Vietnam is covered by U.S. aid and its counterpart funds cover 50% of the national budget of Vietnam. With customs income from commodities imported by the U.S. aid fund added to the above, about 80% of the national income is dependent upon U.S. aid. ... On the other hand, war funds make up a great proportion of the annual expenditure: almost 40 to 50% of the total budget is war expenditure in each fiscal year. With other monies used for military purposes in other budget items and additional outgo added to this, it will be somewhere around 70% of the total budget."

It should be obvious that a regime which is dependent upon a foreign country for more than 80% of its national finance, and which is relying on a foreign country for the bulk of its war expenditure, lacks the autonomous and independent character which is a necessary requisite for recognition under international law.

The Geneva Agreements and the Legal Status of Vietnam

Article 1 of the "Agreement on the Cessation of Hostilities in Vietnam" which was concluded on July 20, 1954, between the Commander-in-Chief of the People's Army of Vietnam and the Commander-in-Chief of the French Union Forces in Indo-China, stipulates: "A provisional military demarcation line shall be fixed, on either side of which the forces of the two parties shall be regrouped after their withdrawal, the forces of the People's Army of Vietnam to the north of the line and the forces of the French Union to the south."

The parties concerned are quite clearly defined in this stipulation. With regard to "political and administrative measures in the two regrouping zones, on either side of the provisional military demarcation line," Article 14 makes those responsible for civil administration quite clear: "a) Pending the general elections which will bring about the unification of Vietnam, the conduct of civil administration in each regrouping zone shall be in the hands of the party whose forces are to be regrouped there in virtue of the present Agreement." That is to say, it is the French Union forces as far as South Vietnam is concerned. Item 6 of the "Final Declaration" issued at the same time by the great majority of the Geneva Conference powers declares: "The Conference recognizes that the essential purpose of the Agreement relating to Vietnam is to settle military questions with a view to ending hostilities and that the military demarcation line is provisional and should not in any way be interpreted as constituting a political or territorial boundary. ..." Item 7 of the same declaration reads: "The Conference declares that, so far as Vietnam is concerned, the settlement of political problems, is to be effected on the basis of respect for the principles of independence, unity and territorial integrity ... (and that) general elections shall be held in July 1956 ... Consultations will be held on this subject between the competent representative authorities of the two zones from 20 July 1955 onwards." This makes it quite clear that the demarcation line between south and north does not at all constitute a political or territorial boundary and that the north and the south of Vietnam are areas to be united peacefully by general elections to be held two years later. From these stipulations and the wordings of the declaration and from the process of their conclusions, it should be noted that the conclusion of this agreement had no effect whatsoever on the sovereignty and existence of the Democratic Republic of Vietnam. This state had already been effectively inaugurated to include all parts of South and North Vietnam. This Vietnam was provided with all functions and ability as a unitary state, and this agreement had provisionally imposed restrictions on the practice of sovereignty as far as the south was concerned.

Violation of the Geneva Agreements

One of the arguments most used as a pretext for armed intervention by the U.S. and its followers is that the Democratic Republic of Vietnam has violated the Geneva Agreements. If this major premise is proved false and groundless, the U.S. allegation must totally collapse and its war be exposed as a war of aggression. It is therefore very important for this Tribunal to lay bare facts regarding violations of the Geneva Agreements by the U.S. and its puppet regime.

Both sides have argued that the other party violated the Geneva Agreements as soon as the ink on the documents was dry. The Democratic Republic of Vietnam, which signed these agreements as the party concerned in the real sense of the word, and which won these agreements after nine years of war, has tried by all means to observe these agreements and achieve peaceful re-unification. Remember that it is the Democratic Republic of Vietnam that would gain the greater advantage from the observance of these agreements and suffer the greater disadvantages by their non-observance. In sharp contrast, the U.S. government, from the very beginning, was opposed to the Geneva Agreements. America's chief delegate, John Foster Dulles, hurriedly left Geneva; the U.S. delegation did not participate in the Final Declaration but merely issued a unilateral declaration and the delegation of the Saigon regime followed suit. Even while the Geneva Conference was still in session, the U.S. made desperate efforts in its preparations for the finalizing of the South East Asia Collective Defense Treaty and concluded this SEATO treaty only six weeks after the signing of the Geneva Agreements. In its protocol, the SEATO treaty designates the three countries or regions of Indo-China, including South Vietnam, as the country or region to which provisions of Article 4 on actions against aggression and on consultations are applicable. This in itself constitutes gross violation of the regulation of the Geneva Agreements prohibiting the inclusion of these territories in a military alliance. All these facts are generally known today and it is obvious that from the very beginning the U.S. had no intention of observing the Geneva Agreements. Take, for example, the unilateral statement made by U.S. representative Bedell Smith, in which the U.S. Government "takes note" of the Final Declaration by the participating countries, but in taking note, the U.S. specifically excludes item 13 of the Final Declaration, which is a very important provision for the implementation of the Agreements. Item 13 of the Final Declaration reads:

"The members of the Conference agree to consult one another on any question which may be referred to them by the International Supervisory Commission, in order to study such measures as may prove necessary to ensure that the Agreements on the cessation of hostilities in Cambodia, Laos and Vietnam are respected."

The fact that the U.S. specially excluded this Item stands as firm proof that the U.S. government had no intention of participating in or cooperating with consultations among the countries concerned with the implementation of the Geneva Agreements, and, indeed, had no enthusiasm for respecting the Agreements. It can be clearly pointed out that the puppet regime of South Vietnam completely sabotaged the observance and implementation of the Geneva Agreements and actively violated them, closely following the will of the U.S. Government.

Violation of the Provision for Implementation of General Elections

Here is a brief survey of the violations by the U.S. Government and its puppet regime in Saigon of the provisions of the Geneva Agreements regarding the implementation of the general elections and the prohibition of reprisals:

On June 6, more than one month before the obligatory date for consultation between North and South Vietnam which was fixed for July 20, 1955, by both the Geneva Agreements and the Final Declaration, the Democratic Republic of Vietnam declared as follows: "The Government of the Democratic Republic of Vietnam declares its readiness to hold the consultative conference with the competent representative authorities in South Vietnam from July 20, 1955 onwards in order to discuss the organization of free general elections throughout the country in July 1956."

But the Ngo Dien Diem Government in South Vietnam, knowing it had no significant popular support in the Vietnamese people, refused to cooperate in the holding of the stipulated general elections.

The late Prime Minister Nehru of India, Chairman of the International Commission for Supervision and Control, condemned the attitude of the Saigon regime in the following words on April 2, 1956:

"The South Vietnam Government has not accepted the obligations arising from that agreement because it says it never signed it. It is perfectly true it did not sign it. It was not an independent Government then. The French Government signed it and subsequently the South Vietnam Government became the successor State to the French Government. The South Vietnam Government gladly accepted al' the advantages accruing from the Geneva Agreement. It only objec to the obligations. ..."

The Democratic Republic of Vietnam lodged strong protests to this breach of the Accords by the Saigon regime and proposed on May 1, 1956, and on other occasions, to hold a consultative conference for the implementation of the united elections, but the U.S. Government and the puppet regime in Saigon continued to refuse these proposals. The foregoing constitute the most serious violations of the Geneva Agreements on the part of the U.S. Government and the puppet regime in Saigon.

Violation of Item "C" of Article 14 Calling for Refrainment from Reprisals and Guaranteeing Democratic Liberties

Item C of Article 14 of the Geneva Agreements requires that there shall be no reprisals against persons for their activities during the war and guarantees their democratic liberties. It states: "Each party undertakes to refrain from any reprisals or discrimination against persons or organizations on account of their activities during the hostilities and to guarantee their democratic liberties". But far from honoring this agreement, Ngo Dien Diem carried out a relentless persecution, not only of former Vietminh liberation fighters, but against all democratic forces without distinction. As a result of this persecution within a short time a great number of assassinations, woundings, detentions and tortures were brought to light. In addition to exposure of the events by the Democratic Republic of Vietnam, these facts were reported by an investigation team of the International Control Commission (ICC) which addressed itself to violations of Item C of Article 14, as well as other violations of the Geneva Accords. The ICC carried out a similar investigation in the territory of the DRV but in contrast, no cases of violation were reported. As ICC investigations proved to be disasterous to the U.S. and its puppet regime, the ICC began to experience obstructionism in its investigations. This is documented in a report dated April 11, 1957 from the ICC to the body's Co-Chairman:

"...Those difficulties have persisted and increased as the Commission has not received the necessary assistance and cooperation from the Government of the Republic of Vietnam and has, therefore, not been able to supervise the implementation of Article 14 (c) in accordance with the Geneva Agreements. In spite of the efforts of the Commission, replies were not received from the Government of the Republic of Vietnam in the majority of pending cases referred to it alleging reprisals and discrimination under Article 14 (c) and involving a large number of persons."

Violation of the Military Provisions

The Geneva Agreements and the Final Declaration stipulate prohibition of the introduction of additional troops, arms and ammunition into Vietnam. It also prohibits the establishment of military bases controlled by a foreign country or the setting up of new military bases. At a cabinet meeting on June 21, 1956, the Democratic Republic of Vietnam decided on the reduction of armed forces by 80,000 men, whereas, in South Vietnam the U.S. authorities which replaced the French Army, carried out arms expansion both openly and clandestinely on a large scale. Already at the time of the conclusion of the Geneva Agreements, 200 members of a U.S. military organ called the "Military Aid Advisory Group" (MAAG) were at work. Since this group was set up by the U.S. in the course of the first Indo-Chinese war, there was no reason for this group to continue its work. But the U.S. Government not only maintained it but also sent additional military personnel to South Vietnam, and also formed a number of new military organizations. As the introduction of military personnel and war material constituted violation of the Agreements, it was carried out by eluding the supervision of the ICC. Yet a considerable number of cases were detected and reported by the ICC. For example: 1) The Fifth Interim Report of the ICC (August 11, 1955 to December 10, 1955) states in part: "28 — The Saigon Fixed Team reported to the Commission that military aircraft including U.S. Navy planes were visiting the Saigon airport regularly. No advance notification of these movements was being received by the team ... 35. — Difficulties were also encountered about the control of the Saigon aircraft, as in August the Team's movements came to be restricted to the VIP stand and the parking area...." 2) The Sixth Interim Report of the ICC (December 11, 1955 to July 31, 1956) states in part: "... According to the reports received from some of the Teams, specially the Saigon Fixed Team, U.S. Naval and Military planes continued to enter and leave Vietnam without notification during the period under review. In a number of cases these planes were seen bringing in and taking out U.S. and Vietnamese military personnel. In the harbour, the Saigon Fixed Team noticed instances where war material was brought in without notifications. ..." 3) The Seventh Interim Report of the ICC (August 1, 1956 to April 30, 1957) states in part: "During the period under review the Commission, after examining Team reports, noted that many notifications from the Government of the Republic of Vietnam were received. Also complaints from the People's Army of Vietnam High Command concerning Articles 16 and 17, amounted to 96 cases which may violate Article 16 and 114 cases which may violate Article 17, in South Vietnam. The Government of the Republic of Vietnam did not, in all cases, give to the Commission advanced notification under Article 16 (f) and 17 (e) of the arrival of military personnel and war material respectively. The said Government did not ask for the Commission's approval, as required by Protocol 23, in any case concerning war material."

In addition to the foregoing violations, a U.S. military organ called the "Temporary Equipment Recovery Mission (TERM) was introduced into South Vietnam in 1955 without the approval of the ICC. 4) The Sixth Interim Report of the ICC states in part: "The Commission was informed that the members of TERM would start entering South Vietnam by the last week of May, 1956. The Commission informed the French Liaison Mission that the matter was under consideration and that pending the decision of the Commission, no entry should be effected. In spite of this, 290 United States military personnel belonging to TERM have been introduced into South Vietnam, thus facing the Commission with a *fait accompli*."

Whereas there were only six air bases in South Vietnam in 1954 at the time of the conclusion of the armistice agreement, the number of airfields had been increased to 57 toward the end of 1960, with naval bases considerably increased and expanded and military roads constructed in all directions. The armed forces of the puppet regime were also increased and strengthened to a great extent and the army, navy and air force.

In April, 1955, the U.S. sent a large number of law enforcement experts recruited and administered by the Mission of Michigan State University (MSUM) to South Vietnam. Although their function was said to be to train civil police for normal law enforcement work, in effect these "experts" trained a paramilitary force which was used as a repressive political army by Diem. The MSU Mission was essentially a device used by the U.S. to circumvent the prohibitions of the Geneva Accords against buildup of armed forces.

113

It is quite clear that all these actions by the U.S. Government and its armed forces constitute serious violations of the military provisions of the Geneva Agreements such as Article 16 (prohibiting the establishment of new military bases), and Article 19 (prohibiting the establishment of military bases under the control of a foreign country).

Formation of the South Vietnam National Front for Liberation

The U.S. Government and its puppet regime in Saigon used repressive measures to stop the general election for the unification of Vietnam, the most important provision laid down in the Geneva Agreements. This was done to suppress the aspiration for unification, the greatest hope of the Vietnamese people, and to forcibly continue the military, political and economic dominance of the U.S. in South Vietnam. Such a betrayal of the desire for unity, such terrorism and arrest, forcible detention, plus the increase and strengthening of U.S. military bases in South Vietnam, led broad sections of the Vietnamese people to form the South Vietnam National Front for Liberation. This is a united front to carry on the resistance struggle of the Vietnamese people in the cause of independence and unification of Vietnam and against interference with and infringement of freedom. It is in fact, a struggle in self-defense against external aggression.

Expansion of the U.S. War of Aggression

It is clear that the construction of U.S. military bases in South Vietnam, the building up and strengthening of the armed forces and police of the puppet regime, and the political and armed repression of the liberation movement are based on a U.S. policy of world hegemony. In particular on the U.S. policy of making Indo-China part of its anti-Communist military bulwark in Southeast Asia. For this same reason, the U.S. has, in addition, turned Thailand into a fortified military base, conducted armed intervention in Laos, and used pressure on Cambodia. It has set up military bases and stationed armed forces in South Korea with increased arms. It has permanently occupied Japanese territory on Okinawa and constructed nuclear and other bases there, in addition to a number of military bases on mainland Japan.

It becomes apparent upon a close examination of U.S. policy on a global and Asian scale, and especially upon examining the history of its military actions in Vietnam, that U.S. actions are not motivated for the defense of the independence of the Vietnamese, but exclusively for the benefit of U.S. interests. Both before and after the conclusion of the Geneva Agreements the U.S. military build-up in South Vietnam coincided with the commencement of aggression. The subsequent construction of military bases and the raising and strengthening of the puppet forces and police were preparations for the aggressive war which culminated in the assaults against the National Liberation Front.

In May of 1961, the U.S. government sent then Vice-President Lyndon B. Johnson to Saigon where he promised the Saigon regime drastically increased military aid. Since that time the U.S. forces have carried out the program of the "Staley-Taylor Plan" which called for "pacification," and the establishment of "Strategic Hamlets" and "New Life Hamlets." In February of 1962, the U.S. set up a Military Air Command in Saigon, expanded and increased their "advisors" and launched a series of large scale operations utilizing napalm, chemicals, planes, helicopters, and amphibious armored vehicles. As these operations met with the stiff resistance of the NLF fighters, the U.S. Government brought their own armed forces directly into the fight. They began the wholesale use of fragmentation and anti-personnel bombs and chemical weapons.

Meanwhile the strength of the National Liberation Front grew and the amount of territory under their control increased. Because of their military losses, the United States began bombing the Democratic Republic of Vietnam and manufactured a completely false incident to justify the escalation. It is now quite clear that the "Tonkin Gulf Incident" had been contrived to gain the assent of the American people and the cooperation of the United States Congress in the escalation which had been decided upon at the Honolulu Conference two months earlier. The immediate incident siezed upon as a pretext to justify bombing of the North was the NLF attack on the Pleiku Air Base on February 7, 1965. It is therefore clear to us that the resistance of the South Vietnam Front for National Liberation and the counterattacks by the Democratic Republic of Vietnam constitute a defensive armed action against aggressive war.

Conclusions

It is clear that U.S. policy and the war in Vietnam presently carried on by the U.S. represent a typical aggressive war. To hide the nature of its aggression the U.S. has used various methods of camouflage, such as establishing the puppet regime in South Vietnam and then ostensibly answering a request for assistance from that very regime. While itself totally violating the Geneva Agreements, it has accused the other side of violating them.

Here we see a typical example of the new form of colonialism, a colonialism more powerful than the older, more primitive, direct colonialism of the European nations. In judging the role of the United States in Vietnam one must not overlook the infringements of the peace, sovereignty, independence, right to unification and territorial integrity of the Vietnamese people which was guaranteed to them in the Geneva Agreements and the Final Declaration. Independence and peace are integral to the Geneva Accords and the U.S. has violated both of these. Seen in this light, merely to define the U.S. war of aggression in Vietnam as a crime against peace would be quite inadequate considering the present stage of development in international law. The fact that a number of Afro-Asian nations gained independence after the end of World War II makes it clear that a respect for national independence and the right to self-determination is universally approved. This finds expression in the provisions of the United Nations Charter. It reads in Article 1: "The purposes of the United Nations are: (1) to maintain international peace and security ... (2) to develop friendly relations among nations based on respect for the principle of equal rights and self-determination of peoples ..." And Article 2, item 4, reads: "All members shall refrain in their international relations from the threat or use of force against the territorial integrity or political independence of any state, or in any other manner inconsistent with the purposes of the United Nations."

Item 12 of the Final Declaration of the Geneva Conference in July 1954 states: "In their relations with Cambodia, Laos, and Vietnam, each member of the Geneva Conference undertakes to respect the sovereignty, the independence, the unity and the territorial integrity of the above-mentioned States, and to refrain from any interference in their internal affairs."

The Declaration on the Granting of Independence to Colonial Countries and People, adopted on December 14, 1960 at the U.N. General Assembly states in part:

(The General Assembly) ... Convinced that all peoples have an inalienable right to complete freedom, the exercise of their sovereignty and the integrity of their national territory, solemnly proclaims the necessity of bringing to a speedy and unconditional end colonialism in all its forms and manifestations; and to this end Declares that:

"1. The subjection of peoples to alien subjugation, domination and exploitation constitutes a denial of fundamental human rights, contrary to the Charter of the United Nations and is an impediment to the promotion of world peace and co-operation.

"2. All peoples have the right to self-determination; by virtue of that right they freely determine their political status and freely pursue economic, social and cultural development.

"3. Inadequacy of political, economic, social or educational preparedness should never serve as a pretext for delaying independence.

"4. All armed action or repressive measures of all kinds directed against dependent peoples shall cease in order to enable them to exercise peacefully and freely their right to complete independence, and the integrity of their national territory shall be respected.

"6. Any attempt aimed at the partial or total disruption of the national unity and the territorial integrity of a country is incompatible with the purposes and principles of the Charter of the United Nations.

"7. All States shall observe faithfully and strictly the provisions of the Charter of the United Nations, the Universal Declaration of Human Rights and the present Declaration on the basis of equality, non-interference in the internal affairs of all States, and respect for the sovereign rights of all peoples and their territorial integrity."

That is to say, in this declaration the independence, sovereignty, self-determination, unification, and territorial integrity of peoples are proclaimed as supreme rights, and its provisions are extended to the people even before they achieve their independence. It is also stated that peace can only be achieved by respect for these rights. "Peace" and a "crime against peace" should not be construed as applying only to peace between great powers and colonial powers nor Should "Peace" be construed as countenancing between these countries and their former colonies merely the *status quo*.

In the judgment of the International Military Tribunal for the Far East on Japanese war criminal which took place about the same time as the Nuremberg judgment, the wars waged against French Indo-China and Dutch Indo-China were condemned as crimes only against France and the Netherlands, which were colonial powers. The Japanese acts were not treated as an infringement of rights to independence and self-determination nor as, crimes committed against the colonized peoples who were the subjects of the war damage. We hold the view that judging the U.S. war of aggression at this present state, a war of aggression as described in the Nuremberg judgment, should be interpreted not only as constituting a crime against peace but also a crime against independence. In this connection, reference should be made to the following statement in the Nuremberg judgment, which states:

"The law of war is to be found not only in treaties, but in the customs and practices of states which gradually obtained universal recognition, and from the general principles of justice applied by jurists and practised by military courts. This law is not static, but by continual adaptation follows the needs of a changing world."[1]

The same judgment also states: "The charges in the indictment that the defendants planned and waged wars, are charges of the utmost gravity. War is essentially an evil thing. Its consequences are not confined to the belligerent states alone, but affect the whole world. To initiate a war of aggression, therefore, is not only an international crime, it is the supreme international crime, differing only from other war crimes in that it contains within itself the accumulated evil of the whole."[2]

*Report from Cambodia
testimony by Bernard Couret

Mr. Couret is a French Journalist

The events which are taking place in the vicinity of Cambodia are disquieting. Prince Sihanouk has openly warned both Cambodian and international public opinion of the threat hanging over his country. What is at stake is not only Cambodia and the example it sets for "strife-torn Asia," but also the possible expansion of the war in that part of the world.

The Cambodian Chief of State has been accused by the U.S. of "threatening the peace," of "playing the Communist game," and even — although his country is said to constitute a "threat to neighboring countries" — of being a "sanctuary of the Viet Cong and North Vietnamese regiments."

It is a well-known fact that Cambodia has never threatened anyone, but it has been proved that the Saigon Government, working

---

[1] International Military Tribunal of Nuremberg Judgment, Vol. XXII, pp. 463-464

[2] Ibid., p. 427

118

with the Americans, has for years been trying to overthrow the neutral regime established by Prince Sihanouk.

Although, up to the present, not one frontier violation by military materiel or by armed Cambodian units has been recorded, violations of Cambodian territory by land, sea and air recorded between 1 January 1961 and 21 December 1961 totalled 1, 608. In 1965, there were 621; in 1966, 1,332, and there were 1,395 at the end of October 1967. Those violations caused the death of more than 200 persons, approximately 400 wounded, and gave rise to the destruction of whole villages.

An intensive "psychological war" against Cambodia has been waged on an increasing scale since 1965. That date marks the beginning of a campaign designed to persuade international public opinion that Cambodia is not militarily and logistically neutral in the Vietnamese conflict and that it offers the protection of its territory to Vietnamese Regiments "operating in South Vietnam". The Saigon newspaper *Tu Do* was the first to speak of Viet Cong bases in Laos and Cambodia, on the borders of Vietnam.

Shortly thereafter, the same newspaper wrote: "Communist troops coming from North Vietnam are concentrated in Cambodia, where they are formed into units, trained and then put across the frontier." The article concluded by stating that the Saigon government had the right to "open offensive action against Cambodia and occupy its territory." Not to be outdone, the American Command claimed the right to "pursue the Viet Cong into Khmer territory if circumstances so require."

That policy statement brought a sharp protest from the Cambodian Government. Mr. Son Sann, who was then Vice President of the Council of Ministers, stated that: "The Royal Cambodian Government has on many occasions given proof of its complete neutrality in the Vietnamese conflict, as evidenced by the absence of foreign bases on its territory, and has renewed its determination firmly to repel foreign troops, of whatever nationality, seeking to violate its borders. That impartiality on the part of Cambodia, and its faithful implementation of the provisions of the Geneva Accords of 1954, have been unambiguously observed and have been noted many times by the International Control Commission for the Cease-Fire."

The statement of the Cambodian Government, along with the disapproval shown by some of the Great Powers, must have given American officials pause. On 6 January 1966, American and South

Vietnamese military spokesmen stated that their troops had been given the order not to violate the international frontier of Cambodia on any pretext, "even based on the right of pursuit." The events of past months have clearly shown that that declaration was buried long ago. On 6 November last, *The New York Times* once again referred to the presence of "Viet Cong forces" in order to state that, for that reason, it was impossible to guarantee the non-violation of the Cambodian frontier by American units. It is true that six months before, on 25 September 1967, the Commander-in-Chief of American forces in the Pacific, Admiral Sharp, had declared: "We have known for some time that various North Vietnamese regiments enter and leave South Vietnam through Cambodia, which they use as a sanctuary when they run into difficulties."

The U.S. Defense Department had denied statements made in May 1966 by General Stanley Lawson, former Commander of the American forces in the Central Region of South Vietnam, who estimated the strength of the North Vietnamese regiments massed along the South Vietnamese border in Cambodia to be around 12,000 men.

It is necessary only to travel along the eastern border of the kingdom to become aware of certain facts. The highway leading to Saigon ends at the frontier post of Bac Vet. Here we are 160 kilometers southeast of Phnom Penh and 80 kilometers from Saigon. Barbed-wire entanglements and South Vietnamese blockhouses bar the road. Across, on the other side, is the war. The jungle-covered mountains are continually being bombed by B-52's and "Skyraiders". Gigantic columns of black and white smoke rise up into the sky. The bombing runs seem to be endless. Over the course of several days — at Moc Bay, Soc Nok, Bathu, Chantrea (in Svay Rieng Province), at Phnom Dem (in Rampot Province), or at Lork, near the coast — we witnessed these intensive, daily bombing raids. "They are bombing us in order to destroy the crops," the captain commanding our escort party told me.

It all too often happens that these bombing raids "spill over" onto Cambodian territory. In some American circles it is said that the Cambodian frontier is "porous". It should be stated at the outset that the Cambodian frontier is not as "porous" as some would have us think. To cite one example. At the frontier post of Phnom Dem, fifteen minutes after our arrival, a reconnaissance plane bearing the United States star fired on us, using a telescopic gunsight. If our presence seemed to give rise to uneasiness on the part of the American and South Vietnam observers stationed a few hundred meters away from us, we are led to wonder how, in this area so rich in rice fields, the NLF troops are able to escape surveillance if they move from one country to another.

Some observers have stated that it was impossible to guard the whole of the frontier. It is more than 800 kilometers long, they say, and twisting, badly marked, contested in some areas; it goes through the rice paddies, swamps, mountains and through the jungle. An operation would require, according to those observers, dozens of helicopters and permanent guard-posts at official cross-points.

The Cambodian Government has refuted the U. S. argument which, it says, is used only as a pretext by those who are planning to escalate the war into Cambodia. It is true that the Cambodian border, like all borders, is not laid out in a straight line. But its exact position is known by both sides.

And yet, the objection is made that the American and South Vietnamese pilots can make mistakes and confuse a Vietnamese village with a Cambodian village. That hardly seems possible. In Cambodia, the villages are built up on stilts and cover large areas, since land is not at a premium, whereas in Vietnam, they are built crowded together in order to free the largest possible area for rice cultivation. If the bombed villages were those in the provinces of Kratie, Mondolkiri or Rantanakiri, regions which are covered with impenetrable jungle, an "error" might be allowed. But in the southern provinces it is impossible to make such an error. The explanation is geographical.

Cambodia is rich in sugar palm trees. Indeed, it is the only country in Southeast Asia in which such trees are found. And it has another special characteristic: the closer one comes to the South Vietnamese border, the rarer the sugar palm trees. Between them and the jungle-infested mountains of South Vietnam stretches a zone of rice paddies, six or seven kilometers in width. Seen from the air, as I was able to verify, that strange demarcation line constitutes an unmistakable frontier. Once the rice zone has been crossed, you are in the territory of the neighboring country, no matter from which direction you come.

It should be evident that the guerrillas — the "best in the world", according to the Americans — would hardly venture into such unprotected regions, thus exposing themselves without hope of being able to retaliate, to the machine guns of the "Skyraiders" which fly overhead constantly.

One must also bear in mind that the Cambodian Government has made great efforts to mark the frontier as precisely as possible. Many methods are used for this purpose, from long bamboo stalks in the rice paddies, bearing the national flag, which also fly from the sugar palm trees, to corrugated tin roofs painted with the Cambodian colors.

As for the people, they live in uncertainty. I saw this in the village of Bathu on the afternoon I was there, when the people fled into the paddies or into the bamboo thickets, or into individual fox-holes, at the slightest sound of airplane motors.

"You have to understand," the village Chief told me, as he anxiously watched the sky from the thicket in which we had sought refuge, "We have been bombed four times; people were killed, wounded, houses were destroyed, buffaloes killed, rice paddies rendered useless . . ."

Night had begun to fall as I arrived the next day at Chantrea, a village situated six kilometers from the frontier and which had been burnt down with napalm by South Vietnamese tanks late in 1964. Although that event was ancient history, relatively speaking, we were met by members of the home guard, rifles on their shoulders. One of them said to me: "Who can tell what tomorrow may bring?" Life has begun again in that martyred village. It has been rebuilt. New houses put up by the Government have risen on the outskirts. I spoke to Kien Pen, whose wife and two children had been killed by the planes. I heard many other tragic stories. I saw little Sourn, with her sad smile and her eyes full of anxiety. She had been marked for life by napalm. Her arms had been stiffened along the length of her body. Her back was ravaged with the scars left by napalm burns. It was a miracle she had survived. The Bonzes[1] of Phnom Den in Takea Province also told me of the horror of the war: "Today, our peaceful life is troubled. Death is always in the sky," one of them said to me.

Leaving the southern provinces, we went looking for the alleged "Command Post of the 325th North Vietnamese Division" in Ranatakiri Province, in the extreme northern protion of the country. This is a swampy region, covered for the most part by impenetrable jungle. Our small military plane landed at the airfield of Labansiek. It was a small strip in a clearing. Here, we were 42 kilometers from the South Vietnamese border and less than 100 kilometers from the Laotian frontier. Our Land-Rover took the only communications route in that part of the country, Highway No. 19 called the "Ho Chi Minh Trail" by some.

That "Highway" is in reality nothing but a long, deeply rutted, red-dirt road, snaking its way through the jungle. Giant bombax trees, vines of every sort, thorn-bushes, iron trees, many varieties of shrubbery — all this vegetation encroaches on the road, often forming a dark green vault overhead. Night and day seem to alternate as one moves along. It took us slightly more than two hours to cover those 42 kilometers. "During the rainy season, it takes a day," said Mr. Mau Sum, the Associate Governor of the Province, who had joined our escort party.

_____
[1] Buddhist Monks.

122

We passed through the village of Bokeo. At the frontier post at O Yadao, the road ends in a river; the bridge was blown up fifteen years ago during the Indochinese War. Previously, the road had gone through the Vietnamese highlands to Pleiku. We walked the remaining seven kilometers to the border. Having waded the river, we followed a narrow trail which twisted through thick jungle and led to a command post, known as an "alarm post", 800 meters from the frontier. Four Cambodian soldiers were keeping watch under difficult conditions. That is all that is left of the prolongation of Highway No. 19, which is being used — according to Saigon and Washington — for "resupplying Viet Cong bases and for the transport of North Vietnamese units in motor convoys."

It should be added that it is inconceivable how large groups of men could escape the attention of the police outposts to be found in each populated area. Furthermore, it is hardly conceivable that a division could be based in such a hostile environment, without means of communication; military maps show no road coming from Laos. Finally, the population, as I was able personally to observe, is unable to subsist without government assistance, which is aimed at alleviating the chronic rice shortage from which these regions suffer. To that, I should like to add the unsolicited testimony of a Lt. Sheerer, of the U.S. 4th Infantry Division, with whom I spoke in South Vietnam during my visit there in December of 1966, when I was serving as special correspondent for *Le Monde Diplomatique*.

I was near Duc Co, west of Pleiku, that is, almost directly opposite Highway No. 19 I asked him the following question: "Does the Ho Chi Minh Trail go across Cambodia?"

"I can't believe it does," he said. "Our helicopters flying over the area would have noticed the troop movements."

As for the "Sihanouk Road," it owes its existence to a *Time* correspondent. According to that weekly magazine, it begins in Siempang, in Stung Treng Province north of the village of the same name, crosses a portion of lower Laos, and comes out in the Vietnamese highlands north of Pleiku.

In light of the *Time* report, six military attaches — from France, Great Britain, Australia, the Philippines, Indonesia and Laos stationed at Phnom Penh, — went to Stung Treng province in the company of the then Minister for Information, Mr. Chea San. Upon their return, they denied the report.

I visited the region some time later. The "road" in question is in reality nothing but a forest path laid out by the former French administrators; it can be found in any good atlas and links the Cambodian province of Stung Treng with Attopen Province in Loas. It is passable only during the dry season, as I was able to see for myself.

Returning to Cambodia on the road after a rather lengthy stay in Laos, I stopped to question some Laotians about the "highway." The Laotian military authorities had heard of its existence through their American "advisers," but no one had seen any trucks carrying men and munitions, nor had anyone heard of any of the bombing of the "highway" — as had been reported by the *Time* correspondent.

In addition, it is hard to see how convoys travelling on that road could leave Cambodia, enter into areas under Laotian jurisdiction — that is, American jurisdiction — and then cross areas controlled by the neo-Lao Haksat forces, to finally come out north of Pleiku. Here, too, an examination of the map — even the map drawn up by the neo-Lao Haksat — shows the regions controlled by him (with which everyone, by and large, in Vientiane agrees,) thus weakening the confidence one should have in a "discovery" of this sort.

Finally, a Parisian weekly magazine pointed out at the time that it had in its archives photographs identical to those in *Time* magazine, also taken by an American photographer. "However," the Parisian magazine added, "at the time those photographs were taken, they were supposed to represent the Ho Chi Minh Trail. It is all too true that from Rangoon to Saigon, from Singapore to South China, all mountain trails look alike. Yet it is on the basis of 'proof' such as this that the escalation has been undertaken!"

Despite the investigations carried out by accredited military attaches at Phnom Penh and the "America Wants to Know" mission of May, 1966, *Newsweek* magazine, in its issue of 23 October 1967, once again took up the myth of the "Sihanouk Road."

Knowing as one does that *Newsweek* articles frequently reflect thinking in the Pentagon, and of those circles in America most committed to carrying the Vietnamese war to the other countries of the Indochinese peninsula, one may well wonder about the reasons for this sudden reopening of talk about the Road, especially since the article appeared at the time when escalation against North Vietnam was being intensified.

One may wonder even more, owing to the fact that *Newsweek* quotes the opinions of Americans in Vietiane, who believe that the "extension of the McNamara line to Laos will create great hardship for the North Vietnamese in getting across the line, perhaps as far west as Thailand." Does this mean that a part of Cambodian territory may be engulfed in an eventual extension of military operations carried over into the western regions? One must also take note of the following statements attributed to the Laotian Prime Minister, Prince Souvanna Phouma by *Newsweek:* "If the United States wants to put up an electric fence in the zone occupied by the Pathet Lao, we will be unable to stop them, since we do not control that area."

The Cambodian Chief of State, with whom I had had a lengthy conversation earlier that month, did not conceal his concern for the future. "International public opinion must be awakened to the threats hanging over my country," he told me. "It's a question of survival."

One has only to visit the port of Sihanoukville to be convinced of that threat. A port under process of development would not seem to be an ideal place for the training of 30,000 Chinese, nor an ideal supply base for armaments destined for the Viet Cong as alleged by the Americans. That this is ludicrous was also the conclusion reached by the members of the International Control Commission.

At the request of the Cambodian Government, on 7 December 1965, the members of the International Control Commission visited the port of Sihanoukville and the surrounding region and carefully inspected the docks and the cargoes of the 258 ships which passed through the port between 1 January 1964 and 14 December 1965. Upon its return to Phnom Penh, the Commission prepared its report and on 10 January 1966 it sent a letter to the Minister for Foreign Affairs which stated, *inter alia*, that "all cargoes arriving over the course of the past two years were addressed only to the Cambodian Ministry of Defense and were barely sufficient for the needs of that Ministry in the effective protection of Cambodian territory." The Commission stated that, as a result, "there were no supplies sent to the Viet Cong" and that it was "convinced that no military materiel intended for the Viet Cong passed through Sihanoukville." The letter added that the Commission "during its investigation, has found no proof of the presence of the Viet Cong in Sihanoukville or its environs," and concluded that the Cambodian Government has "continued to carry out its obligations under Articles 7 and 13 of the Geneva Accords."

In this regard, I might add that, among other foreign observers, my colleague Stanley Karnow of the *Washington Post* shared that opinion, having visited the port installations at Sihanoukville in April 1966, as well as Professor David Schoenbrun of Columbia University and Mr. Paul A. Johnson of the American Friends Service Committee, who came to similar conclusions after their visit to the port on 6 August 1967.

Reference to these reports is not without value, since the same untruths periodically reappear in the American press. The latest are to be found in two articles published in *U.S. News and World Report* on 28 September 1967, and the *Daily News* of 20 August 1967, respectively.

The Refugee Problem

Another little-known problem is worth looking into: that of the refugees. There are at present approximately 20,000 refugees. There is every reason to believe that that number will increase with the intensification of military operations in Vietnam.

The France-Press news agency, in a dispatch dated 7 March 1967, announced that "more than 1,000 Vietnamese, for the most part women, old people, and children, fleeing from the 'Junction City' operation, have taken refuge in Cambodia." They are put into three camps some distance from the frontier in the Minot district of Kampong Cham province. Others have arrived since . . ."

These people are victims of the insane Vietnamese situation. In Kampot province, Lam Sour, a 53 year old refugee, told me: "There were twenty of us when we left. When we got here, there were only ten." I saw an old man, Ta Tim, ninety years old, with horrible napalm burns. His companions had carried him on a stretcher for more than twenty kilometers. Further on, a woman told me that she had seen four Bonzes in her group machine-gunned by American planes.

I asked the refugees at Phnom Den why they had fled. Their reply was nearly always the same: daily bombing raids, defoliation, destruction of rice paddies. One of them, Chan Yen, who acted as interpreter for his group, told me how his village of 400 houses had been burnt down, including its pagoda.

As a general rule, the refugees set up camp near the frontiers; they do not want to go further, since they nourish the secret hope that one day they will be able to return to their farms to cultivate the rice paddies their ancestors have handed down to them over the centuries.

Still others come to Cambodian territory only for the night, in order to avoid search parties, as for example at Lork, which is a small village some distance from the sea. In the daytime, they return to the other side of the border to cultivate the fields and pray in the pagoda. An ever-increasing number of them, tired of that uncertain way of life, are accepting the offer the Cambodian Government has made of a house and newly cleared land, generally in the interior of the country.

There is yet another group of refugees: the Khmers-Loen and the Khmers from the highlands. These are mountain dwellers from the Mgnong and Stieng tribes. There are nearly 5,000 of them in the eastern part of the country in Mondolkiri Province alone. When I was there in November of 1966, a new group of 1,500 of them had just come from across the border at Dakpol.

I spoke to those from Daknam. They had left there because they had lived in an area where bombing was incessant, the highlands area at the center of the Indochinese peninsula. It would seem that new action is being undertaken against the mountain dwellers by the South Vietnamese government and the Americans, as part of their general war effort: the word "Genocide" is commonly used when speaking about infliction of such conditions of life upon a people. Some of them who have been forcibly deported to the lower plains areas, far from their mountains and their simple life, have died of despair; others have fled to Cambodia, where they have arrived with literally nothing.

I will not soon forget my visit to the huts set up in a small valley at the edge of the jungle. These are some tens of meters in length, the whole families of refugees are piled into them, lying on bamboo trestles on either side of the center aisles, which are lined with logs placed at regular intervals. The air is foetid. Their meagre kitchen utensils hang along the bamboo walls. The refugees told me of the horrors of the bombings; one evening, from one of these villages, I myself saw above the jungle the flashes of the dropped bombs. They lasted for an hour and a half. The refugees spoke of defoliation by chemicals, by the scattering of yellow and white powders which cause deathly sickness, as happened in the case of thirty-four Jarai inhabitants of a village in Ratanakiri, in the northernmost part of the country, whom I found writhing in convulsions when I visited the village for the second time in less than a year.

At Snoul in Kratie Province, I saw 200 refugees who had been tortured before they had fled: cigarette burns, the first joints of their fingers broken . . . the war had made them invalids for life. The children were frightened by the sight of a European, I was deeply upset by this. One of the leaders of the group told me: "Many of these people were in the hands of the Special Forces."

It is hard to know what can be done to help them. They live by hunting and gathering fruits, and cultivate the land by the "ray" method, which consists of burning the forest and planting mountain rice on the cleared areas.

The authorities in Mondolkiri Province, in particular the military, have endeavored to deal with the problem with as much humanity as possible, without going against the customs and ancestral life patterns of these mountain dwellers, who have ways of life strange to them, but rather with a brotherly welcome. Their assimilation implies, however, their learning new habits and the abandonment of their semi-nomadic way of life.

On Mondolkiri Province, with a Cambodian population of 14,000, there are today 6,000 refugees. The army is accomplishing the impossible, but that is not enough. Four or five "Colonization Centers" have been set up; the lack of basic equipment is sorely felt. During the rainy season, the time necessary for communication with the capital is three times as long. Elephants are used for transporting supplies to frontier outposts.

Finally, there is the problem of the Bonzes. Approximately 3,600 of them are refugees in Cambodia. Their exodus began in 1961. Many of them told me of their persecution by the Saigon authorities: their schools had been closed since 1961-1962, making Buddhist studies impossible; their Vietnamese identity papers had been taken from them; they had been forced to take their meal in the evenings — Bonzes eat only in the morning; they had been forced to bear arms and to parade before army units; some Bonzes had been defrocked and enlisted in the army by force; some had chosen to be beaten rather than wear a uniform. The exodus had become widespread since the bombing of pagodas began in 1964.

For these refugees, outcasts as the result of a hopeless situation which will prevail as long as the war lasts, the future will depend on the means given them by the international community. The aid given by the Cambodian government is of course infinitely precious. The most noteworthy attempts at regroupment have taken place in the less populous peripheral provinces, such as those near the Thailand border. Temporary buildings have been constructed in those regions by the provincial government. Trails are being cut in the valley which will facilitate the development of cotton and tea plantations. The success of those "Colonization Centers" depends to a large extent on the solution of the refugees' problems. The Centers will give an alternative to those refugees who live close to the border in the faint hope of returning home to their own country. In order to bring this effort to fruition, however, considerable funds are needed.

It is in this context that the campaign undertaken by the Royal Government must be regarded, aimed as it is at arriving at a real international guarantee of the present Cambodian frontiers. Twenty-eight countries already support Cambodia's legitimate demands by adding, whenever mention is made of Cambodian territorial integrity, the words "within its present frontiers:"

128

This means — with Thailand, as set forth in international treaties and confirmed by the International Court of Justice at the Hague in 1962; — with South Vietnam and Laos, following the boundaries marking the territories effectively administered by Cambodia since the 1954 Geneva Accords.

This implies the recognition of Khmer sovereignty over the Preah Vihear Temple, the jurisdiction of which — despite the decision by the International Court of Justice at the Hague — is disputed by Thailand, and the rejection of Saigon's control over the Cambodian coastal islands. Finally, and more generally, there should be a condemnation of any attempt to annex so much as the smallest particle of Cambodian territory. In short, the frontier status quo should be maintained. Nothing could be more clear, no position could be more legitimate, notwithstanding attempts at encroachment.

As a recent example, we might cite the bombardment of Thlok Trach and environs. At this frontier outpost, situated in Kompong Cham Province, members of the International Control Commission and the diplomatic corps were caught in the fire from American planes. The State Department defended that action by declaring that those two groups were on . . . South Vietnamese territory. They presented as proof the best maps they could find. A careful examination of those maps, including those drawn up by American Army cartographers at the time they were still working with the Cambodian armed forces, shows that they were drawn up with the clear intention of including as much Cambodian territory as possible within the borders of South Vietnam. Comparison between the American maps drawn to a 1/250 scale and those (also American) drawn to a 1/500,000 scale, reveals that Cambodia lost a strip of territory some 2.5 kilometers wide. A future edition will doubtless evidence a further advance. For its part, the International Control Commission, after long investigation based on maps drawn up by the French administration in 1929 and reprinted in 1953, concluded that the village of Thlok Trach was really Cambodian.

Report from Cambodia and North Vietnam
by Tariq Ali

Mr. Ali is a Journalist from Pakistan

We spent the first few days in Phnom Penh, the capital of Cambodia, speaking to Government leaders . . . Then we went to Svay Rieng where, after meeting with the provincial Governor, we were taken to the border at Bave — this is the border with South Vietnam. It was interesting to see that in Bave there was a deliberate attempt on the part of the South Vietnamese puppet border guards to create an incident with the Cambodian officers accompanying us. At one stage, when a Cambodian photographer tried to photograph the border, the South Vietnamese puppet officers came to our side of the border with pistols cocked and threatened military action unless the film was handed back to them. Fortunately an incident was prevented only by the tact displayed by the Cambodian officers on the Cambodian side of the border.

We were told that there was a Special Forces camp just across the border and that the Americans flew in with helicopters, strafed Cambodian villages, and then took away villagers for interrogation. In the village of Soc Noc I spoke to a villager named Muy Tith, 29 years old, who had been captured by the United States Special Forces. He told me that he was tortured and beaten by the South Vietnamese Special Forces and also by the Americans, who then asked him whether there were any Vietcong in his village. As the man could not speak any Vietnamese, he kept saying, "No, no, no!" until finally, after tying him up for two hours and beating him consistently, they released him and let him go back to his village. We were also told that others had not been so lucky, and while we were in the village of Soc Noc there were twelve villagers who had not been returned: no one knew what had happened to them.

We visited the village of Ba Thou which had been attacked seven times since 1957. The last attack had been on June 16, 1962. The village had been visited by the International Control Commission, but no tangible results had been achieved. Napalm had been used against this particular village. We met and spoke to a napalm victim, a 10-year-old girl. We saw photographs of the bombing. We saw villagers whose relatives had been killed. There was no doubt in our minds that this was an absolutely deliberate attack on a Cambodian village.

There had been another attack on Ba Thou in October, 1965, and we spoke to some of the victims. We were told by Nguyen Thi Be, 64 years old, that he had lost his two sons: Le Van Tan, 34, and Le Van Dan, 32. We also spoke to Le Thi Dam, 45. She told us that her husband had been wounded in the village, that she had lost a 12-year-old son and that her 14-year-old son had been wounded. Nguyen Van Tron, 24 years old, told us his father Dang Van Cu, 58, had been killed, and his wife, Nguyen Thi Hiem, 58, had also been killed. The list was incredibly long, and it would have taken us hours if we had stayed there and taken every name down. It was clear that the village had been attacked, that its citizens had been terrorised and killed, and that some of its citizens had been taken away for interrogation.

The attack on the village of Chan Trea, which was seven kilometers from the frontier, was even more recent. The village had been attacked on December 22, 1966. We were told by the villagers that amphibious tanks had come in, had destroyed a military post, and had tried to capture the village; but a persistent defense by the frontier guards drove them back. All in all, we were told that ten amphibious tanks and sixteen helicopters had tried to take over the village. Fortunately for this particular village, the Cambodian defences had proved too strong. We met a 22-year-old woman named Tranh Thi Binh, who told us that she, with her family, had been in a shelter when the tanks came to the outskirts of the village. She was chased out, and when she ran she was followed by South Vietnamese troops, who then stabbed and shot her in the back. We saw the wounds caused by the knives and by the bullets and also photographs showing the injuries when they had been more recent. We were also told that there had been cases of rape in the outlying villages when the South Vietnamese troops came in.

After we had seen the villages which had been bombed by the United States, after we had seen the destruction which had been caused by these attacks, and after we had met the victims of these attacks, we went back to Phnom Penh. After two days of talks with officials there, we went on the so-called Sihanouk and Ho Chi Minh Trails, which were long journeys. It was absolutely clear to us from the trails we visited that it would have been impossible for any large force, whether it belonged to the National Liberation Front of South Vietnam or whether, as the United States claimed, it belonged to North Vietnamese divisions, to use those trails. It was

131

impossible for any heavy trucks to go on those trails, and further on the river could not be bridged. We saw the area where the United States said that there was an airport which landed North Vietnamese and N.L.F. battalions when they were coming back or going to the South. It was very clear to us that this was in a clearing, but the rough nature of the ground and the fact that there had been bushes growing on it for over the last two years, would have made it impossible for any plane to land. We also saw near the site of the so-called airport a lot of diamond mining going on, and they had large bamboo sticks sticking up into the sky, which the United States claimed were antennae for an underground radio station.

In any event, there was no doubt in our minds that both the Sihanouk and the Ho Chi Minh Trails could not be used by the North Vietnamese and National Liberation Front Forces, and that the United States was merely using this as an excuse to bomb and strafe Cambodian border villages. This becomes increasingly significant when one learns that at the recent conference in Guam, it was suggested to President Johnson by Westmoreland and other military leaders that two Cambodian provinces be occupied and the war extended to Cambodia to stop the infiltration of North Vietnamese troops. In Cambodia we found (and any other investigation teams that go to Cambodia will find the same) that there was no evidence whatsoever that there had been infiltration by the North Vietnamese forces.

The second investigating team of the International War Crimes Tribunal then went on to North Vietnam. One half of the team, consisting of Dr. Gustavo Tolentino and Lawrence Daly, went to the North; whereas myself, Carol Brightman, an American journalist, and Dr. Abraham Behar, of the Paris Faculty of Medicine, went South. The first group went northwest of Hanoi to Bhu Tho, Vinh Phuc and Bac Thi provinces; while the other group went south to Thanh Hoa and Ninh Binh provinces. The second phase took the whole team to Haiphong and Quang Ninh, where we investigated the evidence of United States war crimes and the total destruction of the mining villages of Ha Tu and Cam Pha, and of Bai Chay sea resort . . . .

We visited Ninh Binh province and spoke to the Roman Catholics there and saw for ourselves the churches which had been bombed. The churches were mainly isolated, with a couple of mud huts next to them. There was absolutely no doubt at all that they were being bombed deliberately. The Roman Catholic leaders we met told us that this was being done to intimidate the Catholic population because the United States belived that it would be easier to break the morale of the Roman Catholics.

But the most traumatic experience was in the province of Thanh Hoa. It was January 29, 1967 . . .We were told that at 2:30 p.m. that afternoon we would be taken to the hospital in Thanh Hoa to meet and interview some of the victims of the' air raids. But the same day, while we were having lunch, we heard the planes roaring overhead and making their way towards the town. Then we heard the bombing and the thuds which have become a feature of life in North Vietnam today. We were told that the trip was off. A major said that they were bombing Thanh Hoa, and however much we pleaded that we wanted to see and experience with the North Vietnamese population the horrors of the bombing, they were adamant.'

At 4:00 p.m. we visited the hospital, the first place on our itinerary. This was the hospital where we should have been at 2:30. At 3:00 p.m. it had been bombed and some of the patients killed. While they were being removed from the hospital and taken to the first-aid station, there was another attack and the first-aid station had been completely destroyed. Incendiary bombs had been used and some houses were still burning. When we visited Thanh Hoa, it was on fire. There were embers and flames everywhere. We saw a large crater caused by an American rocket. Anti-personnel weapons had been used.

Mrs. Nguyen Thi Dinh had rushed out of her house just in time to save herself, but she saw her house and its contents burned to the ground. When I spoke to her, she was weeping silently. She said, "Do you think I will ever forgive them for what they are doing to us? Never! Never! They must be made to pay for their crimes."

Two hundred homes had been damaged or destroyed, and one hundred and twenty-five families were homeless.

Mr. Dang Ba Tao, the local Red Cross organizer and a member of the Democratic Party, had been burned to death. Miss Ho Thi Oanh had been killed a few weeks before her marriage to a young Army officer. We saw her trousseau, her wedding invitations, and a letter from her fiance. . .A hospital with Red Cross markings and a first-aid station had been singled out and destroyed. If the shelters provided by the authorities had not been so effective, the casualties would no doubt have been higher. Half of Thanh Hoa had been evacuated in advance as well, and this too was fortunate. I looked around for anything which could conceivably have been a military target in the town itself. There was no sign of any military object.

The part of the province which had been bombed almost without respite was Dinh Gia district, at its southern extremity. The bombing was so heavy that no one had been taken there before for fear of casualties. We travelled there during the night, crossed a few bridges, and reached Dinh Gia safely. The next day was the most depressing day I spent in Vietnam. I saw bombed school and hospitals. They had been direct hits. There could be no doubt whatsoever that this was deliberate. In the village of Hai Nan, a coastal village not far from the Seventh Fleet, almost every house had been destroyed. The attack which had destroyed the village had taken place four days earlier. The destruction was obviously fresh.

I spoke to Nguyen Thi Tuyen, a 12-year-old girl who had lost a leg. She told me her story in the following words:

"I had just returned from school and was about to have a bath when the aircraft came from the direction of the sea. They dived down and dropped lots of bombs. I grabbed my younger brother and rushed to the shelter, but it was too late. A bomb fragment hit my brother in the stomach and killed him. Another fragment cut my leg off, as you can see for yourself. Our house was burned down. My uncle could not put the flames out in time. Now I live with some relatives. Will you please tell me why they are bombing us? . . ."

This was the story in almost every village I visited. These were no military targets, and the United States could not but be aware of this fact. The schools in the district had been dispersed to avoid casualties. Some of them were in shelters. Hospitals had been dispersed. Hospitals which had been bombed previously were now under the ground. At this stage I think it is fair to point out that the Vietnamese doctors are the most impressive group of people I have met anywhere. They are dedicated, and they have seen more suffering than anyone else, but it has not effected their morale in the least.

Just before I was about to leave, a young woman aged 23 came up to me. Her name was Nguyen Thi Hien. She said she wanted to tell me something about her misery, and she spoke in the following way:

"My 4-year-old son and 24-year-old husband were killed in the last attack. My toes were cut off. I was three months pregnant when I was wounded. I hate Americans. I really hate them! How can you expect me to forgive them? We don't kill their women or destroy their cities, but they come and destroy us. If they come to bomb us again, I will hate them even more. There will be more bitterness and more hatred. What else can I do? If necessary, I will wait for my 2-year old son to grow up and then will send him to avenge his father."

At this stage she broke down completely and wept.

On the same day (January 29, 1967) that they bombed the hospital in Thanh Hoa, they had also bombed a dyke in the province. This too I went and saw. There were over fifteen large bomb craters on the Quang Yen dyke. The engineer told me that if they had bombed it during the flood season, over six thousand people would have died. As it was, they have to build a new dyke before the river floods. The two villages near the dyke had been bombed as well. Houses had been destroyed, and in the case of one village the casualty figures were the largest in the province. Fifty-three people had been killed. Of these, forty-two were women and children.

This was the story in the southern provinces of Ninh Binh and Thanh Hoa. The first things which had been hit were schools and hospitals. In the city of Phat Diem, rows and rows of housing estates had been demolished. Hospitals were destroyed, schools bombed; and it was not difficult to see why the United States was doing this. Its first purpose was to make the Government of Ho Chi Minh unpopular. Their second purpose was to intimidate the civilian population.

We noted that when general purpose bombs and incendiary rockets are dropped on a village or town, they are often followed immediately by the steel pellet bombs which do not harm steel or concrete but only maim and kill the civilians rushing to each other's aid or rushing to the shelters . . .

The interviewee was Bonze[1] Superior, Kan-Kang, formerly Chief
Bonze of a pagoda at (Chum)[2] Kaul (Khum) Vinh Trung, (Srok)
Svay Tong, (Khet) Moat-Chrouk — in Vietnamese Chau Doc and
more recently Chau Phu. The interpreter was His Excellency the
Governor of the province of Takeo. The interviews took place on
September 11, 1967.

Q. *Can you give details of the suppression, by the U.S.-South-Vietnamese
authorities, of the culture, customs and traditions of the Khmer[3] minority
of South-Vietnam?*

A. Yes. They have closed all the Khmer schools, they have forbidden
the population to learn the Khmer language. For example the school
at (Khum) Vinh Trung and also the one at (Srok) Svay Tong.

I know from my contacts with those of my fellow-countrymen who
have fled that the Saigon government has closed all the Khmer
schools. Wherever there are Khmers they have forbidden the population to learn their language. At Vinh Trung and Svay Tong for
example the Khmers form the majority of the population.

The same situation exists everywhere in the province of Moat-
Chrouk. This policy began to be applied from 1960-61 onwards.
The suppression of the Khmer culture has become more and more
rigorous all the time and is increasing even today.

In the schools the children have been forced to learn the Vietnamese language. All the Khmers have been forced to change their
names. People were summoned to the District Office and there they
had to choose Vietnamese names which were written up in the district registers.

---

[1] Buddhist monk.
[2] Both old and new names are given.
[3] Khmers are an ethnic minority group in Vietnam. They are of Cambodian
origin, but live throughout most countries of Indo-China.

Many pagodas have been destroyed, for example at Trapeang Chouk, (Khum) Le Try, (Srok) Svay Tong. Completely destroyed, but dozens of others too. The Bonzes are forbidden to recite prayers. They can only read them from printed texts.

Q. *When did you arrive here and why did you leave your village?*

A. At the beginning of the year 1961, the U.S.-Saigon forces surrounded the pagoda where I was Chief Bonze. The Charek pagoda. they arrested all the Bonzes and the congregation there; they bound their hands and carried them away. Fortunately, I was not there. I had been invited to ceremonies in another village. The authorities interrogated the Bonzes to find out where the Chief Bonze was. They explained that I was absent. They forced the other Bonzes and members of the congregation to come with them to find me. On the way the American-Saigonese forces killed two of the members — the others fled with their hands still tied.

Q. *Why did they want to arrest you?*

A. They accused me of having relations with the Viet Cong.

Q. *Was this true?*

A. I am a man of religion and look after religious affairs.

Q. *Was the pagoda damaged?*

A. Yes. They pounded it with artillery before surrounding it. Afterwards they broke a lot of things and stole kitchen utensils, cooking-pots, etc.

Q. *Are there other Bonzes who have fled because of the suppression of the religion?*

A. Yes. More than seven hundred.

WITNESS

Chau Uon, 55 years old, from the hamlet of (Chum) Sla Dom, villate (Khum) Ang Tuk, District (Srok) Svay Tong.

Q. *Why did you come here, and when?*

A. I came in 1966, to live in peace, to have a little tranquility. The planes came and bombed our village and raked it with machinegun fire. Everything was destroyed, burnt. I fled with my wife. She was killed. I was wounded in my eye by a bomb fragment. (His left eye was destroyed, and there was a large swelling on the left side of the eye.)

Q. *When did you arrive?*

A. At the end of December, 1966.

Q. *Was there much damage in the village?*

A. It was completely destroyed.

Q. *How many dead and wounded?*

A. Thousands, mainly old people, women and children.

Q. *Why was the village bombed?*

A. Because they want to exterminate the Khmer.

Q. *Were you warned before the bombing? Were tracts dropped to warn you?*

A. No. There was no warning.

Q. *When did the attack begin?*

A. It began early in the morning and continued nearly all day.

Q. *Were the Khmer schools in your village?*

A. They were closed a long time ago. There are only Vietnamese schools.

Q. *Besides your wife, were there other relatives of yours who were killed?*

A. My daughter and a nephew were killed.

WITNESS

A woman, Thun, 52 years, from Tuk Chup hamlet, village of Ang Tuk, Svay Tong district.

Q. *When did you come here and why?*

A. I came four months ago. My village was bombarded and raked with machinegun fire several times. We are forbidden to go out and work. The buffalo were stolen. In the last bombing, all the houses in the village were destroyed. Also the two pagodas. It was this bombing that made me decide to leave. There were many killed and wounded. Out of one family — the husband was called Prim and his wife Chun — only one child out of the four stayed alive. All the rest killed. In another family, the father came home only to find small pieces of his family. (She apologized for not being able to remember the names.)

Q. *Were there shelters?*

A. Yes, there were. We tried to go into the shelters when the planes came, but they bombed precisely the shelters and people were buried alive in the shelters themselves.

Q. *Did you see planes dropping powder in the region?*

A. Yes, they dropped bags (she described what looked like a bag of cement) full of white powder. The effect was suffocating. Then

138

they dropped containers of petrol after that, napalm. The bags of powder fell on the roofs of the houses. We did not dare to touch this powder, we suspected it was poisoned.

WITNESS

Chau Hong, 50 years old, from Kiang Duang hamlet, Svay Vong village, Svay Tong district.

Q. *When did you come and why?*

A. I came two days ago. There were a lot of people in my village because all the villages around had been bombed and the people fled to our village. Five days ago the Americans came and attacked our village. They bombed with artillery and planes. Many people were killed, and also buffalo and other animals.

Q. *Did they drop tracts to warn you?*

A. Yes. They dropped tracts, but in Vietnamese. I cannot read Vietnamese.

Q. *What do you think — why was your village bombed?*

A. It is their policy of extermination against our people.

Q. *Have the Khmer schools in your village been shut too?*

A. Yes, a long time ago. It is forbidden to study the Khmer language or to listen to radio programs in the Khmer language.

Q. *Did they try to make you change your religion?*

A. Yes, they wanted us to become Catholics.

During our inquiry, there were about a hundred refugees who followed the inquiry with great interest. Afterwards we asked them to stand, according to their village, and tell us whether the situation in their village was similar to what the Bonze and the other witnesses had described. They affirmed unanimously that these descriptions applied exactly to their villages too. Schools suppressed everywhere, forbidden to speak the Khmer language, obligatory changing of names, villages and pagodas destroyed, etc. . . . The list of villages has been given to the Tribunal.

*Mr. Burchett is a Well-Known Journalist,
Author and Specialist on Southeast Asia*

I have been visiting Cambodia regularly since 1955 and have lived there since September, 1965. I would like first to state that I accompanied the teams of the International Control Commission on their investigations of many of the incidents of which Commandant Kouroudeth has spoken and found the facts exactly as he described. So did the members of the ICC teams either unanimously or in majority.

I would also like to refer to one aspect of the testimony of Madame Rena Cukier-Kahn, relating to the investigation of the Buddhist bonze-superior Thich Kan-Kang, of the Kaul Pagoda, Vinh Trung Village, Svay Tong (now Tinh Bien) district of Moat Chrouk Province.

I interviewed this same bonze in March, 1962, a few days after he arrived in Cambodia. In fact his testimony then was used in the opening pages of my book: *The Furtive War*, published in New York in 1963. At that time I could not use his name or that of the village for fear of reprisals. But the village has been visited since with many reprisals. I would like to quote what he then told me, not only as confirming the evidence given by Mme Cukier-Kahn, but to take the case further and show that this was persecution within a persecution, a case of genocide in particular within the case of genocide in general. Thich Kan-Kang was a victim of "Operation Sunrise" the first big U.S. attempt to herd peasants into "strategic hamlets".

I quote from page 13 of the first chapter of *The Furtive War:*

The next I spoke to was a Buddhist bonze, a dignified figure in his yellow robes, with a sensitive, intelligent face.

"Our people are being massacred right and left," he said. "Peaceful villages are being uprooted; rice fields and orchards destroyed; the people herded behind barbed wire — their pigs and poultry pillaged by Diem's troops. The peasantry is forced to live under the guns of Diem's military posts."

I asked why he had fled.

"I was chief bonze at our pagoda," he said, "and some months ago, I was arrested and accused of having 'ideas' and 'contacts' with the 'Viet Cong'. I was released but warned that if I were arrested again, I would be killed. About a week ago, Diem's militia came to the pagoda to arrest me. I was not there, but they told the other bonzes that unless 15,000 piastres were produced immediately, I would be arrested as soon as I turned up. Of course the pagoda could not raise such a sum. The commander ordered his troops to start firing into the village. They killed two people and everyone fled into the forest. Then the Diemists burned down the village."

"Did you have contact with the 'Viet Cong'?" I asked.

"Who are the 'Viet Cong'?" he replied and then added with great dignity: "I will reply to you as I replied to the Diemist militia a few months ago. Those whom they call the 'Viet Cong' are our own people. Some of them have been forced to take to the jungle to defend themselves. Such people have come to our village at night to get food. They pay for what they take — not like the Diemists who loot and kill. If they come to the pagoda — yes, I will talk to them. That is my duty.

"That there exists what are called 'Viet Cong' is due to the crimes of the Diemists. Although the villages where we come from are 90 percent Khmer, we are forbidden to use our own tongue. Our schools have all been closed — even the Pali language school at Tra Vinh. The Diemists try and force us to change our names. With the slaughter of our people, the destruction of our villages, the repression of our language and culture, it seems our people are to be exterminated . . ."

These are the words of Thich Kan-Kang while the memory of events was fresh in his mind. Genocide was already being committed against the Khmer minority in South Vietnam. Since then, he had elected to stay in Phnom Den, where Mme Cukier-Kahn interviewed him, to give comfort to his compatriots and co-religionists who continued to escape across the frontier with each fresh wave of repression.

Over the years, this included several hundred bonzes. He was in an excellent position to know what was going on over the other side of the frontier. The evidence he gave to Mme Cukier-Kahn, unanimously confirmed by refugees from 17 other Khmer or Khmer-Vietnamese villages, proved that a policy of genocide was still being applied and had been intensified.

141

I would like also to refer to the incident at the village of Chrak Kranh, occupied by U.S. troops between February 24 and March 3, 1967. This typically Khmer village, was occupied, as the Americans tried to seal off the Cambodian border in the preliminary stages of Operation "Junction City" — although it was clearly on the Cambodian side of the border. I visited it on March 5, long before the International Commission did.

Fortunately, because of the noise made by U.S. tanks crunching along the jungle tracks, also because of artillery fire against the village, the whole population was able to get away with what livestock and belongings they could take with them. Over two hundred 105 mm shells were fired into the fields surrounding the village — they were pockmarked with craters when I arrived. Fifty three of these shells had failed to explode and had been stacked in a deep pit by the local people, together with some rockets fired from planes, which had also not exploded.

Leaving aside the question as to whether the Americans had made another of their famous "mistakes in map-reading" and really thought they were in a South Vietnamese Khmer minority village, there was one most striking fact. Every house was destroyed before they pulled out; every buffalo, pig and chicken that had remained were killed, fruit trees cut down. Incendiary grenades had been thrown into every building, as they left, including the little school, the public health clinic and pagoda. Not a single building was spared. It was clear the destruction was not caused by some "accidental" bombing, each house was individually burned, with squares and rectangles of rubble and ashes quite clear from each other. All farm implements and kitchen utensils, ploughs, harrows, enamel bowls etc. were destroyed. Chrak Kranh in fact was an example of the "kill all, burn all, destroy all" tactics which have become standard operating procedure for U.S. forces in South Vietnam.

In my earlier visits to Cambodia, especially in 1955-56, it was obvious that outrageous economic, political and military pressures were being exerted on Cambodia to force her to abandon neutrality. Immediately after the Geneva Conference and in violation of it, the Southeast Asia Treaty Organisation was formed and Cambodia, Laos and South Vietnam were placed under its "protection". But in an interview he granted me in late 1955, the Cambodian Head of State, Prince Norodom Sihanouk said that not only had Cambodia never been consulted about this but he very vigorously rejected any such "protection". Shortly after this declaration, which attracted much attention, South Vietnamese and Thai troops were massed along Cambodia's borders; their planes daily violated Cambodia's air space and Cambodian leaders warned that a "Guatemala-type" situation was developing. To give point to this, the U.S. ambassador who had engineered the Guatemala affair, Mr. John Peurifoy, was transferred to Bangkok.

The grossest form of pressures were exerted on Prince Sihanouk. Invited to the Philippines, he was presented with a ready-made speech, handwritten on U.S. embassy paper, which he was asked to make "to please his Philippine hosts" in which, in effect, he was asked to say that Cambodia was about to enter SEATO. Naturally the Prince wrote his own speech in which he vigorously denounced any such idea. His host, the Philippine President did not even see him off at the airfield on his trip home.

At that time, and for some years to come, Cambodia was receiving U.S. military "aid". But when Saigon troops occupied an area deep inside Cambodian territory and Sihanouk prepared to throw them out. U.S. military advisers backed by the U.S. Embassy in Phnom Penh, refused to permit U.S. — supplied arms or trucks to transport troops to be used "against a friendly (to the USA) power." They could only be used against "Communist aggression". Not against the only two countries which really threatened Cambodia. And it was pointed out that American aid would immediately be cut if Cambodia accepted arms from any other country. Military "aid" — U.S. style — in fact meant that Cambodia was tied hand and foot, helpless against her traditional enemies, who were showing every sign of attacking her.

Later on a consignment of weapons for plotters in one of the many U.S. — backed coups against Sihanouk were found in cases arriving at Phnom Penh as "diplomatic courier" for the U.S. Embassy. U.S. military attaches were linked with the plotters.

In 1963, Sihanouk halted U.S. military aid and expelled U.S. military "advisers". He also halted U.S. economic aid and finally, in 1965, he severed the country's diplomatic relations with the USA, after innumerable U.S.-Saigon violations of Cambodia's frontiers, involving the killing and wounding of inumerable peasants from the frontier villages. Till this day Washington has refused to guarantee to respect Cambodia's territorial integrity within the limits of its present frontiers.

By vigorously and courageously defending Cambodia's independence and the neutrality which is an essential part of that independence, Sihanouk has rendered great service to the peoples of Indochina and Southeast Asia in general. He has consistently supported the struggle of South Vietnam's people, under the NLF and has recognised the latter as the sole, authentic representative of the South Vietnamese people. From the first days, he has energetically raised his voice against U.S. bombing of North Vietnam and has several times proposed solutions to the Vietnamese problem based on an American withdrawal and leaving the Vietnamese people to settle their own affairs.

These are the reasons for the constant U.S. threats to extend the war to Cambodia; the fostering and arming of traitor groups in Thailand; the endless lies about "Ho Chi Minh" and "Sihanouk" trails, "Vietcong bases and sanctuaries", "North Vietnamese divisions" etc. on Cambodian soil. I have searched for evidence of this, in vain, so also has one of the members of the Tribunal, Mr. Dave Dellinger, so also has one of the key witnesses to the Tribunal, Mr. Donald Duncan. The only evidence of foreign interference along Cambodia's borders is that by the United States and its satellites in Thailand and Saigon.

Questioning of a Khmer Mercenary

The following is a report to the Tribunal by one of its investigative teams, which on September 11, 1967 questioned a soldier at the Phnom Parh[?] base in Takeo province, Cambodia, where he had arrived the previous day.

Cambodian officials introduced him as a Khmer soldier from the American-South Vietnamese army who had given himself up with his weapons to the Cambodian authorities. He was middle-aged, with the physical characteristics of the Khmer ethnic group (dark skinned) and was wearing camouflage uniform. On his cap there was a badge showing two wings. He was carrying a Colt AR-15 5.56 mm. automatic rifle equipped with a 40 mm. grenade thrower plus ammunition — registration number of rifle: 134 053. He spoke neither French nor English. We questioned him with the assistance of the governor of the region of Takeo, who acted as our interpreter.

What is your name?
Muong Ponn.

How old are you?
Thirty-nine.

How long have you been in the army?
I have been in the army for nineteen years. At first I was in an infantry battalion of the French Army of the Far East. When the French left they handed me over to the South Vietnamese government. I have been in the intervention forces since 1957. I am a master sargeant.

What was your last unit?
I was in a helicopter unit, known as the "MY" or "Mail Force," stationed to the north of Saigon.

What are the functions of this unit?
It has to carry out "mopping-up" operations in the villages.

How many men are in the unit? Who is its commanding officer?
There are five hundred men — Koreans, Chinese and Khmers. The commanding officer is an American.

So there are no Vietnamese in it?
No, there are none.

Who are the Chinese you mentioned?
They speak Vietnamese. I think they are Chinese from South Vietnam who support Taiwan. There are 180 of them.

What was the unit doing in the region?
It was taking part in an operation to rescue five Americans who were thought to be prisoners on a nearby hill.

Why have you come to Cambodia?
I was disgusted with the massacres of Khmer villages and the Khmer population in villages we had to "mop up."

What is meant by "mopping up"?
We were dropped by helicopters, we fired at everything and killed everyone.

Had orders been given to [do] that?
Yes.

Who gave the orders?
The Americans.

Can you describe a recent operation against a Khmer village?

Yes, On 12th April of this year we took part in an operation against a village, at Phum Oc Yum. First of all the F-105's bombed it. Then we were dropped by parachute. There was a terrible massacre, mostly women and children. There were only a few men, apart from the very old ones. Our instructions were to shoot at everything that moved.

Did Americans take part?

Yes. The commanding officer in charge of the operation was an American, Major Marchand (or Marchett).

What kind of village was it?

It was almost entirely Khmer. It was after this operation that I decided to leave.

Can you tell me other cases of this kind?

There was an operation on My Da [My Tho —?] village in the province [environs —?] of Moc Hoa. Sixty people were killed, nearly all of them women and children. It was a mixed village of Vietnamese and Khmers. We had been given orders to wipe out the whole village. There were practically only women and children. They were the only ones to stay. I was disgusted.

(The Khmer officer from the 2nd Bureau later added that the man had told him that a group of women and children had been lined up and the American officer gave the order to fire. The Khmer soldiers refused and it was the Americans who did the shooting.)

Have you used gas grenades in these villages in the course of operations?
No.

Were there other operations of the same kind against villages?
Yes.

Were there other Khmer soldiers in your unit?
Yes, many.

What was your pay?

Eight thousand nine hundred Vietnamese dongs[1] a month, plus combat rations.

Did you have other reasons for coming to Cambodia?

Yes, I have had enough of being a soldier. I want to have a quiet life. The Americans despised us. We had to salute them whatever their grade. They isolated us. When we returned from an operation we had to stay within barracks. We wouldn't have any contacts with civilians.

---

[1]Popular word for piastres; the sum is not entirely clear in the text and might be "eight to nine hundred." Piastres are quoted at $.0085 in New York City.

Is that all?

No, I couldn't bear to kill my own people, the Khmers. Fortunately, the present operation took us close to the Cambodian border. (At one moment we were transported in a hydroglider.) Then there is the fact that I'm a Buddhist. They refused to let me practice my religion. I had to hide this (he pulled out of his jacket a fairly bulky statuette which he was wearing round his neck on a ribbon). I couldn't go on accepting that.

F. Kahn, W. Burchett, R. Pic and Mme Cukier-Kahn

Extracts from the Summary Report on the Bombing
of the Civil Population in the North
testimony by Abraham Behar, M.D.

Assistant at the Faculty of Medicine of Paris,
Member of the Second Commission of Inquiry

The aim of this report is to answer the third question raised by the Tribunal: "Have purely civilian targets, especially hospitals, sanitariums, dams, etc., been bombed, and, if so, to what extent?"

This report includes, first, historical background, placing the problem of civilian bombings in the general context of the war in North Vietnam. The second part presents data on the bombing of the Democratic Republic of North Vietnam obtained from American Press sources.[1] The third part examines the bombing of hospitals, schools, dams, dikes, religious sites and heavily populated areas.

---

[1]Not included in this extract for reasons of length.

The final part deals with the special problem of distinguishing military from civilian targets.

All four of the Commissions of Inquiry sent by the International War Crimes Tribunal investigated the subject of bombing; but the second team in particular concentrated on this problem. The general method of working was as follows: Comparison of, on the one hand, documents from the United States Press mentioning objectives in North Vietnam actually destroyed, such as railroad yards, ports, large factories, hydro-electric dams, etc. and, on the other hand, documents from the D.R.V. Commission for Investigation of War Crimes, which has meticulously listed attacks and destructions of civilian targets. The findings of this D.R.V. Commission are Judicially valid according to the International Military Tribunal, Nuremberg, Article 21, which reads:

> "The Tribunal will not require proof of facts which are common knowledge, but will take them for granted. It will also consider as valid proof official documents and reports of United Nations governments, including those drawn up by the Commissions established in the various allied countries to investigate war crimes, as well as the minutes of hearings and the decisions of military or other courts of any United Nations country."

The Tribunal's Commissions of Inquiry have verified data on the spot and gathered testimony which confirms a number of the bombings documented by the D.R.V. Commission. In general, comparisons between the destruction reports of the United States and what the Tribunal's Inquiry Commissions actually saw on the spot do not correspond.

For example, on December 31, 1966, on the U.S. aircraft carrier *Enterprise*, Commodore Barry, who had just bombed the city of Nam-Dinh, stated that "he had scored a direct hit on his target, an important railroad junction, and there was not a single victim". But, on that same December 31, Roger Pic, of our Inquiry Commission who was in the same city reported: "Not a single bomb hit the railroad junction; in fact, they all struck the dam which protects the city from floods of the Black River, and a score of straw huts." Other examples of this type are numerous. It was one of the tasks of the Commission to establish, province by province, city by city, the comparison announced by the American forces with our own on-the-spot observations.

A second comparison is also made in the course of this investigation. It is the verification of the reports of the Democratic Republic of Vietnam Commission for Investigation of War Crimes by means of actual observations made by the various Commissions of the International

War Crimes Tribunal. Each of our Commissions has itself been subject to bombing attacks and can therefore testify to their reality. We [Dr. Behar's teams] personally witnessed the bombing of the city of Thanh-Hoa, on January 20, 1967, and in this particular case we personally contributed testimony. While we were in Thanh Hoa, on January 20, 1967, a group of 5 to 8 airplanes attacked at noon. From our shelters we watched the bombing which lasted about ten minutes, then we saw a second smaller wave of planes return five to ten minutes later and bomb for about the same length of time. We were able to reach the spot only a few hours later — this time lapse being due to security measures — and were therefore able to ascertain the real nature of the target. This bombing was aimed solely against a district of Thanh Hoa located about 5 miles from the Ham-Rong bridge, the only possible strategic target in this area. We saw the entire area in flames and completely destroyed; and we also saw the little district hospital demolished by incendiary bombs. On the very spot we saw the craters made by missiles and rockets. By questioning the witnesses we learned the function of the second wave of planes: this second wave machine gunned the rescue teams and the wounded who were being evacuated from the burning hospital.

Testimony of this type — of which this is only one example — can be provided by every Inquiry Commission. Such testimony and others, make it possible to state that from 1965 to the present, in the various regions of North Vietnam, there have been and still are daily bombings of civilian targets. (For the details of this attack, see appendix report IA and documents in appendix.)[2]

The Fourth Inquiry Commission contributed direct testimony confirming the following: (1) It witnessed the bombing of Vinh, on April 5, 1967, at 11:30 a.m. On the spot, at 3 p.m., it observed that fifteen 500 pound-bombs had been dropped in the center of a residential area 300 yards from the cathedral. It recorded the characteristics and U.S. ordnance markings on an unexploded bomb.

(2) On April 9, 1967, the village of Hai Nhan, in Thanh Hoa province, was subjected to naval shelling from 9:40 to 10 a.m. About fifteen rounds were fired, the closest fell less than 200 yards from the Commission team, which reached the spot immediately. The rounds had been fired into the village, amidst the straw huts, and into the surrounding rice-fields. There was no military target in sight. A six year old girl was killed.

---

[2] See Appendices.

Hospitals and Medical Establishments

Our method is to give a general statement and evidence concerning attacks against hospitals, dispensaries, sanatoriums and similar health establishments based on figures supplied by the Commission of Inquiry of the D.R.V. and then we will give comparative statistics between institutions declared destroyed by the North Vietnamese Commission and our own findings on the same institutions.

The general destruction of health institutions up until February, 1967, was 95, with nearly all the technical equipment also damaged or destroyed. There were 87 administrators, nurses and doctors killed and 35 wounded. Of the patients, 262 were killed, 246 wounded, and 65 civilians in the near vicinity were also killed. (Appendix 2)

We can give the details of these attacks and we can cite certain characteristic examples: For instance, that of the Leprosorium of Quyn Lap, the largest center for the research and treatment of leprosy in the D.R.V.; its construction was begun in July, 1956, and was completed in 1959. This leprosorium was situated far from all inhabited areas. This is easily understandable on medical grounds, since one must gather those suffering from leprosy, including the contagious patients, in an area far from any town inhabited by non-infected persons. The Leprosorium of Quyn Lap was for this reason in an isolated coastal area in the district of Quyn Lap in the province of Nghe An. It consisted of 160 buildings and could care for up to 2,600 patients. In the last 5 years, more than 5,000 lepers had been cared for, and more than 1,000 of them had been sent home as cured. (Appendix 3)

The first attack was June 12, 1965, at 8 p.m. Numerous American planes flew over and dropped hundreds of bombs and rockets on the leprosorium; they came back several times to drop more bombs. In these raids, 139 patients were killed, 9 doctors and members of the staff were killed and 100 other persons were wounded.

As far back as July 14, 1965, the D.R.V. Ministry of Public Health had made a public statement drawing attention to this destruction, and to the nature of Quyn Lap as a place set aside for the treatment of leprosy and for research into this illness. In spite of this notice the air raids have continued and even intensified. On May 6, 1966, planes attacked new buildings of the Leprosorium of Quyn Lap which had been relocated to a place close to the Commune of Quyn Lap. This raid resulted in 34 dead and 30 wounded, 10 of them seriously.

The Ministery of Public Health published on May 16, 1966, another statement pointing out that these buildings constituted a leprosorium. Between 1965 and 1966, the Leprosorium of Quyn Lap has undergone 39 attacks. We are emphatic that this leprosorium is situated in a completely isolated area, far from strategic routes, far from any town, far from any industrial center and far from military or so-called military targets. The Quyn Lap Leprosorium, we must also point out to the Tribunal, is internationally known among the medical fraternity who practice in tropical diseases, and it was well and prominently marked with the sign of the Red Cross. (See Appendix 2-a)

Other examples can be given of the destruction of provincial hospitals, notably the main hospital of Thanh Hoa whose condition we have ascertained for ourselves. This hospital has been attacked several times. It is almost completely demolished. Even so, on the 20th of January, 1967, bombs were again dropped on what was left of the buildings. All the main hospitals of the province have been bombed and we can cite those of: Vinh Linh, Quang Binh, Ha Dinh, Nghe An, Son La, Yen Bay, Nam Ha, Fu Li, Bac Thai, Fu Tho, Hoa Binh. We will later give the list of hospitals actually visited by the Tribunal's Commissions of Inquiry confirming the destruction of these centers.

We state furthermore that the attacks on health institutions are not due to target errors or to imprecision on the part of the American planes. Rather, it seems to the contrary, that the hospitals themselves have been the principle objects of attacks. Let us cite, for example, the hospital of Bac Thai attacked on June 22, 1966. Located in a hill-country province, it was completely destroyed by bombs and rockets. Nine patients were killed, one a woman in confinement. This hospital is outside the town, relatively isolated, and its civilian nature could not be doubted.

We will now state, province by province, the provincial and district hospitals destroyed, from a list supplied by the Commission of Inquiry of the D.R.V. We will then see that the findings of different Commissions of Inquiry of the Tribunal corroborate and confirm these data.

Of the 95 health institutions indicated "destroyed" by the Vietnamese Commission, 34 have been personally checked by the Commissions of Inquiry of the Tribunal. This is to say about 36%. The random samples were widely scattered; the 34 hospitals checked correspond to 8 provinces out of 12 exposed to air raids. This sampling seems to us statistically significant because of the scattered nature of the population and because of the proportion examined.

Attacks Against Educational Establishments

Attacks began on August 5, 1964, with the bombing of the primary school of Suag Giang, in the province of Ha Tinh. In the afternoon a second air raid was directed against the secondary school of Hon Gai

151

situated on a hill top. It is important to be aware that these air raids which began on the above date have taken place in a country where since 1954 the effort to stamp out illiteracy and build schools has been remarkable. In the ten years between 1954 and 1964, 95% of North Vietnam's population has become literate. The number of students in schools of general studies reached 3,000,000, with 60,000 in secondary school where the lower and middle grade professional workers are educated. On the university level, the number of students rose from 500 in 1954 to 50,000 now, in 1967.

In North Vietnam, the school system is organized in the following way: first, nurseries and kindergartens; then schools of the first degree, corresponding to our [French] primary schools; schools of the second degree, corresponding to the first part of our secondary school; schools of the third degree which correspond to the last part of our secondary school up to the university entrance level, and the university itself.

According to The Commission of Inquiry of the Democratic Republic of Vietnam there have been a total of 391 schools destroyed in North Vietnam. The schools attacked and bombed are to be found in nearly every part and province of North Vietnam. They are to be found especially in the former 4th Zone, along the route from Vinh Linh to Than Hoa. Vietnamese sources show that practically every weapon of destruction has been used against students and school buildings; including fragmentation bombs, rockets, missiles, incendiary bombs, phosphorus bombs and napalm.

Let us cite a few examples. Two day-nurseries inspected by the Fourth Inquiry Commission, the first at Vinh, had been razed to the ground and only the steps remained. As it had been evacuated, there were no victims. The nursery of the Co-operative of Hong Lac, Commune of Vinh-An, district of Vinh Loe, in the province of Thanh Hoa, had been bombed to the ground on January 29, 1967. Nine of the ten children who were living there and three of the staff were killed.

Other examples must be emphasized, in particular, the bombing of the secondary school at Hong Phue in the province of Ha Tinh on February 9, 1966, at precisely 16:30 hours. The children rushed to get to the slit trenches but the bombs fell directly on them, hollowed out large craters and caused a heavy death toll: Thirty-three children perished as a result of this attack.

The D.R.V. War Crimes Commission has pointed out that a certain number of air raids have taken place during school hours. For example, the secondary school of Van Son in the province of Thanh Hoa was attacked at 8 p.m. at the end of December 1965. This was during the sixth class in which there were 42 pupils, girls from 12-14 years old. The children hastily tried to get to the shelters through the communicating trench; but others rushed out towards the ricefields because the trenches became blocked by the bombings. Mud from the flooded fields filled-in nearly all the trenches, suffocating nine of the children. Three children from the first class from 7 to 8 years old were buried-alive on the school path; they were found only the next day.

We also have examples of attack on children coming out of school — such as the 11 a.m. strike on 17 pupils of a class in the Commune of Hop Thuanh, also in the province of Thanh Hoa. For reasons of safety, they had divided themselves up into small groups — the "normal" practice among the Vietnamese. When they reached the road, they were attacked by rockets from American planes. Some of the children threw themselves onto the ground beside the road, but six others ran for the ditch shelters. The planes released nine bombs killing six of these children, while another was very severely wounded.

The various Commissions of Inquiry of the Tribunal have all documented destruction of schools in the different provinces. We have ourselves in each town visited, sometimes even in each village, found examples of such destruction. In a number of cases the school was only a part of a more widespread destruction. But there are more cases which make me think that there have been specific attacks against schools. It is important to realize that in villages made of bamboo or straw the school is one of the few modern buildings, and therefore perfectly visible from the air. Testimony given by the First Commission of Inquiry that we have since verified on the spot, helps one to understand why we believe schools are specifically targeted. On January 20, 1967, while we were in North Vietnam, the school of Tan Thanh in the province of Ninh Binh was attacked from the air at 12:45. A single plane flying in from the sea released an "air-to-ground" missile. This missile came right into the classroom killing the teacher while he was actually writing on the blackboard. Another teacher and five children who were on a bench near the school and twelve students 6 to 8 years old were killed and seven others were wounded. The Second Commission of Inquiry verified the destruction of this school and found torn books, blood stains, demolished school benches. The purposiveness of this school attack — hit under such circumstances — makes one think that the objective which this plane was aiming for was specifically that school. Often establishments of higher and secondary education are large visible buildings standing apart from the others and clearly distinguishable from the surrounding buildings. Such is the case in the town of Thanh Hoa and in the town of Nam Dinh. In Hanoi, on December 13, 1966, the college for trade union administrators (a very large building) was destroyed in a more systematic fashion than the surrounding houses. We present to the Tribunal, photographs of this damage. . . .

The First Commission of Inquiry saw a whole range of schools attacked in the provinces around Nam Dinh and Nam Ha. The Second Commission of Inquiry has also seen numerous schools destroyed in the provinces of Ninh Binh and Than Hoa.

Part of the Second Commission of Inquiry saw a number of demolished schools in the villages of Viet Tri and Tai Nguyen. Finally, Dr. Krivine who went down to the 17th parallel and crossed several provinces also saw numerous school establishments destroyed. He specifically pointed out the overall nature of the damage in Nghe An province: 92 schools damaged, 1st, 2nd and 3rd degree colleges, 14 professional schools and 25 general schools were completely destroyed, — notably at Nam Dan, Vinh and Thang Giang. In the province of Ha Tinh, 34 schools were attacked — 9 of the second degree, 5 of the 3rd degree, and the 2nd degree school of the Commune of Hong Phuc.

In the accompanying dossiers, clarification will be given to the Tribunal on the schools actually inspected by the Commissions of Inquiry. Upon consideration of the Vietnamese documents and of the findings of the Commissions of Inquiry (especially since the recent bombings) one can conclude that educational establishments in the heart of the civilian areas have been a chosen objective of the air attacks.

Places of Worship Destroyed by American Bombings

Since 1965, according to Vietnamese sources, there have been more than eighty churches and thirty pagodas attacked and destroyed from the air. Priests and monks were killed in these attacks. The majority of attacks against places of worship, especially churches, have taken place in the two main Catholic provinces of North Vietnam, Ninh Binh and Thanh Hoa. The Second Commission of Inquiry visited several of these places of worship, about ten churches in all. We herewith supply photographs and documents on these destroyed churches.

A specific example: the church of Kien Trung, situated near Phat Diem, was attacked on April 14, 1966 at 18:20, precisely at the time of Sunday Vespers. The church was full of worshippers and the result was catastrophic: seventy-two dead, thirty-six males and thirty-six females of whom thirty-four were children. There were forty-six wounded.

Near the church, the school and a dispensary were also destroyed. We collected direct evidence from eye witnesses, and we examined the wounded at this site. In particular, we saw the family of Mr. Trong

154

whose father and four children were killed. We saw the family of Mr. Loi, of which two parents and four children were killed and there remains only a daughter, who at the time of the attack, was in the market place. We saw a child who was wounded on the way to the church; she has had both legs amputated as a result. We saw a Mr. Tunc, of whose large family ten were killed and two were wounded. Only the father is still alive. The family of Mr. Phong, now consists of only one child of eight years old; two parents and two children were killed. Finally we saw young Thang, who now has only one arm: he is five years old and his mother died in the attack on the church.

We also examined the destruction of pagodas in Hanoi itself on raids the 11th and 13th of December, 1966. The main pagoda of Thanh Hoa was destroyed and re-bombed again in several raids at the beginning of this year (1967). In both these cases filmed evidence is attached to the report.

A convent of nuns at the town of Thanh Hoa was attacked at the beginning of this year and the main building was destroyed by heavy bombing. Another example is the Seminary of Bo Lang. This seminary, situated in the district of Tinh Gia on the edge of the Gulf of Tonkin, is a very large building several floors high, completely isolated on the coast with numerous crosses which enable it to be easily identified. Since 1964 the seminary has been attacked from the air nineteen times. In the area we found numerous craters caused by heavy bombs of more than a ton. These craters measure up to thirty meters in diameter. The buildings are almost completely destroyed. There is only one wall left standing which continues to be hit periodically by batteries of the Seventh Fleet which constantly patrols the adjoining waters. This seminary is completely isolated and very far from even a village. There is no objective near the seminary which could be remotely considered military. In this particular case, the recurrence of the raids seems to prove that the objective of the planes was the seminary itself.

The numerous churches which we have visited had been usually built in western style, perfectly visible, with the bell-towers very high, standing out clearly from the neighboring houses which are low and built of bamboo. The frequent attacks on these buildings also seem to indicate that the objective was the place of worship itself. Our opinion is that there is no doubt that the objectives of these bombing attacks were civilian.

The fourth and last Commission visited religious buildings destroyed at: Vinh: the church of the hamlet Quan-Hoa (8 dead). The Buddhist Pagoda three kilometers from the town and 500-1000 meters from the sanatorium, also razed to the ground. Than-Hoa: as well as the main pagoda already mentioned, the Pagoda of the Two Elephants was destroyed in a raid February 4, 1967, (after the visit of the First Commission of Inquiry). Thina Son: (village district of Do Lung); the place of worship has been demolished.

Raids on Heavily Populated Areas

There remains the question of raids taking place on towns, villages and co-operatives; these are very widespread and do not correspond with any military objective.

We visited the towns of Nim Dinh, Phat Diem, Thanh Hoa, Tinh Gia. The other part of the Commission visited the towns of Viet Tri and Tai Nguyen. The First Commission had visited Haiphong and Nam Dinh. Dr. Krivine visited a number of towns in the South, of which the town of Vinh in particular is very important. The town of Thanh Hoa has suffered nearly seventy attacks so far and this town is situated eight kilometers, as-the-crow-flies, as we said at the start of this report, from the only military objective in the region which is the bridge at Ham-Rong. Furthermore, this town has been bombed and bombed again. Also, the town of Nam Dinh has been bombed several times in succession without it being clear what military objective could possibly be there.

Concerning the attacks on these towns, and certainly the most recent attacks which date from the 16th of January, several considerations must be borne in mind, because the sort of weapons used pose special problems. For the town of Thai Nguyen in particular, in the course of the last attack on the 15th and 18th of January, there were dropped eight high explosive bombs of 250 and 450 kilos, and ten "mother" fragmentation bombs.

In the town of Viet Tri, on January 15, at 15:05 hours, twenty-eight high explosive bombs and eight "mother" fragmentation bombs were dropped; and on January 18, Thursday, at 7:05, eighteen high explosive bombs and six "mother" fragmentation bombs were dropped. Now, if it is a question of bombing "concrete and steel", that is to say, the industrial complex, one does not understand the use of fragmentation bombs whose only effect is against human beings and [which are] not at all effective against walls of concrete and steel. Neither does one understand why such a large proportion of fragmentation bombs have been dropped on these two towns.

The Second Commission of Inquiry has verified these findings and the witnesses that it will bring, will inform the Tribunal on this point. Concerning the effect of fragmentation bombs an attached report will explain the important and the legal and medical consequences.[3]

---

[3] See report on steel pellet anti-personnel bombs.

156

Other examples can also be given of attacks on cooperatives. The Second Commission of Inquiry has seen an example completely characteristic of attacks on the isolated cooperatives far from the road and far from any military objective. For example, the Cooperative of Dong Xuan, which is in the province of Than Hoa, is situated in the middle of a region completely remote from all roads and from any objective which could be considered military. This agricultural cooperative was attacked on April 23, 1966, by several planes which dropped numerous bombs. There were many wounded and killed in this cooperative and I would like to report to the Tribunal one particularly moving incident. It is that of Madame Le Thi Tanh who, in the course of the bombing, saw her two children burnt in their house and was not able to go to their aid because three other air raids prevented all assistance by their machine gunning of the town. The Vietnamese wardens urged the poor woman to remain in the shelter with her two smaller children. She is plagued with the memory of the cries of her two children burning in their own house. For me, telling of this shocking affair is as difficult as anything in the course of the whole inquiry.

A short time after they had been attacked, the Fourth Commission visited the following zones: The village of Thinh Som (a district of Do Lung in the heart of the province of Nghe An), absolutely isolated in the middle of rice fields and meadows which was hit on March 24, 1967 at 15:00 hours by twenty-four aerial bombs. There were 10 deaths and 16 wounded. The hamlet of Phong Sinh (Commune of Hung Zung, province of Nghe An) near Vinh was bombarded on the 4th of March 1967, by U.S. Marine artillery. One hundred eighty-five 203 mm shells fell on an area of two kilometers: there were 7 deaths. The Commune of Dinh Tan (district of Yen Dinh, in the province of Thanh Hoa) was bombarded on January 29, 1967, at 16:15 hours by 50 bombs. There were 51 deaths and 53 seriously wounded.

In these last three examples, the Fourth Commission has duly verified the extreme isolation of these areas and the absence of any objective which could be characterised as strategic or military: it has heard witnesses and examined written evidence. There are thus in Vietnam a number of towns, villages, and cooperatives which seem to have been bombed contrary to all logic and against all determinations of a military character. I would like to quote as an example the small fishing village, of Hai Thanh in the district of Tinh Gia, which has suffered (this is a little fishing hamlet of about 10,000 inhabitants whose activity is partly agricultural but mainly concerned with fishing) since the beginning of the aerial bombardments on Vietnam some 152 attacks, of which 21 were specifically directed against the fishing boats.

This fishing village has endured 1,620 bombs, 650 rockets, 12 missiles, and 41 machine-gun attacks. There have been 162 homes burnt and 644 bombed out, 18 junks completely destroyed and 76 damaged. There have been 90 inhabitants killed, of whom 7 were burnt, and 14 villagers have disappeared at sea. There have been 11 children younger than 10 years old killed and 5 new-born babies killed.

Now, this little hamlet with a Catholic majority, is situated on the coast of the Gulf of Tonkin, completely off the main road, far from any objective which could be considered military. The Second Commission of Inquiry visiting this village saw the beach where the fishing boats are tied up. It could not in any case be considered a proper port, but only a simple beach where several junks were pulled up on the sand. It would be difficult to believe that this little fishing village could be confused with a proper port which could have any military activity. All along the coast of the Gulf of Tonkin we saw many small fishing villages that had suffered the same kind of attacks.

Conclusion

This introductory report, supported by testimony of our Commissions of Inquiry, enables us to reply to the third question of the Tribunal concerning crimes against civilians in North Vietnam. In effect, as explained in the report of Maitre Jouffa, crimes against civilians have been delineated, on the one hand, in the following: Hague Convention, 1907; various decisions of the United Nations; Hague Accords of 1923; Statutes of the International Military Tribunal of Nuremberg; and the Geneva Convention of 1949.

In comparing the information from American and Vietnamese sources with the findings of different Commissions of Inquiry of the Tribunal the conclusions are as follows:

1. There have been, since 1964, intense bombings in North Vietnam, premeditated by the U.S. Command.

2. These bombings have hit a certain number of towns, villages and co-operatives in North Vietnam. In these towns, villages, co-operatives and populated areas, civilian habitations and civilian human beings have been killed and wounded.

3. Buildings, of a typically civilian character have been widely attacked and destroyed in the course of these bombings; that is to say, hospitals; educational establishments; places of worship; hydraulic systems, and also the system of water conservancy, as well as markets and meeting places.

4. The use of certain types of weapons, whether or not prohibited by international law, still further characterize these raids as

civilian attacks, particularly the use of a weapon unknown until now: that is to say, the pellet bomb or anti-personnel bomb. This type of weapon, as well as the use of napalm and incendiary bombs of the phosphorus, sodium and magnesium type, result in most serious harm to the civilian population. This is especially the case with children, infants and old people, where the protection which can be provided by the North Vietnamese Government is partly ineffective.

The consensus of all Commissions of Inquiry as represented in this Summary Report conclude in the affirmative to the question posed by the Tribunal.

Questioning of Dr. Behar

SCHWARTZ: *You have informed us that in the bombing of schools and hospitals it was impossible not to have seen the targets. Were those bombings carried out from a low or a high altitude, and during any kind of weather conditions, both cloudy and clear weather?*

BEHAR: In some instances the bombings took place from high altitudes during cloudy weather. At certain times, however — those which we were able to observe for ourselves from our shelter — I can confirm that the sky was clear and that the planes bombed from a very low altitude. . . . It should be pointed out, however, that some of the night bombardments took place without the target having been illuminated. Although the bombings were most usually preceded by the dropping of illumination flares which allowed for target visibility comparable to daytime conditions; we have cited in the annex to our reports a number of examples of night bombings which took place with absolutely no illumination and virtually at random.

DELLINGER: *It would seem from your report that areas with a large Catholic population underwent particularly heavy attacks. Do you believe that this indicates a special punishment, or what is your interpretation of the facts?*

BEHAR: In general, the provinces near the 17th parallel were for the most part the most heavily affected. Having said this, the Catholic regions, too, were far from spared. What is more noteworthy is that in those regions there seems to have been particular attention given to religious installations, most notably churches, seminars and convents. The war has taken a heavy toll in the Catholic provinces and most especially where church property is concerned. I would leave it to the Tribunal to decide whether this is an example of special punishment for those inhabitants, but I can affirm that they do not understand it and that the feeling in the Catholic provinces against the relentlessness of the American air attacks is widespread.

BASSO: *Dr. Behar said that he could give no interpretation of the repeated attacks on the Catholic areas by American bombardiers. During my visit to Vietnam, I too, was struck by this tenacity, and I came to the following conclusion: The American officers have been taken in by the official propaganda of their country. They believe the Catholic peasants to be enemies of the socialist government and that they are ready to rise up against it. It seems to be thought that by destroying their religious facilities, psychological pressure is brought to bear against them which will incite them to rise up against their government...*

BEHAR: That explanation is plausible. It is hard to understand the repeated attacks against religious facilities we have witnessed in any other way: the attacks have sometimes been carried out to ridiculous lengths. For example, although nothing remains of the Ba Lang seminary, bombing raids are still being directed against a piece of wall.

DELLINGER: *The usual explanation given for these attacks in America is that those buildings, the churches for example, are used for military purposes as well as for religious services. Have you investigated this?*

BEHAR: We are aware of this explanation, but we have found no indication, no evidence which would lead us to believe that the churches are being used for any purpose other than religious instruction. Furthermore, church reconstruction is going on; it is solely a question of replacing religious facilities as such. That explanation does not strike me as being very serious.

BASSO: *You have been present during bombing raids. Do you have the impression that the American planes are directed especially against schools, hospitals, and so on? In the bombing raids which you have witnessed, were particular targets being attacked and other avoided?*

BEHAR: During the bombing raid I witnessed, the planes very obviously dropped bombs in a very limited area, in one district of the city of Thanh Hoa. One could conclude that it was that particular area which was aimed at. It turns out that in that area, which we visited immediately afterwards, there were dwellings, the district hospital, a market, and that was all. The fact that the bombs had been concentrated on this area leads one to believe that it was a special target.

Non-Military Targets and Methods of Attack

testimony by Y. Ishijima

The U.S. is carrying out calculated bombings against targets of a purely non-military nature in various parts of North Vietnam. The Investigation Team of the Japanese Commission of Inquiry has amassed three kinds of objective facts and evidence which irrefutably indicates that these bombings are deliberate.

The first evidence consists of damage to such non-military targets as massed residential areas, shops, farm houses, hospitals, schools, public nurseries, kindergartens, churches, temples, and irrigation facilities. The Japanese Investigation Team saw and confirmed this damage directly. Photographs were taken and written and recorded testimonies from victims themselves were compiled by Team members.

The second body of evidence consists of unexploded bombs and reveals that the functioning structure of the weapons themselves — napalm and CBUs in particular — stands as firm proof that these weapons are designed and used by the U.S. with the sole aim of mass slaughter.

The third evidence consists of the confession of a U.S. pilot who was captured while taking part in the bombing.

I. The Japanese Investigation Team witnessed and confirmed on the spot that several cities have been turned into ruins by repeated attacks against the whole cities.

In the cities of Phuly, Vinh, and Dong Hoi all buildings, from houses to small factories and shops, have been destroyed row-on-row. The evidence reveals that the attacks were completely indiscriminate. Hospitals, clinics, kindergartens, churches, and temples were included in the destruction. Even the buildings of the International Commission for Supervision and Control were destroyed by the bombings of the cities of Dong Hoi and Vinh.

Bombings by the U.S. forces have been carried out in four patterns. The first pattern involves the bombing to total destruction, by means of organized and repeated strikes, of cities and villages selected beforehand; the second pattern consists of experimentation in the use-effectiveness of particular weapons; the third pattern consists of systematic attacks against particular targets, such as hospitals; the fourth pattern involves bombing of houses, people, and livestock at random as "targets of opportunity."

As an example of the first pattern, in addition to the ruins of the above mentioned cities, we saw the ruins of several farming villages and villages between mountains destroyed in their entirety by repeated bombings. These were along Highway 1 leading from Hanoi to the 17th parallel.

Typical of the second pattern are the attacks against the City of Vinh Yen and Fu Sa Village of Hanoi City. These attacks were experiments in the use of large numbers of CBUs. On December 8, 1966 on the two villages of Ding Tin and Thanh Van on the outskirts of Vinh Yen, scores of "mother" CBU bombs were dropped in concentration over a 12 square km area; this means that several thousand "bomblets" containing several million small steel balls were dropped. In the case of Fu Sa Village on the outskirts of Hanoi, after the whole village was destroyed by high explosive bombs, 1,200 ball bombs were dropped.

Typical of the third pattern are attacks on hospitals. Of 28 provincial and municipal hospitals in the Democratic Republic of Vietnam, 14 have been bombed; of prefectural hospitals and clinics, 24 have been bombed. In the south of Than Hoa in particular, all the provincial, municipal and prefectural hospitals, clinics and sanatariums have been bombed.

The internationally known Hansen's disease hospital at Quynh Lap in Nge An province, Quang Binh provincial hospital, and Ha Tinh provincial hospital were targets of concentrated and repeated bombings 39 times, 13 times, and 17 times respectively. The weight of the evidence was so overwhelming that we had no choice but to conclude that U.S. bombings against hospitals have been carried out calculatedly and organizedly after especially selecting these targets precisely because they were hospitals.

As an example of the fourth pattern, in Quang Binh province we saw three places where small farming villages surrounded by paddy fields were suddenly attacked by aircraft firing rockets, killing farmers and children. The U.S. planes also strafe and rocket peasants and water buffaloes working in the paddy fields. Completely contrary to statements of the U.S. Government that bombings of the north have been restricted carefully to military targets, the U.S. forces are showering bombs on any and all civilian targets.

II. In bombing civilians and civilian targets, the U.S. Air Force uses various types of bombs in a deliberately chosen deadly combination. Of these bombs, CBUs and napalm in particular, by their very function and structure, demonstrate that they are fundamentally designed to strike civilian targets and civilians.

These two types of bombs and their use as unlawful weapons of mass slaughter in violation of international law has been presented to this Tribunal in detail by our weapons experts. What must be pointed out here is that these bombs, napalm and CBUs, by their very nature and structure, are ineffective against military targets of iron and concrete. But they are devastating against the population in underdeveloped countries such as Vietnam where civilian buildings are made of wood and bamboo. The very fact that these two types of weapons are being used as the main weapons of attack convincingly demonstrates that the U.S. bombings have, from the very beginning, been deliberately aimed at targets of a non-military nature. The Japanese Investigation Team, to substantiate this attack method, has visited Quang Binh province where napalm and CBUs were used in large quantities. We interrogated victims and witnesses; we have obtained splinters of napalm and unexploded CBUs which we submit to the Tribunal in evidence.

III. A statement by U.S. pilot Charles Tanner, whom the Team interviewed in Hanoi, demonstrated further that U.S. bombings of non-military targets are pre-calculated and organized.

According to his statement, which we have submitted to the Tribunal in a recorded tape, Lt. Commander Tanner unequivocally states that the order of attack was to "first destroy dwellings by bombs, then burn out shelters by napalm, and then kill or wound with CBUs all the people who would be driven out of their shelters by the napalm." His formation made successive sorties with these three types of weapons.

These facts, together with the other evidence, clearly delineate the realities of the bombing of the north by the U.S. The manner in which the U.S. is waging air war against Vietnam constitutes not only bombing against targets of a non-military nature, but also criminal acts with the calculated aim of massacring the civilian population.

The Japanese Team confirmed a typical example of this inhuman attack procedure at Ngu Thuy, a fishing village of Quang Binh province, about 10 km. north of the 17th parallel. Three settlements of Liem Lap, Thuong Bac, and Throng Nam of Ngu Thuy Village were completely wiped off the face of the earth by intensive air raids on

July 15 and 16, 1966. The air raids against Liem Lap settlement were carried out from 6:30 p.m., July 15 to 5:30 a.m., July 16, 1966, in four methodical stages. In the first stage three hours were spent in a thorough-going air photo reconnaissance by planes which also dropped flares. For three and a half hours of a second stage, U.S. planes burned-out grasses and trees and turned the earth into a sea of fire with a large quantity of napalm. This tactic was to cut off the roads through which the people would try to find shelter outside the settlement. In the third stage for two hours, bombs and napalm were showered onto the settlement; almost all the dwellings were either burned-out or destroyed.

In their fourth stage, a massacre was carried out for two and a half hours with the combined use of rockets, machineguns and CBUs. The result was that a fishing settlement of 200 houses was obliterated from the earth, including all dwellings, a clinic, a school and warehouses. Then from 5:00 p.m., July 16 to 4:00 a.m., July 17, two settlements of the same village in the northern vicinity of Liem Lap were attacked. U.S. planes first showered these settlements with bombs and napalm for four hours; all 400 houses were burnt out. During the additional seven hours planes kept on showering napalm and CBUs, and machine-gunning from the center of the settlements to the outskirts.

These attacks against Ngu Thuy Village by U.S. planes, which were confirmed by us, constitute a planned massacre against men, women and children in civilian settlements.

Bombardment of Civilians in North Vietnam
testimony by John Takman, M.D. and Axel Hojer, M.D.

Dr. Takman is Director of the Stockholm Child Welfare Board;
Dr. Hojer Serves as Sweden's Delegate to the U. N.
World Health Organization

Our team was in the Democratic Republic of Vietnam from March
10 to March 31, 1967. Despite limited time it was able to carry out
investigations in five provinces. Two previous Tribunal teams had
already done investigations in other provinces. We have not seen
their reports, but understand they have described some of the cities
and villages that were completely or partly destroyed in 1966, and
it would be superfluous to include them in our report. Jointly with
Mr. Manes we have reported on the bombing of Idep Mai Hamlet
in our statement of March 31,1967. There we dealt with the construction and the effects of the global shaped CBU bombs (steel
pellet bombs) which are used as a routine weapon against the Vietnamese people.

It was agreed, for practical reasons, that the medical members
of the team, both living in Stockholm, should make a separate report. It is therefore possible that parts of the reports overlap or
even cover the same investigations. This may be an advantage. In
complex situations different observers may note different things
which may be important to the forming of a comprehensive view.
We hope that the inevitable errors in our report will be insignificant and that more attention will be paid to the content as a whole
than to isolated data which may differ somewhat from the other
reports . . .

Destruction of the Viet Tri Papermill

The city of Viet Tri, in Phu Tho province, is situated about 75
kilometers northwest of Hanoi. We went there on March 15, 1967
to examine the damage and the victims of recent bombings. The
Viet Tri papermill had been bombed on March 12, 1967. The Sec-

165

ond Commission of Inquiry had visited the same plant two or three weeks earlier. Our English-speaking guide, Mr. Dzai, who had accompanied them, also, said that the destruction since then was so great that it was difficult to recognize it as the same site. When the papermill was bombed for the fifth time at 12:20 p.m. on March 12, both demolition bombs and global shaped steel pellet bombs (CBU, cluster bomb units) were used.[1] Most of the buildings were completely demolished by bombs the heaviest of which seem to have been 2,500 lbs. Seven persons were killed this time. Also the dwelling house area situated a few hundred meters from the plant had been bombed, first with demolition bombs, then with steel pellet bombs when the people came out of their shelters to rescue the wounded and extinguish the fires. One of the three-story houses was completely destroyed, the others damaged: 7 persons were also killed here. The mill produced bamboo paper for schoolbooks. The dwellings for workers were built in 1958 and 1959. According to the local authorities the mill had 2,000 employees.

While our team was investigating bombings in nearby Tien Cat Village there was a preliminary alert. Loudspeakers announced that enemy aircraft were 80 kilometers — 10 minutes flight time — from the village but not heading straight in our direction. During our investigations of bombed villages in other provinces this happened several times. The loudspeakers could be heard everywhere in the fields. When they announced that the planes were coming in our direction but at a distance of 80 to 100 kilometers, people would continue their work. After this preliminary alert there would be a final alert or an announcement that the planes had turned in another direction.

The fact that there is a national alert system which reaches into virtually every hamlet, as well as the fact that there are individual shelters close to every home, in the fields and alongside the roads,

---

[1]We avoid using the term "fragmentation bomb". *All* bombs and shells used by the Seventh Fleet and the U.S. Air Force against North Vietnam are, in fact, fragmentation bombs and anti-person bombs. Very little has been written in the U.S. press about the steel pellet bombs which are usually described as fragmentation bombs or anti-personnel bombs. And nothing seems to have been written about the fact that the heavy bombs used for air bombardments and the shells from the Seventh Fleet artillery are made from a materiel which fragments into double edged machete-like slivers. In the bombed or shelled hamlets there are thousands of these slivers left on the ground in and around the craters. We prefer to use the term "steel pellet bombs" or "CBU" for the small anti-person bombs and the term "explosive fragmentation bomb" or "demolition bomb" for the heavy bombs. Also delayed-action bombs are frequently being used against civilian targets in North Vietnam.

has been instrumental in keeping fatalities at an astonishingly low level. Even in hamlets that have been destroyed by demolition bombs and showered with great quantities of CBU bombs, we found that less than one percent of the population have been killed.

The Attack on Xa Viet Hong Village

On March 15, 1967 we visited Xa Viet Hong Village in Phu Tho province, which had been bombed three days earlier. According to the authorities, it had a population of 5,423. Nothing contradicted the information we got that it is a purely agricultural area, far from military targets and remote from communication lines. Prior to the bombing, reconnaissance planes had several times flown over the village. On March 12 at 12 o'clock six planes came from the northeast. Two of them flying at low altitude and four at higher altitude. The first planes dropped four CBU's with "loading date" November 1966 and January 1967.[2] Thirteen persons were killed and thirty-one wounded. Twenty-five houses caught fire and were completely destroyed together with clothes, cooking utensils, farming equipment and other property; thirteen water buffaloes and twenty poultry were killed.

Mr. Bui Van Hguong, 59, spontaneously came to show us a quilt and some clothes, all that was left of his home and property after the raid. At the site of a destroyed home a number of men had cleared the ground and were erecting a new house. The owner, Mr. Nguyen Khac Dan, 30, told us that his wife, 27, had been killed by steel pellets, leaving him with their three small children. We tape recorded his detailed description of the raid.

A few houses from there we met Mr. Nguyen Van Hua, also with three small children. His wife had been running for the shelter when she was hit by a global-shaped CBU bomb which exploded on her head, killing her instantly. A few meters from the spot where she

---

[2]Stencils on the sides of the "mother bomb" — cannisters, which do not explode but merely separate to release the bomblets — are used to convey U.S. Air Force ordnance information. The loading dates are significant. Because of the extended time lag between placement of orders with the manufacturer and receipt of the bombs in the field, the bomb loaded November, 1966, had probably been ordered two to three years before the one labeled January, 1967, shows the ongoing and contemporary U.S. military planning for the use of anti-personnel weapons. According to an article in *Ramparts* magazine of December, 1967, by former Special Forces Sergeant Donald Duncan, sub-contracts for 14.8 billion steel pellets for use in manufacture of anti-personnel weapons for delivery by April, 1968, were placed by the U.S. Department of Defense. — Ed's. Note.

was killed there was one half of a CBU cannister with the following inscription:

FSN1323 — 7/?/29-839H/?/E
Dispenser and Bomb
Aircraft CBU — 24/B
AF Drawing No 65E10875
Cyclotol 122 lbs
Loading Date 1-67
LOT PA-20-82-SERIE . . . / illegible/

We also interviewed Mrs. Bu Thi Sung, 49. She had had six children. Evidently she had not heard the alert. She was boiling water in the kitchen when she heard the planes coming. A moment later a CBU bomb exploded on the thatched roof of their house. Her son, Ban, 5, was killed by a steel pellet through his head and her son, Chich, 7, by a pellet in his neck. A third son, 14, was wounded by a steel pellet in one wrist. Having told us this she said: "The U.S. aircraft have come to kill my children. I'll always carry the hatred of the aggressors in my heart."

The Bombing of Dan Ly Village

In Dan Ly Village, Trieu Son District, about 15 kilometers west of Thanh Hoa City, two hamlets, "Number Five" and "Number Nine" were bombed with pineapple-shaped CBU bombs on March 13, 1967. These bombs were first used against targets in North Vietnam in January 1965, we were told by military experts in Hanoi. They are now replaced by global-shaped CBU bombs. The material is the same in both types, steel pellets cast into a shell of hard, brittle metal. But the pineapple-shaped bombs are loaded in tubes, 18 to 25 bombs in each tube, and 19 tubes in each container (cannister). As distinguished from the cannisters of the global-shaped bombs, which are dropped *in toto* and can be found in all bombed hamlets, the pineapple-shaped bombs are spread directly from the planes: the tubes and cannisters are evidently brought back or dumped somewhere else after the bombing.

We went to Dan Ly Village on March 19, a Sunday[3] . The house closest to the entrance of hamlet "Number Five" was burned down. We heard sobs and moans and in the twilight saw an old man sitting barefoot in the carbonized ruins of his garden. He had been living alone. He had lost everything, including his buffaloes, in the raid. According to the testimonies, two planes came at noon on March 13, and circled the hamlet for a short time. Nothing happened; it was a fine sunny day. At 5:30 p.m., the same day, four planes came which dived and dropped many pineapple CBU bombs.

---

[3]Lelio Basso, Hugh Manes and John Takman took part in this investigation.

In hamlet "Number Five" there were 127 houses of which 12 were completely destroyed by fire caused by high explosive bombs. The raid took place at a time when the children had returned from school and the adults were returning from their work in the fields. Six persons were killed, among them two old women, and seven were wounded. Three of the wounded, all children, later died in the hospital.

The hamlet is in a flat delta landscape and surrounded by immense rice fields. The only military targets to be seen were the rifles which the peasants carry with them to the fields. Only pineapple-shaped CBU bombs had been dropped on this hamlet. The craters had not been counted when we came there. As one plane usually carries four cannisters and four planes had taken part in the attack, the total number of small bombs was probably 6,000 to 8,000 against this single hamlet. Each small bomb contains 240 to 250 steel pellets. The total number of pellets against the population of hamlet "Number Five" was between 1.5 and 2 million. The casings break up into sharp, crystal-form fragments of different sizes. One can safely conclude that the number of fragments from these bombs is probably as great as the number of pellets. We talked with some who had lost family members in the raid. Mr. Tran Van Xuan came with his five children, carrying the smallest of them. His house was burned down. His old mother and his 40 year old wife had been killed instantly.

The inhabitants of hamlet "Number Nine" gave similar information. The planes circled the hamlet on March 13, 1967 at noon. At 5:30 p.m. the same day, one plane attacked the hamlet with pineapple CBU bombs, destroying three houses, killing seven villagers and wounding four. The bombs were dropped from an altitude of 500 meters. Mr. Tran Hoan lost two of his three children, a seven year old girl and a 14 months old boy. "When the planes came the children were playing in the garden; their grandmother was working in the kitchen and did not find them," he told us.

Mr. Tran Van Binh, 33, lost his mother, his younger brother and an 11 month old daughter. He had five children. His mother was carrying his little girl to the shelter when they were hit by pellets. His brother, too, was killed a moment before he would have reached the shelter. In both these hamlets, "Number Five" and "Number Nine", the inhabitants are Catholics.

The Shelling of Ca Lap Village

Ca Lap Village is situated on the coast near Sam Son. This small area has been shelled four times by the Seventh Fleet, the last time on March 5, 1967. On the shore we saw the ruins of Ngo Hun Ky's brick house which was destroyed during the last shelling. He himself was killed by shells on January 26, 1967, while on his way to work in the field. He was 35. Everywhere around these ruins and in the fields we saw heavy double-edged slivers from the shells.

Tran Chi Thuyen, 55, was killed and his brick house destroyed on March 5, 1967. His wife and two of his six children were wounded by shell slivers which penetrated their mud shelter. At our visit, Mr. Vu Dinh Buong, 49, was preparing dinner in the remnants of his brick house, now under a temporary thatched roof. His wife, Ngo Thi Canh, was killed and the house destroyed by three shells on February 26, 1967. He is a fisherman and was working on the sea when the shelling took place. He has four children, 15, 11, 5, and a 4 month old baby. Ca Lap was originally a fishing village but is also a successful producer of sweet potatoes. Its potato fields, now pockmarked with craters from 127 millimeter shells, stretch for several hundred meters in a wide band along the shore. In a modest administrative building Mr. Nguyen Viet Kieu, president of the Village Administrative Committee, briefed us on the situation in the presence of some fifty villagers.

On February 26, 1967, at 9:45 a.m. the village was shelled from the sea, receiving 102 shells. Three persons were killed on the spot, and one died later from wounds. Another three persons were wounded and several houses were destroyed or damaged. Two hectares of potatoes were destroyed. Seven oxen and buffaloes were killed.

On March 5, at 8 o'clock in the morning, three U.S. warships approached the coast and shelled Ca Lap Village from a distance of 10 kilometers. Many shells burst in the air with a blue-black smoke, in all, 397 shells exploded into the ground. We walked through the potato field over a narrow pathway. On each side we counted about 40 craters; at a distance of about a hundred meters they merged into each other, and certainly the total number given by Mr. Kieu was not exaggerated. Nine cooperatives in this village were affected by the last shelling. Three persons were killed and four wounded. Seven houses were destroyed completely, four heavily damaged and another fifteen less seriously damaged. Four oxen were killed. The shells were of the 127 millimeter type ... Shells from the Seventh Fleet often destroy property and kill cattle before they explode. On the flat, horizontal area between the sea and the hills there are potato fields and several houses, now in ruins. Many shells had cut like lawnmowers through the small tree groves and the brush, leaving only stumps standing. We noticed that all buffaloes and oxen were now kept in square shelters below ground level, and we learned that families spend the nights in underground shelters provided with solid covers . . .

Destruction of the Cities

While traveling, we saw several towns and cities, all completely destroyed. As previous investigating teams have described them in detail, we shall not include them in our report, other than to say Phu Ly, Phat Diem and Thanh Hoa have no intact buildings as far as we could see. All dwellings except for some one-story huts, are destroyed or badly damaged. No church or pagoda is intact. The City Hospital of Thanh Hoa is so thoroughly eradicated that it reminds one of the Jewish Ghetto in Warsaw after it had been wiped out by the Nazis. The province hospital in the same city is also destroyed, but remnants of the entrance gate with its red cross and parts of some of the buildings make it distinguishable from the ruins of the residential areas surrounding it.

When we visited Ca Lap Village we passed through the health resort area of Thanh Hoa City. It was created quite recently. One could still recognize traces of its former beauty. Its many modern buildings, gardens and palm-lined streets had been bombed so many times that our guide could not describe them without referring to notes. Every building was destroyed and practically all palm trees were cut off or torn to shreds.

In the provinces of Thanh Hoa and Ninh Binh we did not see one big building intact. In fact, even all one-story brick houses have been destroyed or damaged by bombs or shells, at least all that could be seen from the roads in the regions that we passed through. Now, when brick houses are rebuilt after the bombings, they are invariably provided with thatched roofs to make them look like huts to reduce their attractiveness as bomb targets. This by no means excludes them as targets. When there are no other targets around, the gunners of the Seventh Fleet and the U.S. pilots use any civilian hamlet as a target.

Examination of Victims

We examined 43 victims of bombings and shellings, the majority of them (18 cases) were victims of pellets and/or fragments from CBU bombs. Most of these victims were examined by us in the hospitals after we had investigated the bombings in which they had been wounded. As the Tribunal has the hospital records, photos, etc., it suffices for us to repeat what we have said in our statement of March 31, 1967:

"We have visited many hospitals, functioning in extremely modest houses in the villages, mostly under thatched roofs, since their permanent buildings have been destroyed. At the Quoc Oai district hospital we were impressed, as we have been at all the other hospitals, by the excellent organization of the emergency services and the high standard of the surgery performed. It is to us obvious that the rapidly expanding public health system of the DRV, the highly qualified training of the physicians, the devotion of the physicians and the medical personnel to their patients and their work and the outstanding emergency organizations have played a great role in holding down the fatality rate due to the bombings and shellings and in reducing the rate of chronic disabilities among those who have been wounded."

All records we have seen have been exemplary, nearly always supplemented with X-ray's and drawings and with the extracted pellets or fragments attached to the records in plastic envelopes. We have also examined victims from earlier raids, who had been brought to the hospitals in a state of shock with many pellet holes in their intestines, bones shattered, soft tissue pierced and who are now fully recovered ...

The Resistance, the People and the Morale

We, the medical members of the third investigating team, were appointed to carry out examinations and investigations only in our professional field and give evidence to the Tribunal as to what we actually saw or heard ... Any lengthy or detailed study of the nature of the war or the resistance of the Vietnamese people would have fallen outside our terms of reference and would, of course, be impossible to carry out in a short time.

Nevertheless, we felt it necessary to inquire into the living conditions, past and present, and acquaint ourselves with the general situation. Without the background of the sufferings of the Vietnamese people under colonialism and occupation on the one hand, and the immense development of the northern part of the country since 1954, on the other hand, its resistance and determination to face a long and ever more devastating and ruthless war would be incomprehensible.

A people like our own [Sweden] which has been independent for more than four hundred years and takes its independence for granted cannot easily understand why the Vietnamese prefer agony and death in a seemingly endless war to a peace with foreign troops, foreign bases and a quisling-type government on Vietnamese soil.

We do not intend to make an overall report on what we have seen and heard during our visits. We believe that the background and the development can be described more vividly by a personal history, that of Mr. Ton Viet Nghiem, vice president of Thanh Hoa province administrative committee. He did not mention his position when he briefed us on the situation in his province in the inn near Thanh Hoa City where we spent several nights. But we admired his way of comparing the past with the present and asked him to add something about himself. Here is what he told us:

"I'm an urchin belonging to the Muong minority. The French colonials considered us as a stupid, savage and very backward people. There are 150,000 Muongs out of the two million inhabitants in Thanh Hoa province. Under the French I couldn't afford more than four forms of schooling. I was a farmer. Since then I have passed all 10 forms of preuniversity education and a two-year course at the Political Training School of the Lao Dong Party. I have also finished a university course in literature and a university course in medical organization, both by correspondence. Previously, everybody in my family was illiterate, except for myself. At present in my hamlet of 88 households there are many university students; and those in secondary school are numerous. My eldest daughter, 20 years old, is a student of literature at the pedagogical institute. My 16 year old boy is a 6th form student. My third boy, who is 14, is in the 6th form. The people in my hamlet say that life began with the Party." Under colonialism Mr. Nghiem had been in prison several times.

In 1945, after eighty years of colonial rule, ninety-five percent of the Vietnamese were illiterate. In North Vietnam alone, more than two million people died from hunger in one-half year in 1945. Millions of people suffered from malaria, trachoma, tuberculosis, leprosy. It is said that the entire population had intestinal parasites. Dysentery, typhoid fever, puerperal infections and other infectious diseases were frequent. There were few industries, Vietnam was an underdeveloped country by all standards.

Since 1954, and the expulsion of the French, North Vietnam has been transformed into a country which is remarkably modern and seems to develop despite the tremendous amount of bombs and shells that have been inflicted upon it for more than two years. It is said that illiteracy had been essentially eliminated at the end of 1958, after four years of peace. Through large-scale vaccinations and a nation-wide campaign for better hygiene, smallpox, cholera, plague and many other diseases have been eradicated. Everywhere we could see the results of the hygiene campaign — deep wells, usually with concrete cisterns, septic tanks, the virtual absence of garbage and a scarcity of flies and mosquitoes. Though nearly all schools and hospitals have been destroyed by bombs and shells, all children in the areas we visited go to school regularly, and evidently all citizens, including the victims of the bombings and shellings get medical care of very high standard in provisional hospitals housed in thatched-roof buildings in the villages.

We interviewed five victims of the terror in South Vietnam at length. They were two women who had been subjected to a variety of torture techniques for long periods, two victims of the "strategic hamlet" program [now called "New Life Hamlet" program and "Rural Reconstruction" program], and a victim of toxic chemicals.

The firm determination of the Vietnamese to fight this war to victory, whatever it will cost, must be weighed against this background. One must put in the scales their experiences of colonial enslavement and humiliations, their experiences of neo-colonial terror as opposed to their tremendous achievements in culture, public health and economic development in the brief moment of peace and independence that has fallen to their lot. The costs of a war of resistance must be compared — and they *are* compared by the Vietnamese — with the meaningless and infinitely greater costs of neo-colonial "New Life Hamlet" programs, corruption, torture, terror, ignorance, hunger and disease. The costs of the future must be balanced against the costs of an existence without a future; the costs of national independence with the costs of submitting to the plans of Washington.

We feel that our report would be incomplete from the medical point of view if we failed to stress the necessity for taking action against the destruction, the killing and the maiming that ravages Vietnam every day of the year. A stepped-up campaign against this war and against the senseless bombings, shellings and other atrocities is urgent. At the same time it is necessary to stress that there is no compromise solution for the war in Vietnam. Those who hold the illusion that peace will be accepted by the Vietnamese in exchange for their national independence and legitimate right to handle their own affairs must share the responsibility for the prolongation of the war.

American Bombing in North Vietnam
testimony by Jean Michel Krivine, M.D.

Surgeon at the Hospital Lariboisiere, France

I arrived in Hanoi on an International Control Commission (ICC) plane on February 17, 1967. I stayed in Hanoi until Saturday February 25. During my stay I was briefed on American weapons used against the D.R.V., wounds resulting from fragmentation bombs, burns, and the political and military situation in Vietnam. I visited the hospitals of Viet Duc and Saint Paul.

Monday, February 20, 1967, we visited sites which have been bombed in Hanoi and its outskirts: The hamlet of Phu Xa, Tu Liem district, in the village of Phu Thuong, bombed in August 1966; Phuc Tan Street, Le Van Cau city, attacked on December 13, 1966; its houses have been razed to the ground, its school demolished; the Union School has been cut in two by bombs and surrounded by huge craters; the Polish-Vietnamese Friendship School: bombed on December 2, 13 and 14, 1966. Demolished and studded with craters. Alongside the school, houses are destroyed, as well as a pagoda and the Hoang Liet Commune Maternity Hospital.

On Saturday, February 25, 1967, I departed for the provinces north of Hanoi. Throughout the entire trip, I will be the only member of a special Inquiry Commission for the Tribunal, for the 2nd Commission, of which I was a member, went back to Europe on the ICC plane that brought me here. Following are extracts from my daily journal kept while in North Vietnam:

February 25: arrival in Viet Tri. Morning — visit of places bombed:

1. — The paper-mill: bombed July 19, 1966, November 1, 1966 and November 15, 1966. Still visible is an enormous crater (filled up) in the middle of a workshop (it was left by the first bombing). Fragmentation bombs were later dropped, leaving visible traces all

over — on the walls and on the ground. One authority says fragmentation bombs have left not even one square meter of the factory
untouched. I photographed the groove hollowed out by an unexploded bomb which had not yet been taken care of by the bomb de-
fusing teams. The concrete water-drainage pipes are demolished.
One bomb fell on the dike of the Red River. Two thousand people
work here; production has not slowed down. I spoke with a young
man who had been wounded earlier by a fragmentation bomb: Le
Trung Vinh, 26, operated on for intestinal wound on November 8,
1966, by Dr. Xuan. He has again taken up his work. One person
was killed, and around 30 wounded.

2. — The monosodium glutamate factory: attacked on January 18,
1967, at 7 a.m: one explosive bomb and one wind blast bomb; 2
blast bombs fell farther away. Four hundred workers were working
but had time to seek cover; 60% were women. The roofs are ruined,
and 10 tons of raw materials, Vietnamese noodles, brine, non-
crystallized glutamate, spread around on the ground and unuseable.

3. — The obstetrical surgery department of the evacuated Viet Tri
Hospital: The Viet Tri Hospital was bombed on August 11 and 14,
1966. It has thus been evacuated. This department of the hospital was
attacked again on January 18, 1967, with explosive bombs and fragmentation bombs. You can see fragmentation bomb craters near the
office of the director. The doctor's office is studded with pellets;
closet, X-ray viewer, chair, folding screen, patients' X-ray files; the
sterilizer is pierced. The patients managed to reach shelters (no
killed or wounded).

4. — Nursery school: Placed in a hollowed out part of the ground
and covered with a roof of palm leaves. Destroyed, but because of
the weather there were no classes the day of the attack. Afternoon:
briefing by authorities on the situation in Viet Tri and presentation of the wounded.

On Sunday, February 26, we were in Vinh Yen. After briefing on
the situation in the province, we go through fields in the areas
attacked by fragmentation bombs: the walls of straw huts bear the
signs of the bomb pellets, which left holes, but did not go all the
way through. Then five medical files are presented. 2:30 p.m.: visit
to Da Phuc; we go along rice paddies riddled with fragmentation
bombs; each crater is marked by a pole bearing a piece of white
paper. The warehouse of the cooperative is destroyed, and houses
have been smashed by 3,000 pound bombs. Visit to the school where
the teacher Phung Thi Bich Phung, 31, of first level school of the
village of Tien Duoc, was killed by a fragmentation bomb. The
children had time to make it to a shelter, but the head of the class,

Hoa Van Thinh, 14, was wounded in the shoulder. We were able to speak with this child. A bench still bears signs of the teacher's blood. The attack took place on January 16, 1967.

Monday, February 27, we are in the province of Bac Thai. In the morning we visit the places that have been attacked:

1. — Hospital of the autonomous zone of Viet Bac: planned for 600 beds, it only had 350. Bombed on July 7, 1966, with explosive bombs and fragmentation bombs. Some buildings are still standing, but the roof has been knocked in, and the interior devastated; there are splinters all over. Other buildings are completely flattened, especially the surgery department.

2. — Around the Hospital: a) a group of houses were set on fire by fragmentation bombs on September 28, 1966. Nothing remains of them. According to my companions, there were 16 houses before the attack; b) the area's pharmaceutical center, which was marked with a red cross, was hit by fragmentation bombs; c) civilian dwellings were destroyed by explosive bombs on January 22, 1967. (craters).

3. — Hospital of the Thai Nguyen steel complex: 250 beds. Connected to the Ministry of Heavy Industry, situated 3 km, as the crow flies, from the complex; attacked, while evacuated on January 17, 1967. Hit by five explosive bombs and four fragmentation bomb units: 1 dead, 6 wounded; a headquarters for emergency cases remained operative. I saw the remains of a fragmentation "mother" bomb unit marked "Dec. 1966". The buildings are still standing, but they are riddled with pellet holes and splinters. The rice paddies surrounding the hospital are studded with the small craters characteristic of fragmentation bombs.

Friday March 3, arrived near Vinh, Nghe An province, at 5 a.m., after spending 11 hours to travel 270 km. From 7-7:30 a.m., I can hear the firing of the big naval guns of the U.S. 7th Fleet. We leave around 6 p.m. for Ha Tinh, by way of Vinh. Except for a few services and the self-defense squads, the city is evacuated. The craters on the square in front of the big church, which has been damaged, have been filled-in. The big market has been levelled to the ground; the remains of its facade are on the point of falling. Next we go to see what is left of the Cong Coa Church behind the market. It is a pile of ruins and craters; I picked up a black cross marked with Arabic and Chinese figures. Then go through the devastated populous parts of the city; the Headquarters of the International Control Commission (ICC) is very badly damaged, particularly the Canadian and Polish buildings. Further on is the 3rd level school, modern in its U-shaped architecture. It is destroyed; you can still see one black-board and a chair on the first floor, but the wall has disappeared.

Saturday, March 4, we are in Ha Tinh. Awakened at 7 a.m. by the shelling of the 7th Fleet, U.S. jets flying overhead while the nursery school children are reciting their lessons together. We visit this class where 40 pupils study. Then leave by bicycle to visit the provincial hospital. On the way, I am shown a devastated spot where nothing at all is recognizable: it is the site of the hospital of Huong Khe district, attacked 8 times between March 31 and August 13, 1965. The provincial hospital has been attacked 18 times; it is literally flattened to the ground. Not even pieces of wall remaining, only piles of bricks, roofing tiles, rubbish. The tiling of the operating rooms and the fixtures of the surgery department are recognizable, but the administrative offices, the out-patient clinic and the maternity wards have disappeared. Night falls; on each side of the road lie ruins: this is the residential area, with houses built out of durable materials, cement, bricks . . .We go to the 3rd level school, a big building for 1,500 students: not even a piece of wall is left. The Teachers Training College to the right is razed to the ground.

In the evening, we leave for the province of Quang Binh. We cannot get across the Gianh River because the ferry blew up around 11 p.m. The local authorities think it was a mine, because nobody heard any airplanes. We find refuge in a straw hut some distance from the main town of Ba Don. Sunday, March 5: visit of various places. The village was attacked in September 1966; we find traces of fragmentation bombs and napalm on straw huts and in the rice paddies. There is no military or strategic objective there. There were no victims because the peasants took cover as soon as they heard the airplanes approaching. We go to see the adjacent buildings of Ba Don Sanatorium, and the Hospital of Quang Trach district: they have been destroyed. In particular, we notice a huge crater left by the explosion of two 3,000 lb. twin bombs which fell in June, 1965. Only the ground-level foundation of the 2nd level school remains in this town. All along the road which passes through the regional administrative center, the houses — built of durable material — have collapsed.

Monday, March 6: we are given lodging not far from Dong Hoi in the province of Quang Binh. I am briefed on the situation in the province. The morning of the next day: audience with witnesses (cf. appendix); then a visit by bicycle, of the provincial hospital near Dong Hoi. While passing through the hamlets, where there is an abundance of septic pits designed by the Vietnamese health service, we notice craters in the fields, a demolished pagoda, and burned down houses. The hospital, isolated in the plain, can be seen in the distance, several kilometers away. Everything from top to bottom is demolished. It was attacked 11 times in 1965, and 6 times in 1966.

I can make out signs of pellets, rockets, 20mm cannon, bombs of at least one ton, and napalm. The surgery department has been totally laid waste; a few walls have withstood it all, patches of napalm remain stuck to the tiling. We put a match to a fragment which had not burned; it catches fire, giving off a thick black smoke. A window-pane covered with napalm has been taken as evidence. The garage has burned, as has the director's Citroen, which had been used for transportation of patients. A few hundred meters away were the 2nd and 3rd level schools, of which only a few pieces of the walls remain.

On Wednesday, March 8, we are in the fishing village of Ngu Thuy. On the horizon of the sea, a ship of the 7th Fleet has been cruising for some time; a U.S. reconnaissance plane regularly circles at an altitude of about 1,000 meters. Divided up into small groups, we visit the hamlets of Thuong Nam and Thuong Bac, destroyed by U.S. aircraft on July 16, 1966 (cf. appendix). Everything is burned to cinders, the trees are skeletal, black and leafless; some look as though they had been cut off at the bottom. There are patches of napalm on the sand, and napalm is hanging on the bushes. We stop in front of a crater: on this spot, a napalm bomb burned a woman and her 4 children to death. We speak with the husband, Ngo Vinh, 33, who was on guard duty on August 16, 1966. At Thuong Bac, the Cooperative Offices, built with durable material, have been pulverized. At Thuong Nam, the Commune Maternity Hospital, 25 beds, is a pile of bricks. On the shore is a boat, burned by napalm. Despite these attacks, the inhabitants have stayed in the vicinity. Afternoon: general report and presentation of the victims.

Thursday, March 9: Vinh Linh. After briefing, we leave, at 12:30 p.m., to visit the administrative center of Ho Xa. The road runs around 4 km. from Hien Luong bridge, which we are able to catch sight of spanning the Ben Hai River. We cross Ho Xa without stopping, because the area is dangerous; we are going to the hospital which is situated a little outside of the city as are most Vietnamese hospitals which have been bombed. A particularly hideous detail: the two red crosses over the entrance gate are surrounded by large patches of napalm. The operating room is no longer recognizable: in its place is a napalm bomb crater. On the way back, we stop in front of the 3rd level school, completely destroyed. In front of it are two recent craters, 8 days old: The theatre is badly damaged.

On each side of the road rich fields in perfect condition stretch out; we meet peasants carrying sweet potatoes. After our return to the shelter which serves as our home, we hear witnesses, and I examine a few victims.

At Vinh Linh, bombardment from U.S. artillery dug-in on the south side of the DMZ was especially intense. It will take us 6 days to get back to Hanoi. During this time, I had the opportunity to visit a "sub-district" hospital in Quang Binh province, several straw huts where we make impromptu stops, a cooperative village in the province of Nghe An, Dien Chau district. This village was attacked repeatedly on December 21, 1966 (20 dead — including 10 children and 9 women, 71 wounded, 89 houses damaged) the infirmary was hit. Attacked again on January 15, 1967. We saw the home of the teacher, whose entire family was killed. The teacher, Nguyen Phien, was introduced to us at the evacuated infirmary.

On the Destruction of the Leprosarium of Quinh Lap
testimony by M. Francis Kahn, M.D.

I visited the site of the Leprosarium of Quinh Lap on April 7, 1967, accompanied by Dr. Yen, from the Ministry of Public Health of the D.R.V. and by three members of the Security Commission of the D.R.V. . . .

There had been long discussions on the subject of where to fix the site of this leprosarium before deciding on Quinh Lap. What was required was a spot completely isolated, but which would nevertheless provide a pleasant environment and interesting cultural possibilities for the population of lepers who would live there. The small coastal plain of Quinh Lap, surrounded by a circle of mountains, filled the requirements perfectly.

In spite of its suitability for cultivation, it was so isolated that no road led there until the construction of the leprosarium in 1957. The leprosarium was not a hospital, but a regular city. Leprosy is a chronic disease, now curable but at the cost of long treatment; because of its manifestations in the nervous system, it produces grave infirmities. Finally, as everyone knows, it is contagious. A city of lepers was therefore designed to permit these invalids a life in society as near as possible to the normal, while at the same time offering them the opportunity to be healed, to be reeducated, to learn to readapt, or to adapt to a normal life in society after their recovery. The leprosarium consisted of 160 buildings, mostly residential, designed to house 2,600 lepers; the others being: a hospital, the only two-story building and identified by a red cross, designed for the care of the particular affliction of the lepers; a church and a pagoda; some cultural centers; several schools of general study and trades; a movie theater; a library; and various technical and administrative buildings.

The leprosarium, begun in 1957, completed in 1959, inaugurated in 1960, visited by several foreign delegations, and recognized by the O.M.S., had accumulated 4,000 lepers of whom more than 1,000 returned home cured. It was a vanguard health center, containing a research center on leprosy with a specialized library

That is to say, the leprosarium of Quinh Lap was known throughout the world of medicine and science, and in particular by the international health organizations. No doubt could exist about its existence, its purpose, its location.

After numerous reconnaissance flights in May, 1965, on June 12, 1965, a Saturday, at 8:00 p.m., when the health personnel had returned to their own buildings situated 2 or 3 kilometers from the leprosarium, a first attack took place, with high explosive bombs and rockets. That attack produced only a few wounded and little damage. There were no deaths. The health authorities of the leprosarium were so confident in the identification of the place by the attackers, in the red cross located on the hospital, and above all in the knowledge of the purpose of this town (which the previous reconnaissance flights could not have failed to reveal), that they did not immediately evacuate the leprosarium, *believing the attack was in error* . . .

But the next day, June 13, 1965, at 7:45 p.m., several waves of airplanes dropped bombs of all types causing 120 deaths and more than 1,000 wounded of whom 19 died as a result of their injuries. The last waves strafed with 20mm cannon and with heavy machine-gun fire the lepers who fled the explosions and flames on every side.

The lepers were then evacuated to caves located 5 or 6 kilometers from there, at the foot of rocky isolated hills. The planes attacked again, with rocket, machine gun and cannon fire, causing this time 34 deaths and 30 wounded. The lepers were evacuated deeper into the caves.

This evacuation did not cause the attacks to stop — rather they continued: 13 attacks from June 12, 1965 to June 21, 1965. On June 15, 1965, the Minister of Public Health of the D.R.V. officially addressed a formal complaint to organizations of public health in various countries, and to the International Control Commission which is charged with seeing that the Geneva accords are respected.

Since that attack, however, by official count, 26 new aerial attacks have taken place. The only entrance to the leprosarium is in the region where the missiles strike, which makes access to it dangerous and explains why relatively few journalists or investigators have visited it. It is no longer known, since practically no one stays there, what kind of missiles fall, nor the dates of bombardments. Lists are no longer made, but my companions (who had not come there for six months) questioned two aged persons still present on the premises, one of whom was Mr. Dao Van Tau, who told them that they thought that the missiles recently dropped were the result of shelling from the ships, and that the most recent dated only several days ago.

In the morning, toward 5:00 a.m., just before daybreak, we took the road to Quinh Lap. It rose in sharp turns along the side of a rugged hill, 1,300 meters in height and enclosed in a narrow gorge. After 2 or 3 kilometers, after a final turning, we came to a small pass where we left the bicycles we were riding. At the end of the pass, the small coastal plain of Quinh Lap was visible in the breaking day.

I could thus verify that the isolation which we have indicated was total. The small coastal plain has no other entrance than the road and the pass which goes through the rugged terrain bordering it. From the sea, moreover, this path is not easily seen and one would say that a mountainous circle surrounds it on all sides.

The shore is, along its length, a sandy beach with a gentle slope. It cannot at any point serve as refuge for a boat larger than a fishing vessel. The only two buildings situated on a height were, they told us, the reception building for the lepers and the electric transformer for the leprosarium. No other inhabited site, no other road, artifact or construction is visible outside the perimeter of the leprosarium.

We then verified the total character of the destruction of the leprosarium. We found not one of the 160 buildings intact. One third of the buildings was reduced to rubble without form; the rest of the buildings may be identified by sections of walls still standing. Three buildings have wall sections and fragments of bricks on the ground completely blackened as by fire: their form is fairly well preserved. As for others, they bear the traces of explosion and fire.

Innumerable craters surround these ruins. They are old, and in the leprosarium itself, we did not find any fresh craters. The principal hospital building still preserved wall sections of its two stories, and sufficient planks so that we could climb up part of the stairway and walk along the remains of the first floor. The fragments of walls still intact were riddled with shell holes and round holes which we thought to be caused by machine-guns and 20mm cannons. Here and there, we found the twisted debris of medical implements, some old bottles which had contained antibiotics, plus a bed frame of hospital design.

For almost an hour we explored these deserted ruins, when we were met by a man, evidently leprous, who explained to my companions that he was directing a group of a few lepers who had returned, in spite of the risk, to cultivate the fertile earth of that valley in order to help feed their evacuated comrades.

The presence of that man seemed to greatly amaze my companions, who did not know of their return or that several lepers had rebuilt a straw hut where they lived. At our request, the leper, Mr. Nguyen Van Tan, 42 years old, went to fetch his companions, and we questioned them personally . . .

They are originally from different provinces, and all afflicted with leprosy with open lesions in the extremities with paralysis, retractions, and amputation.

Mr. Nguyen Van Tan was, like his companions, at the leprosarium during the attacks. He remembered very well the first of these attacks, which had disquieted him and some of his comrades a great deal. He remembered vividly the second and large attack, and said: "It was terrifying, the airplanes passed and repassed. Everything shook under us. My comrades tried to flee in all directions, helping each other or trying to. No one knew where to go, and especially where to carry those of the patients who walked with difficulty or who were paralysed." He himself was buried after the explosion of a bomb near him, but he was dug out and saved.

He also remembered an attack on the cemetery of the leprosarium in which the bombs exhumed the remains of the victims of previous attacks.

Questioned on this point, the witness specified that at the beginning there were mostly high explosive bombs, then later fragmentation bombs. The other lepers agreed. Two of them made known by signals that they had something to show us. Dang Van Phac, 54 years old, and Pham Din Xuan, 29 years, went off toward a corner of the ruins and returned with a number of missile fragments: a missile warhead (No. MK 50, Lot 3B) with a rocket propulsion tube . . . and especially an object of cylindrical form, heavy (2 to 3 kilograms), and pierced with two holes. From one of these holes a white smoke emerged when a small piece of wood was thrust into it. One could extract from it a substance which spontaneously flamed on exposure to the air and ignited the piece of wood that we plunged into it. The material seemed to me to be white phosphorus. The object is in the process of analysis at Hanoi . . . I did not find any pieces of fragmentation bombs but, on a wall, a group of impact points were arranged corresponding to the classic pattern of these bombs.

On the way back, I could verify that certain craters that bordered or surrounded the road were very old, and others were quite recent, notably one of them which severed this road completely and contained unrusted splinters.

I saw the small rocky hills, rather rugged and full of caves, one kilometer from the road, located about midway between the leprosarium and the National Route 1, where Dr. Yen told me that the lepers had taken refuge momentarily, and there were attacked after the assault on the leprosarium. These hills also are totally isolated among the ricefields.

From this spot which was 5 or 6 kilometers from the leprosarium itself, the view embraces a wide landscape. One can see that the small network of craggy hills and the coastal valley where the leprosarium was, are totally isolated in the middle of the countryside.

The leprosarium had not undergone very recent attack for the craters looked fairly old; on the other hand, the access route continues to be attacked.

Report on Civilian Bombardment

testimony by Professor S. Kugai

Member First Japanese Commission of Inquiry

. . . The First Japanese Investigating Team stayed in the Democratic Republic of Vietnam for a month from December to January 1967. Mr. Harrison Salisbury of the *New York Times* was also there at this time. He covered the two cities of Nam Dinh and Phu Ly; we traveled more than 2,600 miles through various parts of North Vietnam by jeep and on foot. We carried out investigations and collected evidence in seven provinces and interviewed more than 100 witnesses whose testimonies have been recorded on tapes, films and photos.

After completing these investigations, on January 8, we held an interview in Hanoi with more than 200 people including local and foreign correspondents and the diplomatic corps present. At this conference, it was demonstrated clearly on the basis of the evidence we collected on the spot, of the testimony of witnesses, of films and photos, that there could be no denial that the U.S. committed war crimes in Vietnam. Mr. Salisbury was present at this conference and he is quite familiar with the facts about which we spoke. He is an honest and able journalist and he has every right to report as he likes. Upon his return to the U.S., however, he made no mention in his account of what we had said. He pointed out only that in Nam Dinh and Phu Ly, which he himself saw, civilian targets and the civilian population were attacked. Yet his report caused great repercussions in the United States and the Johnson Administration had to admit that civilian targets had indeed been bombed. Had Mr. Salisbury reported all that he must have learned in Hanoi, all that he heard from us and the evidence we had collected, it would have created a tremendous shock to the people of the United States. The following comprises part of what we stated at the press-conference in Hanoi, part of what I myself said there.

Weapons Used

Bombs most generally found in every spot are CBUs (Canister Bomb Unit). About the nature of these bombs, Prof. Vigier has given an excellent explanation here. Regarding these types of weapons, I would like to add only a few words. CBU bombs are a new type of weapon of mass slaughter that can destroy people over an area 170 times greater than could be covered by conventional bombs of the same weight. Since April, 1966, the new CBU bombs of the ball type began to be used extensively in Vietnam.

CBU bombs are completely ineffective to destroy military targets made of iron and concrete; they are strictly counter-insurgency weapons; weapons of mass slaughter designed to supress people's war. CBUs are greatly effective in killing and wounding people. There is no more powerful answer to the repeated claims of President Johnson and Secretary Rusk who say that the bombing is limited to only military targets, than the fact that CBU bombs are the weapons most generally used in bombing the North.

Secondly, we confirmed that not only in South Vietnam but also in the North, napalm bombs are being extensively used. Napalm turns an area with a diameter of 250 feet into a sea of flame with a temperature of 800-1,300° C. At this high temperature, napalm not only sears the skin and flesh of the victims but even welds the bone together. Four fingers of a patient I saw had been welded together, and only by two surgical operations could they be again made into fingers. The keloid scars from napalm are like those seen in Hiroshima and Nagasaki on victims of the Atom Bomb; the flesh and skin is swollen an inch in dark red blotches.

As napalm burns, it absorbs large quantities of oxygen, and generates carbon-monoxide around the drop zone. Even those people who could otherwise be saved from burning by napalm, become unconscious from the carbon monoxide and find it difficult to escape from the spot, thus increasing the number of victims.

Shutting-off the oxygen by putting sand or a blanket on a flaming wound caused by napalm can put out the fire after some time. But the new supernapalm now used by the U.S. in Vietnam includes 30% of white phosphorus and polystyrenes in the napalm liquid. If this liquid touches the skin, the fire cannot be put out even if the supply of oxygen is cut off. Left as it is, the burn will penetrate deep into the bone. Unless the white phosphorus on the affected part is completely removed, the treatment is impossible. Napalm and supernapalm are atrocious weapons and their maximum use is in killing the civilian population. They have minimal use against military targets.

186

We must also point out that, as seen in the successive use of the latest type planes and helicopters, the "evolution" from "pineapple" bombs to ball bombs and from napalm to "supernapalm", as well as in the extensive use of air-to-surface missiles, the blowing-up of dikes and irrigation facilities, and the spreading of agricultural chemicals, poisonous substances and toxic gases, that the U.S. has made the Vietnamese people test animals for their most modern weapons and most up-to date tactics of mass annihilation. As Mr. Wilfred Burchett told me, in Hanoi, we, as Japanese, cannot overlook the fact that the U.S. has always tested its new weapons against Asians. The U.S., I remind you, first in the history of man, used nuclear weapons against Hiroshima and Nagasaki, bacteriological weapons and napalm against the Korean and Chinese peoples, and CBUs, agricultural chemicals, poison chemicals and super-napalm against the Vietnamese people.

Attacks by Combinations of Weapons

On the evening of January 6, in Hanoi, I met Lieutenant Commander Charles N. Tanner, whose wife and two children live in San Diego, California. A pilot from the aircraft carrier, *Coral Sea*, flagship of the U.S. Seventh Fleet, he was a prisoner of war who was shot down around midnight on October 9, 1966, north of Phu Ly city. His testimony is:

a. After selecting cities and towns as targets, aerial photos of these areas are taken and precise examination is made. Another reconnaissance is made in daylight on the bombing day to confirm the targets.

b. At midnight, when people are sleeping, U.S. planes fly in at a super-low altitude to avoid radar. They drop first ordinary bombs and then wind-blast bombs on the densely populated areas. As it is a surprise attack, made while people are sleeping, considerable numbers are wounded or killed, but those who can, hurry into shelters.

c. The second attack will be with napalm. This causes fire and the people in the bomb shelter try to escape outside.

d. Then a third attack is made with CBU bombs on the people who have just escaped from the shelter.

When asked, "If this kind of attack was used only in the plan to hit Phu Ly city," Lt. Commander Tanner replied, "I have made 95 sorties and this is the method we have always used." Asked again, "If prior reconnaissance can identify hospitals, schools, and churches", he replied, "They can be identified completely. But our targets are the entire town and city."

187

Had he been brain-washed? The charge that his testimony may be false because of his present situation is not valid. We were able to confirm that his testimony was authentic by the evidence we ourselves had found in many spots, embers of napalm, splinters and unexploded casings of ordinary bombs and CBU bombs. We have brought back with us some of this evidence and we submit it herewith to the Tribunal.

Targets

In addition to the fact that urban and rural populations constitute the major targets of bombing, there are some points to be noted in connection with targetting. Dikes, canals, irrigation facilities, and sea-shore breakwaters are systematically bombed, especially in the rainy season from June through October. Testimony on the bombing of dikes and irrigation facilities will be given by Mr. Fukushima, a leading agricultural expert in Japan. It suffices here to quote *I.F. Stone's Weekly* dated July 12, 1965.

"There may be worse in the offing: bombing of the North Vietnamese dikes. These support the irrigation works of the Red River delta. Bombing the dikes has been discussed several times in the French press but has been blacked out of the American. In its July 4-5 issue *Le Monde* speculates whether the dikes will be our next target. In its July 6 issue it carries an article by the famous agricultural expert, Rene Dumont, describing the enormous effort put into the irrigation system to meet the needs of overpopulated North Vietnam. The most tempting moment for our military, especially if they meet serious defeats in the South during the summer, will come at the end of the rainy season in August, when the waters are at their height. Blowing up the great dikes to the North of Hanoi would be comparable to an H-bomb in its effect, flooding the entire delta region, wiping out the summer rice crop and drowning from two to three million people. North Vietnam could survive the loss of the industries it has built up since 1954, but to bomb the dikes would mean starvation. Destruction of dikes was one of the war crimes for which Seyss-Inquart, chief of the Nazi occupation in Holland, was hanged at Nuremberg. The Hague Convention years before had made such action a violation of international law but Goering pleaded at the trial,' In a life and death struggle there is no legality.' Has this become our viewpoint, too, even though Vietnam is hardly a life and death matter for us? The bombardment of the dikes would be genocide."

One more thing about dikes: U.S. planes have even dropped time bombs at the places where the dikes have been destroyed so that repair groups may not be able to get close to the spot. In Quang Binh province, napalm attacks were also made against repair groups.

Hospitals are Targets of Systematic Bombing

Bombing of hospitals are not the result of mis-bombing or bombing of secondary "targets of opportunity." First, hospitals are shown on the maps of targets in the hands of the U.S. pilots who have been shot down and these hospitals are actual targets. For instance, K-71 Hospital, a provincial T.B. sanatorium of Nam Ha is a hospital with 600 beds in about 50 buildings scattered over a large site, with a big red cross marked on all the buildings. All of these buildings were destroyed by continuous bombings over a period of three days. A provincial hospital of Don Hoi, Quang Binh province, was also destroyed in the same way with demolition bombs and napalm bombs. Hospitals and clinics, not only in cities but also in rural areas, have been systematically bombed. Even when a hospital once bombed is moved to a rural area, it is bombed again. This shows that the aim is the deliberate destruction of medical facilities. We cannot but see that the U.S. intention is to make the people of Vietnam feel helpless with no one to treat them even if wounded by the bombing. The same applies to the destruction of schools and churches.

In addition to the indiscriminative bombing and destruction of railways, roads, and bridges, U.S. planes have discharged rockets into straw-thatched huts in rice fields, elaborately blown up even small earthern bridges, and strafed and bombed farming peasants, cow-herding children, buffaloes, and fishing boats along the shore.

All the members of our Investigating Team were unanimous in concluding that, in our estimation, the main aim of bombing of the North is to make the people of Vietnam feel that there is no safe place on earth and so force them to give up their resistance struggle. . .

Report from North and South Vietnam
by Marta Rojas

Cuban Author

. . . . I experienced the U.S. barbarity in Vietnam, during three
months that I stayed there. For 45 days my colleague, Raul Valdes
Vivo, a Cuban journalist and professor, and I lived side by side
with the heroic forces of the National Liberation Front of South
Vietnam.

I arrived in the Democratic Republic of Vietnam in August 1965,
and stayed there for ten days. Later, I moved on to South Vietnam,
where I stayed for six weeks in the liberated zones controlled by
the National Liberation Front. Later I returned to the North, where
I stayed a further ten days in October and November of that year.
During my stay in Vietnam, I saw smoking ruins in the North, as
well as piles of rubble which were the remains of hospitals, schools,
houses and villages. I also saw ruins dating from months before.
The destruction carried out between May and November, 1965,
was worse than for the rest of that year. Dating from the North
American attack after the Gulf of Tonkin, aggression increased
gradually and progressively in its intensity and consequences.
I personally witnessed the atrocities about which other investigation
teams, who went to Vietnam after I did, have testified before this
Tribunal. I do not believe it is necessary to enumerate all this
evidence again. I must repeat that I saw schools, factories, homes
and hospitals destroyed. I spoke with the families of victims of the
bombings, who told me their pitiful stories. I became aware of the
fact that the United States has never declared war on the Democratic Republic of Vietnam, as I am sure all the other investigating
Commissions know. Since there has been no official declaration of
war, the United States imperialists are committing constant and
flagrant acts of aggression against Vietnam.

Then, as now, American planes drop hundreds of thousands of
tons of bombs over the entire area of Vietnam, unless they are
stopped by the wall of fire from rifles, anti-aircraft guns and rockets.

The Vietnamese people have the right to use these weapons to counter American aggression, and they use them well.

I have vivid memories of the time I spent in Hanoi: During the evenings and nights in Hanoi, the women, after a long working day, take pikes and bamboo spades to dig up the pavements and parks and construct shelters. Sometimes they had no implements and dug with their hands. I saw many collapse from fatigue. I saw many of them taken from the shelters they had constructed, almost dead from fatigue. These shelters were made to protect the lives of their children, their compatriots and foreigners. A people who have achieved liberty after so much sacrifice must now endure the most cruel war in history. Victims of the war include children who have died from malnutrition, women who have died building shelters, and those who have been killed by falling machinery while dismantling their factories. They are forced to dismantle factories to protect the national economy. During our stay we spoke with several workers from a dismantled textile factory who were dispersed to 100 different places in order to continue production: they told us how much work they had undertaken in order to protect the factory's machinery.

In July, 1965, the Yankee aggressors bombed and machine-gunned Nan Dinh, the third most populous industrial city in North Vietnam, thereby committing cruel atrocities. For a month, from July 2 to August 3, 1965, this city was attacked six times. The most intense bombardment occurred on August 2 and 3, when the textile factories, residential areas and densely populated streets were attacked, resulting in the death of hundreds of people.

In the rural areas and villages of the South, the people live underground practically the whole time; in the North it is the same. They work in the rice fields at night, to prevent American planes from detecting their presence . . . and the bombing does not even cease at night.

The water in the paddy fields reaches the waists of the women: this criminal war imposed by the United States has interrupted the technical development and mechanization of cultivation. In Vietnam no rubber boots or raincoats are available, nor are there sufficient agricultural machines to improve working conditions in the rice fields. These things do not exist because the Democratic Republic of Vietnam has been obliged to use all its available resources to defend the country. This is also a war crime, as it is aggression against the economy of a country. I have personally worked for an hour in the rice fields, and I must testify before this Tribunal that it is criminal for women to work under these conditions.

Every unborn child who is deformed because his mother is working under the conditions imposed by the war is another victim of aggression. I do not need to explain what happens to a woman who works long hours in swamps full of germs and insects, with water reaching to her waist most of the time. You can try to imagine these conditions, but I do not believe you can picture the reality. A doctor could probably give a better description of these cases . . .

At dawn, September 10, 1965, we found ourselves, for the first time, in the liberated territory of the South. Day broke as we moved through a green and swampy rice field. Everything was quiet until suddenly, from the high trees surrounding this paddy field, we heard voices. These voices warned of the approach of Yankee planes. We were experiencing our baptism of fire in South Vietnam. A wave of B-52s and other planes started the dawn bombing. From then on we were to witness an average of three bombings a day. I experienced 152 bombings during my 45 day stay in South Vietnam. During the whole period we moved through liberated territory inhabited by South Vietnamese people, they were indescriminately bombed.

At about this time the bombings by B-52 strategic aircraft intensified in South Vietnam and simultaneously the aggression increased in the North. The escalation in the North was the North Americans' answer to the victories of the National Liberation Front. We have not the slightest doubt that the North American aggression is a reprisal against the people for their unbreakable spirit of struggle and their unbending resistance.

I have seen the damage caused by the B-52 bombers in the South, I have seen gigantic craters in the jungle and villages from these bombs. I can state to this Tribunal that identical or similar planes have dropped bombs on the Democratic Republic of Vietnam, which produce the same destructive effects.

Judging from the remains of planes and other military objects exhibited in the War Museum of the DRV, it is obvious that the Yankee aggressors have used jet planes of the heavy type, such as B-57, A-3, A-4, A-6, and F-4. Fragmentation bombs, napalm, white phosphorus bombs, anti-personnel and other weapons have been directed against the civilian population. I need not dwell on this, as the report of the Tribunal investigating teams has given sufficient information.

Regarding the bombings by B-52's, the North American pilots have a method, a special system of aggression. The job of the aerial terrorists begins with the visit of a reconnaissance plane or a helicopter which surveys the region to be bombed; this plane drops propaganda, consisting of leaflets showing a photograph of a plane dropping bombs and on the other side a text warning the people to leave the zone where the bombing shall take place. The leaflets exhort the population to go over to the puppet authorities and abandon the patriots, they say specifically that they should abandon the "Vietcong". But before the leaflets have touched the ground, the B-52's appear with a tremendous roar and immediately begin to drop 800 and 1000 pound bombs over the small area. After the B-52's leave, the helicopters appear again, flying low, playing loud music and dropping picture cards and propaganda literature directed to the guerrillas inviting them to surrender or else the bombing of the villages will continue . . .

We retrieved some of these propaganda leaflets and herewith present them to the Tribunal. One reads as follows [literal translation]:

"Friends, officers and soldiers of the Viet Cong, you have experienced terrible and terrifying moments. You have seen with your own eyes the dark tragedy which the Communists conceal beneath their flaming words of Revolution and Liberation in South Vietnam. The actions of the B-52s which you have just witnessed will continue on a larger scale. The war will be extended more and more until the Communist regime of the North makes the decision to accept peaceful negotiations. Stop the war in Vietnam or you will see the rebellion in the South completely destroyed. Think it over. Take this pamphlet to the nearest military post or to the nearest organization from which you have received your orders, help and support."

I shall relate something which is of particular interest to the women of the world. A crime which is not visible in wounds but in human emotions. When we were in Hanoi we received from various sources, letters and photographs of men and women who had in some way learned that we were going to the South. They saw in us a way to send a message of love to their families. "It was twenty years ago that I last saw my wife," one official told us. "Since Geneva I have had no information about my children who were left with their mother in the South," said another, and he added, "How could we possibly meet again?" After we arrived in the South, we began to deliver the letters and thus learned about the fate of many families. The destruction of the family by the war in Vietnam is also a crime!

During an interview that we had with Mrs. Nguyen Thi Dinh, Vice-Commander in Chief of the Liberation Army of South Vietnam, she became grave and sad when we asked her, "Have you any children?" Nguyen Thi Dinh answered us in a dramatic way, "Not any longer. My son would have been 25 years old now. He was in Hanoi. As a child he was evacuated to a northern province during the war with the French colonialists. I remained in the South and after the war resumed, I never saw him again. It was exactly one year ago I learned he was dead." This story is typical of conditions in Vietnam. We heard it from the lips of women in North Vietnam and from the lips of fighters of the great army of women in the South.

Courts, when they are investigating the responsibility of those who commit a crime, take into consideration the perpetrator's background in order to ascertain whether it is a question of an occasional misdeed, or of one who is dangerous because he constantly commits the same kinds of acts. The case of the United States government is precisely that of the habitual criminal. The people of Asia, Africa, Latin America and of the so-called Third World can testify to what I have just said.

I repeat: The United States has been a habitual aggressor. We Latin Americans know this well — in the Dominican Republic, in Cuba, Guatemala, Panama . . . there are many.

Distinguished members of the Tribunal, the day is not far off when a similar International Tribunal will find itself obliged to investigate aggression and crimes committed by the same imperialism in my own land, Latin America.

Extracts from the Testimony of Alejo Carpentier

Mr. Carpentier is a Cuban Author

I come to bear witness before this Tribunal, and I already have the impression that my testimony is outdated, outdated by far. It has been eight months since I was in Vietnam and already the tragedy is greater... In these eight months the North Americans have used every possible method to magnify the destruction to a scale which only technology—their technology—makes possible.

So my testimony is a bit outdated, but I think at the same time it can have a value. The horrors have increased. What I saw eight months ago constituted an introduction, a sort of preview of what would later arrive. This preview was all the more valuable because it reveals the pattern and the method of destruction and extermination which would later become standard operating procedure for U.S. aggression against all Vietnam...

As a witness, I would like to pass on directly to things that I saw and heard with my own senses, and to bypass written and published documents which, without doubt, you already have. This concerns a subject which particularly touches my heart—that of school children burned and disfigured by napalm bombs.

I knew two of them, Ho Van Bot, 16 years old, and the very young Le The Hoa, 12 years old, and on their bodies I saw the napalm scars. I shan't go into detail for it would make interminable testimony. It is hard to measure at what point the horror by accumulation of such detail loses its ability to shock and becomes a monotonous thing. But I think it useful to submit to you the words of Ho Van Bot, whose very brief tale can do without my comment.

"It was July 8, 1964," he told me, "we were in school. A reconnaissance plane arrived and flew around marking out our school. Two rocket shells hit the building. The teacher evacuated us. We ran to the shelters, and while running were in danger from the falling debris. Several students found death there. A little later the Americans sent six planes which flew over and dropped napalm bombs on our school. Three fell near the school and surrounding area, causing a huge fire. Some students were burning like torches; they ran in every direction crying out to the teacher and to their parents. Some threw themselves into the waterholes where they stopped burning. As for me, my face began to burn. I tried to extinguish it with my hands. I made the mistake of putting my arms in the water and I lost the skin. There were some students struck down by the gas exhalations from the explosion. The same planes flew low and machine-gunned the others. Some fell, dead, in the fields; others lost legs or arms. Maddened by the burning I ran to the house before me, jumping over the children's bodies. Then the American planes returned..."

The photographs I took of these young people burned by napalm, I submit to the Tribunal. Names? Yes, I can give them to you, they are in my notebook.

...As for the methods used in general during the American raids, they aim principally at destruction of dikes, dams, and artifacts— at the extermination of the civilian population... Mr. John Steinbeck, in his unbelievable *Letters to Alice,* wrote of his admiration for the American helicopter pilots who maneuver the controls, he said, "with hands as delicate as those of Pablo Casals."

But underneath those hands, so delicate, so sensitive, so musical — to borrow from this writer who has made himself an object of ridicule with such a display of brutal stupidities — there are these people I have told you of. There are children burned by napalm, destroyed schools, massacred adolescents, the ruins of Phu Ly and Nam Dinh, the destroyed cities, and this abominable war waged against a small, poor country by a gigantic military power.

As a writer from a country (Cuba) threatened by the same force of destruction, I have come here to bear witness. This war in Vietnam concerns us all. Our consciences cry denunciation of this monstrosity. This war concerns all men who, in this century, still keep a sense of present realities and who can imagine future realities. Perhaps there is still time to stop on the brink of a catastrophe which will strike all human beings; strike them not only in their spirit, but in their flesh.

Investigations of U.S. War Crimes in North Vietnam
testimony by Lawrence Daly

Mr. Daly is Secretary General of the Scottish Mine Worker's Union

The Second Investigation Team of the International War Crimes Tribunal was in North Vietnam from January 24, 1967, until February 17, 1967. We were welcomed on the evening of February 24 by representatives of the North Vietnamese Government and, on the morning of January 25, we discussed our programme with Mr. Pham Van Bach of the D.R.V. War Crimes Commission. It was agreed that in the first phase of the investigation the team should split into two groups. One group, Dr. Tolentino and myself, to travel northwest of Hanoi and the others, Dr. Behar, Miss Carol Brightman and Tariq Ali, to the south.

On January 27 we met religious leaders and heard details from them of the attacks on churches and pagodas by the U.S. planes.

In the afternoon we inspected areas of Hanoi that had been bombed in attacks which had occurred on December 2, 3 and 14, 1966.

In the Van Dien district, high explosive bombs, rockets and pressure bombs had been dropped. We saw huge craters and destroyed and damaged houses. The Senior High School (named in honor of Vietnam-Polish friendship) had been destroyed. We met two pupils and one teacher (all females) who had been wounded during the attacks. The girls were Miss Hong Thi Ly and Miss Nguyen Thi Giang. The teacher was Miss Nguyen Thi An.

In the Tu Ky quarter of Van Dien, two children were killed in the raid on December 2, 1966. The Tu Ky pagoda had also been destroyed. Most of the 600 pupils had been evacuated and only a class of 44 pupils was in the school when the alert sounded. But for this fact and the nearby deep shelters, the casualties would have been much greater.

We visited the Trade Union Cadres Training School in the Dong Da quarter of Hanoi which had been bombed on December 14, 1966. One student was killed and six were wounded. A large part of the three-storey building was wrecked, as was the student's hostel. Many houses nearby — in Tay Son Street — had been ruined and four people were killed and five wounded. Rockets and high explosive bombs were used.

On the evening of January 27, Dr. Tolentino and I left Hanoi for the north while the others began the journey south to the province of Thanh Hoa and Ninh Binh. We traveled at night by jeeps to the city of Vietri and were welcomed by provincial officials in a jungle headquarters outside the city.

Vietri is an industrial town with a population of 40,000. U.S. planes had made reconnaissance flights over the city on January 12, 13 and 14, 1967 and had then attacked on January 15 at 15:05 hours with twelve F-105 planes which dropped 28 explosive bombs and 4 container bomb units (C.B.U.) (1,200 steel pellet bombs). The attacks were concentrated on Thuan Luong Commune and especially Phuc Theun village and Dong Luc co-operative. two people were killed (one man, one woman). Eleven people were wounded (four male and seven female) including five children. Those killed were the victims of steel pellet bombs. Twenty-two houses had been destroyed or damaged.

On January 18, at 7 a.m., 18 F-105's had attacked with high explosive bombs, pressure bombs, time bombs and C.B.U's. They struck the Roman Catholic Commune of Tien Cat and also the Commune of Minh Dong, including the hamlets of Gia Vuong and Minh Tan. Twenty people were killed (seven male and 13 female), including eight children. Sixty-one were wounded (28 male and 23 female), including 15 children. One hundred twenty-nine houses were demolished and eight were burned down. The school, the hospital and the kindergarten were bombed. Dikes and sluices had also been attacked.

In the hamlet of Doan Det, the church had been demolished and five people had been killed. Mr. Nguyen Van Tho, a peasant, had lost his 39 year old wife and his two sons, aged 15 years and 2 years. They were killed by a direct hit on their shelter. Mr. Le Quing Toai and his wife lost two children, six years and six months old, and both he and his wife coughed blood due to the effects of pressure bombs.

The state-owned bakery shop in Dong Tiem had been bombed. One woman was killed (Miss Do Thi San, aged 53 years) and four other women were wounded. Miss Le Thi Mo, 21 years old, was hit between the eyes by steel pellets. Mrs. Dao Thi Tri, 63 years of age, was also wounded by steel pellets. There was no time to detail all the injuries of all the victims.

We then left our headquarters to visit the bombed areas. The Roman Chatholic Church at Doan Ket was badly damaged, as was the school at Minh Dong. Fortunately, children were not at shool when the raid took place. There were huge craters and there was an unexploded bomb near what had been the state-owned bakery. We spoke to a Mr. Tay whose wife and two children had been killed We visited the hospital which had been transferred from the city centre, where it had been attacked twice previously. Many steel pellet bombs had been dropped on it and the rice fields beyond were covered with small craters left by the guava bombs. We saw many houses that had been destroyed by explosive bombs and others on or near which steel pellet anti-personnel bombs had been dropped. It was explained to us that the normal pattern of attack was to drop explosive bombs first and then to drop steel pellet bombs while people were trying to help the victims of the first attack.

In the afternoon we returned to our headquarters and interviewed the following victims: (1) Mr. Nguyen Van Tho, whose wife and two children were killed on January 18. He described his tragic experience in detail and then answered our questions. His house and property were destroyed. He had another five children, all of whom were now suffering from the effects of pressure bombs. The two dead children included his young son, aged two years. (2) Mr. Nguyen Van Tho of Doan Ket hamlet, aged 50 years. His wife and son, aged seven years, had been killed. He had four children left. His house and property were destroyed. In answer to our questions he said, as had the previous witness, that there was no military target within the vicinity. (3) Mrs. Do Thi Duyen, 66 years of age, worked in the Dong Thien bakery. She described how Mrs. San, aged 50 years, had been killed by a pressure bomb and others were seriously wounded. Her left arm was broken and her left knee was injured. She was a widow and had no children. (4) Mr. Le Qang Toai, 43 years of age, from Minh Tan hamlet, was Vice-Chairman of the Agriculture Co-operative. He described how his wife and two children (one of them five months old) had died. They were crushed as the sides of their shelter squeezed together due to the blast of a pressure bomb.

While we were interviewing Mr. Le Qang Toai, the alert went about 15:40 p.m. and we took shelter. Shortly afterwards, we felt the impact of a missile that struck the hamlet of Hoa Phong only 500 meters away. After these interviews, we visited Vietri city hospital and saw victims who were still receiving treatment. Dr. Tolentino examined these victims, who included:

1. Le Quang Chung, three year old son of Mr. Le Nogc Dang. He was wounded in the right leg and shoulder by steel pellets and he bled heavily.

2. A five year old boy, also named Le Quang Chung. He was wounded by steel pellets in the head and right leg.

3. Mrs. Nguyen Thi Luong, aged 45 years, a peasant's wife from Tan Hong Commune in the province of Ha Tay. She had travelled to Vietri for shopping on January 18 and during the raid she received wounds in the stomach and had been stunned by the bombing. Her legs were paralysed and her bowels were damaged. A bomb fragment was lodged in the spine. She also had an injury to her left arm.

4. Mr. Nguyen Van Binh, aged 51 years, a peasant from Gia Vuong hamlet in Minh Dong Commune. He had head injuries from a bomb fragment. One of his two children had also been wounded.

After leaving the hospital we went to Hoa Phong hamlet which had been attacked while we were taking refuge earlier that afternoon. It had been struck by a "Bull Pup" incendiary missile. Three houses were destroyed. One old woman and two children had been wounded and some animals had been killed. The old lady was named Pham Thi Thau and was 63 years old. A boy, Vu Van Luyen, was 12 years old and the other boy, Le Van Lap, was nine years old....

Next morning, Sunday, January 29, we received a report on the attacks on Phu Tho province. The province has a population of 640,000 and the city of Phu Tho has a population of 14,000 reduced by evacuation to 6,700. Repeated attacks on the city had been made since October 1965. Pilotless planes had been used for U.S. reconnaissance flights. On November 22, starting at 14:15 a.m., 31 sorties were flown over the city. Ninety-five explosive bombs, some weighing 1,000 lbs, were dropped. These made craters as big as 13 meters deep and 37 meters in diameter. Rockets, missiles and C.B.U.'s were also used. Thirty-three people were killed (14 male and 19 female) including one old person and six children. Two hundred eighty-two houses were burned down or demolished. A school, a buddhist temple, a hospital and a medical school had all been bombed The worst damage was done in the area of Coa Bang and Hoa Binh Streets...

On March 4th, 1966, 12 planes had attacked dropping 36 explosive bombs weighing up to 750 lbs. Thrity-eight people were killed (18 male and 20 female) including six old people and 16 children and 24 people were wounded (nine male and 15 female). Ninety-one houses were burned down or damaged; 46 were completely destroyed; 130 meters of dikes were damaged; The Roman Catholic church was severely damaged. 5,300 kilos of paddy were burned; 11 buffaloes and 15 pigs were killed. Over 1,000 banana trees were destroyed.

On October 11, 1966, 12 planes had again attacked. The bombs dropped included six C.B.U.'s — 1,800 guava bombs each containing 300 steel pellets. These fell chiefly on Phu Hong co-operative and on the Second Degree School. Sixteen people were killed (seven male and nine female), including seven old people and four children. Thirty-eight houses were burned down. Animals and rice supplies were destroyed. 1,500 steel pellet bombs fell on the rice fields which were ready for harvesting. One pupil at the school was killed. Victims included: (1) Pham Truong Tho, a 29 year old peasant. Pellets had pierced his body and legs. Part of the bowels had to be replaced by tubes. (2) Mrs. Le Thi Hien, 48 years of age. Pellets had pierced her right shoulder, left leg and right hand. Her nervous system was affected and she was unable to walk. (3) Mr. Nguyen My Tu, 36 years of age. He had lost three children — Nguyen Thi Binh — 10 years old; Nguyen Thi Quang — 6 years; Nguyen Chinh Dong — 2 years. His wife, Tran Thi Thu, aged 35 years, was wounded by a pressure bomb and, as a result, had had a miscarriage. Her brother, Nguyen Van Bang, who was a leader of the local Catholic community, had been killed. (4) Mr. Nguyen Van Chong, 73 years of age, was a teacher of the Roman Catholic religion. He had received head injuries and also a wound on the right wrist from explosive bomb fragments.

On July 27, 1965, two F-105's dropped ten napalm bombs on Co Tiet Commune. A 62 year old peasant, Mr. Ngo Van Huong, had been wounded. Twelve houses were burned down and 2,400 kilos of paddy destroyed. Twenty-nine planes had been shot down in this province, including the 400th to be brought down over North Vietnam. Other planes had been damaged and two pilots had been captured alive.

A local exhibition of war crimes evidence included a piece of cloth carried by U.S. pilots in which an appeal for help was printed in 13 languages. The English version ran: "I am a citizen of the U.S.A. I do not speak your language. Misfortune forces me to seek your assistance in obtaining food, shelter and protection. Please take me to someone who will provide for my safety and see I am returned to my people. My Government will reward you"...

Report on American Bombing of North Vietnam
testimony by Ralph Schoenman

Mr. Schoenman is a Director of the Bertrand Russell Peace Foundation and was Secretary General of the Tribunal

Bertrand Russell sent me to Vietnam to gather first hand evidence concerning war crimes, evidence which was to be used not only in defense of David Mitchell,[1] but in the International War Crimes Tribunal which Lord Russell was in the process of establishing. I arrived in Hanoi on February 21, 1966 and travelled in five provinces under heavy bombardment. South of Thanh Hoa, in Ha Tay, Nam Ha, Ninh Binh and the surrounds of Hanoi, I saw the result of 650 sorties per week, bombs of 1,000 pounds, napalm, phosphorous and a weapon known as "the lazy dog".

[1]Mr. Mitchell was the first young American to refuse service in Vietnam on the ground that the Nuremberg Charter obliges one to refuse to participate in criminal wars. He is now serving a sentence of five years in a U.S. Federal penitentiary.

We travelled by night, a team of eight, including doctors and photographers. We were without light and we stopped often during alerts. The road was pitted, though passable, and the extra-ordinarily beautiful countryside showed the effects of unrelenting bombardment.

On one village and school were dropped 1,000 pound bombs and lazy dogs. At another part of the village I picked up a lazy dog bomb. This was Van Dinh hamlet, Van Hon Village, Thieu Hon district, February 26, 1966. A lazy dog is a grenade-like bomb containing 250 slivers of razor-sharp steel. There are 40 such bombs in a cylinder: 10,000 pieces of steel in a sudden storm of hail, lacerating anyone exposed or seeking shelter from the half ton bombs. The lazy dog has been dropped continuously on the most heavily populated areas of North Vietnam. 10,000 cylinders of lazy dog bombs have fallen on Thanh Hoa province since April 1965. 1,281 rockets have been used. Thirty-seven guided missiles have been launched against villages in Thanh Hoa province. 3,000 bombs alone were dropped on Ham Rong bridge, which still stands. Roads, means of communication, schools, hospitals, the tuberculosis clinic, sanatoria and old age rest houses have been bombed in Thanh Hoa province. I visited all. I picked a lazy dog out of the ruins of a school where it had fallen after a 1,000 pound bomb had made great craters, destroying the shelters and exposing the inhabitants.

I spoke with one of the little school girls who had been wounded in the raid and she said:

"Usually, my friends go to school every day. We like to sing 'Ha Tinh Quang Binh'. My friends are Nhung, Ky, Chau, Nguyen. They are thirteen, twelve, fourteen, twelve. They are all girls. I have a friend who is a boy, named Liem. He was thirteen. My friend Ky liked to play. She would say: 'You go first. You go quickly, or I will step on your heel.'"

(Rhymes in Vietnamese.)

"When the bombs fell I saw Ky's bowel and intestine come out of her body. Her head blew away. Her arm and leg blew away. Nhung was buried alive and was dug out dead. Chau's teeth were broken by stones which shattered them. Nguyen was buried alive. Liem was beheaded. My friend Phuong laughs sometimes; cries; speaks without knowing what she says; she screams; she is twelve. I was buried completely. Teacher Minh dug me out. I have pains in my spine. Canh and Khoa had their chests crushed . . ."

Nguyen Thai Mao was recently twelve. She has been strafed frequently on the way to school. She spoke of a bombing attack on her village on February 9, 1966. Her teacher, a young man of 24 named Thai Van Nham:

> "Fragments of clothing, books and furniture flew so high that all in the vicinity knew the school was bombed. Students were blasted. Many were buried in the earth. I was among those buried alive. I was dug out later and was brought to consciousness. There was nothing left but a bomb crater, 55 feet wide and 21 feet deep. Everything was levelled. Parts of the children were protruding from the earth. We found their heads 20 yards away. Their bowels and intestines were scattered everywhere. Two of my children were spattered on a palm tree and hung from it. Children were pressed to the trench walls. Blood filled the trenches. Children clutched their books tightly to their chests. The books were smeared in blood and ink. Some of them could speak a little when dug out. Then blood shot from their mouths, due to their crushed organs and they died. One little girl, Hoang Thai Nha, twelve, could only be recognised and identified by her rubber shoes. Six of the children were too mutilated to be recognisable to the parents. One dug out became conscious and asked how many of her friends died before haemorrhaging . . ."

The old age and invalid home in Thanh Hoa was levelled. It is a scene of vast craters, filled with water, and the shells of buildings. Mosaics litter the ground — lovely pieces of the floor and walls in soft watercolour design. Out of one crater I picked the tattered pages of books which had once been part of the old age home library. Here, those Vietnamese who had lived through three generations of struggle against the Japanese, the French and the Americans had retired in the ill health of old age to rest. Many of them were feeble through years of brutal labour before the victory of Dien Bien Phu released them from colonialism . . .

The destruction of Thanh Hoa, tuberculosis sanatorium is a study in horror. On Sunday, February 27, the Director gave me the following account:

> "This is the second most important sanatorium in our country. It was set up by our own efforts. We had no help from abroad. We cherish it all the more because of this. The third floor of the tuberculosis sanatorium had very large Red Cross flags hanging outside. There are large Red Cross crosses on the entrance, clear to any aircraft. At 8:00 a.m., four groups of four aircraft came. Among the sixteen were five F-105D jets. The rest were F-101 and F-102. The planes circled several times and attacked. They dove at the clinic. Five F-105D jets dove together. Each dive re-

leased ten bombs per plane, totalling 50. The others dropped two each, totalling 22. Many patients were got to the trenches with difficulty. After the first attack, they circled, and each plane dove repeatedly, strafing everything standing with rockets. There was 30 minutes of uninterrupted bombing, with 1,000 ton bombs, accompanied by rocket strafing, of all who ran out of the buildings. Five doctors were hit and killed instantly. Two of them were women. Physicians and specialists and nurses were killed. Fifty-eight patients were killed almost immediately by strafing. All through the bombing, the shrapnel fragments, lazy dogs and the rockets, doctors and personnel carried patients to trenches. Patients and the sick carried others, while vomiting blood and haemorrhaging. It was only this heroism which kept casualties down.

If we had been dependent upon only the ability of doctors and nurses to rescue patients, the number of deaths would have been infinitely higher. Some of the patients, though weak and ill, tried to save medical equipment: X-ray machines, medicines, implements, files. Throughout these efforts they were strafed. In the surrounding area, people whose own houses were bombed and burning abandoned them, and also the shelters, to help rescue patients and equipment of the clinic.

After the first bombing, the personnel tried to evacuate surviving patients from the ruins. Five days later, the survivors were removed to new hospitals and sanatoria. A few days later, two jets came again and bombed the ruins of the sanatorium. They strafed everywhere in the vicinity. They bombed and strafed the clinic and all buildings of the sanatorium for 30 minutes. Two planes were F-105 jets. Each dropped ten half-ton bombs at a time. Other planes came and fired rockets. Two planes dispersed and returned again to fire rockets. There were three total bombings and strafings. Thus, of the sanatorium and clinic, nothing is left."

As the doctor spoke, I moved amidst the rubble, the great craters, the twisted ruins of X-ray machines and the broken glass of medicines and photo-electric lamps. Occasionally, there were bloodstains. It was difficult to imagine the vast sanatorium, with its many operating rooms and quarters for patients.

The Director continued:

"All of our people understand now that the sanatorium was a clearly intended target of the attack. There was no error. We were hit in three separate and prolonged waves from diving planes. This was a hospital. There were large Red Cross flags flying. Our patients and doctors were strafed, seeking shelter. We realise that the enemy will do anything. The U.S. knows that the treatment of tuberculosis and leprosy is one of our most urgent and difficult tasks, so they destroy. It is entirely in keeping with their bacteriological warfare. The bombing of our sanatorium has affected us profoundly. Every effort has been made by the population to assist in the lodging and treatment of the surviving patients.

They talk about civilisation. It is unimaginable. Our hatred is great. The more we confront this bombing of our leprosoria, hospitals, clinics, sanatoria, schools and villages, the more we struggle."

The K71 tuberculosis sanatorium covered two and a half hectares. There were 30 large buildings and 560 resident patients. There were 425 visiting patients per week and 350 doctors and nurses.

The equipment destroyed included X-ray machines, sterilization equipment, refrigeration facilities, circulatory and respiratory machines, oxygen equipment, distilling and purification equipment, electronic machinery, modern operation rooms and facilities, antibiotics and drugs. I inspected the remnants and ruins of the following stores of drugs: INH (produced in Vietnam); Streptomycin; Rimiforn; Subtilis; Filatove; vitamin compounds; vitamin oils; cod liver oil; sulphur; iodine and various medicines and serums. Medical supplies for the surrounding population were destroyed. Tonics, food supplements, enriching additives for special regimens and diets were all lost in the bombing. Plasma, the blood bank, ambulances, first aid units, the medical library, monographs and notebooks of doctors, microscopes, bacterial cultures, all operating equipment and chambers, tables, electronic devices, lamps and infra-red equipment were all devastated. This was not an isolated event. Wherever I went I saw comparable destruction.

Report on Bombing of North Vietnam
testimony by Charles Cobb and Julius Lester

Journalists from the U. S. and Members of Commission
of Inquiry to North Vietnam

We arrived in Hanoi on March 17, 1967 at 8:30 p.m. and were greeted by the D.R.V. War Crimes Commission, then taken to the Hotel Reunification in Hanoi. We were very generally briefed and told that our trip would be divided into three parts and would end March 31: 1) general briefing in Hanoi; 2) travel to the provinces; and 3) return to Hanoi for further discussions.

On March 22 we met with the head of the N.L.F. Delegation in Hanoi, and in addition to a general briefing on the general resistance and the war in the South, we interviewed victims from the South. The first victim was Hoang Tan Hung, a 46 year old father of four children. He is a native of Quang Ngai Province, Duc Pho District, Pho Minh village, Tan My hamlet. He was a farmer and commercial trader before becoming a victim of napalm.

On May 10, 1965 Hoang and two friends were going to Ba La hamlet in the same province, about four kilometers from a city controlled by the U.S. While they were at this village, Tu Nguyen, two L-19 reconaissance planes flew over. Soon after, four F-86's began firing rockets, forcing him to take shelter in the bush. He told us:

"In a few moments, there was an explosion behind me. I was covered with flames. I ran about 300 meters then fainted due to the extreme heat. Despite the bombing, people in the area came out and gave me first aid, poured sand on my body to put out the fire, then gave me medicine and took me to a hospital 15 Km. away in the liberated zone. I had lost consciousness. I awoke and found my body almost half burned, with the hair all gone, and yellow liquid coming out from all over my body. I was told that my burns were still smoking. I was at the medical station for ten days. My wounds improved a little and

I was brought to a larger medical station and then to the Provincial Hospital, which had 200 beds, filled with U.S. victims. I was there for five months, living in great pain. On the way to the medical station flies had laid eggs on my wounds which were open and giving off an awful smell. At the hospital bits of rotten flesh came off, even in the winter months, and although it was very cold, I felt very hot, and it was difficult to lie down and to eat."

At this hospital, he said, about fifty of the 200 patients were napalm victims and the others were victims of strafing, demolition and phosphorus bombs. A small number of patients were sick with fever or disease. Hoang has been in North Vietnam three months, receiving additional surgery. He showed us his wounds. There were welts and swellings all over his body, which was mostly a pink-brown color. His ears and one side of his face had literally been melted out of shape. The burns covered his whole body with the most severe on his back and neck and left arm. He had to look straight ahead because he couldn't move his neck, and his left arm seemed to be welded from his armpit to his elbow to the upper part of his torso. He said the pain in every part of his body was like constant needles poking at his body, and he couldn't sleep much nor eat much.

Another victim was named Thi Binh Dan, age 18, from Lomz An Province, Ben Tau District, Than Loi village in South Vietnam. He was a farmer. On the morning of March 21, 1966, L-19 reconaissance planes hovered over the village. Later, three F-105's came to bomb and strafe. Then eighteen helicopters — HU 1A type — airlifted into the area U.S., Australian, and New Zealand troops. They shot three persons in the village, more than 20 oxen and buffalo, and burned down more than 20 houses in the village. They took about 100 persons to the helicopters, along with a great quantity of poultry. Thi, along with some relatives hid in a shelter. The troops went away in the afternoon and he returned home. But, he told us, "That evening, while cooking supper, three F-105's came and dropped napalm on the village. There was no time to get to the shelter and my hair and body were burned in many places. I lost consciousness and lay on the ground. I was told later that nearly all my skin had been stripped off by the fire. By that time people had come from nearby shelters and tried to put out the fire. I was rushed to a hospital in a liberated area.

I awoke 13 days later. I black out from time to time, especially when the weather is hot. There's terrible heat in my body. I want to drink very much. For five days I could not urinate. After 48 days new skin began to come out. I was in the hospital for two months. For one and one-half months I could not sleep, feeling like ants were eating my flesh, and pain very acute."

All his fingers were crippled, and two of them were welded together as one. His leg wounds made it very difficult for him to stand and he was escorted to us. He complained of swelling inside of his throat and pus oozing out of it, especially when the weather was hot. His neck also was very stiff, forcing him to look straight ahead. His worst wounds were on his legs, which were all swollen and blistered. Sometimes they'd bleed. His wounds covered his face, back, chest and arms. Of these wounds, he said they were unable to perspire and therefore they were very itchy, but he couldn't scratch them because it caused bleeding.

A third victim was Truong Dui Ba, a native of Thua Thien Province, in the area of the U.S. Phu Bai Air Force Base in Phong Dien District, Hien An Hamlet. He recently has been residing in Duong Hoa hamlet in Man Hoa district, where he was re-located. He has been living as a farmer in this area of Central Vietnam, near Hue, since childhood. In April, 1965, over 3,000 U.S. troops were occupying Phu Bai Air Force Base, which is about 15 Km. south of Hue, close to Highway 1 ("bomb alley" — it runs from Saigon to Hanoi). West of Phu Bai are mountains and agricultural settlements. Under Diem, people from other areas were forced into this area for general resettlement. His native hamlet is located northwest of the air force base, 12 Km. from Phu Bai in a densely populated area at the foot of the mountains. He was forced from his native hamlet in 1963 to Duong Hoa, a "strategic hamlet". He did guard duty at this strategic hamlet in October 1963. His commanding officer, Koh, ordered him to inspect the controls at the gate. He went with another peasant, Tran Lai. It was dark as he opened the door. The door was wired and mined. His friend was killed and he was wounded. Two fragments pierced his left calf and went through just above his ankle. He recovered three months later. The villagers gave him medical care — he didn't receive medical care as part of his military service for the South Vietnamese.

In July, 1964, troops destroyed the strategic hamlet. The U.S. entered the area, and began bombing and strafing. They used L-19 planes with speakers to talk to the people and distributed leaflets appealing to people to leave their villages and live in the cities or towns or near the bases. The U.S. was now beginning its "pacification program" and was replacing South Vietnamese troops at the bases. In May, 1965, the U.S. began terror raids. From May 5-6th there were three raids involving shelling from the air base and jet strafing. Also, after the shelling and strafing, there was a landing of troops who killed and looted. Sixty houses were burned down in three provinces and about ten people were killed. There were repeated raids in July to raze the area. Troops were also used. About fifty civilians were killed and wounded and about 600 men, women and children were taken away. Over 400 houses were burned down, among them the temple and pagoda of Duong Hoa. A Buddhist monk was killed. About 300 hectares (800 acres) of the rice crop the peasants lived on were destroyed. During most of this time, Truong was living in the mountain area. However, there wasn't enough food in the mountains, and he went back to the village looking for sweet potatoes and got caught in a raid. He was hit by a bullet in the right buttock which lodged in the membrane of his intestine. He fell down on his right leg and couldn't move. He was taken back to the mountain area by a friend named Hai, and then to the Province hospital. Since then he has been separated from his family. His right leg is shorter than his left leg. During the eight months he spent in the hospital he learned that his 12 year old daughter had been killed by U.S. troops . . . After eight months in the Province hospital he was brought north for treatment. On the way north he passed through two villages which he believed had been sprayed with toxic chemicals, for he saw dead trees, crops and animals. He is still receiving treatment in the North.

On March 25, we went to Than Hoa Province, North Vietnam, about 200 Km. south of Hanoi. We had to travel at night because of the danger of bombings. We passed through several bombed-out towns, one of which was Phu Ly. We didn't stop, but we could see the outlines of rubble. We arrived in Than Hoa about 2:30 a.m. On March 26 (Easter Sunday) at about 12:30, bombing began 20 Km. southeast of us in the irrigation dike area of Bai Thuong Dam — the largest dam in the province. Looking up into the sky we could see and hear a U.S. supersonic jet.

That day we went to Dan Loi village in Than Hoa in Trieu Son district. The village had been attacked on December 3, 1967, in the evening, when people were either cooking or coming back from the fields. Nine people were killed, 12 houses were destroyed along with farm equipment and large numbers of animals. We stayed in Than Hoa Province through the 28th, visiting Than Hoa City, where we saw a bombed-out hospital of 200 beds, a bombed-out Catholic Church and a bombed-out Pagoda, as well as homes in many neighborhoods that were completely destroyed. All types of bombs were used — high explosives ranging from 500 to 3,000 pounds, fragmentation bombs, and CBU's (pellet bombs of both "guava" and "pineapple" types).

We also visited Liep Mai Hamlet, an isolated rural village where there was nothing even remotely military, unless the rice could be considered that. Twenty-one people were killed in a raid, which involved the use of demolition and CBU's. Next we visited Ham Rong Bridge, where there have been constant bombings nearly every day. 193 U.S. aircraft have been shot down there — twelve of them with infantry rifles. In Tinh Fia District there was a bombing raid on March 14, 1966. All told, there have been 3,145 attacks on Than Hoa Province since the beginning of the bombing in 1965. This province is the location of the Quynh Lap Leprosorium. It has 2,600 beds and 160 billets. It has been bombed and strafed repeatedly. We were not allowed to visit that hospital due to the government's concern for our safety as attacks were continuing.

We returned to Hanoi and on April 6, we visited Nam Ha Province, 60 Km. south of Hanoi. We went to the city of Nam Dinh. The city was mostly evacuated due to the U.S. bombing raids. In one area we visited, literally whole blocks had been completely demolished almost to small stones. Again, we could find no military target nearby. Also in Nam Ha Province we visited Nghia Hung District, the Don Quy Cooperative of Nghia Hung village, which has suffered six raids involving 100 bombs and 2 missiles. The Catholic Church in this all-Catholic village has been bombed, and a mother of five children was killed while working in the fields during one of these raids, most of which involved F-105's.

Effects of the Aggression Against the DRV
on Public Health

testimony by Roberto Guerra, M.D.

Dr. Guerra Practices Medicine in Cuba

In our capacity as medical doctors, we visited the Democratic Republic of Vietnam during the first two weeks of December, 1965, with the purpose of exchanging with our Vietnamese colleagues scientific knowledge regarding the treatment of conventional wounds, the burns resulting from napalm and white phosphorous, and other medical aspects of the war. We travelled to Vietnam to exchange experiences because we do indeed have experience in this matter. We had treated similar cases, though in smaller numbers, between the 17th and the 20th of April, 1961, when Cuba was under attack by mercenaries trained, armed, and transported by the United States.

During our stay in the Democratic Republic of Vietnam we visited hospitals both in Hanoi and elsewhere and we conversed with many doctors, medical assistants, nurses and patients and with laymen concerned with the field of medicine. Before we proceed with our report, we believe it necessary to explain something which shall serve as a basis for understanding the crimes perpetrated by the United States of America against the public health of Vietnam.

The World Health Organization (WHO), organ of the United Nations devoted to world health and numbering the U.S. among its founding members, lists as one of its general principles: "health is an inalienable right of the peoples of the world." Actually, the broader concept of health is concerned not only with illness but also with the protection of health and its promotion. It considers the whole human being, his biological, psychological and social aspects. So that you may appreciate the enormous efforts and achievement of the Vietnamese people in the field of public health, it is important to point out a few facts. At this very moment a barbarous aggression is destroying these achievements.

In 1954 the D.R.V. was an underdeveloped country which had been subjected to a colonial regime for almost a century. Since 1940

211

it had been fighting a hard and cruel war for liberation. When the Geneva Accords were signed in 1954 every aspect of public health conditions in the country was deplorable. Several million people were ill with malaria, 80% of the population had trachoma, and there were hundreds of thousands of cases of tuberculosis and leprosy. Almost the entire population suffered from intestinal parasites and many of the same people had nutritional deficiencies. Large epidemics of contagious diseases such as cholera, small pox, and yellow fever were decimating the population. The mortality rate for mothers at childbirth was 20 per 1000. The first statistical studies of that era noted 640,000 cases of tuberculosis, 11,000,000 cases of malaria, and two cases of leprosy for each 1000 inhabitants. There were only 47 hospitals in all of Indochina; i.e., in Vietnam, Laos and Cambodia together. Most of the hospitals were poorly staffed and nearly in ruins. There was one doctor or one medical assistant for each 180,000 inhabitants — a total of 51 doctors and 152 medical assistants for the entire population. In addition, there were only 1227 nurses and 215 midwives.

From 1954 through 1965, public health programs in the DRV were developed intensively and extensively. Health campaigns reached the entire population, even in the most isolated rural areas. An extensive prevention and cure network was established. Intensive hygiene, local sanitation, vaccination, and anti-epidemic campaigns were waged. Food production and food distribution were increased. Maternal and child care grew extraordinarily and hospitals and child-care centers were built. All this was made possible by the notable increase in technicians and middle-level officials, the creation of many schools and the growth of the Medical Faculty at the University. Seven institutes for scientific research have also been established. The results of this effort can be seen in the following statistics: 3008 graduates of the Faculty of Medicine during the years from 1954 to 1965, with a teaching staff now of 208 full professors and instructors.

According to the statistics published in October, 1964, at that time there were: 2000 doctors, 10,000 auxiliary doctors, 26,378 nurses, 13,374 midwives, 35,550 sanitation teams and hygiene information units, 1500 pharmacists, 480 hospitals and health centers with a total of 28,981 beds.

Cholera and small pox were no longer in evidence and there were only 24 cases of yellow fever. The mortality rate of mothers at childbirth, which in 1954 was 20 for each 1000 had gone down to 0.04 per 1000 in 1965. Infant mortality was only 15.8 in each 1000. These data are evidence of the enormous effort made by this underdeveloped country to promote and maintain the health of its people. Keeping this in mind, we now turn to our visit to the DRV and what we learned from our informants.

We visited the German-Vietnamese Friendship Hospital and St. Paul's Hospital. We saw that 80% of the sick, the doctors and the hospital staff had been evacuated to safe areas. By that time they had learned from the events of December 1966 - when U.S. planes indiscriminately and criminally bombed populated areas of Hanoi. There is no doubt but that the forced evacuation reduced the possibility for giving adequate medical aid to a large part of the population. Nor does it allow those not so seriously wounded to recuperate to the fullest.

Among the patients were some who had been badly wounded by shrapnel. They had been wounded during bombardments in other parts of the country and first treated at nearby hospitals. However, since these hospitals lacked surgical facilities for such serious types of wounds as thoracic, abdominal, head and other injuries, these patients had been brought to Hanoi. There they received specialized treatment. They told us that they were all either farmers or workers — and thus members of the civilian population.

At St. Paul's Hospital we saw several patients with napalm burns - some with serious wounds and others with terrible deformities. Doctors Behar and Takman have already testified and presented evidence to the Tribunal of the terrible burns caused by napalm. Fifty per cent of the people burned by napalm die from these wounds. The survivors suffer third and fourth degree burns which heal with great difficulty and leave the victim with permanent deformities. All those who had been burned were civilians.

Thanks to the heroic effort of the remaining medical attendants, who were few in number at these hospitals, the standard of treatment was high. Most of the staff and facilities had been removed to areas where their presence was vital because of continuous air raids.

In Hanoi we also visited what remained of the Faculty of Medicine. I say "remained" because they were packing the last lot of laboratory equipment to be transferred to a place safe from air raids. There the Faculty of Medicine would continue functioning and preparing physicians.

We also visited some hospitals in hard-to-reach, remote rural areas where there was no electricity or running water. They were camouflaged so as not to be identifiable by the U.S. aircraft. In the improvised hospital operating rooms the personnel was small with, for instance, lamps attached to the foreheads of the staff for lighting. A bicycle was used as a generator. It was turned upside down and by continuously turning the pedals by hand, light was generated. The attendants took turns keeping the small light from fading — the light was so indispensable for saving lives.

From Vietnamese doctors and sanitation officials we collected numerous reports of the raids on the hospitals. Doctors Behar and Takman have already reported in detail to the Tribunal on the enormous damage inflicted on hospitals — hospitals which can easily be seen from the air.

The U.S. imperialist aggression in Vietnam breaks all rules of health recognized by the world. It is a great crime against public health to destroy hospitals and health centers, to wound, burn and kill men, women and children, including women who are pregnant. It is a crime against the health of a nation when medical assistance is disrupted and the sick and wounded must be treated in unlit, humid places, under poor hygienic conditions, in areas difficult to get to. It is also a crime when bombs destroy not only steel and concrete structures but especially when anti-personnel fragmentation, napalm and phosphorous bombs are used to kill and wound non-combatants.

It is an attempt against a nation's health and nutrition to destroy industries and crops, to kill animals, to destroy dikes and flood farming areas. This barbarous attempt to destroy the gigantic efforts made with great sacrifice to improve the sanitary conditions of an underdeveloped country is a genocidal crime against humanity.

By the use of mass destruction and terror the U.S. tries to break down the psychological health of the people. These efforts are in vain. The Vietnamese people are immune to this kind of aggression. Their valor, love of liberty, and unbreakable spirit will triumph.

We have presented to the Tribunal what we have seen and the reports we have collected. We did not go as a Commission of Inquiry, but as interested individuals and therefore did not systematically note down the names of all persons and places. As a doctor who looks after the health of people, and as a human being, I personally felt grief and profound indignation at the pain and suffering brought about by this barbarous and unjust aggression. By its effort to break down the health of the Vietnamese people, U.S. imperialism commits a grave crime against humanity — and genocide in its worst form.

Testimony and Medical Report of Vietnamese Victims

Testimony of Mr. Thai Binh Dan

My name is Thai Binh Dan. I was born in 1949, and am of Vietnamese nationality. I am a native of the commune of Thanh Loi, in Ben Thu district [Long An province, South Vietnam].

My father, Thai Binh Tue, and mother, Pham Thi Tu, are still alive. They are rice-growers. On March 21, 1966, about 4 p.m., while I was cooking, I heard the sound of planes overhead. Immediately afterwards came the explosion of bombs. I ran towards the shelters, but I no sooner reached the door than a napalm bomb exploded nearby. I was enveloped in flames, the heat was unbearable. I called for help, then I lost consciousness.

The napalm had burned my face, and both arms and legs. My house also had been burned. After being in a coma for 13 days, I woke up in a bed in an NLF hospital. According to the doctor, I had a terrible thirst during the first five days. I was given plenty to drink but I had only urinated twice. I alternated between a state of coma and delirium.

After these 13 days I began to feel terrible pain, which prevented me from eating and drinking. After 48 days the wounds began to heal, leaving keloids, and giving me the impression of having been bitten by ants. The keloids on my neck prevented me from moving when I ate or swallowed my saliva. On my right hand the keloids forced me to keep my fingers bent. It is difficult for me to move my body. Even if I only walk a little, the scars on my feet turn white and keep me from bending. When the weather is cold, my scars harden and become purple and numbed. When it is hot, the scars keep me from perspiring, pus collects, and my skin itches terribly when I'm asleep. Other victims of American bombs have been wounded even more severely. Some have become invalids or have died.

To quote the case of the family of Mr. Tan Cuong: in January 1965, seven people were burned by napalm, among them Mme. Tam Cuong, aged 45, four girls and two boys, whose ages ranged from 2 to 18 years. In February 1965, Mr. Nguyen Van Tang was struck by napalm bombs while he was having a meal. His whole body started to burn, and he started to rub himself against the wall. Whole pieces of his flesh fell off. He died soon afterwards.

Testimony of Nguyen Hong Phuong

My name is Nguyen Hong Phuong. I was born in 1930, in Hamlet Five, Phuoc Son Village, Tien Phuoc district, Quang Nam province [South Vietnam]. I am the son of Mr. Nguyen Chay and Mrs. Nguyen Thi The, who are still living. My wife was dead. My occupation is peasant.

I was ploughing my field on the morning of August 8, 1966 when four HU-1A helicopters flew in and hovered again and again over my hamlet. They fired rockets and dropped smoke grenades. Through experience we knew there would be bombing and strafing. That is why I hurried to hide the buffalo and ran back home to save my family's bag of clothes. I nearly reached the house when a U.S. jet plane was seen diving and releasing before me a white bomb, the size of a small sampan. I jumped into a communication trench and sat down, when I saw fire streaming into the trench and on my head. I felt the smelling of powder. I suffocated and covered my head at once with a piece of nylon waterproof that I used to bring always with me. When I began to breathe more easily, I took off the piece of nylon and began to run and cry for help. My shoulders, arms and hands were burnt. My hands were stripped of their skin and turned red. Hardly had I run for a moment than I fell and fainted. On recovering I found myself carried by other people, then I lost consciousness again. Now fainting and then recovering until nightfall I realised that I was in a hospital. A hospital attendant who sat by my side told me that it was the NLF provincial hospital of Quang Nam. My face and eyes were swollen, my hair was burnt and both my ears shrank and were flattened down by the fire. The burns on my arms and on other parts of my body got swollen. I felt acute pain. I could not urinate nor evacuate since my being wounded. At the hospital they gave me mixture of palm-tree roots and maizehair as diuretic. Only three days later could I make water. I could not sleep for one month. Hardly could I close my eyes when I fell into delirium. People around me said I was often delirious. I felt unbearable burning and biting in my wounds. In the hospital they had to soak the bandaged parts of my body with permanganate water, especially my two hands. When the bandages dried up, I felt much pain. In the hospital they changed my clothes, and had them washed. My shirt was burnt into rags, while my trousers were covered with whitish spots. I thought that my trousers were not cleanly washed. The nurse then told me that these stains were left by bomb powder and could not be removed. She rubbed the stains on my trousers and smoke came out and there was a smell of burning. My hair was seriously burnt by the fire. My head skin was blistered and I ached when people touched it. Only twenty days later did they begin to crop my hair which had been burnt. When they cut my hair I happened to feel the smell of burning. The doctor who cut it told me that smoke came out from parts of my hair that were scabs.

I left the hospital after more than two months of treatment. At present I can't move the fingers of both my hands. I am a disabled man. When the wounds of my ears healed up, I used to flatten and stretch the lobes so that they should not shrink. However, I can't hear as clearly as before. My memory is also weakening. Sometimes I can't eat or sleep.

Testimony of Hoang Tan Hung

My name is Hoang Tan Hung. I am 45 years old, of Vietnamese nationality, and I am a native of the village of Tan My, in the commune of Pho Minh, which is in the province of Quang Ngai in South Vietnam. I am a rice-grower and merchant. My father, Hoang Tan Cong, and my mother, Nguyen Thi Trinh, are both rice-growers.

On the 10th of May, 1965, I was on my way to buy goods in the village in the province of Quang Ngai. It is a densely populated sugar-producing region. A wave of American jets appeared, and began to drop rockets and bombs indiscriminately. I heard a tremendous explosion behind me, and was immediately covered with flames. The heat was unbearable. I ran around screaming. Houses caught fire, and the village was hidden by clouds of smoke. Women and children were screaming. I managed to run a little, then I slumped to the ground and lost consciousness.

When I regained consciousness, I realized that I was in the hospital. My wounds were bandaged. I was in a state of semi-consciousness. When the bandages were changed, I saw that my flesh was burned, and there was a yellowish pus oozing from the wounds. I could scarcely see with my left eye. My left ear-drum was burned and mutilated. I was in pain and often in a state of coma. This prevented me from sleeping, and even from resting. When I regained consciousness, the nurses told me what had happened. When I slumped down to the ground, the inhabitants of the village came and put out the flames, and took me to a hospital. An hour later, white smoke, like burning tobacco, was still rising from the burns on the nape of my neck and on my back. I was in agonizing pain. Ten days later I was transferred from the village to a provincial hospital. The road was long, the means of transport precarious, it was raining and my wounds became infected with insect larvae. After six weeks of hospital treatment I was still in terrible pain; I had fever and burning sensations. I suffered from insomnia and anorexia. Often, when my wounds were being dressed, my flesh would come off in pieces, giving off an unpleasant odour. My wounds healed after six months of treatment, but the whole of my left arm remains attached to my body. Keloid scars appeared on my skin. The wounds on my neck became infected again. The keloids on my neck and back made it difficult for me to move.

A few months later, I was taken to the hospital of Duc Pho district to continue the treatment. Two years have now passed, but the wounds on the back of my neck have not yet completely healed. The keloids cause me discomfort. Today I denounce before the Tribunal the barbaric crimes of the American imperialist aggressors, who have brought so much suffering to me and to my country.

Testimony of Do Van Ngoc

My name is Do Van Ngoc, I am 9 years old, from the village of Vinh Tuy, hamlet of Vinh Minh, district of Quang Minh, province of Quange Minh [North Vietnam]. I am the son of Mr. Do Oj and Mrs. Ha Thi Giee; both my parents are rice growers.

On the afternoon of June 16, 1966, I was looking after the oxen with my two friends, named Ha Khec and Do Van Giau, when three American planes appeared from over the sea and dropped bombs on the place where we were. The bombs exploded and the flames reached the bodies of all three of us, causing us very serious burns. Since we could no longer bear the heat, we jumped into a flooded rice field; then the flames were put out and the heat lessened, but when we emerged from the water, the flames broke out again on our bodies.

We asked for help. Then we were sent to a hospital for medical treatment. Then I felt a tremendous pain. Now the burns are scarred, but I still have itching and burning sensations. On my right hand, the thumb is stuck to the other fingers; large scars remain on my stomach and my thighs.

That day the American bombs still set fire to the homes of our family and our neighbours. To my knowledge, apart from the three of us, Mr. Du's family, while having their meal, lost six of its eight members, burned by bombs.

Testimony of Miss Ngo Thi Nga

My name is Ngo Thi Nga, I am Vietnamese, born on the 23rd of June, 1944 in the village of An Lac, Dinh Hoa district, Bac Thai province: I am a fourth-form instructor for the school of general studies of the first degree of the town of Cam Pha, **Quang** Ninh province [North Vietnam]; I am the daughter of Mr. Ngo Van Thieu, 54 years old, and of Mrs. Ngeyem Thi Thin, 51 years old; both of them are rice growers and are still alive.

Since August, 1964, because of the numerous raids of the American Air Force against Cam Pha, my school had to be evacuated to the village of Quang Linh, an agricultural village which is densely populated. The older pupils lived in the homes of the villagers, and the younger ones in the school building itself, together with the instructors.

On October 22, 1966, around midnight, at the very moment when 15 boarding students, a school worker and myself were sleeping, American planes came very quickly. Some bombs exploded, and a burning smell came forth, causing us very unpleasant sensations. I jumped out of bed, and began to lead my pupils toward shelters, but it was already too late. The children cried, while shouting: "Mademoiselle! Papa! Mama! Save Us! Save Us!

At the moment, my colleagues from the neighboring houses rushed to the place where we were staying. When the bombings stopped, I saw little Luu Thi Hoa writhing in pain on her bed — her neck covered with blood. At that moment, I felt a shivering in the nape of my neck. Putting my hand there, I saw blood but, involved in rescuing my pupils, I paid no attention to my wound. And when I had finished leading my pupils to the shelters, I felt a shock in my head, and I fainted. People started to dress the wounds of two of the pupils and my own, and then had us taken to a hospital 2 km. from the school. My head ached more and more. I couldn't sleep, and I vomited all that I was given to eat. From the hospital's diagnosis, I was wounded by a steel pellet in the head: the X-ray showed that the pellet was still there. Considering the seriousness of my injury, the regional hospital decided to send me for treatment to the surgery section of Viet Duc hospital in Hanoi. Little Luu Thi Hoa, 6 years old and a kindergarten pupil, and Vo Thi Binh, 9 years old and a pupil in the second form, both of them very good pupils, died due to the gravity of their wounds.

On November 17, I was told that I had to have head surgery. Some days after the operation, the wound was healing, but the steel pellet of the American aggressor was still deeply lodged in my head, causing me innumerable pains. My sight was failing and I couldn't see anything from certain angles. When there is a change in temperature, I have a tremendous pain in the head, and I am unable to do anything. I am longing to be able to return to my school very soon with my pupils, but till now the steel pellet of the American aggressor forces me to continue treatment.

Medical Examination of Three Vietnamese Victims at the Burn Section, Karolinska Sjukhuset, Stockholm

Do Van Ngoc, age 9 years

Burns of third degree, about 15% of the body. Transplanted with good result. However, some keloid formations in the region of the groin which demands plastic-surgical reconstruction.

Thai Binh Dan, age 18 years

Burns of third degree, about 30% actually vital lesions. Very grave: obvious keloid formations which demand plastic-surgical reconstruction. A certain risk of secondary skin cancer in keloid formations of this type.

Hoang Tan Hung, age 45 years

Burns of third degree, about 25% of the body. The lesions are mainly localised to the dorsum. Gravely diminished function of the left arm, which makes it practically unusable. Also the left ear gravely deformed. A great need of plastic-surgical correction with risk of cancer.

5/5/67 — Sten-Otto Liljedahl — Associate Professor of Surgery, Karolinska Sjukhuset, Stockholm.

220

*Examinations of Wounded from U.S. Bombing
testimony by Henrik Forss, M.D.

*Dr. Forss was a Member of the Fifth Commission
of Inquiry from Finland*

This is a simple report. It is neither long nor exciting and it covers only a very small part of a subject of immense proportions: victims from bombings in North Vietnam.

The Fifth Commission of Inquiry, of which I was a member visited North Vietnam in August, 1967, for about three weeks. We witnessed several savage bombings on the civilian population and it is now my task to try to describe the state of health-or-disease-of some victims of these attacks.

The major part of the wounded suffered from the terrible effects of anti-personnel bombs. The discussion of these arms has been treated in other reports so I am passing directly to the facts about the wounded.

In the province of Ha Tay, district of Quang Oai, we visited the village of Vat Lai two days after it had been bombed on August 1, 1967. To my knowledge there were no military targets in the area. The only type of bombs used were CBUs (Cluster Bomb Units). We examined a few CBU containers, all dated July, 1967. Nine persons were killed and 29 wounded. Of these we saw eleven in the district hospital of Quang Oai. The severely wounded had been removed to the provincial hospital. All eleven patients suffered from wounds caused by CBU fragments. Three children were among the wounded, one had been hit in the head by a fragment that did not penetrate. An old man was wounded in his left hand.

In the province of Nam Ha, I was able to see a few victims from recent bombings. One was Nguyen Thi Nam, a 24 year old woman from Nam Dinh. By the time of the air raid, of June 23, 1967, she had been evacuated to the nearby village of Vuot, Commune of Loc Ha. She was pregnant in her ninth month. Fragments of the CBU penetrated the intestines and the uterus, killing the foetus

221

which had to be removed surgically. Forty centimeters of the intestine had to be removed at the same time. I was able to examine the patient 2 weeks after the operation. She was then still physically weak, pale and tired. It is uncertain whether she can have any more children.

Tran Thi Hieu, an 18 year old girl from the village of Kenh, Commune of Loc Vuong, was wounded by CBU bombs on the same date. Fragments of the bomb perforated the stomach, her left ear and both arms and legs. On examination I found four scars on the right hand and fourteen scars and marks on the left lower limb. One small fragment was still in her body. The patient was anaemic and told me she suffered from insomnia, loss of memory, headache and vertigo. The case of an eight year old girl, Tran Thi Thanh, is very tragic. Her parents and brother were killed during bombings of Nam Dinh in April, 1966. The girl was then evacuated outside the town. On June 23, 1967 she was hit by a CBU fragment in her left arm. Examining the girl, I found that after-effects concisted mainly of psychic disturbances: she was suffering from crises of stupor. I was told, however, that her schoolwork was nearly at normal level. I examined a nineteen year old electrician, Tran Ngoc Hai, who was working in spite of the fact that he was carrying a CBU fragment in his neck. He had been wounded on June 21, 1967 at midnight. The fragment penetrated the region of the left jaw and ear and was later found to be impossible to localise. He is at present suffering from occasional pains in the neck and loss of appetite.

Near Nam Dinh I also examined Pham Van Luan, 38 years old, a chemical and textile products worker. His wife was killed during an air raid on May 25, 1967. At the same time their boy, aged five years, was hit by a fragment of a bomb in his left ankle. Examining the boy, I found a scar 5 cm. in length. However, after-effects are not only measured by the length of a scar. The loss of a mother means more.

In the province of Ninh Binh the bombing of the Commune Yen Lam in Yen Mo district is another example of attacks on the civil population. On June 26, 1967, Ngo Thi Dieu, a 36 year old woman, lost her home during an incendiary and high explosive bomb raid. She suffered severe burns; I was able to examine her August 6, 1967. She was then still in a very critical condition and I speculate on whether she will recover at all. She showed large second and third degree burns on both arms and her head. She was breathing fast, looked extremely exhausted and was not able to answer questions. At the place of the same bombing I met a 22 year old woman, Mai Thi Mien. She indicated the place where her hut had been. She herself showed a partly healed second-degree burn on her left leg, from knee to foot. Her general condition was poor and she might have later difficulties in walking.

In Hanoi, the capital and its surroundings were the target of several heavy bombings during the month of August. These following few examples will reveal, I hope, some of the cruel effects of this air war. On August 15, 1967, I examined an 18 year old girl in the district hospital of Hoan Kiem. Six days later this hospital was to be nearly totally destroyed. Mademoiselle Dinh's house was near the Long Bien Bridge. The very day the bridge was damaged she fell victim to the same attack: she was severely wounded. Her left lower leg had to be amputated below the knee beacause of a complicated open fracture. Her recovery so far is good, but she will be handicapped for the rest of her life.

The Hoan Kiem hospital I mentioned was badly hit by a rocket on August 21, 1967. My colleague, Dr. Doan Tri Cuong, 36 years old, was killed on the spot while on duty. A nurse was also killed and another died later from his wounds. Two more of the staff of this small hospital were wounded. We were able to see them in the Viet Duc Hospital the same day. Le Quan Dan, a male assistant physician, was hit by bomb fragments in his arm and in the neck near the carotid artery. At the time we saw him he was weak, but his condition was not critical thanks to immediate treatment. A female nurse, Le Thi Hao, suffered several superficial wounds in her chest, head and left leg. She will probably recover completely. In Hanoi I was also shown eight victims from bombings earlier this year. Four of these victims were children. All suffered from the after-effects of wounds and scars caused by fire and anti-personnel bombs. Three patients showed extensive areas of thick keloid scar tissue from second and third degree burns. They were undergoing plastic surgery treatment. In their case this is a long and painful procedure and it is doubtful that complete recovery will ever be achieved. In addition three patients had to be operated on for removal of bomb fragments in the abdominal region.

There is much more I could say about the subject I have been describing — the effects of American bombing on North Vietnam. My last impressions are from a district in the center of Hanoi. This region was hit by several heavy bombs on August 22, 1967, the day of our departure. I did not see any wounded, just corpses being carried away from the ruins. I vividly recall this sight; I shall never forget it.

Report on the Destruction of Dikes: Holland 1944-45 and Korea 1953

testimony by Professor Gabriel Kolko

During the final months of the Second World War the Nazis exposed the Dutch civilian population to a form of war crime the United States and English Governments especially designated as crimes against humanity. To prevent the advance of Anglo-American troops, the German High Commissioner in Holland, Seyss-Inquart, opened the dikes and by the end of 1944 flooded approximately 500,000 acres of land. The result was a major disorganization of the Dutch economy and the most precipitous decline in food consumption any West European country suffered during the war. By 1945 the caloric intake in occupied Holland, or the large bulk of the country, was less than 900 a day, and in certain areas 500 calories. As the Allied armies advanced, the Germans threatened to extend the destruction of the remaining dikes to block Allied supply lines and movements.

The misery of the Dutch people, the Prime Minister-in Exile, P.S. Gerbrandy, warned SHAEF Commander Eisenhower, threatened " . . . a calamity as has not been seen in Europe for centuries."[1] The Red Cross issued the same warning, and during April 1945 both Eisenhower and Churchill moved to confront the enormous tragedy resulting from the impact of the destruction of the dikes. On April 10th Churchill wrote Roosevelt that "I fear we may soon be in the presence of a tragedy."[2] To prevent it he proposed the Allies make available necessary food and medical supplies for Red Cross distribution. A warning was to be given to Seyss-Inquart and his

---

[1] Harry L. Coles and Albert K. Weinberg, *Civil Affairs:* "Soldiers Become Governors" ("United States Army in World War Two: Special Studies") (Washington, 1964), 827; also 823ff, and U.S. Department of Agriculture, Office of Foreign Agriculture Relations, *World Food Situation,* 1946-47 (Washington, 1946), 5.

[2] Winston Churchill, *Triumph and Tragedy* (Bantam Book ed.) New York, 1962, 401

subordinates ". . . .That by resisting our attempt to bring relief to the civilian population in this area they will brand themselves as murderers before the world, and we shall hold them responsible with their lives for the fate which overtakes the people of Holland."[3] Several weeks later Eisenhower made an additional proposal along the same lines: ". . . I propose to send a very strongly worded message to the German Commander . . . that the flooding of large areas of Holland with the resulting destitution, starvation and the enormous loss of life to the population will constitute a blot on his military honor . . . He must be told to cease opening the dikes and to take immediate steps to assist in every way possible the distribution of food . . . and that if he fails in this respect to meet his clear obligations and his humanitarian duty, he and each responsible member of his command will be considered by me as violaters of the laws of war who must face the certain consequences of their acts."[4] Confronted by such grave warnings, Seyss-Inquart agreed to stop the destruction of the dikes and cooperate in relief measures.

Nevertheless, the barbarism of Seyss-Inquart in destroying dikes and starving civilians made him appear in the eyes of the Western officers as "one of the worst war criminals," and when General Walter B. Smith met with him on April 30, 1945 to arrange for Dutch relief he also warned the German ". . . you are going to be shot."[5] Of the 185 Nazis indicted at Nuremberg only 24 were sentenced to death. Seyss-Inquart was one of the 24. His crime was considered to be one of the most monstrous of the Second World War, and prominent among the charges against him at Nuremberg.[6]

On May 13, 1953, while armistice negotiations in Korea were bogged down, 20 U.S. Air Force F-4's attacked and destroyed the Toksan irrigation dam in North Korea. The Americans also bombed the Chasan, Kuwonga, and Toksang dams and scheduled the bulk of the remainder for attack — only the signing of the armistice prevented their destruction. The flash flood resulting from the destruction of the Toksan dam resulted in a deluge of 27 miles of valley farm lands. In May 1953, "The production of food in North Korea was the only major element of North Korea's economy still functioning efficiently after three years of war," states the official U.S. account. The Americans were now prepared to destroy it, and quite properly the Air Force concluded that "These strikes, largely passed over by the press, the military observers and news commen-

[3]Ibid., 402

[4]Coles and Weinberg, *Soldiers Become Governors*, 831

[5]Ibid., 832

[6]U.S.: Department of State, *Germany, 1947-49: The Story in Documents* (Washington, 1950), 117

tators in favor of attention-arresting but less meaningful operations events, constituted one of the most significant air operations of the Korean War." "To the Communists the smashing of the dams meant primarily the destruction of their chief sustenance — rice. The Westerner can little conceive the awesome meaning which the loss of this staple food commodity has for the Asian — starvation and slow death ... Hence the show of rage, the flare of violent tempers, and the avowed threats of reprisals when bombs fell on five irrigation dams. ...[7]

Briefly, despite an earlier correct definition of the nature of the war crime inherent in flooding of farm land via destruction of dikes and dams, the U.S. Government within a decade followed the precedent of the Nazis, fully aware of the human and political conseqences of their action. The United States has already begun the destruction of the dams of Vietnam, but it has also clearly defined the nature of the action for what it is — a war crime of the first magnitude.

Significance of the Destruction of Dikes in North Vietnam

testimony by Fujio Yamazaki

North Vietnam is an agrarian country. The main product of agriculture is paddy field rice which is grown on the alluvial flats of the Red River, Chu River, Ma River and Ca River. Of this, the Red River Delta—Tonkin Delta—comprises a major part.

The Tonkin Delta is an immense plain, measuring about 150 km from Viet Tri, at the top of the delta to the mouth of the Red River and covering over 1,100,000 hectares. It is 13 meters above sea level at the highest part and 0.5 meters at the lowest with almost no slope. It is divided into many dike-encircled fields by tributaries and subtributary waters of the Red River. These dike-encircled paddy fields

---

[7] Quarterly Review Staff, "The Attack on the Irrigation Dams in North Korea," *Air University Quarterly, VI* (Winter 1953-54), 40-41

are surrounded by natural dike made by the over flowing of the rivers and by man-made dikes constructed over many years by the work of the peasants. Generally, the relative humidity is low in these dike-encircled paddy-fields. The height of the Red River dikes in the vicinity of Hanoi is 13 meters while that of lower land in Hanoi city is only 4 meters.

The height of ground near the seashore of the delta is only 0.5 meters, as it is reclaimed land with dikes constructed on a tideland. The high tide level rises two meters in the Tonkin Gulf.

The Government of the Democratic Republic of Vietnam attached much importance to river dikes and seashore dikes and made great efforts to have them constructed, thereby extending the total length of such dikes to 4,000 kilometers in 10 years.

The low ground of the delta, including the seashore area, cannot be drained naturally and in the rainy season all the land is flooded, so that growing rice in such a season is impossible unless the land is drained mechanically. In contrast, the high ground of the delta suffers from a water shortage in the dry season, and a rice crop without irrigation facilities is impossible in such a season.

During the days of French Indo-China, irrigation facilities had already been constructed over a considerable area. Since the establishment of the Democratic Republic of Vietnam, the facilities have been greatly and rapidly increased, and 90% of cultivated land is now irrigated. The construction of drainage facilities was undertaken for the first time on a full scale by the Democratic Republic of Vietnam, and was marked by great progress in ten years. As a result of the strengthening of dikes and the completion of water facilities, twice a year cropping has been made possible over a considerable part of paddy fields in the Tonkin delta, remarkably expanding the production of rice. This description of the Tonkin delta can also be applied to the alluvial plain of the Ma River and the Chu River. Destruction of these dikes and water facilities by U.S. shelling and bombing carries the following significance:

(1) The Case of River Dikes

No explanation is necessary to imagine what the results would be should dikes be destroyed in the flood-water season when the river level is higher than the cultivated land and the urban area. In relation to food production, not only farm products would be damaged but the cultivated land itself would be put out of use by the accumulation of earth and sand and by water erosion. In regard to living, houses would either be carried away or destroyed. Damage suffered by the people in both aspects of production and living would be very serious.

227

(2) The Case of the Destruction of Seashore Dikes

If tide-water control dikes along the seashore are destroyed, sea water would flood the land and the cultivated land would be put out of production by sea water, and the crops would die. Even if the dikes are repaired again, and sea water removed, the soil would be salted up and the following season's crops badly effected. If the destruction of dikes should happen at the time of high water, the risk to homes and other buildings and facilities would be great, as they would be destroyed by the force of the inrush of sea water.

(3) The Case of the Destruction of Irrigation Facilities

Destruction of irrigation facilities—dams, water control gates, incidental construction of flumes, etc.—would either damage or make impossible the rice crop in the October dry season. Planting of young rice-plants in the transplanting season is impossible without water, and rice crops would suffer from drought if there is not sufficient water after transplantation. Where dams are high, their destruction would result in heavy damage to men and stock, buildings, and cultivated land.

(4) The Case of the Destruction of Drainage Facilities

Destruction of drainage facilities—drain sites, overflow, etc.—would make rice cropping impossible in the rainy season in May in the rice areas. As is seen above, dikes and water facilities in North Vietnam have a very important meaning in production activity and living of all the people of North Vietnam, because North Vietnam is an agricultural country and rice crops are cultivated mainly in the delta area. The destruction of these facilities by shelling and bombing therefore constitutes an impermissible war crime against the Vietnamese people.

Some Facts on Bombing of Dikes
testimony by Professor Makato Kandachi

. . .The bombs used for the destruction of dikes were of about 1,500 kg, and combined with the use of ball bombs. If the destruction of dikes alone was intended, then demolition bombs would have sufficed; but ball bombs, the exclusive purpose of which is to kill and wound men and beasts, were used in combination. Further, after destroying dikes by bombing, additional bombing was conducted against people engaged in repair work. The dike at Traly, Thai Binh province, was bombed twice in 1967 while it was under repair; 52 bombs were dropped and 32 people were wounded. In Quang Binh province, the tide water control dike was bombed several times, destroying paddy fields of 1,500 hectares. Of late, bombings, were carried out against the Vinh Linh area. These are major examples of U.S. bombing. The purpose is to bring about economic difficulties by the destruction of rice crops through flood, and at the same time to kill and wound men and beasts.

The results of the investigation made by the Second Japanese Investigation Team are given below:

(1) On August 13, 1966, the Red River dike in the vacinity of Hanoi was bombed with a 1,350 kg. bomb, producing a bomb crater 12 meters in diameter and 9 meters in depth. Although the water level of the Red River was at its highest at this time, it was quickly repaired and almost no damage was done.

(2) From October 2, 1965 to June 30, 1967, the vicinity of Bac Giang city, Ha Bac province, was bombed 77 times; Bac Giang city was devastated. In the meantime, the dike in the Thuond river was attacked and destroyed by 100 bombs. Although the destroyed parts were quickly repaired, large scale bombing were done even while repairs were going on. At about 1 p.m. on September 7, 1966, four "mother" ball bombs were dropped.

(3)   Although the Red River dike that runs through the suburbs of Hai Duong city was destroyed for 15 meters, it had already been repaired. The dike is located in the suburbs far away from Hai Duong city, with no military target at all in the vicinity, only a church. This fact leads to the conclusion that the bombing was for the sole purpose of destroying the dike.

(4)   On July 13, 1967, the dike of the Lai Vu river that runs by Ha Thach city, Lami Thau prefecture, Phu Tho province, was bombed by 12 planes. Four bombs hit the dike, and as a result 100 meters were destroyed. A bomb crater 12 meters in diameter and 5 meters in depth resulted. On July 18 the same year Ha Mao was bombed. The investigations of the Japanese team on July 21, showed that there were bomb craters about 15 meters in diameter and 5 meters in depth in 22 places. No bombs had directly hit the dike. It was explained that the height of the dike is about 5 meters and that the water level used to be up to the 4 meter mark at high water. From this, it can easily be seen that the destruction of the dike at high water would bring about serious flood damage. It is also evident that even if the dike itself is not destroyed, destruction in the vicinity of the dike would result in the destruction of the dike because of the nature of the soil in this area which is light and weak in cohesion.

(5)   The case of Da Mai dam, Quang Binh province, as told by Mr. Nguyen Hoan, Minister for Water Conservation, is as follows: The Second Japanese Investigation Team visited the ruins of this dam; The dam is situated in the upstream portion of the Zinh river, about a few score kilometers from the sea. Construction was begun in 1965 and was completed on July 5. It supplies water to 2,000 hectares in Bo Truch prefecture. As soon as the water began to run in the channel, it was bombed. The bombing is being carried on sometimes even now.

Commenting on the denunciation of the Foreign Ministry and the Water Conservancy Ministry of the Democratic Republic of Vietnam that "the U.S. forces are carrying on the planned destruction of dikes, killing and wounding the inhabitants, and are trying to destroy food production and transportation," a U.S. Defense Department spokesman said that "this was done by accident by American pilots and should not in any way be interpreted as intentional" (AP dispatch, July 22). But according to our investigation, the bombing by the U.S. is so accurate that it is inconceivable for places which have no target other than dikes to be bombed by chance. It should therefore be judged that the U.S. forces have carried on bombing purposely to destroy dikes and kill and wound the people repairing them.

Bombing of Dikes and Irrigation Systems
in the DRV
testimony by Tsetsure Tsurishima

Member First Japanese Commission of Inquiry

On our way to Nam Dinh from Hanoi, on the first of January 1967, we, the members of the First Japanese Commission of Inquiry, could see several craters on the dike in Phu Ly, a village of peasants and fishermen, 30 km. from Nam Dinh and 40 km. from Hanoi. The dike was broken up by several craters, each of which was about 7 meters in diameter. Since the water level was so low-during the months of the dry season—that the river bed was visible, the villagers had not filled the craters since the time of the bombardment on October 1, 1966.

On the same day, January 1, 1967, we saw the people repairing the dike in the village of Nam Phong, in the northern part of the province of Nam Dinh. This dike had been bombed the day before our arrival . . .Since the water level of the river running through this village was high enough to be touching the canal dikes themselves, the dike had to be repaired immediately after it was bombed. One crater was visible on this dike, and there were two in the river.

There are many other cases of bombed dikes witnessed by members of the Tribunal investigating commissions. And I have here eight different pictures taken immediately after the bombing of various parts of the irrigation system. But what I would like to draw your attention to is the systematic method in which the irrigation system has been bombed.

According to the report which we were given in Hanoi by Mr. Phan My, Vice-president of the Water Conservancy Commission, U.S. bombings and strafing of the entire dike network were exceptionally violent and concentrated in the months of July, August and September of 1966, when the water level was very high. He explained that the following numbers of raids against the dike system had taken place: From February to June 1966: 55 air raids — In July 1966: 69 raids — In August and September 1966: 136 raids.

He stated that these raids had attacked many sections of the dikes of the Red River, the Thai Binh River, the Ma River, and the Lam River in the provinces of Thai Binh, Ninh Binh, Ha Bac, Hai Duong, Thanh Hoa, Ha Tinh and Nghe An, as well as in Hanoi; many sections of the sea dikes in Quang Ninh province, Haiphong, etc., were also attacked.

The report entitled "Destruction by the U.S. Imperialists of Water Conservancy Projects and Dike Systems in North Vietnam From March 1965 to December 1966," published by the Democratic Republic of Vietnam's Ministry of Water Conservancy, describes the air raids against the dike network in Nam Ha province, for example, as follows:

"The big dikes of Nam Ha were raided 34 times between April and September 1966. Nam Ha is one of the most populous provinces and a big rice bowl of North Vietnam. In April and May 1966, it was attacked by U.S. planes 3 times. In July, it was subjected to 7 air raids. In August and September, when the water level rose highest, the number of air strikes was brought to 24. Typical were the raids on August 1 and 3, 1966, against the Kinh Lung dike and flood gate in Nam Dao commune, Nam Truc district, when the water level was high; a section of the dike was so damaged by U.S. bombs that its surface was only 0.80 meters higher than that of the water, and the damaged dike was the only protection of a populous area of Nam Ha province against the flooding of the Red river. On August 3, 1966, the same dike section was again attacked and the danger of the dike breaking was very serious as some bombs had dug 4-meter deep craters in it. In these two days, the local people had to muster a huge labour force to fill up bomb craters with thousands of cubic meters of earth and stave off the danger of flooding. The air raid on this dike section killed and wounded many people and damaged many houses and much property of the local people." (p. 6)

There are many other similar examples described in this document. For example:

1) *The Water Conservancy System in North Nghe An*

"The water conservancy system in the North of Nghe An province serves 5 districts with hundreds of thousands of people. It consists of a key project, the Do Luong dam, and hundreds of smaller water regulating projects. In June and July 1965, the U.S. imperialists launched raids against 12 projects. In June and July 1965, the U.S. imperialists launched 12 attacks against the Do Luong dam, 10 attacks against the flood gate at one end of the canal and against water regulating projects of the system on June 5, 6, 7, 8, 12, 15 and July 8 and 14, 1965. The system including big and small canals, was hit 137 times. In July and August 1966, when the people made great efforts to repair the damaged projects, U.S. aircraft in 18 attacks used hundreds of tons of bombs and thousands of rockets and missiles against the important projects which had just been repaired. In addition, repeated attacks were also carried out. Between March 1965 and September 1966 the water conservancy system of North Nghe An was attacked 178 times in all."(p. 3)

2) The Dike of the Ma River in Thanh Hoa

"The Ma River is a large river flowing through Than Hoa province. Important dike sections of the Ma River in Thanh Hoa province were subjected to 24 air strikes between March and September 1966. In September 1966, when there were heavy rains, U.S. aircraft bombed and strafed 17 times important sections of dike on the Northern bank of the Ma River; in two days, September 21 and 22, 1966, they bombed and strafed 8 times, damaging sections of dikes and dams which were hundreds of meters long, blasting away 25,000 cubic meters of earth. In these two air raids, U.S. pilots savagely dropped steel-pellet bombs on the people, who were filling up the gaps in the dike and dam network after the bombing, and many peasants working on the top of the dike were killed. From July 27 to 31, 1966, due to the torrential rains during the typhoon Ora, the levels of the rivers were mounting. U.S. aircraft then strafed 14 times many important sections of dike in Tien Lang and Vinh Bao districts, in the vicinity of Haiphong city. Almost all the important dikes in other provinces: Thai Binh, Hai Duong, Ha Bac, Phu Tho, Ninh Binh, Nghe An and Ha Tinh were subjected to hundreds of U.S. air raids in the three months: July, August and September 1966." (pp. 6-7)

3) The Chu River Water Conservancy System

"This system serves a production area comprising 6 districts with more than half a million people. Bai Thuong dam, the key project of the above network was bombed 13 times; the water regulating projects and big canals, 41 times. Typical were the August 21, 22, and 23, 1965, attacks against the Ban Thach water regulating dam, an important project the purpose of which is to carry water to fields on higher ground. The dam was hit 6 times on August 21 and 22, twice on August 23: 236 bombs fell on the dam and about 100 others on the surrounding rice fields, damaging the dam and flood gates, and drying up thousands of hectares of land." (p. 4)

4) The Suoi Hai Reservoir of Ha Tay Province

"The Suoi Hai reservoir is one of the bigger water reservoirs in North Vietnam, with a capacity of tens of millions of cubic meters for watering an area of Ha Tay province which used to be arid. Some days before the attacks, U.S. aircraft had carried out many reconnaissance flights. On September 9, 1965, the main project was bombed 9 times, from 6:45 a.m. to 1:30 p.m., with hundreds of heavy bombs. It was repeatedly bombed on the following days: — September 10: twice; — September 11: 9 times, from 8 a.m. to 5 p.m. — September 12: 9 times — September 14: 3 times — September 15: twice — September 16: once.

Thus, the U.S. attacked the Suoi Hai water reservoir 35 times on 7 consecutive days, destroying a part of the dam, nearly breaking it and damaging a floodgate built across the Tich River, causing serious drought while the crops here badly needed water." (p. 4)

5) *The Be Reservoir in Quang Binh Province*

"The Be water reservoir of Quang Binh province is under construction. Between March 25, 1965, and September 1965 it was attacked 55 times with 1,033 bombs of all sizes, a great number of rockets and 20 mm shells. In 1966, between June 26, 1966, and August 14, 1966, the U.S. launched 57 attacks. In some months as in August 1965, they launched day and night attacks on 30 consecutive days." (pp. 4-5)

6) *Thac Ba Dam in Yen Bai Province*

This was the largest dam under construction in North Vietnam; it was first bombed on September 21, 1965. In 1966, on April 23 and June 22, the U.S. imperialists dropped heavy bombs on the place where workers were working. On July 8, 20 and 21, 1966, they repeatedly bombed the center of the construction site of the main dam where there were numerous workers, killing 30 of them and damaging a large quantity of equipment." (p. 5)

Gentlemen of the Tribunal, as you know, Vietnam is a part of the monsoon area, and the rainy season comes in July, August and September. These are the months when the water level is at its highest. For example, the rivers of Sontay province have an average annual rate of water flow of 3,400 cubic meters per second. During the rainy season, this rate increases to 13,400 cubic meters per second.

One who remembers the great disaster which resulted from the breaking of the dike of the Red River in August 1945 which brought death and famine to two million people, and rendered hundreds of thousands of families homeless, can understand just how serious the bombing of the dikes during the rainy season can be.

One other point on the bombing of the dikes, to which I would particularly like to draw your attention, is that the target of these bombings is nothing other than the dike system itself. The map of the dike system of the Democratic Republic of Vietnam, prepared by the Water Conservancy Commission dealing with the dikes bombed and strafed from March to December 31, 1966, demonstrates very clearly that the irrigation system is one of the main targets of the bombings.

An accompanying map, prepared by the same Commission, which we submit in evidence to the Tribunal, makes it clear that the bombing of dikes has been directed against the most important rivers and canals, and these rivers and canals are not to be found in the proximity of railroads or main roads. Therefore, one can conclude that the bombings of the irrigation system are not the result of error or accident, but have been carried out systematically and deliberately.

The purpose of the bombardment of dikes and the irrigation system in general is not only to cause floods, but also to disrupt economic development and to demoralize the population.

The irrigation system is so important to Vietnam that the success of both the land reform program and the co-operative system depended upon the extent to which they made it easier to build the irrigation system after the abolishment of the landlords. One of the contributions of the co-operatives to the improvement of Vietnamese society has been the mobilization of the people for the construction of the irrigation system. A similar assessment of the success of land reform, based on its ability to improve the irrigation system, can be made for many other countries in Asia as well.

The tremendous increase in the production of rice in the Democratic Republic of Vietnam has been achieved on the basis of the development of the irrigation system since Independence in 1954. The Vietnamese people have moved over 1,200,000,000 cubic meters of earth, and stretched out the network of river and sea dikes over a land surface of 4,000 km during the ten years following Independence (1955-1965). As a result, 90% of the cultivated area was irrigated, and the irrigation of 80% of rice paddies was provided for through hydraulic works. North Vietnam, which had the lowest yield in the productivity of rice of all the Southeast Asian countries before World War II, is now harvesting a yearly average of four tons of rice per hectare. Five tons of rice per hectare per year is its goal, and we know that it is already producing annually more than five tons per hectare in some areas.

The objective of the bombardment of dikes and other components of the irrigation system is to destroy the achievements of the Vietnamese people, to weaken their determination and to prevent them from continuing to develop their economy . . .

On the Law of Land Warfare
testimony by Frank Pestana

Mr. Pestana is an Attorney Practicing Law in California

In ancient times, parties engaged in warfare were subject to few or no internationally binding rules. Treachery and perfidy were permissible and instrumentalities of destruction now forbidden by law were employed without scruple.

An important stage in the development of the idea that the power of belligerents in waging war is not unlimited was reached in the 16th and 17th century when the modern system of international law began to take shape in the treatises of Victoria, Grotius, Pufendorf and others. Stirred by the atrocities of the Thirty Years War and the license which characterized the conduct of the belligerents, Grotius appealed to the "Law of Nature" as a system of law binding upon nations as upon individuals and which set humanitarian limits in the conduct of war.

But aside from occasional stipulations in treaties relating to such matters as the treatment of enemy aliens, etc., the laws of war consisted mainly of customs and usages which were found in the histories and treatises of the text writers. Today, while a considerable portion of the law of war is still based on custom and usage, much of it, especially the law of land warfare, is found in multi-party treaties or guidance of their military forces.

The starting point toward a codification of rules of conduct may be said to have been the adoption of the Declaration of Paris in 1856 at the close of the Crimean War. The Declaration of Paris was followed by the First Red Cross Convention in 1864, which laid down rules for treatment of the sick and wounded in war. Its principles were adopted by one of the Hague Conventions in 1899, and extended to apply to maritime warfare. The Convention of 1864 was replaced by a new and more detailed one, concluded at Geneva in 1906. Finally in 1929, the Convention of 1906 was superseded by a still more detailed convention concluded by an international conference at Geneva.

An important landmark in the law of land warfare was the 1868 Declaration of St. Petersburg framed by a conference called by the Tsar of Russia for the purpose of securing an agreement to refrain from the employment of a type of bullet which inflicted needless suffering. Of special importance is the preamble to the Declaration which asserted the proposition that "there are technical limits at which war ought to yield to the requirements of humanity" and that "The progress of civilization should have the effect of alleviating as much as possible the calamities of war; that the only legitimate object which states should endeavor to accomplish during war is to weaken the military forces of the enemy; that for this purpose, it is sufficient to disable the greatest possible number of men; that this objective would be exceeded by the employment of arms which needlessly aggravate the suffering of the disabled men or render their death inevitable."

The high water mark in the codification of the laws and customs of warfare was in the Hague conferences of 1899 and 1907. The most important was the convention dealing with questions of the law of land warfare at some length. In order to remove the foundation for a claim that matters not covered by the convention might be determined by military commanders without regard to law, the conference inserted in the preamble a statement that it was not the intention that such matters be left to the arbitrary judgment of military commanders and that, until a more complete code of laws should be agreed upon and accepted by the states of the world, "inhabitants and belligerents should remain under the protection and the rule of the principles of the law of nations, as they result from the usages established among the civilized peoples, from the laws of humanity, and the dictates of the public conscience." Importantly, Article I imposed upon the contracting parties an obligation to issue instructions to their armed forces to conform with the regulations of the convention.

A manual dictating conduct for troops, the first ever issued, had already been promulgated by President Lincoln of the United States in 1863. This remained in force until 1914 when superseded by a new manual entitled *Rules of Land Warfare,* prepared by the United States War Department. These were an embodiment of the instructions of the 1863 manual with additions and omissions necessary to conform to the Hague Convention and the Red Cross Convention of 1906.

The Hague Convention of 1899 on the conduct of war on land, of which the corresponding Convention of 1907 was a revision, had been ratified by the belligerents and was binding upon all of them. In addition those provisions of the 1907 Convention which were merely declaratory of existing customs and usages were declared binding as customary law independently of the status of the Convention of which they were a part.

Subsequently there was little sentiment in favor of further attempts to codify the laws of warfare. It was generally felt that world efforts should be directed toward the prevention of war rather than to regulate it. Nonetheless, the horror aroused by the use of certain instrumentalities and methods of destruction during the First World War led to several attempts to outlaw their use by international agreement. Thus by the Treaty for the Limitation and Reduction of Armaments signed at the Washington Disarmament Conference in 1922, the destruction of merchant vessels by submarines was condemned unless crewmen and passengers were first placed in safety. The Treaty likewise condemned the use of asphyxiation, poisonous or other gases and all analogous liquids, materials or devices. Because of France's failure to ratify the Treaty, it never came into force. Meanwhile, by the so-called Poison Gas Protocol, signed at Geneva in 1925, the condemnation of the use of gases, liquids and other materials, mentioned in the Washington Treaty of 1922 was renewed and "bacteriological substances" were added. This Protocol has been ratified by 33 nations, including France. The Senate of the United States, however, refused to consent to its ratification. In spite of the failure of the United States to ratify the Protocol, it has been accepted as binding by the vast majority of civilized nations.

The position of the United States in this matter was authoritatively stated by Franklin D. Roosevelt in his solemn announcement made in 1943: "Use of such weapons as poisonous or noxious gases, or other inhuman devices of warfare has been outlawed by the general opinion of civilized mankind ... I state categorically that we shall under no circumstances resort to the use of such weapons unless they are first used by our enemies."

Another post-war achievement was the signing at Geneva in 1929 of conventions for the treatment of prisoners of war and for the amelioration of the condition of the wounded and sick of armies in the field. The Convention on the Treatment of Prisoners of War is a veritable code whose purpose is to set the highest standard of just and humane treatment of prisoners. Among other rules, the convention forbids reprisals upon prisoners. A stipulation is that in case one of the belligerents is not a party to the Convention, its provisions shall nevertheless be binding as between belligerents who are parties.

At present, there are no international conventions dealing with aerial warfare aside from a declaration adopted by the Hague Conference of 1899 and renewed in 1907, prohibiting for a limited time, the launching of projectiles and explosives from aircraft, and Article 25 of the Hague Convention of 1907 which prohibits bombardments of "undefended" towns, villages, dwellings or buildings.

There also exists the Poison Gas protocol of 1925, which by implication forbids the aircraft of the signatory powers from disseminating gases, liquids and bacteriological substances as means of attack. The U.S. has not ratified this Protocol.[1]

In 1939, World War II started and new barbarities were perpetuated, particularly by the government of Nazi Germany. This time, reactions to war crimes — and retribution for them — were relatively swift. In 1942, the representatives of nine occupied countries met in London and issued the St. James Declaration that war criminals would be "sought out, handed over to justice, and judged."

President Roosevelt of the U.S. agreed that such persons "shall have to stand in Courts of Law . . . and answer for their acts." Prime Minister Churchill of Great Britain agreed that they would "have to stand before tribunals." And the government of the U.S.S.R. declared that such persons must be "arrested and tried under criminal law."

Late in 1943, the concepts underlying these statements received formal sanction at the Moscow Conference of the USSR, Great Britain and the United States, where two categories of war criminals were defined:

(a) "The major criminals whose offenses have no particular geographical location and who will be punished by joint decision of the governments of the allies;"

(b) Those whose offenses against the laws of war can be ascribed to a particular locality. These would be returned "to the scene of their crimes and judged on the spot by the peoples they have outraged."

At the same time, seventeen nations joined in founding the United Nations War Crimes Commission which was concerned chiefly with the second category of war criminals and proceeded to investigate evidence of war crimes and to report to the governments concerned all cases in which there might be adequate evidence for prosecution.

This led, in 1945, to the establishment of the Nuremberg International Military Tribunal by the USSR, USA, Great Britain and France. The Charter of this Tribunal defines as crimes coming within its jurisdiction the following acts:

---

[1]See recall testimony of Professor Gabriel Kolko.

(a) CRIMES AGAINST PEACE, namely, planning, preparation, initiation or waging of a war of aggression, or a war in violation of international treaties, agreements or assurances . . .

(b) WAR CRIMES, namely, violations of the law or customs of war. Such violations shall include . . . murder or ill-treatment of prisoners of war . . . killing hostages, plunder of public property, wanton destruction of cities; towns or villages, or devastation not justified by military necessity.

(c) CRIMES AGAINST HUMANITY, namely, murder, extermination, enslavement, . . . and other inhumane acts committed against any civilian population . . . or persecutions on political, racial or religious grounds . . .

As if to stress the point, Article 6 of the Charter states that there shall be "individual responsibility" for such crimes, and Article 7 provides that the official position of the accused "whether as Heads of State, or responsible officials in the Government Departments, shall not be considered as freeing them from responsibility or mitigating punishment."

The Chief Prosecutor Robert Jackson, an Associate Justice of the United States Supreme Court, in a letter to President Truman regarding the Nuremberg Trial, said:

"By the time the Nazis came to power it was thoroughly established that launching an aggressive war or the institution of war by treachery was illegal and that the defense of legitimate warfare was no longer available to those who engaged in such an enterprise. It is high time that we act on the juridical principle that aggressive-war-making is illegal and criminal.

"The reestablishment of the principle of unjustifiable war is traceable in many steps. One of the most significant is the Briand-Kellogg Pact of 1928, by which Germany, Italy and Japan, in common with ourselves and practically all the nations of the world, renounced war as an instrument of national policy, bound themselves to seek the settlement of disputes only by pacific means, and condemned recourse to war for the solution of international controversies. Unless this Pact altered the legal status of wars of aggression, it has no meaning at all and comes close to being an act of deception. In 1932, Mr. Stimson, as Secretary of State, gave voice to the American concept of its effect. He said War between nations was renounced by the Briand-Kellogg Treaty. This means that it has become illegal throughout practically the entire world. It is no longer to be the source and subject of rights It is no longer to be the principle around which the duties, the conduct and the rights of nations resolve. It is an illegal thing . . . By that very act, we have obsolete many legal precedents and have given the legal profession the task of examining many of its codes and treaties.

"This Pact constitutes only one in a series of acts which have reversed the viewpoint that all war is legal and have brought International Law into harmony with the common sense of mankind, that unjustifiable war is a crime. Without attempting an exhaustive catalogue, we may mention the Geneva Protocol of 1924 for the Pacific Settlement of International Disputes, signed by the representatives of forty-eight governments which declared that a war of aggression constitutes an international crime. At the Sixth Pan American Conference of 1928, the twenty-one American Republics unanimously adopted a resolution stating that 'war of aggression constitutes an international crime against the human species.'

"The United States is vitally interested in recognizing the principle that treaties renouncing war have juridical as well as political meaning. We relied upon the Briand-Kellogg Pact and made it a cornerstone of our national policy. We neglected our armaments and our war machine in reliance upon it. All violations of it, wherever started, menace our peace as we now have good reason to know. An attack on the foundations of international relations cannot be regarded as anything less than a crime against the international community, which may properly vindicate the integrity of its fundamental compacts by punishing aggressors. We therefore propose to charge that a war of aggression is a crime, and that modern International Law has abolished the defense that those who incite or wage it are engaged in legitimate business. Thus may forces of law be mobilized on the side of peace.

"Any legal position asserted on behalf of the United States will have considerable significance in the future evolution of International Law. In untroubled times, progress toward an effective rule of law in the international community is slow indeed. Inertia rests more heavily upon the society of nations than upon any other society. Now we stand at one of those rare moments when the thought and institutions and habits of the world have been shaken by the impacts of world war on the lives of countless millions. Such occasions rarely come and quickly pass. We are put under a heavy responsibility to see that our behavior during this unsettled period will direct the world's thought toward a firmer enforcement of the laws of international conduct, so as to make war less attractive to those who have governments and the destinies of peoples in their power."

The conviction of the major Nazi war criminals did not terminate the activities of the makers of international law. Even when the trials were in progress in Nuremberg, experts at the United Nations were preparing a Convention on Genocide. In December 1946, genocide was declared by the United Nations General Assembly to be "a crime under international law". Two years later, the text of this Convention was adopted by the General Assembly.

The U.N. Convention defined genocide as certain acts done "with intent to destroy, in whole or in part, a national, racial, ethnical or religious group as such." Among those acts are "killing members of the group" and "deliberately inflicting on the group conditions of life calculated to bring about its physical destruction in whole or in part."

Whether committed in time of war or in time of peace, genocide is a crime. Genocide itself, conspiracy or incitement to commit, and complicity in it, are all declared to be punishable and the convention expressly declares that "persons committing genocide . . . shall be punished, whether they are constitutionally responsible rulers, public officials, or private individuals."

Moreover, all governments acceding to this convention are bound to enact legislation "to provide effective penalties for persons guilty of genocide."

The United States and Great Britain are among the few countries in the world which have not acceded to this convention. Vietnam and China are among those which have done so.

Extracts from 'Fundamentals of Aerospace Weapons Systems'

Manual of the U. S. Air Force ROTC, Air University

Chemical and Biological Warfare

Chemical and biological warfare are two types which have not previously been fully developed and exploited. Because of this fact they are relatively unknown and often misunderstood. They, together with radiological warfare, constitute an exotic trilogy of weapons to which the short term "CBR" has been applied.

CBR-the shorthand for chemical, biological, and radiological warfare — may be further defined as toxic warfare against man, his animals and crops, rather than explosive warfare which destroys both man and his material possessions such as buildings and machines. This definition excludes the "conventional" destruction which can be caused by blast and heat from exploding nuclear weapons. Much emotion and controversy has been associated with contemplation of these forms of warfare . . .(Chapter 6).

Chemical Warfare

Chemical warfare is the military use of incendiaries, smoke, and toxic chemicals. Each of these categories consists of agent-munition combinations which may be designed for delivery from high-performance fighter or bomber aircraft. These agents may also be disseminated from cruise or ballistic missiles.

No combat restrictions limit the employment of incendiary, flame, or smoke weapons by local commanders in the accomplishment of their missions. The employment of toxic agents is a different matter, however. Whereas maiming and incineration are acceptable in war, the use of toxic chemicals is unacceptable because man fears most what he cannot see, feel, or hear. Although at the present time the United States has not signed any agreement which prohibits the use of toxic agents, this should not be interpreted to mean that it favors the use of such agents. Also, consideration is given to the position of our allies who have signed such agreements. Both these reasons explain in part the historical reluctance of the United States to employ them.

While the use of toxic chemicals is closely controlled at a high level chemical warfare is very much the business of the Air Force. . . (Chapter 6)

Incendiaries

. . . . Other factors that are vital in planning incendiary operations are the combustibility of the target and the ratio of the built-up area to the total ground area. Naturally, concentrations of wooden buildings will burn, and an empty reinforced-concrete structure will not. Since most incendiary targets are types of structures between these two extremes, a detailed analysis is necessary in order to determine the degree of combustibility. In making such analyses during World War II, professional fire-prevention engineers or persons of similar training and experience gave valuable service.

The type of product manufactured or stored would, of course, greatly influence the vulnerability of targets. A heavy fall of snow or rain would probably decrease the destruction caused by incendiary attack; a light fall of either would have little effect. Snow and rain decreased the effectiveness of attacks on Japanese cities by about 20 per cent. Wind velocity is also of major importance, as brisk air movements cause local fires to spread into a general conflagration.

With the advent of nuclear weapons and their accompanying thermal effects, it is highly unlikely that incendiaries will be employed in any but limited war situations. Such use would probably limit targets to small towns or military installations, where attacks could not assume the same importance as World War II's incendiary strategic attacks against national morale. Nevertheless, the U.S. Strategic Bombing Survey (USSBS), an exhaustive study made immediately following World War II, concluded that attack with fire bombs was an effective psychological weapon against any target, and the effect was heightened by successive attacks . . .(Chapter 6).

Fire Bombs

Considerable use was made of fire bombs against tactical targets during the latter part of World War II and in the Korean War.

Originally the fire bomb was an aircraft fuel tank to which were added two igniters containing white phosphorus. The fuel tank was filled in the field with gelled gasoline which had been thickened with napalm, a mixture of metallic soaps. The present model of the fire bomb, the M116A1 (Fig. 48), was designed specifically for delivery by high-performance jet airplanes. When released at low altitudes, the tank and the igniters burst upon impact. The igniters are filled with white phosphorus, which immediately ignites upon the contact with air.

Figure 48. The M116A1 Fire Bomb

The burning white phosphorous in turn ignites the gelled gasoline. The blazing contents are scattered over an area approximately the size of a football field (Fig. 49). The resulting flash fire ignites readily combustible material and burns or suffocates exposed personnel. It is particularly useful in jungle operations, against troops in lightly fortified positions, and against tanks or other armored vehicles. However, the fire bomb is primarily an antipersonnel weapon . . .

Toxic Chemical Agents

. . . . Because of their nature, toxic chemical agents are of primary value for use against personnel. Other weapons of more conventional nature and of war-proved value, such as fragmentation bombs, are designed specifically to be used against personnel. The toxic chemical weapon must be considered as a possibility, however, because of two characteristics not possessed by other antipersonnel weapons.

From the standpoints of effectiveness and economy, the airplane is the best vehicle for use in delivering and employing toxic chemicals, about 80 percent of the tonnage would be used in Air Force munitions and about 20 percent in ground force weapons . . . (Chapter 6).

Anticrop Agents

Both biological and chemical attack may be made against crops. Crop destruction would affect the food supply of both man and domestic animals, and destroy sources of essential oils, medicines, and industrial raw products.

Among the biological agents are late blight of potatoes, stem rust of cereals, and blast of rice. All these agents are classed as fungi. The plants mentioned may be infected by physical spread of the fungus spores. Control methods are similar, but expensive.

Nonliving anticrop agents are exemplified by such chemicals as 2,4 D (2,4-dichlorophenoxyacetic acid), used against broad-leaved plants such as cotton, beans, sugarbeets, sweet potatoes, flax, Irish potatoes, and soybeans. It may be applied by spraying or dusting. Remarkably small applications are effective. Once applied, and once symptoms of injury appear, plantings cannot be treated . . . (Chapter 6)

Target Intelligence

From the experiences with high-explosive bombs in World War II came a vast accumulation of knowledge about targets . . . New weapons have thus given birth to new target concepts . . .

In common with other areas of military study, the study of targets in warfare has become more complex along with the world's industrial and technological organization. As a consequence, a complete definition of a military target can perhaps no longer be kept simple, but a broad generalization might state that a military target is any person, thing, idea, entity, or location selected for destruction, inactivation, or rendering nonusuable with weapons which will reduce or destroy the will or ability of the enemy to resist . . .

Components of a National Structure as Targets

Targets within a nation fall into four categories: military, economic, political and psychosocial (Fig. 78). In target study, the elements of power grouped within these four categories are structural components of national strength. As targets, such components must be analyzed to determine which should be destroyed in order to cause the entire instrument or organization they make up to malfunction or break down completely. The destruction of certain of the components could render the whole useless to the enemy, and could, in fact, undermine one or more of the others, so closely are all the components of national strength related . . .

Psychosocial Structure

The psychosocial structure of a nation includes the moral strength of the people as manifested in their internal stability, unity, national will, and ability to influence other people. For purposes of target study, the psychosocial structure of a nation or people is often reduced to terms of morale, because morale is something that can be sensed, observed, and influenced.

Before any action designed to influence the morale of the population can be taken, it is necessary to study the population's psychosocial structure. Unless it is harnessed to a strong war machine, high morale in itself has little value; conversely, a strong war machine coupled with poor morale would mean little. On the other hand, both high morale and a strong war machine make a formidable combination; each gains strength from the other. This is not to say that the mutually supporting elements of high morale and military strength are invulnerable to psychological attacks. Following a proper analysis of the state of morale and the military machine of a nation, targets and methods can be selected that will affect that particular combination.

In past wars the morale of the people was an important factor in a nation's ability to fight, since upon it depended the production of materials needed for continuing the war. In fact, in past wars the possession of enough raw materials, industries, and skilled personnel did not necessarily mean adequate quantities of war materials. These had to be produced. Production required efficient organization and direction, cooperation among all the people, their willingness to consume less and produce more, to devote their energies to the production of war materials, at the expense of consumer goods, and at the time to face personal hardships, tragedies, and the dangers of war. In past wars, therefore, if the morale of the people could be weakened, the enemy was deprived of his full war potential.

Some of the conventional targets for morale attacks have been water supplies, food supplies, housing areas, transportation centers, and industrial sites. The objectives of these attacks in the past have been to dispel the people's belief in the invincibility of their forces, to create unrest, to reduce the output of the labor force, to cause strikes, sabotage, riots, fear, panic, hunger, and passive resistance to the government, and to create a general feeling that the war should be terminated. Although the question of how far the will to resist of a given group of people could be weakened or destroyed by aerial bombardment with conventional weapons was debatable, it was an irrefutable fact that a labor force preoccupied with civilian defense duties and the finding of food, shelter, and transportation could not operate at peak efficiency in the production of the materials of war (Fig. 80) . . .

The ability and will of a nation to wage war depend on a combination of military, economic, political, and psychosocial strengths. Attacks against any one of these strengths will have an effect on one or more of the others. In the study of a nation's structure it is necessary to recognize this interdependence and to select targets that will create the greatest adverse effect on the enemy's ability and will to wage war. Therefore, the first order of the day must be to know the enemy.

Strategic and Tactical Targets

By definition, a strategic target is any installation, network, group of buildings, or the like, considered vital to a country's war-making capacity and singled out for air attack; and a tactical target is any physical object, person, group of persons, or position singled out for attack during the course of battle or tactical operations in order to reduce or to destroy, the enemy's ability to sustain his combat operation. Most targets will fall into one or the other of these general categories, with finer distinctions made within them. However, there are no immutable definitions which will place each target in one category forever. In fact, some targets may be correctly placed in a number of categories during the course of a war campaign, and some may even be correctly identified as lying within two or more categories or subcategories at the same time . . . (Chapter 8)

Target Analysis

. . . It is true that a certain amount of target analysis was necessary with the use of high-explosive weapons. Some special missions during World War II and the Korean conflict, such as low-level bombing attacks against dams, required careful preattack analyses in order to assure enough force to breach the structures. But for routine bombing operations, many commanders using high explosives often depended primarily upon intuition for matching weapons against targets. (Chapter 8)

Support of Diplomacy in the Cold War

In considering the peacetime achievements and the expected wartime missions of tactical aerospace power, it is possible to lose sight of a most important immediate mission. In the diplomatic maneuvering of the cold war, the military forces play a very significant and vital role. The presence of powerful U.S. forces overseas give tangible evidence that the United States is ready — and able — to defend its rights and fulfill its obligations anywhere in the world. In its global mission, TAC[1] offers a hand of friendship to its neighbors both here and abroad. Maybe it is a TAC composite air strike force on a training mission to Turkey or a flight to France. Whatever the mission or wherever the location, TAC officers and airmen offer their friendship to the peoples of the free world. In return, our neighbors lay out the welcome mat.

The mutual understanding between TAC and its neighbors is not limited to an understanding of mission and aircraft. For example, doctors of a CASF or TDY to Turkey saved a small boy's life by obtaining plasma for a rare blood disease. In Alaska a TAC troop carrier outfit airlifted sick Eskimos and Indians. At Sewart Air Force Base, Tenn., a unit on a tactical mission included gift packages to Turkish children who in turn sent gifts from Turkey. Other examples of TAC's good-will missions are the airlifting of medicines and equipment to Pakistan following a heavy flood and the airlift of clothing, toys, and books to an orphanage in Athens, Greece . . . (Chapter 12)

---

[1] Tactical Air Command.

Technical Aspects of Fragmentation Bombs
testimony by Jean Pierre Vigier, M.D.

Director of Research at the National Center for Scientific Research; Former Officer-in-Charge of Armaments Inspection of the French Army Under General de Lattre de Tassigny

In Vietnam the Americans are utilizing a new type of anti-personnel arm based on the following principle: a hollow metallic envelope into which is cast certain projectiles such as ball-bearing-like pellets, needles, etc., numbering into the hundreds. These explode on the ground or in the air to fire the projectiles in a sun-burst pattern for many meters. The effects of the projectiles are insignificant on fixed installations. Two types of these weapons are principally in use in Vietnam. The "pineapple" bomb with cylindrically symmetrical explosion: this weapon consists of a hollow metallic envelope made of an alloy of copper and iron with traces of zinc, having a total weight of 800 grams and a thickness of 7 millimeters. Into the envelope, which resembles the shape of a pineapple, are cast 300 pellets of steel 6.3 millimeters in diameter. On the top of the bomblet are placed six "wings" which are folded when the bomb is at rest and which snap-up in flight by means of a spring at their base. These fins stabilize the fall of the bomb in the same manner as the feathers do a badminton shuttlecock. The lower part of the bomblet is closed with a metallic plate pierced by a hole through which penetrates the point of a spring loaded firing pin. Upon impact — if the bomblet falls vertically, as it is supposed to — the spring releases and the percussive causes the explosion of 160 grams of Cyclotol A3 which is composed of 91% hexogene trimethylene-trinitramine and 9% wax, an explosive three times more powerful than T.N.T. The explosion projects the pellets in a sun-burst pattern at an angle of about 20° with the horizontal to a distance of 15 meters; the pieces of the casing are propelled about 50 meters. Craters from these bomblets are small — 30 to 40 centimeters maximum diameter in loose soil and with a depth of 10 to 20 centimeters; their damage to structures is insignificant.

Method of employment: A pod containing 19 cylindrical tubes of a diameter slightly larger than the bomblets is fixed beneath an aircraft's wings and parallel to them. Each tube contains 20 bomblets with the fins folded back. The airplane flies horizontally at an altitude of about 800 meters and fires the "pineapples" from the tubes by means of a directed explosion of several grams of powder. The bomblets disperse in the same manner as a "stick" of parachutists over an elliptical zone about 500 meters long by 250 meters wide. This weapon was first used, to the best of our knowledge, on February 8th, 1965 against Le Thuy, in the province of Quang Binh.

From a purely military point of view, these weapons had two drawbacks: 1. there were numerous "duds" as the bomblet did not always fall vertically as necessary for proper detonation, 2. the horizontal, straight-and-level flight of the aircraft at the low level — no more than 1,000 meters — necessary to assure maximum effective dispersion of the pineapple bomblets rendered the attacking aircraft extremely vulnerable to ground-fire. For these reasons the pineapple anti-personnel weapon seems to have been largely superseded by the:

"Guava" bomb with spherically symmetrical explosion: this weapon is round, resembling a conventional hand grenade and has a total weight of 400 grams. Like the pineapple, it consists of a hollow envelope 7 mm thick of the same alloy and is filled with 50 grams of Cyclotol A3. Into the casing are cast 260 to 300 steel balls 5.56 mm in diameter. Also cast into the casing in meridional direction are four small fins or "wings" which catch the wind and by friction set up a spinning motion along the polar axis. In the center of the explosive filling a new type of detonator is located which operates by centrifugal force. This detonator consists of three small hammers which are cocked by the spinning of the bomblet and which are spring loaded. If the spinning stops for any reason, the hammers fall, exploding the bomblet, and firing the steel pellets into an isotropic distribution in a sun-burst pattern for a distance of about 15 meters.

It is the nature of the bomb that upon touching the ground or even if while in flight, it glances off a roof, a wall, or a branch of a tree — thereby interrupting or changing the axis of rotation away from the original polar axis or, as shown by blast studies in Japan — if the axis changes spontaneously or if the rate of spinning slows, the bomblet explodes. Like the pineapple, the craters produced are small and the effect of the bomblet on structures is insignificant. Method of employment: these bomblets are packed into a hollow "mother" bomb casing about 2.1 meters long by 40 centimeters in diameter which holds roughly 640 "guava" bomblets. The mother bombs have a timing device which separates the container casing at an altitude of about 800 meters. The 640 guava bomblets are flung out and follow a parabolic trajectory and are distributed over the objective in an elliptical pattern about 1 kilometer long by about 500 meters wide.

This weapon was used for the first time on about the 18th of April, 1966, on the village of Moc Chan in the Democratic Republic of Vietnam. Because of the spherical symmetry of the explosion and the tendency for a percentage of the bomblets to explode as air bursts, traditional trenches and open individual shelters are rendered ineffective for cover; these weapons are therefore extremely dangerous. They are usually employed in a three stage raid: first comes observation, then bombardment with high explosives and/or napalm and then by C.B.U. (Cluster Bomb Units) containing the "guava" steel pellet bombs.

Recall Questioning of Professor Vigier

DELLINGER: I'm concerned about the nature of the fragmentation bombs, even though we have Professor Neiland's testimony as to their destructiveness, for what concerns this body particularly is their possible military use and the question of their devastating effect upon civilians. From your analysis and the analyses made at the University of Tokyo, can you furnish us with accurate information as to the number of bomblets in each C.B.U. cannister and the number of pellets in each bomblet?

VIGIER: As I said yesterday, there are two types of fragmentation bombs. One should be careful what exact name one gives to them. At first they were completely classified and all the information relative to the weapons was given two conventional names. They've been called "Lazy Dogs" and C.B.U.'s To our knowledge, the C.B.U.'s, and "Lazy Dogs" are just the two types of bombs which I showed you yesterday, the militarily correct nomenclature of which is "fragmentation bombs." These are bombs which act not through the effect of the explosion, but in which the explosion is made only in order to spray smaller pellets. We must distinguish two stages: first one releases the bombs; in the case of the pineapples they are released directly by the plane. They fall on the ground and explode. In the case of the guavas the release of the bomb is made in two stages: one drops the "mother" bomb which contains 640 guavas; the mother bomb explodes at one kilometer altitude, more or less, and the guavas are spread over a certain zone. One can show by a very simple scientific formula that they fall in the pattern of an ellipse with a big axis oriented along the line of release and a small axis perpendicular to that. The big axis is about 600 meters long and the small axis is about 300 meters wide when they are dropped from an altitude of one kilometer. Each guava then fires out 240-300 small steel pellets. These are multi-stage weapons, similar to the idea of multi-stage rockets.

DELLINGER: The total number of pellets then from one cannister would be 240 times 640 if they all explode.

VIGIER:That would be the number of steel pellets which are blown from one mother bomb.

DELLINGER: You pointed out yesterday that these would be useless to penetrate sandbags or to get at anti-aircraft installations which are generally underground. It seems to me the use of the term "pin-point bombing", which is common in the statements of the White House and the State Department, seems totally out of place in connection with this kind of weapon.

VIGIER: There's no possible application of the term "pin-point bombing." The only way one can use this expression is that such guavas, when they explode, produce very small craters; you can call that a pin-point if you want to. The crater is about 10 centimeters deep and 20 centimeters in diameter on the surface. On walls you can see the trace but the pellets never go through concrete or even ordinary sandstone, they just produce a "pock mark" which is half a centimeter deep. As to the effect of the pellets, themselves, we've made experiments which show that even when the guava explodes 50 centimeters from a sand bag, the steel pellets don't penetrate further than 20 or 30 centimeters within the sand. A sand bag is, therefore, a complete protection against such an explosion. This means that only people who are not protected can be hit; this is why it is strictly an "anti-personnel" bomb. As I said yesterday, they are used after a conventional bombing. The high explosive bomb destroys factories and sets houses on fire and then the fragmentation bombs hit people who have been flushed out of the houses, or who try to dig out the victims. And they have been also used, evidently, to prevent repairs on economic installations. Economic installations can be destroyed by conventional bombing and the fragmentation bombs are then used to prevent immediate repairs.

DELLINGER: There has been talk in the press of timing devices on some of the bomblets so that they don't explode at once. Are any of these fragmentation bombs equipped with timing devices to your knowledge, or do they all explode in a relatively short period of time after being released?

VIGIER: This is a point we were discussing yesterday. We are sure of one fact, that is; after they are released from the mother bomb at an altitude of about one kilometer high, then we are sure that the spinning arms the guavas; namely, it prepares them to be exploded. Now the spinning has a two-fold objective. First, it arms the guavas and second, when the spinning stops, they explode, because the centrifugal force which has spread the three little hammers no longer acts — the hammers fall back and the guava explodes. This means that when a guava falls on the ground, it is spinning; when it hits the ground, of course, it stops spinning and the guava explodes. Now a percentage of these guavas do not explode. One frequently sees peasants collecting these guavas in Vietnamese villages after a bombing. Now the question is why didn't these guavas explode? The only answer the French Scientific Commission has found for that fact is that probably the axis of rotation of the guava as it fell had not coincided with the North Pole-South Pole axis which is the axis around which it should have spun in order to arm the detonator. And so in that case the guavas were not armed and therefore they could not explode.

Then comes the theory we have presented to the Tribunal which results from the Japanese experiments. It shows that under certain critical velocities, the guavas automatically explode without being hit in any sense. Now it's true that a lot of accidents have occurred when peasants were just collecting the guavas on the ground, but I do not think it was because those guavas contained delayed timing devices. It's in the nature of the guavas that just because they had been armed and that by picking them up or jostling them accidently in a non-careful way the little hammers are agitated and the thing explodes.

But as I said yesterday, it's an indiscriminate weapon. You cannot aim any of these weapons with any utilizable precision on the battlefield; you can only cover big zones in this way. You couldn't use them to stop an infantry attack or to protect a military position. You can only throw them at random on cities or hamlets, or on military objectives once you have hit them with a different type of bomb. Another point I'd like to make is that C.B.U.'s can only be effective as weapons over very densely populated regions. This is very clear because if there is nobody in sight the little pellets just spread and are completely useless. Therefore, the use of a "mother" bomb of guavas on an objective is only useful if you use them on densely populated regions. That's why I think that this is a weapon which is meant to be used over very densely populated regions of the world such as, for example, the Delta of the Red River.

COURTLAND COX: I'd like you to expand on one point you made yesterday. You said that you thought that C.B.U.'s or fragmentation bombs are now being used to replace atomic weapons in conventional warfare. In connection with that, I would like you to distinguish between, say New York City, as a densely populated area and some other. I don't think they would use it on New York City, given the industrial nature and all the concrete and steel that exists there. In what type of densely populated areas, therefore, do you envision those C.B.U.'s being most effective?

VIGIER: I was referring to discussions among military experts all over the world on the theory of bombing. One of the points about atomic weapons is that they destroy everything in a given zone; they destroy living beings, military installations and economic installations. If they are used in the way which is being now prepared, it also means that nobody will be able to live for a long period in the target zones. For example, it's very easy to show that if one uses cobalt atomic weapons, no living existence is possible for a period of 30 years in the target zone, not only human beings but any form of beings. So, of course, this is a very dangerous and definitive weapon; and so, from the military point-of-view on bombing, this is not an efficient type of weapen if one envisages occupation or re-population of certain regions. Therefore, the C.B.U., the fragmentation bomb (I propose to call them fragmentation bombs once-and-for-all to designate bombs which explode in many stages and finish with small steel objects. This should be, in my opinion, the correct technical term and we can then distinquish the various types of fragmentation weapons by the symmetries of explosions; namely, the pineapple is a cylindrical symmetry, the guava is a spherical symmetry, and so on), does not harm any type of installation. It does not destroy buildings, does not destroy economic installations, does not destroy fixed military installations; it just hits personnel. It just hits human beings or cattle. So it's very clear that this type of weapon cannot be used against big cities in an industrial civilization, for one simple reason, which is that the houses are generally built of concrete or stone and the pellets do not penetrate. Unless they followed conventional bombing which would have flushed the whole population out of the houses and protective installations, fragmentation bombs would be useless against Western cities. However, the story is very different against underdeveloped countries. In underdeveloped countries the houses are not usually built of hard material. For example, in Vietnamese villages (I can show photographs to illustrated this) you find the steel balls everywhere after a fragmentation bombing by guavas. This is because the houses are generally built with mud walls and covered with straw, therefore, the pellets penetrate everywhere. For this reason you can use the fragmentation bomb as a direct weapon to destroy the population of such a place. As I said, we have evidence of two types of bombing with fragmentation bombs: one which follows conventional bombing and one which uses only fragmentation bombs. This latter is usually performed by the planes of the 7th Fleet with the "lobbing" technique I was describing yesterday.

COX: Would you say, given the scientific knowledge that you have of fragmentation bombs and their effectiveness, that those bombs were specifically developed for what you termed "underdeveloped countries," and that their probable use in the future will be specifically in those areas.

VIGIER: This is my personal opinion. I would like to present in support of this opinion, however, a document which I request the Tribunal to accept as an element of proof. It is an American Air Force document which is called *Fundamentals of Aerospace Weapon Systems.* It is dated May 20, 1966 and it has been published by the Air University of the U.S. Air Force. In that document are two very important points. One is an analysis of the new methods of target intelligence and the nature of modern bombing. On page 205 of this document, you find priority listing of the targets which should be bombed according to modern bombing technique. The priority order represents a very big departure from the target choices of the Second World War.

I will briefly summarize the argument. The document distinguishes four components of national power in a country — the political, the psycho-social (which are schools, hospitals, churches, and so on), the military and the economic. Now the Air Force document explains that in a modern economy all four types of targets are strategically interdependent. Therefore, it is not effective to concentrate only on military objectives if one wants to hit a country very hard. It points out that the suitability of a given target should be chosen in relation to its connection with those four aspects — political, psycho-social, military and economic — and for this purpose a computer technique has been developed in order to give appropriate weight to every type of target. That was the first point. The second point of the document explains that field commanders can no longer be allowed to choose their own targets: the choice of all targets in modern bombing is a question which can only be worked out by computers at very highly technically equipped General-Staff level. I suppose that, for example in Vietnam, they must have a big computer in Saigon to do target selection according to this new technique. It's very clear, considering this, that the specific weight of every target is different according to the type of economy one is dealing with.

For example, let us reason — ignoring for the moment any humanitarian or moral considerations — that if one wished effective bombing, according to these principles, of a country like Vietnam or any other under-developed country, it's very clear that the political aspect of the target is not very important. Why? Because the political centers are moveable; guerilla leaders, the political cadres of popular resistance, move all over the countryside and are not targets in themselves. A place like Paris *would* be a suitable place to bomb if one wanted to bomb France because there you would hit the political nerve center of a modern developed country. So the political aspect of targets is out in a country like Vietnam.

As for the economic aspect of targetting, it also loses specific weight in under-developed countries because the economy is not highly centralized. It has not the modern dependence on a system of communication — which corresponds to a nerve system — as in very highly developed industrial economies. Vietnamese villages are to a great extent self-sufficient. So the economic aspect of target weighting in under-developed lands is also no longer very important, except minimally.

As for the targetting of military installations in Vietnam-type wars, the same argument applies. Namely, that in under-developed countries, military installations cannot be specifically or easily centered at given points. In a guerilla war, the military installations of the nationalist armed forces are non-existent — they are mixed-in among the population. Their sanctuaries are by preference in small villages or in widely dispersed mountain and jungle hideouts. These make poor target objectives for modern technological bombing techniques.

Therefore, only the psycho-social aspect of the targetting remains. And this aspect is tremendously emphasized, assumes a tremendous weight in under-developed countries in comparison to the weight they have in developed countries. This is the opinion of our military technicians, and we have discussed this exhaustively in Paris. In Vietnam the reason why the bombing has been concentrated on the psycho-social objectives, namely, schools, hospitals, churches, and so on, is because this aspect must be automatically emphasized according to modern military bombing techniques such as taught in the U.S. Air Force's *Fundamentals of Aerospace Weapons Systems.*

COX: While in school, I was forced to take "ROTC" — which is reserve officer's training for the military — and one of the things we were taught is that the first task of the army is to destroy the will of the enemy to resist. Now, given the particular emphasis you made on psycho-social targetting, and also given the self-sufficiency of the Vietnamese communities, what types of psycho-social targets do you envision being attacked in Vietnam? What type of targets, from your technical expertise, would the U.S. Government consider effective?

VIGIER: The only rational statement that I can make is that the U.S.'s priority targets correspond precisely to the targets which, as we have seen, have been effectively bombed. You see it's very hard to believe in so many so-called "mistakes". When one states, as the U.S. has in Vietnam, that the Air Force bombs "only steel and concrete", this doesn't sound very reasonable, because steel and concrete exist in a rather limited way in under-developed countries. What is really being done there, I think, is an attempt to break the morale of the population by hitting its psycho-social institutions; namely, churches, schools, medical facilities and dikes. Dikes are especially "good" targets because they are the only economic objective in a nation of peasants with an economy like Vietnam's which rests mainly on the irrigation system. And the dikes are not "concrete," they are just earth. So the objectives which have been effectively hit by the bombing are precisely those which have been meant to be hit. You see, if one tries to construe the bombing of those places such as schools and so on as "accidents" one understands nothing about modern bombing theory. I don't think these are "mistakes". I think that the computers have chosen just the objectives which have really been bombed.

COX: Would you say that the war in Vietnam, or any war that is conducted in colonized countries — which you call "underdeveloped countries — are by nature wars of genocide. That by the nature of the country and by the nature of the war that must be waged against them — in order to destroy their will to fight, that these must be wars of genocide?

VLADIMIR DEDIJER: The matter of genocide is not on our agenda. We will deal with this matter in the second session. So in giving your answer I would like you to take this into consideration.

VIGIER: I'm not going to comment on the word genocide, I'll only comment on the technical aspect. Where under-developed countries are being warred upon by developed countries, the main military objective turns out to be the population itself. It is a battle of machines against people. As the U.S. Air Force document states, the only way to break an under-developed country which maintains a will to resist is to completely destroy the people. There are no military objectives; there are no tactical objectives which can be chosen which can bring that effect in an indirect way. Modern bombing techniques, as this document explains very clearly, require hitting objectives which break the willpower of the enemy. In developed countries you can destroy morale by destroying economic potential. In the case of underdeveloped countries, the primary objective of the bombing is the people themselves. That's, I believe, why fragmentation bombs have been used in such a high proportion; 50% of all bombs falling on North Vietnam are fragmentation bombs. This is not an accident; this is the logical application of U.S. theory of military weapons technique in warfare against an under-developed country.

Combined Report on Anti-Personnel Bombs
testimony by Members of the Japanese Scientific Committee

Japanese investigators have made full analysis of what are called "ball bombs" now being used by the U.S. against the Democratic Republic of Vietnam. Related materials are attached separately.[1] We wish to draw particular attention to the following points.

It is important to note that these bombs are not at all effective in destroying ferro-concrete military facilities, but are designed and used to kill and wound as many people as possible.

Further, these bombs inflict injuries which are extremely hard to treat. They can be compared with dum-dum projectiles in their inhumaneness, doing no major injury on the surface of the human body but causing terrible injury in penetration. Analytical work on the ball bombs is included in this report. This type of weapon is all the more inhumane because once the projectile penetrates the human body, it is extremely hard to remove.[2]

As described in the later reports, the Americans bomb dikes and levees, and later drop ball bombs and napalm bombs to kill and wound farmers as they come out to repair the facilities. What is more import-

[1]Report by Zenkichi Asami
[2]Report by Hidetoshi Shiga and Haruji Nakamura

ant to note, there are standard operating methods of making systematic attacks on doctors who hurry to the scene to minister to the wounded. This unmitigated inhumanity is directed against the few doctors who have come out of the extensive training program of the Democratic Republic of Vietnam, which since its foundation, has worked hard to improve medical and health services.

Construction and Performance of the Pineapple Bomb

The pineapple bomb is so called because it looks like a pineapple. It is an improved version of the fragmentation bomb for the purpose of killing and wounding. It is packed with slugs in its case, this variation is called a Cannister Bomb Unit (CBU) in America. Figure 1 shows the bomb; the cup-shaped body of the pineapple is 6.7 cm. in diameter and 6.8 cm. in height. With its four vanes, each 7.0 cm. long, the bomb weighs 0.8 kilograms. The cup-shape part is filled with 160 grams of explosive. About 250 steel balls (each 6.3 millimeters in diameter) are buried in the zinc-copper alloy of the approximately 7.mm thick walls of the cup shaped part. Upon explosion the bomb walls break into fragments and scatter the steel balls with high velocity. The effective range of the scattered steel balls is a 10 to 15 meter radius. The four blades are to stabilize the bomb in falling, and to hold its detonator (fixed on the bottom of the bomb) facing the ground. Folded until dropped, the blades spring open automatically as soon as the bomb is released. As the blades unfold, the fuse is armed.

Release and the range of spread — A special release apparatus is provided for the pineapple bomb. The release apparatus is a cluster of tubes which contain 19 cylinders packed with a total of 360 pineapple bombs. When triggered, compressed air blows loose the pineapple bombs through an outlet on the side opposite the aircraft's course of flight. A survey group of the Democratic Republic of Vietnam, reported that a U.S. F-105 flying at an altitude of 600 meters could drop 300 pineapple bombs over an area 500 meters in the direction of flight and 100 meters on each side. In other words, 500 x 200 square meters of ground would be strewn with 360 x 250 — 90,000 steel balls, to kill or wound any man or beast within reach.

Construction, Performance of the Ball Bomb

Developed from the pineapple bomb into a ball shape (see figure 2) the ball bomb has a substantially increased killing and wounding power. It is about the size of an orange, 6.8 centimeters by 6.1 centimeters. The charge is 100 grams of Cyclotol A^3. Its round case, made of zinc-copper alloy, is inlaid with 300 steel balls, each 5.56 millimeters in diameter. A fuse in the center detonates the bomb on landing, and the explosion covers a radius of five to ten meters.

Release and range of spread — The parent bomb is a cigar-shaped container (Figure 3). These bombs come in two sizes, the larger one containing 640 ball bombs and the smaller 300. At a certain height from the ground the case splits into two by operation of a time fuse. The bombs then scatter on an individual flight downward. At an altitude of 600 meters, the ball bombs spread over one kilometer in the direction of flight and 100 meters on each side of the effective range, exactly twice the range of the pineapple bombs. Any man or livestock within the vast 1,000 x 300 square meter expanse are killed or wounded. As is evident, these two types of bombs are solely designed for killing and wounding human beings. They are strictly prohibited by international law.

The shape of the ball bomb is elliptical, a slightly compressed sphere. Its diameters are 67mm and 61mm. The shell is of die-cast zinc alloy, 7mm thick. Each one contains 280-300 steel pellets 5mm in diameter. Total weight of the bomb is 450 grams including 100 grams of explosive. The detonator functions by centrifugal force generated as the bomb falls. The bomb is fitted with four cast-in vanes which spin the ball in falling; at a certain rotational volocity, the safety is released and the charge is ready to explode. The landing impact or ceasing of spinning explodes the bomb. Experiments were conducted to test this data.

Ball bombs are not dropped individually; they are carried in a streamlined steel container. On release, the container divides into two and the ball bombs are scattered. Two types of steel container called the "mother bomb", are in use in Vietnam. The Japanese investigation team saw one of these containing 300 ball bombs. Its maximum outer diameter was 400mm, and total length 2,400mm. The other type carries 640 ball bombs. A time fuse is attached to the top of the mother bomb to vary its timing from 0 to 90 seconds. When the mother bomb splits in the air, for instance at an altitude of 600 meters, the ball bombs spread over an area 1,000 meters in the direction of flight and 200 meters on each side. The 90,000 steel pellets (300 times 300) fly in all directions over this range. Anyone caught within this area will be stuck by some 30 pellets from all directions.

The conventional individual cannister Bomb Unit (CBU), or "bomblet" consists of a fragile shell imbedded with many steel pellets and an explosive charge. The slaughter range of the conventional CBU of 170 kilograms is reported to be a circle of 30 meters diameter. By contrast, the killing range of a "mother" ball bomb is 1,000 by 200 meters. In addition, the "blind angle" of the balls is far less than that of conventional CBU's so the killing range is 30% greater from this alone.

In Vietnam, the Americans have used conventional fragmentation bombs such as the butterfly bomb, and have now developed new types of CBU. The pineapple bomb, which was formerly used in great numbers is one of these. It is like the ball bomb except for large wings on the tail which stabilize the bomb in descent. Now the improved CBU ball bomb is used more because it is a more effective killer.

The U.S. has many other new weapons designed to massacre a great many people. A portable land mine used in South Vietnam has many pellets or tiny steel balls, imbedded in it, and a mere touch causes instant explosion. A new type of bomb called a parachute bomb was devised to kill occupants of foxholes or dug-outs covered with thin roofs. The upper part is a small parachute and the bomb part is made of duraluminum. There are two types, delayed-action and instant-action. As the explosion is "shaped" to concentrate downwards vertically, it breaks through the thin roofs of dug-outs and shelters to kill people inside. Dumdum bullets were also found by the second Japanese Investigation Team to be used by the U.S. in spite of their prohibition by the Geneva Protocol. . . .

—*Zenkichi Asami, science journalist; member of First Japanese Commission of Inquiry.*

Chemical Analysis of the Ball Bomb

The explosive used in the ball bomb is a light brown colored chemical known as "RDX". It has other names such as "hexogen" and "Cyclonite" and has been used as a high-powered explosive since the latter part of World War II. Its scientific name is trimethylene-trinitramine $C^3H^3N^3O^3$). Chemical analysis shows that the charge is 91% of RDX and 9% wax. This composition is known as A^3. Detonation velocity (i.e. the ignition speed through the explosive) is 7,500 m/sec. This can be raised to 8,500 m/sec. by compressing the explosive. It generates heat of 1300k cal/gram. Conventional TNT has a detonation velocity of 7140m/sec and combustion heat of 1000k cal/gram.

The pellets in the shell of the ball bomb are steel. The shell in which the tiny steel pellets are embedded, is an alloy of zinc and lead, with some copper and iron as an impurity. The following chemical analysis was done at the University of Tokyo. Chemical analysis of the CBU by per cent — Pineapple bomb: zinc, 73.50; copper, 3.22; iron, 0.38; lead, 22.90. Ball bomb: zinc, 62.45; copper, 4.46; iron, 0.25; lead, 22.84.

It can be surmised that the manufacture of such zinc alloy bomb shells is done by die-casting, the most suitable and efficient mass-production method. Dozens of units per minute can be made from a permanent mold. Die-casting machines have high productivity, and no machining is needed, so this mass-production method is cheap and rapid.

Under microscopic inspection, metallic structure shows a petal shaped part and a hexangular part over the matrix of zinc and lead. The former contains copper and zinc, and the latter zinc only. The petal-shaped part ensures that the whole body will be comparatively fragile, so that on explosion, the steel balls will fly out freely. The pineapple bomb is of a different shape in the copper section, but the structure of the alloy is, on the whole, the same.

Professor Zenshiro Hara, University of Tokyo.

Bodily Suffering Caused by the Ball Bomb

It is important to bear in mind the following points when considering the damage done to the human body by ball bombs. Penetration: The formidable penetrating nature of a ball bomb is evident from the fact that the small steel balls can cause complicated fractures of thigh-bones and other large bones, or go right through them, and that the steel balls pass through many internal organs.

Conventional demolition bombs burst into complicated shapes which do not fly straight, but lose their momentum quickly from air resistance. Their penetrative force in the living body is much less than the balls of ball bombs. The tiny pellets of the ball bomb, on the other hand, are designed deliberately to overcome this defect of conventional demolition bombs: they fly straight, they face less air resistance, and retain velocity. Because of their small surface, the steel balls meet little resistance from objects they strike. Their light weight (0.70–0.72 grams) means they will not penetrate hard objects, but are deadly against soft human bodies.

Numbers: Over a bombed area steel pellets are of saturation density and spread in all directions; they are not aimed at a particular target. Not one steel pellet, but vast numbers, make entrance into human bodies within the range of the bomb. Typical cases are recorded of victims receiving averages of 30 pellet wounds, the worst case received 100. In addition to all these tiny steel balls, bomb splinters and ground debris thrown up by the blast penetrate the victims.

Variety and Complexity of Wounds: The complex paths traced by the steel pellets striking a body simultaneously from all directions make it impossible to trace which pellet took which course and affected which internal organ. It is difficult to determine which wound is the most dangerous. In the case of internal organs, a single traumatic wound can be fatal; surgery and treatment are difficult.

Residual balls: Some pellets occasionally can not be extracted. In fact, it is very difficult to remove all these tiny pellets from the intricate organs and muscles of the human body. Even a full series of X-rays is often not sufficient to locate and extract residual pellets and splinters. And yet residual balls may well have an unexpectedly great effect both mentally and physically. There is strong evidence that the alloy of the pellets and that fragments of the iron-copper-zinc-lead casing are incompatible with human tissues and body fluids and that they cannot be allowed to remain *in situ* in inoperable cases because of the certainty of supporation. Prognosis, therefore, for patients with inoperable residual pellets in vital organs is generally negative.

In the Democratic Republic of Vietnam a test explosion of a ball bomb was done. A dog weighing 10 kg. was placed one meter from the spot of the explosion. One of the seven pellets that struck it stopped in the forefoot and six others went through its body. A cervical vertebra was broken by a ball. These revealed the great power of penetration of a ball in soft tissue and bone.

These are the characteristics of ball bomb damage, which inflict a great variety of grave wounds to the human body. Some concrete cases examined are given below:

(1) Nguyen Van Tho, 36, male-worker of the Than Lon tobacco factory in Hanoi. Killed in a bombing raid on May 12, 1967. An autopsy case. Ball bombs exploded both in front and behind the victim and steel balls penetrated both front and rear. An enormous number of balls penetrated his back, leaving many entrance wounds. Some entrance wounds were from bomb splinters. One ball entered the middle, right back, penetrating the main artery, then crossed his heart diagonally from the rear lower right side to the upper front, stopping at the inner chest wall. Post-mortem examination showed the ball had passed through the main artery and the heart. Another ball had pierced the cranium from front to rear. Skull dissection showed that the steel ball made an entry hole in the front and an exit hole in the rear. Midway through the skull in the projectiles path were a number of fissures. The two tiny steel balls were fatal. This death was instantaneous.

(2) Do Thi Dung, three months old, female. — Baby victim in Tran District near Hanoi. Bombed May 14, 1967. Burned by bomb flames on both legs. A ball bomb caught the little victim in the right shoulder. The pellet came to a halt right beneath the skin, causing no fractures.

(3) Do Duc Thinh, 48, male. — Peasant on the outskirts of Hanoi; bombed on May 20, 1967. Fractured skull from small steel ball pene-

trating the head from the rear, with a subdural hematoma right beneath the fractured part. Eleven additional pellets were found in neck, right side front, chest right-front, right forearm, left hand at the forefinger and right foot, the last was fractured. Victim underwent surgery to remove subdural hematoma, but he suffered the after-effect of nervous paralysis on the left side of the face.

(4) Tran Danh Chien, 20, male. — Mine worker in Ha Bac Province. Bombed on May 26, 1967. Raid occurred while he was at work and he was struck just before he reached a shelter. One of the numerous steel pellets hit him in the lower thoracic vertebra and inflicted a spinal wound, causing paraplegia in the lower part of the body, plus sphincter disturbances. Though provided with an artificial anus and an artificial urethra, this victim has no chance of recovery because it is impossibe to remove the pellet from the spinal column. Other similar cases were reported with impeded kinetic functions of the lower body from single ball spinal wounds.

(5) Trinh Dinh Ty, 25, male. — Worker. Bombed on May 22, 1967. Two small steel balls penetrated from the upper right part of the chest into lungs. Hemorrhage was found in the right pleural cavity.

(6) Nguyen Thi Lieu, 20, female. — Student nurse. Bombed in Ha Bac Province on April 20, 1967. Wounded while ministering to other wounded. A ball penetrated from the chest to the abdomen. Path of projectile went through right twelfth rib, liver and transverse colon. Victim underwent rib surgery, partial removal of the liver and transverse colon was repaired.

(7) Doan Thi Thang, 42, female. — Peasant. Bombed on June 17, 1967 while at Cooperative Society. Tiny steel balls penetrated abdomen and lower right leg; the pellet that entered the abdomen made 12 holes in the small intestines, and abdominal dropsy started 40 hours after the bombing, when she was admitted for surgery. Many other cases similar to this — where a single steel ball makes many holes in the intestines as it follows a zigzag line through the intestinal tract.

(8) Tham Thi Tung, 10, female. — Elementary schoolgirl. Bombed in Phuu Tho Province on June 11, 1967. A ball bomb burst in front of the victim while she was helping bring in the rice harvest. Unconscious when carried to hospital with many steel balls in the abdomen. Exploratory surgery revealed 14 affected places, including the diaphram, pierced by one ball. Three holes were found in the small intestines, and four in the large intestines. All wounds were sutured.

(9) Nguyen Thi No, 18, female. — Peasant. Bombed while working in the fields near Hanoi. Steel balls caught her in the abdomen; one penetrated the epigastrium into the abdominal cavity. A surgical operation revealed a great number of holes in the small intestines

over an area extending 63 centimeters. The damaged intestines had to be removed. Pellets which passed through the abdominal cavity still remain in the pelvic cavity. (Confirmed by X-ray)

(10) Nguyen Tien Toan, 11, male. — Elementary schoolboy. Steel ball entered from right side of the abdomen. Passed through the extreme end of the right lobe of the liver, then through duodenum, perforating two holes in the jejunum. Partial removal of the liver and suture of the perforated parts of the small intestines were performed.

(11) Vu Thu Hao, 23, female. — Institute teacher. Bombed in the suburbs of Hanoi on May 22, 1967. A great number of tiny steel balls pierced right shoulder and both legs. The right leg was struck with one of the pellets which lodged in the joint cavity. Splinter of the ball bomb hit lower part of the thigh but caused no fracture; another splinter hit the left thigh coursed through the flesh and ended by fracturing the tibia. This victim is one of the many cases hit by both the small steel balls and ball bomb splinters.

Dr. Masahiro Hashimoto, member the Second Japanese Commission of Inquiry.

Effects of Anti-Personnel Bombs on the Human Body
testimony by F. Mazas and J. Zucman

Members of the Faculty of I.N.S.E.R.M.

Documents were brought from North Vietnam by two French doctors who had visited there for several weeks: Dr. Behar, radiologist, and Dr. Krivine, surgeon (Head of the Clinic of the Faculty of Medicine, Paris) who have had numerous contacts with Vietnamese doctors, examined many wounded, and have studied hospital and X-ray reports.

Although the medical documents which they were able to bring with them are too few to allow for a statistical study, they give a good illustration of the new trauma pathology created by anti-personnel pellet bombs. Further documents have been provided by Dr. Vu Ngoc Thu of the Republic of North Vietnam...

The round shape of the projectiles has two effects: they maintain a high speed and travel up to 15 metres in a straight line; they have a high capacity for penetration into the human body.

On the other hand, their small size and light weight makes them useless against a wall or a roof; they have no destructive effect on dwellings, factories, etc. They are therefore clearly anti-personnel weapons. These characteristics of anti-personnel bombs indicate the special seriousness of the injuries they inflict.

(a) Multiple wounds, some of the wounded having been hit by many projectiles. (b) The apertures of the wounds are very small. (c) The paths of the projectiles are long, often very irregular due to ricochet, and give rise to deep multiple wounds in internal organs.

Two results for the surgeon: Diagnosis is difficult since entrance apertures may be overlooked; it is often necessary to X-ray the entire body in order to find some of the projectiles and then, beginning with the point of entry, to retrace the possible trajectory and therefore the probable wounds — presuming there are several projectiles — the outward signs of which are often difficult to discern, given the smallness of the wounds caused. However, the gravity of these wounds, even though minimal at first, increases if the organs affected are not treated immediately.

Difficulty in treatment: lengthy operations are necessary in order to discover all the organs which may have been injured; the extraction of deep-seated multiple projectiles (as many as 10 to 15 throughout the body) is extremely arduous. Furthermore, the soft steel balls corrode, suppurate, and can give rise to later complications. Those which are undiscovered may shift position within the organism.

Lastly, wounds from fragments of the bomb itself must be considered along with wounds from the projectiles as such. These fragments are exactly similar to those from a hand-grenade: though they have a shorter trajectory and a weaker penetrating force than the projectiles, they are of an irregular shape and their wounding capability is more grave.

Several facts are noteworthy: 1. The frequency of wounds to the nervous system, since neither the skull nor the vertebrae are usually able to stop the projectiles: as a result, there is damage to the brain and the spinal cord. The irreversible nature of such injuries to the central nervous system is well established.

2. The eyes are particularly vulnerable; many cases of blinding of one or both eyes have been pointed out.

3. Frequency and gravity of injuries to the internal organs, in particular: A single projectile may give rise to multiple intestinal per-

forations, which are operable only on condition that they are all detected; they are small, hard to see, and necessitate a complete examination of the entire abdomen, the seriousness of which is considerable from a surgical point of view. The overlooking of one intestinal wound can bring about peritonitis and death.

4. The seriousness of bone damage: The projectiles, like all high-speed projectiles, give rise to bone fragmentation.

5. The penetration power of the projectiles is attested to by observations of foetal injuries in pregnant women.

One of the reports concerns a cheek wound inflicted on a foetus in the womb. The fragment was removed at birth. At the age of eight months, unfortunately, the child showed evidence of retarded neurological development. It is conceivable that a splinter may have reached the central nervous system, or that the latter was injured by concussion during the bombardment.

Conclusion: The projectile fragmentation bomb has profound wounding capabilities with regard to the human body but no effect whatsoever against solid buildings. The effects of such wounds have not as yet been described in world medical literature, but it is established that aside from the immediate lethal effects, the bomb can frequently give rise to irreversible after-effects and disabilities.

Statement on the Pentagon's Denial of the Use of CBUs
by Vladimir Dedijer

Tribunal Statement of May 6th, 1967 in Answer to U.S. Department of Defense Declaration Denying the Use of CBU's in North Vietnam on Civilian Targets, Read by Vladimir Dedijer

The United States Department of Defense in a statement to the press declared yesterday that it is not using cluster bomb units (CBU's), or anti-personnel bombs on civilian targets in North Vietnam.

We are absolutely astonished that the Pentagon can deny this. General Westmoreland himself has proudly declared:

"We shall just go on bleeding them . . . to the point of national disaster for several generations."

We shall continue to give evidence demonstrating Westmoreland's words. Over the past five days we have presented a vast quantity of direct evidence to the public on this subject, information gathered by our scientific experts in Vietnam. We have shown that CBU's have been repeatedly used in North Vietnam against civilian targets in violation of legally binding and conventionally accepted rules of war. In forthcoming sessions we shall present further evidence on the use of CBU weapons, napalm and chemical weapons against strictly civilian targets and in violation of rules of war.

Our eveidence is irrefutable. If the Department of Defense believes its statement is correct, we shall be happy to present all of our evidence and witnesses, American, French, Vietnamese and others, directly to a Congressional Committee or any official body designated by the U.S. Government. We are certain the American people desire to know whether or not their Government is committing war crimes in Vietnam, and we await the reply of the United States Government to present our vast collection of evidence to a public session in the United States so that the American public itself may decide the truth of the conflicting allegations. Whether the United States Government accepts or rejects this offer, we shall continue to release our full documentation to the world press.

Report from North Vietnam on Civil Bombardment
testimony by J.B. Neilands

Professor of Biochemistry at the University of Southern California at Berkeley; Member Third Commission of Inquiry

Probably all Americans who have returned from inspecting war damage in the Democratic Republic of Vietnam have been confronted with these questions: "Isn't it possible that the U.S. military made a mistake?" "Were you brainwashed?" "Did you actually see these bombs dropped by U.S. aircraft?" Members of the Third Commission of Inquiry were aware of the skepticism displayed toward charges of atrocities on the part of U.S. forces in Vietnam. Consequently, we made every effort to carry out a critical and objective survey. Whenever possible, we attempted to make a personal, on-the-spot examination and evaluation of the evidence.

All visitors to the DRV have remarked on the exceptional morale and fighting spirit of the people. This persists and appears to intensify even after two years of heavy bombing. I offer the following for those who need a rational and logical explanation for this remarkable *espirit de corps*.

As our team went from hamlet to hamlet we were inevitably surrounded by large numbers of villagers. The particular incident under examination was usually described in Vietnamese by a victim or by an eyewitness. Translations were shouted out simultaneously in both French and English. If the evidence had been faked it seems very unlikely that the government could maintain the high level of morale which is everywhere evident in the population. Furthermore, the Vietnamese say they cannot afford the luxury of exaggerated claims. They argue that the truth is their strongest weapon and the U.S., with its enormous arsenal of death, still has the physical resources to carry on the war in spite of the erosion of its moral position through flagrant falsification of gains and losses.

The best evidence reported herein concerns the deliberate bombing of civilians with anti-personnel weapons. On March 15, 1967, in the Viet Tri area, we interviewed the victims of steel pellet bombs and we were able to see the X-rays and complete medical records of these patients. Additional evidence was furnished to us by authorities of the DRV. In each case we have indicated the source and nature of this material.

Anti-Personnel Bombs

1. Public Statements: During the past several months all Western visitors to the DRV have reported the use of various types of anti-personnel bombs over that country by the U.S. air force. Special interest is centered on this matter since U.S. officials have repeatedly disclaimed the bombing of the civilian population of North Vietnam.

As early as June 1, 1966, the *Washington Daily News* reported: "Reliable sources said the American planes dropped a powerful anti-personnel bomb among their explosives. It has been used before against North Vietnam but its use was not made public until today. The bomb shoots out thousands of steel pellets. They were designed for use against such targets as clusters of Communists manning anti-aircraft guns and missile sites." Accounts of a similar nature appeared in the *Philadelphia Inquirer* of June 2, 1966, and the *Washington Post* of December 29, 1966. On June 28, 1966, the *New York Times* (International Edition) ran this item: "Vietcong Face 'Exotic' U.S. Arms — Clusters of Bombs Scathe Mountains Like Giants Beating Kettle Drums. The sound of it is terrifying and stupendous . . . This is C.B.U. , a military abbreviation that stands for 'cluster bomb unit' . . . The United States Defense Department and White House seem ashamed of C.B.U. and of other so-called 'exotic' weapons, including a new and better brand of napalm . . . A cluster bomb unit is a cannister containing more than 800 little bomblets with fat orange noses and folding silvery tail fins . . . Now, a new and better C.B.U. has been developed that spews both napalm and lethal steel pellets from the bomblets . . . The C.B.U. is part of the most impressive arsenal of conventional firepower ever brought to bear in warfare . . ."

President Johnson persistently maintained that American bombs are directed against "steel and concrete." The *New York Times* of December 28, 1966, reports as follows: "Former President Eisenhower said today that he knew United States bombing operations in North Vietnam are aimed exclusively at military targets'. A few days later (December 31) President Johnson told his press conference: ". . . . it is the policy of this Government to bomb only military targets." On January 2, 1967, the *New York Times* ran an editorial which denied ". . . . that there is even a shred of evidence to lend credence to the Communist propaganda that the United States is deliberately bombing civilian targets . . ."

President Johnson spoke to the Tennessee Legislature on March 15, 1967, and he is reported by the *New York Times* to have said: "Now, as to bombing of civilians, I would simply say that we're making an effort that's unprecedented in the history of warfare to be sure that we do not. It is our policy to bomb military targets only. We have never deliberately bombed cities nor attacked any target with the purpose of inflicting civilian casualties . . . ."

In a dispatch from Hong Kong, the *San Francisco Chronicle* on April 11, 1967, reported that a group of Quakers en route home from the DRV had charged the U.S. with killing and wounding civilians with "bombs specially designed for that purpose." The change was immediately answered by the military command in Saigon: "Sure, we used C.B.U. in North Vietnam" — *Evening Sun,* Baltimore, April 10, 1967. The latter item goes on to say that the C.B.U. is used only against "thin-skinned" military targets. A parallel account ran in the *San Francisco Chronicle* on April 11 under the head: "Cluster Bombing Admitted by U.S.." Commented Royce Brier, a columnist for the *Chronicle:* "So the Big Lie is flattened again. The Pentagon dragged out the inevitable "spokesman", who said we have been using such bombs for over a year. He said they are used against anti-aircraft guns and crews, convoys and the like. Having confessed this, the "spokesman" hopes you'll forget it. Will you? Do you believe him? Why?" (April 14).

2. Findings in the Viet Tri Area on March 15, 1967:

On March 15, 1967, I accompanied other members of the Third Commission of Inquiry to the Viet Tri area, a region lying perhaps 50 to 100 km northwest of Hanoi. We inspected several hamlets which had been subjected to bombing with the C.B.U. The baseball-size grenade which is dropped from the C.B.U. cannister makes only a six inch deep pockmark in a dirt roadway and the pellets penetrate probably less than an inch into wood. The best traces of the pellets are left on masonary walls or on the apparent targets, namely — people. We visited a field hospital and saw the X-rays, medical records and patients. These were all victims of the steel pellet bombs. Herewith follows a brief description of some of the cases:

17 year old youth, victim of January 18, 1966 raid, riddled with pellets in arm, buttock, stomach and intestine.

14 year old girl, victim of August 14, 1966 raid, with pellets in chest, intestine, upper arm, finger, lip and a pellet remains under the skin of the forehead.

35 year old farmer, victim of January 18, 1967 raid, pellet lodged in left side of cranium and patient paralyzed down the right side of the body.

5 year old son of victim just described, struck in the same raid, suffered a 2 cm pellet penetration in the brain (removed by surgery), also struck by pellets in the hand and right leg.

21 year old woman, victim of January 18, 1967 raid, struck and blinded in the left eye, also struck in the torso.

34 year old mother of five children, the most serious case. Struck by a single pellet in the August 11, 1966 raid. Pellet entered the forehead and lodged at the base of the brain. It could not be removed. Patient was essentially moribund. Almost total paralysis. She can swallow but cannot chew and is kept alive by her son who puts soup in her mouth daily.

7 year old boy, victim of March 12, 1967 raid, with a flesh pellet wound which had entered under the arm. The pellet had lodged near the spine; also had a pellet in the left leg.

Most of the bombed hamlets inspected by us in the Viet Tri area appeared to be surrounded by agricultural land and there was no military target of any kind in evidence. Several of the hamlets had relics of the C.B.U. cannisters. The latter seemed to be of identical manufacture to those seen in the armaments exhibit in Hanoi. (See photo). The cannisters were painted in olive drab and carried a stenciled inscription, in yellow paint, which with minor variations stated:

Cyclotol 125 lbs   FSN 1325-N- . . . (illegible)
Loading date 11-66   Dispenser and Bomb
Lot PA — 20-19-Ser. 15   CBU

One cannister gave the weight of cyclotol as 139 lbs. and the loading date as 7-66. Conflicting reports were obtained on the number of bomblets per cannister and figures from 200 to 800 have been mentioned. The number furnished by the armaments experts was 640. The Vietnamese call the C.B.U. "mother" bombs, and the bomblets are sometimes called "guavas". The walls of these bomblets contain steel pellets — the figure we obtained was 265 pellets per bomblet. The pellets measure 5.56 mm in diameter. In the armaments exhibit we saw the "pineapple" bomblet which has slightly larger pellets, 6.3 mm in diameter, The pineapple is launched from a dispenser which carries several hundred of the bomblets.

Chronological Account of Experiences Within the DRV

March 10, Arrived Hanoi. March 11. Briefing from DRV Commission for Investigation of War Crimes. March 12. Inspection of bombed sites in Hanoi. Visit to town of Phu Xa which had been devastated by various types of bombs including C.B.U. Visit to the Polish-Vietnamese Friendship School which had been completely destroyed.

March 13. Briefings, March 14. Visit to a hospital to inspect records of Ngoc Boa, a child wounded by a bomb fragment while still in her mother's womb. At the same hospital a visit with Tran Thi Minh, an 8 year old girl with spinal cord severed between the shoulder blades by a bomb fragment. She was paralyzed from the waist down and had bed sores on her heels. March 15: Visit to Viet Tri Area. Inspected a paper mill complex hit with a variety of bombs including, probably, 3,000 lb. demolition explosives. The living quarters of the workers, about one-half mile distance, was devastated in the same raid with excellent precision. We inspected a Catholic hamlet in which the small church had been destroyed. We saw a field hospital struck with steel pellet bombs. The X-ray screen, sterilizer and other equipment had been damaged. We saw a youth who had been wounded in the arm with steel pellets. March 16: Briefings at the Weapons Committee and visits with captured American pilots. March 17: Visit with the leaders of the DRV and appearance at a press conference. We were furnished with various pamphlets, documents and photographs depicting U.S. atrocities in Viet Nam.

Notes and References from U.S. Sources

Napalm: "Civilian Victims of Napalm" — *New York Times,* April 9, 1967;

Chemical and Biological Warfare: "Medical Ethics and Biological Warfare" — *Perspectives in Biol. & Med.,* Summer, 1963; "Chemical and Biological Warfare" — *Science,* 155 p. 175 & p. 299, 1967; "Crop Destruction in South Vietnam" — *Christian Century,* June 29, 1966; "Chemical and Biological Weapons" — *New England J. Med.,* January 6, 1966; *Tomorrow's Weapons* J. H. Rothschild, McGraw-Hill;

War on Civilians: "Medical Problems of South Vietnam" — Jan. 1967, Physicians for Social Responsibility, Suite 17, 416 Marlborough St., Boston 02115.

The Bombing of Dai Lai
testimony by Gerard Chaliand

I arrived in Thai Binh province on November 3, 1967 in connection with an inquiry which I carried out among the peasantry of the Tonkinian delta. The bombing of Dai Lai[1] had taken place the day before, and at my request the local authorities conducted me to the locality, forty-six hours after the bombing, at dawn on November 4th.

It should be pointed out that the province of Thai Binh, in relation to the country as a whole, is a zone comparatively seldom bombed, because the objectives that could be classified as strategic are few. In fact, the province is exclusively agricultural, and its geography—uniformly flat and sparsely wooded—does not favor dispersion.

Nevertheless, the American air forces attacked the province 230 times from 1965 to the end of 1966, according to the local authorities, and 491 times in 1967 up to the end of October. Its capital, which was bombed in 1966, is almost totally destroyed, as I was able to confirm. The dikes, which are of vital importance in the delta, because they are a protection against flooding and a safeguard against drought, have been attacked forty times, while one third of all the bombing has, to a greater or lesser extent, affected the civilian population.

I was not given the figure for the total number of victims, as this is classified under military secrets....

Three Village Bombings

For my part, I can add that during the five weeks I spent in North Vietnam—October 6 to November 10, 1967—Dai Lai was the third village bombing that I was able to confirm personally. The first was the village of Tuy Hoi [?], Gia Vien district, bombed on Octo-

---

[1]Apparently in the neighboring province of Nam Dinh

ber 8. I went there on October 9, together with the French journalist, Olivier Todd. The bombing, done at 12:30 at night, had left seven dead and eight wounded. There was nothing in the vicinity of the village, not for several kilometers around, that could be taken for a strategic objective, not even an antiaircraft defense. The second was the village of Kim Bai, Thanh Oai district, situated on route 22. On October 26, several waves of aircraft destroyed about twenty concrete buildings there, including a pharmacy and a nursery. I arrived in the village on October 29. The bombing had left seventeen dead, and twenty-two injured. Thus the case of Dai Lai is not an isolated incident.

There is no strategic objective of any kind near the village of Dai Lai. It is situated between two arms of water, at about one kilometer from the provincial road, five kilometers from the nearest bridge, in a flat countryside of canals, rice fields and ponds. I did not see a single antiaircraft defense unit in the area.

Fifteen Explosions

There were two American airplanes on the bombing raid. It was very light. It could not be argued that there had been a technical fault or that the bombs had been dumped in order to lighten a damaged plane which was trying to avoid coming down in Vietnamese territory. We visited the village in the early hours of the morning. In some places the ashes were still hot. Men and women were busy clearing away the debris. The planes had released chains of incendiary and explosive bombs. The witnesses agreed that they had heard about fifteen explosions. That was at 1 p.m., November 2. There were 255 inhabitants in the village of Dai Lai. The bombing killed fifty-one and left thirty-nine injured. Out of a total of forty-one homes, thirty-four were destroyed, many razed to the ground.

Men were weeping quietly. A young woman squatted, supported by two elderly women, and wailed loudly. Another woman was weeping as she swept debris from the floor of a house which was no longer there. She burst into sobs as we went past, saying: "He couldn't escape because of the heat, and I could see his arms reach out of the flames!"

Most of the peasants of the cooperative were already in the fields at 1 p.m. on the day of the bombing for the harvest of the tenth month. In the village some peasants were shelling the rice on the threshing floor. When the planes were heard, everyone went down into the trenches or into individual holes. The children went into the holes dug inside the buildings. Some buildings exploded under the bombs. Fire enveloped the thatched roofs of others. Fire spread

275

throughout the village, making rescue difficult. However the militia was able to save some people. In the holes were found charred bodies, burst open by the heat. Some mangled bodies were beyond identification. Out of fifty-one dead, thirty-nine were under the age of 15.

Survivors' Accounts

Bui Thi Tinh, twenty-two years old, the vice-president of the administrative committee of the commune, who conducted the work of identifying bodies and placing them in coffins, told me:

I was one kilometer away from the village. From the single hole I occupied, I saw two planes, one flying lower than the other. The one flying low dropped its bombs first. It was after the meal; there were already workers in the fields, others were preparing to leave. The old people and children were taking their siesta. I could count sixteen bombs exploding in a chain. Huge flames shot up to the tree tops. They dropped the bombs and left. It all happened very quickly.

Then the militia rushed forward and the people came with buckets, ropes and shovels. They tried to put the fire out, they fetched water from the pools and formed a chain. They made a passage right through the fire to get to the trenches. Some of them used shovels to dig people out of caved-in trenches. A blast of wind stirred up the flames. Some rescuers were burnt to death.

A co-worker from a neighboring village—a man called Them— came to the rescue and was able by himself to save seven injured victims. He ran to and fro carrying them on his back. The family of a co-worker called Roan had four children down in the trench of their house. Halfway there Roan was torn to pieces by bomb explosions as he ran to save his children.

I ran forward with two other girls. I had some gauze bandages in my bag and some cotton-wool which I passed out to friends. On the way we saw a body buried under a pile of straw. We hastened to drag it out and then we realized that all there was of it was the two legs. The upper part of the body had been scattered about elsewhere.

There was a lot of flame and very thick smoke. You could not see five yards in front of you. There were a great many of us, and we were falling over each other in the attempt to rescue people There were blood and corpses on the threshing floor. Meanwhile they carried bodies on stretchers. I had lost my sandals and my feet were burning, so hot was the earth near the fire. As soon as the bombing was over, the families ran in from the fields. Some of them were shouting and weeping as the flames rose high into the air and they were there trying to put the fire out.

Roan's wife tried to jump into the flames to save her children. She had just seen her husband blown to bits before her very eyes. When we tried to restrain her, she tore her clothes like a mad-woman; she fell upon me and cried, "Take me into the fire." I said to her: "If you love me then you must come with me." Then she said: "Why do you want me to come, and whom will I live with, they are all dead." And she repeated: "Who, who am I going to live with?" And she tried to jump into the fire again, and I said: "You are going to live with us," and they led her away.

I saw the five children of the Ru family—all killed in the same trench along with their mother. They were among the first to be pulled out. The Nguu family—the husband and wife were in the field—they have one child left who was not in the village, the other four are dead, three in the trench and the eldest, they only found his trunk and his left leg. Just beside them was a fa-mily of four—the husband and wife were out in the field, the two children are dead. The entire family of the co-worker Khoi was killed—he was out in the field alone—his two children, his wife who was eight months pregnant. His mother's corpse was flung up into the branches of a jack tree and the blood trickled down the trunk to the roots of the tree.

When we got the fire out, I stayed to direct the work of putting the bodies in coffins. The state gave four meters of cloth per coffin. It was 2:30 p.m. when we began to collect the bodies. I saw sights which turned my stomach. There were burnt bodies which were nothing but skin stretched over bones and entrails running out of burst bellies. They no longer had a human shape. We collected parts of bodies—arms, legs—sometimes we could make out that it was a woman because there were tufts of hair. While I registered the names of the dead, others wrote their names or presumed age in chalk on little placards to be placed on the graves. There were bodies which could not be identified, but they estimated the age by the size of the foot, and wrote "Child, five to ten years old, no name" on the coffin.

I saw, among these shreds, a heap of flesh which they reckoned to be a fifteen-year-old girl, because of the cluster of hair and her neck. It was horrible to see, in the midst of this mass of flesh, a thigh still plump and brown. There were bodies of children that looked like stunted dogs.

I also recorded the accounts of six relatives of victims. Here are some extracts:

Tran Thi Sai, peasant woman, thirty years old, relates:

At that moment I was on my way to the field for the harvest, I was with some friends. When I heard the planes, I went down into a single hole to shelter, and right after the bombing ran toward my house to see what had happened. As I approached the village, I could see that the whole village was in flames. Then I threw off my bucket yoke to get there more quickly. My second child, a boy, was able to escape out of the fire. His little brother of 5 followed him but he could not run fast enough and was burnt in the yard. And my mother fled carrying my youngest child, twelve months, but they were burnt alive at the door. My ten-year-old daughter was out watching the cooperative's buffalo, and she I still have now. My husband was the head of a group of workers—he was in the village at the threshing floor of the cooperative. He was pulling the stone roller to husk the rice. At the time of the bombing he stayed outside the shelter till the last minute, to get the others back in, and he was killed. The bomb explosions opened his head.

I began to scream and cry, while other members of the cooperative jumped into the fire to save their relatives. Then I wanted to jump into the fire too and save my mother and my children, but I was held back. They led me away to where I could not look on, and then they carried away the bodies of my relatives.

I have lost my mother along with the baby she was carrying in her arms, my five-year-old child and my husband. Now there are only three of us left, my two children and myself.

Bui Van Nguu, peasant, forty-six years old, relates:

At that moment, I was at home making brooms for the cooperative. Over in my kitchen there was a grinding mortar. There my two daughters were pounding meal and their two little brothers were with them, having fun. My wife had left my little girl of eighteen months asleep in the hammock at home and had gone to the pond to wash clothes.

When my wife saw the planes coming she ran towards the house, but on the way there she was knocked down by the blast of a bomb. Meanwhile a bomb exploded in the kitchen, burying our three children. The house also collapsed and caught fire. The roof fell on me, and the baby in the hammock began to cry. I got up and went and took her. Then I came through the fire with my daughter. In the yard I saw my wife stretched out on the ground, half buried by the ruins of the wall. She called out to me. I placed the baby in the hole to go and help her. When I came towards her, she tried to get up. Her clothes were all torn and her face was bleeding. I handed the baby to her for her to carry it away, and I ran to try and pull my children out.

I rummaged in the debris looking for my children. I found mangled limbs, shreds of flesh. I only found three bodies by collecting fragments and a leg. I couldn't find the body of my big girl.

It was only yesterday that I found her body—it had been thrown into a garden seven yards away. Her body was buried under a pile of ashes, and it is thanks to the people who came to clear the debris that I found her. At first I thought it was someone else, but I looked and realized that it was really her ear—she was 13.

Hoang Ban, peasant, forty-four years old, relates:

I was on the way to the harvest along with some other workers. I heard planes and I looked, but did not see anything. Suddenly I heard explosions and saw our village in flames. We were one kilometer away from the village. We ran and when we arrived the fire had spread all around the village.

I saw my sister-in-law also coming from the fields carrying in her arms her two-year-old child, its head burst open. She called to me to come and help her children. My house is 300 yards from my brother's. I had not yet reached my own house and I hastened to my brother's house. The house had not been burnt, it had exploded, and both the roof and the walls had gone. I ran to the house's trench—under the bed. Over the hole there had been a cover. At the edge of the hole there lay half of the body of a little girl of 2, my niece. I took the half of the body and placed it out in the yard and came back to search in the hole. I pulled out one of my nieces, ten years old, with her head burst open by the fragments of the cover. One of her arms was broken and her whole body was blackened. And again I carried the body out into the yard, and then I called for help. Then the militia and other people came and they brought out another little girl of 8, also with her head burst open because of the cover. This one had a broken leg. Afterwards, they dug out of this hole two more little girls, both five years old, my nieces from next door who had come to play. They were not injured but suffocated. Six children are dead.

As for my brother, only remains of him were found. In the kitchen they found his two arms. His two legs were caught on the bamboo wall. They also found his ribs, but not his head. Only his wife is left; it is as though she were insane. She is at my house at present. She screams and cries and no one can speak to her.

I would like to add that I was able to visit the five seriously wounded victims in the provincial hospital—the others received attention at the district or commune level. The Dai Lai massacre—for how else can one describe this bombing?—was also reported on November 5, 1967 by Sven Oste, a Swedish journalist from *Dagens Nyheter*, a Liberal daily newspaper of Stockholm, and by Antonello Trombadori, an Italian journalist, special correspondent of *Unita*.

Summary of the First Two Charges
by Lelio Basso

The first aspect of our meetings which may strike the external observer, whose opinions we must bear in mind, is the absence of the defense. Although this absence is not the fault of the Tribunal, which invited the American government to make itself heard, I have felt it my duty to study the arguments on the American side as they are presented in many official publications, of which the most important would seem to be the White Papers of 1961 and 1965, the memorandum of the Legal Adviser of the State Department published in March 1966, under the title *The Legality of American Participation in the Defense of Vietnam* and the speeches of President Johnson and Secretary of State Dean Rusk. I have read these documents and I shall take the arguments developed therein into account as I deal with the various questions we must consider in order to give a satisfactory answer to the two charges we have before us in this session of the Tribunal, namely the first and second questions contained in the constituent act of the Tribunal.

The first of these questions is: "Has the United States government (and the governments of Australia, New Zealand, and South Korea) committed acts of aggression according to international law"?

Here we are immediately faced with a problem of international law, which I shall no more than touch upon, since otherwise we would never come to any conclusion. No comm ¬ly accepted definition of aggression exists in international law, although the question has been debated at least since the end of the First World War. Attempts have been made to arrive at an agreement on such a definition at the League of Nations; at the time of the Nuremburg trials, and particulary at the United Nations; but all these efforts have simply served to point out the difficulties of a theoretical definition, without producing any definite results. Nevertheless I should like to set down two conclusions on this problem:

1. Although it is very difficult to arrive at a theoretical definition that covers all possible cases of aggression, "the existence of the crime of aggression can be deduced from the circumstances of each particular case" (resolution 599 [VI] of the United Nations General Assembly of January 31, 1952). As has been underlined during endless discussions at the UN, while aggression can be considered an abstract, theoretical and distant notion, the aggressor, on the contrary is a concrete, personal and tangible reality; we therefore do not need a definition of aggression to identify the aggressor, as demonstrated by the Nuremburg trial.

2. In any event, the efforts made to define aggression, and particularly those of the UN, are an aid to defining the aggressor, since although we do not have a definition, we do have many useful indications which allow us to take a relatively precise approach to the problem. To determine the aggressor in the present case and to define, if necessary, the crimes committed, we cannot limit ourselves to the Nuremburg verdict as our only point of reference. Politics evolve, situations change, as do ways of acting; and law must follow this evolution or be by-passed by events. Aggression is a typical example of these changes. As the human conscience and international laws have increasingly come to condemn direct armed aggression without reservations, the aggressor has turned to new, more subtle and underhanded forms. Vietnam is an example of this, and I believe that we can accept, by simply reversing its direction, the assertion of the second American White Paper that entirely new forms of aggression are being used in Vietnam. Obviously, we must use a more modern concept of aggression, such as is commonly accepted today, a concept which includes indirect aggression and even a negative aggression, arising from the failure to submit to legally made decisions. As rightly stated by the Nuremburg Tribunal, international laws "are not static, but, through a process of continual adaptation, they conform to the needs of a changing world". I shall examine the behavior of the United States in the Vietnamese question in this light.

I shall attempt to be brief, without, at the same time, leaving out any essential evidence.

To answer our first question adequately and completely, I shall attempt to prove not only that there has been an American aggression, but that it is necessary to distinguish four different stages within this aggression, each of which can be considered a crime in itself:

1. A concerted plan to violate the fundamental rights of the Vietnamese people;

2. Political and military intervention aimed at arbitrarily creating a separate State of South Vietnam, despite the Geneva agreements;

3. Direct participation in the war of the South;

4. The attacks on North Vietnam.

The Nuremburg verdict spoke at great length of a concerted plan directed towards aggression as a crime in itself, set apart as Charge No. 1. A similar stand has been taken by the authors of a draft of a code for crimes against peace and the security of humanity. To establish whether there was a concerted plan of aggression against Vietnam or whether the war is the inevitable outcome of a series of events for which no one can be considered clearly responsible, we must quickly review American policy of the years 1945-1954, in the light of the reports submitted to us and the facts we have at our disposal.

I agree with those persons who hold that there is a continuity in American policy in Vietnam from the end of World War II to the present, despite the existence of apparent contradictions. We must, however, distinguish two basic policy lines within this continuity. The first is aimed at retaining within the capitalist sphere all those countries not recognized at Yalta as being within the Soviet sphere of influence and therefore at causing the downfall of all new socialist revolutions; the second, at ensuring American predominance over the other capitalist powers in every country within the capitalist sphere. At times, these two lines have been superimposed one on the other in Vietnam, giving the impression of an apparent contradiction.

The second of these lines — the desire for predominance in all the non-communist countries of the world — has driven the Americans to support the downfall of classical colonialism, this being a preliminary condition for beating out the monopoly of European power in the colonies and opening up the way to American penetration with the methods of neo-colonialism. Within this framework, the United States took a quite brutal position against Holland in connection with the independence of Indonesia. But since this anti-colonial policy arises from a simple desire to step into the colonizing power's shoes, it has given way to the defense of old style colonialism whenever the alternative to the latter has been not neo-colonialism resting on a so-called independent government, but rather communism, as in the case of Vietnam. This explains why the United States furnished a considerable amount of aid to French colonialism in Indochina; at the moment, this was the only way to combat, with other people's lives, the advent of a communist regime. In this case, the first of the policy lines I have mentioned — to retain all the countries in the capitalist sphere and block communism — seemed to be the more urgent. Having established this, however, we must immediately add that, if we take these two general lines of American policy into account, the position of the American government towards Vietnam is clearly consistent; that is, it is the result of a precise plan aimed at depriving the Vietnamese people of their right to self-determination. The stubborness of the Americans in following this plan was undoubtedly strengthened by the victory of the Chinese revolution and the Korean war.

It is in this context that we must view the attempt to turn the administration of North Vietnam over to Chiang Kai-Chek, the later overtures to Ho Chi Minh, the agreement with Bao Dai, once it became clear that Ho Chi Minh was a convinced communist and, finally, American aid to French colonialism, as a stop-gap while arranging a new so-called nationalist solution. Such a solution eventually appeared in the person of Ngo Dinh Diem, but as time passed, this too proved incapable of providing the sort of total domination desired by the United States.

These facts are well known, and I shall spend no more time on them. I merely wish to recall your attention to the massive aid given to the French for the war in Indochina and the plans for direct American intervention prepared at the time of Dien Bien Phu, but opposed by the British government.

After Dien Bien Phu, when France was thinking seriously of pulling out of the war and the Geneva Conference of May-July 1954 had been called, the position of the United States was instead clearly oriented towards blocking any further communist advance. At the very time when the Vietnamese people, after a long, hard fight, had finally obtained international recognition of their basic national rights, the United States, acting in the most evident bad faith, did everything possible to sabotage the agreements being prepared and to nullify the results of the Vietnamese victory on the battlefield and at the conference table. Our historians have called our attention to Foster

Dulles's declarations against any territorial concession to the communists and to Eisenhower's attempts to stop the Conference. They have also pointed out the very ambiguous behavior of the American delegation, which demanded a new method of final protocol and refused to endorse the Final Declaration, while stating America's intention to abide by the clauses of the agreement, with the exception of the last article. This last article provided for later consultation by members of the Conference to supervise the application of the agreements, and refusal to accept it meant the elimination of the only international body capable of effectively controlling this application, since the International Control Commission (India, Canada, Poland) alone did not have sufficient authority.

This was a clear indication that the United States had no intention of abiding by the agreements at the very moment it committed itself to do so. This ambiguity was confirmed on the same day by President Eisenhower, who stated, "the United States did not participate in the Conference and is not bound by its decisions", a statement reiterated several days later by Foster Dulles.

The meaning of these words becomes clear when we turn to the content of the agreements. At the time they were approved, the People's Army was victorious everywhere; it had already occupied three-fourths of the national territory and nothing stood in the way of its continuing its victorious march, since France no longer had any desire to continue a war that had led to the disaster of Dien Bien Phu. In accepting the agreements, the Vietnamese accepted not to exploit their victory on the battlefield, by taking over the whole country, but the agreements, by providing for elections within two years, guaranteed them the same result, while permitting the French to withdraw peacefully. Substantially, the Vietnamese agreed to substitute political means (the elections) for military means to reach the same goal: the unification of the country under the leadership of the forces that had brought the war of liberation to its victorious conclusion. No one had any doubt that this would be the outcome of the elections. Eisenhower himself has clearly stated in his memoirs that Ho Chi Minh would have polled 80% of the votes.

The Geneva agreements therefore made up an indivisible whole: the cease-fire, the provisional nature of the military demarcation line along the 17th parallel, the reaffirmation of the unity of the Vietnamese State, the guarantee of democratic freedom in preparation for the elections, the bar on the introduction of arms or men and the construction of military bases during the interim period and, at the end of this period, free and internationally supervised elections. All of these dispositions were interdependent and aimed at the reunification

284

of the country. The violation of one of these clauses meant the destruction of the whole structure worked out at Geneva, a structure which had to be accepted or rejected in its entirety. The bad faith of the Americans lay in the fact that they accepted the immediate solution, that is, division; but rejected its provisional character and consequently all the other commitments regarding the military *status quo,* freedom for adversaries of the regime, and particularly, the elections. This rejection comes out very clearly in all the texts and statements of the period, some of which have been cited in the reports and documents submitted to us.

It is also evident in a series of actions on the part of the American government, whose meaning, in the light of later events, is now quite clear. I shall mention only two: the choice of Diem as Prime Minister and the organization of SEATO. Our attention has been directed to Sheer's study of the circumstances and reasons prompting the choice of Diem, a choice imposed on Bao Dai by the Americans; but we might also mention another American work, *The Invisible Government,* by Wise and Ross, centered around the activity of the C.I.A., which gives us a version of these events that, although slightly different in detail, is identical as far as the points that interest us are concerned. The aim in the choice of Diem was to provide a leader who could represent an alternative to Ho Chi Minh and had the strength to embark on the dangerous road of non-application of the agreements. I remind you that this choice was made during the Geneva Conference and that Diem accepted the nomination a few days before the end of the Conference when the substance of the agreements was already known.

The other manoeuvre to sabotage the agreements was the Manila Pact establishing SEATO. Although the Pact was signed a few weeks after the Geneva Conference, the United States made every effort to reach an agreement during the period of the Conference itself. In this Pact, there is a protocol guaranteeing the territorial integrity of South Vietnam, against both the letter and the spirit of the Geneva agreements for two obvious reasons: 1. the Geneva agreements, which the United States had committed itself to respect, forbade the participation of Vietnam in military alliances and blocs under any form, and therefore also under the passive form of accepting a guarantee; such a guarantee constituted an alteration of the military *status quo;* 2. according to the Geneva agreements, South Vietnam was only a provisional military zone, destined to last no more than two years, and therefore not a State; to guarantee it a territorial integrity to which it had no right meant to consider the Geneva agreements as mere pieces of paper.

This bad faith and this duplicity, with which the Americans pretended to accept something that in reality they did not accept, and with which the Vietnamese were misled into exchanging the military victory that was within their reach for a political solution which the United States had no intention of allowing them; this bad faith and duplicity with which the Americans sought only to gain two years' time in which to concentrate the forces necessary to gain the upper hand once more, are the proof of the existence of a concerted plan of aggression against the fundamental rights of the Vietnamese people. And I ask you to declare in our verdict that this plan was an international crime.

This plan of aggression was put into action without hesitation immediately after the signing of the agreements. Once again, I do not intend to review the history of the events of this period, but simply to set forth those elements which constitute the crime of aggression.

First of all, I shall touch on the legal aspect of the problem. I have already mentioned the evolution that the notion of aggression has undergone since Nuremburg and the concept of indirect aggression introduced into international law after the constitution of the United Nations. Article 15 of the Bogota Charter of the Organization of American States condemns not only the use of armed force, but also the use "of every other form of interference or action damaging to the personality of the State and the political, economic and cultural elements that compose it". Among the new forms of aggression dealt with by international law, we find the refusal to abide by an international decision. At the present time, the United Nations is debating the problem of South-west Africa, and, although I am not sure whether the debate is finished or not, I do know that during the discussions a large number of countries — I believe the majority — demanded that the Union of South Africa be declared guilty of aggression because of its attempt to turn a provisional situation into a permanent one — that is, its refusal to turn the administration of a territory obtained only provisionally over to the United Nations and to grant the right of national self-determination to the population of South-west Africa.

I believe that the sense of this evolution in the concept of aggression is evident. It is now fully accepted in international law that there can be aggression without armed attack. The crime of aggression is constituted by an attempt to change a legitimately established situation in international relations whether this is done through the use of threat of force, through internal subversion, through heavy economic pressure, through a refusal to abide by an international decision, or any other illegal means. Let me make it clear that I have not given you a definition of aggression; that would be impossible. I have merely attempted to examine the problem that interests us a little more closely.

Now, what happened in South Vietnam after the Geneva agreements? A provisional administration, intended by the agreements to last no more than two years, arbitrarily transformed itself, with the support of the United States, into a permanent authority with a claim to independent statehood — a thing which the agreements formally excluded. In doing so, it consciously disrupted the legal mechanism created by the Geneva Conference, again with the support and even under the leadership of the United States. Here is an act that has the characteristics of aggression.

I do not need to go into detail to bring you proof of this systematic and total violation of the agreements. These agreements, as I have said, were a coherent structure, whose parts were mutually interdependent. If the division into two temporary military zones of the opposing forces was a consequence of the cease-fire, reunification was the goal of the whole mechanism. The elections constituted the necessary instrument for the expression of popular will, and the guarantee not to permit reprisals or discrimination was a necessary condition for these elections. Finally, the ban on the introduction of new troops, military personnel, armaments, munitions, and bases was intended to guarantee the maintenance of the balance of power between the opponents until the final application of the agreements — that is, until reunification by means of elections.

The political persecution of adversaries, military reinforcement, and, above all, the refusal to hold the elections destroyed the agreements and created a new situation that was contrary to international law. This is exactly what happened. I shall limit myself to recalling your attention to the information on this matter contained in Kolko's, Chesneaux's and the Japanese Committee's reports and to the extremely useful Chronology presented by the delegation of the Democratic Republic of Vietnam, information which is confirmed in the interim and special reports of the International Control Commission abundantly cited in these documents.

Thus we have official proof of the many violations by the Saigon authorities of two essential points in the agreements: the persecution of former resistance fighters and the importation of American arms, war equipment and military personnel. I shall not attempt a complete list of these violations; for that matter, such a list would be impossible, since, as the I.C.C. has denounced, both the Saigon and American authorities made it practically impossible for the control body to carry out its function. The Commission was permitted to control those things which were its right and duty, according to the powers conferred on it by the Geneva agreements, only to a very small degree.

The most serious violation, however, and the one that sabotaged the entire Geneva structure, was the refusal to hold the elections. According to the Final Declaration of the Conference, the elections were to take place in the month of July 1956, and preliminary consultations "between the competent representative authorities of the two zones" were to begin by July 20, 1955. The Saigon authorities refused to submit to this disposition and also declined to take part in the preliminary consultations, repeatedly requested by the Hanoi authorities and urged by the co-Chairmen of the Conference. No one denies that this was a major violation of the agreements.

To justify their position, the Saigon authorities and the American government resorted to two arguments: 1. the situation in North Vietnam was not such as to permit the holding of free elections, such as foreseen by the Final Declaration of the Conference; 2. South Vietnam had not signed the Geneva agreements and was therefore not bound by their stipulations nor obligated to respect them. The memorandum of the State Department Legal Adviser uses the same arguments.

They are both totally invalid. The date of the elections was set for the month of July 1956, two years after the signing of the agreements "in order to ensure" — as the Final Declaration states — "that sufficient progress in the restoration of peace has been made and that all the necessary conditions obtain for free expression of the nation's will". Obviously, the authors of the Declaration felt that such conditions did not exist at the moment of the Conference, but that they would progressively be prepared over the intervening two years. Through the preliminary consultations, due to last for one year beginning on July 20, 1955, each side had the opportunity to demand and ensure that the necessary conditions of freedom called for in the agreements actually existed in the territory under the authority of the other side. In refusing to take part in the preliminary consultations a year before the date set for the elections, the Saigon authorities could not invoke the lack of freedom in the North. Even admitting that in 1955 complete freedom did not yet exist — and no proof was produced in this regard — there was still plenty of time to change the situation, and the preliminary consultations were intended to fulfill just this need. The government of the DRV made concrete proposals in this direction and naturally accepted control by the I.C.C. as foreseen in the agreements. We can therefore conclude that this argument was nothing more than a senseless cavil against the DRV; it only proves that the Saigon authorities were looking for excuses to avoid the elections and not allow the necessary freedom in their own territory.

Saigon's other argument carries no more weight. In accordance with the agreements drawn up between the French government and the Emperor Bao Dai, France represented the latter in international relations. The "Independence Treaty" signed by France and Bao Dai's regime on June 4, 1954 — during the course of the Geneva Conference — specified that the Saigon authorities were to assume all the rights and obligations of France with regard to Vietnam. The French authorities legitimately signed the agreements on the cessation of hostilities in full exercise of this right of representation; article 27 stated that "their successors in the exercise of their functions will be responsible for the application of these agreements".

In any event, there is no way of escaping this dilemma: either the Geneva agreements are binding on all sides or they are not. If they are not, then the hostilities did not legally cease, and the Vietnamese People's Army has the right to march below the 17th parallel and continue fighting in the South. It is absolutely inadmissible from a legal point of view for the Saigon authorities and the American government to demand that Hanoi totally respect the Geneva agreements when they themselves refuse to respect them. However, not only have the Saigon authorities constantly invoked the agreements to denounce alleged violations on the part of the government of the DRV, but President Johnson himself claims that the Americans are fighting to enforce these agreements.

There can thus be no doubt about Saigon's obligation to apply the agreements integrally and therefore about the flagrant violation it committed in refusing to hold the elections, which were the keystone of the entire situation. This opinion was shared, for that matter, by both the French and English governments, as stated by the French Foreign Minister M. Christian Pineau, to the *Conseil de la Republique* on February 23, 1956, and by Harold MacMillan to the House of Commons on June 15, 1955. This was also the opinion of President Nehru, who signed a joint statement with Pham Van Dong calling for the elections, and of the co-Chairmen of the Conference.

But although the Saigon authorities had no legal grounds for refusing the elections, the practical reason behind their position is well known: their certainty of losing at the polls.

"The outcome of Western-style elections for the country as a whole could be a provisional coalition government strongly influenced by the Viet-Minh. This is exactly what Ngo Dinh Diem wants to avoid, and this explains the police persecution and wave of arrests in the South. The fact that ten thousand Vietnamese soldiers, many of them officers, and four thousand politicans, among whom top officials and intellectuals, are being held in South Vietnamese prisons, is sufficient to illustrate the uneasiness within the Saigon regime".

(Le Monde, May 2, 1956, cited by Charles Fourniau: Le Vietnam face a la guerre, p. 92)

"If the elections, had been held immediately after Dien Bien Phu, the South would have voted 80% for Ho Chi Minh. Impartial observers estimate that it would still vote 60% for Ho Chi Minh. Not only the communists are against Diem. There are also the super-patriots, faithful to the goatee — the symbol of Uncle Ho — and proud of Giap's victory. There are also all the hard feelings caused by Diem's police-state dictatorship." *(Murray Bromberger in France Dimanche, May 16, 1956, cited by Charles Fourniau: Vietnam face a la guerre, p. 50)*

"Most reports suggest that unless a miracle happens the Communists are likely to win free elections in Vietnam which, of course, would be a severe humiliation for the West. It need not have been so. The anti-Communist Forces had the opportunity in South Vietnam to pull themselves together to try to win these elections in July next year, but they have so far lamentably failed to grasp their opportunity . . . The Saigon regime will not make any agreement about an electoral law at all. They do not even seek agreement. They can claim that legally they are not bound to reach agreement on the electoral law. They know that so far as they are concerned free elections will be the end of their regime". *(Christopher Mayhew to the House of Commons, June 15, 1955, Hansard, vol. 524, no. 7, p. 705)*

I have dwelt on this problem because, by violating this point of the Geneva agreements and refusing to submit to a free expression of the popular will, Diem in effect usurped power and carried out a secession of the South from the united State of Vietnam as envisioned by the Geneva agreements. This act of secession and usurpation, which gave birth to the pseudo-State of South Vietnam, was the outcome of the aggression I mentioned above.

Can we speak of a direct responsibility of the United States in this act of aggression? Without a doubt. The facts already presented to the Tribunal in the reports are sufficient proof: Eisenhower's letter to Diem, the SEATO guarantee, the frequency of American missions and the volume of aid granted by Washington to the pseudo-Republic of Vietnam, without which it could not have continued to exist. It is also interesting to note that the American government moved rapidly to ensure their own domination in South Vietnam and rid themselves of the French, whose job it was to guarantee the application of the Geneva agreements, by drastically cutting back their aid to France at the beginning of 1955 and thus forcing the French and General Ely, their commander, to withdraw in all haste.[1]

---

[1]Eden, *Towards Peace in Indochina,* London, 1966, p. 5.

In practice, the American government completely controlled the Saigon authorities, who were entirely dependent, both for the daily subsistence of the country and their administrative budget, on American aid. And since nothing of any importance could take place without its consent, the American government must be held responsible for the deliberate breaking of the Geneva agreements and the secession carried out by the Saigon authorities, in strict accordance with the American plan I have already mentioned above. We must, however, add that the American government in taking this position knew that it was creating a serious threat to peace. By violating the cease-fire convention, it knowingly reopened the process that had brought on the war of liberation against France, which the Geneva agreements were intended to end.

Proof that the American government knew it was provoking a new conflict lies in its behavior during the two years following the Geneva Conference and prior to the final breaking of the agreements, when it deliberately set about organizing and reinforcing the army and police of the so-called government of South Vietnam, and when, at the same time, it prepared the Manila Treaty with a particular eye to the war it was about to unleash against the Vietnamese people. As I have already said, an additional protocol to this Treaty states that "the free territory placed under the jurisdiction of the State of Vietnam" (this is the expression used in the text) is protected under the dispositions of the Treaty regarding armed attack or simple aggression, and an interpretative declaration of the American government adds that these dispositions apply only "to communist aggression", so far as the United States are concerned. Under this cover, plans were already being made to intervene militarily against the population of South Vietnam and crush their spirit of independence and their desire for unity.

We are therefore dealing with an aggression on the part of the American government in the truest sense of the word.

Direct Intervention in South Vietnam

History has its logic, and events developed as could be foreseen. Diem's puppet government had no popular base whatsoever, and his persecution of former resistance fighters and democrats, rather than strengthening his position, swelled the ranks of the discontent. The resistance movement began to organize in 1959, and the National Liberation Front was set up in 1960.

The only real forces on which Diem could count were the American armed forces, since his own army was increasingly plagued with desertion. To prevent the total collapse of their puppet government, the Americans were obliged continually to increase their presence and take an ever more direct part in the fight against the popular movement. But since they knew very well that in this way they were violating international law, they disguised their participation in the struggle under the hypocritical formula of so-called American "advisers". Later, when they could no longer hide their intervention behind this veil, they admitted it openly, resorting to another hypocrisy: the alleged armed aggression from North Vietnam. Recently, in the memorandum of the State Department Legal Adviser, the United States has finally attempted to provide a complete and legal justification for its acts. But before arriving at this point, it had shifted its arguments around a number of times, providing the world with a deplorable demonstration of its own bad faith.

I shall now examine the document which is intended to demonstrate the legitimacy of United States participation in the war in Vietnam (the document naturally speaks of "defense" of Vietnam). This justification is supposedly derived from the violation of the Geneva agreements by the DRV, but the document provides no proof of this alleged violation. The legality of Saigon's refusal to hold the elections is still supported with the argument of lack of freedom in the North; naturally, nothing is said about the very real lack of freedom in the South, and above all, nothing is said about the fact that Diem and Dulles rejected the elections from the very beginning and refused to take part in the negotiations which were to provide reciprocal guarantees, a full year before the date set for the elections.

The figures cited by the memorandum to prove the existence of an attack from the North are clearly false. It states (Department of State Bulletin, March 28, 1966, p. 474) that in the three years running from 1959 to 1961, around 10,000 men infiltrated South Vietnam from the North, that another 13,000 entered in 1962, and that by the end of 1964, an estimated 40,000 "armed and unarmed men" had moved from North to South. If the category "unarmed men" includes any citizen who happened to travel from one region to another for reasons of his own, it would be difficult to deny this figure, but I do not see how this peaceful migration can be considered an "armed attack" justifying, as the State Department Legal Adviser would have it, "legitimate self-defense".

If we limit ourselves to the number of men that the American government claims were sent into the South to take part in guerrilla warfare, then we must compare the figures given in the momorandum with those furnished by the State Department in its second White Paper, published in February 1965. According to the White Paper, these figures were: in 1959-60, between 1,800 and 2,700 men, and in 1961, 3,700 men. This means a total of between 5,500 and 6,400 men, less than two thirds of the 10,000 mentioned in the memorandum. For 1962, the

White Paper lists 5,400 instead of 13,000: for 1963, 4,200: and for 1964, a figure between 4,400 and 7,400. The total at the end of 1964 works out to about half the figure given by the Legal Adviser.

I have made this comparison simply to show the low level of validity with which the official American documents can be credited. The same can be said of the figures given in the White Paper, which have most certainly been manipulated for reasons of propaganda. We must not forget that the second White Paper is entitled *Aggression from the North* and was intended to prove the existence of such an aggression. But this is not all; even if we accept the figures included in the White Paper we must remember that the authors themselves admit that a large part of the men involved were Southerners who had been grouped in the North during the application of the Geneva agreements and who had obviously counted on returning to their homes after the elections and reunification. When circumstances worked out differently, they returned just the same, but in a new situation, to take up arms again, if they wished, or simply to rejoin their families. The White Paper states that the 90,000 men moved from South to North after Geneva created a vast reservoir of manpower for supplying the guerrillas in the South; and, in fact, most of the personal examples cited in the White Papers (and the examples are not very numerous — only a few cases) refer to persons born in the South. The Mansfield Report of January 3, 1966, states that beginning with the end of 1964, units of the regular North Vietnamese army began to penetrate into the South. In summary, even if we were to accept the information given in official American sources — which to me seems highly dubious — we would conclude that in the course of six years, between 1959 and 1964, a total of about 20,000 men passed from North to South; most of these were Southerners returning to their homes. Under these conditions, can we seriously speak of an armed attack from the North?

The picture does not change if we take arms as well as men into consideration, since the two White Papers concord in admitting that the arms used by the NLF are, for the most part, French or American weapons captured in battle, or arms rudimentally constructed in the jungle. Using Pentagon figures, Stone has calculated that in a period of 18 months, NLF forces lost about 7,500 weapons, of which only 179 were made in the socialist countries and sent in from the North.

The embarrassment of the State Department Legal Adviser when forced to admit that there is some uncertainty about the exact date on which the aggression from the North became an "armed attack" justifying "legitimate defense", is obvious. Nevertheless he sets this date at some time prior to February 1965, in an evident attempt to justify the bombings of North Vietnam which began in a permanent manner in just that period. He seems to forget that, at the time, the bombings were justified as retaliation for a specific incident and not as a measure of self-defense against aggression. His position is false, in any event, since according to the Mansfield Report, "units of the regular North Vietnamese army" began to move into the South during this period, around the end of 1964; and a few units of the regular army do not represent an armed attack in the true sense of the word. They certainly do not represent an attack of the sort that would justify a reaction on the level of the massive American bombing of the North, which has not ceased since that date.

The fact which the Legal Adviser completely ignores is that, at the time when these infiltrations are supposed to have begun, there were already a great many more American troops actively participating in the fighting in the South; therefore, the possible infiltration of DRV forces would have been nothing more than an understandable reaction.

According to the Mansfield Report of January 3, 1966, there were 10,000 American soldiers in Vietnam in 1962, 34,000 in May 1965, and 170,000 in December 1965.

If I do not take the trouble to analyze the figures furnished by American sources in detail and, at the same time, I do not discount them, although I doubt their authenticity, it is because these figures clearly prove that the aggressors in Vietnam are the Americans.

In fact, even if the presence of DRV forces in the South could be proven (and the Americans have never furnished any proof for their charges and figures), this presence would be legally justified by a series of factors, which can be briefly summed up as follows:

1. The breaking of the Geneva agreements determined by Saigon's refusal to hold the elections, and therefore the negation of the very substance of the accord, necessarily nullified the cease-fire convention, which represented an indivisible whole. No party can expect another party to abide by an agreement which it itself tramples upon; the North Vietnamese army therefore had the right to re-open hostilities.

2. According to the Geneva agreements, Vietnam is a single State; thus the North Vietnamese can never be considered invaders in the southern part of their own country. Had the Geneva agreements been respected, units of the North Vietnamese army crossing the demarcation line would have violated the cease-fire convention, but they would not for this reason have become invaders, and even less could they be considered so after the violation of the agreements by Saigon relieved them of any obligation to respect the cease-fire.

3. In any event, American troops came into South Vietnam and took part in the fighting first, and the role of priority in international law in such cases is well known.

On the other hand, there was no plausible justification for the presence of American troops. This was contrary to the Geneva agreements, which forbade sending foreign troops into Vietnam, and contrary to the United Nations Charter, to which I shall return shortly. To justify their own intervention in the war, the Americans have invoked Article 51 of the Charter, which, under certain conditions, authorizes self-defense against armed attack, but not against just any sort of aggression. The State Department Legal Adviser himself admits that no date can be established for the beginning of such an attack and limits himself, for obvious reasons, to general references to February 1965. At that time, around 30,000 Americans were already active in the fighting in South Vietnam, without any plausible justification.

We can, therefore, conclude that the American participation in the fighting in South Vietnam constitutes a crime of armed aggression, a crime against peace, in violation of the fundamental rights of the Vietnamese people.

The Bombing of North Vietnam

We thus come to the fourth stage of the United States aggression, which is the bombing and shelling of the DRV. In this regard, I shall again rapidly analyze the legal arguments invoked by the American government and the criticism that can be moved against them, much of which has already been called to your attention in the legal reports. Other criticisms can be found in the important analysis by the Lawyers Committee on American Policy Towards Vietnam included in the dossiers of the Tribunal. [2]

Mr. Rosenwein has already reviewed the official American position, as set forth in the memorandum of the State Department Legal Adviser. I shall limit myself to reminding you that the American action in Vietnam is presented as a case of collective self-defense, as foreseen in the SEATO pact and in the commitments the United States has assumed towards South Vietnam and as authorized by Article 51 of the UN Charter. The argumentation contained in the memorandum raises a whole series of legal problems, but I feel that I would be belittling the force of the DRV's cause if I sought to combat this argumentation on the strength of juridical subtleties. I shall therefore limit myself to only the most important arguments. It is easy to deal with the reference to the United States' commitments towards the Saigon puppet government, since no member country of the U.N. has the right to make commitments contrary to the Charter. Article

---

[2] *Vietnam and International Law: The Illegality of United States Military Involvement.* O'Hare Books, Flanders, New Jersey, 1967

103 of the Charter expressly states that in the case of conflict between obligations arising from the Charter itself and those derived from any other agreement, the former must always prevail. The same principle is contained in the Manila Treaty. We have, therefore, only to ascertain whether the American action in Vietnam is compatible with United States' obligations under the UN Charter.

The Charter forbids all its members to take up arms and resort to war, whether declared or not, except in two cases: when the action is in conformity with the decisions of the Security Council or in cases of self-defense. The American government can only invoke this second exception, as we have seen it does. But the right of individual or collective self-defense, permitted by Article 51 of the Charter as a natural right, cannot be applied in this case for a number of reasons. Outstanding among these are:

1. The right of self-defense presupposes the existence of an armed attack, which has not occurred.

2. Even if one accepts the American position that an armed attack has actually taken place, this attack would have had to be so violent and unexpected as to leave the victim no alternative than to act and no possibility of choosing his means nor time to negotiate. This is, in fact, the definition international law gives to armed attack justifying self-defense, without preliminary appeal to the United Nations.

3. The defense must be in proportion to the attack; otherwise, it becomes an attack in itself. Even if we accept the American position without question, the U.S. reaction of massive bombing and shelling of the DRV is totally out of proportion to the alleged "infiltration".

4. Self-defense is admitted only if the attack is directed against a Member of the United Nations.

Even if we accept the possibility of participating in collective self-defense with non-Members, we must still remember that, in the present case, South Vietnam is not even a State, and this is a much stronger objection. It would take too long to analyze this question in detail; I simply recall your attention to the fact that the DRV alone is the legitimate heir of national sovereignty, as sanctioned, on the one hand, by the abdication of Emperor Bao Dai and, on the other, by the agreements signed with France in 1946. It is true that France later attempted to regain its rights and fought a war lasting until 1954 to this end, but this attempt was an arbitrary act and could in no way create a new sovereignty, particularly since France lost the war and the Geneva agreements confirmed the loss of all French claims to sovereignty.

The Geneva agreements invested the Command of the French Union Army in the South and its successors with a *de facto*, limited and provisional authority, which did not give birth to a new State. This is particularly true, since the South has never attained the necessary condition for the existence of a State; the capacity to lead an independent and sovereign national life. The Saigon authorities have always survived thanks to American aid; their power has never been more than a facade and, without ever increasing American intervention, they would long ago have collapsed Thus there is no South Vietnamese State; there is no war between States, and it is impossible to invoke a non-existent war as a justification for external intervention.

We must add at this point that, not only is there not a war between the two States of Vietnam, there is not even a civil war in the South. This war is being fought by the people on one side and by the American army and mercenary troops on the other. The number of desertions, documented by Western sources, shows that the puppet government does not have the support of any part of the Vietnamese people. It must be made clear that we are dealing with a second war of liberation, in which the United States has replaced France as the colonial power attempting to impose its own law and authority on the Vietnamese people. Since the motives invoked by the United States to justify their intervention have proven to be without validity, we can conclude that this intervention is in violation of Article 2 of the United Nations Charter and the Kellogg-Briand Pact. And since this violation is directed against the basic national rights of the Vietnamese people, it also violates Article 1 of the Charter (the right to self-determination) and the General Assembly Resolution of December 1960.

Having spent so much time on our first question, I shall deal more rapidly with the second. I can more easily afford to do so, since the reports and testimony submitted to us in the course of our hearings provide crushing evidence for an affirmative answer.

For the legal aspect of the problem, I shall simply refer to Maitre Matarasso's introductory report and Maitre Jouffa's special report on the laws of war, to which I have nothing to add. After an accurate and scrupulous investigation, we can conclude that the laws of war have been violated, that there has been and continues to be a wide use of arms against human beings and deliberate bombing of civilian targets, such as hospitals, schools, sanatoria, churches, pagodas, dams, etc. In the case of some of these targets, such as hospitals, the bombing has been systematic; in other cases, I believe it has been less systematic, but no less deliberate.

I should like to say to my colleagues who may still have doubts about some of these targets that, unfortunately, even the most faithful testimony cannot give any real idea of the actual situation. Before going to Vietnam, I had read all that I could about this country and I thought that I knew what was happening there. But my idea was an intellectual one, filtered through the printed word, and far from the living eloquence of the facts themselves, far from the overwhelming force of the ruins and the victims, seen and heard. After having lived in the DRV for three weeks, after having seen the bombed hospitals, churches, and dams, after having observed their position, their construction, their relation to the landscape, and the nature of the bomb craters surrounding them, after having seen the precision of certain bombings of small targets (certain bridges, for example, also mentioned by Dr. Krivine), after having talked with many witnesses living in different places and totally unacquainted, but all with the same story to tell, I can no longer have any doubts.

Above all, I can understand what J.P. Vigier has said so well in his report on the nature of this war and the psycho-social character of the American bombing. This is, as I said earlier with regard to the act of aggression, a war against a people who are defending their basic rights, their right to self-determination, and who refuse to accept the law of the jungle. And when such a war is waged against a people like the Vietnamese who are firmly aware of their historical personality and determined to protect this personality, their culture, their historical values, and their right to progress along the road they themselves have chosen; when such a war is waged against a proud, independent and determined people, it necessarily becomes a war against all the people, against the men, the women, the children, and the aged, a war aimed at morally crushing and physically destroying this people. The more resolute the people's resistance, the more criminal the conduct of this war of aggression necessarily becomes. The crime of aggression against the basic national rights of a people and the crimes of war are closely connected. And as the Nuremburg verdict has already stated, this first crime includes the others.

I believe that the answer to our second question must be affirmative.

We must still deal with two other questions.

The first involves the other countries, besides the United States, mentioned in our first charge. I believe that with regard to the presence of Australian, New Zealand and South Korean troops in the war of aggression, these are facts admitted by the countries themselves. Their complicity in the crime is obvious. The same thing must be said of Thailand, which has opened its bases to the American Air Force for the purpose of murderous bombing missions.

The last question regards the crime of aggression against Cambodia. In this case as well, the evidence is clear, and the U.N. itself has already deplored these acts of aggression. The documentation submitted to us by the Cambodian delegation, Commander Khouroudeth, Mr. Vuthi's oral summary and Mr. Matarasso's report are sufficient to convince us of the existence of a crime of aggression.

Having examined the major problems before us and having, for my part at least, given an answer, I could end my report at this point. However, I fear that the presentation of so many different arguments together may have given a rather fragmentary impression of the basic problem, and that therefore a few more general remarks are necessary before concluding.

I spoke a short while ago of a war of liberation — that is, of the war of a people against a foreign power which is trying to impose its own law. At the beginning, I mentioned that American policy which consists of preventing any new State within the capitalist sphere from leaving it. This was the principle behind the Truman doctrine, even though officially it was couched in terms of defense against aggression. The formula has remained the same, and the concept of defense against aggression is still used, but reality stands clearly before us: the aggressors are the imperialists. The thing they call the "defense of the Free World" is nothing more than aggression against the peoples of the world who would prefer a socialist, or simply non-capitalist, form of development and also against those peoples who choose a policy of real neutrality, as seen in the example of Cambodia.

What is the "Free World" for the Americans? In this regard, we have a very interesting telegram sent by President Eisenhower to the President of the French Republic at the time of Dien Bien Phu, in which the American Head of State salutes the courage and resistance of the soldiers and officers defending Dien Bien Phu and expresses his admiration for these troops who, as he says, are defending the freedom of humanity and providing a shining demonstration of the qualities on which the salvation of the Free World depends.

I feel that Eisenhower's words in this message help us to understand the meaning of the term "Free World". At Dien Bien Phu, the French were still defending classical colonialism, that colonialism which, from that time on, all the countries of the world, except, I believe, Portugal and the Union of South Africa, have condemned in the General Assembly of the U.N., as contrary to the principles of international morals and law. It was just this colonialism that the President of the United States termed "Free World".

You are aware that over the gate at Auschwitz the Nazis wrote the phrase, which can still be read, *Arbeit macht frei* (Work makes man free). There is little difference between this phrase and Eisenhower's position when he called that immense concentration camp that was the slave world of colonialism "free". Today, still in defense of this "Free World", the Americans have again turned South Vietnam into a terror-ridden concentration camp and are using all their vast resources and powerful means of destruction to spread death in North Vietnam.

What is this "freedom", if not the freedom to carry out one's own business, freely to exploit other peoples for the greater profit of what is called "free" enterprise, the freedom for American imperialists to force their own laws and social relationships on other peoples, the freedom for them to oppose any other way of life and human relations, particularly if this way of life is socialist and could become contagious? What is this "freedom", if not the freedom for American imperialists to bar the way to peoples who, after so many years of oppression and colonialism, want to start down the road to independence, democracy and social progress.

I hold that, above and beyond the particular economic, political and strategic reasons that can and have been invoked to justify or explain the American aggression in Vietnam, the thing that most characterizes the imperialism of the United States is this drive towards world domination, this drive to set itself up as master of the earth and impose the rules of life it finds most convenient on all humanity. For this reason, the war being waged in Vietnam is, at the same time, a war of national liberation of the Vietnamese people and the struggle of all the world's peoples against the most serious threat that has ever hung over their future, since no other imperialism has ever accumulated such a vast power of aggression and destruction in its own hands.

In these days, I have heard American imperialism compared with Nazism several times; I made the same comparison myself a short while ago. I agree that on the level of internal politics, such a comparison is not possible at the moment, although we know that to reach its aims imperialism is capable of stirring up the worst possible sentiments within its own people and that war and national pride always bear the seeds of Fascism within them. However, the fact that many Americans are here at this Tribunal, as witnesses and members, and that they are able to organize vast mass movements against the war within their own country, shows that certain freedoms are still respected within the United States more perhaps than in some other Western countries with which I am acquainted.

Nevertheless, it must be said with the same sincerity that on the level of international politics, the Americans have the same disregard for law and the same cult of power as the Nazis. They will commit any sort of arbitrary act against those countries which are not strong enough to defend themselves. This power cult, this arrogance always presents itself under the hypocritical mantle of a democratic mystique, the mission of the American people, and it is probable that a large part of this people is fooled by this mystique. We must not forget, however, that the Nuremburg judges considered the fact that the Nazi leaders had given their plan of aggression and conquest the appearance of a mission and a historical destiny as a part of their crime. In doing so, they gave us further arguments for our own sentence.

The whole world knows, in fact, that the American imperialists are in Vietnam to carry out a mission of freedom and democracy, that they are bombing, destroying and killing in their role as "good Samaritans", as Cardinal Spellman has put it. But the Cardinal was only repeating the official position of this country's leaders: the American imperialists are fighting in the interest of humanity, in defense of the free world and to teach the rest of the world the American way of life, just as Hitler's soldiers fought to fulfill the historic mission of the Germanic race. Every conqueror attempts to destroy the personality of other peoples in order to impose his own laws, his own way of life, his own concept of peace. *Pax Americana or Pax Germanica:* both mean a violation of the freedom of other peoples, of their right to self-determination, of what we have called their fundamental national rights.

We have thus come to the heart of the problem. The war in Vietnam has by now become a test-war. If the Americans win it, the *Pax Americana* will be established over all countries, since it will have been shown that a nation is not free to choose a future different from that chosen for it by the Americans. It will be a dark future for all countries, not excluding the Western nations, who will no longer be masters of their own destinies, any more than the others. But if the Americans are beaten, a ray of hope will once more light our troubled world. The peoples of three continents, now emerging in the midst of so many struggles and sacrifices from their colonial condition, will finally know that no power on earth is capable of barring the road to a country that means to build a future of democracy and progress, that attempts to throw off the yoke of neo-colonialism. The Western peoples themselves will also discover that they too can have a better future.

The future of the world for many years to come is at stake in Vietnam. President Johnson's stubborn drive to escalation cannot be explained by the pressure of the coming elections alone; Johnson is perfectly aware of what this test-war has come to represent for American imperialism. Hence this furious escalation, this disregard for humanity, this moral degeneration that accompanies it day by day and that cannot but arouse the indignation of the human conscience.

It is our task to give this conscience a voice.

The International War Crimes Tribunal, during the session held at Stockholm from the 2nd to the 10th May, 1967 studied the two following questions included in its programme, adopted in London on the 15th November, 1966:

"Has the United States Government (and the Governments of Australia, New Zealand and South Korea) committed acts of aggression according to international law?"

"Has there been bombardment of targets of a purely civilian character, for example hospitals, schools, sanatoria, dams, etc., and on what scale has this occurred?

Having heard the qualified representatives of the Democratic Republic of Vietnam and noted the official refusal of the government of the United States of America to make known its point of view, and this despite the various appeals addressed to it.

Having heard the various reporters, the experts, numerous witnesses, including members of the investigating teams which it had itself sent to Vietnam, as well as Vietnamese victims of the war.

Having examined several written, photographic and cinematographic documents, together with numerous exhibits.

Having heard the summation of Mr. Lelio Basso, considers itself able to take the following decisions:

ON THE FIRST QUESTION

Resort to force in international relations has been prohibited by numerous international agreements, the chief of which is the 1928 Pact of Paris, known as the Briand-Kellogg Pact.

In its Article 2, the United Nations Charter solemnly recalled the said principle immediately after the Second World War.

Article 6 of the Statute of Nuremberg qualified as crimes against peace "the conduct of, preparation for, starting or pursuit of a war of aggression or a war in violation of international treaties, pledges or agreements, or participation in a concerted plan, or plot for the accomplishment of any of the foregoing acts".

Finally, it must be recalled, as in the United Nations resolution of December 1960, that all peoples have fundamental rights to national independence, to sovereignty, to respect of the integrity of their territory, and that breaches of these fundamental rights may be regarded as crimes against the national existence of a people.

The accession to independence and to national existence of the people of Vietnam dates back to 2nd September, 1945. This independence was called in question by the old colonial power. The war of national liberation then embarked upon ended with the victory of the Vietnam Army.

The Geneva Agreements of the 20th and 21st July, 1954, intended to put an end to the previous conflict, created in Vietnam a state of law, the respect of which was incumbent on all, and particularly on the United States. These Agreements recognised the guarantees, independence, unity and territorial integrity of Vietnam (Articles 6 and 7 of the final Declaration). Although a line of demarcation divided the country into two parts on a level with the 17th parallel, it was expressly stipulated that as the essential aim of this division was to settle military questions, it was of a provisional nature "and could in no way be interpreted as constituting a political or territorial boundary". (Article 6 of the final Declaration.)

The Geneva Agreements stipulated that general elections should take place over the whole of the country in July 1956 under the supervision of an international commission, and that consultations on this subject were to take place between the competent representatives of the two zones as from July 1955.

The Agreements specifically excluded all reprisals or discrimination against persons and organisations by reason of their activities during the previous hostilities (Article 14 of the Armistice Agreement). They formally prohibited the introduction of fresh troops, of military personnel, fresh arms and munitions, as well as the installation of military bases (Article 16 of the Armistice Agreement) and the inclusion of Vietnam in military alliances, this applying to the two zones (Article 9 of the final Declaration).

This state of law, intended to create a peaceful situation in Vietnam, was replaced by a state of war in consequence of successive violations and the responsibility for the passage to a state of war lies with the government of the United States of America.

It transpires from the information of a historical and diplomatic nature that has been brought to the knowledge of the Tribunal:

— that numerous proofs exist of the American intention prior to 1954 to dominate Vietnam;

— that the Diem government was set up in Saigon by American agents several weeks before the conclusion of the Geneva Agreements;

— that the Saigon authorities, subservient to the United States, systematically violated the provisions of the Geneva Agreements which prohibited reprisals, as has been established on several occasions by the International Control Commission;

— that in defiance of the Geneva Agreements the United States, has, since 1954, introduced into Vietnam increasing quantities of military equipment and personnel and has set up bases there.

The elections that were fixed for July 1956 and which were to be the subject of consultations in July 1955 did not take place in spite of numerous diplomatic notes from the government of the Democratic Republic of Vietnam calling for the said consultations. Information from United States sources make it possible to ascribe to the U.S.A. the refusal by Saigon of the most essential provisions of the Geneva Agreements.

In this manner there was created in South Vietnam a situation of foreign intrusion by force against which the people of Vietnam had to launch a struggle of national liberation in a political form until 1959 and in the form of an armed struggle since that date, a struggle led by the National Liberation Front of South Vietnam since 1960, which has succeeded in controlling vastly greater territories than those controlled by the United States.

This attack against the South was followed by an attack against the North, begun in 1964, and intensified since 1965 in the form of aerial bombardments and naval and land shellings in circumstances which form the subject of the second question studied by the Tribunal. The United States has not ceased to increase the power of these attacks by practising what it has itself called a policy of escalation.

The Tribunal has made a point of examining scrupulously the arguments put forward in American official documents to justify the legality of their intervention in Vietnam. Special attention has been paid to the document entitled: "Juridical Memorandum on the Legality of the Participation of the United States in the Defence of Vietnam", which document was submitted to the Senate Foreign Affairs Committee on the 4th March, 1966. The main argument formulated by this text consists in claiming that the American intervention in Vietnam merely constitutes aid to the Saigan government against aggression from the North. Such argument is untenable both in law and in fact.

In law, it is hardly necessary to recall that Vietnam constitutes a single nation which cannot be seen as an aggressor against itself.

The fact is that no proof of this alleged aggression has ever been produced. The figures stated of infiltration of personnel from the North into the South, often contradictory, mixing up armed men and unarmed men, are thoroughly disputable and could in no case justify the plea of legitimate defence provided for in Article 51 of the United Nations Charter, an Article, moreover, none of the other conditions of which are complied with.

From the foregoing it follows that the United States bears the responsibility for the use of force in Vietnam and that it has in consequence committed a crime of aggression against that country, a crime against peace.

It has therefore violated the provisions of International Law outlawing the use of force in international relations, in particular the Pact of Paris of 1928, the so-called Briand-Kellogg Pact, of which it was however the author, and the United Nations Charter (Article 2, para. 4). This violation of the general principles has been accompanied by violation of the special agreements relating to the territory in question, Vietnam — that is to say, the Geneva Agreements of July 1954.

In acting thus the United States has undeniably committed a crime against peace within the meaning of Article 6 of the Statute of Nuremberg, a provision sanctioned by international jurisprudence (Judgments of Nuremberg and Tokyo) and acknowledged as international law by all, the the unanimous resolution of the United Nations of the 11th December, 1946.

The United States has furthermore committed a crime against the fundamental rights of the people of Vietnam.

It should be added that States such as South Korea, Australia and New Zealand, which have in one form or another provided aid to the American aggression, have rendered themselves accomplices.

The Tribunal has concerned itself with the situation in Cambodia. It has heard the report of the investigating teams which it sent to that country and the depositions of a qualified representative of the General Staff of the Cambodian Army. It considers that the forces of the United States and those of the governments subordinate to it at Bangkok and Saigon are engaging in continuous and serious acts of aggression against the Kingdom of Cambodia. This aggression constitutes not only an attack on Cambodian neutrality and independence but also an extremely serious threat to the peace in South East Asia and in the world.

ON THE SECOND QUESTION

The Tribunal has gained the conviction that the aerial, naval and land bombardments of civil targets is of a massive, systematic and deliberate nature.

The massive nature of these bombardments is attested by innumerable reports from American sources on the tonnage of bombs dropped and the great number of American aerial sorties.

The systematic and deliberate bombardment of civil targets is established by extensive evidence to the effect that in the vast majority of cases they are preceded by reconnaissance flights: according to a report of American origin, the aircraft stationed at a single base in Thailand alone utilise 300,000 metres of film every month to photograph Vietnam. If it is borne in mind on the one hand that most of the aircraft are equipped with automatic firing devices and, on the other hand that the aircraft return persistently and furiously to the same targets, which are sometimes already almost completely destroyed, no doubt is possible as to the deliberate intention to strike the targets in question.

Besides the aerial bombardments, intense pounding by the artillery of the U.S. 7th Fleet is progressively ravaging the coastal zones.

All of the witnesses heard, in particular the members of the investigating teams, have confirmed that the greater part of the civilian targets (hospitals, sanitoria, schools, churches, pagodas) are very obvious and very clearly distinguishable from the rest of the Vietnam countryside.

The extent of the bombardments is considerable and the Tribunal has had a close study made by its investigating teams of the results published by the Democratic Republic of Vietnam. Proceeding by the method of sampling, the investigating teams have been able to verify at places of their choice the information received. Thus, for example, so far as hospitals are concerned, out of 95 establishments mentioned as destroyed by the Vietnamese Commission of Inquiry into War Crimes, 34 have been verified by the Tribunal's investigating teams, i.e. 36%. The great value of these samplings lies in their dispersion, since the 34 hospitals checked relate to eight provinces out of the twelve involved in the bombardments.

Apart from the extensive private evidence submitted to it, the Tribunal has heard general reports on the distribution of the various categories of civilian targest: hospitals, schools, places of worship (pagodas and churches) and dams, as well as of the bombardment of the civilian populations of urban centres and in the countryside. It has also heard combined reports on the bombardments in the two provinces of Nghe-An and Thanh-Hoa. All of these reports were accompanied by documents, statements and material evidence.

The Tribunal ascertained the vital importance to the people of Vietnam of the dams and other hydraulic works, and the grave danger of famine to which the civilian populations were exposed by the attempted destruction by the American forces.

The Tribunal has received all necessary information in the diversity and power of the engines of war employed against the Democratic Republic of Vietnam and the circumstances of their utilisation (high explosive bombs, napalm, phosphorus and fragmentation bombs, etc.). Seriously injured victims of napalm bombs have appeared before it and medical reports on these mutilated people have been provided to it. Its attention in particular has been drawn to the massive use of various kinds of anti-personnel bombs of the fragmentation type, also called in American parlance, C.B.U., and in Vietnamese parlance, pellet bombs. These devices obviously intended to strike defenceless populations, have the following characteristics:

— containers, called by the Vietnamese the "mother bombs", release hundreds of small, oblong or spherical bombs ("pineapple" or "guava" bombs) which in turn release hundreds of small pellets. A single "mother bomb" can therefore cause the dispersion of nearly 100,000 pellets; these pellets can cause no serious damage to buildings or plants or to protected military personnel (for example, civil defence workers behind their sandbags). They are therefore intended solely to reach the greatest number of persons in the civilian population.

The Tribunal has had medical experts study the consequences of attacks with these pellets. The path of the particles through the body is long and irregular and produces, apart from cases of death, multiple and various internal injuries.

The Hague Convention No. 4 of the 18th October, 1907, laid down the principle that belligerents may not have unlimited choice so far as the means of injuring an enemy are concerned (Article 22); the said Convention specially prohibits the use of arms, projectiles and material deliberately destined to cause pointless suffering (Article 23); attacks on or bombardments by any means whatsoever of town, villages, dwellings or undefended buildings are prohibited (Article

307

25). During bombardments all necessary steps must be taken to spare, so far as possible, buildings devoted to religion, art, science or charitable purposes, historical monuments, hospitals or places where sick and injured persons are assembled, provided that these places are not used for military purposes (Article 27).

Article 6 of the Statutes of the Tribunal of Nuremberg has qualified as war crimes the destruction without reason of towns and villages or devastation not justified by military requirements.

The Geneva Convention of the 2nd August, 1949, also laid down the principle of absolute prohibition of attack on civilian hospitals (Article 18) and private and collective property not rendered absolutely necessary by the conduct of the operations (Article 53).

The government of the United States cannot override such Treaties, to which it has subscribed, whilst its own constitution (Article 6, para. 2) gives them preeminence over domestic law. Furthermore, the Official Manual (Department of the Army Field Manual) entitled "The Law of Land Warfare" published by the U.S. Defense Department in 1956, under reference F.M. 27-10, refers to all of the foregoing provisions as being obligatory on all members of the American Army.

In consequence, the Tribunal considers that in subjecting the civilian population and civilian targets of the Democratic Republic of Vietnam to intensive and systematic bombardment, the United States of America has committed a war crime.

Apart from condemnation of this war crime, the Tribunal makes a point of declaring that fragmentation bombs of the C.B.U. type, which have no other purpose than to injure to the maximum the civilian population, must be regarded as arms prohibited by the laws and customs of war.

Meeting with the resistance of a people who intended to "exercise peacefully and freely its right to full independence and to the integrity of its territory" (United Nations resolution of the 14th December, 1960), the government of the United States of America has given these war crimes, through their extent and frequency, the character of crimes against humanity (Article 6 of the Statute of Nuremberg).

These crimes cannot be regarded merely as a consequence of a war of aggression, whose prosecution is determined by them.

Because of their systematic employment with the object of destroying the fundamental rights of the people of Vietnam, their unity and their wish for peace, the crimes against humanity of which the government of the United States of America has rendered itself guilty, become a fundamental constituent part of the crime of aggression, a supreme crime which embraces all the others according to the Nuremberg verdict.

FINDINGS OF THE TRIBUNAL

1. Has the government of the United States committed acts of aggression against Vietnam under the terms of international law?

   YES (Unanimously).

2. Has there been, and if so, on what scale, bombardment of purely civilian targets, for example, hospitals, schools, medical establishments, dams, etc?

   YES (Unanimously).

We find the government and armed forces of the United States are guilty of the deliberate, systematic and large scale bombardment of civilian targets, including civilian populations, dwellings, villages, dams, dykes, medical establishments, leper colonies, schools, churches, pagodas, historical and cultural monuments.

We also find unanimously, with one abstention, that the government of the United States of America is guilty of repeated violations of the sovereignty, neutrality and territorial integrity of Cambodia, that it is guilty of attacks against the civilian population of a certain number of Cambodian towns and villages.

3. Have the governments of Australia, New Zealand and South Korea been accomplices of the United States in the aggression against Vietnam in violation of international law?

   YES (Unanimously).

The question also arises as to whether or not the governments of Thailand and other countries have become accomplices to acts of aggression or other crimes against Vietnam and its populations. We have not been able to study this question during the present session. We intend to examine at the next session legal aspects of the problem and to seek proofs of any incriminating facts.

Endorsed "ne variatur"
The President of the Tribunal
Stockholm, 10th May, 1967   *Jean-Paul Sartre.*

Closing Address to the Stockholm Session
by Bertrand Russell

The International War Crimes Tribunal has been subject to abuse from people who have much to hide. It has been said that the conclusions of this Tribunal were known in advance. The conclusions of our Tribunal are built out of the evidence. The evidence is abundant. It is precisely because the knowledge of crime is a cause for enquiry that we are holding this session. When the evidence on aggression and the systematic bombardment of the entire population of Vietnam becomes known this evidence will be compelled to reach the same conclusions.

During recent days the United States has been bombing residential quarters of Hanoi and Haiphong with steel pellet bombs. These facts are reported in newspapers throughout the world. These actions are criminal. They must be investigated because of the evidence that they are occurring and because of their criminality. Those who are prepared to investigate these new crimes against the people of Vietnam will be men of sufficient public spirit, moral concern and personal integrity to be prepared to consider the crimes in Vietnam cause to abandon private work, endure public abuse and risk personal harm.

We have heard evidence for many days on the sustained aggression by a great power against a small, heroic people. A large power has occupied an impoverished nation to subdue a popular movement seeking land, independence and social advance. It is not the evil which is new; nor is it the crisis which has changed. We have celebrated in history the struggles waged by oppressed people against large, cruel and powerful invaders. The sense of identity with the small victim of a cruel and large tormentor touches our deepest impulses and is part of our mythology, religion and literature. The concern for the weak struggling after long suffering against the strong for their simplest rights is the source of our ethics and the great moments in our common history. David and Goliath, the Greeks at Salamis, the Vietnamese and Genghis Khan — the partisans of Vietnam and the United States air force and mechanised army — are part of a continuous tradition.

The International War Crimes Tribunal defies the powerful rulers who bully and butcher with abandon. Who would compare the 100,000 tons of napalm with a peasant holding a rifle. Who can fail to distinguish the power which destroys hospitals and schools of an entire people from the defenders who attack the airplanes carrying napalm and steel fragmentation bombs. The difference between the victims and the criminals who oppress them is part of the evidence before us compelling honest men to speak loudly and to risk much.

The United States is using fascist states to facilitate its plans for new levels of crime. Each day bombers leave Thailand to saturate Vietnam in steel pellets and liquid fire. Has one American city been attacked? Are Canada and Mexico bases for the destruction of America by a power on the other side of the world? If one American city suffered two hours of bombing such as has been inflicted for two years on Vietnam the world press would inform us rather fully. This imbalance is a clear indication of the great injustice we are investigating. The difference in power is matched by the indifference of the powerful and those who serve them or depend on their favour.

During the 1930s when millions of people could see the nature of Adolf Hitler and Nazism, there was too little understanding and insufficient will to act in time. In Germany there were no great strikes or mass demonstrations. The large political parties opposed only in words but did not mobilise their large support. Even now the great political parties fail to act and the nominal opponents of the aggressive violence of the United States satisfy themselves with pious complaint in institutions dominated by the aggressor.

Nazism emerged from a nation unable to stabilise itself and degenerated to unforeseen limits of depravity. The policy of aggression in Washington has brought a comparable degree of scientific extermination and moral degeneracy. The International War Crimes Tribunal must do for the peoples of Vietnam, Asia, Africa and Latin America what no tribunal did while Nazi crimes were committed and plotted. The napalm and pellet bombs, the systematic destruction of a heroic people are a barbarous rehearsal. The starving and the suffering will no longer die in silence. We must discredit the arrogant demand that they protect our comfort with their quiet agony. Our social institutions, impregnated with racism, must be reconstructed. The Tribunal must begin a new morality in the West, in which cold mechanical slaughter will be automatically condemned. The Tribunal must inspire a new understanding that the heroic are the oppressed and the hateful are the arrogant rulers who would bleed them for generations or bomb them into the stone age. The Tribunal must warn of the impending horror in many lands, the new atrocities prepared now in Vietnam and of the global struggle between the poor and the powerful rich. These are themes as old as humanity. The long arduous struggle for decency and for liberation is unending. A Tribunal such as ours will be necessary until the last starving man is fed and a way of life is created which ends exploitation of the many by the few. Vietnam struggles so others may survive. The truths we must declare are simple truths. Great violence menaces our cultural achievments. Starvation and disease can not be tolerated. Resistance at risk of life is noble. But we know this. Western Europe and North America are drenched in the blood of struggle for social change. Feudalism, the reduction of men to starving hulks, the purchase of their minds, the eradication of their spirit — these are blights on human culture. These are vicious forms of aggression at once more fundamental and more pervasive than the crossing of frontiers by foot soldiers. Wherever men struggle against suffering we must be their voice. Whenever they are cruelly attacked for their self-sacrifice we must find our voices. It is easy to pay lip-service to these ideals. We will be judged not by our reputations or our pretences but by our will to act. Against this standard we too will be judged by better men.

Bertrand Russell
May 10, 1967

APPENDIX A

U.S. Air Attacks on DRV Medical Facilities — 1965-1967

YEAR 1965

Date	Names of Establishments Raided

FEB.
- 7   Hospital of Quang Binh province (1st time)†
- 8   Infirmary-Maternity of provincial capital of Ho Xa, Vinh Linh (1st time)
- 11 Hospital of Quang Binh province (2nd time)
- 20 Infirmary-Maternity of Vinh Thai village, Vinh Linh (1st time)

Monthly total or raids: 5

MARCH
- 3   Hospital of Huong Son district, Ha Tinh (1st time)†
- 19 Health Station of Thanh Chuong district, Nghe An (1st time)
- 19 Pharmacy of Thanh Chuong district, (1st time)
- 21 Infirmary-Maternity of Quang Phuc village, Quang Binh (1st time)
- 22 Infirmary-Maternity of Huong Lap village, Vinh Linh (1st time)
- 26 Infirmary-Maternity of Canh Duong village, Quang Binh (1st time)
- 31 Hospital of Huong Khe district, Ha Tinh (1st time)

Monthly total of raids: 8

APRIL
- 4   Consultation and Health Station of Dong Hoi provincial capital (1st time)
- 4   Infirmary-Maternity of Phu Bai, Dong Hoi (1st time)
- 6   Hospital of Huong Khe (2nd time)
- 13 Infirmary-Maternity of Hai Trach village, Quang Binh (1st time)
- 14 Infirmary-Maternity of Duc Trach village, Quang Binh (1st time)
- 23 Infirmary-Maternity of Dai Trach village, Quang Binh (1st time)
- 28 Infirmary-Maternity of Thanh Trach district, Quang Binh (1st time)

Monthly total of raids: 7

MAY
- 4   Vinh Linh Medical Center and Hospital (1st time)†
- 16 Pharmacy of Cam Xuyen district, Ha Tinh (1st time)
- 23 Hospital of Nghia Dan district, Ngh An (1st time)
- 23 Hospital of Duc Tho district, Ha Tinh (1st time)
- 23 Infirmary-Maternity of Vinh Long village, Vinh Linh (1st time)
- 27 Huong Khe Hospital (3rd time)
- 28 Huong Khe Hospital (4th time)

Monthly total of raids: 7

Date	Names of Establishments Raided

JUNE

3   Huorg Khe Hospital (5th time)
4   Tuberculosis Hospital, Nghe An (1st time)†
10   Duc Tho Hospital (2nd time)
10   Nghi Loc Pharmacy (1st time)
10   Vinh Pharmacy (1st time)
10   Cau Giat Pharmacy (1st time)
10   Pharmacy of Nghe An province (1st time)
11   Huong Khe hospital (6th time)
12   Quynh Lap Leper Sanatorium (1st time)††
13   Quynh Lap Leper Sanatorium (2nd time)
14   Quynh Lap Leper Sanatorium (3rd time)
14   Quynh Lap Leper Sanatorium (4th time)
14   Hospital of Quang Trach district, Quang Binh (1st time)†
14   Ha Dun Sanatorium, Quang Binh (1st time)†
15   Quynh Lap Leper Sanatorium (5th time)
15   Quynh Lap Leper Sanatorium (6th time)
15   Quynh Lap Leper Sanatorium (7th time)
16   Old Age Home of Nga Ba Mai, Thanh Hoa (1st time)†
16   Quynh Lap Leper Sanatorium (8th time)
16   Quynh Lap Leper Sanatorium (9th time)
16   Quynh Lap Leper Sanatorium (10th time)
17   Quynh Lap Leper Sanatorium (11th time)
18   Huong Khe Hospital (7th time)
18   Hospital of Sen La province (1st time)
21   Quynh Lap Leper Sanatorium (13th time)
26   Hospital of Viet Trung, Quang Binh (1st time)
27   Hospital of Ha Trung district, Thanh Hoa (1st time)†
22   Hospital of the Autononomous Northwest Zone†
22   Medical School for the Autonomous Northwest Zone†

Monthy total of raids: 28

JULY

1   Hospital of Tuyen Hoa district, Quang Binh (1st time) *
8   T.B. Hospital of Thanh Hoa province (1st time)
9   Hospital, Medical Center and other medical
10   stations of Yen Bai province
11   (5 times in 3 days)
10   Quynh Lap Leper Sanatorium (14th time)†
11   Cua Lo Sanatorium, Nghe An province (1st time)†
14   T.B. Hospital of Thanh Hoa province (2nd time)
20   Hospital of Ky Son district, Nghé An (1st time)
24   Hospital of Quang Binh province (3rd time)
25   Hospital of Tuong Duon district, Nghe An (1st time)
25   Hospital of Con Cuong district, Nghe An (1st time)†
25   Hospital of Nghe An province (1st time)
25   Quynh Lap Leper Sanatorium (15th time)
27   Hospital of Quang Binh province (4th time)

Date	Names of Establishments Raided
28	Hospital of Do Lueng district, Ngha An (1st time)
29	Hospital of Nam Dinh province (1st time) *
30	Hospital of Ha Tinh province (1st time)†
31	Quynh Lap Leper Sanatorium (16th time)

Monthly total of raids: 19

AUG.

1	Hospital of Ha Tinh province (2nd time)
3	Quynh Lap Leper Sanatorium (17th time)
4	Quynh Lap Leper Sanatorium (18th time)
7	Quynh Lap Leper Sanatorium (19th time)
7	Medical-Maternity of Son Giang village, Ha Tinh (1st time)
12	Hospital of Thach Ha district (1st time)
13	Hospital of Huong Khe district (8th time)
13	Hospital of Ha Tinh province (3rd time)
14	Hospital of Vinh (Polish Equipped) (1st time)††
14	Quynh Lap Leper Sanatorium (20th time)
15	Hospital of Ky Anh district, Ha Tinh (1st time)
16	Hospital of Ky Anh district (2nd time)
16	Hospital of Ky Anh district (3rd time)
16	Hospital of Ky Anh district (4th time)
16	Hospital of Ky Anh district (5th time)
17	Quynh Lap Leper Sanatorium (21st time)
17	Medical-Maternity station of Huong Loc district, Ha Tinh (1st time)
20	Quynh Lap Leper Sanatorium (22nd time)
22	Quynh Lap Leper Sanatorium (23rd time)
21	Tuberculosis Hospital of Thanh Hoa province (3rd time)
˜5	Quynh Lap Leper Sanatorium (24th time)
27	Duc Tho Hospital (3rd time)
29	Quynh Lap Leper Sanatorium (25th time)

Monthly total of raids: 23

SEPT.

5	Quynh Lap Leper Sanatorium (26th time)
6	Hospital of Quang Binh province (5th time)
10	Hospital of Ha Tinh province (4th time)
11	Hospital of Quang Binh province (6th time)
13	Hospital of Quang Binh province (7th time)†
22	Hospital of Tinh Gia district, Thanh Hoa (1st time) ††
23	Hospital of Quang Binh province (8th time)
24	Hospital of Quang Binh province (9th time)
24	Hospital of Ha Tinh province (5th time)
25	Phu Ly hospital, Nam Ha province (1st time)†
27	Medical station of Cam Nhuong village, Ha Tinh (1st time)

Monthly total of raids: 11

Date	Names of Establishments Raided

OCT.

5 Hospital of Ha Tinh province (6th time)
6 Tuberculosis Hospital of Ha Tinh province (1st time)
8 Quynh Lap Leper Sanatorium (27th time)
8 Hospital of Ha Tinh province (7th time)
9 Hospital of Quang Binh province (10th time)
10 Hospital of Ha Tinh province (8th time)
10 Ha Tinh Tuberculosis Hospital (2nd time)
11 Quynh Lap Leper Sanatorium (28th time)
12 Health Station of Vien Thanh village, Nghe An province (1st time)
13 Hospital of Ha Tinh province (9th time)
14 Hospital of Quang Binh province (11th time)

Monthly total of raids: 11

NOV.

3 Health station of Xuan Truong village, Ha Tinh (1st time)
5 Health station of Xuan Hoi village, Ha Tinh (1st time)
11 Ha Tinh Tuberculosis Hospital (3rd time)
18 Ha Tinh Hospital (11th time)
19 Ha Tinh Hospital (12th time)
22 Hospital of Phu Tho province (1st time)*

Monthly total of raids: 7

DEC.

2 Hospital of Nghia Trung district, Nam Ha (1st time)
6 Uong Bi hospital (1st time)
16 Health station of Hoang Que village (1st time)

Monthly total of raids: 3
1965 : 129 bombing and strafing raids.

YEAR : 1966
FEB.

1 Health Center of Vinh Tan village (1st time)
3 Quynh Lap Leper Sanatorium (29th time)
5 Hospital of Nga Son district, Thanh Hoa (1st time)†
12 Hospital of Nga Son district, Nghe An (1st time)
15 Assistant Doctors' School of Nghe An (1st time)

Monthly total of raids : 5

MAR.

5 Quynh Lap Leper Sanatorium (30th time)
14 Health station of Ky Ninh village, Ha Tinh (1st time)
16 Health station of Hung Hoa, Nghe An (1st time)
20 Quynh Lap Leper Sanatorium (31st time)
20 Health station of Nghi Hai village, Nghe An (1st time)

Date	Names of Establishments Raided
21	Health station of Huong Thuy village, Ha Tinh (1st time)
28	Huong Lap Hospital, Vinh Linh (1st time)
29	Huong Lap Hospital, Vinh Linh (2nd time)

Monthly total of raids: 8

APR.

5	Quynh Lap Leper Sanatorium (32nd time)
13	Duc Tho Hospital (4th time)
16	Health Center of Dien Than village, Nghe An (1st time)
19	Health Center of Dong Xa village, Cam Pha (1st time)
20	Hospital of Ha Tinh province (13th time)
21	Quynh Lap Leper Sanatorium (33rd time)
24	Quynh Lap Leper Sanatorium (34th time)
24	Health Center of Dien Van village, Nghe An (1st time)
27	Health Center of Dien My village, Nghe An (1st time)
29	Health Center of Lien Thanh village, Nghe An (1st time)
29	Hospital of Ha Tu Coal Mine (1st time)†

Monthly total of raids: 11

MAY

6	Quynh Lap Leper Sanatorium (35th time)
6	Quynh Lap Leper Sanatorium (36th time)
8	Hospital of Ha Tu (2nd time)
10	Hospital of Ha Tinh province (14th time)
11	Hospital of Ha Tu (3rd time)
12	Hospital of Ha Tinh province (15th time)
14	Hospital of Ha Tinh province (16th time)
21	Hospital of Ha Tinh province (17th time)
22	Hospital of Ha Tu (4th time)
26	Hospital of Phat Diem district, Ninh Binh (1st time)†
29	Hospital of Ha Tu (5th time)
22	Sanatorium of Vinh (250 beds)††

Monthly total of raids: 11

JUNE

1	Provincial Hospital, Center for the Mothers and Children and Assistant-Doctors' School of Thanh Hoa province (1st time)*†
12	Quynh Lap Leper Sanatorium (37th time)
13	Health Center of Huong Linh village, Ha Tinh (1st time)
19	Quynh Lap Leper Sanatorium (38th time)
22	Hospital of Bac Thai province (1st time)†
24	Quynh Lap Leper Sanatorium (39th time)

Monthly total of raids: 6

Date	Names of Establishments Raided

JULY

25   Hospital of the province of Hoa Binh.
25   Medical Center of the province of Hoa Binh.
25   Medical School of Hoa Binh province.

Monthly total of raids: 3

SEPT.

19   Medical School of Naur Ha province (situated in the center of the city of Nam Dinh)*
25   Medical School of Naur Ha province (situated in the center of the city of Nam Dinh)
29   Maternity-Infirmary Commune of Vu Lam (Vu Tien, Thai Binh provinces)

Monthly total of raids: 3

OCTOBER

4   Medical School of Nam Ha province (2nd time) (situated in a Commune of Xuan Troung district).
27   Medical service of Thu Tri district (Thai Binh province)

Monthly total of raids: 2

DECEMBER

6   Medical school of Nam Ha province (3rd time) (situated at Phu Ly)*
3   Hospital of Thanh Tri district (Hanoi suburb)t
14   Hospital of Thanh Tri district (2nd time)

Monthly total of raids: 3

JANUARY 1967

17   Hospitals of Viet Tri and Thai Nguyen†

Total of establishments attached: 95
Number verified by Tribunal Commissions: 34

1. Total: 95 medical establishments raided:
   1965 . . . . 131 raids
   First half of 1966 . . . . 54 raids

   From February 7, 1965 to June 30, 1966 . . . . *185 raids*

2. Peak months in bombing raids:
   June 1965 . . . . 30 times
   July 1965 . . . . 19 times
   August 1965 . . . . 23 times

3. Peak Days in Bombing Raids:
   a) May 23, 1965:
      Hospital of Duc Tho district (Ha Tinh)
      Hospital of Nghia Dan district (Nghe An)
      Medical station of Vinh Long village

b) June 16, 1965:
   Old Age Home of Nga Ba Moi (Thanh Hoa)
   The 8th attack on Quynh Lap Leper Sanatorium (7 hours)
   The 9th attack on Quynh Lap Leper Sanatorium (13 hours)
   The 10th attack on Quynh Lap Leper Sanatorium (24 hours)

c) July 9, 10 and 11, 1965:
   Medical Center of Yen Bai province
   Hospital of Yen Bai province
   Anti-Epidemic Station of Yen Bai province
   Anti-Tuberculosis Station of Yen Bai province
   Medical Center for Mothers and Children of Yen Bai province
   Medical Technician's School of Yen Bai province

d) July 25, 1965:
   Hospital of Tuong Duong district (Nghe An)
   Hospital of Con Cuong district (Nghe An)
   Hospital of Nghe An province
   Quynh Lap Leper Sanatorium (15th time)

4. Repeated Attacks in One Day, on One Establishment:
   June 15, 1965:   4, 10 a.m.
                     6:30 a.m.   Quynh Lap Leper Sanatorium
                     1:50 p.m.
   August 15, 1965: Hospital of Ky Anh district (Ha Tinh)
   August 16, 1965: 1:30 a.m.
                    3:15 a.m.
                    5:00 a.m.   Hospital of Ky Anh district (Ha Tinh)
                    9:00 p.m.

5. Kinds of Establishments Bombed and Strafed:
   Province hospitals: 12 (3,610 beds)
   Specialized hospitals: 7 (3,950 beds)
   District hospitals: 22 (1,150 beds)
   Village Infirmary-Maternity Homes: 29 (362 beds)
   Other medical establishments: 10
                                Total: 80 (9,072 hospital-beds)

6. Medical Establishments Repeatedly Raided:
   Hospital of Quang Binh province (11 times)
   Feb. 7, 1965   Sept. 19, 1965
   Feb. 11, 1965   Sept. 23, 1965
   July 24, 1965   Sept. 24, 1965
   July 27, 1965   Oct. 9, 1965
   Sept. 6, 1965   Oct. 14, 1965
   Sept. 11, 1965

   Hospital of Ha Tinh province (17 times)
   July 30, 1965   Nov. 11, 1965
   Aug. 1, 1965   Nov. 18, 1965
   Aug. 13, 1965   Nov. 19, 1965
   Sept. 10, 1965   Apr. 20, 1966
   Sept. 24, 1965   May 10, 1966
   Oct. 5, 1965   May 12, 1966

Oct. 8, 1965	May 14, 1966
Oct. 10, 1965	May 21, 1966
Oct. 13, 1965	

Hospital of Huong Khe district (Ha Tinh province) (8 times)

Mar. 31, 1965	June 3, 1965
Apr. 6, 1965	June 11, 1965
May 27, 1965	June 18, 1965
May 28, 1965	Aug. 13, 1965

Quynh Lap Leper Sanatorium: (39 times)

June 12, 1965	Aug. 17, 1965
June 13, 1965	Aug. 20, 1965
June 14, 1965	Aug. 22, 1965
June 14, 1965	Aug. 25, 1965
June 15, 1965	Aug. 29, 1965
June 15, 1965	Sept. 5, 1965
June 15, 1965	Oct. 8, 1965
June 16, 1965	Oct. 11, 1965
June 16, 1965	Feb. 3, 1966
June 16, 1965	Mar. 5, 1966
June 17, 1965	Mar. 20, 1966
June 17, 1965	Apr. 5, 1966
June 21, 1965	Apr. 21, 1966
July 10, 1965	Apr. 24, 1966
July 25, 1965	May 6, 1966
July 31, 1965	May 6, 1966
Aug. 3, 1965	June 12, 1966
Aug. 4, 1965	June 19, 1966
Aug. 7, 1965	June 24, 1966
Aug. 14, 1965	

*First Commission
†Second Commission
††Fourth Commission
**See testimony of Dr. Abraham Behar page 147*

APPENDIX B

Schools Attacked by the U.S. up to the End of December 1966

Provinces and Cities	Number of Schools Attacked	Schools of the 1st and 2nd Degree	Schools of the 3rd Degree	Kindergarten Schools	Primary Schools	Technical & Professional Secondary Schools	Universities	Miscellaneous Other Schools
Vinh Linh	16	13	1		1			
H-Bac	1	1						
Quang Binh	43	42	2	1		2		
Ha Tinh	74	65	4	3		2		1 Primary Seminary
Thanh Hoa	98	81	4	5	5	2		
Nghe An	64	37	4	14		6	1	1 Primary; 1 Advanced Seminary
Nam Ha	17	11	2	2		2		
Ninh Binh	4	3				1		
Thai Binh	7	6						
Hung Yen	1	1						
Bac Thai	3	2	1					
Ha Tay	1	1						
Tuyen Quang	3	3						
Phu Tho	12	9	1		1	1		
Nghia Lo	1		1	1	1			
Son La	13	7	2	1	1	2		
Yen Bay	13	8	1	1	1	2		
Quang Ninh	4	4						
Vinh Phuc	3	3						
Hanoi	6	2	1	1			2	
Haiphong	2	2						
	391	301	24	29	10	20	3	3

PART III

The Evidence Of Copenhagen

The Fourth, Fifth and Sixth Questions:

4. Have prisoners of war captured by the armed forces of the U.S. been subjected to treatment prohibited by the Laws of War?

5. Have the armed forces of the U.S. subjected the civilian population to inhuman treatment prohibited by the Laws of War?

6. Do the combination of crimes imputed to the Government of the United States in its war in Vietnam constitute the crime of Genocide?

The second session of the International War Crimes Tribunal was held at Roskilde, Denmark. The proceedings began on November 20th and terminated on December 1st, 1967.

Since the end of the Stockholm session on the tenth of May, 1967, the war not only continued, but escalated in intensity. More American troops arrived in Vietnam; Hanoi and Haiphong were being subjected daily to a massive bombardment. By this time more bombs had been dropped on Vietnam than had been used in the whole Pacific Theater of Operations during World War Two. Before the end of 1968, at this rate, it became certain that bomb tonnages used against North and South Vietnam would exceed tonnages dropped in all Theaters — Europe and the Pacific — in World War Two. The larger proportion of these bombs continued to be the murderous CBUs, which the Stockholm Tribunal Session had forced the Pentagon to admit were being massively used.

It was evident that the civilian population of this tiny country was enduring carnage. But there was more to come.

There was no more dramatic moment during the whole Tribunal than on the third day of the Copenhagen session. It was on that day that three American ex-GIs were called in person before the assembly. All were young, all were, in some way typically American — all had committed war crimes. What they related were confessions in every sense of the word. It took courage for them to have come and suffering to tell.

Their testimony was irrefutable. Familiar phrases like "But you see, it happens all the time...," "It was standard operating procedure...," "I had to obey orders...," were often heard.

Opening Statement to the Second Tribunal Session
by Bertrand Russell

As we meet in quiet comfort, the people of Vietnam are made to suffer new and greater crimes. Hour by hour, day by day, the horror intensifies, inflicting wanton pain and torment upon a nation which has known no peace. We are calm and unhurried. We have carried on our work these many months in the tranquility of our laboratories and reading rooms. We have studied the war through the means which are customary to us as scholars. The written word, pictorial evidence, the material remains of incinerated villages — all these are transported to us for examination at our convenience. We form our judgement as we would judge right and wrong in a war of antiquity. The anguish of the Vietnamese people is as remote from our lives as that of a people who are removed from us by centuries.

We have not shared their suffering. Our judgement does not vindicate them, but vindicates ourselves. The idle man has no right of judgement over those who support the concepts of morality and justice by their active struggles against cruelty and injustice. Our words are a small charity, causing us to endure no hardships. Ours is a meagre role in history. Can we consider ourselves actors when the drama of our epoch is a life and death struggle between the peasants of Vietnam and the mechanized slaughter perpetrated from Washington?

The course of history is being shaped in Vietnam. We shall not alter it much by our words. It is the people of Vietnam who refuse to submit to United States hegemony who are altering history. They are proving the might of men inspired by ideals. They face the richest armies and the most modern instruments of extermination. America spends seventy million dollars per day to enact mass murder, but the impoverished nation of Vietnam cannot be deterred. The power of this example will be felt in every continent where the poor have been cowed before the military prowess of their oppressors. The power of their example extends even to the affluent nations of the West, where their heroism has stirred politically inert peoples to massive protest against the new barbarism of the Pentagon. What we may say counts for little beside their deeds. By examining and exposing American war crimes in Vietnam, we do no more than ask to be counted on the side of those who are struggling in a just cause. By fulfilling the minimal obligations which we recognize, we seek merely to avoid moral impotence.

We have already presented conclusive evidence of the aggressive character of the United States intervention in Vietnam. As we proceed, we must recognise how profoundly the concept of aggression covers all of America's crimes in Vietnam. We are not examining a border dispute between Great Powers to determine which is the aggressor, in the sense of the first party to transgress the frontiers of another. In such a case, I should be reluctant to say that the incident of aggression would constitute the totality of all war crimes in the ensuing battles. I do not agree with the rigorous adherence to formal definitions which prevented our placing the bombardment of Hiroshima and Nagasaki on the same moral plane as the crimes of the Axis in World War II. Japan's aggression does not exonerate the United States for using the atomic bomb against civilian centres. But I believe firmly that America's aggression in Vietnam is a pure crime of conquest, delineating precisely between aggressor and victim. I cannot remember any way within my own lifetime in which the term 'naked aggression' so profoundly explained the full meaning of the bloodshed.

In Vietnam there is a race of men who, in modern times, have never been free and who have never known peace. This explains why the war knows no middle course between national salvation and genocide. Men who have known only war, injustice and suffering can make no compromise, for they possess nothing to concede. They may lose their lives, but these were already taken from them. Their culture may be brought to ruin, but it was already perverted and abased by the power of alien forces. Their wealth may be wasted, but it was already stolen. A century of Western oppression forms the prelude to a quarter century of violent strife. The struggle aims not to restore the past, but to create the future. The epic struggle of Vietnam continues so long as one man survives, embodying these hopes, demanding to create a new life, free of impoverishment and fear, with dignity and courage. Every man of this race, who has not been bought by the United States, carries this hope. Each threatens America; for each must be exterminated if America's will is to prevail.

We meet in the coming days to consider the extent to which America is already guilty of genocide, in the most exact juridical sense of the term. America's intent is plain; the logic is unmistakable. Our task is to hear the evidence, document the atrocities, and declare the extent to which this—the most heinous of crimes—has been committed.

Vietnam has much in common with other struggles for justice. Although it is not the task of our Tribunal to consider these other struggles, we cannot forget them. They are the *raisons d'etre* of new tribunals and future enquiries. By our modest effort, we wish to affirm the duty of those who have sought only to contribute to civilisation to stand with the men and women who struggle to uphold its values. Let this remind the complacent that the crimes against the American Negro will also receive the most exhaustive examination. Let this warn the arrogant spokesmen of the "American Century" that the crimes against the people of Latin America will also be exposed.

We are not judges. We are witnesses. Our task is to make mankind bear witness to these terrible crimes and to unite humanity on the side of justice in Vietnam.

Bertrand Russell
November, 1967.

Opening Address to the Second Session
by Jean Paul Sartre

So the second session has begun. I would remind you that we have three principal accusations to consider:

Have the American Forces used or experimented with new weapons, or weapons forbidden by the laws of war, such as gas, special chemicals, etc?

Have Vietnamese prisoners been subjected to inhuman treatment, in particular, torture or multilation, forbidden by the laws of war?

Have there been unjustified reprisals against the civilian population, in particular, execution of hostages? And have camps for forced-labor been created, populations deported, or other acts committed which contribute to the annihilation of the population and which can be legally characterized as acts of genocide?

315

I do not think we need here reconsider our aims, or the problem of the legitimacy of the Tribunal, because all that has been explained at length during the first meeting. I will say that if there is no American here to defend the position of the American government, it is because the American government, which was invited several times to send a representative, refused to send one. Therefore it is not that the Tribunal is one-sided, but that it cannot bring the accused here by force. We asked them very nicely to come, and they have not come. However, if in essence there is no dividing line between the first session and the second session, if we renounce our intention to have a single session, it is because it would have been too lengthy, and been under too difficult, and too costly, conditions. But the two questions to which we responded in the first session are tied to the three questions which we are going to consider this time.

In particular, when we speak of the bombing of civilians, of the systematic and deliberate bombing of the civilian population, we have at hand something which was proved during the first session, something which we have condemned, something which since the first session has been so intensified that our condemnation has been outdated. Having said that, we cannot withdraw the condemnation, because it is complete, but we shall devote this afternoon to the development of the bombings since the condemnation we made in May.

Consequently, and to give you an example of the change, I am bringing to your attention a telegram sent from Hanoi on the 19th of November, 1967, which speaks of the bombing of Hanoi on the 17th of November:

On the 17th of November, the American imperialists once again committed extremely grave crimes against the Vietnamese people.

They launched violent attacks against several residential districts and in the center and in the suburbs of the capital, Hanoi, and in other provinces of North Vietnam. In attacking the capital Hanoi three times, at 7:15, 9:00, and at 10:55, they mobilised planes of the U.S. Navy and the U.S. Air Force, which made 76 attacks, dropped 56 explosive bombs, more than 30 of them being delayed-action bombs, 12 containers containing 200 ball-bombs, including delayed-action ball-bombs, fired 50 fragmentation missiles, thereby killing 33 civilians and wounding 158 more, and destroying numerous dwellings and property belonging to the people. Each of the four urban districts of the capital, Hai Ba Drung, Hoan Kiem, Ba Dinh, Dong Da, as well as the several villages attached to the suburban districts of Gia Lam, Thanh Tri, and Tu Liem were attacked. Just in the Hai Ba Drung district, from the market of Hoah Binh to the market of Mo, on an area of about one square kilometer, U.S. planes dropped six containers containing some 3600 ball-bombs, thereby

killing more than 100 civilians, and setting fire to and damaging hun-
dreds of dwellings. They dropped a great number of ball-bombs and two
explosive bombs of 750 pounds each on the Bach Mai hospital, the biggest
hospital in Hanoi, killing a patient and wounding a doctor, a nurse and
an assistant nurse while they were at work. The ward for infectious di-
seases, the neuro-psychiatric ward, and lodgings reserved for the per-
sonnel of the hospital, were seriously damaged.

The Hai Duong hospital was also attacked. They also dropped ball-
bombs on the Polytechnical School, the Economy-Plan High School, and
on the Music School and its grounds. Just on the Polytechnical School
and on the Economy-Plan High School above, they dropped more than
1000 ball-bombs, killing and wounding more than 25 people. They fired
lacerating cube-missiles on the residential district where the diplomatic
corps are located, in Ba Huyen street, Than Quan street, and at the office
of the International Control Commission at 12 Rue Phan Chu Trinh.
Assistant Officer Mangal Chand, 25 years old, of the Indian Delegation,
was killed by a missile fragment, and another member of the Indian Dele-
gation was wounded. On the same day, American planes also attacked
several residential districts in the city of Haiphong, in the provinces of
Hung Jen, Thai Binh, Nam Ha, Hai Duong, Ninh Binh, Hoa Binh, Ba
Thai, Ha Bac, and numerous places in Thanh Hoa, a region bordering
on the demilitarized zone. Before Vietnamese and foreign opinion, the
commission of enquiry on the war-crimes of the American imperialists in
Vietnam denounces the new grave crimes of the American imperialists.

You see our second session is tied to the first. At bottom, they are
but one. Therefore it requires few words.

Greetings to the Tribunal from American Supporters
address by Carl Oglesby

Mr. Oglesby is an American Playwright and Former President of Students for a Democratic Society; Tribunal Member

I'm very happy to be able to bring greetings to the Tribunal from a new and different America — an America which stands apart now from that America which chooses to wage such an intolerable war on the people of Vietnam. If you would allow me Mr. President, I should like to take a moment or so to describe the situation as it now exists in the United States. It is of interest to this Tribunal to know that it is not what it was when we first convened. It has changed markedly, and it is of importance to this Tribunal to understand that partly through its own work, a radically new situation now obtains.

It is of course difficult to know what's exactly the best way to describe a phenomenon which at bottom is cultural and very complex. There are for one thing, the statistics, which even though they begin to grow a bit dry, nevertheless retain some of their descriptive power. The statistics now speak of the capacities of the American people, once certain facts begin to be at their disposal, to change their views, to develop a resistance against a government which has at its disposal the most compelling, one always wants to say the most monstrous means of controlling thought that have ever been available to any masters of a modern nation state. In spite of the management of the news and the almost unrelieved sycophancy of the media, the truth about the war in Vietnam begins to come home to the American people; and when that truth is known, the American people exhibit again that kind of capacity for courage and dissent which has characterized their most noble moments.

We know today for example, that only 23 percent of the American people approve of the presidency of Lyndon Johnson and his conduct of the war, and that of those who disapprove, the clear majority

318

wants *less* war, not more. The primary difference now seems to be tactical: Should the American withdrawal be unilateral and precipitous or on the contrary should it be handled through negotiations? It is clear in any case that over the last six months Americans have begun to see that the war is a very bad war and must be stopped. They differ now primarily as to the most appropriate and effective mechanism for disengagement.

This new mood is reflected in the opinion polls and in several referenda on the war which have been held recently in several American cities. The most interesting of these was held not long ago in San Francisco, where the people voted on a proposition calling, not for negotiations, but for immediate unilateral withdrawal, pending no negotiations, pending no saving face, pending no rescue of badly damaged American prestige. And even when the issue was drawn in such stark terms, over one-third of the people still voted in favor of the proposition.

It is also important that since we were last together what may prove to be a powerful movement has developed on the inside of the Democratic Party to unseat President Johnson at next year's convention in Chicago. Senator Eugene McCarthy stands at the head of this movement. It is impossible at the moment to say how much to expect from it, but it is clear that it is at least real, it's important, it has the support of powerful leaders in the Democratic Party, and it is sure in some way to combine politically with a similar movement that takes place more quietly within the Republican Party.

But while the statistics can be interesting and while the stories of what happens on high in the United States intrigue us, the new meanings that unfold from the inside of the American culture are sometimes much more acutely discernable in the small events. In this respect, one of the most sharply revealing incidents involves the first leg of President Johnson's recent tour, which this month took him 5000 miles throughout the United States to seven different speech-making stops. It is important about this speech-making tour that it took him not to American cities, but to American military bases. That in itself would be revealing enough. But one detail in particular will draw out the meanings of the present situation still more sharply. Not more than a week ago, I talked with a girl from Students for a Democratic Society who had been in California on November 9, 1967, when President Johnson arrived to make a speech at El Toro Marine Base. She went to his speech intending to do no damage, but merely to see the President in the flesh. Nobody in her car looked especially suspicious. There was no especially long hair. There were no especially bearded faces or ferocious eyes. Nevertheless, her car was stopped and searched at the base, and only when the Marine MPs had satisfied themselves the car carried no anti-war signs was it allowed to pass. Once inside the compound, all automobiles were directed to a parking area, and their passengers were loaded onto buses which shuttled them from the parking area to the place where the speech was to be made. When each bus was filled, a Secret Service man stood up in front and ordered all female passengers to open their purses for inspection. When this Secret Service man saw an SDS button on the girl's collar, he ordered her off the bus. Completely without explanation, she was placed under MP guard, put into a military jeep, and driven off the grounds. Her description was radioed to other entrances, along with an order that she was not to be allowed in. It is a strange land indeed whose President feels so isolated and threatened by his people that such precautions have to be taken.

There are other such incidents. One in particular I think deserves the attention of the Tribunal. It happens to be an intellectual incident. Everyone who knows the main American theory about the Vietnam War understands that the pacification program is considered basic to the military program. The theory is that the United States has to bring the Great Society to Vietnam. The ideology presupposes that all we good Americans want for this Vietnam which we are so badly battering with our pellet bombs and napalm, is a future filled with Fords, split-level suburban homes, and a people as neurosis-ridden and ulcerated as we Americans ourselves. But just recently that liberal view of the war against Vietnam has suffered a setback from another intellectual circle, The Rand Corporation, which you perhaps know is the major Air Force "think-tank". The Rand Corporation has recently concluded a study of pacification efforts in Vietnam from 1960 through 1966. The conclusion reached by the hard-headed analysts of the Rand Corporation is that these widely advertised pacification programs have in fact played into the hands of the National Liberation Front. The study showed that Saigon is not stronger in those areas where its CIA-run "revolutionary programs" have been carried out, but weaker. Saigon's power holds only in those areas of Vietnam where peasants are poorest, structures most oppressive, the culture most feudalistic. In the light of this study, one wonders how much longer the liberal pacification experts can maintain their dreadful fictions.

It seems to me that this report is important particularly for the reason that it represents something much larger. One searches for a phrase that can encompass the potential meanings of what is going on now in America. I would suggest that it does not exaggerate the situation to say that the United States, for the first time since the 1930s, is at this moment undergoing a traumatic "world-view" break-down, the meaning of which is that the people no longer have confidence in their old prophets. It is perhaps a time in which the people are in the process of breaking faith with the shared propositions that have held the culture together and provided the basis for the on-going national consensus. That is to say, the ideas that are in the mainstream today, the ones that were put into place by the New Deal of the '30s, are no longer ideas which can account for the experience which the American people are undergoing. The liberal ideas of the welfare-warfare state cannot explain the American frustration in Vietnam. These ideas cannot explain the rebellion of the black Americans in the ghetto colonies of Chicago, Newark and Detroit. These ideas cannot explain why, in a time of unprecedented prosperity, poverty should continue to grow. Moreover, they cannot explain why the most prosperous generation in America's history, the young white middle class, should also turn out to be the most rebellious.

The student movement is the political form taken on by rebellion of America's post-war generations. That movement has been building since 1962. In 1963, doubling its size, it was still much too small to be seen, although the kinds of work that were ultimately going to produce the present dissent in America had already become basic life patterns for a great many of the country's best young people. And what has happened just this fall has been the coming of a very important pay-off — a preliminary pay-off to be sure, one of uncertain consequences — of that work which has been going on for about five years.

From such military bases as Fort Dix and Fort Hood in the United States, there comes a steady rumor of widespread disaffection from the war, and more and more often the rumor is of rebellion and riot. There are at least 10,000 young Americans in Canada today, refugees from conscription into an unwanted war. Hundreds of deserters are finding asylum in Europe. These events only repeat the obscure but haunting stories one hears everywhere of uneasiness among the American troops in Vietnam, very few of whom appear to understand and accept the Administration's descriptions of its purposes. Beyond all this, however, there is the still more important steady movement of Americans who, like the Vietnamese themselves, are only demanding the opportunity to make their own destinies, to live out their lives on terms which seem to them good, a movement of people who no longer believe it is in their interest to go about in the world like fools, ruining the lives of people who mean them no harm and whose primary struggle is merely to come into contact with the resources and possibilities of their countries.

Just this October, that movement of the young has reached some kind of crescendo and has exhibited a militant anger which last spring was foreign to it. In October, in one blow, a thousand young men turned in their draft-cards. At Brooklyn College there was a most militant rebellion, less militant only than the rebellion which followed by a few days at the University of Wisconsin, in Madison, where hundreds of students staged a three hour-long pitched battle against a special corps of riot police. At the same time as this was going on, there was a week of sustained militant action against the draft-board involving thousands of people in Oakland, California. The entire movement, a machine gun burst in the American calm, culminated in the mass action in Washington, D.C. on October 21, where among other things, one saw the flag of the National Liberation Front being planted on the lawn of the Pentagon and even carried inside its doors.

The Tribunal has played an important role in the developing of the consciousness which instills this militancy among America's young people. For one thing, the Tribunal has established a clear legal base for that mass refusal of induction which in the U.S. we call the Resistance Movement. Even more important, however, is the fact that the Tribunal has been the clearing-house of information on the war. You understand that it is not easy always for us, unless we probe with great care, to get an accurate picture of what actually happens in Vietnam. The Tribunal's capacity for pulling together and then developing in a most public and conspicuous way the elements of the war's reality — this function has been very important to us in the United States. Everybody in America these days knows about the anti-personnel bombs (CBU), and a good many of those who have heard have been moved to revulsion and then rebellion. Perhaps even more important in the long term as a specific Tribunal function is that it creates in the very heart of the West a window on the Third World. We who live among the oppressors and who try to fight them in our lives need as acutely to know what happens in Bolivia, in Argentina and in Ghana as well as what happens in Paris, London and New York. This represents a most vital role for the Tribunal to fill in the building of an internationally solid New-Left movement.

Finally and most generally, the one important message I want to bring the Tribunal from the American movement, is that it is no longer necessary for you to think that it is one monolithic America which is waging war against the Vietnamese. America is a deeply divided place. Indeed, there is a small but very visibly growing America, an America which grows more visible and larger every minute. That smaller but growing America has declared peace with the Vietnamese and war against their enemies. It is for that America that I speak now and it is from those very brave brothers of mine who have met the mobilization orders with anger and contempt, from those who have the audacity to refuse to be criminals in a criminal America that I bring to the Tribunal greetings, gratitude and a strong sense of fraternity.

Report on the Law of War
testimony by Yves Jouffa

Attorney of the Court of Paris

In order to answer the second question of this session, the Tribunal will have to decide if the character of the American counter-insurgency activities is immense, indiscrimate and destructive and, in consequence, is in violation of the fundamental rules of war that figure in International Law, at least after the formulation of the Convention of the Hague of 1907.

The principles posed by the Convention of the Hague are very important. The Preamble of Convention No. IV respecting the Laws and Customs of War on Land — 18th of October, 1907 states:

"Until a more complete code of the laws of war has been issued, the High Contracting Parties deem it expedient to declare that, in cases not included in the Regulations adopted by them, the inhabitants and the belligerents remain under the protection and the rule of the principles of the law of nations, as they result from the usages established among civilized peoples, from the laws of humanity, and from the dictates of the public conscience."

Article 22: "The right of belligerents to adopt means of injuring the enemy is not unlimited."

Article 23: "In addition to the prohibitions provided by special Conventions, it is especially forbidden: . . . e) To employ arms, projectiles, or material calculated to cause unnecessary suffering."

Article 25: "The attack or bombardment, by whatever means, of towns, villages, dwellings, or buildings which are undefended is prohibited."

Article 27: "In sieges and bombardments all necessary measures must be taken to spare, as far as possible, buildings dedicated to religion, art, science, or charitable purposes, historic monuments, hospitals, and places where the sick and wounded are collected, provided they are not being used at the time for military purposes. It is the duty of the besieged to indicate the presence of such buildings or places by distinctive and visible signs, which shall be notified to the enemy beforehand."

The most important problem in the air war is that of bombing; that is, the protection of the civil population and of non-combatants. Prior to the outbreak of the Second World War a number of attempts were made to establish an authoritative code of air warfare. The most important of these was the draft drawn up by a conference of jurists, convoked by the Governments participating in the Washington Conference, that met at The Hague from December 1922 to February 1923. This commission embodied its findings in a convention which allowed the bombing of military forces, military establishments and factories engaged in war production *(Art. 24/3)* but forbade aerial bombardment for the purpose of terrorizing the civilian population. *(Art. 22)*. The general principle followed was that air attacks are, "legitimate only when directed at a military objective — that is to say, an object of which the destruction or injury would constitute a distinct military advantage to the belligerent" *(Art. 24/1).*[1]

The question had also been examined by the League of Nations. The Assembly of September 30, 1938, for example, "considering that a new consecration had to be given to these principles, recognizes the following principles as a necessary basis for any subsequent regulation: 1) The intentional bombardment of civilian populations is contrary to Law. 2) The objectives aimed at from the air must constitute legitimate military objectives, and must be identifiable. 3) Any attack on legitimate military objectives must be carried out in such a way that the civilian population in the vicinity not be bombed through negligence. (Document A.69 of the League of Nations, 1938, unofficial translation from the French.)

These general principles were repeated in Article 6 of the Statute of the International Military Tribunal at Nuremberg:

Article 6: "The following acts, or any of them, are crimes coming within the jurisdiction of the Tribunal for which there shall be individual responsibility: . . .

---

[1]Quoted in Arthur L. Goodhardt, *What Acts of War are Justifiable?* Oxford, 1940, p. 16. The complete draft convention is reproduced in Spaight, *Air Power,* 1947, pp. 498-508.

b) War Crimes: namely, violations of the laws and customs of war. Such violations shall include, but not be limited to, murder, ill-treatment or deportation to slave labor or for any other purpose of civilian population of or in occupied territory, murder or ill-treatment of prisoners of war or persons on the seas, killing hostages, plunder of public or private property, wanton destruction of cities, towns or villages, or devastation not justified by military necessity."

This is very noteworthy since it is a point where the Allies were the most vulnerable.

Article 18: "Civilian hospitals organized to give care to the wounded and sick, the infirm and maternity cases, may in no circumstances be the object of attack, but shall at all times be respected and protected by the Parties to the conflict. States which are Parties to a conflict shall provide all civilian hospitals with certificates showing that they are civilian hospitals and that the buildings which they occupy are not used for any purpose which would deprive these hospitals of protection in accordance with Article 19."

Article 53 "Any destruction by the Occupying Power of real or personal property belonging individually or collectively to private persons, or to the State, or to other public authorities, or to social or cooperative organizations, is prohibited, except where such destruction is rendered absolutely necessary by military operations."

The Constitution of the United States Art. VI, Cl. 2, establishes:

"This Constitution, and the laws of the United States, which shall be made in pursuance thereof; and all treaties made or which shall be made under the authority of the United States, shall be the supreme law of the land; and the Judges in every State shall be bound thereby, anything in the Constitution or Laws of any State to the Contrary notwithstanding."

Chapter 1, Section 1, Paragraph 9 of the "Law of Land Warfare, Manual of the Department of the Army, F.M. 7-10 July, 1956", establishes that the treaties relative to the "war enter in force, also in the absence of formal war declaration."

This principle has been applied in the "High Command Case" cited by *The American Political Science Review:* "Superior Orders, Nuclear Warfare and the Dilemma of Military Obedience in the Atomic Age." March 1961, page 16.

The Principles of Humanity

The judgment in the *"High Command Case"* declared that "under international law, criminality may arise not only because an act is forbidden by international agreements, but also when it "is inherently criminal and contrary to accepted principles of humanity as recognized and accepted by civilized nations." This finding was based on Article 6 (c) of the Charter of the International Military Tribunal and the corresponding clause in Control Council Law No. 10.

Therefore the Tribunal, without violating International Law ought to decide if the texts, the essence to which I have referred, have been literally violated. But, referring to these proper texts, it will be able to recall the requirements part of the Convention IV of the Hague, 1907, before the promulgation of the Kellogg-Briand Pact that, in 1920, condemned war as such.

Thus, the Law requires the highest moral preoccupations such as Lord Bertrand Russell and the President of the Tribunal, Jean-Paul Sartre, recalled them in their introductory messages.

I would like to end with a remark that I believe very important. If you answer in the affirmative to the first question, if you believe that the U.S. war in Vietnam is a war of aggression and by its nature constitutes a severe violation of International Law, you have to decide, as I see it, that the other crimes and notably those that are the object of the present report necessarily follow from the first one.

An imperialist aggression inevitably produces resistance by the people in the aggressed country. This is why you cannot condemn resistance by the people aggressed against, and if, during the war, the aggressor finds himself "in danger" or is "very menaced," the danger in question comes from himself. You therefore ought to refute the theory of "necessity of war" that already was refuted by the Nuremberg Tribunal as expressed:

"The theory on the necessity of war can only be used, if it leads to a demonstration that the act has been realized precisely in order to avoid a more severe and irreparable accident, that there does not exist any other way to avoid it and that the losses derived thereof are smaller than those that one has succeeded to spare."

This is precisely the profound meaning of the question posed to the Tribunal and it is, as I see it, in this way that the Tribunal shall work, not only for Peace in Vietnam but shall also create jurisprudence for the future.

Incendiary Weapons, Poison Gas, Defoliants Used in Vietnam
testimony by Abraham Behar, M.D.

Principles and Methods of Work of the Scientific Committee

The Tribunal has assigned us the task of assembling a commission of experts in order to make the necessary elucidations concerning the question: "Have new or forbidden arms been used in Vietnam?"

During the Session in Stockholm, proof was already given that new weapons, the ball-bombs, were in wide use against the civilian population of Vietnam.

We shall now consider, in particular, poisons, forbidden by written and unwritten laws that have been sanctioned by usage and custom, such as poison gas and weed-killers, whose toxicity affects human beings, animals, and crops. In this connection, we shall also study new incendiary weapons, not because of the mechanism employed, but because of their massive use by the United States against the population. Here we should like to: 1) Explain why our study is divided into three headings — poison gas, weed-killers, and incendiary products. 2) Give an account of the methods of investigation and of experimental study. 3) Emphasize what directly answers the questions posed in the three chapters.

1. *Justification of the Division*

Concerning incendiary products, we can say that by their effects (the destruction by fire of people, animals, plants, and inanimate objects) napalm, supernapalm, magnesium bombs, and white phosphorous all have a common characteristic. By contrast, if we consider the two groups of substances used in chemical warfare, poison gas on the one hand, and "defoliants" on the other, then there are two separate concerns:

   a) One is the legal question, since the condemnation of the use of gas in warfare seems, at least for a number of countries, to be well-established, while the destruction of crops by the use of chemical products is not specifically covered by the law.

b) The second is a scientific matter, because gas and weed-killers work differently. Gas is an anti-personnel weapon used directly against people and animals, while the weed-killers used against the crops only affects living creatures indirectly (above all by famine, but also by the consumption of contaminated food).

However, I draw the attention of the Tribunal to the fact that all these products, including white phosphorous, are poisons . . .The notion of toxicity, that is to say, impairment of health with the possibility of death, is applicable to both groups of substances. But the threshold of toxicity, i.e., the lethal dose, the minimum concentration of the substance necessary to kill a man, varies depending on the substance.

2. *Methods of Study*

The Scientific Commission collected and analyzed data systematically from official American sources, and from the results of scientific work published in the United States relevant to the subject-matter considered in the three chapters of our report. We did the same with information and testimony from Vietnamese, Laotian, and Cambodian sources. By Vietnamese sources we mean the DRV and the NLF.

This analysis was compared with the testimony of Commissions of Inquiry of the Tribunal which made on-the-spot verifications of the veracity of the facts as reported by the two parties. Finally, the Scientific Commission conducted and directed experiments of a scientific nature on certain specific points. Thus you shall be called to judge the totality of our work. It must however be said that the methods of scientific evaluation were different according to which of the three chapters defined above is being considered.

a) *Incendiary Weapons*

Pricrity was given here to proving deliberate and massive use outside the battle areas. To assist the Tribunal in this respect, the Scientific Commission would like to clarify the effects on living creatures of napalm, supernapalm, and phosphorous. Their effects are not limited to immediate ones, to wounds only. When napalm burns it releases a poisonous gas, carbon monoxide, the effect of which is quite significant on the victims. White phosphorous has a direct effect on the organism which contributes greatly to a slow death. Professor Dreyfus, of the Medical Faculty of Paris, shall amplify these points.

b) *Defoliants*

Two approaches were taken in this connection by the Scientific Commission.

i) A description of the mechanism by which defoliants act on vegetation, and an explanation of the selective destruction of food crops, such as rice. It was important to show that phytotoxic substances are also poisonous to living creatures, i.e., humans and animals. For example, the acid 2,4,-D (2-4-dichlorophenoxy-acetic) has a lethal dose of 50 mice at 275 mg/kg. That is to say, if we take different lots of mice, injections at a concentration of 275 mg. per kg. of weight of the mice, will result in a 50% mortality on the avarage. Another example: DNOC (4.6 Dinitro-C-cresol) has a lethal dose of 50 mice at 10 mg/kg. That is to say, thirty times more poisonous than in the first example.

ii) A precise determination of the massive extent of the use of phytotoxic substances in South Vietnam seemed to us important. Important both on account of the use of airplanes to spray these products, and on account of Vietnamese testimony, and the declarations of American specialists. As an example, I ask the Tribunal to consider the following statistics, furnished by the NLF of South Vietnam: 1961 — The spraying of weed-killer in 6 provinces — 500 hectares of crops destroyed (hectare - 2.47 acres). 1962 — 12 provinces sprayed; 11,030 hectares destroyed. And the latest figure we have of 1966 — 32 provinces sprayed; 876,490 hectares of crops destroyed.

Such an attack against the agriculture of Vietnam naturally has grave consequences in regard to the feeding of the civilian population of the liberated zones. The Commission, in particular Professor Minkowski, will bring you the necessary facts.

c) *Poison Gas*

A first difficulty ought to be mentioned — poison gas is manufactured in the form of a powder. In fact (to use the excellent definition provided by the *New York Times* of 3 January 1966), it is a powder which is transformed into a gas when agitated. On this subject, it is not difficult to demonstrate the reality when we speak of the use of gas in Vietnam, i.e., in South Vietnam. This has already been officially admitted by the Pentagon. We shall be able to show this poisonous powder to the Tribunal, a poison that was collected by the Commission of Inquiry, and whose properties were verified by a scientific laboratory in Paris. We shall consider the following two aspects of the problem at hand in order to clarify the situation for your judgment:

1) *Degree of Toxicity of Gases*

This demonstration is of importance, since it establishes that, under the specific conditions as used in Vietnam, the gases are not only harmful to the health of the population, but also result in death.

For example: C.N. (chloroacetopheneone), in an air suspension, produces a transitory irritation of the cornea and the appearance of tears at the weak concentration of 1/10,000 mg. per liter of air; a serious irritation of the eyes and of the respiratory tract at a concentration of 2/1000 mg. per liter; and death through acute inflammation and pulmonary edema at strong concentrations of 10 to 15 mg. per liter of air. The same demonstration will be made for D. M. (Adamsite) and for C.S. (chlorobenzylidenemalononitrate).

Toxicology and results of experiments in laboratories on animals will thus be of great importance for you in understanding the consequences of these gases on human lives.

2) *Uses of Toxic Gases*

The use of powder as a vehicle is important since it illustrates the massive and indiscriminate nature of the attacks on the civilian population. Whether this powder be delivered by cylindrical grenades, oval grenades, or cases containing ten packets of the products weighing 8 pounds each, this is an indiscriminate delivery system. This characteristic indiscriminateness becomes even clearer when we consider the launching method which uses rocket ramps having 16 projecting tubes, each containing four gas powder-loaded missiles.

In the case where the toxic product is effectively delivered by nebulising apparatus which selectively vapourises the gas into the tunnels and underground shelters where the population has sought refuge, this application under pressure produces lethal concentrations which you will see reprodced in the laboratory.

The case in which the hamlet of Vinh Quang in Binh Dinh province was cleared on the 5th of September 1963, is an example of this lethal use. The spraying of 48 toxic gas containers into the shelters there resulted in the death of 35 persons and seriously poisoned 25 others. Out of the total of 60, it should be mentioned that 28 were children and 26 women.

Grave Problems Imposed by these Types of Weapons

These weapons are poisons, they are a terrifying means of destruction, but above all:

a) incendiary weapons, napalm or phosphorous, inflict indescribable suffering on those persons burnt; their special use against the civilian population only adds to their horror.

b) the phytotoxins imperil the present and future state of South Vietnamese agriculture and the natural balance of its ecology.

c) the toxic gases are most often lethal in their effect, capable of causing death to living beings; and the method of their use in tunnels and shelters is a further factor of toxicity.

The Scientific Commission wishes to emphasize to the Tribunal its report on these three points. Also it is important to realize that these efforts have only been possible through the contribution of American journalists and scientists who have publicised all these facts, through the contribution of Japanese scientists who have worked long and in detail in their laboratories in order to make these phenomena comprehensible, and finally through the remarkable work of the Commissions of Inquiry of the DRV and the NLF. A confrontation with the official viewpoint of the United States spokesman can be made in full clarity of these facts . . .

On Chemical and Biological Warfare in Vietnam
testimony by Alexandre Minkowski, M.D.

Professor of Pediatrics, Paris Faculty of Medicine; Director of Biological Research of Port Royal Hospital, Paris; Rockefeller Fellow to Harvard University; Visiting Professor at Harvard, Yale, Stanford, University of Illinois; Professor University of Colorado

I'm particularly happy that this session is being chaired by an American [Dellinger]. Part of the documents which I shall use are of American origin. I would like to recommend that members of the Tribunal read *Science and Citizens,* Vol. 9, No. 7 of September 1967. In it there is an excellent article by a Professor of Nutrition from Harvard, John Mayer, which is called "Starvation as a Weapon: Herbicides in Vietnam."

In presenting a summary of the effects of defoliant products in Vietnam, I shall not go into the biochemical details, as that is covered in the numerous reports, but I would like to stress the consequences of defoliation.

I think that it's obvious that a product which, at the start, is meant simply to make the leaves of a tree fall is not *per se* noxious. However, it seems that in the long run, and on a long term basis, this might be one of the most dangerous and terrible forms of biochemical warfare. In principle, the aim of defoliation is to destroy the cover of the land and therefore to make troops easier for airplanes to see. Another of its aims is to starve those who are fighting.

But, it was very quickly realized that these weapons, when they are used on a large scale, are toxic for the population and particularly for the children. And even though I'm not a specialist in biochemistry, this is one of the reasons why I was asked to summarize this report. These products destroy the food supply, and among the populations which are famine struck, the children are the weakest and first to fall.

I would like to proceed by recalling the background of this problem, then I will briefly speak of the products which are used and the way in which they are used. I will furnish evidence that such products are used, and most importantly, discuss the consequences of their use. That is, I will draw certain technical conclusions concerning these products and their toxicity and their influence on nutrition.

Now these chemical products are used in agriculture to kill weeds and to make leaves of the cotton plant fall in order to facilitate mechanical harvesting. During the Second World War the United States and Great Britain attempted to develop chemical products capable of destroying the rice fields of Japan to starve the population to the point of surrender. It was then that one of the products currently being used in Vietnam, 2,4D, was developed. In Great Britain, MCPA, that is, 2 methyl—4 chlorolphenoxyacetic acid was prepared. And then there were others which I shall not list here. But there are mineral substances which penetrate into the plant, particularly during its growing life; and these herbicides lose their efficiency during the dry season. Today organic herbicides are being used. We have two types of these on the table here; we gathered them on the spot in Vietnam. One is 2,4D which I mentioned a moment ago, the other is 2,4,5T, and finally, DNOC which we also gathered on the spot.

Some herbicides act in the following way: there are certain chemical products which stimulate the growth of plants, but when they are used at extremely high dosages they become defoliants. And finally, there are certain herbicides which are more particularly absorbed by the roots of the plant. This is the case with the triasins and substitute urias. With regard to the way in which intoxication of the plant is brought about, the defoliants absorbed by the leaves do not entirely intoxicate the plant and vegetation can continue if the recommended dosage is respected. This is precisely the problem, as you will see when I go into the method of use of these products. If one uses them at dosages which are 10 or 100 times higher than that which is necessary for simple defoliation, this is another matter. And, as my report will show, they are not used according to the recommendations which are given, and therefore all vegetation is killed, the area of damage becomes extensive, and lastly, these products become toxic for human beings.

And so, the claim of some who say that the war is being waged in a "humanitarian" way with these chemicals, because one is simply using defoliants to make leaves drop off, is invalidated when the dosage is changed to the toxic level. I also want to mention that arsenic products are being used and the word alone recalls toxicity.

On the action of herbicides, if one uses the normal dose for simple defoliation, the plant is still damaged, for if the leaves are no longer there, photosynthesis will cease. The product will penetrate into the plant and it will become intoxicated. The effect of herbicides is not always immediate. In some cases, with 2,4D, for instance, it is only the next year that one notes characteristic deformations of the plant. DNOC, which you see here, and all chemical agents of the same type make the leaves drop simply because they kill the plant. The persistence of active chemical products can be seen to remain in the earth where the destroyed vegetation was formerly growing. If one changes the type of crop, the sensitivity of the new crop may not necessarily be the same, and this can lead to very serious damage. This is because defoliants have a marked effect on some types, while others are more or less resistant. Even if they have not been aimed at directly, the large scale spreading of defoliants often destroys food plants because these toxical products poison large areas by spreading through the water. Wind also causes mis-application of the sprays and they can have an effect as much as ten kilometers from where they were originally spread.

The spraying is usually done in the morning and each aircraft can carry about 4,000 liters of herbicide and spray about 30 liters per hectare. I have taken these statistics from the American press. The spreading process takes about five minutes, but if necessary for tactical reasons, the whole 4,000 liters in the reservoirs can be jettisoned in 30 seconds...

Sometimes the planes dive down to spray at tree-top level, about 50 meters in altitude, at a speed of about 750 kilometers. When spraying begins, one can smell an odor reminiscent of a hospital smell. When one returns a few weeks after the spraying he can begin to see the change in the countryside. It looks as if Fall were come, the plants are dry and the leaves crackle and crumble to the hand.

This indiscriminate spraying has had very serious consequences for the culture of rubber trees in Vietnam. When I speak of rubber trees, I mean the *Hevea* and *Jacquiers,* and other similar species. The rubber plantations in Vietnam have experienced a drop in production on the order of 30% and it will undoubtedly get larger. It is probable that rubber culture in Vietnam is permanently jeopardized by this kind of warfare.

I would like to refer you to my written report, and then speak of the destruction of the equilibrium of the human environment that is also jeopardized by these sprayings. This again, arises because of the violation of the recommended dosages and the subsequent toxicity and nutritional deprivation.

A series of scientific observations have shown that forests have a regulating role in maintaining the balance in the biological and human environments. It is quite obvious that when the environment is modified, the climate is modified, and above all, the destruction of food crops will result in enormously diminished nutrition and will lead sometimes to complete starvation in the population. Here again, I will refer you to the article of John Mayer in *Science and Citizens.* Mayer recalls that destruction of crops began in the Spring of 1965 when 2,4D and 2,4,5T were sprayed by C-123 "Providers." The U.S. Army realized that rice is extremely difficult to destroy, but if you try hard enough you can do it.[1] The use of herbicides for defoliation before ripening is quite effective, however, and can lead to losses as high as 60 to 90% of the harvest.

---

[1]It has just been learned that U.S. scientists have been successful in developing a specific biological agent for destruction of rice in the growing stage. It was developed under the direction of the U.S. Army Munitions Command Headquarters at Picatinny Arsenal in Morris County, New Jersey. Research and development was probably with the cooperation of the Edgewood Arsenal in Edgewood, Maryland, and the Fort Detrick, Frederick, Maryland, CBW facilities, plus numerous University and corporate laboratories. The new weapon is based on an extract and culture of "Rice Blast," a rare natural disease of rice plants. This new bio-weapon is stable, resistant to cures, has a long shelf-life, and can be easily spread over large paddy-field areas. A weapon of this nature is of no use except in countries such as those of Asia, where rice is the primary staple food of the population. It is probable also, that the "Rice Blast" bio-weapon has already been tested in Vietnam. The consequences of extensive tactical use of this new weapon for the Asian continent would be catastrophic. Ed. Note.

Dr. Mayer has pointed out that the enemy military are apparently not affected by this, because when the Americans take NFL prisoners, they are seldom, if ever, suffering from insufficient nutrition and are quite capable of continuing their soldiering. On the other hand, as is always so with people who have a low nutritional level to begin with, it is the people who suffer the most, the old, the children and pregnant women. I'm not going to catalogue the dangerous nutritional diseases of children, but two diseases that strike children frequently and have a high mortality prognosis result from insufficient nutrition. They have a series of symptoms, the belly swells, the liver is attacked and leads to death if treatment is not begun at once. Even where treatment is possible nutritional deficiency residual effects can be left on the brain centers and emotional development. So much for the children.

Now, because of the state of famine, there occur large scale migration of the people in search of food. There are certain diseases which attack such a migratory population — diseases which had been wiped out in certain parts of Vietnam and which are now reappearing, particularly (and here I quote Doctor Tach, Minister of Health of the D.R.V.) cholera and the plague.[2]

We realize now too, that these herbicides are toxic for animals and human beings; again I refer you back to my written report. Substances which are not noxious at the start, can become noxious and lead to different kinds of lesions, the most important being burns on the skin and irritation of the lungs which can be lethal. The action can be through direct or indirect contact, as has happened with children — I have a Vietnamese report on this subject which is enlightening — who have eaten meat or fish which had been contaminated. All these products are extremely dangerous.

If one takes 2,4D, for example, one of the products most frequently used, one finds by laboratory tests that it is toxic for 50% of an experimental batch of mice at 375 milligrams, at 686 milligrams for the rat, and only 100 milligrams for the dog. It is spectacularly toxic for fish, and fish, I remind you is the second most important food in Vietnam. Some other effects of these products are chromosomic disturbances which can lead to genetic complications. Ingested residues of these

---

[2]According to recent information, Picatinny Arsenal has also developed a strain of *Pasteurella pestis* (the bacillus of Bubonic Plague) that is resistant to common antibiotics. This information was furnished by research of the New Community, of Madison, New Jersey, for which we thank them. Ed.Note.

products inhibit thyroid activity and we have even noted lesions which are very comparable to those which one can see in the experimental inducing of cancer with cancer-producing hydrocarbons. It is apparent that when you use herbicides in this massive way you must expect very long term catastrophes. For figures concerning this massive spraying, I refer you to my written report [readers of this volume may see the Report of the Sub-Committee on Chemical and Biological Warfare by Edgar Lederer.] . . .

I will conclude with a short personal comment. It is my belief that this war, which is a particularly terrible one, uses products of this type because in this way it is possible to reassure American public opinion and assuage the conscience of the average American, whereas in actuality we are tending toward one of the most devestatingly imaginable forms of chemical warfare. I will answer questions, which I prefer to be of a medical rather than a biological nature.

DELLINGER: *I'd like your comment on Professor Neilands statement that the defoliation program is being escalated from a $6 million operation last year to a $60 to $100 million operation this year.*

I think it's obvious that the medical and other human effects of such an increased program must be greatly intensified.

PETER WEISS: You mentioned the effect on the cattle in Vietnam. We all know the importance of the water buffalo, as an essential animal in the life of the peasant. Will the effect of this chemical destruction always destroy the cattle or is it only sometimes?

I think it varys. In some cases of simple defoliation they are not affected. It depends on the quantity and speed of the drop plus the dosage. In some cases it effects only a part of the cattle, in others almost all are destroyed. If you permit me some time, I can make abstracts from my statistics and I will give you figures which may be of some use.

DELLINGER: *Perhaps you made this clear, Professor Minkowski, and I missed it, but you make a connection between the use of herbicides and the incidence of cholera and plague in Vietnam. Also, are you speaking of South Vietnam or North Vietnam?*

There are two factors. First of all, it has already been mentioned that when food crops are destroyed the population must migrate a great deal and migration in itself increases the incidence of epidemics. There's always a little bit of plague, of cholera and of malaria present in South Vietnam. This always, refers to South Vietnam. I believe Dr. Tach could inform you of the conditions in the North. So as a result of this migration, diseases which formerly had been confined to certain areas, become epidemic in a wider area.

Secondly, in answer to your question, famine — and you don't have to be a doctor to realize this — greatly decreases the individual's resistance to these diseases. I repeat, that plague and cholera, while they existed endemically, have now become disseminated widely and are of epidemic proportions in the South.

In the North the problems are not the same. I think this is because of the high level of organization of the preventive medicine in the North. I am particularly familiar with Chinese preventive medicine and I would like to point out that this is one of the most extraordinary organizations of preventive medicine in the world. A great many Western countries, even the United States and France, could take this as an example. Now, in the North, I think that I can clearly say these diseases are extremely rare, precisely because of the strides in public health and preventive medicine. This does not mean that in the South, in areas controlled by the National Liberation Front, there's no preventive medicine, but the dispersion of populations and the conditions under which they must work make it much more difficult.

CARL OGLESBY: *Doctor, just for clarification at this point, do you know of any instances of the use of herbicides or defoliants in the North, or are all of these instances from the South?*

Of course, predominantly the reports I have cover the South. But as far as I know at the moment herbicides have been used in the North, but not so extensively. It must have been used in the North, but how much I don't know. If you want exact figures. I think I could supply them in the afternoon.

OGLESBY: *I'd be especially interested, too, in the attacks on rubber plantations as we've heard that production had been driven down approximately 30% because of herbicidal attacks on the rubber plantations. If you could, perhaps in consultation with Dr. Tach, I'd like a comment on what possible military use there could be in attacks on rubber plantations.*

I don't think I can answer that last part of your question . . .

Report of the Sub-Committee on Chemical Warfare in Vietnam

Compiled by the Biochemists and Nutritionists of the Region of Paris, Under the Direction of Edgar Lederer, Professor of the Faculty of Sciences, Paris-Orsay

Chemical warfare is condemned in several international agreements:

1. A protocol for the prohibition of the use in war of asphyxiating, poisonous or other gases, and of bacteriological warfare, was signed at Geneva on 17 June 1925. The text of the substantive part of the protocol reads as follows:

"Whereas the use in war of asphyxiating, poisonous or other gases, and of all analogous liquids, materials or devices, has been justly condemned by the general opinion of the civilized world, and,

"Whereas the prohibition of such use has been declared in Treaties to which the majority of Powers of the world are Parties; and,

"To the end that this prohibition shall be universally accepted as a part of International Law, binding alike the conscience and the practice of nations,
"Declare:

"that the High Contracting Parties, so far as they are not already Parties to Treaties prohibiting such use, accept this prohibition and agree to extend this prohibition to the use of bacteriological methods of warfare and agree to be bound as between themselves according to the terms of this declaration.[1]

---

[1]The United States delegation proposed the ban on gas. The protocol is in force with respect to most countries, including the United Kingdom, France, the Federal Republic of Germany, Italy, the Peoples Republic of China, and the U.S.S.R. The United States and Japan signed but did not ratify the protocol.

2. United States policy on gas warfare was expressed in the statement made on June 9, 1943, by President Roosevelt, who was reportedly under military pressure to use gas in the Pacific. "Use of such weapons has been outlawed by the general opinion of mankind... I state categorically that we shall under no circumstances resort to the use of such weapons unless they are first used by our enemies."

3. The XXth International Conference of the Red Cross, on October 1965, in Vienna, adopted a resolution concerning the "protection of Civilian populations against the dangers of indiscriminate warfare. It ends as follows:

"Expressly invites all Governments who have not yet done so to accede to the Geneva Protocol of 1925 which prohibits the use of asphyxiating, poisonous, or other gases, all analogous liquids, materials or devices, and bacteriological methods of warfare."

4. The General Assembly of the United Nations in its 148th Plenary Meeting on December 5, 1966,

"1) *Calls* for strict observations by all States of the principles and objectives of the Protocol for the prohibition of the use in war of asphyxiating, poisonous or other gases, and of bacteriological methods of warfare, signed at Geneva on 17 June 1925, and condemns all actions contrary to those objectives;

2) *Invites* all states to accede to the Geneva Protocol of 17 June 1925."

Nevertheless, some (for instance, General J. H. Rothschild, who has served as Chemical Officer of the U.S. Far East Command) argue for the use of chemicals which "are bringing some degree of humanity into warfare."

In a letter published in *Science*, 1967, *156*, J. T. Edsall and M. Meselson, Professors at Harvard University, answered these arguments and emphasized the damage caused primarily to the weakest, women, children and old people. "Is it 'humane' to make persons emerge from protective cover" [after gas has been employed] "to face saturation attack by fragmentation bombs?" In the same letter the authors continue: "...We would like to quote the strategic analyst T. C. Schelling in *Arms and Influence,* Yale University, Press, New Haven, 1966, p.131, on possible agreements for preventing the use of gas in warfare:

" 'Some gas' raises complicated questions of how much, where, under what circumstances; 'no gas' is simple and unambiguous. Gas only on military personnel; gas used only by defending forces; gas only when carried by projectile; no gas without warning—a variety of limits is conceivable... But there is a simplicity to 'no gas' that makes it uniquely a focus for agreement when each side can only conjecture at what alternative rules the other side would propose and when failure at coordination on the first try may spoil the chances for acquiescence in any limits at all."

Combat Gases in Vietnam

a) Tear gases and other gases

On March 28th 1965, *The New York Times,* quoting McNamara indicated the three principal products spread from helicopters and bombers on "enemy territory".

DM (diphenylaminochlorarsine which causes in progressive order; irritation of the eyes and mucous membranes, viscous discharge from the nose, sneezing, coughing, severe headache, acute pains and tightness of chest, nausea and vomiting. *CN (choroacetophenone)* Lachrymatory. Also irritates upper respiratory passages. In high concentration, irritates the skin, especially on moist parts of the body. *CS (chlorobenzalmalononitrile)* which causes extreme burning of the eyes and a profuse flow of tears; constricts respiratory tract; burns moist skin; induces nausea. Incapacitates at 1-6 mg/per cubic meter; at 20 mg/per cubic meter, it causes irreparable lesions.

When asked if cyanides and arsenical compounds were used in Vietnam, Cyrus R. Vance, Undersecretary of State for Defense, declared at a Washington conference on foreign policy "we are using them in a limited way in South Vietnam, but not yet in the North" — *Daily Pennsylvanian,* November 1st, 1965. Even as early as 1964, incidents of the use of gas took place in Cambodia[2]. From *Vietnam;*

---

[2] Cambodia placed complaints before the Security Council concerning incursions of South Vietnamese troops and machine-gunning against the national territory, denounced more than once, particularly on July 29th, 1964, the use of chemical warfare in the course of American-Vietnamese air raids, five times between June 6th and July 23rd, 1964 (after M. Sakka, *Vietnam Guerre Chimique et Biologique,* p. 15, Editions Sociales, Paris, 1967).

N.Y. Times, April 12, 1965 (Tokyo, UPI) April 11: Cambodia states that Thailand drops "noxious chemicals." A Cambodian report said the chemicals were dropped late in March over villages in the Pailin region of Battambang Province in west-central Cambodia. More than 100 persons died after similar incidents last June and July in a province that borders South Vietnam."

Documents sur la Guerre Chimique et Bacteriologique," a pamphlet edited by the *Comite National Suisse d'Aide au Vietnam,* Geneva, 1967, we know that "gases of the type CN or DM have been used in South Vietnam since the end of 1964" (December 23'rd, 1964 at Ca Mau and December 15th, 1964 at Tay Ninh). In Jan. 1965 they were used at the same time as explosive and napalm bombs against the population of the village of Phu Lac.

The use of gas in South Vietnam released a wave of indignation throughout the world. Washington then promised to prohibit the use of toxic gases, but the prohibition was of short duration. In fact, in the course of the raid made on September 5th 1965 against the village of Vinh Quang, province of Binh Dinh, a battalion of Marines under the command of Lieutenant-Colonel Leon Utter flooded the civilians taking refuge in air raid shelters with 48 containers of poison gas, killing 35 and wounding 19 (26 women and 28 children).

The Pentagon at first threw the responsibility for this act on Lieutenant-Colonel Leon Utter as having acted on his own. Nevertheless, the Pentagon, at the end of September 1965, modified its attitude and gave full power to General Westmoreland to use poison gas in South Vietnam, *New York Herald Tribune,* September 1965; also *New York Times,* October 5th, 1965.

Ever since this date gas has been used habitually to evacuate shelters and tunnels where many civilians were taking refuge. According to the *Wall Street Journal* of January 5th, 1966, "most peasant houses have underground shelters designed to protect residents from typhoons and wars. Now, when American troops are entering South Vietnameses villages, they generally throw grenades in the shelters. Of course there are innocent victims." [3]

Many reports have since appeared in the U.S. and world press concerning the use of gas. Let us quote an A.P. dispatch from Saigon, *Le Monde,* January 5th, 1966:

"U.S. specialists in chemical warfare are studying the actual use of new methods with lachrymatory gases which the Commanders have authorised in certain sectors against the Liberation Front. The most recent method consists of drops, from low-flying aircraft, of clusters with an irritant gas in 'aerogel' form."

---

[3] See Report of Jean Bertolino in this volume. Ed. Note.

This same dispatch mentions cylindrical grenades thrown by hand or fired from rifles (rifle grenades). The effect of the gas is "to cause violent mucous membrane irritation and causing salivation. The victims get a burning sensation in the lungs and at the sweat gland areas of the skin. But above all, the gas produces an insurmountable desire to run—says a U.S. officer."

"Grenades of this type were used during the last weekend," The *Le Monde* article continues, "during 'Operation Marauder' in the North Mekong Delta, and many Vietcong were routed from their hideouts by this method. The U.S. specialists are at the same time studying the effect of 'Mighty Mite,' an air pump which sends out a jet of gas at about 200 mph to penetrate into tunnels and hideouts."

According to the *New York Times*, of March 23rd,1964—Washington March 22, by Max Frankel: "U.S. Reveals Use of Nonlethal Gas against Vietcong. The United States disclosed today that it was giving the South Vietnamese some temporarily disabling 'types of tear gas' for combat use against the Vietcong... The use of gas in Vietnam was first reported by unspecified official sources in Saigon and then quickly confirmed by an American spokesman there. His statement was also distributed by the Defense Department. It said: "In tactical situations in which the Vietcong intermingle with or take refuge among non-combatants, rather than use artillery or aerial bombardment, Vietnamese troops have used a type of tear gas. It is a non-lethal gas which disables temporarily, making the enemy incapable of fighting. Its use in such situations is no different than the use of disabling gases in riot control.

The State Department then added that, 'tear gas in standard form, as well as tear gas inducing nausea, has been supplied by the United States and used by Vietnamese forces in a few instances—for example to meet riots and in technical situations where the Vietcong have mingled with innocent people.' Apparently this meant that 'standard' tear gas had been used for riots while gas 'inducing nausea' had been used in combat operations... One source said he believed the gases had been used twice, once in December and once in January, in areas where rebels had mingled with civilian populations to avoid bombing attacks.

"The blister gases widely used in World War I had a delayed rate of action, destroying tissues and injuring blood vessels several hours after contact. They sometimes led to death. The gases used in Vietnam apparently have an immediate but temporary disabling effect that wears off after several hours."

342

"Officials, obviously sensitive to the propaganda problems posed by the disclosure, insisted that the use of 'nauseous gases' was not contrary to international law and practice."

Again the *New York Times* of March 23, 1965, (Saigon, March 22) "Saigon Reveals Tactics—A military spokesman disclosed today that gas of a 'temporary disabling type' had been used against Vietcong guerrillas in South Vietnam recently.

"He said this gas, which was similar to that used in quelling riots, had been employed against Communist guerrillas to flush them out of hiding places."

"This was usually done when the Vietcong were taking refuge among non-combatants, he said. The gas had been released by South Vietnamese troops from dispensers carried in helicopters, he added."

"Gas of the type described by the spokesman was reported to have been used recently along the central coast of South Vietnam against an area where the Vietcong were known to be numerous. But atmospheric conditions were not favorable and the gas was reported to have hung on the ground exerting little effect."

"The military spokesman emphasized that the gas used was of a type that caused only nausea and was not permanently damaging to a person enveloped by it."

Here are the opinions of officials and combatants given in the *New York Times* of October 9-10, 1965: (Saigon, October 8, by Charles Mohr) "Some of the troops engaged today carried grenades resembling baseballs and containing a tear gas designated as 'CN' and 'CS'.

"In briefing reporters, American officials have been at pains to stress that the gas is only temporarily incapacitating and is only ordinary tear gas, which causes weeping and difficulty in breathing. Asked if any nausea-causing agent was in the gas, the reply was an emphatic 'no'.

"In the field today, a sergeant in a weapons platoon was asked to describe the difference between 'CS' and 'CN'. He said that 'CN' was stronger—it makes you nauseous, it makes you feel like your stomach is coming up."

The official view (*New York Times*, March 23, 1965) that the use of such gases was permissible under codes of warfare was challenged by Senator Wayne Morse, Democrat of Oregon, an international lawyer and vigorous critic of the Administration's Vietnam policies.

He said he was sure that gases inducing nausea were among those that the United States, as well as other nations, had in the past described as 'justly condemned by the general opinion of the civilized world'.

"It is interesting to see, "Mr. Morse said, "how easy it is, once we depart from the principles of international law, to violate more and more of them."

But what is *the real effect* of gas on those who had to suffer from it? A well known case is the death of Corporal Botwell:

The *National Guardian* of January 22, 1966, reports that in an incident that may revive the world-wide outcry against U.S. gas warfare in the Vietnam war, "non-lethal" gas killed Australian Cpl. Robert William Botwell, 24, of Casula, New South Wales, during "Operation Crimp" in Haunghia Province. Botwell was killed by a combination of gas and smoke despite the protection of a gas mask. The *Brisbane Courier Mail* (January 13) reported that Botwell "died of asphyxiation" when he became trapped in a tunnel into which the Australian forces had thrown "tear-gas" grenades and smoke bombs in an effort to destroy NLF guerrillas.

The *Courier Mail* continued, "Two other Australian Soldiers were overcome by the gas when they attempted to rescue Botwell and were rushed to a hospital; four Australian engineers were "overcome by carbon monoxide poisoning" during the same operation. Army dogs brought in to help in the tunnel were also overcome."

Le Monde of January 14, 1966, reports on operations involving U.S. Marines (AP, Peter Arnett) "Trung, Lap, January 13th, 1966. It was a long and bloody kilometer we covered on Wednesday. Gas filtered down from the trees and burned our skin. The wounded writhed in the sun, looking like monsters with their grotesque gas masks. Then came helicopters dropping gas on Liberation Front positions. When the Commander saw the strike coming towards us, the order was 'gas masks on'...

"The Commander called to the medics 'keep the wounded covered, get them dressed, the gas will burn them' In any case, the gas was catching bare arms and the exposed neck area, leaving men with the same pain as when burned."

The *New York Times* of March 24, 1965 comments as follows upon the three types of gases which the United States admits having employed: "Even this kind of gases can be fatal to the very young, the very old and those ill with heart and lung ailments."

The *New York Times* of March 26, 1965, published a letter to the Editor from David Hilding, M.D., Yale University, School of Medicine, New Haven, Conn., written on March 23, 1965: "Can anyone imagine any greater bitterness than that of the parents of little children choking away their last few moments of life after being poisoned by 'humane nauseating' gas spread by our military leaders.

"The weakest, young and old, will be the ones unable to withstand the shock of this supposedly humane weapon. They will writhe in horrible cramps until their babies' strength is unequal to the stress and they turn black and blue and die. This may be a more humane weapon than shells and napalm; but its legacy of bitterness will be even more lasting.

"It seems that Vietnam has been a problem too great for even the finest of our military thinkers to solve, and they have resorted to tactics devoid of any hope for anything but hatred. The same revulsion which many of us felt toward Senator Goldwater's belligerent attitude has suddenly been earned by the actions of the Administration.

"Horrible drugs such as these that we are turning over to the Vietnamese Air Force to spray from helicopters wherever they decide, probably produce the designed effect in a few persons of the proper weight, height and general condition, but the dosage for others will be wrong. Those of us with experience with these dangerous substances know that lethal consequences result from haphazard administration.

"There is absolutely no possibility that everyone sprayed with the poison gas in the civilian villages of Vietnam escaped permanent harm. Even the smog of Los Angeles effects a few of the helpless."

However, we may read in the *New York Times*, September 8, 1965: "Marines Use Tear Gas in Caves to Oust Vietnamese Civilians — A United States Marine unit has used tear gas to remove women and children from tunnels and caves where Vietcong suspects were believed hiding. . ."

The French journalist, Madeleine Riffaud, writes: "It is very difficult to save the children, particularly the babies from chemical warfare; they are the first victims." (Madeleine Riffaud, in *Maquis du Vietcong*, Juillard, Paris, p.123).

Since the beginning of 1966, the use of tear gas has been improved and intensified in different ways:

New York Times, February 22, 1966 (Washington, February 21):

"U. S. Explains New Tactic — Defense Department officials explained today that the new tactic of a helicopter-borne tear gas attack was designed to flush Vietcong troops out of the bunkers and tunnels before the attacks by B-52 bombers. One of the limitations of B-52 saturation bombing attacks was that little or no damage was done to the

Vietcong troops unless a direct hit was made on a tunnel or bunker in which they were hiding. The purpose of the gas attack was to force the Vietcong troops to the surface where they would be vulnerable to the fragmentation effects of the bomb bursts."

New York Times, February 23, 1966 (Saigon, February, 22):

"Before the bombers struck the area, 12 miles southwest of Bong-son, hundreds of tear-gas grenades were dropped from helicopters. The first soldiers to enter the zone wore gas masks. Similar tactics were used in the area yesterday, apparently to flush the Vietcong from fortified positions so that the bombs would have maximum effects."

Very little recent news is to be found in the press since the beginning of 1967 concerning the utilisation of chemical warfare. However, the *Asahi Evening News* (Tokyo, August, 18th, 1967) writes: UPI, Danang, August 17, 1967: "Marine helicopter gunships dumped thousand of gallons of combination tear-nausea gas on a suspected Communist position last Thursday, the first use of the gas this way in Vietnam."

And now a conclusion from the *New York Times* of May 3rd, 1965 (Washington May 2, by Jack Raymond): "Defense officials do not like the terminology, but they readily concede that Vietnam has given the United States armed forces a 'laboratory for war' . . . Many weapons have been modified on the basis of experience and many are 'gimmicks'."

Damage by Toxic Products in South Vietnam (Information from North Vietnam Sources)

The *New Bulletin* of February 26, 1966 summarized the effects of the chemical war in South Vietnam as follows:

1961: Attacks were made 11 times, 6 provinces affected, 182 persons affected, 120 animals killed, 560 hectares ruined.

1962: 40 times, 12 provinces affected, 1,220 persons affected, 448 animals killed, 11,040 hectares ruined.

1963: 192 times, 16 provinces affected, 9,000 persons affected, 4,500 animals killed, 320,000 hectares ruined.

1964: 192 times, 19 provinces affected, 11,000 persons affected, 7,511 . animals killed, 500,230 hectares ruined.

1965: Number of attacks not yet available, 26 provinces affected, 146,247 persons affected, 700,000 hectares ruined.

In a more detailed North Vietnamese document entitled: *U. S. Imperialist Crimes in South Vietnam* (February 22, 1966) are given some incomplete data concerning the use of toxic chemicals and poison gas on a large scale in South Vietnam, with indications as to places, dates, observed facts and damage. It is not always easy to distinguish between the use of weed killers and toxic gases: (see also *Vietnam Agency*, 18.3.1966 and 24.6.1966).

January, 25, 26, 1965: On Phu Lac (Phu Yen prov.) U.S. planes dropped gas bombs with napalm and explosive bombs; poison gas alone killed 80 persons and affected hundreds of others.

February 27, 1965: Gas pellets on Binh Hoa and Thanh Phuoc. Many children played with these pellets and were intoxicated.

March 9, 1965: Toxic gases loosed on the Tan Uyen area by a chemical warfare unit. Many deaths among the civilians.

End of March 1965: poison gas spread on the Boi Loi area. Hundreds of persons intoxicated, some are dead.

April 3, 1965: Poison bombs on Phuoc Tan village (Quang Nam). The explosion produced a high column of white smoke which turned yellow and dissipated after 24 hours. 72 persons intoxicated, many of them fell unconscious for a long time.

May 13, 1965: Toxic gas employed during a raid against "Terrorists" in Vihn Chan area. Hundreds of civilians intoxicated. 30 dead.

September 5, 1965: Vihn Quang hamlet (Binh Dinh province): 48 bottles of poison gas sprayed into air-raid shelters killing 35 persons, most of them women and children, more than 100 wounded.

September 8, 1965: Ba Long An area (Quang Ngai province), U.S. troops threw gas grenades into shelters killing 74 civilians.

September and October 1965: Gas grenades were thrown into shelters occupied by civilians in Kim Thac hamlet, village of Nhon Phong, An Nhon district: 40 persons killed.

November 22 and 23, 1965: Quang Ngai, U.S. aircraft dropped gas bombs and fired gas shells and grenades on the vicinity of Thach Tru area, intoxicating a great many persons.

December 17 to 30, 1965: In Long Xuyen province, during a poison spray drive, thousands of persons were affected, 13 of them, mostly women, children or old people died instantly. During four poison sprays on different areas in and around Can Tho provincial capital in recent months, 13,200 persons were intoxicated and 97 hectares of rice fields and gardens devastated.

From December 31, 1965 to January 7, 1966: in Tan An and Cho Lon during a big raid against Bau Trai area, besides showering napalm and white phosphorous bombs and using B-52 aircraft for massive bombing, the U.S., on many occasions, used "Mighty Mite" sprayers to spread toxic gas and threw gas grenades on civilians killing hundreds of persons.

January 2, 1966: During a raid on Bau Tray area, the U.S. for the first time, used a kind of sprayer named "Mighty Mite" capable of spraying poison gas or powder at velocities of 200 mph.

January 9 to 14, 1966: In Gia Dihn, 9,000 American, Australian, New Zealand and South Vietnam puppet troops doused people's shelters with strong poison gas, killing hundreds of persons inside.

February 3 and 4, 1966: During operation "White Wing" in Bong Son area (Binh Dinh province), U.S. aircraft dropped more than 800 gas grenades causing the intoxication of a large number of persons.

Defoliation and Crop Destruction

- *Introduction*
- *Recognized aims of defoliation*
- *Organization of research aiming at the intensification of CBW*
- *The type of agents used*
- *What becomes of herbicides when they are sprayed on plants*
- *Effectiveness and tonnage of the agents sprayed*
- *Defoliation of hevea [rubber] plantations*
- *The equilibrium of human environment destroyed*
- *Crop destruction; Nutritional aspect; Creation of a state of famine*
- *Toxicity of herbicides for man, livestock, game, fish, insects, and micro-organisms*
- *Conclusion: References and Bibliography*

Introduction:

As an article published in *Le Monde* on the 10th of November 1965 points out, no one can possibly ignore the use made of chemical agents in Vietnam, for the purpose of destroying forest, jungle and food crops, a fact which has been frequently and vigourously denounced by American scientists. Although confirmation of the aerial dispersion of toxic compounds in Vietnam can hardly be said to have provoked an unanimous outcry in the United States, a considerable number of petitions have been addressed both to President Johnson and to the Administration, in an attempt to put an end to this new form of warfare which "of all war crimes, constitutes the most cruel and the most inhuman" (1).

Following an article by Charles Mohr, published in *The New York Times* on the 21st of December 1965, — "U.S. Spray Destroys Rice in Vietcong Territory," 29 scientists from Harvard University, MIT, and other Massachussetts institutions, signed a declaration urging President Johnson to prohibit the use of chemical and biological weapons (CBW) by the American army and to oppose their use by the South Vietnamese and their allies (2).

At roughly the same time, the Rev. Peter J. Riga sent a letter, published on the 27th of December 1965, to the editor of *The New York Times,* stating—"There are certain actions which are so criminal in intent and execution that one simply cannot remain a Christian and not protest with one's whole soul. The spraying of the rice crops by United States planes is exactly one of these crimes.
"... It is an indiscriminate act of total war...
"... It is not 'by accident' that food is destroyed, with the result that thousands of the innocent must suffer and die...
"... Far better a prison where we can live with our Christian consciences than the silence of Christian betrayal." (3). R.B. Fosdick also wrote to the editor of *The New York Times* on the 25th of December 1965, saying that the article on CBW is the saddest Christmas story he had ever read, and deeply ironical, since these military operations were being carried out in the name of "peace."

On the 18th of February, 1967, 5,000 scientist, including 17 Nobel Prize winners, sent a letter to President Johnson, asking for a public declaration about the government's policy with regards to CBW and its control. They drew particular attention to the relatively low cost of this type of warfare, consequently accessible to the nations which do not possess nuclear arms. They also pointed out that expenditure on CBW is now seven times higher than in the late 1950's (4).

An article published in *Scientific Research* reported an acute shortage of defoliants (5). The Army alone could make use of four times as much as available at the present moment.

President Johnson therefore issued an order to his Office of Emergency Planning to insure that the military orders for 2,4,5,T are fully met. At the same time, he said that he appreciated the petitioners' concern and was deeply impressed by their prestige and knowledge. Meanwhile, the Pentagon decided to intensify the defoliation of Vietnamese jungles. The military increased the dose of herbicides to be used during the current fiscal year to 5 million gallons, (costing 32 million dollars), and announced (6) their intention of spending $57,690,000 more for that purpose during the fiscal year beginning July 1, 1967 (for the fiscal year 1966, the bill amounted to 10 million). The Dow Chemical, Diamond Akali, Uniroyal Chemical, Thompson Chemical, Hercules, Monsanto, Ahsul and Thompson Hayward companies agreed to provide the required defoliants.

This intensification of crop-destroying by CBW took place during the year that the civilized nations decided to launch the "Freedom From Hunger Campaign" and a great many authorities concerned have pointed out far-reaching and inevitable effects of defoliation. The purpose of this section of this report is to sum up the articles already published on CBW, adding more recent information when necessary.

The Recognized Aims of Defoliation

1. The stated aims of defoliation are to guarantee the safety of the zones in the vicinity of roads, and prevent Vietcong movements from Central to South Vietnam.

2. To prevent the Vietcong from using foliage, as cover.

3. To reduce the Vietcong to starvation (guerillas and "unfriendly" civilians) in what is termed the "food denial program."

Defoliation carried out by the American army is therefore openly recognized by the government (7) and certain officers, for example Brig. Gen. J.H. Rothschild go so far as to recommend it (8). The results of this defoliation program arouse such animosity, that Truong Dihn Dzu, the civilian candidate for the South Vietnam presidency, thought of including in his electoral program a promise that he would intercede in favour of the interruption of American defoliation missions.

Research for Intensification of C.B.W.

In 1964, the author of *Tomorrow's Weapons* stated (8) that a number of the chemical agents available at that period required too much time to produce results, and were unsatisfactory from a tactical standpoint. Moreover, certain agents proved ill-adapted for use in tropical regions. Brig. Gen. Rothschild went on to say that an energetic research program could provide anti-guerrilla forces with a number of defoliants which would be effective, regardless of climatic conditions.

The government, with this aim in view, proposed subjects for classified research which many American and foreign laboratories under contract to the government accepted. As the results achieved are not made public, it is difficult to discover of what, exactly, these research programs consisted. American scientific circles only became aware of the existence of these programs when the suspicion of several people was sufficiently aroused to lead them to ask a few indiscreet questions (9,10,11,12). When it was no longer possible to harbor any doubt as to what these programs were aiming at, conflicts broke out between University Administration and certain members of various faculties. Early in September 1966, the President of Pennsylvania University, G.P. Harnwell, announced that an advisory committee would be set up to help the university steer clear of future contracts (for which a grant of a million dollars a year is provided) in which there would be a ban on publishing research results. Twenty-four hours later, Professors G. Kolko (History), R. Rutman (Chemistry), E.S. Herman (Finance) and A.S. Milvan (Medicine), announced that the following principle had to be discussed: should universities be involved in research, whether classified or not, concerned with the development of CBW?

Several other universities raised the same problem. Cornell University, a subcontractor to Pennsylvania University for the projects "Summit" (contract with the Army) and "Spicerack" (contract with the Air Force), carried out under the control of the Institute for Cooperative Research — ICR —, found themselves faced with the decision of whether or not to publish results. While both Professor Kolko and President G.P. Harnwell himself held that the results should be published, Dr. Knut Krieger, in charge of those projects, begs to differ, "My findings are not of general interest, they are highly specialized. And, in the second place, I don't think it's the kind of work that ought to be published. It's a matter of national security." It should be added that Dr. Krieger receives information directly from Vietnam, and can therefore test the efficacity of new defoliants very quickly.

As the CBW program had acquired a bad name for Pennsylvania University, and had been the occasion of dissension between the various faculties, students, and the Administration, the latter attempted to have the laboratories working under government control transferred to another Philadelphia research center, where there would be sufficient room to house them. (University City Center). The trouble was that the Quaker members of this group of colleges refused to have anything to do with the CBW program.

The decision to encourage research on CBW was taken in late 1950 (10,11) and research under contract has been going on now for about 12 years. In addition to determining the most efficient manner of carrying out CBW on subsistence crops, including rice, these programs study the repercussions of CBW on the economy of developing countries, and on the political and social climate in Asia. A large-scale CBW research center has been built for this purpose at Fort Detrick, Maryland, providing, as reporters said, excellent working conditions for research on herbicides and defoliants. The testing ground for this research center is situated in Utah. It occupies an area greater than the state of Rhode Island and employs more than 900 scientists. In the United States, the budget for CBW rose from 36.3 million dollars in 1959 to 170 million dollars in 1964 (*Le Monde*—March 1967). In addition to specialized American research groups, foreign laboratories are also actively involved in CBW research, probably on behalf of the U.S. Department of Defense.

An article in *Le Monde*, published on the 27th of April 1966, reports a resolution adopted by the Japanese Council of Sciences calling upon all the Academies of Sciences throughout the world to oppose the use of Japanese defoliants in Vietnam. Dr. Funazaki energetically denounced the collusion existing between the Japanese and American governments. At the present moment, there is good reason to believe that the herbicides used in Vietnam are effective in all seasons, rapidly effective, even if the results obtained are not quite as spectacular as those hoped for. *The doses of defoliant sprayed per acre are much stronger than that recommended by the herbicide manufacturers* (13).

The most recent information provided by the Pentagon reveals that in 1966, more than 500,000 acres of jungle and bush land, and more than 150,000 acres of harvest land were "treated with herbicides"—*New York Times*, 25 July, 1966). The Pentagon considers however, that this represents only a negligible fraction of Vietnam's arable land, and that the scope of the program should now be tripled (12).

Type of Agents Used

Chemical agents are frequently used to keep fields clear of weeds, to provoke the fall of cotton leaves, to render a harvest by mechanical means possible, or again, to destroy old or contamined crops. At the beginning of the century, the only agents known were Bordeaux mixture and sulphuric acid. When the problem of the selective destruction of broad-leaved plants (dicotyledons) which grow among cereals, arose, it became necessary to use dinitrophenols.

During the second World War, the United States and Great Britain set out to discover agents which would destroy the Japanese rice plantations and thus reduce the population to starvation; but the Atom Bomb put an end to research on chemical agents just when the laboratories had succeeded in producing substances, with very high biological efficacity. A large budget was granted for the first synthesis in the U.S. of 2,4D (2, dichlorophenoxyacetic acid) M.C.P.A. (2 methyl, 4 chlorophenoxyaceticacid) was prepared in England under similar conditions.

The number of herbicides then increased with great rapidity. Herbicides are of mineral or organic origin. The mineral substances penetrate the plant, mainly during the period of active vegetation (this is probably one of the reasons which led Brig. Gen. Rothchild to believe that herbicides cease to be effective during the dry season). Organic herbicides of the 2,4D, M.C.P.S., or 2,4,5T type, have taken the place of the aforementioned without, however, eliminating them. Research carried out both in the United States and in Great Britain has made it possible to provide synthetic substances with the properties of naturally occurring hormones (14) found in plants—the most important of which is IAA (indol-3-acetic acid). Auxins which normally exists in plants at minute concentration, promote cell division and elongation, and partly control, cell differentiation. An infinitesimal dose of auxins prevents leaf fall. On the contrary, however, synthetic substances which imitate the effect of auxins become harmful because they are employed at higher concentrations. They then produce leaf fall. To give example, at the concentration 10-8 to 10-6M, the 2,4D stimulates the cell division of vegetable tissue cultures. At the concentration 10-4M, it becomes highly toxic. Herbicides are generally mixed at a solution of 0.1 per cent for agricultural use.

At the period when the American Army began to spray herbicides over Vietnam in accordance with the Stayley-Taylor plan, i.e., in 1961, a long list of effective agents had already been established. (15). Considering the well known efficiency of American laboratories, there can be no doubt that the present list of herbicides is rapidly becoming longer and longer (16). Although the authors will restrict the possibility of their being widely used, it is unlikely that the Joint Chiefs of Staff refuse on this ground to try out one of the agents, considered to be more "completely successful" than those employed until now. A considerable number of new agents are being tested daily in control laboratories. Not all of them such as basamid, herban, benzomarc, methoxymarc, cotoran, carbetamide, casoron, amethyne, norfamquat, tordon, (4-amino, 3,5,6-trichloropicolinic acid, which is 10 times more effective than 2,4D) are put on the agricultural market, but certain have been already tested in Vietnam.

What Becomes of Herbicides Sprayed on Plants

Certain herbicides applied in a given molecular form, become active in another chemical form. Others are absorbed, translocated, and accumulated in the same molecular form (18). Most of these substances are translocated (19), and rapidly metabolized, and this process transforms a relatively harmless molecule into a herbicidally active molecule. Certain herbicides accumulate in the leaves and inhibit photosynthesis. The plant dies of starvation, since it is no longer able to fix carbonic anhydride (20).

Some compounds move with the stream of photosynthesis and assimilation; they therefore become widely distributed throughout the plant and generally accumulate in young expanding tissues. In that case their toxicity could be caused by the synthesis of another volatile hormone, ethylene, which provokes a considerable increase in respiration (21).

Results and Tonnage of the Agents Sprayed

Herbicides do not always produce an immediate result. In some cases, the charateristic distortions are only visible the following year (15). The arsenites, arseniates, dinitrophenol, dinitrocresol and all the other chemical agents which are translocated, cause leaf fall because they kill the plants (17).

The presence of active agents has been found to continue to exist in soil where plants have been treated. If the variety of crops grown is changed, the new variety may well have a more violent reaction to the agents, and this sometimes results in considerable damage (15).

In spite of the tons of herbicides sprayed over Vietnam by squadrons of C-130 or C-123s, effective or total defoliation of the jungle continues to be a problem. Certain plants are affected by the defoliants, but others resist. Although it would appear that the military have not achieved their acknowledged aim, the haphazard spraying of toxic substances which are not entirely destroyed by microorganisms undoubtedly contributes largely to the destruction of subsistence crops, even if these are not the primary aim of defoliation missions. Toxic agents, carried by running water, poison crops situated at a distance from where the spraying actually took place. The wind scatters volatile defoliants and makes them effective at more than six miles from the point of spraying. From January to September 1966, the 12th Air Command Squadron defoliated 1,000 square miles (U.P.I. *New-Haven Register*, 18th Dec. 1966). Early in 1967, the 309th Air Command Squadron carried out operations in the demilitarized zone of the 17th parallel, and on the borders of Laos and Cambodia.

Each plane carries roughly 1,000 gallons of herbicide, spraying approximately three gallons per acre. The spraying takes place very early in the morning (*National Observer*, 28 February 1966). The target is sprayed for about five minutes. If it should prove necessary, the 1,000 gallons stored in tanks could be sprayed in 30 seconds. According to the *New York Times* of the 10th of Sept. 1966, there were in:

1961: 60 defoliation missions (rice, sugar-cane, and vegetables were included in the spraying).

1962: 107 missions to defoliate canals and rice plantations in the Mekong delta and in the Central Highlands;

1966: 1,324,430 gallons of herbicide were sprayed on half-a-million acres;

1967: It was recommended that missions be carried out by 18 planes; the targets are chosen by American and Vietnamese officers.

From Vietnamese sources 320,000 acres of crops are said to have been destroyed in 1963, 500,000 acres in 1964 and 700,000 in 1965. Sometimes planes drop down until they are just above the trees, (at a height of 150 feet). Their speed is then 110 miles per hour. The tail of the plane releases a fine blue mist which has a strange smell reminding one of hospitals (ether). This spraying seems too slight to cause serious harm to the vegetation, but if one flies over the treated region a week after the spraying, one can observe the first changes, and the first signs of an artificially produced autumn. Three months later, there is nothing left of the country but a dried up stretch of land, which is lost to all intents and purposes. Each plane only requires four minutes to destroy 300 acres of forestland.

The defoliating planes are universally hated by the Vietnamese and they are constantly shot at. The herbicides are carried in barrels painted dark red, and the planes that carry them are nicknamed "Purple Hearts."[4] The crew jokingly call each other "magnet-asses" because of their propensity to attract bullets from fierce ground-fire. Each member of the crew who has been shot or shot at is awarded a mock medal, the "Order of the Purple People Eater," which is worn with great pride. The Code name for defoliation is "Operation Ranch Hand."

A series of reports of USOM Agriculture and of the South-Vietnamese administration concerning the defoliation situation in the Bien Hoa area, state that when damage done to the farmers is officially estimated, compensations have to be paid. It is, however, difficult to evaluate the damage in a serious manner because the farmers are

---

[4]Medal awarded to U.S. Servicemen wounded-in-action. Ed. Note.

afraid to sow and because they harvest before maturation because they fear indiscriminate sprayings. The compensation procedure is long and complicated and often, especially for rapidly growing crops, estimations are quite impossible.

Defoliation of the Hevea Rubber Plantations

After repeated requests from planters, worried because they had noticed that the appearance of hevea foliage had been abnormal for some time, a survey was carried out in order to define the scale and the initial causes of this phenomenon. It is possible to draw the following conclusions:

The occurrence of rubber tree foliage poisoning is exceptionally serious, (concerning a rectangular band running NW by SE of more than 130 kilometers long x 40 kilometers wide) and involving more than 25,000 hectares of heveas. The latex plants, (heveas, jacquiers, kainitiers, and papayas) are the most seriously affected, as they react more violently to the defoliant than forest species. When the agent is wind-born it is still sufficiently concentrated at a distance of ten kilometers from the point of spraying, to be harmful. The toxic activity of the substances is manifest on every tree, although it does not appear in a spectacular manner on all leaves. This could explain the considerable drops in production observed during 1965-66 which cannot be accounted for by mere defoliation.

At the present moment, it is necessary to leave the defoliated trees dormant and unproductive until they recover. However, the renewed application of defoliants will, in all liklihood, threaten the very existence of hevea culture in Vietnam.

For a while it was thought that it was an especially heavy attack of the oidium on the hevea. Yet this disease is seen in general only on adult or aging trees; but the symptoms stated by the Vietnamese concerned the latter as well as (but above all) the young trees, one or two years old, which are often completely defoliated. In addition, they observed necrosis oriented in a SE direction and this necrosis follows the tree to the ground. If it were a question of cryptogamic disease, the stated symptoms would not be evident; the petiole would stay on the terminal stem and moreover, new leaves would appear at the end of two or three weeks.

After spraying, harmful substances are taken by the wind and contaminate plantings far away from the originally sprayed zone as much as six miles in some cases. This is, probably, a defoliation by pulverization of a mixture of paraquat, in a concentration five times higher than that recommended for the destruction of weeds, and of 2,4D plus 2,4,5T. In this case defoliation is almost complete. When the product is transported by winds, the result is just as harmful. The defoliant is translocated rapidly bringing on latex coagulation in a belt 4.5 to 15 feet high, always oriented with the prevailing winds. Latex trees are hit the hardest; when defoliation is diffuse, bamboos, coffee and tea plants are later hit.

The defoliation of heveas creates serious economic and social problems for Vietnam. In the period extending only from April to June 1967, the latex production decreased by about 30 per cent. This drop in rubber production affects a population of around 100,000 people, including workers and their families; even if the planters continue to pay half salary and half rice ration, it would be necessary to exact a compensation for the loss in earning that the workers underwent.

Equilibrium of Human Environment Destroyed

Our attention has frequently been drawn to the fact that woodland has a regulating influence on the pedological and hydrographical equilibrium of human environment. Dr. M. Sakka states "that in a given region, one cannot modify without danger one element of Nature without serious consequences for the other elements which live there."

Professor G. Lhoste (23) gave several examples of the modification of flora. When herbicides are employed to clear rivers, the immediate results are positive, but, generally, the following year, another type flora appears which eventually completely blocks the river.

Crop Destruction — Nutritional and Social Aspects, State of Famine.

In a series of recent articles (24,25,26) Dr. Jean Mayer, Professor of Nutrition at Harvard University and Dr. Victor W. Sidel, Chief of Preventive Medicine at Massachusetts General Hospital in Boston, point out that the destruction of harvests began in the spring of 1966 with spraying of 2,4D and 2,4,5T. The spraying operations were carried out by C-123 transport planes ironically called "Providers." The soldiers discovered that rice is one of the most maddeningly difficult substances to destroy. Using thermite incendiary grenades it is almost impossible to make it burn and even if one succeeds in scattering the rice, this does not prevent its being harvested by patient men. And so, it is easier to use herbicides, since defoliation before the rice is ripe means a 60 to 90% loss of the harvest. (*New York Times*, 21 Dec. 1965). And yet it would appear that even defoliation is not the ideal solution, for recently they have started throwing harvested rice into the rivers. New methods are also being employed to rapidly destroy subsistence crops. The spraying of toxic substances now consists in dropping barrels of herbicides which are machine-gunned full of holes, or else which seep into the water of the rice paddies. This was first observed in the province of Vinh Long in December, 1966. This type of attack is quite different from the spraying of forests. The airforce also drops something resembling a coloured bladder on subsistence crops. On hitting the ground, this bursts and releases herbicides (Can Tho Province, December 1966).

Without debating the moral issues of using chemical products in time of war, it seems obvious that the present situation in Vietnam caused by the destruction of crops and food supplies poses a very real human problem. The aim is to starve the Vietcong by destroying the fields which provide food for the insurgents. As a nutritionist who has studied the effects of famine on three continents, Professor Jean Mayer states flatly that there has never been a famine which has not first and foremost affected small children and old people. Pregnant women abort and lactating mothers can no longer feed their babies. Children under five years are the most vulnerable and in Vietnam always on the verge of *kwashiorkor* (a protein deficiency syndrome) or *marasmus* (a combination deficiency of calories and of protein). Another result of famine is that people leave home and go elsewhere in search of food. Families are split up, children lost and probably die. Adolescents fall ill with tuberculosis. Some migrants go on to form marauding bands, which adds to the general state of social decay. It is difficult to eradicate this form of banditry. Though adults have greater resistance to famine, its effects in mature populations can also be very spectular. The first noticeable effect is the wasting a-way of adipose tissues, then internal organs are affected: the size of the liver diminshes, the intestinal lining becomes thin and ineffective, food is absorbed with ever increasing difficulty and diarrhea results. Starvation is a self accelerating process especially in children. In extreme cases diarrhea does not respond to medical treatment, cardiovascular collapse occurs and infections set in.

Plague and malaria are endemic in South East Asia but these diseases seem to be on the increase recently. Moreover, a new form of malaria which does not respond readily to traditional drugs has appeared. Cholera and smallpox have always followed in the wake of Asian famines, as have influenza and relapsing fever.

In time of famine the armed forces consider that they have a perfect right to seize whatever food remains in order to continue the struggle. The destruction of foodstuffs has never hampered military operation, but it does victimise great numbers of children (26 bis). And Professor Mayer is extremely alarmed of what must be a steadily developing famine in Vietnam since the efforts towards crop destruction are being increased.

Toxicity of Herbicides on Man, Livestock, Game, Fish, Insects and Micro-Organisms.

According to the State Department (9th March 1965) these herbicides are not toxic, especially since the "innocent" populations are warned before spraying takes place. They are advised to leave the district encouraged by promises of food in plenty if they agree to regroup themselves in refugee villages *(New York Times* Dec. 21, 1965). Without querying the very definition of the term, one cannot but wonder how innocent persons can be effectively warned before the spraying of herbicides in regions where there are neither telephones, newspapers, radio nor television and even if such warning were possible, one wonders where these peasants whose only means of subsistance has been this one piece of land, could possibly go? (25).

Moreover the chemical substances poured over Vietnam are far from being harmless (30). A glance at the instructions for the use of weedkillers sold by the Dow Chemical Co. is enough to convince one. The suppliers warn potential users of Esteron 245 OS (2,4,5T):

- Even small quantities of 2,4,5T can cause serious damage to plants which are to be preserved, both in dormant periods and periods of growth.
- In hot water the product volatilises and can contaminate neighbouring plants.
- Care must be taken not to contaminate drinking water or irrigation ditches.
- Keep out of the reach of children; the agent can cause skin or eye irritation.

The herbicide sold under the name of Formula 40 (2,4D) has such a high toxicity that one is advised not to go on wearing shoes contaminated by the product.

When it is known that cacodylic acid (dimethylarsenic acid) has 54% arsenic in it and when one reads in the *New York Times* 10th September, 1966 that this product is being used on elephant grass and rice, it becomes evident that there exist serious risks of toxicity. In 1953 the Stationary Office (Ministry of Agriculture and Fisheries, London) published a recapitulative table showing the residues of herbicides present in plants (27). The concentration of 2,4D can be considerable in cereal straw especially in maize and sorghom (23) and when this fodder is given to cattle there is a risk of 2,4D being secreted in the milk.

Numerous experiments have been carried out on laboratory animals to determine the toxicity of herbicides. Thus (29) the "LD5O" (dose necessary to kill 50% of the experimental batch) of 2,4D is: 375 mg/kg for mice, 666 mg/kg for rat, 800 mg/kg for rabbit, 1000 mg/kg for guinea pig, 100 mg/kg for dog.

The doses then vary with the species and also with the herbicides. Professor R. Truhaut (31) stresses the mitotic poison characteristic of maleic hydrazide (dihydro 1,2-pyridazinedione 3,6) with the risk of chromosomic aberrations. ATA (3-amino, 1,2,4-triazole) is a thyroid inhibitor (32); it is secreted slowly from the organism where it persists as long as two days after ingestion (33). — Dipyridile compounds are easily absorbed by soils to maximum C.A.F. (capacity absorption force). Micro-organisms apparently destroy diquat and paraquat completely. It would appear that not the slightest accumulation of those products has ever been discovered in any alimentary canal, i.e. the substances are retained and not eliminated as waste. (34).

The toxicity of paraquat has been well described (35). For the laboratory rat the dose of paraquat is lethal at a level of 0.25% in the diet. At necropsy pulmonary lesions are found to exist with cellular proliferation. Such a proliferative process has been observed after an administration of carcinogenic hydrocarbons (36). Similarly in human poisoning by the accidental ingestion of paraquat (the lethal dose is probably some several mg) of body weight. One can observe all the symptoms of the condition of "fibrosing pneumonitis" described in dogs. (U.S. Biotest. Lab. (37,38).

The effects of paraquat after daily application to the skin of the skin of the rabbit are the secretion of a brownish saliva, loss of appetite followed by death in a state of cachexia with pulmonary lesions. Applied to the skin, paraquat forms a reservoir for oral contamination of the animal through grooming, hence the symptoms observed. A dose of 286 ppm of the substance makes drinking water poisonous.

There have been many known cases of suicidal or accidental posioning from herbicides. The following table shows that synthetic hormones are extremely poisonous (39). The symptoms described are an acute and extremely rapid ataxia, neuromuscular irritations, convulsions and renal and hepatic damage.

Substances	Approx. dose mg/kg	Age	Sex	Time between ingestion and death (hr.)
Ethyl, 1,2,4D	500	49	F	54
MCPA (verdone)	400	32	M	20
2,4D (herbatox)	80	23	M	found dead
MCPA (verdone)	250	65	M	20

No antidote exists. Hydrocortisone can have a comparatively beneficial effect. The carcinogenic properties of maleic hydrazide have been described many times. Quite recently (40) a series of experiments on mice has clearly shown that this herbicide provokes a high incidence of hepatomas as well as various other tumors. A simple calculation of the amount of herbicide ingested per annum from potatoes suggests that "normal" human ingestion of maleic hydrazide is quite comparable to that which is carcinogenic for mice. The Swiss National Committee for Aid to Vietnam asked four doctors to collect documents about CBW. They stated that the effects of certain weapons in authorized use are the irremediable destruction of plants and the poisoning of animals. If man is exposed to these substances he runs the risk of pulmonary edema and digestive disturbances. Chemical substances used in agriculture which, unlike medicines and products for veterinary use, are not subject to a strict sanitary control, sometimes possess an acute toxicity. Further proof of this has just been provided after an accident in France which cost several technicians their lives (from inhaling hexafluorodichlorobutene because they had been wearing inadequate masks). The autopsy revealed pulmonary lesions similar to those described previously *(Le Monde* 19th Sept. 1967).

The North Vietnamese Commission on War Crimes has issued a list of damages suffered in 1965 in South Vietnam by the local populations and their livestock after the spraying of chemical products (41). And the Vietnamese newspaper *Sang Kum* published (August 1967) a set of rules to be observed in case of contamination by defoliants. Doctors Tran-Ky and Keo Sang Kim recommend urgent treatment in all such cases.

Herbicides are not only dangerous to man and his surroundings but also to livestock *(Le Monde,* 23rd April 1966, reports that 50 to 60% of bovines are affected) as are sheep (42), game, fish, insects and micro-organisms.

Dr. R. Vermeyen (43) points out that certain birds abandon eggs if contaminated by phytohormones. The hatching rate is, incidentally, considerably reduced since herbicides are poisonous to the embryon in infinitesimal doses (5 to 7.5 mg per hen's egg). Paraquat would appear to be the most dangerous of all the herbicides tested (44) since it causes the death of the embryon when injected into the egg at concentration lower than 0.15 ppm.

The effects of herbicides on fish cannot be deduced from their effects on animals. Monuron, for example, is mildly toxic for rats (LD50−3500); whereas it is dangerous for fish in dilutions weaker than 1.2 ppm (45). Moreover the toxicity of herbicides is much higher in tropical temperatures than in temperate climates, which further stresses their toxicity. According to Cope (46) it is approximately 130 times higher at 29%C than at 7%C. After being exposed for thirty days to the effects of dipyridyle compounds or a sodium arsenite, the herbicide residues to be found in fresh water fish are as follows:

Species	Herbicide	Locality	Amount in water ppm	Amount of residue in animal. ppm
Rainbow Trout	Para-quat	Denver (Col)	1	0.11
Green Sunfish	"	"	1	0.05
Bluegill	"	"	1	1.21
Channel Catfish	"	"	1	0.37
Bluegill	Na arsenic	La Crosse (Wis)	0.23	0.40
Bluegill	Diquat	"	1	0.09

The effects of 2,4D on fish are the following: hepatic glycogen is no longer to be found. Brain vessels are congested. Embolisms occur, and lesions in the liver and testicles are noted. In four days casoron causes intense vascular disturbances around the gills; and fusion of the lamellae occurs. (47). The toxicity of herbicides for Daphnia, small fresh water crustacea on which fish feed, is higher than one would think according to experiments on laboratory animals (48).

All insects are affected by herbicides (49). Fortunately, bees have a strong repulsion for these substances and usually stop gathering honey from flowers in fields which have been treated, but their "pastures" are thus reduced (50,51). Direct contact kills them more or less rapidly. The symptoms are not always evident immediately after returning to the hive and sometimes a whole week passes before death occurs (53). During the 1950 summer season in Denmark and Sweden the poisoning by herbicides of an extensive bee population was noted after dandelions and mustard had been treated (53).

Normally the destruction of chlorophenoxyacetic derivatives by microorganisms takes approximately 2 to 15 weeks for one application of herbicide, although some derivatives persist for more than one year (2,4,5T is more resistant than 2,4D). Phenolic compounds poisonous to both plants and microorganisms of the soil are to be found as end products of this process. The activity of microorganisms is of importance for the preservation of tropical soils.

Conclusion

Despite the denials of General J.P.O'Connel, Commander-in-Chief of the Air-Force, in Washington on the 3rd February, 1967, before the Senate, there can be no doubt that defoliation of the forests, the jungle and the bush are already having dangerous repercussions on the conditions of human environment. In fact, it is a question of something much more pernicious than defoliation in the strict sense of the term in Vietnam, since the chemical substances which merely cause the leaves to fall without damaging the rest of the vegetative cycle are still at an experimental stage at the present time. This term, therefore, cannot be applied to operations which consist in pouring tons of herbicides and arboricides over forests and crops. Defoliation is but an euphemism for destruction of the vegetation. Although the Political Committee of the United Nations has refused to condemn the United States, the use of chemical warfare is in danger of provoking wholly unsuspected biological devastation in the very near future. The immediate effect on the destruction of rubber plantations and food harvests is a spectacular example of such dangers.

In the absence of information about the repercussions on civilians (Dean Rusk assured Senator Pell that is not possible to assess them at the moment), Dr. Mayer, Professor at Harvard, recalls the effects of earlier famines (24) — "My point is not just that innocent by-standers are hurt by such measures. My point is that *only* bystanders will be hurt. The primary U.S. aim — to disable the Vietcong is not achieved. Our proclaimed secondary aim — to win over the civilian population — is made a hollow mockery"

At the present time the Pentagon no longer knows how many times, nor for what reason the Air Force has carried out this kind of operation. It denies the danger of escalation in the field of food destruction. And, yet we have seen that what was once unthinkable sometimes becomes standard policy (12). It can now be feared that bacterioligical warfare agents may be directed against the vegetation in Vietnam if such is not already the case.

To quote Professor Mayer once more (24) — "If crop destruction efforts are successful, they constitute a war measure primarily, if not exclusively, directed at children, the elderly, and pregnant and lactating women . . .The rice crop destruction program is a blot on our national honor and should be stopped immediately. Those who destroy forests calm their conscience when they get back to the U.S. by collecting money in certain parishes in order to buy fruit trees which are then sent to South Vietnamese villages. The results of this "Program of Civic Action" are, according to the Air Force Public Relations Office, very positive, since fruit trees rapidly became a source of profit to the civilian population and replace the jungle. Commander Dennis (from Yakima, Washington) expresses satisfaction at the fact that "defoliation" is not an entirely destructive process. "I like to feel, he said, that someday, we will have made farm land out of what once was jungle . . .Even now there are some benefits; in some places they've started a charcoal industry using the trees we've killed".

According to Mike McGrady (54) . . ."defoliation is just one small aspect of this dirty war. Whether people are killed directly or simply starved off their farm, whether animals are slaughtered or simply forced to leave their natural habitat — the final results are roughly the same. . . .We can buy $492. worth of fruit trees, but that's not even down payment on conscience money. We can hang up signs that say REMEMBER, ONLY YOU CAN PREVENT FORESTS,[5] but the joke is a bad one."

REFERENCES

1. *Le Monde*, 23 April 1966; Agence France Presse, Hanoi, 22 March, 1966

2. Petition printed in *Science*, 21 January 1966, p. 309

3. Protest of Rev. Peter J. Riga, Professor of Theology, University of Notre Dame, Indiana; *New York Times*, Letter to Editor, 21 December, 1965

4. Petition of 5000 Scientists, United Press International, Washington, 18 February, 1967

5. *Scientific Research*, 2, 39, 1967

6. Washington, 11 July 1967; *Le Monde*, 12 July 1967; *Science*, 1967

7. Dixon Donnelly, Assistant Secretary, U.S. Dept. of State, 28 September, 1966

[5] The exhortation, "Remember, Only You Can Prevent Forest Fires" is the slogan of conservationists in the United States. The mythical forest-ranger "Smokey the Bear" utters these words on television and posters; they are widely known to American children. The C-123 defoliation squadrons flying out of Tan Son Nhut airport have perverted this slogan into "Remember, Only You Can Prevent Forests." It is impossible to comment on the cynical callousness this attitude represents. Ed. Note.

8. Brig. Gen. J.H. Rothschild, *Tomorrow's Weapons*, New York, McGraw-Hill, 1964

9. *Scientific Research*, 1, 11 and 17, 1966

10. *Science*, 155, 1967, 174

11. Ibid, 177

12. Ibid, 299

13. W. Pruden, Jr., *National Observer*, 28 February, 1966

14. A.C. Leopold, *Plant Growth and Development*, New York, McGraw-Hill, 1964

15. P.E. Pilet, *Les Phytohormones de Croissance*, Paris, Masson, 1961

16. D.E. Moreland, *American Review of Plant Physiology*, 1967, 18,

17. Heller, *"La Defoliation et ses Consequences,"* Colloquium, Associacion Amitie Franco-Vietnamienne, 19 Novembre, 1966

18. J.L. Hilton and L.L. Jansen, *American Review of Plant Physiology*, 14,353, 1964

19. M.H.M. Goldsmith, *Science*, 1156, 661, 1967

20. E.A. Davis, *Weeds*, 14, 10, 1966

21. S.P. Burg and E.A. Burg, *Proc. Nat. Acad. Science*, 55, 262, 1966

21. (bis) Excerpts from reports U.S.O.M. Agriculture, April 14, 1965, May 4, 1965, January 15, 1966

22. M. Sakka, *Vietnam, Guerre Chimique et Biologique*, Paris, Ed. Sociales, 1967

23. J. Lhoste, 30eme Sem. Sociale Universitaire, Universite Libre, Bruxelles, 1963, p. 278

24. J. Mayer, *Science*, 15 April, 1966

25. J. Mayer and V.W. Sidel, *The Christian Century*, 20 June

26. J. Mayer, *Ramparts*, 5-10 and 50, 1967

26. (bis) Madeleine Riffaud, *Dans Les Maquis du Vietcong*, Paris, Ed. Julliard R., 1965, p. 12

27. "Toxic Chemicals in Agriculture," *Publ. Ministry of Agriculture and Fisheries*, H.M. Stationary Office, London, 1953

28. A. Bevenue, G. Zweig and N.L. Nash. *Journal American Oils and Chemical Society*, 1962, 42, 99

29. V.A. Drill and T. Hirastzka (?), *Arch. Industr. Hyg.*, 1953, 7, 61

30. R. Truhaut, "Journee Inf. Subst. Croiss., Fed. Nle. Group Project." *Culture*. Paris, 30 May, 1967

31. R. Fabre and R. Truhaut, *Toxicite des Produits Phytopharmaceutiques,* Sed. E., Paris, 1954

32. T.H. Jukes and C.B. Shaffer, *Science,* 132, 4322, 1960

33. S.C. Fang, S. Khanna and A.V. Rao, *Agr. Food Chem,* 14, 262, 1966

34. W.R. Boon, *Endeavour,* 1967, p. 27

35. D.G. Clark, T.F. McElligott and E.W. Hurst, *British Journal of Industrial Medicine,* 1966, 23, 126

36. L.V. Ackerman and J.A. Regato, *Cancer, Diagnosis, Treatment, Prog.,* 2nd Edition, St. Louis, 1954

37. C.M. Bullivant, *Brit. Med. Journal,* 1967, 1, 1272

38. C. Almog and E. Tal, *Brit. Med. Journal,* 2, 721

39. D.I.R. Jones, A.G. Knight and A.J. Smith, *Arch. Environ., Health,* 1967, 14, 363

40. S.S. Epstein, J. Andrea, H. Jaffee, S. Joshi, H. Falk, and N. Mantel, *Nature,* 1967, 215, 1388

41. *U.S. Imperialists' Crimes in South Vietnam; Incomplete Data About the U.S. Use of Noxious Chemicals and Poison Gas in* 1965, Hanoi, 1966

42. J.B. Jackson, *Amer. Journal Veterinary Research,* 1966, 27, (118) 821

43. *La Presse Medicale,* Paris, 1957, 65, 1352

44. J.F. Dunachie and W.W. Fletcher, *Nature,* 1967, 215, 1406

45. J. Lhoste, *Phytoma,* 1959, 11, 13

46. O.B. Cope, *Proc. 18th Ann. Meeting Southern Weed Conference,* 1965, p. 439

47. O.B. Cope, *Journal of Applied Ecology,* 196

48. D.G. Crosby, and K.R. Tucker, *Science,* 1966, 154, 289

49. A. Gall and J.R. Dogger, *Journal Economic Entomology,* 1967, 60,

50. T. Palmer-Jones and I.W. Forster, *New Zealand Journal Agri. Res.,* 1958, 1, 620

51. T. Palmer-Jones, *New Zealand Journal Agr. Res.,* 1960, 3, 485

52. C.C. King, *Gleanings in Bee Culture,* 1964, 92, 230

53. E.E. Leppik, *American Bee Journal,* 1951, 91, 462

54. M. McGrady, *San Francisco Sunday Examiner and Chronicle,* July 30, 1967

Extracts from a Report on Agricultural Chemicals Used in Vietnam

testimony by the Japanese Scientific Committee

After the First Japanese Investigation Team made its report, Vietnamese experts on chemistry prepared evidence on the five kinds of farm chemicals spread by the American forces. The Second Japanese Investigation Team confirmed that the methods of chemical identification adopted by the Vietnamese experts are correct and the results are reliable. These are: (a) Substances containing arsenic: (arsenic was not identified as to whether organic or inorganic); (b) Calcium cyanamide; (c) DNOC (Dinitrophenol-O-cresol); (d) DNBP (Dinitro-6-sec-butylphenol); (e) Dinitrophenol.

These chemicals, added to the 2,4-D and the 2,4,5-T listed in the First Investigation Team's report, bring the total to seven kinds of agricultural chemicals used by the U.S. in its chemical war against Vietnam. Poison gases used include CN (Chloroaceto-phenone), Adamsite and CS (Chlorobenzyl-malononitril).

The spread of chemicals was carried out by modified C-123 and C-130 transport aircraft flying above ground between twilight and 8 to 9 a.m., both on fine days and on other than rainy days, when there was only light wind. The planes were preceded by a reconnaissance plane escorted by fighters. Several planes, two or three, would come in echelon formation. Chemicals in a mist-spray or powdered, were spread by these planes from both wings and tails. Observation of the spread, most frequently aimed at heavily bombed areas and remote places, was done mostly by local people rather than specialists whom it would take two or three days to reach the target area. This meant that it was extremely difficult to retrieve samples of the chemicals, and difficult to observe the immediate after-effects on the crops. There were many occasions when the liquid dried in two to three hours, withered the leaves in a day and made them fall in a week.

The arsenic chemicals, among others, were found to have left white or white-gray powder on the surface of the affected crops. People who breathed it in were affected in the mucous membranes of eyes and nose, had a headache and felt itchy over the whole body. Those who swallowed it vomited, had stomach ache, muscle convulsions and lost the use of limbs. The spread in June, 1966, over Cocong, Ben Tre Province, led to approximately 10,000 men and women casualties; 5,000 of them developed toxic symptoms and 900 were so seriously affected that they took high fever, with violent purging, loose bowels, and some of them died.

The calcium cyanamide gave off an acetylene smell; victim's eyes reddened, as well as face and lips. Symptoms were aggravated if the patient drank beverages containing alcohol.

Following are some examples of meticulous observation. The following description is based on a report by Dr. Luong Dinh Cua of the Agriculture Ministry and the report of Tran Kim Ho, vice chairman of a district Investigation of War Crimes Committee. Dr. Luong stayed in Japan for a long time as an expert on the improvement of plant breeding. The Second Japanese Investigating Team saw in the DRV some of the samples of damaged farm products, and took specimens and photos.

The civilian villages of Vinh Son, Vinh Zang and Vinh Tai were immediately affected in an area 20 kilometers wide on May 3 and 12, 1967. A C-123 plane arrived from the eastern sea and raided a six kilometer long and six to eight kilometer wide area along the Ben Hai river, on both north and south banks. Damage was done to 700 hectares of taros, 22.2 hectares of watermelons and 1,547 pepper plants, as well as paramits, bananas, papayas, pumpkins, snake gourds and potatoes. Heavily affected were the villages of Vinh Son, Vinh Lam, Vinh Huy and Vinh Hung. The affected area extended to 200 square kilometers.

Damage to Vegetables in Vietnam

1. Tapioca: (a) The leaves shrink, then wither. The stalks swell and break down. (b) The trunk swells and looks as though cracked. It will no longer grow upright. Its cracked parts develop new buds. Knobs grow out of the lower part. (c) The roots, usually small in number, grow extremely numerous and produce no tubers where they should grow. The trunk grows, but produces no tuberous roots. The skin of grown-up tuberous roots, if any, are cracked, turn black and go bad.

2. Taros: The leaves grow yellow; the stalks swell and tear in places. The ripped part breaks off if pulled. The corymbs are no more fruitful than the tapioca. There are no longer corymbs where they should be.

3. Papayas: The leaves shrink, turn yellow and wither. The stalks begin to bend. The trunk gradually sinks and develops no fruit.

4. Bananas: The leaves shrink, and become unsymmetrical. The buds rot, and are replaced by leaves instead of fruit. The leaves swell at the joints and break down. The skin of the trunk tears off and grows knobs, breaking as they develop cracks. Fruit, if already grown, becomes straight or bends in the opposite direction to that of natural growth.

5. Water Plants (mora for pig-feed); The stalks bend in all directions. The leaves shrink and immediately fall off.

6. Water Plants (*Reu muong*, the edible *Ipomea aquatica* — an important vegetable); The leaves shrink and thicken, increasing the number of veins. The stalks do not grow longer. If pruned four times to grow all over again, they develop the same phenomenon.

7. Pumpkins and Snake Gourds: Both withered in two days. The stalks developed knobs and cracks.

8. Pulses: Red beans, among others, would produce no fruit but only leaves. Their roots grow thick but the plants bear no fruit.

9. Mit (a fruit): The trunk is blasted on the side facing the east. The leaves turn yellow and branches become easy to break. The fruit will not become round but long and thin; contents no good to eat.

10. Orange and Shaddock: All withered up.

11. Cayenne-Pepper: The leaves shrink, with joints grown far away from one another. Fruit would grow up only to half size, and develop thorns.

12. Sweet potato: Runners were spoiled. Potatoes swell, the skin tears off and they go bad.

13. Peppers: The leaves turn yellow and fall off.

14. Hilao Trees (a windbreak): Is blighted. Heavy damage.

The effects of 2,4-D and 2,4,5-T were confirmed through both local damage in South Vietnam and experiments; it was difficult to determine the exact nature of the poison. Experiments were conducted with the use of Mit leaves. The 2,4-D alone would not have a blasting effect, but mixed with 2,4,5-T, the result was the same as in the actually affected areas. Neither amount nor density of the used chemicals was known. These examples of poison used have yet to go through further chemical analysis.

In addition, it was reported that two unknown toxic substances were spread over the Vinh Linh district. These are:

1. Report of Tran Kim Ho, vice-chairman of the district investigation committee. He stated that:

   Toxic substances were spread over Con Co Island on April 25, 1965, its nature was unknown.

   A spread over Hmong Lap on the Laos border did damage to hundreds of hectares of farms, destroying, in particular, all the tapioca crops. No poison was able to be examined from this remote district inhabited by a minority group.

2. Report of Tran Van Hin Hien, head of the District Agriculture Department.

   Two AD-6 and T-28 planes spread a liquid with a vile smell over the village of Hmong Lap on January 18, 1967 — doing damage to 120 hectares of fields. Also, escorted by jet planes, C-123 modified transports raided at about 2 p.m. on March 15, 17, 18, 20, 22, 27 and 29, 1967.

Experiment on the Excessive Use of Farm Chemicals

An experiment was made in Japan from August 15 to 21, 1967, with a 1/1000 solution of DNOC which is commonly used in Japan as a herbicide of comparatively little virulence. Usually it is diluted to a 1/500 or 1/1000 solution. In this experiment, DNOC was used on sweet potatoes at ten times the usual concentration. On the fourth day after application the plants withered.

The next experiment was done with 2,4-D, one of the common herbicides used in Japan as well as America. A 1/100 solution of 2,4-D was applied on sweet potatoes. They withered in the characteristic way. The stalks bent and became crooked while withering, a result which completely agrees with the testimony given in Vietnam. Other experiments were done on soy bean, rice plants and weeds. Most of these withered and became yellow, but the process of withering differs according to the species.

— Report of Professor Mokoto Kandachi, University of Tokyo, Department of Agriculture, Member of the Second Japanese Investigating Team.

Effects of So-called Farm Chemicals on the Human Body

Vietnamese experts have not yet determined whether the arsenic contained in these substances is organic or inorganic. In Japan several sorts of arsenic containing organic chemicals are used as fungicides. They are specified as poison. But the chemicals spread in Vietnam may be surmised to be inorganic chemicals such as lead-arsenate or lime-arsenate, because after the spread a white powder remained. Lead arsenate is white powder, hard to volatilize or dissolve after being spread.

Arsenic, which used to weigh most heavily in pre-war Japan among agricultural chemicals; specifically among insecticides, is a deadly poison to both man and livestock — poisonous enough to kill a man if he takes 0.13 grams of the arsenious acid which constitutes the raw material of the lead arsenate. The lead arsenate is said to be six times less poisonous, requiring 0.8 grams to kill a man.

A person taking such arsenates orally would be poisoned acutely, suffering chest trouble, vomiting, dizziness, headache and convulsions. If the amount taken is sufficient to cause malignant loose bowels, low blood pressure, dead sleep, jaundice or anuria, he will die. One whiff is enough to make it hard to breathe and cause coughing; a touch of it on the skin would cause inflammation. A chronic patient of poisoning would complain, first of all, of nervous disorders, such as violent headache, paralysis of sensation, abnormal feeling in the limbs, kinetic paralysis, and the so-called arsenical brain malfunction which develops the symptoms of disinterest and idiocy. As for his skin, he would be blackened around the neck and eyelids, and have callouses develop in the palms of the hands and on the soles of the feet. The affected skin would also develop a circular shaped depilation: liver trouble, chronic nephritis, anemia and loss of weight follow. If taken into the blood, the arsenic sticks to the walls of the liver, kidney, stomach and intestines, thus making it slow to discharge. Once spread over agricultural crops, the lead arsenate powder is likely to remain there for a long time, so it is dangerous to eat the crops. It is forbidden to spread it, at least, one month before harvest.

Lime arsenic is another kind of arsenide, but less stable than lead arsenate. When it turns acid, in particular, it develops arsenic and may do harm. Comprising 40 per cent arsenic, it makes a no-less deadly poison, remaining effective as long as lead arsenate. It develops its arsenical poisoning manifestations and symptoms in much the same way as the above-mentioned lead arsenate does.

As to calcium cyanamide, in Japan, farm chemicals containing 60% of calcium cyanamide are called nitrolime and used as a sort of fertilizer. A man would have his liver affected by it, stopping the working of oxidase. Specifically, it causes failure of oxidization and dissolves alcohol, he would have a headache, feel sick, complain of severe palpitations, feel dizzy, feel oppressed in the chest, have difficulty in breathing, and eventually begin to talk in delirium with his senses blurred. His face would turn red, his blood pressure would plunge to a sharp temporary low. If nitrolime touched his wet skin, he would develop a rash. Inhaling it, he would suffer from bronchitis. His eyes being affected, he would have conjunctivitis, and his nose would be inflamed. Crops, of course, will be poisoned and withered up if their stalks and/or leaves are touched with it.

As the experience in Vietnam is similar to these experiences in Japan, it is considered that in Vietnam American troops use calcium cyanamide as poison for men and crops.

Japanese farmers use DNOC in general as a weedicide, with which they are apt to be poisoned. It is highly poisonous to men and live-stock; even if it does not enter through the mouth, but only touches their skin. It must also be handled with care, being combustible. In Japan, a weedicide containing DNBP is called "Premerge", which is also specified as poison. At several scientific symposiums many examples of dermatitis due to DNBP have been reported.

Dinitrophenol, the last among the five kinds of farm chemicals identified as in use by the U.S. in Vietnam is also a poison and its toxic character is similar to DNOC and DNBP.

2,4-D and 2,4,5-T are hormone types of herbicides which would not do much harm to the human body, but does seriously affect plants as the chemical penetrates into its roots. This action results in the plants promoting irregular fission, arresting its formation of chlorophyll and excessively expediting its respiratory function, eventually to end in malformation and withering. This chemical is most effective when used at a temperature of 24° C. It is used to eliminate weeds in paddy-field, but farmers must be careful not to let it fall on nearby vegetables and fruit-trees.

Our conclusion is that some of the farm chemicals used contain virulent poisons and others have comparatively little, though all are commonly considered to be useful. Even in Japan, virulent farm chemicals are sometimes carelessly misused by farmers in the busy season, although they are always being instructed how to use them and how to avoid accidents. The government is being pressed to forbid the use of some of these substances as farm chemicals. It seems completely against humanity to scatter these poisonous chemicals over fields indiscriminately. Some of them cause chronic poisoning as does arsenic, and leave terrible effects long after the time of acute suffering. Farm chemicals can work as poisons if they are spread wrongly, at the wrong time, in wrong quantities or at the wrong concentration. Damage is done not only to crops but also to people in their environment in general. Poisoning fish and cattle, which are then eaten by people, is another danger. Both by direct and indirect suffering, the whole lives of the people are damaged. As a doctor, I would like to repeat and emphasize that in the cause of humanity we should not allow the spreading of these poisons which do long-term invisible damage. War which destroys all plant life indiscriminately and uses chemicals which are virulent poisons should of necessity be called war of "annihilation".

—Shunichi Wakatsuki, M.D.

Amount of Chemicals Used

The American agricultural magazine *Farm Chemicals* says in its June, 1966 issue, that the Deputy Commander of U.S. forces in South Vietnam declared that he had, "spread weedicides over 200,000 acres (approx. 80,000 hectares) of jungle or bush," and that he also had "spread defoliation agents over arable land of the Viet Cong-controlled areas."

This year the U.S. Government declared that $100 million (36,000 million yen) worth of farm chemicals would be used in Vietnam in fiscal year 1967. This $100 million worth of farm chemicals is equivalent to Japan's total production as used on Japan's arable land of 6 million hectares. The chemicals spread over the Vietnamese 80,000 hectares are therefore 100 times as much as the Japanese use in terms of quantity per unit area.

The Vietnamese say that target areas covered are more than 700,000 hectares, which is evidently the right figure. Even so, the amount of farm chemicals used would be ten times higher than the Japanese use per unit.

—Prof. Yoichi Fukushima, Member of Japan Science Council

Napalm and its Effects on Human Beings
testimony by Gilbert Dreyfus, M.D.

Professor of Biochemistry at the University of Paris Medical School

The word "napalm" is derived from the two words "naphthene" and "palmitate." Napalm itself is a jelly obtained from the salts of aluminum, palmitic or other fatty acids, and naphthenic acids. The property of these acids is that they give a viscous consistency to gasoline so that an incendiary jelly results. We have developed the habit of calling "napalm," not only the napalm itself, but also the material resulting when it is mixed with gasoline to form the incendiary weapon.

The generic precursors of this weapon go back to the flamethrowers first used In World War I. These flamethrowers had a limited effective range because of the fluidity of the liquids. Therefore an attempt was made to diminish fluidity and render the liquids more adherent. An example of primitive success in this area is the early Molotov cocktail where a simple fragment of cotton was added to adhere to a tank and to render the combustion of the gasoline more effective.

The first napalm was developed by American technicians of the Chemical Corps during World War II. They observed that latex mixed with gasoline took on a viscous consistency which gave good results. But as the sources of latex were blocked after Pearl Harbor, they had to find a synthetic. They sought a jelly which could be prepared at low temperatures, which was easily handled, stable and not too costly. A soaplike aluminum mixture — aluminum salts with fatty acids — met these requirements, especially the acids having from 10 to 16 carbons, like palmitic acid and oleic and other unsaturated acids. Napalm comes in the form of a gray-white powder resembling soap powder; it can be made usable by mixing with gasoline right on the field of combat.

The use of fire as a weapon by soldiers is very ancient, but the technology in modern terms really began, in a rudimentary way, during World War I and became generalized during World War II. Napalm conferred on a flammable substance the properties necessary for extended use and the airplane furnished an efficient delivery system.

Until the beginning of World War II, magnesium was the incendiary substance most frequently employed by all belligerents. But from 1942 on, it was recognized that magnesium was costly and in too short supply for massive use. Therefore, as napalm was developed, it became the prime material in the manufacture of incendiary bombs. The first model in service, the M-69 bomb weighing six and a half pounds, was utilized in great quantities against Japan. The models which followed were developed too late to use against Japan, but they were used during the Korean War and then by the French in Indochina and Algeria.

To utilize napalm effectively large target areas are preferred. Flamethrowing aircraft have proved ineffective because conventional aircraft fly at too great a speed to be accurate. On the other hand, excellent results are obtained by dropping fire bombs made from launchable drums filled with gasoline jellied with napalm. The napalm drums have exterior ignition devices consisting of small incendiary bombs or phosphorus grenades.

There exist a number of different containers for napalm. Those most frequently used contain nearly 500 liters of gasoline, jellied by an addition of napalm varying from 6 to 13 per cent — 6 per cent seems more often used. Such a bomb will cover with flames a surface 75 feet wide by 270 feet long. To obtain the best results the bomb should fall as rapidly as possible, giving, by momentum, a greater length to the surface covered. Therefore the best delivery is not to drop the bomb vertically, but to launch it from low altitude — about one hundred feet — from a "hedge-hopping" aircraft.

At the present time the Americans use two types of napalm and several different means of delivery. The two napalms are "ordinary," which produces a temperature of 800° to 1200° C. [1472° to 2152° F.] and "super-napalm," enriched with polystyrene, sodium, magnesium or phosphorus, with which the temperatures reach 1500° to 2000° C. [2732° to 3632° F.]. These two napalms are principally used in drums of from 60 to 630 liters capacity and in bombs weighing from one hundred to two hundred kilos [220 to 440 lbs.]; the U.S. Seventh Fleet also uses napalm missiles.

Since napalm is essentially an incendiary product it sets fire to any combustible matter with which it comes in contact. A human being in the open cannot protect himself against it. Napalm acts not only by burning but has an equally devastating effect which consists of a complicated process whereby shock, absorption of oxygen from the air [deoxygenation], smoke and noxious gases become lethal. The Surgeon-General of the French Army has described the massive poisoning by carbon monoxide after a napalm attack and points out that none of the burned in the cental strike area survive because of this phenomenon. Victims who are able to survive the massive deoxygenation are those who have been on the periphery of the strike zone.

An examination of some of the methods of execution practiced during the Middle Ages sheds some light on these effects. In executions by burning at the stake, when large fires were used, the victim died rapidly from carbon-monoxide poisoning before being actually burned by the flames; when small fires were used a longer and much crueler death by flame resulted. (From this has come the popular French expression for being on tenterhooks: *brûler à petit feu*, to roast over a slow fire.)

During the Second World War, troops reported finding Japanese shelters which had been struck by napalm bombs in which all the occupants were dead without having been burned at all. These soldiers had died, apparently without pain, and had an expression of fright and surprise frozen onto their faces; they had been instantaneously and massively poisoned by carbon monoxide. The only way to escape the asphyxiating effects of napalm is to flee into the open air — where the direct destruction by burning from flaming splashes is greatest. In a strike zone it is almost impossible to escape the effects of napalm by taking shelter, for one cannot hold one's breath for the time it takes napalm to burn off. The very carbon-monoxide poisoning itself paralyzes the will and robs the victim of the ability to move.

From the preceding it can be seen that a napalm bombardment has two principal effects: incendiary and asphyxiating. When napalm strikes human beings the resulting burns are distinguishable from ordinary burns by the fact that they are covered with a viscous black magma resembling tar. The depth of the burn is always considerable. The extensive fires caused by the combustion of flammable structures in contact with napalm prolong the effect of the primary burning.

The asphyxiating effect of napalm is due to the incomplete combustion of the compound, which produces carbon monoxide. This phenomenon has been reported in areas ravaged by the fire storms caused by bombardment of cities with conventional bombs during the 1939-1945 war. The lethality of carbon monoxide is well known and it was tried by the Nazis for use as a destructive gas for the mass executions of civilians. The source of this gas was the exhaust of diesel motors which was either directed into an enclosure built onto a truck or into a gas chamber. The method was too primitive and was abandoned in favor of cyanide derivatives.

We now turn to the poison and burn pathology of napalm. Carbon monoxide poisoning is most effective. Carbon monoxide dissolves rapidly into blood plasmas.

Combined with hemoglobin, it imparts to the red corpuscles a very stable combination of carboxy-hemoglobin, which is more stable than the combination with oxygen. The combining with hemoglobin is powerful and rapid, occurring within a few hundredths of a second. It is 250 times more rapid and powerful than the reaction with oxygen. The elimination of carbon monoxide, on the other hand, is much more slow and difficult. Once combined with hemoglobin, carbon monoxide suppresses the oxygen-carrying capacity of the blood pigment, thereby inhibiting the function of hemoglobin in supplying oxygen to the tissues. Carbon monoxide also seems to have an effect on the iron-containing cells and combines readily with the respiratory enzymes, bringing about direct disturbances of cellular respiration in addition to those caused by the lack of oxygen.

The chemical effects of carbon monoxide depend on its concentration in the surrounding air. With as little as 1 per cent it is toxic. With higher concentrations, ideation is disturbed and there are hallucinations. Concurrently there occur motor disturbances and paralysis which prevent walking and all desire to escape. Beginning with a saturation of 15 to 40 per cent of the hemoglobin, encephalic disturbances, cardio-respiratory failure and fatal coma appear. Survivors of poisoning who have received emergency treatment exhibit permanent neurological after-effects which range from mild to very severe. Prognosis for coma depends in large part on the therapeutic facilities. The immediate use of oxygen therapy is called for since the symptoms are reversible with a forced intake of oxygen. Modern resuscitation equipment is imperative. One can imagine the unavailability of such equipment in a target area in Vietnam.

The second and most evident effect of napalm is the burn. The explosion of a 200-liter napalm incendiary bomb precipitates massive destruction by flames in a circle about 240 feet in diameter. In that zone the heat is from 1800° to 3600° F. and the carbon-

377

monoxide release is massive; within this zone, there will be no survivors. Outside this zone nonsheltered individuals will suffer burns from flaming splashes of napalm of a gravity in proportion to the amount of cutaneous surface affected. Parts not protected by clothing — face, hands, often the upper and lower members — will be burned. The fire affects the clothing also, which can contribute to localized burning, rendering the effect worse.

After bombardment of a human group by napalm, the wounded — in need of immediate treatment if they are to survive — will be found around the periphery of the strike zone. The possibility of treatment is a function of the gravity of the burn. Besides the extent and depth of burning, age is a determining factor since the effects are more severe on children and the old. Also, burns of the face and neck are more serious for a child than for an adult. Gravity is expressed in terms of percentage of the body surface affected. Any adult burned on more than 10 per cent of the body, or any child burned on more than 8 percent, is considered critically burned.

Doctors also distinguish between superficial burns — burns of the first and second degree, where the thermal lesion involves only the epidermis — and the deep burns of the third degree, where the destruction of all skin, epidermis and dermis, renders any spontaneous healing impossible. Burning which goes as deep as the tissues [third-degree] develops scabs which, when they fall off, leave an open wound susceptible to infection. A third-degree burn will never heal aseptically. Because of napalm's adhesive quality, the burns it causes are almost always of the third degree. It is estimated that a napalm burn affecting as little as 5 per cent of the body surface is grave.

A serious burn progresses through successive stages: first of shock and poisoning; second of infection; and third of healing. Any grave burn becomes a generalized illness due to the loss of body fluid and the breakdown of the body's mechanism for fluid balance. Immediately after burning there is shock due to pain and fear. Toward the sixth hour and for three or four days thereafter, true physiological shock due to the leakage of liquid plasma from the burned areas sets in. The amount of this fluid loss is proportional to the amount of burned surface. Some loss occurs at the exterior but mostly in the subcutaneous tissues, causing edema which is sometimes considerable. The direct consequence of the plasma leakage is a hemoconcentration from diminution of the blood mass. The diminution of the blood mass leads to a circulatory slowing and often to cardiovascular collapse, which in turn compromise the oxygenation of the tissues and cause multiple metabolic disturbances.

Beginning with the third and fourth days a reverse phenomenon of reabsorption of the exuded liquids takes place. The tissues and the red corpuscles release their liquids into the circulatory system bringing about a hemodilution causing anemia, and hypertension with crises of cerebral and pulmonary edema. Also around the third day the consequences of liver and kidney damage appear. This is an anoxia of the tissues due to the buildup of toxic products coming from the reabsorption into the blood stream of the destroyed tissues. Later, nutritional disturbances appear which are a result of the nitrogen loss following nitrogen destruction. Thus within ten days such a burned person loses about eleven pounds from fluid loss alone.

In addition to the foregoing, every profound burn is a wound that is susceptible to infection. This is especially true since the initial inadequacy of general resistance facilitates the multiplication of microbes. Once established this infection further inhibits nutrition and blocks healing. Thus a vicious, often irreversible circle is created which is responsible for more than 50 per cent of the secondary deaths from burns. Such death can often appear months after the trauma.

Finally the healing process develops with elimination of the necrotic tissus. A second-degree burn heals in a few weeks. By contrast, in a deep burn, the epidermatization [growth of new skin] can only start from the periphery of the wound, if one has been unable to make a graft, to build a fragile scar tissue. This tendency to heal from the periphery causes granular, sclerotic tissue to form on the wound, further inhibiting healing.

In napalm burns, a final element is of great importance; this is the gravity of facial burning. Eye burns can lead to loss of one or both eyes. Nasal and ear passages involved develop extended suppuration and necrosis which abcess with unbearable pain to the patient. The visage becomes hideous with psychological trauma of formidable proportions. There are other lingering damages: lesions of the bones, which do not show up on X-rays, and appearance of cysts of certain joints and bones of the hand — for instance, the metacarpus — which persist for many years after the initial burning.

The treatment of the burned is symptomatic, directed at those symptoms we have just enumerated. It is simple and generic, but requires that treatment be undertaken immediately, that treatment be prolonged and attentive and that it be given by a very advanced medical organization. At the bombardment site, extreme care must be taken not to take any action which will increase the risk of infection. The patient should be wrapped in a sheet and be given antipain injections, and antibiotic injections and antitetanus serum to combat infection. If possible, an infusion of glucose or saline solution should be given and the victim evacuated immediately to a medical facility of the "general hospital" level. Every burn victim should be treated as an incipient shock case and should receive emergency treatment without delay. This is of extreme urgency; if shock is not prevented it will establish itself and become irreversible. If so treated, the burned person will pass the crisis in from six to ten days. It can be seen that in medically advanced countries with good medical organization available it is possible to reduce the mortality from severe burning. In underdeveloped areas or during great cataclysms such as war, this is something else.

In medical summation then, treatment consists of compensation for liquid loss by blood transfusion, plasma substitutes, saline solutions, (especially at the time of hemodilution), prevention of infection by antibiotics, oxygenation under pressure and high calory intake. After these emergency treatments follow long-term care, dressing, antiseptic cleaning of the wounds, excision of necrotic tissue and if possible, grafting. Grafting requires good general health, clean wounds and an availability of skin from nonburned donor sites. The present state of medical science does not allow us to take grafts from any donor other than the recipient himself. It is evident from the foregoing that the treatment of a burn victim is difficult, even with specialized personnel and the most modern equipment. Even with this, the suffering of the patient is intense and onerous.

It is obvious that under repeated bombardments which destroy structures which could be used for evacuation — when medical personnel are overworked and subject to lethal attacks themselves — these ideal conditions we have described are impossible. There is no resemblance between conditions prevailing when treating accident victims during peacetime and victims of deliberate attacks. The emergency treatment of a mass of burn victims in areas remote from medical centers and without adequate means of evacuation presents insuperable problems. It is therefore inadvisable in such conditions to attempt to save the worst cases, which will, no matter what is done, die within a week. One ought to concentrate efforts upon the less gravely burned with between 10 and 20 per cent of the body surface affected and without impairment of the digestive tract.

In Vietnam a limited number of gravely burned persons can be treated in general hospitals, especially those in Hanoi, but the majority of victims are treated in the village maternity infirmaries and the district hospitals where skin grafting is not possible. Instead of grafting, wounds are left to heal by slow skin extension from the wound periphery.

I do not have definitive statistics, but it seems that only about 30 per cent of those wounded by napalm and not killed outright can be saved. If the victim does survive, the dermatological consequences of napalm burns are especially serious. After the surgery there exists extreme risk of superinfections. Poor grafting also leaves serious aftereffects. Retractile skin and contraction of scars form huge welts which will require further treatment. Keloid and hypertrophic scars will form to limit and inhibit the normal elasticity of the skin, which in turn inhibits the normal movement of the member. These scars are prone to pyodermic and microdermic infections. The new skin is extremely fragile, and scleroatrophied skin will always be susceptible to minor infections that a normal skin would easily combat.

Lastly, concerning the medical effects of napalm recovery, there is the specter of secondary cancers. Old burn scars show a frequency of skin cancer out of proportion to such appearance in normal skin. This cancer consists of a spino-cellular epithelioma with a negative prognosis because of the rapid invasion of the malign cells to the related ganglion areas.

Napalm, to conclude, whether it is used strategically on the battlefield or in the bombardment of urban areas or village collectives, is a means of extensive, nondiscriminatory destruction. It effects primarily human beings, livestock, crops and light flammable structures such as habitations. Its employment in heavily populated areas will produce immense loss of life from burning and asphyxiation. In survivors, corporal injuries of the greatest gravity with functional sequels which prevent the resumption of normal life are the rule.

Though some of the victims may partially recuperate after long and costly treatment, for the majority of napalm-burned persons nothing much can be done.

Patterns of Bombing Civilians in the North
testimony by Wilfred Burchett

I arrived by road from Hanoi at about 11 p.m. on October 17, 1967, and was immediately taken to see the destruction of civilian housing in Hong Bang ward, the most densely populated of Haiphong's three city wards. We had to make a quick visit because Thanh Tam, Deputy-Chief of the Haiphong Provincial War Crime Commission warned that raids now took place at night, starting around midnight. There was considerable damage to civilian housing; one whole residential quarter built up since 1956, on the western perimeter of the ward was entirely wiped out, as were a large section of housing around the Central Market, a fishing smack repair yard, an automobile battery plant and several streets of shops.

I was warned that because of the proximity to the sea where U.S. aircraft carriers patrol, at times only 30 kilometers off the coast, and also because of sneak tactics employed by American pilots, there was usually not more than one minute between the sounding of the alert and the actual attack. In fact, at just 30 minutes after midnight, there was the simultaneous explosion of bombs and anti-aircraft guns and the sounding of the alert. It was a bright moonlight night and there were two more raids at 1:30 a.m. and 2:30 a.m. and again later . . .

Thanh Tam gave me a briefing on the situation as of October 12, 1967. He stated: "Regular bombing raids on Haiphong started on June 29, 1967, one year to the day after the first attack on June 29, ostensibly against oil storage depots but in which the village of Cam Lo on the outskirts of the City was wiped out and the ward of Hong Bang also suffered.

"In Haiphong province, of which Haiphong city is the capital, there are 161 communes of which 150 have been bombed. The district capitals of An Lao and An Hai have been completely wiped out. Throughout July and August, 1967, attacks were intensified, especially in that part of the province situated midway between Haiphong and Hanoi.

"In the first eight months of 1967, over 6000 High Explosive bombs were dropped, 400 CBU's ("mother" bombs each containing about 300 "guava" fragmentation bombs), 130 missiles were fired and over 4000 rockets. The above applies to Haiphong province as a whole, with a total population of about one million.

"During August 1967, some 760 High Explosive bombs were dropped of which by far the greater part were in the urban area of Haiphong city. Of the latter, 206 were delayed-action bombs; 102 CBU's and a large number of rockets and missiles were also used.

"From August 31, until October 12, 1967, an action named by the Americans "Operation Thunderclap" has been continuing. This is aimed at exterminating life in the residential areas, at isolating Haiphong city from the rest of the province and from the other provinces; it is meant to paralyse all communications, to prevent aid from socialist countries from reaching the DRVN and from being distributed. During "Operation Thunderclap" one third of the residential area of Haiphong city has been destroyed. A new feature has been the widespread use of new types of delayed-action bombs. These are of three main types having either vibration fuses, magnetic fuses or time fuses.

"These are dropped among ordinary bombs to delay rescue workers or extract a high cost for rescuers in human lives; they are strewn alongside roads and rivers to halt traffic. We have had to find special means to explode them so that traffic can keep moving and people may go about their daily life. A time table of attacks during the past month on the city itself, shows the extent of the raids and their increased tempo."

September 11: 50 sorties in three raids; 95 HE bombs of 500 to 2000 lbs. on the residential area. *September 12:* 68 sorties, including some with A-6A night-bombers at night. 163 HE bombs, lots of missiles and rockets on targets already bombed the previous day. Residential targets in the Le Chan ward were also attacked, including No. 8 Secondary School and the French Martyr Memorial. The school had already been evacuated. *September 18:* 110 sorties in three waves; 105 HE bombs, apart from objectives of Cua Cam and the Tam Ky Children's Clinic which forms part of the Czech-Vietnam Friendship Polyclinic Hospital; the Children's Clinic had been evacuated. *September 21*: 74 sorties in two attacks; 62 HE bombs and 16 CBU's. The latter were dropped along and around the intersection of two main streets, Lach Tray and Dinh Dong and along another section parallel to and about 10 meters from the eastern side of Lach Tray street; also along Cau Niem street and around the TB hospital in that street. *September 26:* 22 sorties; 76 HE bombs, 4 CBU's, 84 rockets and 22 Bullpup missiles against 14 different spots within the city limits. Typical of this raid was the indiscriminate firing of rockets and missiles. For example, against the Ky Dong Hospital in the street of that name, Hong Bang district. I had visited this site and interviewed witnesses. *September 28:* 28 sorties; 40 HE bombs, 60 rockets, 2 missiles against similar targets as on the 26th, plus several zones in and around the newly built working-class quarter. I visited here earlier in the day but could not stay for long because of the presence of delayed-action bombs. *September 29:* 24 sorties; 52 HE bombs, 4 CBU's, rockets and missiles. *October 3/4/5/6/7:* Altogether 227 sorties in 9 attacks; 620 HE bombs, 45 CBU's, 527 rockets, 32 missiles. Most of these were aimed at buildings damaged in other raids, and at Kien An, an industrial and commercial town in Haiphong province not far from the port city. *October 8/9/10/11/12:* Night bombardments, including three I witnessed on the night of October 11-12: 124 HE bombs, great number of missiles and rockets. During October, up to the 12th, 450 delayed-action bombs had been dropped on waterways, dikes, rice fields, roads, railway lines, ferryways, on all approaches to urban centers."

Vibration fuse bombs can be detonated by trains, trucks, buses tractors in the fields, steamers or motorboats. *Magnetic fuse bombs* by anything metallic passing near them. Dropped into rivers, they can be detonated by any craft with metal parts passing over them. *Time fuses* are set to explode at varying times after the bombs are dropped. The delayed-action bombs look exactly like each other and like ordinary 500 lb. to 3000 lb. impact-detonation bombs.

The United States intended with all this to paralyse the port and demoralise the population by day and night raids, also by harassing raids at night to prevent people sleeping and thereby reducing their working capacity next day. But in fact normal activities continue — as I was able to see for myself . . .

Escalating Bombardment of North Vietnamese Cities
testimony by Antonello Trombadori

Mr. Trombadori is a Correspondent for Italian Catholic Newspapers

The characteristic of the U.S. Air Force attacks, verified by everyone who undertook investigations in the period from May to October 1967, has been the intensified bombing of civilian targets, especially in heavily populated zones. As of May 1967, all of North Vietnam's six large cities, Hanoi, Haiphong, Nam Dinh, Thai Binh, Viet Tri, Vinh, 20 out of 30 important provincial towns, 59 out of 97 district towns and villages, as well as hundreds of communes and hamlets have been systematically attacked.

From May until October 1967, the American Air Force has concentrated on the following targets:

— Hanoi, the capital of the RVD (bombed in August, October, and November of 1967). As a result of the bombardments of Hanoi's residential quarters in August of 1967, there were 76 dead and 151 wounded civilians.

— Haiphong: For 44 days in a row, in July and August of 1967, the city was attacked with more than 1000 bombs of various sizes, more than 100 CBU's containing over 30,000 individual fragmentation bombs, and hundreds of rockets. These air raids were intensified in September of 1967. Material damage: More than a third of the city destroyed, including 600 houses, 3 hospitals, 3 schools; 156 of the 161 communes have been subjected to air raids. The towns of Tat Ba and Cau Lao have been completely razed to the ground. The official number of victims is more than 100 dead and wounded.

— The Vinh Linh zone: B-52's and other aircraft have destroyed whole villages.

Other cities and provincial centers severely attacked were Nam Dinh, Vinh, Thai Binh, Dong Hai, Than Hoa, Phu Ly, Ninh Binh, Hai Duoag, Lang Son — the last lying very near to the Chinese border. Also hit were dikes and pumping stations in the rainy season, particularly the Traly dike, which on August 23, 1967, was hit with 70 high explosive bombs and 4 CBU bombs. Destroyed were hospitals, schools, social-cultural institutions, religious places, and 18 hospitals and sanatoriums such as the TB hospital at Viet Tiep, and the district hospital in An Lao. A total of 130 hospitals and schools have now been attacked in the DRV. The seminary in Haiphong (120 bombs) and the school in Ha Phu, where 33 students from the age of 8 to 12 years died and where 28 others, including two teachers were wounded, were attacked. Also 73 churches and 13 pagodas, which raised the number of bombed churches and pagodas in Vietnam to 307 and 116 respectively.

The methods and line of action which are used by the US Air Force can allow us to draw the following conclusions: Gradually, as the bombings are intensified, the number of bombing missions has risen to 150 per day on the average. Fragmentation bombs (anti-personnel weapons) are in widespread use. Delayed-action fragmentation bombs have appeared. The use of fragmentation bombs combined with explosive bombs of great size has been intensified in order to achieve the maximum effect on the civilian population. The use of weapons with vibration fuses, magnetic fuses, and delayed action fuses have permitted nightly attacks of devastating effect.

After an absence of 11 months, I visited the DRV for the second time from October 17, 1967 to November 10, 1967. I traveled more than 1000 kilometers along Route No. 1, from Hanoi to the 17th parallel, Route No. 5, from Hanoi to Haiphong, the route between Hanoi-Viet Tri, and that from Hanoi to Thai Binh. I visited the cities of Hanoi, Haiphong, Than Hoa, Viet Tri, the village Bai Lai and the province of Thai Bhul.

From the 30th of August 1967, 80% of the American bombing missions against the DRV have been directed against Haiphong. On the 30th August 1967, the Americans initiated operation "Thunderclap" directed against Haiphong. What primarily amazes a stranger visiting Haiphong is that the harbor, docks, and estuary, where Soviet, Chinese, Polish, English, Greek, and ships from other countries lie at anchor, have never been massively attacked. Until now the Americans have been afraid of provoking serious, international political complications. Therefore, the aerial attacks have been directed much more concentratedly against other zones of the city with the aim of paralysing the harbor and paralysing the lines of communication to the hinterland and breaking the peoples' morale.

More than a third of Haiphong has been seriously hit and practically obliterated. Out of 161 communes in Haiphong province 156 have been seriously attacked.

If one takes into consideration the fact that the number of U.S. aircraft shot down over Haiphong by the Vietnamese air defense was about 16 in 1965, 45 in 1966, and 107 up until only October 23, 1967, one can get a precise picture of the increase of the American aggression against the largest port in the DRV. At the same time one can also get an idea of the Vietnamese air defense's increasing strength.

Here are some facts on the latest American bomb attack against Haiphong and its suburbs:

11 September 1967: 50 planes, in three waves, attack the city's west zone. 95 high explosive bombs and an undetermined number of missiles, rockets, and fragmentation bombs are counted. 17 September: 68 planes, still in the west zone. 163 high explosive bombs counted. The children's hospital is seriously damaged as well as school No. 8 in the city. 18 September: 110 planes, still over the west zone, in three waves; 105 high explosive bombs. 21 September: 74 planes in two waves, 60 high explosive bombs, 16 fragmentation bombs, still over the west zone. The tuberculosis hospital is seriously hit. 26 September: 30 planes in two waves, 76 high explosive bombs, 4 fragmentation bombs, many air-to-ground missiles and rockets, still over the west zone. 28 September: 28 planes, 40 high explosive bombs still over the west zone; school No. 8, and other places which were hit before were hit yet again. 29 September: 24 planes, 52 high explosive bombs, 4 fragmentation bombs, air-to-ground missiles rockets: the village Dong Ke in the city's eastern suburb was razed to the ground.

On October 3, 4, 5, 6, and 7, the same places were attacked again. Our statistics show that 220 planes participated with 620 high explosive bombs, 45 fragmentation bombs, 530 rockets, and 30 "Bullpup" and "Shrike" air-to-ground missles.

On October 8, 9 and 10, 1967, there were numerous nightly attacks on the city's east zone, with 124 high explosive bombs, rockets and missiles. On October 12, 14 and 16 the attacks continued on the east and west zones of the city. On October 14, 113 high explosive bombs were dropped on the east and west zones of the city. That day more than 60 houses, three schools, 4 hospitals and nursing homes, two factories (coal and furniture) were destroyed; more than 1500 families became homeless. The number of dead and wounded was officially 200.

On Sunday, October 22, at 2 a.m., I was personally present at the day's first air attack, and, at 3 p.m., the second. The first lasted a half hour, the second about the same time. Route No. 4, which goes to Hanoi, was seriously hit, as well as the residential quarter which surrounds it at the western gate. I saw one of the enemy planes in flames falling into the sea.

The planes which take part in the attacks on Haiphong practically all come from the Seventh Fleet. They are mostly planes of the F-4 and A-4 types. If they transport bombs of 250 kg., then each plane can transport 15-18. The F-4's have two pilots, the A-4's one. Usually they come in groups of 15 — 20 from two directions — the northeast and southwest. Those which come from the ships in the Seventh Fleet need only 1.5 minutes flying time.

I visited Quarter No. 1 in Haiphong. The first thing I thought of were documentary films of the Second World War from Berlin, Warsaw or Coventry. The quarter was completely razed to the ground. There was not *one* single important road in the vicinity of this area, and not *one* single transportation installation which in any way — could justify "military grounds" for the American aggression against the DRV. Only the application of the principle of "psycho-social" attack on the civilian and working population can explain these bombings. The intended target is very obvious.

I herewith give the Tribunal a list of the wounded which were treated at Thong Ke hospital in Haiphong from September 9, 1967, to October 14, 1967. It lists 75 wounded, of which 49, that is to say more than 50%, are seriously wounded by fragmentation bombs with delayed-action fuses, the use of which has become more frequent in the last escalation on the DRV.

From the 5th of August, 1964, until the end of 1966, the city of Than Hoa has been exposed to 212 American aerial attacks, of which 155 took place during the day and 57 during the night; 5110 high explosive bombs, 210 incendiary bombs, 934 rockets, 163 missiles, and 5 floating mines calculated to hit the Ham Rong bridge over the river Ma, which had proved impossible to hit and until now has not been destroyed; Many rounds from 20mm cannons: no fragmentation bombs in the first period.

The results: 2522 dwellings completely destroyed and 300 heavily damaged; 4 hospitals (all the existing ones) destroyed, 3 infirmaries destroyed, 16 schools and 3 kindergardens destroyed, 9 pagodas destroyed.

From the 1st of January 1967, until September 30, 1967, Than Hoa was exposed to 213 attacks, of which 165 took place during the day and 48 at night. But the number of planes which took part in every attack rose by 20 on the average. 3715 high explosive bombs. 115 missiles, 1687 rockets, 5 "mother bombs" (CBU — fragmentation bombs), 42 rounds from 20mm cannons. The aircraft which were used are of the following types: F-100, F-101, F-102, F-8, F-4, A-3J, F-105, A-4, A-6.

The results: 710 houses completely destroyed, as well as 174 heavily damaged; 8 hectares of rice fields destroyed; 2 hospitals, which had been restored, were attacked again; one Catholic church destroyed; the cloister, *Le Monastere Catholique des Adoratrices du Saint Sacrement,* was heavily damaged; the theater and cinema completely destroyed; the state library destroyed; the central post office was destroyed; the two electrical and water works destroyed; all the city's administration buildings as well as a number of craftsmen's cooperatives were destroyed; 27 meters of irrigation canals and 22 meters of dikes were either destroyed or heavily damaged.

All this I have seen with my own eyes. And I have also seen with my own eyes the results of the bombardments which occurred after the 30th of September until the day I left, October 27, 1967. There was an entire group of straw huts which were unable to withstand the powerful explosive bombs and were ignited. In this area the inhabitants of Thanh Hoa were in the process of planting vegetable fields.

I shall now give some information on an attack on September 3, 1967 at 7:50 a.m.: 32 planes in 15 minutes; 100 high explosive bombs, one missile; the planes were of the A-4, A-6, F-4, and F-8 types. They dived and shelled the Phu To quarter in the surburban district. One hectare of rice field was destroyed, one buffalo and one ox died, three stone houses with straw roofs were destroyed, 5 people, including three children were killed, and 26 were wounded. This is a typical example of an attack the Americans continued after the city itself is destroyed, in order to annihilate all the life which might be left in the city and its neighborhood.

I visited the outlying mobile first aid station near the city of Than Hoa. The buildings were straw huts, the operating theater consisted of a larger straw hut than the others draped with white sheets. But the leader of this first aid station, the surgeon, Doctor Nguyen Xun Khue, who is 32 years old and educated in Hanoi, most often operates right on the spot where the Americans have bombed and killed. I visited some of his patients and I submit a list of their names and the medical data to the Tribunal . . .

I will refrain from describing in detail the results of the American attacks on the Viet Tri zone in the years 1965 and 1966. It is sufficient to know that in this period Viet Tri has been the target for 20 bombardments of massive character with over 150 attacks, 241 high explosive bombs, 57 "mother" CBU bombs, a large number of rockets and 20mm shells. 53 targets were hit: densely populated areas, factories, electricity works, the province hospital, the co-operative crafts concerns, etc., etc. It can be said that not one of the most important production centers had been spared. Here are some figures from 1967: Up until October Viet Tri was exposed to 23 attacks; 58 Squadrons took part (174 planes) in 263 sorties. 578 high explosive bombs were dropped, which was double the number in 1966; 61 "mother" CBU bombs, an unknown number of missiles rockets and 20mm cannon shells. The bombardments took place night and day regardless of weather conditions. I have been given these official figures of dead and wounded: 94 dead and 222 wounded from January 1967, until October 18, 1967, when the last attack against the Viet Tri area took place.

It can be said that during the bombardments in 1967 all of Viet Tri's industries were destroyed or made unusable. Some were of great importance. For example, the factory which produced foodstuffs. It was bombed on January 15, and 18, March 12 and 19, April 29 and July 18. It took 26 high explosive bombs and two "mother" CBU bombs. There were 10 dead and 20 wounded. The paper factory was bombarded seven times in 1967 using 63 high explosive bombs and 35 CBU bombs; there were 25 wounded and 16 dead. Work shops, machines, the workers' homes, the canteen, meeting hall, kindergarden, infirmary — all this is now a heap of ruins, which I confirmed on November 2, 1967.

Allow me to give two more examples: the village Doan Kiet — which is far from all factories, roads, railways — received at 7 a.m. on January 18, 1967, five demolition bombs. Four of the houses were completely destroyed and there were five dead and five wounded. The little Catholic church, Saint Jean, had its roof destroyed and the wall broken. The custodian of this church lost his wife and two of his small children.

The second example: The large out-patient clinic in Viet Tri was opened in 1964, and staffed with eight doctors, 10 assistant doctors, 60 administrative personnel and male nurses. It had been necessary to evacuate the out-patient clinic in the beginning of the escalation against Viet Tri. Nevertheless, some installations remained — the X-ray room and hospital dispensary.

On August 11, 1966, the offices and kitchens at the hospital were bombed, and thereafter on August 15, 1967, the quarantine building for the contagiously ill was completely destroyed. I myself have seen all of this. What made the deepest impression on me was to see this large, modern building closed and unused. In addition it was greatly threatened and still in danger of being razed to the ground. This is a characteristic of the escalation — to attempt to annihilate the whole infrastructure of the DRV.

For more than a month, from the middle of September until October 24, 1967, Hanoi's center and suburbs were not bombed by American planes. On October 24, 25, 26, 27 and 28, greater Hanoi and the city's center were exposed to one of the most violent air attacks the capital of the DRV has experienced since the beginning of the escalation.

I visited practically all of the heavily populated areas of Hanoi which were attacked during the last week of October. Two attacks took place on October 25. At 6 a.m., 20 F-105's and F-4's came and dropped a large number of high explosive bombs and CBU bombs over the Gia Lam area. At 4:25 p.m. 28 F-105's and F-4's dropped some 3000 round shaped CBU anti-personnel bombs, that is to say, over 1.5 million small pellets with a diameter of 5.6 mm sprayed the area; these were dropped over various streets and city complexes in the central quarter of Hoan Kiem. Hoan Kiem has a population density of 14,000 inhabitants per square kilometer. I have myself seen evidence of the pellets everywhere. They had hit business signs, the large posters celebrating the October revolution's fiftieth anniversary, and the poster type newspapers on walls; house facades looked as though they suffered from smallpox. If the population had not heeded the alarm loudspeakers' there would have occurred a terrible mass murder.

On the 26th of October at 11:45 a.m., more than 20 planes again attacked the Hoan Kiem quarter and the Ba Dinh quarter in the middle of the city. I saw three and four story stone houses completely destroyed, and whole streets which were completely razed. A complex of workers' dwellings, Hanoi's quarter 32, no longer exists. I saw in place of its 90 houses an enormous area of dust, ruins and rubble; everywhere there were traces of CBU bombs.

On October 27 at 4:10 a.m. there was yet another time in which a large number of bombs with delayed-action fuses was dropped over the Gia Lam area. At 8:10 a.m. of the same day the suburbs of Than Quang, Yen My, Mai Lam and Duyen Ha were exposed to a massive attack from 36 planes which dropped high explosive bombs and missiles. At 6:45 p.m. many demolition bombs and bombs with delayed-action fuses were dropped over Thanh Tri.

On the 28th of October there were four attacks from various planes directed against the city's northern quarters. It is known that 30 American planes were shot down during the attacks on Hanoi in October, and that various pilots were taken prisoner. Of the city's inhabitants more than 200 were dead and wounded following these five days of attacks, and more than 150 dwellings were destroyed.

I have personally been present during two of these attacks — the first and the last, perhaps the mildest. In comparison with the attacks of the 13th, and 14th of December 1966, which were the first attacks of a comparable extent directed against the capital of the DRV and which I personally experienced, I can only say that this new escalation appears to me to be yet more blindly murderous.

Juridical Report on the Treatment of War Prisoners
and Civilians
testimony by Solange Bouvier Ajam

Advocate of the Court of Paris; Member of the Legal Commission

The second and third questions to be decided by the Tribunal are: 1. Have Vietnamese prisoners been subjected to inhuman treatment prohibited by the rules of warfare, in particular torture or mutilation? 2. Have unjustifiable reprisals been taken against the civilian population, in particular the execution of hostages? Have forced-labor camps and methods of deportation been instituted?

Our opinion is that the fundamental, general rules set forth in the Universal Declaration of Human Rights and in the Judgments of Nuremburg and Tokyo apply in both these cases. I must reiterate in a general way those rules of international law which are particularly applicable to these two questions and demonstrate to the Tribunal that those rules apply fully to the aggressive war being carried out by the American Government against the Vietnamese people. In this regard the decision of the Stockholm Tribunal, after detailed investigation, clearly established the fact of American aggression against all of Vietnam.

This aggression carried out by the United States of America is the major, underlying element on which the evidence to the Tribunal is based. That aggression is what determines the international character of this war.

What Particular International Laws are Applicable in the Present Context?

Essentially, they are the four Geneva Conventions of August 12, 1949 which supersede the Geneva Convention of July 27, 1929: the first concerning military wounded and the sick; the second concerning shipwrecked wounded and sick; the third concerning war prisoners; the fourth dealing with the protection of civilians in war time.

Although the first two are also important with regard to the Vietnam war, our examination will be devoted to the Conventions concerning prisoners of war and the protection of civilians. With regard to the protection of civilians, attention should be drawn to the International Convention on the Laws and Customs of Land War of October 18, 1907, which is still in effect and which the Fourth Geneva Convention of 1949 merely modifies. All of these Conventions have been ratified by the United States.

Prisoners of War

If one takes a look at the past, it is clear why, in the face of the murderous developments in the art of warfare, the trend of international law concerning prisoners of war has taken place along humanitarian lines.

After Grotius and the Treaty of Munster of 1648, Jean-Jacques Rousseau wrote, in the *Social Contract*: "when the combatants put down their arms and become simply men, no one should any longer have any power over their lives." We owe to Lieber, an American, the laws referred to as the "Lieber Laws," promulgated during the U.S.'s Civil War, which decreed in Article 74 that the "prisoner of war, as a belligerent, is the prisoner of the Government which has captured him." The *Instructions to Armies in the Field* constituted a detailed body of laws. It became effective in 1863, was revised in 1914, and enables the United States to lay claim to having been in the vanguard of humanitarian war legislation. The barbarity of the methods employed by the present U.S. Government thus becomes more reprehensible from a moral point of view.

The development of these laws in the course of contemporary history, is marked by various high points, such as the Hague Convention of 1907, the Geneva Convention of 1929 (extended and improved in 1949); it goes hand in hand with the evolution of humanitarianism, to arrive at a concept of the prisoner of war as "not a criminal, but merely an enemy prevented from rejoining the fighting, who should be liberated at the conclusion of hostilities, and treated with respect and humanity as long as he is a prisoner" — (Red Cross).

The basic elements of the law, make mandatory the duty to provide the prisoner of war with the basic, normal necessities possible within the limits of his confinement, limits defined solely by the need for removing him from combat.

1. These elements include the satisfactions of so-called "primary" necessities, or at least: — respect for his physical well-being: prohibition of mutilations, tortures, and extreme penalties; — the right to elementary physical care: nourishment, and all necessary medical attention.

Articles 13 and 15 of the Third Geneva Convention stipulate: "Article 13: Prisoners of war must at all times be treated humanely. Any illicit act or omission on the part of the detaining power leading to the death of, or seriously threatening the health of, a prisoner of war under its jurisdiction is forbidden and will be considered as a serious breach of the present Convention. In particular, no prisoner of war may be subjected to physical mutilation or to medical or scientific experiments of any kind whatsoever not called for by the medical treatment of the prisoner in question or which are not in his interests . . . "

"Article 15: The detaining Power responsible for prisoners of war shall be responsible for providing free of charge for their physical needs and for making available to them free of charge any medical care which their state of health may require."

Those imperative and unqualified provisions are also set forth in Article 3, which excludes any forcible renunciation of beliefs based on a difference of opinion as to the legal character of the war. We will return to this last point. In any event, the Tribunal must consider the extent to which the American aggressor has fulfilled these important conditions.

2. Secondly, the dignity of the individual must be respected in every sense of the word, and that gives rise to several important considerations: — the kind of questioning: the forbidding of any physical or moral constraint which would tend to obtain information or cooperation (Article 17): — general living conditions: respect for personal belongings, decent living conditions (Articles 18 and 22); — with regard to imprisonment: transfer from the com-

bat zone to surroundings of safety and well-being (Article 19); — penal or disciplinary sanctions; the rule protecting prisoners against all arbitrary decisions and assuring rights and means of recourse (it is to be noted that in this case a prisoner of war, if he has committed a crime or a misdemeanor, can be judged provided that he is assured a legal trial before a military court) (Articles 82, *et seq.*)

Here again, the Tribunal will have to decide whether it is proved that the aggressor has fulfilled the least of its duties in a particular place or at a certain time.

3. Given the actual conditions the war has imposed on the people of Vietnam, I hardly dare mention the obligations relating to the respect of human dignity, in the most subjective sense. These concern: — the forbidding of all humiliating treatment. I quote:

"Articles 14; Prisoners of war have the right in all circumstances to respect of their person and their honor. Women must be treated with all the respect due their sex . . . war prisoners maintain their complete civilian competence as it prevailed at the time they were taken prisoner . . ."

— the minimal work provisions for prisoners: type, length, renumeration for work (Articles 49 to 57);

— the freedom to write letters (Articles 69, 73, 74, 75, 76, and 77) and to transfer or to receive monetary resources (Articles 58 to 68).

Now let us examine those cases in which the category of "war prisoner" can be applied to the combatant. In this regard, one must consider the proposition that has been held, that the N.L.F. in South Vietnam is not a co-signer of the Geneva Conventions. This point does not bear up under scrutiny. It is enough to point out briefly that unanimous opinion agrees that humanitarian agreements drawn up according to the dictates of world conscience are binding unilaterally on the contracting parties which have ratified them and, more generally, on anyone subject to public internation law, to the extent that they are an embodiment of common law and custom.

Article 2, which is also repeated in the Four Conventions, makes redundant the American position which holds that the United States is not engaged in a declared war. Thus in the Four Conventions, Article 2 states: "...the present convention is applicable in the case of a declared war, or in any other armed conflict taking place between two or more Contracting Parties, even though a state of war is not recognized by one of them..."

As for those persons to be designated as prisoners of war, they are precisely defined in Article 4 of the Third Convention, as follows:

1. members of the armed forces of one of the warring parties, as well as members of the national guard and voluntary bodies forming part of those armed forces;

2. members of other units and members of other voluntary bodies, including those of organized resistance movements belonging to a party to the conflict and acting outside or inside their own territory, even if that territory be occupied, providing that the units or voluntary bodies, including organized resistance movements, fulfill the following conditions:

   a) have at their head an individual responsible for his subordinates; b) have a fixed and distinctive emblem recognizable at a distance; c) openly carry arms; d) conform in their actions to the laws and customs of warfare.

Among the parties engaged in Vietnam, we should underline the fact that the National Liberation Front of South Vietnam, representing the Vietnamese population in that region, completely fulfills the criteria set forth above. It has a program uniting all levels of the population; it has political and military organization and recognized leaders; it is publicly known to control two-thirds of the territory, a large part of the population and its influence is a controlling factor in the remainder of the country. It openly bears arms and conforms to the laws and customs of warfare. As for the question of a distinctive emblem, it must be stated that such use by regular units of the N.L.F. singles the combatants out for immediate assassination and not for protection under international law.

Further, the International Hague Convention on Laws and Customs of Warfare, summed up in the Third Geneva Convention (Article 4, section 6), recognizes as belligerents those who spontaneously rise up against an invader, even though they lack all the organizational criteria mentioned above, if they openly bear arms and if they respect the laws and customs of warfare. The concrete conditions in the struggle of the Vietnamese people, its combativeness and its endurance, must be seen in the light of this legal requirement.

But the Geneva Conventions went even further, taking into consideration the problems presented by a non-international war. As we have seen, Article 4, section 2, singles out "organized resistance movements" and defines their treatment should members become war prisoners. Article 3 sets aside any equivocation concerning the formal character of the conflict (international or non-international, etc.), and guarantees the minimum rights applicable to any armed political conflict. Indeed, in what other case could the terms of Article 3 be applicable, as it is stated here and repeated in the Four Conventions? The fact that Article 3, governing conflicts of a non-international character, was repeated in the Four Geneva Conventions emphasizes the importance attached to it by the Contracting Parties, among them the United States. The text is as follows: "In the case of armed conflict of a non-international character arising in the territory of one of the Contracting Parties, each party to the conflict is bound at the minimum to adhere to the following provisions:

1. Persons not directly participating in the hostilities, including members of the armed forces who have laid down their arms and persons made unfit for combat by illness, wounds, imprisonment or for any other reason, will be in all circumstances treated with humanity, without any unfavorable distinction being made as to race, color, religion or creed, sex, birth or wealth, or any other similar criteria. In this regard, the following actions are and remain forbidden in connection with the persons mentioned above: a) attempts on life or bodily well-being, in particular murder in any form, mutilation, cruel treatment, torture or corporal punishment; b) taking of hostages; c) attempts on human dignity, in particular humiliating or degrading treatment; d) sentences pronounced and executions carried out without benefit of trial before a duly constituted tribunal or without those juridical guarantees recognized as indispensable by all civilized peoples.

2. The sick and wounded shall be received and cared for.

It is thus clear that civil wars and internal wars of national liberation are covered by those provisions, which are seen as the minimum necessary to the application of common law. The theory according to which the Vietnam war is a civil war has quite justly been set aside by the Tribunal. But it is still supported by many courageous opponents of the war undertaken by the United States in Vietnam. We stress, in this connection, that international law contains formal provisions covering the American Government's actions, which purport to be in aid of one of the participants in that so-called civil war.

Civilian Populations in Combat or Occupied Zones

It would be simple to show that the evolution of international law from conventional or doctrinal sources has tended towards a more humanitarian position.

The Fourth Convention of August 12, 1949, concerning the protection of civilians in war time, does not contravene the International Convention on the Laws and Customs of Warfare signed at the Hague on October 18, 1907, but rather, according to the formula adopted by the Conference, complements it. Articles 22 *et seq.* are still applicable. They forbid:

1. Murder in any form: assassination, summary executions, tortures, extreme punishment, or cruel treatment (Article 23 B, Hague Convention, repeated in Article 3 of the Geneva Convention);

2. The taking of hostages and all affronts to human dignity, such as: a) the suspension of the application of internal law in occupied territories (Article 23 H, the Hague); b) collective punishments or reprisals (Article 50, The Hague).

The events leading up to the Judgments of Nuremburg and Tokyo should clearly indicate the deplorable situation which arose from the absence of an international Convention for the protection of civilians in war time, outside of those few contained in the Hague Convention. The Fourth Geneva Convention of 1949 attempted to fill this gap by better discerning and defining the necessary provisions.

In order to make clear the intentions of the Contracting Parties who signed the Fourth Convention in 1949, we quote this sentence from a French-Finnish draft preamble: "respect for the dignity and value of the individual must be assured by a full definition of those rights which are, in essence, due him and of those liberties without which he loses his reason for existence."

Under this heading are set forth some *general measures* for the protection of the population against certain effects of war which , the purpose of Part II of the Convention. These measures are applicable to the population as a whole, without any distinction (Article 13). To protect civilians in time of war, sanitary and security zones and locales are provided for the wounded, the sick, invalids, old people, children under fifteen years of age, and pregnant women (Article 14), as well as neutral areas of refuge (Article 15).

Such neutral or protected zones cannot, in any case, be set up directly, or through the intervention of a neutral State or Humanitarian body, without the formal agreement of the conflicting Parties (Article 15). Those provisions made a juridical fiction of the illegal "strategic hamlets" to which the N.L.F. has always, and for good reason, been opposed, and the concentration camp character of which has been well established. Furthermore, Article 49 (Section III, on occupied territories) forbids the transportation of groups or of individuals.

The occupying power may undertake the total or partial evacuation of a fixed occupied region if the security of the population or over-riding military considerations demand it, but only in clearly-defined conditions.

"The occupying power, in undertaking transfers or evacuations, should carry them out so that in so far as possible the persons to be protected will be received in installations providing proper cleanliness, hygiene, security and nourishment."

Here again, the Tribunal must decide on the extent of the violaions committed by comparing these texts with the tragic reality.

The fourth Convention forbids *in all cases* the use of physical or moral constraint to obtain information (Article 31); it forbids murder, torture, mutilation and all other forms of brutality (Article 32) and repressive measures (Article 33); the occupying power must respect the rights and freedoms of workers. Articles 51 and 52 may be quoted in this connection:

"Article 51: The occupying power may not force protected persons to serve in the armed forces or auxiliary forces; it may not employ any pressure or propaganda aimed at encouraging voluntary enlistments . . . In no case may requisitions of workers take the form of a mobilization of workers under military or semi-military regime.

"Article 52: No contract, ruling or agreement may prevent the worker, voluntary or involuntary, wherever he may be, from exercising his right to call on the protecting power for its intervention. Any provision tending to create unemployment or to restrict the working opportunities of laborers in an occupied country in order to force them to work for the occupying power, is forbidden."

Possessions and property must also be respected, except in case of absolute military necessity (Article 53); food supply (Article 55) and civilian hospitals (Article 57) must remain in civilian control except in case of urgent need.

Children are the subject of particular attention (Article 50) with regard to their education according to the laws of their country and preferential measures for their benefit prior to occupation are specified. Communication between and reuniting of families should be facilitated.

As summed up by Article 27: "Persons in custody have a right to respect for their persons and their honor, their family rights, their convictions and religious observances, their habits and their customs, in all circumstances."

These duties have an imperative character which goes beyond the framework of an international convention: they arise out of general and universal principles which are set forth at the end of the Fourth Convention, in the last paragraph of Article 158.

It is stated there (with regard to possible abrogation of responsibility under these Articles) that such renunciation "will have no effect on the obligations which parties to the conflict are bound to fulfill by virtue of the rights of people arising out of the established custom of civilized nations, the laws of humanity and the dictates of the public conscience."

That mention of the Martens Clause, along with Article 3 cited above, in my opinion, makes any controversy over the question of formal adherence to the Fourth Convention unimportant. The Tribunal will have to decide on the culpability of the American aggressor in violation of these regulations.

Guilt of the American Government

The responsibilities of the American Government must clearly derive, in the field of international law, from the provisions of documents to which it has expressly subscribed or which it has ratified.

The American negotiators themselves, during the preparatory meetings for the Four Geneva Conference of 1949, proposed the inclusion in the draft laws of each of the Parties the necessary means for "determining" the penalties applicable to those persons who commit or order to be committed serious infractions, such as intentional homicide, torture, taking of hostages, and all illegal, deliberate and widespread destruction of property not justified by military necessity.

In fact, internal law of the United States followed suit by faithfully including the four Geneva Conventions in the *Law of Land Warfare*, a manual of the Department of the Army, dated July 20, 1956, which refers expressly to the international agreements here mentioned. The United States Government, bound by its own law, cannot bring forward any valid argument against the application on that law, nor can it invoke the legal fiction that the American armed forces are merely assisting the puppet Saigon Government. This argument is not supported by facts: the proof of this was brought out in the first session of the Tribunal; it is a question of a war of agression and, from the beginning, the war was thought out, waged and enlarged by the American Government. Who is making war? Is it the handful of accomplices in the Saigon Government, who would not survive a single day if the Americans pulled out, or is it the American Government which continues to declare through its leaders that the war will be fought to the end?

What General Staff is directing operations? Whose are the Marine and the Air Force personnel who ravage Vietnam, whose over-equipped army of 500,000 men? Whose is the destruction? Who is taking prisoners, who is organizing strategic hamlets?

The mere existence of a mixed General Staff of Americans and puppet Vietnamese as officially set up in 1964, does not lessen the culpability of the United States Government. Without the presence of the U.S. there would be no war. If common sense is a determining factor in international law, we are faced here with a perfectly clear situation which enables us to state categorically that the American Government is the principal party to the conflict, and thus that all criteria of belligerence, with the legal obligations they entail, apply fully to its armed forces.

Admissions to that effect can be found in American statements. For example, here are three statements which give rise to important legal questions:

1. August 10, 1965; *Reply of the American Government to a Letter from the International Committee of the Red Cross* asking for clarification of the intentions of the former with regard to the 1949 Conventions. — The Government of the United States unequivocally stated that it did not question the *International nature* of the war. This reply, in our opinion, definitely excludes the possibility of any restrictive interpretation of the Geneva Conventions.

2. February 8, 1966 — *Communique Published After the "Honolulu Meeting"* between Lyndon B. Johnson and the representatives of the *de facto* Saigon Government stressed the intention to respect the Geneva Convention, in all cases, particularly insofar as it concerns the rights of innocent civilians and the treatment of war prisoners (N.E.D. No. 3381, p. 11, point 9.)

3. September 30, 1967 — the President of the United States set forth the *immediate war aims* he envisaged after the customary reference to communist expansion. He stated: " . . .the key to everything we have done is our own security."

In conclusion, I feel it necessary to draw the Tribunal's attention to the especially serious breaches of the Geneva Conventions, since they bring out not only the bad faith of the American Government but also its premeditated plan of destruction.

Firstly, there is the flagrant violation of Article 12 of the Third Geneva Convention, which was based on Lieber's American legislative practice. It states:

"War prisoners are under the control of the enemy Power, not of the individuals or units which have captured them. Notwithstanding individual responsibilities which may exist, the detaining Power is responsible for the treatment meted out to them. Control of war prisoners may not be transferred by the detaining Power to any but a Power Party to the Convention and when the detaining Power is assured that the Power in question is willing and able to implement the Convention."

In this regard, the complete illegality of the American practice of turning prisoners taken by the American military over to the puppet authorities in Saigon is clear. In light of the quotation above, it is obvious that the Geneva Convention has been violated over and over again.

Secondly, we must stress the general and widespread implementation of the policy of "strategic hamlets", a policy which condemns the Vietnamese people to choose between death and the concentration camp. In conclusion, the Tribunal must decide, on the basis of the facts set before it, whether the total and extent of all these crimes gives rise to a further crime, that of genocide.

Testimony and Questioning of David Kenneth Tuck

*Former Specialist Fourth Class with the U.S.
25th Infantry Division in Vietnam*

VLADIMIR DEDIJER: *Mr. David Tuck, please do take the stand. Your
name, sir, please.*

My name is David Kenneth Tuck.

DEDIJER: *How old are you?*

I am 25 years old.

DEDIJER: *Where were you born?*

In Baker, West Virginia.

DEDIJER: *Are you married?*

No, I am single.

DEDIJER: *Are your parents alive?*

Yes, both of my parents are alive.

DEDIJER: *Where do they live?*

In the U.S.A., Cleveland, Ohio.

DEDIJER: *Ohio. What are their occupations?*

My father is a bricklayer, my mother is a housewife.

DEDIJER: *And what is your occupation?*

I am a U.S. postal mail clerk.

DEDIJER: *And you were in the U.S. Army in Vietnam? In which unit
were you?*

I was part of the 3rd Brigade of the 25th Infantry Division. My
smaller unit was A Company, 1st Battalion, 35th Infantry Regiment.

DEDIJER: *And when did you go to Vietnam?*

I was in Vietnam from January 8th 1966 to February 9th 1967.

DEDIJER: *Thank you very much for your answers and, Maitre Halimi, I ask you to please pose the questions to Mr. Tuck and, Members of the Tribunal, after the cross-examination by Maitre Halimi, I think that our task will be to make by our questions some points more precise and more clear. We also have to keep in mind to keep on the agenda.*

GISELE HALIMI: *Mr. Tuck, ... in New York I posed a certain number of questions to you about the deeds to which you were directly a witness in Vietnam. I would like you to, before the Tribunal, tell me about these things. Particularly about what you told me about having witnessed one day in the Month of October 1966 how American soldiers killed wounded South [?] Vietnamese prisoners with machetes. Is it possible that you can confirm this to me before the Tribunal and give details which maybe you did not give earlier?*

Yes, I can confirm this. But the only thing inaccurate as to this question that you asked me was the date. This did not happen in October of 1966. It happened March 2nd, 1966 at a place about fifty miles north of Ban Me Thuot, near a Special Forces camp — Bam Brain [Buon Brieng — ?]. On this date, in the 3rd Brigade of the 25th we had our first casualties. We lost eleven men that day and the enemy lost one hundred men. After the battle was over there were several wounded North Vietnamese, you know, laying around on the ground, see, so everyone was angry because this was our first battle and we had lost a lot of our friends, see. So one Japanese-American, his name was Sergeant Takahatchi, I believe he was a staff sergeant, he took his machete and beheaded this wounded soldier. The soldier was wounded in the chest but he was still alive. So after he beheaded the man, he threw his head down the hill to serve as warning to other N.V.A. elements, if they were still in the area, that we meant business. And I was standing nearby when this occurred.

HALIMI: *Can you witness about other cases that are analogous about war prisoners or civilians that were killed by the American forces or by the South Vietnamese in the presence of American forces?*

Yes, I could also testify to other incidents of mistreatment of prisoners by U.S. and South Vietnamese forces. Shortly afterwards, after we got over there in February 1966, I happened to be on a work detail to a place called Camp Hollaway which is right outside the town of Pleiku, and while I was there I saw a V.C. being tortured by the South Vietnamese under the direction of U.S. forces. When I got there they had the man tied on the ground; he was spread-eagled. They were using a knife to sort of pry under his toenails and the soles of his feet. When this· got no results they went on to other more sensitive parts of the body. Well, this still got no results, because evidently this man was, as we say in America, a tough nut to crack. So then after that they put the knife under his eyeball in another endeavor to make him talk, and he still would not talk. So then what they did, they put him in a barbed-wire cage in which he was on his hands and knees. And if he made any moves the barbs of the barbed wire would press into his flesh, so they kept him there for two days. And I had to go back on another detail, and when I got back the man was gone. I assume that they had turned him over to the South Vietnamese to execute him. Now all of this torturing was done by the South Vietnamese, because there were very few U.S. forces who were able to speak Vietnamese, so a U.S. officer, I believe it was a captain at that time, he was giving orders to the Vietnamese interpreter and he was relaying them on to the man who was doing the actual torturing. It is common procedure over there to turn over all prisoners to the South Vietnamese for later disposal and I believe invariably they execute them after they get the information that they receive. Other acts of mistreatment of prisoners that I saw was in November 1966. We were operating in an area near Plei Jrirang Special Forces camp. Now it was the practice of our outfit to rotate men back and forth to base camp to give them a few days' rest. So on that day, I believe it was about at 1400 hours, on that day I boarded a "Huey" helicopter. On this helicopter there was the pilot, the copilot, the machine-gunner, myself. There were also two dead American soldiers and two North Vietnamese prisoners. Well, while we were on there, one of the North Vietnamese pointed to one of the U.S. dead and started to laugh about it, see. So the shotgunner, he saw this, and he told the pilot about that, and the pilot said: "Throw that S.O.B. out." So he picked up the man, the man was tied anyway, bound, and threw him out of the helicopter. Well, immediately after, the other North Vietnamese soldier kept quiet.

So then when we got back to base camp, you know, such a thing is an everyday thing. You know, we did not think too much about it.

Another time was near the Cambodian border. It was called Duc Co. We had surrounded this village and we noticed that there was this one woman that had not lined up with the others, see. So, this officer who was with me said that this woman looked suspicious. So he went up to the woman and said something to her, and she reached into a pile of wood. We did not know what she was reaching for, so then he ordered me to shoot her, which I did. I am very sorry that I had to do this, but I was acting under orders.

HALIMI: *I would like to return to your testimony about the helicopter . . . I would like to know if the officer responsible had to make a report on the missing prisoner?*

Well, yes, it is true that he would have to write a report saying that one of the prisoners had disappeared. But, you could always get around this by saying that the man attempted to escape and we had to shoot him or the man was suicidal and he jumped out of the helicopter. Even if one prisoner was missing, it would not have mattered all that much because, unless the prisoner was an officer or something like this, no one would really have cared anyway. It was standard policy in my outfit not to take any prisoners. We were told by the officers that we had better not take any prisoners unless it was a North Vietnamese officer.

HALIMI: *Can you specify for the Tribunal the orders that you had? Did you have orders to shoot prisoners when they became obnoxious?*

No! We were ordered to shoot, to take no prisoners just as a matter of standard operating policy, especially wounded prisoners anyway, because a lot of our officers were sort of fanatical on this. They believed that the only good Vietnamese was a dead Vietnamese, and so forth. And a wounded man stood very little chance of being evacuated to medical aid anyway.

HALIMI: *I would like to inform the Tribunal that in the testimony of the witness Campbell, whose deposition you have, he speaks of similar actions — that is, the ejection of prisoners from his helicopters. I hope you will be able to hear Mr. Campbell's deposition on these actions, if you follow up these questions.*

The ears of Vietnamese, for certain Montagnard tribes, are reputed to be valuable. Can you confirm instances of American bounties paid for Vietnamese ears?

Well, ah, as far as the cutting off of the ears, when I was over there it was a practice for a while of the 173rd Airborne Brigade to, after the battle was over, to cut the ears off of dead Vietnamese and to use them as a souvenir. Also this was a practice of the 1st and 14th of the 3rd Brigade of 25th. This was more or less a passing fad. The person who had the most ears was considered the number one V.C. killer, and also when we would get back to base camp the one who had the most ears would get all the free beer and whiskey that they could drink. But it was more or less the passing fad, but they did cut the ears off of dead V.C. to show as souvenirs.

HALIMI: *Mr. Tuck, you have told me of seeing refugee camps. Can you specify for the Tribunal the conditions of life inside them?*

Most of the refugee camps that I saw were invariably near a Special Forces camp. From what I could see from these people they looked just like they were starving; they were in rags. Shortly after we got over there I was on a work detail to dump some garbage into a sump, which is a hole dug in the ground for that purpose. As soon as we had dumped this these refugees — a whole lot, a horde of children, it seemed — literally jumped into this sump and fought like animals for the garbage. The refugees — I got the impression from what I saw — were left to eke out their own living. They also had to be in their refugee camps at a certain time, because if they showed up outside our perimeter or outside the South Vietnamese perimeter they were liable to be shot as V.C. A lot of the women in the refugee camp had to turn to prostitution to earn a living.

HALIMI: *Mr. Tuck, do you know how they separated the population? That is, how did you decide who was Viet Cong, who was a civilian, and so on, and what did you do after you had distinguished them?*

It was standard operating policy when in what we call V.C. country; that is, areas which were under control of the V.C., to surround a village and to go in and assemble the inhabitants in a bunch in the center of the village. All young men who looked like they were able to bear arms we sent them away in helicopters to be interrogated by the South Vietnamese. The women and the children we sent to a refugee camp. Also it was common practice that if we received any shots from a village to have what we call a "mad minute." This means that for one minute everybody would cut loose tanks, machine guns and everything that they had into this village, because the way we had assumed that until proven otherwise every Vietnamese was a V.C.

HALIMI: *Mr. Tuck, you have spoken of helping American troops spray gas into tunnels. Can you specify what you mean?*

It was frequently when we were on an operation we would find a whole lot of tunnels and, a lot of times we did not know whether there were V.C. in there or not. My outfit did not have such men as they have further south as they call the "tunnel rats." So what we would have to do, we would have to use tear gas to bring them out. A lot of times it would be women and children besides the V.C. in there. But most — but then again a lot of times it would only be women and children. The tear gas does not kill anyone as long as they can get out to the fresh air, it just irritates them. Uh — as far as I know, tear gas was the only chemical agent being used to bring these people out of the tunnels.

HALIMI: *The Tribunal can question him on specifics, but I would like to ask Mr. Tuck two general questions. The first. You are black, and I would like you to tell the Tribunal if you sensed, during operations, a segregation — a discrimination between yourself and the white soldiers in the American Army. In particular, could you explain the advantages the others had over you?*

407

I would say that that while there was not any segregation, if anything it was overintegrated. What a lot of people do not realize is that most of the soldiers fighting in the infantry over there are black soldiers. In my particular outfit it was 117 out of 156 were black soldiers. It is a common practice to put the people whom they consider expendable in the infantry. This is the black soldier, the Puerto Ricans and the hillbillies. The reasoning behind this I believe is that if these people are killed no one is going to miss them, because after all black people are always complaining, so if they complain about being used in the infantry, no one in the U.S. is going to listen to them. The war is very popular in the United States and if the Johnson administration use the middle-class white people, then the parents of these people when they sustain casualties would be complaining about this and would demand that the war be over with. So, therefore, they put the expendables, the black people, the Puerto Ricans and our poor rural whites that we call "hillbillies." They put the expendables in the infantry, but I noticed that when I came back from the war and saw on T.V., I saw very few black soldiers. It always seems to be mostly white, but I know with my own eyes this is not true.

But other than that there was not any segretation. There was discrimination as far as lining up men to be the point man. The point man is the man who always goes some meters ahead of everyone else. He leads the way and is always on the lookout. He is usually the man who first gets killed. And invariably it seems like the soul brothers — or the Negroes — were the ones who were on the point. And so that is one way in which they discriminate.

HALIMI: *I have explained to you that the Tribunal, above all, is concerned with the question of, "Has the United States committed genocide?" I think I have explained to you that one can consider that "genocide" can begin with the words of officers and their method of inspiring their men's attitude toward a race or a people. Can you say if, before battle, your officers' words indicated that they wished you to fight a purely defensive war, or that they wished you to exterminate the Vietnamese people?*

My outfit was stationed in Hawaii before we went to Vietnam. Shortly after we heard we were going to Vietnam, we were given orientation — little pamphlets saying that we were fighting to save the Vietnamese from Communism. We should always treat the Vietnamese as our equals. When it came time to giving them the right of way we should always give the Vietnamese the right of way. Everyone went along with this, but then when we got to Vietnam it was a different story. All at once the officers referred to the Vietnamese as "gooks." When we got there, we were told not to associate with the Vietnamese, whereas before we got over there we were told to make friends because unless we win the hearts and minds of the people we will lose the war. But, once we got over there our officers told us otherwise: that the only good Vietnamese was a dead Vietnamese, that they were no good, that they would not fight. So, on March the 23rd, when we first went into our first really combat operation, the commander, Lt. Colonel Saul A. Jackson, gave us what he considered an inspiring speech. He said, "I want you to keep these Vietnamese on the run so much, so hard that I want to see Vietnamese blood flowing upon the earth." Everyone was surprised because before then we thought we should distinguish between Vietnamese and Viet Cong. After all we were supposed to be saving the Vietnamese people from the Viet Cong. So, everyone remarked on how bloodthirsty that man was. The officers referred to them as "gooks," and we were told to consider all of them no good, and the only good one was a dead one. I was very shocked because I had assumed we were fighting to save these people from Communism, and now all at once it came to me that perhaps these people were going to practice genocide after all, because here we are lumping all Vietnamese together. I thought we were only to fight the Viet Cong, who were supposedly preventing the South Vietnamese from having their freedom.

DEDIJER: *Thank you, Mr. Tuck. Members of the Tribunal, please begin with your questions.*

SARA LIDMAN: *A couple of times you referred to the captured or the dead enemy soldiers as North Vietnamese. Now, how did you know, how could you know that they were born in North Vietnam?*

I do not know that they were born in North Vietnam, but they had on the uniform of the North Vietnamese Army. Documents were found on them showing that they were in the North Vietnamese Army. The North Vietnamese Army wears a khaki uniform, as you know.

LIDMAN: *I see, and the second question is whether you before going to Vietnam or during your stay were given to read the Geneva Agreements from 1954?*

I see, I would like to say that U.S. soldiers were never given a history of South Vietnam or the results of the Geneva Agreements of 1954.

LIDMAN: *Have you read the accords later?*

Yes, I read them this year.

DAVE DELLINGER: *I want to ask a couple of questions. First of all in the incident in which you described a prisoner who was tied and bound, being thrown out of the helicopter, could you give an estimate about how high off the ground the helicopter was at the time?*

I would say that we were about two thousand meters in the air. This is just an estimate, I could not be sure.

DELLINGER: *But there is no question that he could not have survived. He was way up in the air?*

No, he could not possibly have survived.

DELLINGER: *Secondly, you spoke about a "mad minute," that is, after there were shots from a Vietnamese village, everybody would let loose with everything that they had. I wondered if, for example, how many shots it took to provoke such a "mad minute," I mean, if there was an isolated shot from a village, could this happen?*

Well, no. It would have to be more than one shot. If we got a series of rounds fired at us and if the bullets came close to someone or they hit somebody, we would do this more or less as an act of revenge. Then, after the "mad minute" we would move into the village and see how much damage we had done and whether we had gotten anybody. But usually in most cases the V.C. was gone anyway. So we never caught them.

DELLINGER: *Was there any attempt to find out if there were women or children?*

We knew there were civilians in the village, but as I say, we did not give a damn. We just intended to show them that we were not playing.

DELLINGER: *One final question. You spoke to Mrs. Lidman, if I understood you, that although there was very little said ever about what you were not allowed to do, at some point you were given a card which said what was illegal?*

Yes.

DELLINGER: *Could you tell us more about that? You remember what it said on the card and at what point in your service were you given the card: in the United States or in Vietnam?*

I was given this card when I was in advanced individual training. This is the second eight weeks of training in the U.S. Army. I was given this at Fort Sill, Oklahoma. Among other things it said on the card that stuck out in my mind was that we were to treat the enemy humanely. And this was sort of a surprise to me, because I had myself always assumed that anything goes in warfare. But that was the thing that stuck out in my mind, to treat the enemy humanely and not to use him in any construction of fortifications or so forth.

DELLINGER: *But then did you carry these to Vietnam with you and was there any reference to the card after you were there?*

There were some people that carried their card. Most of the men, because it was not emphasized, they threw them away. You know, like they do most of these cards that they gave to them. When we were over there in Vietnam I did not hear any reference to the Geneva Conventions of Warfare. I might have heard them among the enlisted men, but I did not hear any from the brass or, you know, the officers.

DELLINGER: *Thanks.*

PETER WEISS: *Mr. Tuck, referring to the incident when the prisoner was thrown out of the helicopter. You say this was an "everyday incident," and it could happen often, and nobody was really seriously concerned about that. And the person who threw this prisoner out of the plane would not be punished and perhaps he would not even be asked about what happened. Could you from your experience tell the Tribunal an approximate figure of incidents of the same kind that you have witnessed? Other cases where prisoners were just sort of killed, or left to a certain death, with nobody caring for it?*

Well, in the first place I would like to say that the enemy prisoners were never left to die by themselves, they were always executed, but they were never left to die of their wounds. I have also seen other cases in which a wounded prisoner was laying there supposedly waiting for an evacuation helicopter, and I have seen several G.I.'s just go over and shoot him in the head just to be done with it.

WEISS: *Without any special order?*

No, well, in some cases they had orders, and in other cases, since it was the standard policy in my outfit not to take any prisoners, that is what we did. Occasionally, if we had a wounded officer and there was an American officer around, then he would tell us, do not kill the man, but to send him on a Medevac, to be later interrogated. But if the man was not an officer and he was wounded, we just got rid of him.

WEISS: *And this happened several times?*

This happened all the time in Vietnam, it is a common thing.

WEISS: *Is it a rule?*

Yes.

WEISS: *Mr. Tuck, you were speaking about the villages. When it was just a wild shooting, afterwards what happened to the villages? Were they torn down by bulldozers, or what happened to the villages when you landed, when the troops landed in the village, the population was sent away? Could you tell us a bit more specifically what happened around this event?*

Immediately after a "mad minute" we would surround a village and then we would send a party in. We would always have a Vietnamese interpreter with us. He was assigned to our outfit. And then we would line the villagers up and interrogate them, and depending on the battalion commander, we would have to radio back in for instructions whether to turn in all the villagers, whether to destroy or just warn the villagers about such activities. In some cases we would send for helicopters to evacuate these people and send them to a refugee camp and we would burn the village.

WEISS: *Have you seen people from a village being sent to a refugee camp?*

Yes, I have.

WEISS: *Could you describe the refugee camps?*

Well, the refugee camp as I said before is usually located near a Special Forces camp. You have a lot of wooden and tin huts, you know, just built together haphazardly. Usually the ground is bare: no vegetation or anything, no trees. So there is also a barbed-wire fence surrounding them, and only one entrance. And as I said before, at night they have to be in before dark, you know, before about 1800 hours anyway. And they eke out their living as best as they can.

WEISS: *They lie on the ground, they have no beds?*

No, no, I am not saying that. They have beds, but what I mean is, the ground around, in the little village, is usually the poorest type of ground. It is just mud; in other words, all the grass and vegetation has been worn away. In other words, the soil is not fit for farming and so forth.

WEISS: *How do they get their food?*

Well, like I said, they have to beg from the U.S. troops. In other words, they have to eat a lot of the food that we throw away: our garbage and so forth.

WEISS: *So there are not immediately afterwards coming special troops with supplies, with food, to help the people who are being driven away from their villages?*

Not that I know of. If they get any food, they certainly do not show it, because all the ones that I have seen they looked like they were starving, and they were dressed in rags.

WEISS: *So it is the American soldiers who might give them food if they want to, but it is not necessarily done?*

No, it is not necessarily done.

WEISS: *May I ask one more question?*

DEDIJER: *Yes, please.*

WEISS: *Mr. Tuck, you spoke about the speech which a General Jackson — a fiery speech — which he gave to the troops before entering into the battle. Have you witnessed other speeches like that by other officers?*

Right, I would like to say that these speeches . . . usually we were getting them when we were going on a combat operation. And after a while, such things sink into the minds of the men, because then I noticed that a lot of my fellow G.I.'s started referring to the Vietnamese people as "gooks." "Gooks": G-O-O-K-S. "Gooks." This is a derogatory term.

WEISS: *For the moment, I have no more questions.*

LAURENT SCHWARTZ: *Mr. Tuck, you have said that you had the order to shoot [prisoners] and that you could not oppose it. Now, the American soldiers who are sent to Vietnam — do they know about the judgments of the Nuremberg Trials; that is, that they have the right — or even the duty — to resist inhuman orders? Do you know of any soldiers who have been punished for committing war crimes?*

Well, I would like to say I have never heard of any G.I.'s who were punished because they committed acts of war. Most of us had heard of the Geneva Convention of war. We knew that we were not supposed to do certain things. On the other hand we realized that we had to be realistic, because if you disobey an order, sooner or later they will get rid of you. I mean, what I am saying is, like for instance if I had decided to refuse to fight the Viet Cong, my friends, my own friends, and the officers would get rid of me. I mean, they would have killed me — there is no doubt about that. Therefore you go along with the program.

SCHWARTZ: *You have told us about eating conditions in the refugee camps. Have you seen people who died of starvation in these camps? Have you seen sick people who were refused medical care? What were the medical and sanitary conditions in these camps?*

I would say that the medical and sanitary conditions are very primitive. I mean by anyone's standards. I could not say that I ever saw anyone *die* of starvation, but I saw people who looked as though they *were about* to die of starvation. People who looked like they were on their last legs, and every now and then the U.S. forces were sent, the S-5 section, this is the section which is involved in civil affairs. We would send a medic to give out pills and shots and so forth. But this only occurred about once a month anyway. Most of the time our S-5 section was in the field anyway.

SCHWARTZ: *There could have been regular medical visits, but there were not?*

As far as I know, no.

SCHWARTZ: *You just told us that most of the time, or quite often, that you gave prisoners to the South Vietnamese for interrogation. But on the other hand, Mr. Martinsen told us yesterday that there was usually an American interrogator along with a South Vietnamese [interpreter]. In your opinion, did the Americans do most of the torturing, or the South Vietnamese?*

Well, I cannot dispute what Mr. Martinsen says, I am only going on what I saw. In the case that I saw it was an American who gave the orders, who asked the questions. He passed it on to a South Vietnamese interpreter and then he was the one who interrogated the man, but the actual torture that I saw was being done by people in the South Vietnamese Army.

GUNTHER ANDERS: *Repeatedly you quoted the sentence, "the only good Vietnamese is a dead Vietnamese." Did you vary the famous words, "The only good Indian is a dead Indian," or was this sentence generally known, was it like an order given to you by the officers?*

Well, I mean, this was a statement which the order, which the officers gave to us, and a lot of the men, as I said before, this indoctrination sank in. They also believed this because after all most Americans have heard that saying, you know, "the only good Indian is a dead Indian."

ANDERS: *Yes. The same applies to, "don't take prisoners." Was this an order or was it an anonymous custom everybody knew, that this had to be applied, or did you ever hear the command, the order, "Never take prisoners"?*

Well, I would like to say this. The order was "Never take prisoners" as well as "Don't take prisoners," because there had to be exceptions if there was an enemy officer — because we considered the officers more important than the enlisted men. Therefore there had to be exceptions. This was not a written order. This was an order, but it was a spoken order; it was not a written order.

ANDERS: *Yes, that is just what I wanted to know. And I have a third question. You spoke about this terrible collection of ears, and there I would like to know if you would say that this is a crime which everybody would recognize as a crime. Was there anyone among the American soldiers who objected to this crime or who refused to cooperate in this sad sport to collect ears?*

Well, I am quite sure that there were individuals who did not go along with it. If they did not want to take any ears they were not under any pressure to do so. This was something dreamed up by the brass to inspire the men to help the morale.

ANDERS: *This is what you call inspiration?* [*Laughter*]

Yes. [Laughter]

ANDERS: *Do you know of any case that this macabre collection of ears was brought home by G.I.'s to the United States?*

Well, I would like to say that I don't know of any case, but in the first place, they would have to put it in alcohol in order to do this, so the only ones who might have done this would be the medics, because they would have access and the time to preserve the ears. But the ordinary G.I., he wouldn't know how to preserve them anyway.

ANDERS: *He just showed the ear to get his free beer?* [Laughter] *Good, thank you.*

DEDIJER . . . *because during the Second World War in Yugoslavia it was a habit of some quisling troops who were under the command of German officers to do the same thing of cutting the ears and even the eyes. I witnessed myself several of these cases and I wonder have you met in Vietnam any German or Yugoslav national who was, perhaps not an American citizen, but as a kind of adviser?*

No, I can say that I have never met any German or Yugoslav nationals, but the only thing German I have seen was German rifles left from World War II used by the V.C. That's all.

DEDIJER: *Thank you very much.*

JEAN-PAUL SARTRE: *You've told us that black soldiers are used more often than white soldiers in combat operations. Did your black comrades realize that there was this sort of racial discrimination? In general, do black soldiers sense they are being used on dangerous operations just because they are black?*

Well, I would like to say that in this respect he wasn't used for the more dangerous work. Let's say that more black soldiers were used. I mean both white and black were used, but more black soldiers out of proportion. Most of the black soldiers in the Army are the same as they are in civilian life: they have been brainwashed and they believe that they are fighting for the freedom of the South Vietnamese — forgetting completely that in many parts of the United States they do not have freedom, see? But on the other hand the few who do know this are very realistic. They know that if they refuse to do something they would be killed anyway, and in order for the black soldier to prevent their being used in such a manner it would take a sort of an uprising in order to get this practice to be stopped.

SARTRE: *Did they also sense that this racial criterion was also being used with regard to the Vietnamese?*

Well, there was a lot of black G.I.'s including myself who realized that here they looked upon us the same as they did the Vietnamese. But on the other hand they thought that they really had no choice in the matter, that they had to fight or else.

SARTRE: *Thank you.*

MAHMUD ALI KASURI: *Mr. Tuck, you refer to the practice of cutting their ears. Did it extend to only killed Vietnamese or also to those who were injured?*

Well, as far as I know I only saw it being done on those who were killed.

KASURI: *You have referred to a distinct change in indoctrination while you were in Hawaii and after you reached Vietnam. Would you say that its object was that people in the U.S.A. should not know what the American forces in Vietnam were doing, and that is why in Hawaii the ordinary practice was being taught and in Vietnam the actualities were being brought before the troops?*

I would say that this was precisely the case.

KASURI: *Now, you referred to tear gas being the only chemical reagent which was used. Now may I know if you have any knowledge of chemistry?*

No, I have very little knowledge of chemistry.

KASURI: *And you would not be able to distinguish between various reagents?*

Yes, but on the other hand, we were given training in detecting such as mustard gas, chlorine gas and so forth. So, the only gas that I saw being used was tear gas.

KASURI; *Now, you have referred to a certain kind of interrogation, and we have had other evidence of interrogation, and I just like to sort out the points. When you are referring to interrogation I believe it is the interrogation that was conducted by actually fighting troops.*

416

In this interrogation that I saw at Camp Holloway, yes. It was by military men, yes.

KASURI: *It wasn't by the intelligence staff who were specially appointed, who are in quite large numbers, white and black Americans who conducted the interrogation? It wasn't by those?*

No, it wasn't.

KASURI: *It was by the ordinary regular infantry unit?*

Right.

KASURI: *So that if there is a difference in the matters of intelligence staff and infantry staff, it is perfectly understandable?*

Right.

KASURI: *Now, you referred to this "mad minute". In how many cases while you were present in Vietnam was this practice indulged in? Three, four, five, twenty?*

Well, I would like to say that this practice was indulged in so many times that you might say it's numerous, you know. This is a common practice. You know, everyone starts firing for one minute — approximately one minute.

KASURI: *So it is not an unusual thing to which you are referring, this is the ordinary thing?*

Yes, this is an ordinary thing.

KASURI: *This is the ordinary thing. Now you said many times that "the good Vietnamese were the dead Vietnamese," and on another occasion you said this sentiment had evolved out of a sentiment that the Vietnamese were not good soldiers. Then do I take it that in killing some discrimination was made between men and women or children and adults?*

Well, I would like to put it this way: a lot of times when you have to assault a village you shoot at the first thing that moves. In some cases, inevitably, it was women and children that got killed.

KASURI: *So that it wouldn't be necessarily right to say that this practice is the result of the refusal of the Vietnamese to fight on the side of the Americans?*

Right.

KASURI: *Now you referred to the composition of your own unit and you said that out of the 156 people in it, 117 were dark.*

That's right.

KASURI: *Now was it an unusual kind of a unit or the ordinary composition of infantry units?*

This was a regular infantry unit.

KASURI: *No, but I mean, did you notice similar composition of other infantry units?*

Right, right, also noticed this in the 1st Battalion of the 14th Infantry Regiment. This was the same practice. Most of the infantrymen were black G.I.'s. Then after that you had Puerto Ricans and what we call "hillbillies."

KASURI: *Would it then be right to assume that in the casualties the majority would be black?*

That is correct to assume.

KASURI: *Now, would it be right to assume that the things you are referring to: namely, that the Vietnamese should be shot, that the good Vietnamese was a dead Vietnamese, or that it was common to cut the ears off the killed Vietnamese or that the practice of the "mad minute" existed — is within the knowledge of the higher military officers of the U.S. Army?*

There is no doubt that it is within the knowledge of the higher U.S. authorities.

KASURI: *Thank you.*

CARL OGLESBY: *Mr. Tuck, you said that you were trained in the use of mustard gas and chlorine gas.*

No, we weren't trained in the use, we were trained how to detect them, how to put our gas masks on before thirty seconds and so forth. They do have army units, you know, in ordnance who are trained in the use of such agents.

OGLESBY: *You know that from personal experience, do you, that Army units are trained in the use of lethal...?*

Oh, yes, this is well known within the U.S. Army, you know.

OGLESBY: *Do you know whether or not any units with that kind of training were seeing active duty in Vietnam?*

Well, as to that I don't know. When we used the tear gas, there was always one man, you know, who was an expert in chemical warfare. He directed the other G.I.'s on how to use this. But as to whether there were any units of such, I really don't know.

OGLESBY: *On the question of the executing of prisoners I'd just like to follow a little more Anders' line of questioning on the way in which you knew that it was standard practice to execute prisoners. Did you find out that that was standard practice from speeches made to your unit by your superior officers, or was it more of a matter of word-of-mouth circulation among the soldiers?*

Well, it was circulated among the soldiers but it was also what our company commander told us, you know. He didn't put it in writing, of course, but he told us this. He said, "You better not take no prisoners." You see, that's the way he said it, in that spirit.

OGLESBY: *What would happen if an American officer, a veteran of Vietnam, would come and testify to this Tribunal that he knew nothing about this? Would there be any way to settle an argument between ...?*

Well, it depended upon what type of outfit the officer was, what his experiences were. You know, I couldn't say yes or no. If he was in an infantry outfit I would say — and he denied it — I would say the man was lying.

OGLESBY: *How did you first find out that it was standard practice to take no prisoners?*

Well, you see, shortly after we got over there we heard from these other outfits, the 1st Air Cavalry, 1st Brigade, 101st Airborne, they told us the same thing and then our officers, they told us that would be our policy. That we weren't going to take any prisoners unless we happened to capture an officer and then there was an American officer there to decide that he should be saved; otherwise we were to get rid of him.

OGLESBY: *Besides the refugee camps which you talked about do you know of the existence in Vietnam of any prisoner-of-war camps?*

Yes, I know of prisoner-of-war camps. Right outside of Pleiku there is a prisoner-of-war-camp on Highway 14.

OGLESBY: *Are there nothing but officers in that prisoner-of-war camp?*

That I couldn't say. I would presume it.

DELLINGER: *I just wanted to clear up one point. If I understand Mrs. Halimi's French properly she mentioned a rumor that officers were paying a thousand dollars for Vietnamese ears, which I won't explain why but it seemed unreasonable to me and ... oh, anyway I'd like you to clear up this point. You spoke of it more as a fad or as a way of getting free beer.*

Well, in the case of the thousand piastres this was strictly a rumor, you know.

DELLINGER: *You have no evidence of this.*

No, no evidence.

DELLINGER: *Now the other thing is the sound was very bad on the film yesterday, but if I saw and heard correctly you referred to the practice of cutting the tips off bullets before a battle, and I don't believe you said anything about that today. Can you give us some details on this and possibly how common a practice — if it was a practice — and also if there was any relationship discussed between this and the Geneva Conventions?*

DEDIJER: *This is so-called dum-dum, you see. It was a British custom first used in India.*

I want to say that this is a common practice among many units to cut the tips off of the cartridges because we found out that a lot of the V.C. and North Vietnamese dope themselves up with morphine and you could hit them in the chest they would still keep coming so while you were hitting them they still had time to kill you. So then, we got into the habit of shooting them in the head to stop them, see, and then some guy had the bright idea of cutting the tips of the bullets — the end of the cartridges — and then putting a notch in. This would cause the bullet to expand and expend more energy inside the body because with the regular military bullets it would just make a clean hole through the man and also the energy would be expended going through him. But with these bullets it was found that they would expand and cause much more damage and this was the only way to stop them, cause all the time you could not get a shot at the head. The officers knew about this but they never said anything about it. It was one way or the other, you know.

DELLINGER: *When you say the officers knew about it, did they ever instruct you to do it, or did they observe the soldiers doing this, or how did they know?*

Well, I would like to say that they never instructed us to do this, but they observed us doing this. The G.I.'s who didn't know how to do it, they were taught by their friends, how to do this.

DELLINGER: *Thank you.*

KINJU MORIKAWA: *I have information from a press correspondent that if there happens to be an explosion of mine, the Americans soldiers usually kill almost all villagers that could be seen nearby. Is that true or not?*

Yes, yes, this is a common practice, but I would like to say that all the time they wouldn't kill *all* the people, but they would go into the village shooting, better say this, and if any innocent people got killed, well the attitude was, "That's war."

ANDERS: *Did you meet the experience that ordinarily the number of Vietnamese civilians who perished in course of the war was greater than the number of Viet Cong soldiers who were killed? If yes, wouldn't you be forced to say that the fight is mainly being fought against the civilian population?*

I would like to say that there was as many civilians killed from what I've seen as the V.C., but I don't think I'm qualified to come to the conclusions that it was a fight against the civilian population. It would seem that way, but I couldn't really say that this was a rigid policy of the U.S. government.

DEDIJER: *You are here to give the answers to the facts not to express opinions.*

WEISS: *Mr. Tuck, you said that if you disobeyed an order they will get rid of you. You mean, have you seen any cases where American soldiers were shot because they disobeyed orders?*

Well, you would be surprised at the number of people who are killed by their own troops. Now, I know two sergeants who happened to get drunk while they were out in the field, see, so they set these men further out with the artillery outfit that had just been hard hit, see, hoping that they would get knocked off. And when they came back alive the brass were unhappy about it, see.

WEISS: *This was deliberately done?*

Right, and also in my own case I was sent to a line outfit for punishment anyway. When I first came to Vietnam I was the battalion mail clerk, but myself and a sergeant-major did not get along so they sent me out with the infantry as an R.T.O., hoping that I would get killed of course. That is the way they punish you in a lot of cases.

WEISS: *To come back to a detail you mentioned in the beginning, you said that Vietnamese prisoners were put into a barbed-wire cage.*

Well, I didn't say prisoners, I said I saw one prisoner.

WEISS: *This was only one case you saw?*

Right.

WEISS: *And the incident when one prisoner was tortured with the knife on the toenails was one case?*

This was the same prisoner who was put into the barbed-wire cage.

WEISS: *So you have seen this sort of torture only once?*

Yes.

DEDIJER: *No more questions?*

DELLINGER: *Yes, on that business of the cage, again remembering back to the tape, you described yesterday something about the closeness of the barbed wire to him, which I didn't get completely, and I don't think you referred to that today.*

421

The barbed wire was sort of an oval-shaped barbed wire, you know, in that shape, the man was on his hands and knees and if he attempted to move to relieve his discomfort the barbs would cut into his flesh, and that was the type of cage he was in.

DELLINGER: *In other words it was a matter of being within an inch or two of his flesh, is that what you're saying?*

Well, yes, it was even closer than that.

DELLINGER: *Was an American interrogation officer present?*

Yes he was present.

DELLINGER: *Did the American officer ask questions of him while he was in the cage?*

Right, but I must say that this man must have been a superman or something because he never talked.

DELLINGER: *He was there did you say for about two days?*

Right.

SCHWARTZ: [in French] *You said that it was the only case in which you saw a Vietnamese prisoner in the cage. However, the cage already existed. It was not constructed for him. What had it been used for?*

I would assume that the cage had been used before.

DAVE DELLINGER: *... You spoke yesterday of the practice of cutting the tips off the bullets in order to make dum-dum bullets. On the other hand, Sergeant Duncan spoke of the effect of the M-16 as being in the same direction as the dum-dum only stronger with a tumble quality; he described how it had torn the chest off a person and thrown him three feet, and other terrible things of that kind. I'm wondering in view of this why you found it necessary to cut the tips off the bullets; maybe you can explain.*

When we first went to Vietnam, we had the U.S. Army rifle model M-14; this is 7.62 mm. caliber. This particular rifle it was necessary to cut the tips in, but in the case of the M-16, which was given to us in March of '66, this was not necessary because the bullet would tumble in flight.

DELLINGER: *So this would give our Tribunal to think that the M-16 in itself exceeds the conventions of war by this tumble effect?*

I guess you could say that. It does have the same effect as an expanding bullet, probably a worse effect.

DELLINGER: *Now, one other question here. I've been told by recent visitors to South Vietnam that a great deal of the firing of shells, mortar and so forth is indiscriminate; that is they pick out a certain target area, a very generalized area, and during the night, without any knowledge of really what the shells are hitting — that there's a great deal of firing of this kind. I have no idea whether that's accurate or not, but I'd be interested, from your experience. We've heard of the free-fire zones, where everything that moves is shot; are there also free-fire zones that are just sort of blasted at random this way?*

The U.S. Army has a policy of what they call "H and I"; this is harassment and interdiction; the idea is to keep the enemy on the move, so that he is unable to rest. So what they do is to select a set of co-ordinates, and they fire a certain number of shells at night. This war has been called a "6400 mil* war," because the enemy is everywhere. So therefore the artillery guns are placed roughly in a 360-degree circle so that they can fire in all directions. I wouldn't say that it is a policy not to know what they are firing at, but I do know that my own outfit killed about fifteen people at a village about twenty miles north of Ban Me Thuot in March of 1966. I can't say that this was deliberate, but the effect was the same anyway. I would also say in the settled areas they are bound to kill civilians accidentally anyway. But in the Central Highlands it's not as densely crowded as down around Saigon.

DELLINGER: *Just one final question about the execution of prisoners that you referred to. This is not necessarily a conflict, but some difference of testimony between that and some of the evidence of the taking of prisoners. I wonder if you could be more specific. And you spoke about the general attitude of the officers: "the only good Vietnamese was a dead one," and various factors of that kind. But could you be more specific, in terms of actual instances in which you saw prisoners executed?*

I've seen several instances in which men, wounded men, were waiting for an evacuation helicopter, and some of the enlisted men said, "Well, why wait for a helicopter, we'll just shoot the S.O.B. right now." So therefore when the Medevac arrived, there wasn't anything to pick up. But this is very common, the shooting of the prisoners. Like I said before, the only time that our officers wanted us to keep a prisoner was if it was an officer, because we figured that he can tell us something. But we figured that if he's just an enlisted man, he really can't tell us anything, so if he's wounded and we're in a hurry to move on, then we just executed him anyway. So that's the way it is.

DELLINGER: *What if he's not wounded?*

Well, in the first place, the only prisoners that we are going to get when we're out in the jungle and the forest will be the wounded. The unwounded always manage to slip through our fingers anyway.

---

*mil — a military unit of angular measurement equal to the angle subtended by 1/64000 of a circumference. — *The Random House Dictionary of the English Language.*

DELLINGER: *When Mr. Duncan spoke of receiving orders to get rid of the prisoners, he was behind the lines so to speak, although I realize there are not regular lines, but he parachuted in. There was a problem in getting back. Now were there circumstances of this kind when you saw prisoners executed, or did you have some kind of direct line back to the base camp?*

Well, there's always a line of communications back to our rear area as we call it; we can always contact them on the phone. But a lot of times it wasn't necessary for them to give us direct orders to execute the men, because we knew ahead of time that we were expected to execute these people. And it wasn't a matter of the prisoners preventing us from moving on, because the U.S. Army travels by helicopter anyway, in this operation. So it wasn't a matter of the prisoners hindering us.

PETER WEISS: *One additional question please. Mr. Tuck, you just mentioned this village where there was shooting going on and the number of casualties that were found there; these people when they were killed, later on was there a report made and were they all called V.C. then?*

I couldn't honestly say that there was a report given to higher headquarters. The higher headquarters in the II Corps area is called Military Assistance Command; that is located in Pleiku. But I couldn't honestly say that a report was sent to higher authorities. We knew about it and the artillery knew about it and I'm sure the brigade commander knew about it, but other than that I couldn't honestly say.

WEISS: *Was it just in this special case that there was no report given or was it a rule that in this sort of incidence there was no report given?*

As far as the accidental hitting of this village by artillery fire, I can't speak for other units, but in my unit we tried as much as possible to avoid hitting these villages with H and I's, because our outfit believed, just like the V.C., that the idea was to win the hearts and minds of the people. So I couldn't say that this was a regular thing.

WEISS: *Have you any experience from reports given where you could say that the killed people were not only [those] belonging to the Liberation Front, but [extended] to the population of the cities, and they were reckoned as killed V.C.?*

This, again, I could not say. I do know that when we go into action, when we count the number of killed, this is a confirmed body count. And we figure this way, if there is a woman or child lying there, depending on who makes the count, they may or may not count them as killed. It all depends on how successful we are in the battle. If we take a lot of casualties and inflict only a few on them, the commanding officer does not want to look bad to his superiors, so he includes these civilians in the count. It depends on how well the battle went.

Testimony and Questioning of Peter Martinsen

Former Prisoner of War Interrogator with the 541st Military Intelligence Detachment in Vietnam

VLADIMIR DEDIJER: *First, I would like to identify the witness. How old are you?*

I am 23 years old.

DEDIJER: *And where do you live?*

In Berkely, California.

DEDIJER: *And what is your occupation?*

I am a student, a junior.

DEDIJER: *Well, thank you very much, and thank you for your willingness to come here to give witness. Maitre Halimi, please direct your questions to the witness.*

GISELE HALIMI: *Mr. Martinsen, please tell to the Tribunal your role in the Army: your grade, your branch of service, the date of your enlistment — I believe you were a volunteer — and afterwards we will speak about Vietnam.*

I enlisted in the Army in June 1963 and was trained initially as a cook. However, I was then sent to a foreign-language school, where I learned Italian, and from there I was sent to the U.S. Army Intelligence School in Fort Holabird, Maryland, where I was trained as a prisoner-of-war interrogator. The Vietnam build-up began, and I was assigned to a unit, the 541st Military Intelligence Detachment, which was to go to Vietnam. The 541st Military Intelligence Detachment was attached to the 11th Armored Cavalry

Regiment. We left for Vietnam in the middle of August 1966 and arrived in September. I was in Vietnam from September 1966 to June 1967, as a prisoner-of-war interrogator.

HALIMI: *Did you, in 1965, go to a training school, called U.S.A.I.N.T.S., and could you please indicate to the Tribunal what you learned there?*

The U.S.A.I.N.T.S., or "U-saints" as it is called in the Army, is the U.S. Army's intelligence school. There were several curricula there, and I was trained to interrogate prisoners of war. This training involves certain classified things, which are not really relevant, and a mass of techniques taught at the school which are not in any way illegal.

HALIMI: *Did you receive any decorations?*

Yes, I have several decorations. Should I present them?

HALIMI: *No. No, just specify which ones you have got.*

I have the Vietnam Service Medal, the Vietnam Expeditionary Medal, the Army Commendation Medal, the Good Conduct Medal, the National Defense Medal and several marksmanship medals.

HALIMI: *So you were a "prisoner-of-war interrogator." Could you tell the Tribunal that during your entire stay in Vietnam you did nothing except interrogating Vietnamese? You did not have any other activities . there?*

Aside from my normal Army life, such as "details" and such, my occupation was to be a prisoner-of-war interrogator. I performed several hundred formal interrogations. I probably did several thousand screenings.

HALIMI: *Could you please indicate to the Tribunal the structure of the detachment to which you belonged? How many men were you? How many men and officers directly took part in the interrogations (and presently I will ask you, in what manner)?*

The intelligence detachment is made up of four sections: the counter-intelligence section, the prisoner-of-war interrogation section, an order of battle section and the photo-interpretation section. The interrogation section had only four interrogation officers and nine enlisted men. The detachment itself had a strength of thirty-two men. It was assigned to the 11th Armored Cavalry Regiment. Every large independent combat unit in Vietnam has a military-intelligence detachment. These are Army units, I don't know about Marine units. The function of these units is to provide intelligence support in one of the four areas.

HALIMI: *Mr. Martinsen, you are here to testify about two series of facts. I am well aware that it must be very difficult for you to say exactly what you yourself did while interrogating prisoners. But you understand that we need to get your direct testimony. You told me (because you remembered this particularly) that the first time you had interrogated and tortured a Vietnamese was in Lon Giao camp. It was on your arrival in Vietnam in November 1966. I wish you to please repeat to the Tribunal the account you already gave me.*

This was some time after I arrived in Vietnam. We established our base camp in Lon Giao, which is in Long Kien [?], twelve kilometers south of Xuan Loc, and during this time we were receiving quite a few prisoners. The troops were very nervous and arresting just about everyone in sight, and we were interrogating these prisoners. While we were moving our base camp to this area, one of the men of the detachment was killed in an ambush. Later on we received a group of prisoners, eight or nine I believe, I don't remember exactly. I interrogated one and I had no data on where he was captured or what he was doing. He was just presented to me. I started to question him and he kept saying that he was not a Viet Cong, that he didn't know where the Viet Cong was, etc. I was quite sure that he was lying. I was not certain if he belonged to the Viet Cong, but I was quite sure he was lying about not knowing where they were. I decided to beat him. This did not help. I struck him with my hand. This did not produce anything except a long string of "I don't know's", . . . and then — as was often the case — another interrogator took my place, an interrogation officer. I told the officer, a lieutenant, that I couldn't get anything out of the prisoner.

The lieutenant proceeded to do the same thing as I had been doing, finally beating the prisoner, and this did not work. The lieutenant had an Army field telephone, which runs on batteries and a generator. You crank it and it gives a nasty shock, a very nasty shock, quite painful. The interrogation commenced with the prisoner being tortured by field telephone. The telephones were first placed on his hands and then the field telephone wires were placed on his sexual organs. I left, I could not watch it.

HALIMI: *Later on you witnessed torture done by an American lieutenant on a captain from the Viet Cong — particularly electrical tortures and torture consisting in inserting bamboo splinters under his nails. Could you please explain this to the Tribunal?*

Yes. This particular case occurred on Operation Cedar Falls. This was a very big allied operation in the so-called "Iron Triangle" to the north of Saigon. A North Vietnamese Army captain was captured. He admitted he belonged to the North Vietnamese Army.

He was not a Viet Cong. I was to interrogate him and they kept telling me: "You must get information now. *Now!*" While I interrogated him, my section leader, who was another enlisted man, was torturing him with a field telephone. When I could not get anything out of the prisoner they replaced me by another lieutenant. The lieutenant kept interrogating him with the field telephones. Finally he became quite frustrated; he then inserted bamboo splinters under the man's fingernails.

This brought about a reaction from our unit commander, because he had left marks. The electrical torture generally does not leave marks, and beating generally does not leave marks, but the use of bamboo was forbidden, because it left marks and there was blood. After that the use of extreme forms of electrical torture became less frequent. But it was understood that if we did not leave marks we could do exactly as we pleased.

We had absolute power over our prisoners — absolute power, we were the judge, the jury and the god. We had the power of life and death over the prisoners. I never did this, but it is quite possible that a prisoner could be killed in anger or out of carelessness or for a special reason — perhaps to intimidate other prisoners. On the other hand it was possible that nothing might ever happen to them.

HALIMI: *Mr. Martinsen, you told me that one day you saw a Vietnamese die after torture. You said that you were not yourself present during the torturing, but that you saw the Vietnamese enter the neighboring tent, where he was interrogated by an American captain. I should like you to indicate to the Tribunal who did the interrogation, and that afterwards the American captain came out of the tent saying: "He is dead." You also told me that you saw yourself the dead body of this man in the same place where he had been tortured. Could you add other details to the Tribunal in order to complete this declaration?*

Yes. The case referred to occurred during Operation Cedar Falls, when I witnessed more torture than I had seen on any special operation in Vietnam. We were cooperating with the 172nd Military Intelligence Detachment, which is attached to the 173rd Airborne Brigade. We received a large group of prisoners, and we had a "Chieu Hoi." A Chieu Hoi is a deserter from the Viet Cong. He is generally used as an informer to give information about his former comrades. A certain prisoner was pointed out by the Chieu Hoi as being some sort of local cadre in the Iron Triangle — and this also goes for Ben Suc by the way; this was during the same operation that included Ben Suc. The prisoner was taken into the tent in the afternoon. Our unit stopped interrogation in the evenings because our

428

tents were so full of holes from bullets and other things that our light seeped out and attracted enemy fire. Anyway, another unit continued to interrogate at night and all of a sudden an enlisted man from that unit came over and said: "We just lost a prisoner." I said, "What?" I couldn't believe it. And he said, "We have. The captain was wiring him, and he just fell over and died." The captain came over a little later and said: "Yes, I was wiring him. He was just about to break. He was just on the verge of telling me something when he died."

There is a log which must be kept in regard to the prisoners. It is a very informal thing but you have to fill in the disposition of the prisoner. In this case the prisoner was dead, so a doctor was called, a brigade surgeon, as I recall, in the 173rd Airborne Brigade. He diagnosed the cause of death of the prisoner as being heart failure, which is logical. The man had been electrically tortured to death. He probably had a weak heart.

HALIMI: *Could you indicate whether the man in charge of the interrogation was an American captain? And that South Vietnamese translators were present?*

In one hundred percent of the interrogations performed in our unit and in other units I watched, there was always a Vietnamese interpreter present, because Americans do not speak the language well enough to conduct a complicated interrogation. This creates much difficulty and a lot of misinterpretation during the interrogations. It probably leads more to the use of torture, because one becomes angry with the interpreter and the prisoner. Yes, there was a Vietnamese interpreter present. There had to be and there always is. The captain couldn't speak Vietnamese. I can say that I did not personally see which interpreting sergeant was there but I know that one was there. The captain was, I believe, a section leader of either the counterintelligence section or of the interrogation section of the 172nd Military Intelligence Detachment. I don't recall who he was. The captain said he had "wired" the prisoner and we were waiting for information from the prisoner that would implicate other prisoners. There were more prisoners — and this was documented by press reports — taken during Operation Cedar Falls than in any other, literally thousands of people.

HALIMI: *After the death of this prisoner, did the officer give a report?*

There was no formal report concerning the death except for an informal prisoner log kept by the military police who guard the prisoners. The disposition of a prisoner can involve one of several things. For example, he can be recommended for further interrogation. In that case he goes on to another unit, a higher unit in the echelon — at that time it was the 1st Infantry Division. A prisoner can also be recommended to be a civil defendant, meaning he is guilty of a civil crime and that you don't believe him to be a Viet Cong. A civil crime can be not having an I.D. card or traveling without travel papers or anything you want — it is a catchall phrase. He can be an innocent civilian (in that case he's released) or his can be a doubtful case. In the latter event, he is interrogated further, and this is marked under "disposition" in the record book. In this case, disposition was "death due to heart failure" — and very simple! No one ever reviews it. No one cares. The International Red Cross is not there. I don't know where they are, in fact. They were not on any operation except for their recreational girls. They were not present at any operation I was on, and I was on every major operation in III Corps Tactical Zone during that time that I was there.

HALIMI: *You also told me about an interrogation which you conducted yourself a few kilometers from a Michelin plantation, when you were given a prisoner who you took to be a Viet Cong cadre. Would you please tell me, repeat for the Tribunal, the methods you used to make him talk?*

That was during Operation Manhattan which was in May of this year. We were carrying out a village "sweep." The village was surrounded, all the people were herded into one area and screened. The people we thought should be interrogated were interrogated. A certain prisoner had been found hiding in a drainage ditch with a weapon, so immediately I knew he was a Viet Cong. There was still the question of determining his rank, second, if he was important or not. We were about four kilometers south of the Michelin plantation of Yan Tieng [?]. I started the interrogation. My interpreter was beating this man with a wooden mallet that he had found in the house we were working in. He beat the man on the knee-caps and the shoulder blades and I did not stop the interpreter. This didn't yield much information. We were being watched by my commanding officer and I got very frustrated. I decided to try out a new idea.

I had the man dig his own grave with a gun at his head, and he dug his grave until I counted off the minutes that he had to live. I counted them off in Vietnamese so that he knew I wasn't kidding. He broke down and cried. This is the absolute power the interrogator has. The prisoner was quite certain he was going to die. I described what death he was going to have. He had a rifle or an M-79 grenade launcher being pointed at him the whole time. The interpreter occasionally beat him while he was digging his grave. He was quite certain he was going to die. This is what is known as "breaking the prisoner." After he was "broken," to keep him broken I just kept reminding him, in Vietnamese, that he was not yet dead. I have read the 1949 Geneva Convention on the treatment of prisoners of war. Coercion is quite illegal. It is a war crime. It is specifically stated that prisoners must not be harassed or coerced.

HALIMI: *Mr. Martinsen, in the brief time that we spoke together, you enumerated a number of cases of torture in which you and other Americans participated. I also remember that you declared, "If I am going to be questioned seriously and for a long time I could speak of many cases, many hundreds of cases, of torture." Would you confirm it?*

This is quite true. Electrical torture was very common for a while in Vietnam but was not common toward the end of our assignment. Beatings were extremely common. An interrogator came to me and said, "My hands are getting tired from hitting this man in the mouth." It was something that occurred in almost every interrogation and it was tacitly condoned by the officers. The commanding officer of the unit stated for the record that there must be no torturing or the use of force during an interrogation. However, he allowed it to continue and watched it. He knew of it. The commanding officer, the section commander, knew of it.

HALIMI: *I would like to ask you to give some details concerning that young girl of 17 years who was not tortured but who was gassed. You remember that you said to me that the Americans threw tear gas into a tunnel ten kilometers long that you believe was occupied by the Viet Cong. You said that there were many wounded, including several young girls. You said you were a witness to the case of a young girl of 17 years who was badly wounded and who was not given medical aid in time because they wanted to get information from her. You said her condition worsened and the doctor was called. She died while you were there. Would you please confirm this for the Tribunal?*

This was a particularly odious thing. I heard that it involved several girls. I was not there when the people were captured but there are "capture circumstances" tags that each prisoner has. There were some people in a tunnel, and the Americans found the tunnel entrance. They looked inside the tunnel and found it was occupied. They immediately gassed the tunnel with tear gas. It might have been "antiriot" gas. Then they proceeded to chase the people from the tunnel. The tunnel was so long they chased the people for twenty-four hours, until the people came out the other end of the tunnel very badly gassed and coughing. All of them sounded as if they had serious damage to their lungs. The prisoners were brought in to us, and I only looked once. Four or five of the prisoners were girls between the ages of 16 and 20. They were nurses and laborers.

The girls were brought to us in very bad physical condition. They were coughing, wheezing and gasping, as if they had bad — very bad — asthmatic attacks. I took one look and called the doctor. The doctor gave them all injections and dosages of adrenaline. The prisoner compound was nothing but a tent with barbed wire around it. The prisoners were not segregated by sex as the Geneva Convention calls for. The prisoners were not given proper bedding. The girls were lying on the ground, which was rather damp, and one girl grew more ill. It was the policy that all prisoners must be interrogated. I kept calling the doctor to say "Doctor, she has pneumonia." I knew that because I have had pneumonia. The doctor kept saying: "No, No. She'll get better," and she kept getting worse. She was finally evacuated to Lai Khe, to the 3rd Brigade, 1st Division field hospital, where I hear she died. I denounced the stupidity of the doctors and the stupidity of the commanders for trying to keep her there to interrogate her, and I almost got court-martialed for it. That was one of the most odious things I saw there.

HALIMI: *Mr. President, I have finished asking my questions about the torture. You can ask Mr. Martinsen directly about the use of weapons such as white phosphorus, the M-16 rifle, tear gas and antipersonnel weapons like canister and beehive, which are fragmentation weapons. I think it would be better now to ask the witness questions directly concerned with the question of torture.*

DEDIJER: *Thank you very much. In accordance with our rules the questions posed by the President will come last. Members of the Tribunal are invited to present their questions to Mr. Martinsen. I would propose that each member of the Tribunal present the whole list of his questions, so that everybody will get a chance to question the witness.*

GUNTHER ANDERS: *Do you think, or do you have evidence, that many of your compatriots, your comrades or former comrades, are feeling the way you are feeling about the events, and the American acts, in Vietnam and are being encouraged to open their mouths? Do you think that there are thousands who feel the way you are feeling?*

Yes, I'm studying psychology and writing a paper on guilt manifestations caused by war crimes. The paper isn't as good as I would have liked. It's much too general. I just don't have enough knowledge of psychology to have studied it carefully, but there have been definite manifestations of guilt.

People are saying "I'm guilty." They had been trying to rationalize and say: "I'd rather torture one Viet Cong than have one of my friends die because we didn't get some vital information." This was a very common rationalization. But you don't get the information anyway. If you torture a prisoner, a prisoner will tell you everything he thinks you want to know, to keep you from giving him pain. He will tell you anything that he thinks you will believe.

PETER WEISS: *Mr. Martinsen, you said during your experiences in Vietnam you became acquainted with the Geneva Conventions about the treatment of prisoners of war. When you went through your military schooling, did the officers speak to you and to your comrades about the Geneva laws?*

Yes, it was stressed in the school that torture was not permitted in the Army but that was before the Vietnam war got very large. That was in July and August of '65, I forget exactly when Johnson made his speech for the escalation but it was at that time. Our troops did not arrive until after large amounts of interrogations had been completed. After I went to school, they may have changed policy, but I doubt it. They didn't teach us about the Geneva Conventions. They taught that war crimes must not be committed, that prisoners must not be tortured nor mishandled, nor harassed, coerced or forced into doing anything. The instructors say privately, "Yes, I know they do it in Vietnam, but we don't officially admit it."

WEISS: *May I continue with some more questions? When you came to Vietnam, is it true you found that in practice the prisoners were tortured? Was it a sort of rule? Was it quite common that the prisoners went through this procedure?*

It was a pattern of the interrogations. The Army had classified field manuals on interrogation. Several different techniques are discussed but, without saying anything classified, I would say you begin by being nice to the prisoner. If you start out by torturing the prisoner where do you go from there? It's only logical. You must start out by being nice to the prisoner. Afterwards it depends upon the information that you get. I cannot think of an interrogation that I saw in Vietnam during which a war crime, as defined by the Geneva Conventions, was not committed. I cannot think of one without harassment or coercion. Even where force was not used, coercion, such as beating, torturing and harassment (such as screaming and yelling) was used. This was coercion, and it was specifically stated that one not do this. The Army, has a field manual called the "Law of Land Warfare," I forget the number, and it's the entire 1949 Geneva Convention. This field manual is easily obtained but no one ever reads it. I read parts of it, but it was not required that it be read.

WEISS: *Mr. Martinsen, I think you must have gone through a tremendous moral development when you came to Vietnam. When you changed your views, you went through a lot of experiences and you have a different view on these experiences now, than when you came to Vietnam?*

When I went to Vietnam, I was for the Vietnam war, I thought it was an open case of Communist aggression and that the majority of the Vietnamese people wanted us in Vietnam. I received a short course in the Vietnamese language before I went. Then I always tried to speak to my interpreters as much as possible, and speak to the people as much as possible. I developed a small knowledge of Vietnamese, and I understood that the government in Vietnam, which states that it supports the Vietnamese people, does not really. If this government wants us there, the people don't. I know this and the Vietnamese people have told me this. This is the major absurdity of the war, not the fact that the war crimes are committed. War crimes are committed in every war. War has war crimes, by definition.

WEISS: *When you were schooled, you and your comrades were convinced that what you had to do in Vietnam was for a right cause and that it had to be done because it was a war — and that in war everything has to be done to conquer the enemy.*

None of us ever thought that we would actually torture, or even beat a prisoner. There was not much force used — coercion and harassment, yes — but not much physical force until after members of the detachment were killed and death became a reality. You see, we knew, other people were dying, but when one of our friends was killed, death became a reality, and we realized that a certain amount of force does work.

WEISS: *Most of your comrades had the same opinion, of course. You all went in a group. You didn't go there alone. Did you discuss what was ahead of you when you left the United States for Vietnam?*

Yes. We were certainly very anxious on the ship going over, and we were certainly very anxious when we landed. We didn't know what to expect. We were armed to the teeth and we landed in Vung Tau, which was a very secure area. We were constantly looking for Viet Cong and there weren't any. Then, we became more sophisticated to the war, as we found out what was happening there. The first thing you realize is that the Vietnamese are not welcoming you as their liberators. This may be because they don't talk about anything. If you learn to speak their language, you learn that they don't like you at all. In fact I don't think of any people they like less, except, perhaps, the French.

WEISS: *Were you taught that the Vietnamese people were of less value than the Americans, for example, or the people of Western nations?*

The general viewpoint of the American troops was that the Vietnamese were apathetic, ignorant, dirty and were really not worthy of our efforts to be there. That was the general feeling, and the general feeling was, "Well, we might as well be here and show them *the* right way, clean them up, build them suburbia houses, and put two cars in every garage." That's the American dream for Vietnam.

WEISS: *So you really thought you had some good things to do there?*

There are a lot of good things to do in Vietnam, in the fields of education and health, but it's certainly not the killing of Vietnamese.

WEISS: *Mr. Martinsen, could you tell a little about the development you went through? How did it happen that you changed your attitude?*

My development came about with a number of things. It has partly to do with seeing all the little things in a war. If you've read Joseph Heller's *Catch-22*, you may think it is pure fiction, but that such things don't really happen. Then you see things happen constantly. If you encounter a man who likes to shoot water buffaloes, you may ask him, "Why do you like to shoot water buffaloes?" and he says, ' Because I like to shoot water buffaloes." It's so absurd. I remember a man who was a helicopter door-gunner and he likes to kill people on the ground, but only after playing with them like a cat plays with a mouse with his machine gun, chasing them around, etc. I saw rice captured from the Viet Cong, in American bags, and you don't really know if the rice is American rice but the bags are American bags. They have "U.S. NATO rice" written on them. It's all these ten thousand things. It's also the torture, the torture that shouldn't really happen. Then you realize, because everybody participates in the torture — unless we have a special group of sadists working as interrogators, which I don't believe; I believe they are just normal people — you realize that there is an innate capability to do harm to your fellow man in proper circumstances, and these circumstances are provided by the war in Vietnam. It's so horrifying to recall an interrogation where you beat the fellow to get an effect, and then you beat him out of anger, and then you beat him out of pleasure. That is what is horrible to say.

WEISS: *Have there been others of your comrades who had the same experience as you did?*

I don't think they talk about it. A lot of the men are still in the Army and if there is ever any kind of trial they'll be subpoenaed of course. This would affect their careers. So I won't name any names. I will not ruin careers, but someone has to say that Americans believe that an American doesn't commit any war crimes, simply because he is an American. They must understand that it does not take a Nazi to commit a war crime, it does not take a Nazi to kill six million Jews. They must understand this and no one is willing to speak because there is quite a bit of pressure. In my case it was mainly family pressure, dragging the family name through the mud or losing my inheritance, etc. — and the fact there probably is going to be a lot of pressure on my family from the press, etc. But even they don't think Americans do wrong. Even they misunderstood what is happening. Even they say, "My country right or wrong." In this case it's wrong, and I can't accept it if it's wrong, and they still say, "My country right or wrong." That's the way they think and this manner of thinking must be changed.

WEISS: *One final question: You mentioned an expression used by an officer who tortured a prisoner, the prisoner who was killed. He said, "I was 'wiring' him." Later on it was stated that the cause of death was heart failure. If one has studied the German concentration camps, there were methods of killing people by phenol, by gas, and other means, and the death certificate used the same phrases. I suppose you were too young to remember what happened during the Second World War, but did you, before you left the States or perhaps when you returned and were more concerned with this problem, did you know anything about the Germans? About the killings by the Nazis during the Second World War?*

Yes, I came across some of it while doing research. But I don't see what inference you're trying to draw. I'm quite aware of what the Nazis did.

WEISS: *I am referring to the terminology: "I was wiring him," and then: "death by heart failure." This phrase "I was wiring him" was exactly the same term the Germans used, "Ich hab ihn eingespritst."*

This is true. The common term is "wiring" or "phoning him up," one or the other — and at least the Germans used a death certificate. This man, no one knows he died. No one even knows if he was ever alive. He probably didn't have a birth certificate and he cetainly didn't have a death certificate.

WEISS: *Thank you very much, Mr. Martinsen.*

DAVE DELLINGER: *As you'll probably be able to tell from my accent, I'm an American too. And even before you mentioned the pressures that your family was subjected to, I just wanted to congratulate you for your courage. Although I know there will be many pressures I think the day will come when not only many Americans, who will do it today, but all of the American people will hail you as a hero and thank you for helping their country to get its better self back. Now on this question of pressures, you mentioned that after the girl was not given medical treatment, and after several girls were brought in coughing and gasping and put into interrogation, you considered this odious and you complained about it, and almost got court-martialed. Could you tell us a little bit about the circumstances of that? What kinds of pressure were brought on you? What makes you say that you almost got court-martialed?*

Well, you see I was being insubordinate. It doesn't matter what you're being insubordinate about. If you're insubordinate, you're insubordinate, I called it foolish. I called it stupid. It was so obvious to me that the girl was very ill, that there was no reason for her to die. When I heard that she died, the evening that she died, I just got so angry that I went around telling every officer in the place what I thought of him, what I thought of his personal stupidity for keeping the girl there while there was a possibility of her dying.

DELLINGER: *Did you file a complaint, or did you simply mention it?*

Would that I had had the courage to file a complaint or to go to jail for my beliefs then.

DELLINGER: *Secondly, I'm wondering... if you know what happened to the prisoners after the interrogation was completed. Did you ever see them, or do you know what happened to them, the ones who did survive?*

Yes, I know exactly what happened to them. They were separated into categories, for intelligence purposes. The people who had information of strategic value were taken to the central command. These prisoners were generally high-ranking people, like the North Vietnamese army captain we captured. He is kept in U.S. hands until he gets all the way down to Saigon, where there is a joint interrogation center run by the C.I.A., the Vietnamese special branch of the national police, Vietnamese military intelligence and Army military intelligence. That's where they finally got information out of this particular captain. There are other prisoners who may or may not have information. If we felt they were suspicious we could always treat them as if they were civil criminals, civil defendants. You're supposed to have the "concurrence" of the Judge Advocate staff in this, but their agreement is a mere formality and generally we didn't do it anyway. The Vietnamese have to have their traveling papers for travel from one province to another, and if a man does not have any travel papers he is guilty of a crime and for this he can go to jail. It is quite easy just to take him to the provincial capital and give him to the national police, and they are thrown into the filthiest dungeons imaginable.

DELLINGER: *In other words, if you did not find out any information you could still consign them to jail on the basis of their not having their travel permit or something of that kind?*

Yes. A lot of Vietnamese do not have any identification cards. They don't carry their identification with them, because they are afraid they might lose it. So these people are guilty of a crime. I got tired of seeing people with no identification cards. They were arrested by the American troops, since the American troops have that power. We call it "detained." And the people who are arrested are called "detainees." Until they are interrogated and their status is determined, they remain detainees. Draft dodgers are in another category. When I was at Cedar Falls, before it was turned into a "free-fire zone" (where anyone found would be killed) and while the refugees were still being moved out, I was screening every man between 20 and 30, to be taken into the Vietnamese army. I had the power to induct men. A U.S. citizen has the power to induct men into the Vietnamese army.

DELLINGER: *Without any procedures at all! I wonder if you have any idea of what happened to people who gave testimony — testimony which for one reason or another was interpreted as being correct. Excuse me, I don't think I made myself quite clear. I was thinking of what category they would be put in, if they would be rewarded or not, or whether they would be treated any better for this. I know in American prisons an informer is not liked or treated well even by the guards even after they have gotten the information. I have no idea of what the pattern is here. I also wonder if, from seeing them afterwards, you have any idea of what happened to them psychologically — if they were broken by torture? Did they then give any information?*

Of the Vietnamese prisoners, those determined to be high-ranking Viet Cong were generally taken to the superior authorities. And they probably ended up in the Saigon interrogation center. It is called C.M.I.C., Combined Military Intelligence Center. Generally, high-level people were taken there. For low-level guerrillas, low-level V.C., we had two policies because we changed policy at a certain time. We were evacuating him, this low-level V.C., to 2nd Field Force Headquarters, which is III Corps Tactical Area, where he was placed in prison camp until the Vietnamese decided whether or not he was going to remain dangerous, then he was moved to another, slightly less prisonlike camp, which was called "Chieu Hoi village." And [they would] say, "Here you are. You are on your own. You must take care to defend yourself against Viet Cong attack, you are on our side now," etc. In reality, this is a concentration camp.

DELLINGER: *I have three more questions. I believe that in all the instances you talked about, or at least the majority of them, the American was either doing the torturing or the beating or supervising the interrogation. In the United States, when instances of torture have been revealed, the explanation usually given is that it is the Vietnamese committing it and that the Americans either couldn't stop them or weren't even there. You mentioned there is always a Vietnamese present. Is it possible that in these reported instances the Vietnamese acted as the interpreter and the American was conducting the torture?*

It could very well be. At every interrogation there has to be an interpreter and there are many hundreds of interrogators in the country.

DELLINGER: *Many hundreds of American interrogators?*

Yes, and each one of the American interrogators has a "pool" of interpreters to choose from. All of our interrogators had participated in actual torture.

DELLINGER: *They had all participated?*

They had all participated at one time or another. It is foolishness and lies to say that only the Vietnamese torture. I never saw an interrogation conducted by Vietnamese. I don't know what they do when they interrogate. I assume they do exactly what we do, but I don't think they have any compunctions about leaving marks.

DELLINGER: *Did you hear of any cases, among the hundreds of interrogators, where people insisted on interrogating without beating or torture? Did you hear of cases where people refused to do this, and if so do you know what happened to these people?*

No, I don't know of a single case. I almost refused, but unfortunately I was too cowardly to actually refuse. I don't know any percentages, but what is torture? Is torture electrical torture or is torture beating? I don't know. Personally, I had a lot of success when I learned to speak Vietnamese. I had a lot of success with pure coercion, because I'm a fairly large person. I was able to intimidate the rather small Vietnamese, especially when I learned to speak their language. I was able to tell them "I know you're lying," and in their language.

DELLINGER: *I want to ask another question. One of the soldiers from Fort Hood, Texas, who refused to go to Vietnam and who is now serving a sentence in the penitentiary at Fort Leavenworth, testified at his court martial that in his training in the United States he was told that it was his duty "to kill the little brown Asians." According to Gisele Halimi's summary report this morning, one of the people who has testified, I think on tape, said that he was told, "You can kill anyone with slanted eyes." Concerning this whole question of interrogation, were there any instructions or indoctrination or common talk that would have implied that to use torture wasn't so serious because of race, because of Asian qualities?*

The common American G.I. term for a Vietnamese was either a "gook" or a "slant." Our unit was not a typical unit; it was a military-intelligence unit. The people were more intelligent, and the unit was small. It was more or less a family, and I spent most of my time with the unit. Concerning the line troops, during Operation Cedar Falls, I was in the Iron Triangle. I had a prisoner who had volunteered to lead us to tunnels. I had to use force on him: I didn't beat him but I interrogated him for eighteen hours. I finally broke his resistance. We took him to find the tunnels in the 173rd Airborne's territory, and we found them. The men there told me they weren't taking prisoners. They said, "We aren't taking prisoners, because one of our platoon leaders was killed three days before." One fellow, 18 years old, I think he was, said to me with a grin, "You should've seen the girl I shot yesterday." This is the absurdity of war: an 18-year-old telling me about killing a girl. They wired the dead with explosives so when the Viet Cong came to get their dead, they were blown up.

DELLINGER: *As I understand it, the Vietnamese place a particular significance upon a proper burial and keeping the graves of their ancestors. Is that common knowledge among those who wire the bodies with explosives?*

I don't think so. Normally the soldiers going over there are given a short orientation on things you should and shouldn't do in Vietnam. You know, don't pat people on the back and things like that. But the soldiers generally ignore this, because to the soldiers the the Vietnamese people are whores to sleep with, servants to supply the cold beer and the Coca-Cola. They're the people who make the beds and sweep the floors and shine the boots. But they aren't thought of as real people. Their status is that of a Negro in the United States in, say, 1850. It's incredible. I was constantly complaining that I couldn't speak Vietnamese and that I wanted to speak Vietnamese better. The common line troops would react to this by saying "Oh, they should learn to speak our language." Why should they learn to speak our language?

DELLINGER: *I just have one other question. You referred to the fact that you were surprised to discover, when you got there, or after you'd been there a while, that the Vietnamese don't like the Americans very much and don't want them to be there. Are you speaking of the people in areas under U.S. control, or are you speaking of prisoners from so-called Viet Cong areas?*

Surprisingly enough, most of the prisoners, I believe, actually liked the Americans more after they were captured, and perhaps even after they were tortured. They had been told that the Americans kill all their prisoners. This is to keep them from defecting. The Viet Cong are relieved to find out that they aren't going to be killed. The prisoners, I believe, liked the good food and I think they liked not having to be in the jungle. I am referring to low-ranking prisoners. I'm not talking about our North Vietnamese Army captain. I'm certainly not talking about him. I'm not talking about political cadres.

DELLINGER: *On that point, I can remember the relief that American antiwar demonstrators sometimes feel when they end up in jail and sit down perhaps and finally have a meal. They feel glad. There's a psychological pressure to feel grateful to the very person who may be your jailer, but who is now bringing you food. In a sense one feels that the ordeal is over.*

Yes.

DELLINGER: *Do you think the prisoners feel grateful because they've been told they will be killed?*

Yes, several prisoners told me they had been told that. When I interrogated the prisoner who broke down after eighteen hours, he constantly confessed to a higher rank. He was a private soldier, he said. Then he said he was an assistant cell leader, then a cell leader, then a squad leader, then a platoon sergeant. It took about an hour or so to break down a psychological barrier. He was told that everybody above a certain rank is killed. When he finally feels safe, he will talk. You get more flies with honey than you do with vinegar. Interrogations were generally more successful if they didn't use a great deal of force, yet force was used. Why?

DELLINGER: *Did you find that the Vietnamese in the American-occupied areas did not like the Americans much?*

You can only say an area is American-occupied if the Americans have placed a barbed-wire fence around it. But in areas where the American control is more strong, you can say that the Vietnamese don't like us for several reasons. First of all is the indiscriminate shooting and bombing. The Americans have a policy of "free-fire zones," where the Vietnamese provincial chief sets off an area and says it's a free-fire zone. Then he tries to tell all his people not to go into that area — then of course the logic being that he'll tell the people on the right side not to go in there. But, invariably, innocent people do get killed. I heard this in a report. Two peasants were riding in an ox cart, it was spotted in a free-fire zone and they called for permission to fire on an ox cart loaded with rice, as they later found out. They fired and killed the Vietnamese. The Vietnamese hate us also because the whole thing is turning into a big brothel. Fulbright was right. Saigon is a large whorehouse. It is. I was there. I saw it. Bien Hoa is too. Xuan Loc is too. You can still see the French heritage there in Vietnam where, I understand, the French used Sudanese soldiers, so you can see mixed Negro-Oriental babies — no longer babies now, but children, and, in another three or four years you're going to see a tremendous amount of mixed caucasians with the Vietnamese. A tremendous amount. We're corrupting the whole country. The money a prostitute in Vietnam can make is three hundred dollars a day, whereas the average wage I believe is thirty to forty dollars a month. How would you feel if your daughter or your sister became a prostitute?

DELLINGER: *I visited both Saigon and Hanoi and it was my impression, my experience, that the Vietnamese in Saigon felt more hostility to the Americans than the Vietnamese in Hanoi, because they experienced the unconscious arrogance that we Americans too often display, and the race prejudice and the things of that kind, directly and personally.*

Well, it's not only the race prejudice. There's nothing more obnoxious than a drunk G.I. And there are thousands of drunk G.I.'s in that country, whistling at the pretty schoolgirls — and the Vietnamese women are really pretty. And the students, the high-school students, wearing an *ao-dai* are really a very charming sight. An American G.I. when he arrives there, and probably even when he leaves there, thinks that that woman is a prostitute. He'll proposition to her, lay his hands on her, and expect the Vietnamese to like this.

DELLINGER: *Thanks a lot. I think I'll give someone else a chance.*

MAHMUD ALI KASURI: *Mr. Martinsen, please forgive me for asking some questions which may appear to you to be very ordinary — but I want some basic facts.*

May I know if you were in many camps, or only in one camp?

We had a base camp which was in Lon Giao . . . This is where the unit was headquartered, but every time they had a major operation the unit was attached to a larger unit — one of the infantry divisions — for support. You see, we were an armored unit. We had tanks and armored cars — armored personnel carriers actually. And these were excellent weapons for shock value — tremendous firepower, etc. So we were attached to an infantry unit to provide convoy support, to spearhead attacks, etc. If you're in any way familiar with the operation there — Operation Attleboro and Operation Cedar Falls, Operation Junction City and Operation Manhattan — all very big operations involving forty, fifty, sixty thousand troops in the III Tactical Corps Area, Second Field Force Area. And these were all over the area. I was in Bien Hoa. I believe it is, where they just had that recent battle. Loc Ninh — I was very close to Loc Ninh. I was throughout. I was every place in the III Corps Zone where you could take a tank.

KASURI: . . . *What were the names of the four major operations you were in?*

Operation Attleboro . . . Operation Cedar Falls . . . Operation Junction City . . . Operation Manhattan — which carried on into early June of this year.

KASURI: *And apart from . . . these four major operations, you were in a number of smaller operations?*

Yes.

KASURI: *Smaller. And would it be right to understand that what you have testified about in a number of cases was the common practice in all the places you were in?*

It was the common practice in every operation except Junction City. In Junction City we did no interrogation. We had no prisoners. We were there, but there were no prisoners in Junction City, in our area. There were prisoners in other areas, but in the area that we were in, we had no prisoners. And from what I observed and from the other units that I worked with, the 172nd Military Detachment — I worked with them — the 4th Military Intelligence Detachment, which is attached to the 4th Infantry Division (I worked with them on Operation Manhattan, and I *know* they torture, well . . . they said they did . . . I'd have to say it's hearsay) . . . They said, "Why don't you wire him up a little?" They had a special field-phone apparatus, as a matter of fact, that they showed me, for placing wires on.

KASURI: *And you did, I suppose, visit Saigon on a number of occasions?*

I didn't visit Saigon often. I was in Saigon twice. Once I went on leave to Saigon. That was after our unit had established itself and everyone was tired. I was given a two- or three-day pass to Saigon. In fact, it was illegal. General Westmoreland wants all the troops moved out of Saigon because they are such an obnoxious presence in the capital, except for some troops [that] must be there. The M.A.C.V. (Military Assistance Command Vietnam) headquarters are in Saigon.

KASURI: *I merely asked if you had visited Saigon. I wanted to know if you had met people in other units.*

Unfortunately, I had no contact with interrogators from other units. I can say nothing about the interrogators from the interrogation centers, what they did there, whether they had torture devices, or anything. I do not know.

KASURI: *Can you give us an idea of the number of prisoners who were captured in the first major operation — Attleboro?*

We had only one squadron, a thousand men, including an interrogation team, participating in that operation. Our unit was running road convoys and we had practically no prisoners. That was on Route 13 between Lai Khe and Loc Ninh or the town just south of Loc Ninh. We were helping the 1st Infantry Division in Lai Khe.

KASURI: *What about Operation Cedar Falls?*

During that operation we were just outside Ben Cat. We were working closely with the 173rd Airborne Division. It was during that operation that the Iron Triangle was taken. Thousands of people were moved out of the Iron Triangle. Thousands upon thousands. My task was to "screen" people, to select individuals for questioning from among the refugees. This is a tremendous power to be given one man. The Iron Triangle is bordered by the Saigon River and another river whose name I forget. It has been a V.C. area for years and it is heavily fortified by the V.C. They even have concrete bunkers. The population was "evacuated." We had helicopters and psychological-warfare specialists. We took some Chieu Hoi's, that is deserters from the Viet Cong, and they flew over the villages, and we said, "Come out. Lay down your arms and come over to our side." This was quite effective. We got quite a number of Chieu Hoi's during Operation Cedar Falls. There were also several hundred people running around, who didn't want to leave the Iron Triangle. These people were shot on sight.

KASURI: *You said that during Operation Attleboro there were not many people captured by your unit. Were there many people captured by other units?*

Both *Time* and *Newsweek* reported that a tremendous number of prisoners were taken during that operation. Reports of interrogations are not always made if it is unimportant and we decide to release the prisoner, but during Operation Cedar Falls our detachment made over one hundred reports of interrogations. There were also hundreds and hundreds of "screenings" which took place. Sometimes, during "screening" you just look at a person and you say, "You, come with me." The refugees were kept in a barbed-wire enclosure and they were passed in front of me, an interpreter, maybe a few interpreters. The Vietnamese national police were there. Anyone could be selected for interrogation. The thousands of refugees had their belongings with them, their oxen, chickens, pigs and all they could carry. The people were sent on army flat-bed trucks to Phu Loi. Afterwards, according to *Life*, they were placed in a refugee camp, which was just another concentration camp, with barbed-wire fences and guards.

I was in the battle zone in the Triangle on two occasions. At the time there was little fighting. Many of the domestic animals — livestock like water buffaloes, oxen, as well as chickens — were running around free. The villages were being demolished. I watched Ben Suc being demolished. I saw the remains of the villages. The bulldozers just came through and tore everything down. Livestock and personal possessions were left behind. There may have been people in tunnels beneath the houses. "Tankdozers" — a tank with bulldozer blade — were also used. On both sides of the road crossing the Iron Triangle, Army Engineers cleared the area back to 400 meters off the road, to decrease the chances of ambush. The area was pockmarked with bombs. A thousand-pound bomb makes a huge crater up to fifty feet across and forty feet deep. You can hear a B-52 raid from a distance of twenty or thirty miles. It sounds like distant thunder. You wonder what the hell they were bombing.

Our unit had something called a "Zippo," named after the American lighter. It was a flame-throwing armored personnel carrier. We used it to burn away the foliage. I don't know if it was ever used in combat but it was a very destructive machine. It can fire napalm for a distance of almost one hundred meters. It fires a thick spray of napalm, which clings to everything and burns rapidly. I saw napalm being dropped from planes. I saw it at a distance, and I don't know what it was being used against.

KASURI: *Were you also in Operation Junction City?*

Yes, I was there during phase two, but not during the first phase.

KASURI: *In that operation did the unit you were operating with capture many prisoners?*

This time we were again assigned to road-reconnaissance security. I and an interpreter worked as an interrogation team. In Vietnam, interrogators do not exhibit their ranks, as they normally should on their arms. If the prisoner has a higher rank than the interrogator, it is harder to interrogate him. We wore the "U.S." collar insignia which has no rank significance and represents quite a bit of power of intimidation. For example, I might be a captain. I had complete freedom and I conducted the interrogation as I wanted to. They arrested seven rubber workers for not having identification, but I released them very quickly. It was obvious that they knew something, but it wasn't worth going after.

There were no regiments where we were, about ten kilometers from the Cambodian border, at a small plantation called Xa Cat. We had seen some action in War Zone C, but at Xa Cat there was no action at all. There was no sniping and there were no mortar attacks. The captain who had rounded up the prisoners said he had just become bored and threw them in the tank and delivered them to me. It was obvious they were rubber-plantation workers. If they were also

Viet Cong I could not determine. You never can know that. So I just released them. They had been brought to me for interrogation because they didn't have I.D. cards, and many people were arrested for that reason. In Operation Junction City there were many prisoners, but not many in our area. In Operation Manhattan, there were again many prisoners. This time our unit, because of increasing experience, also took many prisoners. Many of them had been classified Viet Cong and admitted to being Viet Cong. This was when I had the prisoner dig his own grave. There was no "wiring" done on this operation, but there was quite a lot of beating. It was then that I heard the remark, "My hand is getting tired from beating this prisoner." We had perhaps fifty or sixty interrogations.

KASURI: *This was during Operation Manhattan?*

Yes. I am just speaking about our unit, of course. Our unit was the smallest unit on a low combat echelon, and I had a great amount of freedom. I could do anything I wanted to do. I knew that if a prisoner happened to die, then there would be no formal report and nothing would ever happen to me. There would be perhaps an explanation such as, "Shot trying to escape" or "Died of heart failure." My unit never killed a prisoner under torture, but if it had happened, there would have been no official action.

KASURI: *What was your rank?*

I was a specialist of the fifth class; that is equivalent to a sergeant.

KASURI: *In the various operations, is interrogating done every day or just for a few days?*

We interrogate as the prisoners come. Interrogation has to be rapid and the information has to be accurate, especially at our level. It was very important to provide our command with tactical intelligence for planning. The common term is "hot poop."

KASURI: *You stated that you questioned one man for eighteen hours. If that is the case how long would you question one hundred prisoners?*

That would take months.

KASURI: *Did you interrogate for months?*

Yes, I did. Some interrogations are done very rapidly. Eighteen hours was unusually long for an interrogation. The only reason the prisoner talked is that it was such a long interrogation. If I got tired someone else could always take my place. If necessary I could take a stimulant pill. While the interrogation proceeded I was constantly filtering the information. The information only had to be obtained, and it was. As the interrogation proceeded, the man confessed to a higher and higher rank.

446

KASURI: *In my country, the police first make the prisoner comfortable before they begin the interrogation. Was that also your experience?*

Yes. If you begin by torturing the prisoners, where do you go from there? . . . You begin by offering him a cigarette and a drink of water. You ask, "Have you eaten lately? Would you like to eat?" "Well, you'll eat as soon as you tell me what I want to know," etc.

KASURI: *Now, you have mentioned three methods of getting information, or three instruments of torture: human hands, electrical wire, and bamboo sticks. Were there any other methods?*

There were kickings, there was beatings. This kicking could be done in any way. The beatings could be done in many ways. But I never saw clubs used, or rifle butts, because rifle butts leave marks. The same prisoner that I was taling about, during the eighteen-hour interrogation, was beaten in the face when he was captured, by rifle butts, by the capturing unit and he was very heavily bruised, scarred, and he didn't feel much like talking. When he got to me, I was at a disadvantage right there.

KASURI: *We heard about some experience with water torture. Did you have such experiences, or did you hear about any?*

No, I haven't, except from Robin Moore's book. I think he wrote about it. I may be libeling him, maybe he didn't. But I never heard of it being used there. Of course I am only familiar with the III Corps Zone. What they do in the I, II and IV Corps, I don't know. I understand from what I have heard from other people that the Marines are quite brutal in their interrogations. They have much more freedom to do as they please.

KASURI: *May I ask you a few question about something slightly different. You were in South Vietnam and you referred to the attitude of the South Vietnamese people and that you understand the Vietnamese language.*

To a certain extent . . .

KASURI: *To a certain extent. I would like to know, what in your estimate is the area of South Vietnam which is under the occupation of American troops?*

I don't know. I don't even know how I could hazard to guess. I would say about fifty percent. There are extremely large areas where the Americans only spasmodically enter into. These are the so-called "unsafe zones"; these are called war zone D, war zone C, the Iron Triangle, etc. In many jungle areas there is a heavy undergrowth underneath the double, triple jungle canopy . . . It is a disagreeable place for the population to be, and there are places like that where nobody lives. South Vietnam is not, of course, entirely covered with jungle, but wherever there is jungle is a safe place for the Viet Cong. Nevertheless, quite a bit of the country is covered by jungle, and that is why the Viet Cong probably control fifty percent of the country. At least it is under their influence.

KASURI: *In the fifty percent which is under American control, what is the relationship between the South Vietnamese government and the American forces?*

That relation depends on the T.A.O.R. (Tactical Area of Responsibility). The "areas of responsibility" are given units according to the size of the unit. Our area was bordered on the south by Australian 5th Royal Regiment and on the north by the 18th A.R.V.N. Division Army, in the west by the 9th Infantry Division, and to the northwest by the 199th Infantry Brigade. The areas that are considered under control are divided in the way I just described. It does not mean that the U.S. has complete control there, not at all. In our tactical area of responsibility there were few villages. In the area assigned to the Vietnam Division, two striking things occurred. The Rural Development Force was trying to establish two model villages there. They were close to Xuan Loc. One of them was called Song Bay, and was fifteen kilometers from where we were. One night a large Viet Cong unit came to Song Bay and brutally killed three young girls belonging to the Rural Development cadres. The 18th Vietnam Division did not respond, although they were only five or six kilometers from Song Bay. I thought it was strange, but the Vietnamese Army doesn't like to go out at night. They don't like to call for American help, and one night on Route 1, between Xuan Loc and Gia Ray, they lost almost an entire battalion. There are large regiments of the Viet Cong in that area — this is not classified information, incidentally, I read this in *Time* Magazine — and they penetrate your T.A.O.R. and are able to mortar your camp. There is no place where you are really safe. The only place we were certain of controlling was the interior of the base camp, some three or four square kilometers.

KASURI: *In how many categories do you divide the prisoners after interrogation?*

The policy was changed while we were there. There was a card which had to be filed for each prisoner, I think Department of the Army Form 343, it was later changed. There are many categories. He may be someone captured, who is a Viet Cong prisoner. He could also be a Chieu Hoi, someone who has deserted the Viet Cong. You might have a civilian, an innocent civilian. You may have a civil defendant. Any person can be placed in the category of a civil defendant. It is a catchall. For this you must have theoretically a Judge

Advocate's concurrence, from the army lawyers. You send a "343" interrogation report to the Staff Judge Advocate. The report states that without his concurrence, the person must be released. The concurrence, is, practically speaking, automatic. I never saw it denied. The concurrence may be based on the fact that the person has broken a Vietnamese law. He may not have travel papers. He may be in the wrong place. He may have broken curfew. He may be avoiding induction into the army. He may be a murderer. He may be a thief. The civilian defendant (and I am not speaking of political crimes here) will eventually be handed over to the Vietnamese authorities. During his detainment he is interrogated at every place he is held. The Vietnamese Third Corps runs a prison camp in Bien Hoa. It is just a barbed-wire concentration camp with tin huts. It is a camp for those who are "hard core," who are not expected to cooperate, to give information. I know nothing about Vietnamese law. I don't know if these prisoners receive a trial or not. If they have been sentenced, I don't know how long the sentences are, but I had the impression that they were to be kept in prison for the duration of the war. Less important prisoners or civil defendants go to provincial jails, which are incredibly filthy, medieval-like dungeons. The International Red Cross visits the camp for political prisoners, but they have nothing to do with the provincial jails, even though the people there might really be political prisoners. It's almost a matter of chance where a detainee will be sent.

KASURI: *What happens to those who are cleared?*

They are released.

KASURI: *Can they then go where they like, or must they go to a camp?*

That depends on the operation. In Operation Cedar Falls the refugees were moved to Phu Loi. I remember seeing a refugee camp there with thousands of people. They had been loaded into flat-bed trucks with as many of their possessions as they could carry, and they were taken to the camp. When people are released they are not just taken out through the gate of the base camp and told they are free. They are instead taken to the provincial center, which in our case was Xuan Loc, and let out at a bus stop. They could be a good twenty or thirty kilometers from home, and they must make their way home as best they can. This happened hundreds of times. When we first arrived, the combat units were not selective about whom they arrested. We had too many people and we had no facilities for keeping them — or to guard them. We didn't have enough interrogators or interpreters. Professionally speaking, this was rather frustrating. They were all released at Xuan Loc. There was something else that made me think. If a person could not be classified as a civil defendant, but if you still wished to have him detained, he would just be released in front of the national police station at Xuan Loc, because they don't have to have a reason for making an arrest. They are a very powerful force in Vietnam. They are called paramilitary. They have over 100,000 members who are armed with submachine guns, grenade launchers, machine guns and hand grenades, if you can imagine police armed that way. They are so fascistic, they drive around in black Citroens like the Germans used in the Occupation.

DEDIJER: *Please stick to the questions asked from your own experience.*

KASURI: *You said officers were sometimes present during interrogations.*

Yes. In the interrogation sessions you have four officers, a captain and three lieutenants. The captain never interrogated.

KASURI: *Were there any superior officers higher than captain present who performed interrogation?*

Perhaps. I don't know. Our unit had a major as a commanding officer and a captain as section leader. The other officers performed some of the most brutal interrogations I witnessed. The only time I saw electrical torture applied to the sex organs it was an officer who was doing the torturing. The only time I saw bamboo placed under fingernails was by an officer.

KASURI: *Would it be correct to say that the superior officers are cognizant of what occurs during interrogation?*

No.

KASURI: *Why do you say no?*

They aren't. The interrogator's job is to obtain information. The superior officers do not care how the information is obtained. I don't know if the command in Saigon knows about the torture, but the commanding officer of lower echelon units do know and they condone it tacitly. It is not expressly forbidden. General Westmoreland might have gotten a hint that torture was being used to get information, because he sent out a directive reaffirming the Geneva Conventions of 1949 concerning the treatment of prisoners of war. So in Vietnam they know it, this is at "M.A.C.V." level. But I don't know if the officers in the Pentagon know about it and that is why I'm here.

KASURI: *I was not concerned with the officers in the Pentagon. I wanted to know if officers with a rank much higher than captain or major know that torture is used during interrogation.*

Lieutenant-colonels knew about it.

KASURI: *Do they know about it for sure?*

They know about it because they are the squadron commanders, and occasionally they witnessed interrogations in which beatings occurred. I can't speak for our regimental commander. I don't remember him ever witnessing an interrogation. Interrogations are private affairs. You don't have officers looking over your shoulder. You have complete control and you don't want people distracting you.

KASURI: *Now just one last question: Do you know any officer or soldier of the United States who has been punished for using torture?*

No.

CARL OGLESBY: *Were you selected for training as an interrogator or did you volunteer?*

I volunteered for the language school, and after I finished my language training I was sent to the intelligence school. I wanted to get into counterintelligence training, which is not exactly like James Bond. Instead I was placed in interrogation training; after that I was not used because I had a useless training. I was trained to interrogate prisoners of war, and at that time there wasn't a big war. I was also trained to speak Italian and the army has very few persons in Italy. So I was not used.

OGLESBY: *Did the Army direct you into interrogation training?*

Yes.

OGLESBY: *Was this training generalized or was it intended for interrogation in Vietnam?*

While I was there they were changing the curriculum to include Vietnamese-style interrogation. The training had formerly concentrated on Soviet interrogation; we had to memorize Soviet terminology and so on.

OGLESBY: *When they began to train you for Vietnamese interrogation did you notice whether or not any new attitudes appeared? Was there any kind of racialist cast to the training for Vietnamese interrogation?*

I can't say: I believe that there were four hours devoted to Vietnamese interrogation and that was all.

OGLESBY: *What kind of person, generally speaking, found himself in this sort of school? Was it a more-than-average intelligent soldier?*

Yes. Military intelligence is correlated with tested intelligence. In the Army tests you have to have a score of 110, with 100 being the average, to get into the intelligence school.

OGLESBY: *Do most of the people have college education?*

The officers did. But most of the people did not have a college education; I think one hundred percent had high school education. Some, like me, had some college education; but I can't think of anybody in interrogation training with a college degree. In counter-intelligence training there were many people with college educations.

OGLESBY: *So far as you know, how many Negroes were doing interrogation work in Vietnam?*

None.

OGLESBY: *You never saw any Negroes interrogating?*

No.

OGLESBY: *Do you know of any Negroes doing that kind of work?*

I have to change what I just said. A Negro captain in the 172nd Military Intelligence Detachment was working as an interrogation officer, although I never saw him interrogate. I believe we also had a Negro in our interrogation class; I don't know if he went to Vietnam or not.

OGLESBY: *You mentioned a field manual on interrogation which you said was classified. I can't ask you for its contents, but could you answer this question? Can you explain to the Tribunal, in general terms, what could be classified in a manual on interrogation?*

That was my greatest thing. The Army is entangled in "overclassifications" of everything. It takes a tremendous amount of bookkeeping, people with security clearances, money and time for this overclassification. Everything having to do with interrogations is classified "confidential." The fact that I can tell about war crimes is that war crimes were illegally classified as being "confidential," because by Army regulations you cannot classify a mistake to keep the mistake from being known. That is why I'm doing this. Now the interrogation — I don't know why the manual was classified. It was fairly general and I can tell you it did not specifically advocate the use of torture.

OGLESBY: *What are the ways in which you learned how to torture?*

The ways were there.

OGLESBY: *It was passed on by word of mouth?*

Everyone is subject to violence in our society. Everyone can think of some nice fiendish ways to torture people, I think.

OGLESBY: *How did you learn to use a field telephone?*

A field telephone is part of the equipment of the interrogation team.

OGLESBY: *How did you learn to use the field telephone in the interrogation process as an instrument of torture?*

I heard about it before I went to Vietnam. I asked others, "How do you interrogate people?" I asked people who had been in World War II and the Korean War, people who had performed interrogations under combat conditions. They said, "You get a little field telephone, and you ring him up and he always answers." That was an overstatement; it's very untrue, but it's a common belief, that pain can elicit information promptly.

OGLESBY: *If that torture doesn't work, can you explain why that technique continues in use?*

A man is given the order to get information and it is irrelevant *how* he gets the information. In the case of a recalcitrant prisoner one gets angry and the anger can degenerate into a strong wish to torture.

OGLESBY: *I understand that, but you said torture isn't really an efficient way of getting information; torture nevertheless continues to be employed. Is there another purpose that the torture begins to serve?*

I don't know, I can tell you how it is rationalized. There can be a rationalization about torturing to get information that might save lives: torturing that *might* yield information which *might* save lives. The probability of getting information decreases the more you torture a man. Generally, torture doesn't work.

OGLESBY: *From the things that you say I can draw the following picture: People who torture know that torture doesn't work. They know that the information they are likely to get from the victim is probably bad information given just in order to avoid being tortured. As a way of acquiring information it seems bad on its own terms without even raising the moral issue.*

Yes, without raising a moral issue at all.

OGLESBY: *Do the interrogators begin to use torture as a mechanism of revenge against the people?*

I don't think it's used to take revenge against the Vietnamese people. I think it's an expression of revenge for being placed in Vietnam in the first place. Vietnam is a disagreeable place to Americans: it's hot; the people are trying to kill you; snakes are trying to kill you, etc. It's really unlike America. A person is bound to be resentful about being in Vietnam. I can't analyze it. I haven't studied enough psychology to analyze it. I have tried to analyze it in my research and I've reached a dead end.

ANTONIOLLI: [substitution for Lelio Basso]: *You told us that you have taken many prisoners. Were they taken in battle or because you occupied some villages without battle?*

It was more common to detain someone without combat, although I did see wounded prisoners.

ANTONIOLLI: *Do you think that after being a witness here, when you go back to the United States, you will be faced with some personal difficulties?*

Yes, I definitely do.

ANTONIOLLI: *Have you come here to be a witness for your conscience's sake or because you think it is in the interest of your country and in accordance with the principles of your country's constitution?*

By coming here I want to show several things. But the main thing I want to do is to show that an American isn't necessarily good because he's an American. If I told the average American that I committed war crimes, he would say it was horrible; but it doesn't reach any level of consciousness. To the average American a war crime is something incomprehensible. To him, it is inconceivable that Americans commit war crimes. Frankly, I'm the sterotype of an American college student; I want to show that it's not perhaps some long-haired freak from Berkeley campus with a beard who commits war crimes, but it's perhaps Mrs. Jones' son down the street. I'm hoping to develop that consciousness. I'm hoping to get someone to honestly consider that war causes war crimes and that all wars are bad because they cause war crimes.

HALIMI: *I would like to supplement what Mr. Martinsen has said by explaining the circumstances in which he agreed to come. He wanted to know about the Tribunal and its orientation. He indicated that he did not wish to serve any political line, and more particularly he said that he did not want to serve the Communist line. I told him that he would be able to speak quite freely and that he would be able to express any opinon he held. I said that we would only question him on the facts. I would like Mr. Martinsen to confirm this.*

This is quite true. Everything you have said is true. You see, Americans try to find Communists under every rock they pick up. Of course, the Tribunal will be used for Communist propaganda. Personally, I do not embrace Communism as an ideology. I don't like Communism and what it does. But neither do I like war. But this is an antiwar issue that may be used for Communist propaganda. That it is antiwar is the important thing. It's not necessarily important that it may be used for Communist propaganda.

DEDIJER: *Thank you very much, Mr. Martinsen. Are you going to be available to the Tribunal?*

I was going to go back to the States on Sunday. But I'm having more and more doubts about going back. Frankly, I'm frightened — of official harassment and unofficial harassment for myself and my family. The harassment of my family will continue if I return or not. I can avoid it for myself if I don't return. So I may not return. I don't know. I shall be available.

DEDIJER: *I fully understand you. Many of us here have had times where we were faced with the same kind of decision. Thank you very much...*

PETER WEISS: *Did you ever see children in these [prison] camps?*

Yes, there were occasionally children, children with their mothers. You see, on these village-sweep operations that we often went on, there were women prisoners taken who had children and there's nothing to do with the children but take them along. These were young children, children still at the breast-feeding stage, and there were no sanitary facilities... Several times while we were interrogating, women would be breast-feeding the child during the interrogation.

DAVE DELLINGER: *I'm trying to explore this question of the execution of prisoners which Mr. Tuck told us about yesterday I believe it was. According to his testimony, in the infantry unit of which he was a part, it was a common practice — it was expected — that the prisoners would not be returned but would be killed. I wanted you to give us any information you have about the number of prisoners — what kind of actions they came from. Did they come, for example, from some of these infantry actions?*

....We operated with tanks and armored personnel carriers... So we would be involved in the same sort of thing as the infantry, but slightly more limited because you cannot always take a tank where a foot soldier can go. The prisoners taken were mainly in village sweeps without combat. In other words we had very few wounded prisoners — I can only think of maybe four or five wounded prisoners — and for these wounded prisoners it was the policy to see if the prisoner would talk first before he was treated. And then the treatment could be withheld as a promise: you will be treated if you do talk but you certainly will not be treated if you don't talk. This was a method of interrogation.

DELLINGER: *I'm wondering if you have any idea on what type of occasion it would be decided to execute a prisoner, or he might be executed, and what kind of occasion he might be brought in.*

I can offer no opinion on that because I know nothing about the execution of any prisoners.

DELLINGER: *Did you ever interrogate a juvenile?*

Well, I've interrogated people down to probably 8 or 9 years old, maybe even younger. Often a child, a young child, can be used to incriminate his parents. For instance, if you ask a woman, where's her husband, and her husband isn't there and she'll say, "My husband was killed by an American bomb," and then you ask the child, "When was the last time you saw your Daddy?" and he'll say, "I saw my Daddy two weeks ago."

DELLINGER: *Did you yourself participate in or observe any torture of women or children — and differentiate between what you did and what you saw.*

I saw and have participated in beatings of females; this is females down to the age of I think — I'm not very proud of this of course — but one time I beat a Chinese girl, I think she was 15 years old. This was with my hand. I just want to clarify. I was approached by a member of the press, and they said I talk of beating prisoners and I seem to have given a connotation of beating prisoners with rifle butts. I want to stress that I beat prisoners with the flat of my hand and other people beat prisoners with the flat of their hand; this is because it does not leave marks. I just wanted to make this clear again, because obviously it is not clear to the press and this upsets me very much.

DELLINGER: *Did you use the field telephone on women or children?*

No, but I saw it used on women. I saw it used on several women.

DELLINGER: *Did you ever see a child tortured?*

No, But — well, how young is a child?

DELLINGER: *Well, you mentioned a 15-year-old girl; that would be the youngest I take it — other than this business of asking them about their parents.*

No; I've never seen a child tortured.

LAURENT SCHWARTZ: *... Have you ever seen any strategic hamlets?*

The strategic hamlet concept is no longer used in Vietnam as it was a failure; they now call them New Life hamlets. I don't know if the New Life hamlets are the same as strategic hamlets or not. A New Life hamlet is supposed to be a place that is government secure. This is very incongruous: we ran several village sweeps in New Life hamlets, which by definition are supposed to be government controlled. Yes, I have been in New Life hamlets, and they didn't seem to me appreciably different from any other kind of hamlet.

SARA LIDMAN: *A small additional question to the fact you mentioned — you had seen a woman breast-feeding her child being interrogated. Was she able to protect the child during the ... ?*

She was not tortured.

LIDMAN: *She was not tortured. In what way was she then interrogated?*

It was an interrogation without force.

LIDMAN: *Do you think that the fact that she had the child there made her more bent to talking than she would have been without the child?*

I don't know the Vietnamese mind that well that I could comment. I know that having the child there definitely affected the interrogator, by the fact that he wasn't going to harm a mother with a child at her breast.

LIDMAN: *Did the woman talk?*

No. Well she spoke; she didn't speak to our satisfaction.

LIDMAN: *But then she was allowed to leave?*

Yes, she was.

Testimony and Questioning of Donald Duncan

Former Special Forces 'Green Beret' in Vietnam

DEDIJER: *Mr. Duncan, where were you born, please?*

I was born in Toronto, Canada, in 1930.

DEDIJER: *Are you a Canadian citizen?*

No, I'm an American citizen, naturalized.

DEDIJER: *Naturalized, when were you naturalized?*

I was naturalized in 1955 in Junction City, Kansas, while I was a member of the United States Army.

DEDIJER: *And what is your education, please?*

I was educated in Canada, elementary and high school, and my college training in the United States in various colleges around the country near army camps and so on. My specialty is political science, and I do not have a degree.

DEDIJER: *There are many good scientists without a degree. But please do tell me which military courses you attended.*

Specifically I was an operations and intelligence specialist and I was trained in these things both in and out of Special Forces at special schools, and I in turn, used to teach these subjects.

DEDIJER: *You teach?*

Yes, I was an instructor.

DEDIJER: *Another thing. You served in Vietnam. How long, when did you go?*

I went to Vietnam in March of 1964 and returned from Vietnam in September of 1965.

DEDIJER: *In which unit did you serve?*

I was in the United States Army Special Forces, sometimes referred to as the Green Berets. I essentially had four different jobs while I was in Vietnam which took me from the northern provinces south of the 17th parallel to the Ca Mau peninsula.

DEDIJER: *Would you tell us about your decorations and citations?*

I have two Bronze Stars, one for valor. I was recommended for the Legion of Merit, the United States Army Silver Star. I was presented with the Vietnamese Silver Star, the U.S. Army Air Medal and various and sundry service decorations: Combat Infantry Badge, and Master Parachutist, and so on.

DEDIJER: *And you are also an author and have published a certain number of books and articles.*

Yes, I am.

DEDIJER: *And excuse me for asking you this question because this question is not a habit of European courts but is a habit of your mother country, the United States. What are your political beliefs, general ones?*

I don't belong to any political parties, if you specifically mean am I a Communist or something. . . .

DEDIJER: *No, no, I just ask what are your political parties.*

If I had to put a label on it, I suppose I would say I'm an Independent Radical, meaning, (I feel I should possibly define this term, because it is one misunderstood in our own country), somebody that is upset at things that are happening and doing something about it.

DEDIJER: *And, Mr. Duncan, after the questioning of Miss Halimi, the Tribunal will question you, but due to the fact that you were not only in Vietnam for four and a half years, but you were also in other parts of the World as well. In your books, you state how policies in Vietnam were decided. So the members of the Tribunal will also ask you questions on this. Are you willing to answer them also?*

Yes, certainly within my area of competence.

DELLINGER: *There's just one question I would like to ask him along these lines, because I don't know what the situation is but I heard or read somewhere something about when Secretary McNamara came to Vietnam you were called in to consult with him or something of that kind?*

Yes, I was called on to brief him on certain operations there as I also have been called on to brief General Westmoreland and General Throckmorton, the Ambassador at that time, Mr. Lodge and Mr. Taylor.

DEDIJER: *Well, thank you very much for warning me of that because this is a very important issue.*

HALIMI: *Mr. President, I would like to ask you, to finish identifying the witness, to read to the Tribunal and the audience this piece of testimony which is in connection with what Dave Dellinger just pointed out. It is a letter of congratulations addressed to Sergeant Donald Duncan, which comes from the Headquarters of the Fifth Special Forces Group of the U.S. Army, because this will finish the witness' identification.*

DEDIJER: *I will read it. This is from the Headquarters Fifth Special Forces Group Airborne First Special Forces, APO US Forces 96240, 22 July 1965. Subject: Letter of Appreciation,* to, M/Sgt. Donald W. Duncan, Headquarters, Fifth Special Forces Group, ABM, First Special Forces, APO U.S. Forces 96240: I wish to express my appreciation for your outstanding presentation of facts and information of Special Forces activities to the Honorable Robert C. McNamara on 19 July 1965. 2. Throughout the entire presentation your knowledge of Special Forces activities and lucid oral expression employed were exceptional. 3. The salient points which you so aptly presented to the Secretary of Defense may have significant results of future support of Special Forces in the Republic of Vietnam. You are to be congratulated for a job well done. This letter will be made a permanent part of your military 201 file. William A. Mac Kean, Col. Infantry Commander.

HALIMI: Mr. Duncan, I may warn you that I will ask you a series of questions which will be numerous in connection with your experiences in the Army because as an instructor your competence will allow the Tribunal to grasp the principal points that went into that instruction. I would like to ask you first if you are in fact the author of the book, The New Legions, *and if this book, the resume of which I gave to the Tribunal yesterday, is, as you say, the hard truth on Vietnam, on the military practice there and on the foreign policy which has made more enemies than friends for the Americans.*

Yes, the facts presented in the book are just that, facts. It is not a work of fiction. There are parts of it, as you know, that are, perhaps, polemic, in other words, opinion, when I'm talking about politics, per se, but the actions, the specifics of any action in there is as it did occur.

HALIMI: Mr. Duncan, another preliminary question. I met Mr. Robin Moore in New York, who is the author of two books, The Green Berets *and* A Country Team, *and I asked him if he would come and testify before our Tribunal. He told me, after having accepted, that a publishing contract committed him to stay in the States. The important thing is that we have his book here, that we know that this book is not a work of imagination, that it cites methods employed by American parachutists in Vietnam, and I know, because I read it, that you wrote a review of this book in Ramparts. Do you have any objection to being questioned on the methods which are described by Mr. Robin Moore in his book, and at the same time verify them?*

Yes, I will testify to that.

HALIMI: Mr. Duncan, I would like to start with the first part of your military career when you were an instructor at Fort Bragg. You described in your book [The New Legions]... *how an effort was made to depersonalize and psychologically break down the recruits to prepare them for antiguerilla fighting, teach them interrogation methods, torture and the manner in which to get rid of prisoners. Would you indicate briefly to the Tribunal what were the methods used from the moment the recruits arrived until the time when they were sent to Vietnam?*

These methods which you discuss are not something peculiar to Special Forces. This is the standard method of training all young soldiers. I don't even believe it's peculiar to the United States Army; it's essentially a method of depersonalization, isolation, the changing of a value system, the disorganization of an individual, a reorganization of an individual — and finally with a new value system he does become a soldier. This is in his first, let's say, eight weeks of army life. When he goes on to such places as the United States Army Special

Forces or an airborne battalion, the training, of course, becomes much more severe, and essentially it's an extension of what's taught in basic training, just more emphasis, more physical. The main purpose, of course, is to take a man from civilian life, to give him a new set of values, to make him amenable to do things which normally he would not allow himself to do or would not be willing to do. In other words, it's a means of giving him a different rationale or a philosophy. This is all of course psychological; it's a method used not only in the army. It's a method used in prisons. It's a method used in insane asylums.

HALIMI: *I would like to ask you ... how you, yourself, instructed the recruits on the methods to be used in antiguerrilla warfare and, in particular, methods of interrogating a prisoner.*

Fine. Now we're getting into a different area ... into specialized training and the area to which you refer is at the United States Army Special Warfare School at Fort Bragg, North Carolina, the Special Forces school. ... I was an instructor at this school for a year and a half and I was teaching intelligence training, both conventional and unconventional, as well as interrogation techniques. There was such things as clandestine communications, the organization of guerrilla nets, escape and evasion routes, and so on and so forth ... They were trying to teach not only the methods, but an appreciation for the psychological methods of interrogation. By this I mean the nonphysical methods of interrogation, an appreciation for how this type of interrogation produces the most valuable intelligence, the more accurate information. Essentially it follows the training, for instance, of a lawyer — a trial lawyer — through communication, using the tools of entrapment and so on for soliciting certain information ... You can appreciate ... that in ... classes of thirty or more people ... over a period of one week, it would be impossible to make each and every one of the students an expert in psychological interrogation techniques. He would know the methods, but he would not himself be a trained psychological interrogator. The specific purpose for teaching this is so the student in turn, once he is put in another country, can teach these methods to what we refer to as an "indigenous counterpart," somebody indigenous to the country. And he in turn then would become the interrogator.

Very realistically, they admit that there are going to be those times and conditions when it will be impossible to conduct psychological methods of interrogation and ... also ... that it's very difficult to train any number of people in these techniques to the point where they are effective. Right after this block of instruction, there is another course taught as a subcourse which was the countermeasures to hostile interrogation. One of the references used in this particular course was the N.K.V.D. manual, the manual used by the secret police in Russia, where are detailed quite specifically any number of methods of torture . . . When I was a student, . . . it seemed a little unnecessary to use this as a reference source, except to perpetuate the myth that the other people do this but we don't . . . In any event, throughout this course it becomes very apparent that, in fact, given a determined interrogator, given the methods of interrotation — that there are no real countermeasures to interrogation . . . In fact, we used to teach that the only person who could resist interrogation would be a fanatic, religious type or whatever — someone who would rather die, and his brain actually cuts off his senses so they don't feel the pain. . . . Having convinced us now that there were no real countermeasures to interrogation, it became the question then, well, why is the course being taught? This is a very highly classified class. By this I mean it has a security. There are guards on the doors, and strangers aren't allowed to walk in and hear this, and all the reference material to it is classified. Still and all, they cannot tell you that *you* are supposed to do this . . . If I had only been a student, I would say: Well, perhaps I just got something from the class that I was not supposed to get. However, I in turn became an instructor in this course, and this was what I was trying to teach, because this is what I was told to teach, and this was how to imply it. Leave no doubt in anybody's mind that there are those times when you will have to use "other" . . . methods of interrogation. Other methods, of course, are discussed beyond the N.K.V.D. manual, but again, you know, it's always the other person supposed to be doing it. Now there's a very important reason for this — why they have to be so careful even in their own classrooms. This is possibly more true of Special Forces than other elements of the Army. They are very conscious, first of all, of the Rules of Land Warfare. And very conscious that they can be brought to task for these things. So they bend over backwards to at least, give the outward appearance of legality and adherence to such things as the Kellogg-Briand Pact and the laws of land warfare.

The Army itself spies on itself We used to make a joke of it at Fort Bragg: Who is the C.I.A. agent in the classroom? Or who is the man from Army Security Agency that could be pretending to be a student, but was, in fact, there to take notes to make sure what is taught. This carries over into our radio communications, and later on I will testify to an occasion in Vietnam where certain words are used on the radio that in fact mean something entirely different because our own Army Security Agency is monitoring these calls, and if there's a legal proceeding the man can say: "Well, I didn't say that, I said this," and they can check the record and yes, that's what he said; but the words, in fact, mean something else . . . .

HALIMI: *You have indicated that the young recruits did not under-stand very well those methods of interrogation taught to them, and the methods were justified to them by telling them that that is exactly what would happen to them if the Communists would take them prisoner in Vietnam. Would you like to confirm that?*

No, I won't confirm that. They were not trying to justify it. That's what they were saying for the official record. But in fact it was pre-sented in such a way that it left no doubt in anybody's mind that, if you need the information, these are other methods and you cer-tainly can use them. In other words, they were not trying to justify to the troops. For the official record, if somebody said: "you're teaching methods of torture," they say, "no, no, no, no, all we're teaching is what the enemy does." Again, it's for the official record. There's no doubt left in the student's minds. When you say, "young soldiers," the people in this class were not all that young. First of all, there was an age limit at that time to get into Special Forces. You had to be a Regular Army Soldier, and you had to pass certain mental qualifying tests and a physical test to get into Special Forces, and you had to have a mimium rank of sergeant to attend that class. So there were not naive 18-year-old boys that were sitting in this class as students. These are mature men, in years at least.

HALIMI: *Mr. Duncan, in your book on page 158 and 159 you write a dia-logue between a recruit and his sergeant instructor, Sergeant Lacy, and this young recruit doesn't understand something. He says, "You are teaching me about countermeasures, but at the same time you tell me that there are none. Why don't you tell it like it is and say that we could actually use those meth-ods?" And you indicate that the sergeant answers with a sarcastic air, "Yes, but we can't tell you directly because the mothers of America wouldn't ap-prove." Is this true or did you just make up the dialogue?*

I have reconstructed that dialogue as accurately as I possibly could; the actual quote, "We cannot teach you that because the mothers of America would not approve," is a word-for-word quote. It is accurate; in fact it became almost a classic catchall throughout training in dis-cussing other things. It became a common phrase. It was used in the book to point out the . . . cynical way in which these subjects were taught.

HALIMI: *Now, Mr. Duncan, will you tell us very specifically which meth-ods were taught at Fort Bragg to those who would have the job of interrogat-ing or teaching interrogation methods to their indigenous counterparts in Vietnam?*

Speaking just specifically of the N.K.V.D. teaching such things as the squashing of the male genitals, putting buckets over people's heads and beating them (they had various names for all these things which escape me right now); suspending a man from a chain or a rope with a wide belt around the waist and spinning him around. Also, complementing this manual there were certain other references which we were encouraged to read, detailing . . . interrogation techniques used in such Communist countries as Hungary . . .: the isolation, the hot-and-cold treatment, the confusing of the man's mind, making it impossible for him to relate time, for instance when is night and when is day, . . . and how you break the person down. We were encouraged to read these things, and as a matter of fact, we were, in a way, interrogated or tested on these subjects. Of course, other methods that were discussed were such things as the use of electricity, field expedient methods such as using the double E-A telephone, just a standard Army field set — battery operated — attaching the lead wires to the genitals, or genital areas, for shock, and so on. And, of course, because we were an unconventional organization, we were encouraged to use our imagination. The specific thing was always suggested that you do not mark a person. In other words, don't leave physical evidence on his body. Use those types of interrogation where if somebody were to see the prisoner immediately afterwards you couldn't tell that he had been abused.

Now, I think that for the record I should state something more about the training. The training in Special Forces breaks down into two categories: there is the guerrilla warfare category and the counter-insurgency category. The methods of interrogation as taught, were taught within the guerrilla warfare section of the training. I ask the indulgence of the court here — perhaps not too many people are familiar with the specific mission of Special Forces in a guerrilla war. So, I would like to explain that, perhaps we'll put it into some sort of context then. There was a theory back in the fifties that attack from the Eastern European countries, Russia specifically, was somewhat imminent. It was realistically posited that, given an attack by the Eastern countries, we could not hope to hold them much short of the Atlantic Ocean. In other words, there would have to be a gradual pull-back until reinforcements could arrive and so on. To complement this pullback, then, Special Forces were trained, as we used to say, to be used as soon as the balloon goes up, so that they would jump in behind the advancing enemy, into these Eastern countries. These would be 12-man teams, essentially. The theory was that since these are Communist countries, everybody is unhappy, so it's a very ripe ground to start a guerrilla war. In other words, the people would flock to you, and you're automatically in business. To go on with that, of course these teams are trained in area studies: each team has a particular area right down to and including the town and the village that he will be in or near, and they're studying the habits of the people on the ground in those countries. So the idea would be that this 12-man team, 2 officers and 10 enlisted men, would go in. And these subjects that are being taught, such as interrogation, such as the organization of guerrilla units, assassination teams, sabotage teams, and the like, would be taught in turn to the people in this country, and they in turn would do the actual fighting. So the methods of interrogation were taught specifically with the idea that they would be used in a guerrilla context. As stated in the Special Forces Manual, one of the missions of Special Forces is to subvert foreign governments unfriendly to the United States. It's a stated admission, I have a copy of that manual here if you care to see it. Quite obviously, now, when we talk about Vietnam, we're talking about an entirely different thing. We are now talking about counter-insurgency, as it is called. We were talking about the guerrilla warfare aspect as compared to the counter-insurgency aspect. Now I just completed saying that our purpose was to go in and organize people against a government. Quite obviously, the rule is somewhat reversed in Vietnam. We're helping a government, the Saigon regime. So the whole structure had to change, quite obviously. We worked through the government. So, interrogations for the most part were done by the Vietnamese, the Saigon government troops, if you will. Now, we did, starting back in the fifties, train these people. We helped set up their police, we helped train their Rangers, we helped train their own Special Forces or the Luc-Luong Dac-Biet as they are called in A.R.V.N., that's the Army of the Republic of Vietnam . . .

The specifics of interrogation techniques sort of backfired on us, inasmuch as we were getting very bad information. It became very difficult to motivate these people into using psychological methods of interrogation, because they were not interested in using them, they weren't properly motivated to use them, they were tremendously unsuccessful using them, and . . . they reverted to the physical methods of interrogation. And of course, we got very bad information as a result of this. It became, I think, a runaway situation, to the point where the information was getting so bad that it was hurting us. However, I don't even know if we were really interested in stopping it. Because we found out that even when we sent our own interrogators who spoke Vietnamese to carry on psychological methods of interrogation, they were relatively unsuccessful also. So everything sort of degenerated on that thing. We started using or developing our own means of gathering intelligence directly, instead of trying to get it through interrogation methods. The interrogation methods, I don't mean to imply, were stopped. You always keep hoping that something will turn up . . . My specific job in Vietnam was gathering intelligence. We had to form a special unit to gather it, because we no longer could depend on Vietnamese intelligence sources for any accurate information. This was called Project Delta.

HALIMI: *What were the roles of Special Forces units in Vietnam when you were there? I read in your book and in your testimony during the Levy trial that there were three kinds of team: "A"-Teams, "B"--Teams and Robin Moore, author of The Green Berets, speaks particularly of the achievements of "C"-Teams at Nha Trang. Can you explain these categories?*

Yes, the A-Team, that's the team I've talked about, is a team of 12 men. Special Forces do not — first of all let me precede my remarks by saying they would never, commit a Special Forces company as a company — they're always deployed in small teams; one team in this area, and so on. The 12-man team is composed of a captain, a lieutenant, and 10 enlisted men. There's one operations sergeant, an intelligence sergeant, but in fact they do the same job, each one is trained in operations and intelligence. Two weapons men, two demolitions men, two radio men, and two medics. It's so designed that the team can be split down the middle. In other words, you can send six men, and the skills are compatible. Each man in turn is, theoretically at least, supposed to be trained in two other skills than his own. In my own particular case, I was a demolitionist, a radio operator and weapons specialist in addition to my primary specialty of operations and intelligence. The B-Team is an enlargement of the A-Team. Essentially they are supposed to do the same things as the A-Team. But they have additional personnel and it is commanded by a major, rather than a captain, and the major in turn has four captains under him, where they set up what we call the S-1, S-2, S-3, and S-4 sections — Administration, Personnel, Intelligence and Operations, and Logistics. The idea would be that for every three A-Teams in the field, you would then commit a B-Team for operational control and coordination of the three A-Teams. But also within that B-Team, they would have an A-Team. In other words, there would be about 19 people on a B-Team rather than 12. The other's for operational control. And then for each two B-Teams you would have a C-Team. Again an enlargement of the B-Team. To make this specific for Vietnam, each of the camps that we had in Vietnam had one A-Team. And then back further, away from the border, towards the larger urban areas, you had a B-Team. For instance, we had a B-Team at Quan Tho which directed the operations of the A-Teams along the Cambodian border and in the Delta. Their headquarters, in turn, was in Nha Trang to control the four B-Teams in the country. The potential of an A-Team, again theoretically, is that they have the capability of directing, controlling, equipping, training either guerrillas or counter-guerrilla units of regimental size. Each 12 men can supposedly control one thousand men.

HALIMI: *Mr. Duncan, can you explain what you and Robin Moore call "C.I.D.G.'s" [Civil Irregular Defense Groups]? And will you also tell us whether there was a direct liaison among these teams, and explain the workings of the information network between them and A and B teams?*

The primary job of Special Forces, up to the summer of 1964. was the field-implementing arm of the C.I.D.G. program. This program was started back in 1961, I believe, as a means of organizing ethnic groups within Vietnam, such as the various Montagnard tribes, and eventually it came to include the Hoa Hoa and Cao Dai and some people of Cambodian extraction within Vietnam. The main purpose of this was, starting with the Montagnards, to nuetralize their struggle against the Saigon regime. There have always been problems between the Montagnards, and the ethnic Vietnamese and the Saigon government. Hopefully, the idea was to build them into self-defense units, for village self defense. It had the added advantage (I happen to have read this in an official report), of being one way of circumventing the Geneva Agreements of 1954. The Geneva Agreements of 1954 prohibited the establishment of new military bases within the southern zone of Vietnam. So, by calling these things village-defense units, or self-defense units they in fact circumvented that provision of the agreement. Of course, the camps that they set up are not in the village.

They are invariably set up next to the village, isolated from it by mine fields, punji stakes, barbed wire, etc. In fact, in many areas the villagers are not allowed into the camp for security reasons, meaning they don't trust the people in the village that they're defending. And in many cases the strike force, the combat group of the civilian community-defense effort, was not even from the village itself. In other words, they were imported from other areas of the country. To give a specific example, I remember the Special Forces camp at Tan Phu, which is in the Delta. We could not recruit any what we call "strike force" from the local area, so we had to bring them from another area in there. The camp lasted for about six months. It became an untenable position and they moved out. Again I say, this was the primary job, or the biggest, not necessarily, but the biggest that the Special Forces had up to 1964. In addition to their role with the CIDG program they also had other functions within Vietnam forming special little units. They had Project Delta, Project Omega, people were sent off with what was known as SOG, and they trained the MAAG forces, and they're also on detached duty for various purposes. The one thing we haven't mentioned, I don't know whether you want to go into it or not, is the origin of this program called CIDG. Originally it was, and it remained so up until 1964, a C.I.A. program. The CIA having come up with the idea, of course, did not have the field personnel to conduct the program in the field. Special Forces, then, were made available to the CIA for this purpose, of running it in the field. All the funds, the money for the program, came from CIA sources, directly or indirectly. Another purpose of the CIDG program was to try to set up intelligence nets throughout the countryside emanating from these camps. Again the funds, the money for the agents, came from CIA sources.

HALIMI: *Mr. Robin Moore said, in his testimony during the Levy trial, and reconfirmed it when he spoke to me, that there existed "assassination teams." He told me that Americans trained and paid Vietnamese for them. He said, for example, that the assination teams passed out black cards with white eyes on them, designed to frighten the enemy. Can you tell the Tribunal first, exactly what the assassination teams were; and second, what was their relationship to the American forces and especially the C.I.A. ....; and third, the methods used by these teams?*

The assassination teams, as they were called, grew out of Project Delta, which was the program I helped start over there. Men who had worked with Delta were detached, and helped to train these assassination teams under the auspices of the C.I.A. They are organized as part of the overall organization — what they call the Rural Revolutionary Development Team, part of the pacification program in the southern zone. In 1965 it was decided that something had to be done to break up the infrastructure within the villages in the southern zone. In other words, defeating the armed forces of the National Liberation Front on the battlefield, essentially, was not going to accomplish too much if in fact all they did was retreat back in the villages and consolidate its infrastructure. Possibly for the first time there was tacit admission of the success of the National Liberation Front within the villages, because it was declared, at the time, that the way to work in the village was to use the same methods that we claimed the National Liberation Front was using .

In other words, to use the same instruments. It was realized of course, that Americans themselves could not implement this program. It would have to be Vietnamese. So Americans were detached from Special Forces Units to train the Revolutionary Development Cadres. After encircling a village, and making it secure from outside influence, they would go in there, and use psychological methods, and reeducate the people. It was realized, even in the planning stages, that there would be intransigence on the part of the people and there would be those within each village, very determined to see this plan not work. The idea was to find out who these people were and try to remove them from the village and imprison them, or, if that was not possible to do without upsetting the village (in other words, they might be respected members of the village and people would rebel if you took them out) there was always the method of removal by assassination. Provisions were made to train assassination teams. The methods they used are unlimited. There are a large number of ways to kill people. The training, the support, the transport and the weaponry of these teams are controlled by Americans. There are Vietnamese counterparts involved. When it was first announced that we were going to use these new methods, we talked about the Revolutionary Village Development Cadre. The American military didn't speak about the assassination teams. It was said at the time it was run by the C.I.A. It was in our own newspapers. The rationale for this — why the C.I.A. and not some branch of the military was in charge — was that the C.I.A. had men in the field, on the place, and that they had the organization ready to go. As a matter of fact, this is much like the C.I.D.G. program when it first started. The fact is that with the C.I.A. there is no accounting for what they do, or the money they spend or where they get their money.

So it can be a rather clandestine operation. Had it been just the Revolutionary Development Cadre going in to reeducate people, there would have been no need for clandestine methods. Since the assassination teams were part of this, the C.I.A. was brought in. The white card that you referred to was a form of psychological warfare. In the initial stages, each time somebody was assassinated, a calling card would be left which varied from area to area. One of these calling cards was a card with a white eye on it. The plan was that in the future you wouldn't have to assassinate the people, leaving a card would be sufficient to stop them from trying to do what they were trying to do. Variations of this are used in other countries where Special Forces operate, in Guatemala specifically. In Guatemala, they use a black hand. You leave it as a little calling card to warn the people not to help the guerrillas.

HALIMI: *Mr. Duncan, I believe your official title was "operations and intelligence officer," and that you changed your role... and your operations thereafter were other than those in the first period. In the third period, the last one, I think it is important to emphasize that you especially and officially wrote a history of the "Green Berets," the Special Forces. As a result, you had access to documents and secret information. I think it is very important that you specify your duties in Vietnam, to allow us to ask questions about the actions of American forces in Vietnam. So, can you be specific about the role of the Special Forces in Vietnam, and especially about your three different roles during your service there?*

Yes, it can be divided into three phases, with one subdivision in the second phase. The first assignment I had in Vietnam was with the Headquarters 5th Special Forces, as one of the three area specialists for III and IV Corps tactical areas. This would be characterized as the southern half of the southern zone of Vietnam. Specifically, there were two captains and myself. We were responsible for the briefing of teams coming into the country and the briefing of teams going out of the country. We were the coordinator between the various camps in this area. Of course, we were also in charge of the briefings for visiting dignitaries, V.I.P.'s and so on, and as part of this job it was our duty to go to the various camps and in my case to actually take part in patrols and combat actions, in order to evaluate the worthiness or the unworthiness of the various companies. These are again the C.I.D.G. camps, the strike forces. In the second phase, which is subdivided, I was operations and intelligence officer in a group called Project Delta. In fact, I helped form this project from scratch. This project was initiated originally for the specific purpose of infiltrating teams into Laos. Later on the program was enlarged, and in addition to being an operation and intelligence specialist I was also a team leader, actually going with the teams. These are eight-man teams, consisting usually of two Americans and six Vietnamese, essentially started out as an intelligence-gathering agency and later developed into something that was given the name "hunter-killer team." In other words, you went out and you hunted information but you also got involved in commando-type raid tactics. As I became more and more involved in the field and the operational end of that, I did less and less of the office work, and although I was still in an advisory capacity, that particular function was taken over by a major. And in the final phases I was assigned for the purpose — this is in the last six to eight weeks in Vietnam — of writing the official history for Special Forces in Vietnam, in addition to which I was also doing staff study papers, analyzing various field situations, and submitting solutions to problems for study . . .

MAHMUD ALI KASURI: *Would you, Mr. Duncan, give us the dates to which these three periods are related?*

The first period was sometime in the middle of March 1964, in fact, from the day I arrived . . . and that period ended on the 24th day of May 1964. It was one month and a half. And then from 24th May 1964 through August, I was with Project Delta. I never was really officially separated from Project Delta. In other words I was still — after I was writing this history — I was still in advisory capacity to the project; although I was no longer taking part in the field operations after August of 1965. And my service in Vietnam terminated somewhere around September 15, 1965.

HALIMI: *I would like to ask you a question about prisoner treatment in Vietnam. Almost all the witnesses agree on this point: the instructions that were given, after the capture of prisoners, to the Americans was to kill them if they became bothersome. You said it in your book,* The New Legions . . . *Peter Bourne said the same thing at Captain Levy's trial. Also, Robin Moore in his book,* The Green Berets, *confirmed very forcibly that there were formal instructions to kill prisoners that were definitely considered dangerous — or Viet Cong, in most cases. Can you answer this first point?*

Yes. I think, in the interest of brevity, I may be improper here on procedure. You have mentioned the Levy trial. The problem as I see it here, is to show pattern and practice in the treatment of prisoners, in other words, to separate pattern and practice from isolated, individual incidents. Perhaps I can clarify this by saying that between Peter Bourne, Robin Moore and myself, we have visited and been in at least seventy-five percent of Special Forces camps that existed in Vietnam at that time. I myself have been at perhaps twenty-five such camps. Of course I could not see all of these things myself. I will talk about things I actually have seen myself, but of course in my capacity of reading the intelligence reports, the after-action reports that came from these camps that was part of my duty, I have knowledge that, in fact, these are the practices throughout the country at Special Forces camps. Now, in the book, I related two incidents in some detail — one, in which a prisoner was disembowled with a knife under interrogation, and another event, where civilians were picked up along the route of march and abused. Both these incidents took place in Tay Ninh province, by a company of strike force stationed at Camp Trang Sul, which is a camp, an old French fort, as a matter of fact, just outside the city of Tay Ninh. This particular company was composed primarily from an ethnic minority group, the Cao Dai. The company leader was given the normal rank of lieutenant. His name was Dam. I understood that he was a former major in the now-defunct Cao Dai army. The strike force, like all strike forces, brings in another problem — who controls these teams? And if I may, I'd like to digress here, just for a moment.

It was contended by the U.S. Army at the Levy trail that, in fact, these strike forces are under the command and control of the Army of the Republic of Vietnam, the Saigon government. At Fort Bragg, North Carolina, it is taught as doctrine, that either in guerrilla warfare or counterguerrilla warfare, when you are working with indigenous groups of people, you control these people by controlling the money, by controlling the supplies and by controlling the communications. At all of these camps, without exception, the money is supplied by the United States; the strike forces are paid by the United States through Special Forces; in fact, the supply base at that time was Nha Trang, and it was either funneled through the B Team to the A teams, or directly from Nha Trang to the A teams.

The communications, both equipment and the operators, are controlled by the Americans. So, in fact, to say that the Vietnamese Special Forces are running these camps is an evasion on the grandest order; yet is a convenience that when something goes wrong it works conveniently both ways. The Vietnamese can say: we can do nothing, it was the Americans who are in charge. The Americans can say: we can't do anything because we don't have control. One hand rubs the other . . . I have a specific example on by whom and how these camps are controlled. In the case of this story and this disembowelment, both of these patrols . . . were led by this Mr. Dam.

Both cases, the Special Forces people were there. A captain, excuse me, a first lieutenant — American — and two American N.C.O.'s. There was one Vietnamese Special Forces present, a sergeant. He was just there for whatever reason, more like an observer; he did not give orders. The orders were given through the interpreter, or indirectly from the lieutenant or one of the American sergeants to this Mr. Dam. These acts were performed from this particular camp. In fact, the American Special Forces were able in the space of two months to have three camp commanders relieved. The one camp commander was relieved because he tried to put Mr. Dam in jail. This is the Vietnamese camp commander, his official title. He tried to put Mr. Dam in jail, and as a result of that — and I have personal knowledge of this because I happened to be there for the changing of the guard ceremony when one was relieved — the new commander came in. They try not to interfere, in other words, as long as everything is going the way the Americans want it to go. Then, of course, the Vietnamese are given great sway as to how they conduct the camp. As soon as it does not meet with American approval, the pressure is put on and the man is relieved. As a matter of fact, United States Special Forces themselves were instrumental in getting the commander — the overall commander of the Vietnamese Special Forces — not only relieved but sent out of the country, which was Colonel Lamson, who I understand right now is in Laos, Vientiane.

As for the specific incidents referred to in the book, in both cases Americans were present. All the instructions were: get the information. They knew what methods would be used to extract that information, and the thing is, then the Americans would turn their backs, light a cigarette, you know, until the nastiness was over. Now, this type of thing is very common throughout. Special Forces, perhaps more so than other organizations within the United States Army, are very sensitive about the ethnic differences. For instance, in training, you are told that you should never torture a prisoner; let your counterpart do it. You should never kill a prisoner; let your counterpart do it. This is the indigenous counterpart; in Vietnam, of course, that would be the Vietnamese. Now, there is no morality; this doctrine is not put forth on a moral issue, but a very pragmatic issue.

The idea being that, since you are an American, it could be resented — your torturing or killing these people. In other words, you don't want the charge of prejudice or racism thrown at you.

HALIMI: *Mr. Duncan, I would like to ask you about torture of prisoners by the South Vietnamese, in the presence of Americans. I would like to ask you about blanket orders given to the troops to get rid of prisoners. I ask this because in your book, in the testimony of Peter Bourne, in the testimony of Robin Moore which the Tribunal has, and in the deposition of Marion Campbell — which the Tribunal will hear — we find references that indicate there were orders to execute prisoners. Can you say whether you know if there are general orders of this kind given to American forces?*

I personally have never heard a blanket order of this type given. However, such orders are given to individuals in specific circumstances, and I will relate a personal one.

This was in the An Lao valley in 1965. We went into this area — again, a team of eight men — this was an area that had been controlled for some time by the National Liberation Front. As a matter of fact, there hadn't been government troops in that area in a couple of years at least.

Our mission was to last five days in this area, to put the valley under surveillance or whatever, and hopefully, on the way out, to pick up prisoners, if we could, for interrogation. As these things do happen when you are working in somebody else's territory, we inadvertently had to take prisoners. In other words we were in a position where we had to take prisoners for our own safety because they had walked in upon us. We would try to let them go by, but it just didn't work that way. However, we were faced with the problem: we were in this valley; we have four prisoners, there are only eight of us. Quite obviously, we can't carry these people around with us, we can't let them go. I radioed back to base, informed them of the situation, and my instructions over the radio were to "get rid of them." I asked for a repeat on that, and they said, "get rid of them." I pretended to ignore — not ignore — pretended that I didn't understand the communication (of course I fully understood the communication) and effected a helicopter transport out of there. When I got back to our base camp, the people were very angry, and when I say people, I am talking now about the commander of the project at that time, because I had brought the prisoners back and had not stayed in this area for four or five days. He made it very plain to me that what he meant by "getting rid of them," of course, as I well knew, was that they were to be murdered, and to carry on with the mission. I think that two other people were present at the time when that conversation took place. It would have been the standard practice in a situation like that to get rid of the prisoners, and the only way to get rid of them is, of course, by murder.

This comes back again to something I said this morning. The captain that gave the order would not in all good sense, ever say directly over the radio, to "kill the prisoners." Because again, these radios are monitored, and if there should be some legal ramification later he could always deny that he ever gave them such an order. It would be considered an illegal communication, in the Army, to say such a thing.

HALIMI: *I would like to ask you — I think that you have your text in English — what you wanted to say in your book on page 161, when you say: "There is a time to take prisoners and a time to dispose of them . . . . " and so on. You have the page. Could you explain what you wanted to say?*

This particular page, I assume you mean where it starts: "this means of course, that you have a disposal problem. Prisoners who have not learned too much, can be turned back to their own, as propaganda weapons" and so on and so forth. Again, you are referring to this portion where I am talking about getting rid of prisoners. First of all, to put it in context, I have tried to reconstruct as closely as I could, an actual class at Fort Bragg, North Carolina.

It was very easy for me to reconstruct this because this is the same class I taught; in fact, I helped make up the lesson plans for it. This is in the context of a guerrilla warfare and counter insurgency operation. In all of these things, one, is perhaps applicable to the other. It in fact, means that if you were in a guerrilla warfare area, for instance, if these teams were operating — let us say, in North Vietnam — and you took prisoners — quite obviously you could not set up a prisoner-of-war camp in North Vietnam. So, what do you do with the prisoners? Of course, you would have to dispose of them somehow, for security. It's a problem all guerrilla units have. Their existence is dependent upon mobility and it's very hard to be mobile when you're pinned down with a prisoner-of-war camp. So it is in that context that that information is given.

HALIMI: *But Mr. Robin Moore as well as Captain Bourne and as well as the Marine, Campbell, speak only about the war in South Vietnam and say that their instructions in South Vietnam, not in counter guerrilla operations, were to get rid of prisoners if they became burdensome.*

Yes, Now we are referring to a combat operation. In the process of a combat operation you're on, maybe a one-week patrol and you pick up a prisoner here, or a prisoner there, and it is pretty well decided that he is "hard-core" — the expression that is used there — "hard-core VC" — that of course, the man is jeopardizing the security of the patrol. There is nothing else to do, if he is inconveniencing the patrol, then of course, the thing to do would be to dispose of those prisoners, which of course, would mean killing. Perhaps I should add that the Americans, like any other army, are well aware of the value of prisoners as a source of information, and, if possible, they would bring them back to camp for interrogation — proper, thorough, interrogation. The exigencies of battle do not always allow that of course. That would mean, that they would be in the middle of a battle, but they would be on a military operation and there would be no convenient method of sending these prisoners back. So in that sense, they would have to get rid of them.

HALIMI: *Mr. Duncan: you, Robin Moore, as well as Captain Bourne, Carl Campbell and Jones, whose testimonies will be heard on tape, said that it was in fact the Americans who taught the South Vietnamese the interrogation techniques they practice. Could you verify this? And then could you talk about the two incidents of turture that you yourself saw that are described in your book?*

Yes, it was the practice, at least certainly at the time I was there, when you did have prisoners, after a rather superficial interrogation — and by this I mean a direct in-the-field type interrogation of a prisoner — that they were turned over to the Vietnamese (I'm talking now of the Saigon elements) for interrogation. Sometimes they were turned over at the camp level, sometimes at the — what they call — the province, or district, level. In any event, the type of treatment that they would receive in the process of interrogation and incarceration, was well known to the Americans; there is report after report of such things in the files in Saigon. There have sometimes been remonstrations against it, again not on moral grounds, but due to the fact it wasn't eliciting very good information. As far as I know it generally still is the practice, although we do now have our own interrogators. Specifically, it was done for two reasons: One, contrary to popular myth, very few of the Special Forces people in Vietnam spoke Vietnamese, of which I'm no exception. The other reason was that it helped to perpetuate the myth that in fact the Vietnamese were in charge of the operations. Interrogating anybody through an interpreter is a very awkward method of interrogation and . . . it takes a very highly trained interrogator to ever get any good information this way. So they were turned over to the Vietnamese with full knowledge of the treatment they would receive. More often than not, or — let me correct that — quite often the prisoner did not survive the interrogation.

To answer specifically the second part of your question, which is an elaboration of these two incidents in Tay Ninh province, the one took place after a battle; there was . . . what we call a fire fight — both sides shooting — the strike force was pinned down in a rather open area; airplanes were called in. You couldn't actually call this a hamlet — it was maybe a collection of twenty huts — twenty-five huts perhaps, many of which were destroyed; it was recognized that there would be many civilians in that village . . . (we get a relative value problem here: Who is it better to have killed, a few civilians that we don't know, or, us?)

After the fire fight stopped, . . . the strike force went on into the village. Those houses that were still left standing were searched; all material taken out of them that had any value at all, souvenirs mostly; and then the houses were put to the torch. In the process of this of course, as you might fully understand, the people who owned the houses weren't too happy to see their houses burned, and in a couple of cases they protested to the soldiers and were beaten, and, in fact one woman was shot by one of the soldiers. And finally, one prisoner was brought forward with a broken leg. He was tied with what we call communication wire. It's a very thin wire with a plastic coating and with a steel core in it and it bites very deeply into the flesh. His arms were tied twice; once at the biceps and once at the wrists, behind his back. He was dragged into the center of the village.

First of all he was interrogated by what would be called the executive officer of the strike force, without any results. When I say interrogated, I mean that questions were shouted and screamed at him, while simultaneously one of the other soldiers was kicking the broken leg to the point where the bone finally was pushed through the flesh. During this interrogation a lieutenant had a knife in his hand — a type of knife called a "Kabar," an item that is issued to the United States Marines, very popular with Special Forces in Vietnam and a treasured item amongst strike forces — and he was teasing the prisoner with this knife: drawing — not actually cutting — but scraping with the point, tracing marks on his chest and stomach.

As time went on, of course, the prisoner was not speaking and finally the prisoner was literally pinned to the ground with this Kabar knife. A Kabar knife has a blade on it about nine inches long. It's like what we would call a hunting knife. The knife was pushed straight through his stomach. Then another platoon leader jumped on the prisoner, who was now almost in a state of shock, and he proceeded again to attack him with a knife, only this time ripping the stomach cavity open and going into the cavity and extracting the gall-bladder, which he treasured as a trophy. As a matter of fact some three weeks later he was still wearing the gall bladder around his neck in a little plastic bag as a good-luck token. I have been told — I have no way of verifying this — that he would probably eventually sell that gall bladder to a Chinese, to make some Chinese medicine, evidently valued for some reason.

The other situation: again it was the same company, in Tay Ninh province. Different advisers this time — different Americans with them. We were not involved in a battle initially, but on the second morning we were out, as we progressed along the route of march — going generally east, toward a village called Suoi Da — we started picking up civilians. These were unarmed people, working in the fields with their water buffaloes, or with their little carts, going off somewhere. A couple of them were, I guess, of military age. But the others were older — older men. In fact one man was almost the stereotype of the venerable elder, with a long beard, and so on. When I asked why they were being picked up, I was told, "because they are suspected Viet Cong."

Whether they were sympathizers with the N.L.F. or not, who can say? The fact that they were living in peace in that particular area indicates that at least they were somewhat sympathetic to the National Liberation Front, but if you picked up everybody in South Vietnam who felt that way, you really would have a lot of people. In any event, during the next three days, as we picked up more and more people, the civilians were pressed into service as ammunition bearers. They had one carrying a machine gun, another one carrying the ammunition and another man carrying what is called a Browning automatic rifle, not of course to use but as a convenience for the soldiers. And eventually, on perhaps the third morning, perhaps the fourth morning (I'm not sure which now), we did engage in an attack on a suspected village and these people were passed into the battle along with the soldiers. They had no weapons to use, they were just carrying other supplies along, sharing the same exposure to the shooting as the soldiers. And certain of the soldiers were detailed to keep pushing them in with the other soldiers. Shortly after the battle was over the patrol also was considered over. By this time these people were many miles from home. And having been picked up as Viet Cong sympathizers or suspects, they were then turned loose to make their own way back home. Also, during this period some of these people were treated very badly. One was beaten with a rifle butt, the old man was thrown to the ground and beaten again by this Mr. Dam. I think that the significant thing about this is that this was considered one of the finest companies that we had operating at that time amongst the strike forces. And it was hoped that we could bring every company up to the standards of this company . . .

HALIMI: *Before passing to questions on the treatment of the civilian population, I would like to ask you to finish your testimony on the torturing of prisoners by confirming what you have already mentioned in your report — that these are not isolated incidents which you describe but occur on a large scale — in order that the Tribunal be convinced that this is in fact established practice.*

Yes, I will confirm this. It was brought out at the Levy trial. Capt. Peter Bourne, Robin Moore and myself have discussed similar things in at least 75% of the camps that existed at that time. It's interesting to note here too, with Robin Moore, Peter Bourne and myself, when you put our times in Vietnam together, cover about a three-year period of time. So this is not something that went on one month but not the next month. It was consistent for at least three years.

HALIMI: *Would you describe to the Tribunal how you proceeded to arrest civilians during an operation, how they were screened and classified, and how they were put into camps_ . . .*

Well, first of all there was no arrest in the proper sense of the word. The people were just forcibly taken away from whatever they were doing and there was an initial interrogation at that point. For example, "Are you a member of the National Liberation Front?" or, "Are you a Viet Cong?" As you might suspect not too many people admit to that, under those circumstances. And then the following question would be, "Do you know where they are?" or, "Do you know who is?" And more often than not this is accompanied by violence, especially if you're operating in an area of contention or a known National Liberation Front stronghold or controlled area. The people are eventually broken down roughly into the categories of suspected hard-core V.C., sympathizers to the National Liberation Front, or possibly innocent.

HALIMI: *I see, that's what you call innocent civilians?*

Yes, innocent civilians.

HALIMI: *During the Levy trial, you were questioned on the existence of, and the conditions in, the refugee camps. You have said that these camps are "garbage pits." Could you explain this and tell the Tribunal how many camps you have seen and what has led you to make this judgement?*

I have seen three or four such camps. I used the word "garbage pit" for lack of a better euphemism, I suppose. The conditions under which these people are forced to live are, by any standards, appalling. There is usually a grave shortage of water, perhaps one water point for two hundred people. In other cases water has to be brought in, if there is any water at all. They are fortunate to have enough water for cooking and drinking, leaving very little over for sanitary purposes. The latrine facilities, if they exist at all, are of the worst order. There is very little for these people to do, no form of creative work. It's simply a matter of sitting around and letting time pass by. I didn't, myself, see any evidence of physical abuse, in the sense of people going in there and just systematically beating up refugees, but there was overcrowding, in the number of people living in one cubicle, for instance, in the provisions made for beds, which are usually nonexistent. You could usually smell these camps long before you came to them, because of the lack of sanitation facilities.

HALIMI: *Orville Schell, in an article not yet published but brought to the attention of the Tribunal yesterday, has written not only of the screening of civilians but also of the methods of displacing them, taking them by truck from their homes and throwing them into these camps with neither beds nor food. Could you tell us if you have any knowledge of these practices?*

My information from this comes from documents rather than from first hand. I haven't actually seen the physical displacement headquarters, and there are documents in American headquarters, for instance, going back talking about the strategic hamlets when that program was first initiated. There is an essential difference I suppose, between what we used to call the strategic hamlet and what are now known as the new life hamlets. The strategic hamlet from the documents that I read, and this was in the process of writing this history, were essentially nothing more than concentration camps. The people were forcibly removed. The idea came, of course, from the British experience in Malaya. The idea of, we're going to take the "sea away from the fish." To deny the National Liberation Front access to information, supplies, recruiting, etc. The new life hamlet theoretically, at least, these people are supposed to be given something to do and in other words it's a new home. The responsibility for this sort of thing lies with the Vietnamese, who are in charge, or the Americans. The idea for, the funding for, the supplies, come from American forces. The Vietnamese are supposed to do the actual handling of this. In other words, they are supposed to be the ones physically controlling these camps. More often than not it is the common thing that much of the money, food, clothing supplies, etc., never get to the people. It ends up in the black market or wherever. It's siphoned off. The provisions that they are supposed to get are minimal but then they only get the smallest percentage of that. When complaints are made, the Americans say well, the Vietnamese are in charge and we can't interfere.

HALIMI: *Would you give us your opinion on the report of David Tuck this morning? David Tuck described how some prisoners were locked up in cages in which there was no room to stand. First, could you tell us if you have seen these cages yourself, and secondly, whether these cages have been specially made for interrogating Vietnamese in these camps or whether they were already in existence?*

The cages are made specifically for prisoners. I can't even imagine what other use they could be put to and I have seen them. I have seen prisoners in them. In fact, referring to Robin Moore's *Green Berets*, there he talks about a camp . . . called Tinh Bien, named after the village close by. It's in the Seven Mountains area, very close to Cambodia, and I have seen prisoners in those cages. In fact, they had two cages there for that purpose. It was made from wood. Very close together and of such size that it's impossible to stretch, lie down, or stand up, exposed to the direct sunlight so a man almost bakes in there. There is another type which is an adaptation of something we call a "conex" container. This is a steel container and it has a door on it, and of course, placed in the direct sunlight it becomes a virtual oven.

HALIMI: *Mr. Robin Moore, testifying at the Levy trial, told a most extraordinary story. He was, besides, proud to tell it and I would like to ask you if you have any knowledge, from the documents you examined, which would confirm the facts presented by Mr. Moore. He said that while he was following the operations of the Special Forces, it was noticed that medicines were being stolen during the night by the Vietnamese. There was a large supply of medicines and in particular a supply of penicillin. Then the commandant of the camp decided to play a dirty trick on the Vietnamese and replaced the penicillin with strychnine. Robin Moore justified this incident by saying that 'if they steal from us, it's natural to try to kill them' Do you have any comments on this story or on other similar stories?*

I have knowledge of such practices. There are other examples of course, booby-trapping hand-grenades and other things like this so that if they are ever used they will explode prematurely. The thing about the medicine I have never actually seen in a document, in the sense that a report of it actually was made. I have seen it in note form as a suggested thing to do only, but it was conversation amongst the soldiers that this was being done, or had been done.

HALIMI: *Robin Moore testified to this during the trial of Captain Levy but perhaps you did not hear it.*

He has also told me the same thing, yes.

HALIMI: *And he also told it to me when I saw him in New York. Understandably, a lot was said during the Levy trial about the role of the doctor in the Army, about the roles of American doctors when they are in Vietnam and the role of the medics. I would simply like to ask you to affirm what has already been affirmed at the trial but in a very lengthy form. Could you tell us much more briefly what was the role of these doctors? First, did the medics actually do the nursing, or, as Peter Bourne and Robin Moore said very precisely and clearly, were they trained to destroy and plunder? Lastly, were they armed and did they in spite of this treat the sick?*

Most of the testimony at the Levy trial was not specifically about doctors. It was about Special Forces medics. Special Forces medics are a little bit more than a normal aid man. A medic's training lasts approximately one year and goes far beyond the first-aid type of medical practice. At Fort Bragg, for instance, they are even taught how to perform simple operations, amputations, appendectomies and so on, and how to treat wounds, quite an extensive course. This is essentially because it is planned that they will be working in areas where doctors will not be readily available, either American or indigeneous. The testimony centered around defining the primary role of a medic. Is he in fact a doctor, or a doctor-substitute, or is he essentially a surgeon? This has to do with the Geneva Accords on the treatment of medical personnel. First of all, Special Forces medics are used as a political weapon, the idea being that a medic may often get into an area where other military personnel would not be allowed to go. There have been many examples of this in Vietnam, where a medic has been allowed to go into a village, for instance, and treat people, and gain their confidence — the "we're only here to help you" type of thing. This of course makes an entree then for the other soldiers to come in. This, of course, is done deliberately, and is taught as doctrine in Special Forces training. One of the reasons the man is so well trained is that he can't afford too many mistakes, if he loses too many patients he is not going to gain the confidence of the people, quite the opposite. They are armed, they carry a rifle just like anybody else in Vietnam, they go out on regular patrols, not essentially as medics but as soldiers, taking their turn. Each time a patrol goes out, two Americans must accompany it. The reason for two and not one is a lack of faith in their Vietnamese counterparts — strange things can happen — so two Americans go. Of course, with only twelve men, your turn on patrol comes up very· often. The medics take their turn just like anybody else. There are two medics on each team, only one medic goes out at a time. In the CIDG camps, they are not there specifically to be doctors to the American troops, they give limited medical aid to the strike force soldiers, but Americans who are seriously ill or wounded are evacuated to Saigon. They are there to treat Vietnamese civilians.

HALIMI: *Mr. Duncan, during the trial of Captain Levy, both you and Robin Moore talked about special weapons. I will now ask you one or two questions which you can answer briefly, and the Tribunal will be able to recall some of the other witnesses who are still here to find out whether they, as well, have used certain weapons considered by international law to be illegal, or if they know of the use of such weapons. Mr. Duncan, I would like to ask you about the weapons you used. You and Robin Moore have talked about the M-16 rifle, describing its cruel effects. You have also talked about the explosives which were put in hand grenades, you talked about these in your testimony at the Levy trial. You have talked about the use of white phosphorus and other witnesses have explained the destruction this weapon is capable of causing. Lastly, I would ask you about the use of two weapons which are specifically classified by the Americans as anti-personnel, according to general documents, and which are called in English 'cannister' and 'beehive'. I would like you to tell the Tribunal if you have used them yourself, whether the Special Forces used them, or whether they were used by other units in the U.S. Armed Forces. Do you know, after the research you undertook to write your book, whether they were widely used?*

The M-16 is the standard weapon of most Americans. The Special Forces were the first to use it in Vietnam. At that time it was called the Colt Armalite AR-15. It fires a .223 calibre bullet. In fact, it is mandatory now for the Special Forces to carry them. At one time there was a choice, you could carry that, or any other weapon you so desired. But now, for reasons of standarization and logistical purposes, everyone carries the same weapon, which is the M-16. White phosphorus: Every Special Forces camp, at the time I was there, and I assume it's still true, had a basic load of white phosphorus for their mortars. The cannister I am not familiar with. The beehive, I am. It's not used by Special Forces, it's an artillery round, and, of course Special Forces has no artillery other than various sizes of mortars. It has been used. The beehive is a shell that contains literally hundreds of 'flechettes'. Each flechette is approximately the length of a standard paper clip. It's pointed and then has three pins on it, so that it acts like a little needle. It's also crude and shaped roughly enough so that it penetrates the body, and after it goes in the wound closes behind it. Because the pins themselves, as they come back off, round off again, so that they go in and the wound will close. A person in the path of such a round could literally receive hundreds of these things in his body. Each one of them would require surgery for removal, they would penetrate deeply enough so that they couldn't just be picked out, like slivers. I'm sorry, I could have brought a picture of these to the Tribunal I didn't know I would be asked questions along these lines. If at a later date you would like a photograph of these flechettes, I could certainly supply it to you. They are currently being produced by a company very close to San Francisco, where I live, in San Jose, and the pictures are available.

HALIMI: *The cannister you are not familiar with?*

No, except by definition. It's not classified material, as far as I know. If I could add something about the M-16, concerning my testimony at the Levy trial. Specifically, what they were asking was the effect of a bullet from an M-16 on the human body.

Whether by design or not I have no way of knowing — as I was not one of the designers — the hitting effect of the M-16 rifle is essentially a circumvention of the law prohibiting the use of dumdum bullets. The bullet is very small in diameter — 22 caliber — but very long proportionately to its diameter, and it has a shell casing on it which would look more at home on a 7.62 cartridge than it does on this little .22. Because of its length and because of its shape and because of the high velocity with which it travels through the air, when it strikes the body — whereas a 7.62 round, which is the standard NATO round, would continue through, essentially in a slanted direction — with the M-16 bullet, the bullet hits but does not have the tendency to penetrate, rather as it hits it tumbles. So in effect what we have now is a very big object trying to go through sideways. The effect of this, of course, is quite devastating. It's possible for a single bullet, if it hits a bone, to shatter that bone completely — one bullet now. If it hits a bone, let's say in your leg, the shock itself could kill you. It would not be necessary to kill a person in a vital area such as the heart. To give you an idea of its hitting effect, on one combat operation at a relatively close range, I hit a man in the chest with one of these. It literally picked him up and jurled him back till he was stopped by a tree. He must have traveled about three or four feet off the ground and, of course, there was no chest left on the man. It was completely demolished. With a dum-dum bullet, which is an expanding bullet, though it would penetrate the body, it certainly would not have such a great effect. It's not only a circumvention, it's a magnification of the dum-dum effect.

HALIMI: *You have in your book, on page 95, alluded to a form of racism which exists even within the Special Forces, in their recruiting as well as in the destruction they carry out. And you have said that this racism took definite forms, for instance, your officers told you not to recruit any Negroes, and that you must find some excuse for rejecting them. Could you give us an explanation of these racial prejudices?*

Within the United States Army, and Special Forces is no exception, officially there is no such thing as prejudice, for whatever reason. However, individuals within the service bring the prejudices from civilian life with them and, as I stated in the book many times, people with these prejudices get in rather high or official positions. Possibly (this is opinion) the ones that very emphatically and quite honestly state that they have these prejudices or racist attitudes perhaps are more honest than many of those that deny it. One is just a little bit more obvious. It is a fact that at the time I was sent out recruiting for Special Forces, the captain directly in charge of that program made it quite clear and he used the term "Don't send any niggers." He quite definitely did not want any Negroes at all, any surplus of Negroes, in the Special Forces. Again, this is not an official policy, but the prejudice does exist and it exists throughout the Army. It shows up in peculiar ways. I've seen it with the American Army in Germany, I've seen it with the American Army at home, and I've seen it with the American Army in Vietnam too. One white and one black worked together, perhaps fixing a truck or as airplane mechanics. But at five o'clock the duty day is over, the white man goes to a white bar and the black man goes to a black bar. Now, in Vietnam . . . It's a strange phenomena . . . .I just assume it still exists, it existed when I was there. Now these bars are not segregated by the Vietnamese. They are segregated, unofficially, by the American soldiers. A black man walking into a white bar is made to feel very unwelcome and in a few cases I have actually seen them thrown out of the bar. Now, two men from the same unit, if two men sharing combat hazards, one white and one black, were to go to town and go in to the same bar, of course, nothing would be said. But a stranger, let's say a black man from a strange unit, coming into the bar, it could cause trouble. At least it did while I was there. Now this manifests itself in a very strange way in the relative value put on life in Vietnam. One rifle shot from a village is an excuse to wipe out a village. The idea being, to use the words that they would use, "there isn't one of those slopes, there isn't a hundred of those slopes, worth the life of one of my men. So better to shell the village rather than risk getting one man shot." And of course, they believe ... it's a commonly held opinion, that most of these people are VC anyway, so what the hell.

HALIMI: *While working for our Tribunal, I heard strange revelations, and most of these deal with the penetration of the CIA into the Special Forces. I must say that the principal source of information is Captain Peter Bourne, who, as far as I know, is an apolitical doctor. He has explained objectively the role the CIA plays in the Special Forces in Vietnam, and it was especially the CIA who decided the location of the refugee camps, not according to military or to strategic criteria, but solely according to political criteria. On the other hand, Mr. Robin Moore, who defended this viewpoint, answered very peremptorily that the CIA was in the Special Forces. That throughout the world where Special Forces are found, it [CIA] takes men from the Special Forces, uses them, and puts them back into uniform. Questioned on the extent of this penetration, Robin Moore said, (I think this is his exact phrase) "They are all over the world." He even gave details of the penetration of the Army of Peru, of the Tenth Group of Special Forces at Battols in Germany, and I believe that the only exception he agreed to make was Mexico. He said, "I am not sure whether we have this form of organization in Mexico." So the question I would like to ask you, and this is my last question, could you explain to the Tribunal what are the official ties between the CIA and the Special Forces? Would you first describe the connections between the CIA and the Special Forces in Vietnam?*

Yes, I testified, I believe it was this morning, that the whole C.I.D.G. program from the time of conception was a C.I.A. operation, and Special Forces was the operation arm of the C.I.A. in running the C.I.D.G. camps. This is one aspect. This would be an overt operation. Within Vietnam, and this is especially true when Special Forces first went there, many of the Special Forces men traveled in civilian clothes, out of uniform. They entered the country on civilian passports and were working directly with and for the Agency. However, they were still in Special Forces, still being paid by Special Forces. This would be a covert operation within Special Forces itself. This was a means of again circumventing the Geneva Agreements. At that time the number of American soldiers in Vietnam was restricted by the Agreements and this was a way to have them in the country doing the job and being able to say they were not soldiers.

Now in the operation I was on, Project Delta, we worked very closely with the C.I.A. We coordinated operations. We exchanged equipment: communications equipment, radio equipment. Project Delta ... was initiated for the initial purpose of infiltrating Laos, and of course we would have to cooperate or coordinate with the Central Intelligence Agency, essentially because they already had people in Laos and were we to go in there without coordination we might have compromised their operation. In other words, we could have jumped people in on top of their people. Their teams were called "Hardnose" teams at that time in Laos. There is another operation called SOG [Special Operations Group.]. Its main base is at Bien Hoa, and they have forward operational bases at Kai Sahn [Khe Sanh], Da Nang and a new camp just south of Da Nang . . . This particular operation, in 1964, was for the purpose of infiltrating teams into North Vietnam, north of the 17th parallel. This was more or less a continuation of a program started quite a while back by Colonel Lansdale, who was the head of the C.I.A. at that time in Vietnam. The training, the direct training of the people on these teams was done by Special Forces personnel, who were put on detached duty to the C.I.A. for that purpose.

The Project Delta itself branched out and had a satellite organization called Project Omega — again both a combined military and C.I.A. operation. Project Omega was formed and its primary duties are to infiltrate teams into Cambodia. Complementary with that they have a similar operation in Thailand for infiltrating Cambodia from that border. They also infiltrate people into Laos from Thailand, again a combined C.I.A. and military operation. Most of the funds for these operations came from C.I.A. . . .

And I have already discussed the strike force operation and the assassination teams. Now this is a little different. The man is taken out of Special Forces, and it would amount essentially to a reassignment within the government. He would no longer be drawing his pay from Special Forces, he would be drawing it directly from the Agency. Special Forces then are both in covert and overt operations with the CIA, but still within Special Forces, and they are detached and reassigned directly to CIA, and then often after that particular mission is completed they will come back to Special Forces. Training for the Bay of Pigs invasion in Cuba was done this way. The men were taken from Fort Bragg, North Carolina, and sent to Latin America for training the Cuban invaders, and when that operation was over these people came back to Special Forces.

HALIMI: *Mr. Duncan do you know if the Combat Studies Group, has given orders to the CIA to place teams in Vietnam?*

CSG is just one of the names used for the CIA there, sometimes they are called "embassy officials" too, but CSG, CAS and SOG are all CIA of various echelons. The CSG was in control of the CIDG program and in fact, as you asked earlier, were responsible for the actual location of many of the CIDG camps. The location of them was not always picked out by the CIA, but in many instances and especially in the earlier stages they were. If I may anticipate your next question, why they were placed in certain positions, in many cases it was for political reasons. In fact many times these camps were placed, from a strictly military point of view, in incredible and very untenable places. I could name for instance the camp of Ban Sar Pa, which is directly west of Ban Methuot, very close to the Cambodian border, and which was sitting at the base of a hill with trees, large trees and dense foliage growing right up to one edge of the camp. In other words, no field of fire for gunners, and somebody wanting to attack the camp could virtually crawl right up to the wire without being seen. Of course the reason for the location of this camp which was in Montagnard area, was that they wanted those people at least pacified, to stop them from harassing the government or stop the government from harassing them.

You may recall this is a camp that went out of existence in 1964. This is one of the camps where the Montagnards' revolt took place against the South Vietnamese government. The camp was destroyed by the South Vietnamese Rangers, a company attached to Project Delta at that time.

HALIMI: *Mr. Duncan, do you have any more to say to the Tribunal regarding the penetration of Laos, Cambodia or other countries?*

As a matter of fact we did remove the overt element of Special Forces from Laos at the time of the Geneva Accords, but we left the covert there and of course have put additional people in since that time. Again in Laos, even when they were initially in the relatively overt operation, they traveled on civilian passports and for the most part wore civilian clothes. Of course this is a pattern of Special Forces. It was repeated again in the Dominican Republic. Long before the American Marines landed in the Dominican Republic there had been Special Forces teams there. They had been recruited from Spanish-American people within the United States, in other words people that could blend very well with the people of the countryside, and they were there to pick up intelligence, and, to use the expression, "win the hearts and minds of the people" in the countryside. This first came to my attention when a couple of people from the Peace Corps complained that Special Forces was also trying to enlist or recruit people from within the Peace Corps to supply them with information. These individuals took exception to that. The same was true in Guatemala. Special Forces are in Guatemala and have been for some time. Like any other type of military personnel, American military personnel in Guatemala, at least when they are in Guatemala City or any of the larger towns, do not wear uniforms. This is also true of the Air Force there. Of course they are in Panama, in the Canal Zone, where we have our own school called the School of the Americas, where we take people from these countries, such as Guatemala, Peru, Bolivia, Venezuela and so on, and we send them to that school for training by Special Forces. All of these things are very closely coordinated, of course, with C.I.A.

SIMONE DE BEAUVOIR: *Mr. Duncan, could you explain to the Tribunal what has brought you here today? I would say that your attitude had changed very much between the time when you took part in Project Delta, and the time you gave evidence at the Levy trial. Would you explain to us the reasons for this change?*

DEDIJER: *Mr. Duncan please feel free to answer it as much as you wish. This is a complex question.*

It's complex and it's very long. First of all, I'll refer you to the book. Having experienced these things, having been aware of the things that I have written about in the book, there was a certain matter of conscience involved of course. There was no one thing that ever occurred in Vietnam that made me change my way of thinking. It was an accumulation of events, obvious contradictions between what was being told, and what in fact existed. I was in a very peculiar position on Project Delta, something that doesn't, I suppose, happen too often to an enlisted man, in that, on the one hand, I was in a policy making position, privy to high councils in Vietnam, policy making councils, and, at the same time, was an operator in the field. In other words, I would be making out operations orders, and then I would put on my pack and I would go to the field and actually perform that operation, usually two entirely separate functions. It was also incumbent upon me, as the man not only making out the plans, but also performing the operation, to very carefully study and evaluate the intelligence that we had available. Obviously there was quite a discrepancy between these intelligence reports, the intelligence that we were able to gain ourselves, and what in fact was being told to the American people, and our so-called 'stated aims' in Vietnam. If I wanted to be facetious I could say perhaps as an intelligence specialist they overtrained me. I'm going to relate just different incidents now, all of which had an effect, and they're cumulative.

DEDIJER: *The value of your evidence lies also in the motives which moved you to make it.*

First of all, when I first went to Vietnam, the opinion prevalent amongst the American soldiers there at that time, most of them regular Army soldiers, was very bad concerning the Vietnamese. In other words, "all Vietnamese were thieves, they were rotten, and they were cowards." And of course this was an opinion I had to revise from direct contact with fighting against them. I possibly would never have changed my opinion had I stayed in the frame of reference in which most soldiers work. Had I stayed in that same frame of reference, my opinions I'm sure, would have stayed virtually the same. Being on this project, which took me the whole length of the southern zone of Vietnam, and meeting people from all over South Vietnam and fighting all over South Vietnam, again had an influence.

On these operations that we used to go on, these were very small teams, isolated with no direct support in NLF-controlled areas. As you might well expect, it would be very tense while you were in the areas, a better way to put it perhaps, is that while you're in there for four or five days you're damned scared. When you come back from these operations, you have been working at a very high pitch for five days, and almost immediately you're in a very peaceful situation, you're sitting down, you're having your gin and tonic or your whiskey, and there's a certain bit of unwinding involved. I was fortunate in having a young Vietnamese officer working with me. In fact, I had been responsible for making him an officer; originally he had been a sergeant. He was very competent at his job, his motivation was peculiar, perhaps, but at least he had it, and we shared a lot of hazards together. And as was our custom we used to unwind together in the evening; in other words, drink ourselves stupid when we came back from these things, as a means of being able to sleep and unwind. And for the first time since I had known him after I had been in Vietnam about 10 months, this man got so drunk, he forgot to control his tongue. He said things to me that normally he would never have said. Much of it was detrimental to Americans, what Americans were doing there, why Americans were there, and his opinions of Americans in general. And keep in mind this is not a member of the National Liberation Front, this is a man I had great respect for as a soldier. Of course, I was drinking myself and tended to pass off the whole thing as drunken talk, and put it out of my mind. About four or five days later, he came to my villa, where I was staying, and invited me to his home — something that doesn't happen too often to an American soldier in Vietnam; they seem to get in a lot of houses, but not too many homes — to meet his family, to meet his children, his mother and father, and so on. And these people — I will point out again — were not members of the NLF, nor as far as I know were any others I was introduced to. These were people, who had no affiliation with the NLF, to the best of my knowledge, but by the same token, they were very unhappy with the situation in their country, specifically they were very unhappy with the Saigon regime. And they gave me certain insights into how people felt, whether they were Communists, non-Communists or whatever, in Vietnam. At first, I had a tendency to dismiss this as a sort of a deliberate attempt to dissuade me and so on. It became very apparent, of course, that they were very resentful of the American presence. They would take me around and show me things, that possibly I would never have seen by myself. This is not the one factor that made me change my mind, but this is one of the factors. Meeting people and looking, trying to look, at their country as best I could, through their eyes instead of through the eyes of an American who is in Vietnam for a short period of time and who will shortly go back home. Again, I was in Vietnam during the 1964 elections, when President Johnson was making certain statements relative to the war. He was in fact asking people to support the American official position in Vietnam — which it is certainly within his right to do — but I felt, in fact I had the visual proof, that he was not giving the facts to the American people on which they could make a reasonable decision. For instance, he was talking about getting ready to come home and getting out as soon as possible, and while he was making that same speech, the huge port facilities at Cam Ranh Bay were already well along in construction. He was talking about infiltration from North Vietnam and here in fact I was very closely involved with an operation where we were infiltrating North Vietnam, instead of North Vietnam infiltrating us. He talked about violations of the Geneva Agreements by the National Liberation Front and or Hanoi.

DEDIJER: *Mr. Duncan all these facts influenced your motivation to do as you did?*

Right.

DEDIJER: *This is important for us.*

So anyway there was, I felt, an element of dishonesty. Now we all know that every war has its propaganda, and each side has its propaganda, it's an inherent part of warfare. But for the first time the American people were actually being given the propaganda before they knew there was a war, and war had been going on for some time. And now, after it had become a much larger affair, they were asked to support it. They were never asked when it first was started. If I can just digress from that for a moment, first, it gives me no great pleasure to come here and to say these things that I said here today. I don't think it gives *anybody* any great pleasure to come here and to say these things that I said here today. I don't think it gives anybody any great pleasure to say things against their own country. I happen to love the United States very much. Things are being done in its name and I'm a part of that country; I must say something. I feel that my main motivation is in fact that what we are doing in Vietnam, as horrible and tragic as it is for the Vietnamese, is equally horrible and as tragic for what it is doing for our society at home.

I feel very strongly about this — that we are in fact dangerously close, if we have not already arrived at that point, to becoming a military nation that thinks, and can think, only in military terms. We have become so powerful and our thinking is so military, or militaristic is perhaps a better word, that we seem loath and reluctant to come up with alternatives for people in these other countries. We, on the one hand, say that Communism is bad, that Communism is the enemy, and then we seem to take action that is bound to guarantee the survival and long life of Communism in many countries. If Red China is the enemy, it's a very peculiar way to fight it, by forcing people into the arms of Red China to ask for help. Well, again I'm getting very long here, Mr. Chairman.

SARTRE: *In the* International Herald Tribune, *23 November 1967, General Westmoreland stated that the Vietnam War's major objective was to show to the world that guerrilla war did not pay. Consequently there is a current military doctrine of anti-guerrilla wars in the USA. Could you tell us what it is, and, more precisely, how it raises the problem of repression of the people supporting the guerrillas?*

The doctrine — perhaps I would prefer to use the word policy — I think, has been stated many times by Mr. Rusk, President Johnson, Mr. McNamara and other officials in our country: that they're determined to make sure that wars of national liberation will not work, will not succeed. And of course, the whole counter-insurgency program of the United States is set up to follow through with that program, that John F. Kennedy set up, for special warfare: the School of the Americas in Panama and so on. It works, as so often happens, from what I consider a false premise. For instance, we have never admitted officially that the guerrillas, or the National Liberation Front in Vietnam, for instance, are anything other than just a very tiny minority of the population of South Vietnam. We justify our actions by saying in fact, given a free choice the people would support us or support the government that we are backing at any given time. The ironic part of this policy is that it is tied-in very closely with the economic systems in these other countries, what is to our economic and political advantage in these countries. I think if you will make a study of it, that in every country in Latin America where we are involved and certainly in South Vietnam, it becomes readily apparent to even a casual visitor that these people are in grave need, long overdue need, for some type of social-political-economic revolution. Invariably they are being run by oligarchies, dictatorships or juntas of one sort or another. Instead of going into these countries and giving these people a revolution, by dealing directly with the people, the policy always is to go in and help the government; in other words, to help the people through existing government. The rationale for this is, of course, that the government we're helping is anti-communist. And so we are willing to overlook many of the imbalances, injustices, in many cases the corruption, of these governments, and in fact, I ought to use an American colloquialism, it becomes a policy of "eating soup with a fork." Because in fact what you are doing is helping the very people that are responsible for the very conditions that exist and that made it necessary for you to get involved in the first place. We are determined to say that wars of National Liberation will not work. We realize on the one hand that they are indigenous but we claim that they are directed from outside the country and this is the rationale for that. Does this answer your question completely?

SARTRE: *What you said much interested me, but I wanted to ask it more precisely about the Vietnam War. That is, the Vietnam War, if one believes General Westmoreland, has a demonstration aspect. In military operations, there are military forces and a population. In anti-guerrilla operations, could you tell us whether the US Army has the enemy armed forces or the civilians which support it bear the bulk of its effects; that is, on the NLF fighters or on the popular base which supports it?*

The program in the United States — I have seen it variously estimated but it seems to average out — that for every dollar spent in the so-called pacification program dealing with the civilian populace, that there are 20 dollars spent on the military effort. Again that is an estimate. The program working with the populace is large but certainly not as large as the military operation. The policy is that first of all you must pacify the country or an area of the country before you can deal with the people. I'm sure that the contradiction here is very important — that you have to wage psychological warfare, that you have to wage a battle to win the hearts and minds of the people that you say are already on your side if given a free choice. To answer your question directly though, of course the military effort far exceeds what we are trying to do with the people. The theory being that once the fighting stops or slows down, then we can spend a proportionate amount back on the civilian populace, for winning their hearts and minds.

SARTRE: *From your point of view, how did the participation of Special Forces on the field in Vietnam evolve, and does it increase or does it tend to decrease?*

Special Forces in Vietnam started off with just a few teams and then eventually they expanded up through the First Corps area down into the Delta. They started off in the II Corps area. Are you familiar with these terms? One, two, three, and four Corps?

DEDIJER: *Just for the sake of the members of the Tribunal do explain.*

The Southern zone of Vietnam, for tactical purposes and control pruposes, is divided into four tactical zones, I Corps, II Corps, III Corps, IV Corps; the IV Corps being the southern-most. The II Corps area is the central and highlands area. This is where the Special Forces program started and then it came down into III Corps and then lapped over into IV and so on. It then got a C Team and we went through the structure of Special Forces. It got large enough to have its own C Team. Then that further expanded, actually displacing a whole group. In other words, these are all the companies of a Special Forces group with all the administrative paraphenalia that would go with the group, all the non-combat personnel, engineers, doctors, and so on. As far as I know it has not decreased their operations. The CIDG program has decreased, but that has been taken up by Special Forces being responsible under MACV, Military Assistance Command Vietnam. The popular Forces and Regional Forces program do much of the training for them.

SARTRE: *As you covered much of Vietnam, do you have any idea of some figures, for instance, the number of executed prisoners and the number of people interned in camps.*

I would have no idea how many prisoners have been killed, other than to say a substantial number. This, of course, is not something that people publicize and if such reports would exist in document form, they would be at a very high level indeed to give any kind of accurate picture. In other words, they may have a report from here, and a report from there, and a report for someplace else, but these would be combined at the very highest level, probably the J-2 or J-5 level, the Joint Operation level. And the other part of your question, Sir, was on the number of people in refugee camps? At the present time I don't know, or again I can only tell you what I've been told, but this is not direct information and it's been variously estimated at 1/3 of the population. That figure, as I understand it, comes from government sources or people working with the government. Mr. Don Luce, who worked for the International Volunteer Services in Vietnam and has subsequently quit that organization, I believe, has used that figure. He would have been in a position to know, since the refugee problem was one of the problems given to him and essentially, it was the main or primary reason for him leaving the organization. To use his own words: "how can you solve a refugee problem, when you take care of ten people and next day the United States Army makes a thousand more," or something like that.

SARTRE: *Do you think that these methods used in this war, were un-avoidable, or that they are inevitably linked to this type of war wherein there is on the one hand a guerrilla, and, on the other hand, the bulk of the population which sympathises with guerrilla forces? Do you think that torture inevitably appears in those cases, as well as the extermination of an important part of the population, and a war related to genocide?*

The methods could be avoided. They could have been avoided from the beginning. You get a cause-and-effect relationship. The excuse for many of the things done by the United States' military personnel or by those people under their charge or control is usually, "look what the National Liberation Front does, look at the terrible things they do." Again I think there's a cause-and-effect here. The methods that first started this displacing of the population, things like the "Strategic Hamlet" programs, perhaps might have had some validity in Malaya, given an entirely different political situation, given ethnic groupings, and of course a different people, different terrain and so forth. Certainly it was a tragedy in Vietnam and one of the things that led to the situation that exists in Vietnam today. In other words, a self-defeating thing. It's common, when you're dealing with Regular Army people or with military people that they always think in terms of the last war, the one that preceeded this one, and you make all the mistakes and then you try to learn something. And in this case they made many mistakes and now, in my own opinion, it's impossible to rectify them. And to answer your question directly again, no, I don't think these methods were necessary, because I don't think it was ever necessary for the United States Army to be there in the first place.

CARL OGLESBY: *A picture that's grown very familiar to us, as we're been hearing about the torture of prisoners, is one in which an American inter-rogator passes a question through a South Vietnamese interpreter and then looks on as South Vietnamese torturers inflict their torture on the prisoner. I think that because of the familiarity of this picture, we need to know some-thing about the formal authority relationship that exists between the Amer-ican interrogator and the South Vietnamese torturer. What kind of formal authority if any does the American have over the South Vietnamese? What would happen if a South Vietnamese torturer decided for example not to torture any more?*

Within Special Forces, and again now I'm talking directly of the years '64 and '65, of which I have the first-hand, direct, eye-witness know-ledge, the interpreters used by Special Forces were hired by Special Forces directly. In other words, they were not hired through even a government agency. They were paid by, clothed by and supported by the Americans. They were working for the Americans, as opposed, let's say, to the camp commander. As a matter of fact, a Special Forces interpreter, in the pay of Special Forces, is exempt for military duty in the army of the Republic of Vietnam, and if he chooses to remain with Special Forces for a period — I think it's three years — then he has no obligation with the Saigon forces. In other words, it's another way a man can get rid of his military obligation there. It's a much sought-after job in Vietnam. So we have direct control over that interpreter.

OGLESBY: *Do you know if that same kind of relationship exists outside the Special Forces, for example in the infantry?*

It would be very common. Of course, the Vietnamese government prefers that you accept one of their interpreters. And so, he becomes something a little bit more than an interpreter; he's sort of like an integral spy, if you will, you know, passing information back and forth: what are the Americans saying today, what are the Vietnamese saying today. It's the practice, and the preferred practice, to hire your own interpreters.

OGLESBY: *Is this interpreter the man who carries out the actual torture?*

Often, yes. Not necessarily. For instance, there could be a third person involved here; well actually, there would be a fourth person; there would be the American, an interpreter, a member of the strike force or a member of the Luc-Luong Dac-Biet and the prisoner. The American could — this is one way of doing it; again these things vary — the American would pose the question to the interpreter who in turn would translate it to Vietnamese to the member of the strike force or the Luc-Luong Dac-Biet. He in turn then would present the question directly to the prisoner.

OGLESBY: *Let me put the question like this: what power would an American interrogator have to bring torture to a stop?*

In the circumstances I've just stated, it is completely within his power to stop it.

VLADIMIR DEDIJER: *Mr. Oglesby, may I in connection with your question, just put, in the good old American tradition, a straight question to Mr. Duncan for you? Who is responsible for these crimes? Who is the initiator — the American instructors or the South Vietnamese? If you could just make a — in the good American tradition — just in a nutshell.*

To put it in a nutshell, the American.

OGLESBY: *Another witness like yourself has testified that as a mechanism for acquiring information, torture is simply not very effective. At the same time, it seems that the torture goes on and on. I wonder if I could have your view on why an ineffective means of acquiring information is pursued so obstinately.*

It's used persistently as an alternative to no information at all. First of all, again, to conduct proper psychological interrogations requires an expert, and by this I mean a man who has been trained for a long period of time in these methods of interrogation. It requires certain sophisticated surroundings over and beyond what would be found under field conditions. And of course it takes time, and it certainly would require a great knowledge of the language on the part of the interrogator himself.

OGLESBY: *Let me put it this way: in your experience, do American field officers commit themselves to action on the basis of information they acquire from tortured prisoners?*

All information that is developed into intelligence is given a rating, from A1 through D4 or D6, for reliability. The rating would depend not necessarily on the direct testimony of a prisoner that had been tortured, but it would be weighed against other available information, the circumstances of the interrogation; in other words, the rating would not be given on just the one item alone. At least, if it was, it would be a very improper procedure. And of course, action would be taken, either negatively or positively on the basis of that information.

OGLESBY: *My final question has to do with the American giving of bounties on ears of Vietnamese whom the Montagnards for example have killed. It surely must occur pretty soon to anyone doing this that an ear can come from anybody, an innocent civilian, and that there's no difference between an innocent civilian's ear and a Viet Cong's ear.*

Yes, I believe I [have] tried to present this traditional, I used the word "animosity" between the Montagnard and the ethnic Vietnamese — and that for the first time in his life the Montagnard has been given essentially a license to kill Vietnamese legally.

OGLESBY: *But the Americans must know this . . .*

Yes, right . . . there is no way of attaching politics to an ear.

OGLESBY: *Do you think that the Americans are conscious then of unleashing an angry ethnic group against the Vietnamese population as a whole?*

As a matter of fact, it has been a problem for some time over there. The Vietnamese are very nervous — I'm talking about the Saigon government now — they're very nervous about these C.I.D.G. strike forces — and witness the Montagnard rebellion in the Ban Me Thuot area in 1964. I believe it was September or October of 1964. This is a thing they predicted would happen; as a matter of fact, of course, the action on the part of the Luc-Luong Dac-Biet counterparts of the United States Special Forces more or less guaranteed that it would take place, because of their treatment of the Montagnard. So this is

496

a problem, and it's one the American government is very conscious of, that it is a force that could conceivably get out of hand. Again, the control we have is by controlling the supplies and their money.

OGLESBY: *I'd just like to know, in your experience, what the attitude of the American officers is about this.*

There's a peculiar thing here. Most of the Special Forces got along very badly with the Vietnamese, especially the Vietnamese Special Forces. But for some reason they had a rather good feeling about the Montagnard. And the Vietnamese was held up to be a dishonest person as compared to the Montagnard who was essentially a very' honest man. And they think of the Montagnard as a much more — generally speaking now, given a comparable amount of training — a better fighter. And so, there may be some unfortunate incidents, but that can't be helped, these are the best people to work with. Certainly in the mountains, reason tells you, they would be the best people to use, since they live in that area. So the unfortunate incidents have to be overlooked, or are overlooked.

OGLESBY: *Let me just pursue this one more second. You see, we have to decide at this Tribunal whether or not the United States is committing genocidal acts against the Vietnamese. One of the considerations that we have to make has to do with "intention," malevolent intention to do ill to the Vietnamese people, and the business about the ears and the reward for the ears seems to at least contain the possibility that American officers who give bounties on the ears — aware of the fact that ears can come from any Vietnamese — might also be aware that they're terrorizing the population by setting up this bounty system. And I wanted you to comment on that.*

I won't answer to the question directly: "Do I think we're committing genocide there?" I will relate my answer directly to the specifics. We have intent here. I don't think that even though they're aware they could be coming from anyone — soldier, civilian, N.L.F., pro-Saigon, or whatever; they are aware of these things — the intent is a means of keeping score of how many people are killed. The intent is not just to eliminate the Vietnamese people per se. For instance, the United States Army has made an effort there, or has tried to make the Vietnamese Special Forces or other groups accept certain numbers of Montagnards into their ranks in non-commissioned officer positions. There's been a little of this done; of course it's not the habit there. But strictly from the position of intent, in reference to the ear business, no, I would say that genocide is not the intent in that case.

OGLESBY: *But don't the Americans care to whom the ear belonged? Is it a matter of indifference to them that it might come from an innocent civilian?*

It's not often talked about, but it's very little different from the policies we had in '64 and '65 of free-bomb zones. If a person runs when a helicopter appears, it's a V.C. or it's legal game, and as a matter of fact I've seen helicopters going across the rice paddies deliberately trying to make people run, and as soon as they run of course that was the — it sort of gave them the tacit approval to themselves to be able to shoot that person, and of course that went in on the kill count at the end of the week. I've seen similar things being done with the boats on the rivers and so on and so forth. They're always listed, of course, as V.C.

DEDIJER: *. . . Although we made the rule that I should have the last question, I just would like to explain why I asked you the straight question: it's because I relate the events in Vietnam with the events in other wars . . . This is an explanation to you, more of a personal character: in Yugoslavia during the last world war there were killed about 1,700,000 people. And these crimes were originated by the policies of the German and Italian facist governments. But they found the quislings — and I must stress that we had no doubt a very great resistance movement, but we had at the same time perhaps more quislings than any other occupied country.* `Now after the war, some German historians are writing such big books, telling "we had nothing to do with it; these are over there a savage people cutting each other's throats;" and this is against all the historical facts, you see. And that was the reason why I put that question to you, Mr. Duncan. This is just my personal opinion, I don't ask any answer of you.*

Thank you. I didn't have an answer, but I would have a comment on that. The business of control and responsibility I believe was presented in testimony yesterday, when I detailed the actual organization of the Special Forces camp, I will say this: that for every one of those things that I said, the United States Army will produce for you, upon request, a piece of paper or a document saying that this is not true. They will show you pieces of paper also that will show you that as official policy as stated in documents, we do not torture prisoners.

DEDIJER: *Well, the Germans at least were more honest, you see, they didn't produce papers, but tortured and killed prisoners, and killed thousands of wounded and so on.*

LAURENT SCHWARTZ: *Apart from torture, torture with a view to get information, which is not very efficient as you said yourself, would you say that there is a generalization of ill treatment and systematic cruelty to prisoners, not even to terrorize people but simply because war easily develops this kind of sadism and useless cruelty? Have you ever witnessed massive acts of cruelty of this type? On the other hand, these acts of cruelty or torture: are these committed by others than South Vietnamese, for instance South Koreans?*

In answer to your first question: yes I think this is quite true; as a matter of fact, in the book I tried to point out, or tried to recreate the atmosphere showing that it became rather apparent to the men actually performing the brutality that they really didn't expect to get any answers. There was a certain psychological effect; it took place after a battle: these people had been very scared. It was perhaps a method of regaining their manhood; it's a vengeful thing; it's a number of factors; and of course I suppose these acts become easier and easier to the individual the more often he goes into combat, the more often he is scared. It's been well documented by people more competent in the psychiatric and psychological fields than myself, the brutalizing effects of this type of war. In answer to your second question about the South Koreans, again I only have second-hand testimony on the South Koreans. When I was in Vietnam, the only South Koreans there were in a hospital, a surgical field hospital in Vung Tau. If you're interested, I can say yes, second-hand information about the South Koreans is full of acts of brutality; in fact people coming back say they've really got a great pacification plan, because after the South Koreans go through a village there's nothing there to leave any trouble; it's just an elimination of the population. Again, this is not a direct eye-witness. One of the people, if I may relate an anecdote, . . . this was in a village north of Saigon, where it had been a combined operation: South Koreans had one element and Americans had another element and there were Americans in reserve. The South Koreans had gone into this village, and the following day were to be relieved for further action elsewhere. The Americans, when they came in, found, of course, a completely devastated village, no people remaining in the village, and the South Koreans left. As they preceeded to search for weapons, tunnels, supplies of any kind, they did find one woman, a very old woman, who was hiding under some old rice sacks and so on. When she saw the Americans, she thought they were her liberators, because of the treatment at the hands of the Koreans. She had difficulty deciding even who was the enemy now. She didn't realize that they were our allies there.

DAVE DELLINGER: *I want to take the question of control and responsibility one step further. Now we've heard testimony here of court-martials of Americans who have refused to commit war crimes — that is, have refused to go to Vietnam because they understood that this would involve their committing war crimes. Professor Greenspan in his treatise*

The Modern Law of Land Warfare, *states the law as follows: "In accordance with the general principles of criminal law regarding complicity, the accomplice is accountable for crimes committed in furtherance of the common purpose, even though he himself did not commit the actual crimes." So my question is in two parts: do you know of any soldier who was court-martialed for the direct commission of war crimes, and do you know of any case in which an American officer has been court-martialed in accord with this law of land warfare?*

Yes, well we've had a case not too long ago, I believe it was a Marine, who was convicted by courts-martial for killing a prisoner or prisoners. His defense at that time was that he had been ordered to do so by his commanding officer. The officer also stood courts-martial, or at least a pre-trial investigation under article 32, and to the best of my knowledge — the latest information I have — he was not convicted, whereas the enlisted man was.

DELLINGER: *Do you know of any other cases of court-martials of soldiers for committing war crimes in Vietnam?*

Not directly. No. This is not to say that such things have not happened. I do know of the danger of it happening to the individual. Perhaps that's a bad choice of words, and I'll explain. If the act became known and, let's say, publicized by the American press, the military officials would obviously at least have to go through the formality of a court-martial or a pre-trial article 32 investigation. Of course they don't want to publicize that fact that even individuals are performing these acts, and of course it would have a bad morale effect on the troops in the field. I do know of an instance where a man known to me, a man that I worked with in Vietnam, just cold-bloodedly with a Browning 9 mm. pistol, just killed, just out of hand killed a Vietnamese. And fortunately for him at the time, although he was in Special Forces, he was working for the Agency, the C.I.A., and so in fact this was kept very quiet, and it didn't become public so there was no investigation.

DELLINGER: *I'm wondering if it would be a fair conclusion of your point of view on this, and thinking also of your testimony yesterday that there were certain practices of torture that one could do as long as one didn't leave marks, and that you must leave the impression with the interrogators that this was what they were to do but you mustn't directly tell them; would it be a fair inference that the possibility of a court-martial would depend upon either executing the prisoner or torturing him in a way in which it came to the knowledge of the public and would look bad?*

Yes, I would say that would be paramount in the consideration of a court-martial. The fact of a prisoner complaining that he had been beaten and had no marks to show for it would have no weight whatsoever.

DELLINGER: [Dellinger recalls that Duncan, during Halimi's questioning, declared: "Every Special Forces camp . . . had a basic load of white phosphorus for their mortars."] . . . *but you didn't give us any details. Can you tell us how this is used, what type of targets it is used against, that is if you ever saw it used, how far away perhaps it is projected, how precise the targeting can be, this type of amplification?*

White phosphorus is a standard basic load in all C.I.D.G. camps, to my knowledge — at least any that I was at. The normal method of delivery of course is by mortar round, 60 mm., 81 mm. mortar; the exact ranges of those I don't have — I could look it up, I have it. The way in which it is used: officially white phosphorus is a marking round for directing subsequent fire. In other words, you put one white phosphorus round out; you can see it because it burns very brightly and so you can tell where your rounds are hitting. and now you can go on with your other firing. As a matter of fact, it's used quite commonly in what they call "H and I" firing: harassing and interdiction, interspersing the white phosphorus with the normal HE [high explosive] rounds. It of course is used against villages, because of its incendiary effect. It's a fine means not only of seeing where your rounds are landing, but of course it removes any cover that may exist in a village, against a potential enemy. Of course, the effect on people is devastating and there's a terrible moral issue involved in the use of white phosphorus against personnel. It's extremely painful, painful to the highest degree, essentially because white phosphorus doesn't stop burning after it gets on the body; it continues to burn until the substance itself has completely dissipated.

DELLINGER: *Yes, we had medical testimony on that; I know the effects. I was interested in the targets. And is there real precision possible?*

There are also white phosphorus grenades, but normally this would be used after you were already in a village, to burn down structures, and it would also be used as a marking round. For instance if you were calling in an air strike, you would throw one of these grenades to let the airplanes know where they're supposed to hit.

DELLINGER: *You say that the phosphorus grenades were useful, or used at least, in burning down villages. In your capacity with the Special Forces, do you have any idea on what basis it's decided to burn down a village or not?*

As a matter of fact, this was a question I had when I was over there. Because on some combat operations I went on it was decided that after you went through the village you would burn it and other times not to.

DELLINGER: *Who made the decision?*

It was made by the commander of the team of Special Forces. The one village in the Suoi Da area of Tay Ninh province that we went into — for some reason, although it was a known N.L.F. encampment or village, was left untouched. About two weeks later, we went practically in the same area but a few miles away, and this time the village was burnt. What the pattern and policy on it was, I never was able to fathom . . . I might add that this village that we did not burn, there were absolutely no people in it, because of the battle. By the time the battle was over, everybody was either dead or gone; and they had left some weapons there, not too many, and other supplies. We took the supplies, picked up the weapons, and left the village.

PETER WEISS: *Mr. Duncan, you spoke yesterday of the time when you trained Special Forces. May I ask you when you yourself were trained for the Special Forces?*

1960-1961.

WEISS: *May I ask you further — of course you needn't answer to this question — were you before this time already engaged in some other activities, as we know that in 1954 the counterinsurgency was already planned and built up in South Vietnam. Did you have any relationship to some of these groups that planned this?*

Prior to my entry in the Special Forces, I was an artillery operations and intelligence sergeant. My foreign duty had been in Europe. I was drafted in December 1954; I had three years of service in Europe, which is where I first met Special Forces, in Badholz in southern Germany. But no, specifically, no, only through normal information channels in the army, but not as a matter of policy or practice.

WEISS: *Mr. Duncan, you were trained for the Special Forces, which had as its main aim the antiguerrilla warfare and the counterinsurgency. Was it built up with the ideas of fighting especially against liberation armies, liberation movements?*

Yes, that was part of the orientation; any time we ever talked about aggressor or aggression and so on — if not stated specifically, which it often was — it was at least implied this referred to such things as insurgent operations, wars of liberation and so on.

WEISS: *In this training was it ever discussed if in the struggle of the liberation movement, if the whole population would be suggested as being part of this liberation movement, or would the fight be directed towards these special groups who are to be considered liberation movements?*

Official[ly] — when I say "official" I mean both in the sense that this would be in their information booklets and in information given to students in a class — the possibility of the whole or a major portion of the population siding with the forces of national liberation was, you know, it was just an impossibility. It was not considered possible, except that the people had been duped or misled, and if given the truth they would not be with them. This is the premise on which all training is given.

WEISS: *I'm going into this question because of course we have to decide where are the limits between the liberation movement and the population. And I wonder if you could give some more specification on that, if possible; if you in your training and even in Vietnam, if there would be the problem to ask or to discuss the question: Is the whole population to be regarded as being part of the liberation movement, or do you clearly divide these two groups?*

In the reality of the war on the ground as opposed to the war in the classroom back at Fort Bragg, North Carolina, this was the greatest difficulty of the United States Army and specifically Special Forces the time I was there: How do you tell the enemy from somebody other than the enemy? It was a problem that was never resolved; it was more or less considered impossible. You build up certain criteria; in other words, if it was possible to go into a certain village without having to shoot your way in, then you could say that at least it was not under N.L.F. control. Other villages where you knew it was going to be extremely difficult if not impossible to get into, that area would be considered N.L.F. area and was considered a free-bomb zone. In other words, anybody could bomb in that area; a man given a primary target who for some reason couldn't drop his ordnance on a primary target, he's authorized to drop it in that area. Some of these areas are very close to Saigon and Bien Hoa, and one free-bomb zone was just south of Bien Hoa. In fact it was a matter of continual frustration — all the soldiers in Vietnam in 1964 were professional army, regular army, rather than the type of soldier that's there now, younger men, draftees for the most part — there was a cynicism that prevailed amongst these people, to the fact that the realities of the field at least had the individual soldier convinced that you couldn't trust any of them, that they were probably all Viet Cong or N.L.F. sympathizers.

WEISS: *We have heard the expression by the other testimonies that "everything that moves is a V.C." but we have not had any clear definition if this expression came from some higher sources — if it is really directed to the troops to shoot at everything that moves.*

In a battlefield situation, quite often such an order would be given: that if it moves, it would be V.C., or if it runs it would be V.C. The An Lao valley is a good example; it was just considered that anybody in the An Lao valley was sympathetic to, a member of, a full-time guerrilla, a part-time guerrilla, of the N.L.F. And as such, anybody in that valley was fair game.

WEISS: *So in the military orders, you couldn't say there was any clear distinction between V.C. and population?*

No, as a matter of fact, the only way this can be determined in most cases is through interrogation. You know, after you — as we used to put it — "have the man's attention."

MAHMUD ALI KASURI: *Mr. Duncan, would you tell me some rough estimate of the strength of the U.S. troops at the time when you went to Vietnam?*

At the time I first went to Vietnam, the strength was approximately 14,000. At the time I left Vietnam, the troop strength was, roughly estimated, close to 100,000 — 80,000 plus.

KASURI: *Now, what was the strength of the South Vietnamese army at the time when you went there?*

Approximately 400-500,000. Now, this is a very difficult number to pin down, because you have popular forces, regional forces, your strike forces and so on. Regular army, under their own command, I would estimate that would have been about 350-400,000.

KASURI: *And would it be right to say that these South Vietnamese troops were paid by American funds, that the American government provided the funds?*

Not directly to the regular army. The money is given to the Vietnamese government, and the Vietnamese government pays the army.

KASURI: *And if the Vietnamese government were not paid the money it would not be able to pay its army?*

That's correct. In fact, we have Congressional testimony to that effect in the United States.

KASURI: *And since the United States was the paymaster of the Vietnamese army, is it in fact and in law responsible for what the Vietnamese army does?*

Absolutely. I think the first evidence we ever had of this was the time back in 1954 when the army itself objected to the imposition of Ngo Dinh Diem as the president of the Saigon regime. And in fact we told them we would — and this is in official testimony in the United States — to paraphrase it: if they didn't support him we would cut off their money, so in fact they did support him.

KASURI: *Now, the next question. Would it be right to say that if the Vietnamese army wasn't paid, there would be no possibility of the Vietnamese army — the so-called Vietnamese army — to make these cruelties upon the Vietnamese people?*

We are positing that if they did not get paid they would not in fact do anything? Well, as a matter of fact, we've had proof of this, because due to certain corrupt officials, certain units within A.R.V.N. have not been paid for significant periods of time. In one instance of — I think, a company of airborne rangers who billeted themselves in Nha Trang, they had not been paid at that time for something like three months — they did refuse to go to the field and spent their time harassing the citizenry of Nha Trang, the people they were supposedly protecting; in other words, going in and taking food and refreshment and so on.

KASURI: *Mr. Duncan, we have some evidence and knowledge of the various phases through which American operations in Vietnam have been passing. And would it be right to say that when you went there, it was the period of special warfare, and that when you came back, the period of limited war had already started, that there was a change in American policy during the time that you were in Vietnam?*

Yes, it was definitely the transitional phase; the plans for it I was of course aware of in 1964, and we knew it was going to happen. We were told to hang on with what we were doing and to continue our normal operations until we could get this thing organized in 1965. In fact, there was a transitional phase; this essentially is why a large portion of the C.I.D.G. program was phased out. Operational control of Special Forces C.I.D.G. program, the popular forces program, the regional forces program — operational control for that was relinquished by the C.I.A. and direct control of many of these programs was put under Military Assistance Command Vietnam — General Westmoreland's office. In other words, there was a whole command structure change at that time.

KASURI: *Now, Mr. Duncan, we've had evidence from some American witnesses, who have given facts about a large number of Vietnamese being directly tortured by American interrogators or in the presence of American interrogators; and from your evidence one gets the impression that these were limited cases of torture in the presence of American troops or*

American officers. Now if I were to conclude now that there are more num-bers of American troops in Vietnam, the evidence which has been given that there are more cases of direct barbarities by American troops should be believed, would you have anything to say against it?

I can only express an opinion on that, because I was not there at the time that that started. Again, I've already explained, I believe in some detail, the pattern and practice up to and including September '65. Again, I've read testimony, soldiers coming back from Vietnam have told me of these things, but I have no facts and figures and I certainly have no first-hand knowledge of it.

KASURI: *But you wouldn't be in a position to say that this could not be true?*

Oh, no. I would say this: there's a difference in training between a member of the United States Army Special Forces and a member of a regular army unit such as the 101st, 82nd Airborne or the 4th Division or any of these units. It is not planned that these people would be working directly with indigenous personnel. They would not be working in small teams in a prospective hostile area; they would be working in large units. So this idea that, you know, you do not mistreat indigenous personnel, you let a counterpart do it — in the first place, the regular units do not have indigenous coun-terparts, except on the very highest level, the joint chiefs and so on. For Special Forces people to have engaged in these activities as a matter of practice would have been against all doctrine — again, as I explained yesterday, not on a moral basis, but on a pragmatic basis.

KASURI: *A few more questions. I'd like to know from you, what is the difference between a concentration camp and a prisoner of war camp, because we sometimes read of concentration camps and sometimes of pris-oner of war camps.*

I don't know what the dictionary definition is. Just by common us-age, I would think of a concentration camp as a place where political refugees — civilians essentially — are incarcerated and a prisoner of war camp being a place essentially where soldiers are incarcerated.

KASURI: *While you were in Vietnam, were any concentration camps run by the Americans?*

Not directly.

KASURI: *Not directly. But there were many camps run by the govern-ment of Vietnam?*

Oh, yes.

KASURI: *Now, we also read of concentration camps and prisons. Now, would you tell us the difference between prisons and concentration camps?*

A prison would be a place where people not thought to be guilty of being NLF — prisoners or political prisoners necessarily — but acts that would be considered criminal under the criminal code, such as stealing, robbing, manslaughter, and that sort of thing. This is not necessarily true, of course, but that would be the normal interpretation of a prison; something run by the civilian authorities, let's say in an urban area, such as Na Trang, downtown Saigon and so on. Of course, we do know that political prisoners are put in these things.

KASURI: *Now I have read that there are about half a million prisoners in South Vietnamese prisons. Would you be in a position to confirm this? What was the position when you were there?*

No, I would be in no position to confirm that figure, one way or the other.

KASURI: *Would you say that the prisons were extensively overcrowded?*

Yes. I had occasion to visit one in Nha Trang one time, and it certainly was overcrowded. As a matter of fact, just the threat of prison to many of the citizenry of Nha Trang, the Vietnamese people, was enough to put the fear of whatever into them. The treatment and the overall conditions were that severe that just threatening them with jail was enough to bring them into line.

KASURI: *Now I want to know from you, if you would confirm it on the basis of your knowledge, what I have read elsewhere, that in South Vietnam, that which is controlled by the government of South Vietnam, there is no normal process of law, and anybody can be put in prison at any time without any trial. Would that be right?*

This is true.

KASURI: *So that the entire country is in fear of being imprisoned?*

I think that's a fair statement, yes.

KASURI: *Now, one more question about these prisons. If you have visited any prisons, what would be your estimate of the food arrangements and habitation arrangements and medical arrangements and sanitary arrangements in these so-called prisons?*

In most cases, if the prisoner does not have some personal funds or if he has no one on the outside that will bring him food or medication if he requires such, he just more or less does without. In other words, there are theoretically provisions made to feed these people, but more often than not the money is spent elsewhere, put in somebody else's pocket. The food is not of a quality that would be considered a normal diet in Vietnam — of course, this is not something that happens only in the prisons; it was a problem we had with our own strike forces when in fact we left the food arrangements in the hands of the Luc-Luong Dac-Biet. And we had trouble in our own Project Delta camp in this way; in other words, they would steal the food a lot and so on. . . . It's common knowledge to any official in Vietnam, both American and Vietnamese, that these people are living under deplorable conditions and that they are in fact incumbent upon outside help for food and other necessities.

KASURI: *So that the Vietnamese government not only imprisons people, but compels their family to maintain them while they are in prison?*

This is the general rule, yes. The main exception to this — this is true of the refugee camps, it's true of certain jails and so on — they do have certain showplaces that they keep for visiting dignitaries, where the people fall out and wave little flags, and so on.

KASURI: *You mentioned about having visited a certain number of prisoner of war camps. Now I just wanted to know the number of people, the largest number of people in a single prisoner of war camp and the smallest number.*

The one camp I was at perhaps had 300 or 400; the other one I was at was quite a bit larger and it was very hard for me to determine if it was just purely a prisoner of war camp or if it was also a political prisoner camp; and this was a camp right next to the border I forgot the name of the town now — but it's where the highway runs from Chipone (?) over through into South Vietnam, it's very close to the Laotian border there, and quite large, quite extensive. I had occasion to see this at the time that we were staging the infiltration of Laos from the camp at Kheson; it's not too far from Kheson, in fact. . .

KASURI: *We've had some references to strategic hamlets. Would you be able to give us your idea of the number of people who were in "strategic hamlets" in 1964-65?*

The strategic hamlet program as such had been phased out by that time; we no longer called them strategic hamlets, although in fact there were still a few existing; one I think of specifically was Godaha (?) which is near Highway 1 very close to the Cambodian border. My knowledge of strategic hamlets comes essentially from documentation; the Special Forces commitment in significant numbers to Vietnam coincided with the start of the Strategic Hamlet program. There are various estimates of how many people were ever in these camps at any one time; I have heard as much as 20 to 30 per cent.

KASURI: *20 to 30 per cent of the total population?*

20 to 30 per cent of the rural population, excluding places like Saigon, Na Trang, the major urban areas. The figure to me sounded like an exaggeration.

KASURI: *We've also heard of these Strategic Hamlets being followed by what are known as "New Life Hamlets."*

Yes, that's the new term.

KASURI: *Yes. Have you any idea of the number of people who might be in these New Life Hamlets? From documentation, if not from personal knowledge.*

Again, I've heard 20% as a figure used; I've heard other people use other figures, but 20% is the one commonly heard. There are such people as Don Luce and so on, who have used these figures; he was very much involved with the refugee program as part of his duties with the International Volunteer Services; he was essentially a para-government or para-official arm of the AID program at that time.

KASURI: *You were connected with Special Forces. And generally at the time when you went to Vietnam, the intention was that the commando duties, the Special Forces would not operate directly but they would make the South Vietnamese do things?*

Again, and for a matter of clarification, their primary job at that time, that job or those duties that utilized the bulk of the Special Forces troops there was within the CIDG program. I don't know if it's the proper thing to do; we always made a difference between Vietnamese and Montagnards — although they're all of course, Vietnamese citizens — but we used to think of them by their ethnic groupings. Our program was essentially dealing with the Montagnards and other minority groups to the exclusion for the most part of ethnic Vietnamese. Now, twelve men in a camp obviously cannot by themselves mount combat operations of anything other than an intelligence patrol type operation. The plan was, of course, to recruit as mercenaries as many of these ethnic minorities as we could and use them as a strike force.

KASURI: *I've heard it said that by 1964 the NLF was in control of about 80% of the area of South Vietnam. Was that correct?*

I would say that that was a correct estimate. As a matter of fact, in 1964 — if I may make a brief comment on that, the war as such in South Vietnam in the early part of '64, was, as far as we were concerned, was in a deplorable condition in that there was no war going on. Part of my duties as the Area Specialist for III and IV Corps, was to brief the Commander of Special Forces each morning on what had happened in these Corps areas. Other people were responsible for briefing in I Corps and II Corps. The idea of these briefings is to give the idea that the Teams in your area are in fact doing something or that there is a lot going on in your area. It became extremely difficult at times to project the idea that there really was something going on. The man in I Corps, for instance, was almost at a complete loss every morning; his briefing would possibly take two minutes for the whole briefing of what had happened in I Corps. Any action that was going on, in the main, was either NLF initiated according to our intelligence reports, or it was something initiated directly from a Special Forces Camp, a camp or area directly under American control. In other words, if a camp had three companies of strike force in it, the standing orders were that one company would stay in camp, one company would be out of the camp on local patrol or security, and the third company would be out of the camp on a longer range operation. Specifically for the purpose of trying to keep things going, stirring it up, if you will. But in the main, ARVN had virtually ceased to be a fighting force at that time; the desertion rate was appalling of course.

KASURI: *Yes, that's what I was coming to; that there were extensive desertions from the South Vietnamese army at the time, and people were going over to the NLF, the soldiers were going over to the NLF. Now what were the means used by the government of South Vietnam and by the United States forces to stop this kind of attitude?*

As a matter of fact, they really haven't stopped it. I understand the conditions have improved somewhat, but they certainly haven't stopped this desertion rate. As a matter of fact, if a man deserted and was willing to come back, very little was ever done to him; they were just happy enough to see him back. I'll give you a specific example; on Project Delta, where I was working, a very highly classified operation, the very day of the night that we were infiltrating the people into Laos — you can imagine the security necessary for such an operation, to even hope for success — people that had been in on the final briefings for that operation deserted a matter of hours before the operation took off the ground. They came back one way or the other, either by military police supervision or had just walked back, and they were given something like three days in jail and put back to work again.

KINJU MORIKAWA: ... *Concerning assassination teams, do you have any cases in which the assassination teams assassinated Saigon regime officers or other people under the cloak of the N.L.F. to arouse sentiment against the N.L.F.?*

Yes, I do have knowledge of such type operations. It wasn't a widely known thing, but it was known; it was part of the C.I.A. program — I might add that it was at that time, now the assassination teams that are around today are not necessarily working on that basis, ... but back in '63-'64, such was the case: assassinate an individual, and blame it on the N.L.F. I believe it was Senator Young of the United States government who also gave testimony to this, which he claimed he got directly from a C.I.A. officer in Vietnam.

ANDERS: *You will remember Mr. Duncan, that yesterday you opened your report by telling us about the manipulation to which the American soldiers are subjected, about the depersonalization. Now, my first two questions have to do with this problem. Do you think that this transformation of human beings, for instance, of students in the Special Forces school in Carolina where you were teaching in conventional and non-conventional warfare, that this training, this depersonalization was so successful that the students when arriving in Vietnam and confronted with the criminal requirements which they had to fulfill, that they immediately were able to fulfill them, or were they shocked or startled?*

Perhaps I should preface my remarks by saying first of all, I am not a pacifist; that will put my remarks in some sort of context. Given a direct attack on the United States, or whatever country of which I was a citizen, given a direct threat to the country, as an attack by an invader, given the necessity of having to fight a guerrilla war, many or most of the things taught at Fort Bragg, North Carolina and the cruel discipline required to fight that kind of a war. I would consider necessary, and you would need these types of people to defend your land. Where it goes awry in Vietnam, as applied to Vietnam, is that it is part of our whole upbringing, the whole society — that in fact, somehow, we are being threatened by the Vietnamese people; that our society is threatened by the Vietnamese people. Now whether this is real or imaginary is irrelevant. Most of the young soldiers going to Vietnam feel that in fact a real danger does exist to the United States from the NLF and from Hanoi. So this is the justification for their acts; they're not pleasant; they realize they're not pleasant, but they do believe they are threatened. No army is drafted or recruited from the Quakers or other pacifist organizations. These brutal acts become the very part of war . . . What can I say?

ANDERS: *Thank you. I'm very much satisfied with your answer, because it is an answer in another sense than you think. The very fact that the American boys were convinced that America was attacked by the Vietnamese, although no Vietnamese plane or Vietnamese soldier was ever on American soil; this proves that actually the depersonalization and the trans-*

formation of personality was extremely successful. Now a second question which has to do with the psychological problem with which you opened your report too. Do you think that the transformation of human beings which is being performed by the training, that this will be a final one? Do you think that people who come back from Vietnam will live as "Vietnam Veterans" so to speak, in the same way as certain people who came back from the First World War, the generation of Hitler for instance, and were unable to readapt themselves to civilian life, and tried time and again to lead a soldier's life within the civilian world. This is a very important question I think, because if this training is successful it means that another crime is being committed: the crime of transforming normal and average human beings into criminals, and I'm asking you whether you think this crime is being committed in these training schools.

My answer has to be in two parts. A well-trained soldier is not just a man who knows when to shoot; he also is trained when not to shoot. It's a much finer point, given a combat situation; it's a higher degree of training, knowing when not to shoot. And these people, even while in training in Fort Bragg, North Carolina, do have certain contact with the population outside of their training camp. If you were to meet these people, I'm sure you wouldn't be offended by them; they make car payments and have families and so on. I hope this doesn't sound too familiar to some other things I've heard, but they are very nice to their own children, and so on. I think what you have, and this is of course one of the things I have written about at some length, and even within the Army there have been sociological studies made on this program — what does happen to the man when he comes out? It's not so much the fear that he's going to run amok with weapons, and start shooting people on the streets just because he has nothing to do on a Saturday night. Essentially it's in his thinking itself, what makes sense to him, or what doesn't make sense to him, given a particular situation. The man that is willing to admit to the transformation that has taken place, has become aware of it, I think, will naturally readjust himself. I think the majority of people who came back from World War II, or many of them at least, made a fair adjustment, even without realizing — I'm talking about the United States now — made a fair adjustment without admitting that they had actually gone through this transformation. The general attitude of a man when he gets out of the army, let's say a draftee, is that somehow he beat the army, you know, they didn't get to him. And yet he's got an honorable discharge to prove that he did exactly everything they wanted him to do. So this man is not going to admit that in fact they have gotten to him. Now this is going to affect his thinking in this way: he is going to be able to accept what I call a military rationale for such things as Vietnam or foreign policy or internal affairs in the country. For instance, if I can give you a specific, that idea that we — and by "we" I mean the United States — cannot withdraw unilaterally from Vietnam because it would result in a loss of national prestige, is not a normal civilian reaction. That is a military rationale, or let's say it's more common to somebody used to thinking in military terms than it would be for somebody not exposed to the military. I think we've already seen the results of this in our country, because we've now had a draft for 25 years; we've had literally millions of such people coming back into our society; where are they now? They're in the Rotary Clubs, the Junior Chambers of Commerce, they're working for newspapers, they're doctors, they're lawyers, and they're government officials; they are both the elected and the electorate. And then the other people — let's take another group of our society — you have them put under pressure indirectly by the military, through the Selective Service System which we have in the United States; by their own admission, the least function of the Selective Service System is the supplying of manpower to the military; by their own admission, their own documentation, their primary function is, to use their own word, "channeling" manpower into other directions, specifically in areas related to defense industries and so on. Now, whether that means forcing them into school with the threat of the draft hanging over their head so that they will become physicists — again, you create a milieu of war orientation. And it's not that, as an individual, you have created a monster in the normal sense of the word. But it's the whole atmosphere you generate.

WEISS: *Just one final short question, Mr. Duncan. Would you confirm the question, if Vietnam could be regarded as an example for an experimental field, for further activities against liberation movements in other parts of the world, from your experience?*

This is quite true. New weaponry, new technology being developed, modification of tactics and techniques, and of course some have been implemented other places already; witness, the first groups of Special Forces people sent to Thailand were specifically and deliberately picked from people that had worked for some time in Vietnam. And of course all reports, all after-action reports and everything, these are forwarded to the Special Warfare Center at Fort Bragg, North Carolina, and in fact they are adapted to Special Forces activities in such places as Guatemala, Peru, Bolivia, and so on.

Report of the Commission of Inquiry to the United States testimony by Gisele Halimi

Advocate of the Court of Paris; Member of the Legal Commission

This Commission of Inquiry was composed of Gisele Halimi, Attorney at the Court of Appeals of Paris and President of the General Commission of Inquiry of the Tribunal, and Mr. Loup Verlet, Director of Research at C.N.R.S. The Commission was to: 1) Make a census of and gather American witnesses — Vietnam veterans, journalists, reporters, doctors and historians, who were willing to come and give evidence to the Tribunal at Copenhagen. 2) Record on film or magnetic tape the depositions of witnesses who, for important reasons, could not leave the U.S. to go to the Tribunal. 3) Complete the documentation by reporting to the tribunal on the latest works, articles, reports, scientific, legal or historical studies, appearing in the United States which related directly to the three questions Serial No. 1993167; a combatant in Vietnam from 1962 to 1964. Carl prisoners of war, on the treatment of the civilian population and whether the combination of alleged acts constituted the crime of Genocide. In each case, the commission has authenticated the sources and content of the elements gathered.

Depositions Recorded on Magnetic Tape

Carl Campbell: 25 years old, of Detroit, Michigan, U.S.A.; former Marine PFC of Delta Company, 1st Battalion, 7th Marine Regiment; under examination by the Tribunal — namely on the treatment of Campbell was interviewed by Mr. Eric Bosckstael, journalist.

Three tapes have been deposited with the Tribunal. Two of them of a duration of about an hour and a half contain the entire statement of Mr. Campbell. The Commission of Inquiry abstracted from this recording a third tape of a duration of 20 minutes, the content of which precisely and directly concerns these questions under examination by the Tribunal. The interview of Mr. Campbell can be summarized thus:

Speaking of his basic training in the Marines, he declared: "They told us, that if we took prisoners and they became a burden to us, we should kill them."

Question: "Do you know that this is contrary to the Geneva Conventions?"

Answer: "They didn't teach us in the Marines what those Conventions are. The people who taught us did not occupy themselves, I believe, with the Geneva Conventions."

Again on the subject of training and on the subject of ambushes, Campbell relates that an officer asked the trainees: "What would you do when you are on an operation if you see civilians or children in your line of fire?"

No one answered. The officer then roared out: "Kill them!"

At Chu Lai, in the summer of 1965, his group left on an operation. Before entering the first village on their route, the officer said to them, verbatim: "You can kill anything with slanted eyes." The first Vietnamese they saw, an old man of about 80 years, was killed by a Marine. The Marine was immediately congratulated by the lieutenant and promoted two months later. The lieutenant slapped him on the shoulder and said, "That was a good shot, very well done." The officer added that the staff the old man was holding could have been a gun. Several months later this same soldier killed an old woman just as harmless.

Campbell also stated: "When we entered the village we warned the people to leave their homes and to assemble at a certain place; we were then ordered to throw grenades into each house." Having entered the village, the soldiers burned the houses. They amused themselves by tearing the thatch from the roofs and setting fire to it. A Marine had been killed by the Viet Cong the previous day; therefore, the soldiers threw themselves upon the village with a vengeance and devastated it.

Carl Campbell relates what happened to one of his "buddies" from another Company, who had taken part in a difficult operation: "The Viet Cong had been cornered by the American forces with their backs to the sea. They had been furiously bombarded by air and artillery. When the bombardment ceased, my friend was one of those who went into the bombarded zone to see the effects. They found hundreds and hundreds of dead but all of them in civilian dress and only 40 rifles in the whole zone. The estimation of the number of dead varied between 600 to 1,000 civilians. And in other cases as well, those who are killed are called Viet Cong. Thus, they kill no civilians."

The rest of the tape concerns Campbell's own evolution, his crisis of conscience about the political problems of the Vietnam War, the reactions to this subject by his friends, and finally his return to the United States.

James Jones, of the Bronx, New York, U.S.A., fought in the infantry in Vietnam from February, 1965 to May, 1966, in the region of Ben Cat. His deposition was taken in New York by Mr. Loup Verlet, member of the Tribunal Commission.

He testified to facts directly under investigation by this Tribunal: 1) He saw two Vietnamese prisoners thrown from a U.S. helicopter. 2) He saw a woman burned by napalm, to whom medication was refused until she would talk. 3) He was present at the interrogation of a prisoner who had been bound and placed under the wheels of a truck. The truck was to start and crush him if he persisted in silence. Mr. Jones declares that though the tortures were the doing of Vietnamese functionaries, they were working under supervision of American officers who gave the instructions

He added that the American troops had themselves: 1) burned villages; 2) executed a group of civilians; 3) destroyed an underground hospital in which all the patients perished.

On the same tape is recorded the deposition of *Alex Hubbart,* of Staten Island, New York, U.S.A., who spent three years in Vietnam from 1964 to 1966. The American pilots returning from a mission, told him tales of machine-gunning of civilians, destruction of villages, etc. His testimony seems to us imprecise. The Tribunal will have to evaluate its suitability.

Depositions Taken Verbally by Maitre Gisele Halimi

James Clark Child: 29 years old. He was a bomber pilot and served in Vietnam for 18 months from 1966 to 1967. He is presently a seminary student in Theology.

The *San Francisco Chronicle* of Nov. 1, 1967, under the headline "Vietnam Pilot Returns Medal," notes that James Child had returned his war decorations to Secretary of Defense McNamara.

To the journalist who interviewed him, Child explained that these decorations represented "something of which he was less than proud," and that he wanted to provoke in the American public a shock which would cause it to become conscious of the "immorality" and the "futility" of the Vietnam War.

516

The Tribunal Commission member, Gisele Halimi, with Saul Landau, American author, immediately made contact with him and gathered his deposition.

His deposition included these statements: "I served well as bombing pilot for nearly 18 months in Vietnam (1966-1967). I completed 17 bombing missions. Twelve of these missions were deliberately directed against civilian targets. I myself dropped high explosive and incendiary bombs against farms, villages, forests.

"I became aware that I was killing women and children, and I went to protest to my officer, indicating that I would refuse any future missions of that kind. He answered me that it was necessary to obey orders from Washington. Soon after my gesture of protest, I was sent home.

"I am a Christian and I am an American and for these two reasons I would want neither to hurt my country, nor to accept without protest the pursuit of this inhuman and futile war.

"In my letter to McNamara, I declared verbatim: 'My friends and the Vietnamese are dying every day for the ideologies held by leaders who do not understand the proportions of this foolish and agonizing war in Vietnam. I cannot, in my soul and conscience, uphold the policy of escalation and of massive incessant bombardment of North Vietnam.''

"I can give you an example of how this formidable war machine is put to work in order to crush non-strategic objectives: In one of my missions three jet bombers furiously attacked a tiny bridge in a woods, of which the surrounding area had already been attacked. We dropped 18 large bombs and were never able to hit it; all we hit was the river and the surrounding countryside.

"I never personally discharged any napalm or fragmentation bombs, but I can confirm that they are currently used by the American forces.

"I was not witness to the creation of forced labor camps or to deportation of the civilian population, but I knew of the existence of strategic hamlets.

"I would not want in any way to harm my country, which I deeply love, but I wish to help awaken the conscience of my compatriots who must unite their efforts to stop this war.

"I don't believe I'll be able to accept to come to testify before your Tribunal. I shall think about it. But I want, in every way possible, my position to be known."

Mr. Child later made known that he could not go to Copenhagen.

John Hartwell Moore: 28 years old, of St. Louis, Missouri. A former U.S. Army PFC, Serial No. RA 18647. He served in the infantry in Vietnam from December, 1963 to May, 1964. He is presently a student of Sociology at the Ethical Culture Center in New York.

In the province of Quong Duc, Mr. Moore was assistant to a captain advisor to the South Vietnamese. The witness could only testify on the question relating to inhumane treatment and torture inflicted on prisoners.

He stated: "In January, 1964, I was present when a Viet Cong was captured. The South Vietnamese Soldiers, in the presence of American officers, beat him violently about the face until he collapsed.

"Sometime during the month of February, 1964, although I cannot say exactly the day, a prisoner of war was brought into our area. He was bound, hand and foot, and brutally hit with blows of the fist and rifle butt. This prisoner was reputed to be withholding important information. They had to make him talk at any cost. In the presence of an American officer (a Captain), five South Vietnamese soldiers set upon him furiously. He was beaten unmercifully on the chest and the face. Then they lifted him up and carried him, his hands and feet tied, to the edge of a canal. They attached a cord to him which permitted him to be dipped regularly in the water. Each time that he began to choke, they would pull him out by the cord to allow him to talk if he could no longer hold out. The prisoner did not talk.

"It was horrible to see - the body filled with water, the chest bloated; he lost consciousness several times. This torture lasted two hours. Then the South Vietnamese soldiers, on the instructions of the U.S. Captain, gave up the interrogation and took away the prisoner.

"The American officer contented himself with giving instructions and superintending the operation. He did not himself participate in the implementation of the water torture.

"I do not know where this prisoner was taken or what became of him. I did not witness any other things which might enlighten the Tribunal on the other questions you told me about."

Conclusion

. . . In summary we should like to review our method of constructing our evidence to this body. It consists of testimony presented in person by witnesses on the stand before the Tribunal; of filmed testimony; of testimony recorded on magnetic tape; of verbal testimony gathered into depositions by members of this Commission of Inquiry. It included journalistic accounts which impress one with their authenticity and which, thanks to this Tribunal, will be brought to the attention of world public opinion. We have, in addition, made analyses of works by American authors, of Vietnam veterans, and of American citizens directly and personally involved in this war. Finally we present in evidence transcripts of the significant testimony of the proceedings of the court-martial of Captain Howard Levy, which took place in Columbia, South Carolina, U.S.A., in May, 1967.

Our conclusion from reviewing this testimony is that criminal acts have been committed *deliberately, massively* and *systematically* by the U.S. forces and their allies in Vietnam. We further conclude and recommend to the Tribunal that these acts, from a juridical, historical and scientific point of view, can be said to constitute the crime of Genocide by the government of the United States against the sovereign people of Vietnam.

Study on the Erosion of Moral Constraint in the Vietnam War testimony Compiled by Clergy and Laymen Concerned About Vietnam [1]

Eight months ago, as the Vietnamese war continued to widen, discussions in our Executive Committee meetings more and more centered around reports in reliable journals, newspapers and on television which seemed to point to a breakdown of constraint by the United States and allied personnel in military operations.

By constraint we do not mean an adherence to broad and general moral precepts. Norms of constraint are defined as rules in international treaties, ratified by the Government of the United States and therefore part of the supreme law of this land. These "norms" comprise "laws of war" and laws protecting civilians in time of war binding upon all American citizens, civilian and military.

---

[1]Submitted in evidence to the Tribunal by the Committee to the United States headed by Gisele Halim.

It should be made clear that we neither had the expertise nor the climate (cessation of military conflict) for making a formal legal study. However, it did seem appropriate to compare the reliably reported conduct of American operations in Vietnam with the laws of war. As religious leaders we felt an urgent obligation to see if our suspicions were born out by facts.

We were interested to see if there was a general breakdown of constraint and further, to see if it appeared to be accidental and/or followed a pattern.

We initiated the study in early November of 1966. Along with our Executive Secretary, The Reverend Richard R. Fernandez, we asked Dr. Seymour Melman, Professor of Industrial Engineering at Columbia University to serve as research consultant. The project was to proceed in several stages.

•Mr Fernandez and Dr. Melman, working closely together, secured the services of five graduate students at Columbia University.

•The researchers were charged with specific responsibilities.

•The background, purpose, and possible significance of the study was explained to the researchers in some detail.

•Researchers were aware that their work would be viewed by consultants.

•The researchers were first assigned the arduous work of collecting and familiarizing themselves with relevant sections of international law, codes, and regulations regulating activities between nations at war.

•As this was to be a general study and not an attempt to "prove" anything conclusively, researchers were instructed not to collect and/or solicit first hand eyewitness accounts of possible violations.

•We asked the following persons representing the three major religious traditions in this country to act as co-chairmen: Dr. Robert McAfee Brown — accepted; Rabbi Arthur J. Lelyveld — accepted; Father John Sheerin — accepted.

•We will send the co-chairmen the document, the letter of transmittal of the consultants, and ask them to read it and draft an opinion for the approval of the entire committee.

•We will ask the following distinguished religious leaders to accept the role of committee members: (partial list) Bishop Harvey D. Butterfield (Episcopal); Dean John Bowen Coburn, Episcopal Theological Seminary; Bishop Robert L. Dewitt, Jr. (Episcopal); Father John S. Drinan (Roman Catholic), Dean, Boston College Law School; Rabbi Roland Gittelsohn (Reformed), Temple Israel,

Boston; Bishop Charles F. Golden (Methodist); Dr. Dana McLean Greeley, President, Unitarian-Universalist-Association; Rabbi Wolfe Kelman (Conservative), Executive Vice-President, Rabbinical Assembly; Dr. Martin Luther King, Jr. (Baptist), Executive Director, Southern Christian Leadership Conference; Bishop John Wesley Lord (Methodist); Dr. Martin Marty (Lutheran) Professor, Divinity. School, University of Chicago; Dr. James I. McCord (Presbyterian), President, Princeton Theological Seminary; Bishop Kilmer Myers (Episcopal); Bishop J. Brooke Mosley (Episcopal); Father John Courtney Murray (Roman Catholic), Professor, Woodstock College; Dr. Reinhold Niebuhr (United Church of Christ) Professor Emeritus, Union Theological Seminary; Dr. Frederik A. Schoitz, President, American Lutheran Church; Bishop James Shannon (Roman Catholic); Dr. Eugene Smathers, Moderator, United Presbyterian Church in the U.S.A.; Rabbi Jacob Weinstein (Reformed), President, Central Conference of American Rabbis; Bishop John Joseph Wright (Roman Catholic).

*We will circulate the document, the letter of transmittal, and the *Opinion* of the co-chairmen.

*The religious leaders will then be asked to read the document in its entirety. Following a careful reading they will be asked to sign, with the co-chairmen the *Opinion*.

*With the three co-chairmen we will initiate a press conference in New York City to disclose the results of our study, the opinion of our committee, and ask that both the Executive and Congressional branches of our Government take such steps as they deem necessary to rectify such breaches of constraint as indicated in the study.

*We intend to publish the document in its entirety.[2]

---

[2]This study was published as *In the Name of America* by Clergy and Laymen Concerned About Vietnam, 475 Riverside Drive, New York, N.Y. 10027, in January, 1968. It constituted an indictment of the United States' conduct of the war.

A Doctor Reports from South Vietnam

testimony by Erich Wulff

Dr. Wulff was for Six Years a Member of a West German Medical Mission to Vietnam and Taught Medicine at Hue Hospital

Ladies and Gentlemen ... I have just arrived from South Vietnam and I have had no time to draft a text. I decided to come here before this Tribunal for two main reasons. One, because in the six years I spent in Vietnam, I saw a certain number of things which revolted me; and when the opportunity occurred to come here, I seized it immediately. Secondly, because a number of my Vietnamese friends who are rendered silent at the present time, asked me to come here and speak in their stead. It is particularly difficult now to continue after this film that you have just seen, which illustrates to you much better than I could do, what is happening at the present time in South Vietnam. I was not able to bring much photographic evidence: the export of this kind of thing from South Vietnam is difficult. I have not so much seen the actual events, as the effects that these have produced. I shall begin by giving a general and rather superficial view of South Vietnam at the present time, especially, to show you the present reality of South Vietnam. It is recongizable to everyone, without the necessity for a great intellectual effort. You have just seen the South Vietnamese landscape; you have seen the bomb craters. Everyone who flies over South Vietnam now can see that the landscape resembles a human skin that suffers from smallpox. There are eruptions everywhere caused by bomb craters which are especially close to isolated habitations, little hamlets, little valleys. Everyone who flies over the land can see it and can draw his own conclusions. In flying over the country, also, you see vast areas which are destroyed and devastated by chemical products. It is a grave landscape — a landscape of ashes. You see, especially in the coastal region, in the province of Quang Nam, close by Phou Yon, chains of villages, habitations, and rice fields, that have been abandoned — a blanket of death — a landscape of death. One need not be an expert to draw conclusions.

In the towns controlled by the Saigon administration and the Americans, you see whole artificial forests of barbed wire. The American troops, the province heads and the district heads have surrounded the house of every person who collaborates with the Americans with a hedge of barbed wire. The isolation of the Americans and the South Vietnamese officials from the population is immediately visible. There is a desolate chasm between the populated streets and the habitations of the Americans, of the American officers and the South Vietnamese civil servants. For anyone who knows how to look, this already gives a rather clear picture of what is happening in Vietnam. When one goes a little more deeply into events and into the techniques used by the Americans, one can distinguish several main ways by which the war is conducted. The most standard technique is "search and destroy" operations. That is what you have seen just now on the screen. What happens is that a number of helicopters will land in a village. The soldiers enter the houses, they take a certain number of people who live there, especially young ones and women. They arrest them on the pretext that they are suspected "Vietcong" and they take them to interrogation centers. The rest of the population has endured this ceaselessly. It is a nightmare of the thirty years war. After a time the helicopters fly off, and the population remains, stricken with terror and fear.

Now what happens to these prisoners? I have had occasion while working at the Central Hospital of Hue to see about fifty prisoners from the neighboring prisons who were sent to the hospital in extremely serious condition, sometimes just before they died. I can testify to a certain amount of medical data on these prisoners and especially relate material from dossiers which concern their stories and the manner in which they became prisoners. Many Vietnamese medical students helped me — as much as they could — to establish these files. I shall read to you two examples from these original dossiers that I have before me. I shall not publicly name the prisoners because they are still in prison, and I don't want to risk their further suffering. But the names will be in the file I will submit to the Tribunal.

Mr. "X", a farmer of thirty years, is living in Pen Dim, in the Province of Quang Dien. He has been an orphan since childhood. He is married with two children. Condition: poor. He had been in prison three years before being sent to the hospital with a condition of beriberi. The man had been arrested in a raiding operation without any evidence of his guilt. He was suspected of being a Vietcong. He was tortured by kicks on his chest, head, his belly, and then by electric wires wound around the forefinger. After this, he preferred to sign the confession that was presented to him already written. Penalty: four years of prison. After this he was evacuated to the prison of Hue, where he was imprisoned.

The second example, a young girl of 20, living in Top Ku, in the province of Tun Tang, a farmer's daughter, unmarried, living with her parents in a large family. She had been in prison for two years. The arrest was quite identical with the first case — she had been arrested in the course of a raiding operation as a Vietcong suspect. She was tortured, beaten with sticks and given the electric torture. She was made to drink soapy water. The result was that she signed an avowal and was convicted to two years in prison. These are typical cases, and I shall submit them to the Tribunal. There are a few others There are also, of course, some men and women who do not confess and their stories are much worse. They are tortured for a much longer time. No judgement by a court is usually pronounced, and they remain in prison or in a prisoner's camp for an indefinite time. This, in a few words, constitutes the raiding operations, the so-called "search and destroy" operations by the Americans. This is what happens to the people when they are caught up in them. I am convinced therefore — I convinced myself rather — when I spoke with these unfortunates among the poor fifty, that I could suspect that perhaps at least two or three of them had participated in the fighting. But most of them were simple peasants who lived quietly at home, and whose only wrong was of not having fled in time.

The success of these raiding operations from the American point of view has been very limited. In the last two years, the year 1967 especially, another method has been invented. This other process has as its objective to destroy all potential bases for the Liberation troops in such a way that certain areas or districts are stripped of all the inhabitants who happen to live there. This process is especially used in regions where raiding operations have had no lasting effect. In the minds of the Americans, then, the only alternate solution is to remove the entire population. To settle them elsewhere, and during this process of resettlement, to try to find the people who were collaborating with the Liberation Front and put them into prison, into so-called refugee camps which are well-controlled and distributed in groups and within which a confidence man is placed. But one cannot succeed in eliminating a whole population from an area; the people won't go of their own volition. They are attached to their rice fields, to their villages. The mass worship of ancestors plays an important role in the Vietnamese culture. Every peasant Vietnamese wants to live, to marry, to have his children, to die, in the place where he was born — in his own village. So people do not leave. To make them leave they have to be driven, they have to be forced to become refugees. To do this, the Americans use various procedures. According to a relatively recent vocabulary, all this is called to "generate refugees." This expression is used by most of the American civil service; it is, of course, not used at press conferences.

How does one generate refugees? First, one declares a certain region to be a "free fire zone", or a "free strike zone", or a "free target zone", which are the technical terms for this. The Americans then send over planes; the planes drop leaflets in which the population is warned to go to the district headquarters or the chief town. Then because of a "military necessity", real or imaginary, on the part of the Americans, there will be napalm bombing, and machine gunning at will in such a zone which explains the official designation "free fire zone". Despite all this, only a part of the inhabitants leave. If the bombings become intensified, after a few weeks of increased bombing, two thirds of the population can no longer endure life in such a "free fire zone"; they then come to these urban centers. But some still stubbornly remain and the third procedure (the first was the invitation, the second the bombing) is forced evacuation. Forced evacuation is not possible everywhere, there are regions where the forces of liberation are too strong for the helicopters to land, but nonetheless the Americans try. Two provinces where forced evacuation has been practiced are Quong Sin and Pu Yen in central Vietnam. There more than half of the population was turned into refugees. The planes and the helicopters take these people at the point of a gun. They have no possibility of taking their possessions with them. This is a kind of punishment because they did not accept the invitation of the Americans initially. In these provinces massacres occurred. In these two provinces the South Korean divisions the Americans brought are operating. I base this testimony not on my own experience, but on the experience of an American friend, who has lived for two years in these provinces and who was a witness to all this. I cannot mention his name because he is still in Vietnam. Several times there were cases, when, in the course of a raiding operation an NLF soldier fired on a Korean and total massacre of the village was the response. There have been new "Ouradours and Lidices" in these two provinces on several occasions. To give you some figures on the extent of this technique, in the province of Binh Dinh, an American told me that in the month of February 1967, there were 173 evacuated towns, in other words, about half the population of this province. The same is true of the province of Phou Yen. In all, one can count about 2,000,000 refugees in South Vietnam, and I need no longer explain what the term refugee means. Other estimations go as high as 4,000,000. Before, 80% of the population lived in the country, now only 55%.

Now I would like to speak of some of the psychological and material effects of this process. In a rural culture, when the people leave their homes, the cohesion of village life is broken; the people no longer have their rice fields. They are settled around the great American bases; they have to be settled there, because these are the only places where at least a few of these unfortunates can find work. These unfortunates, almost all of whom had land — albeit small plots — in central Vietnam, now have to work as coolees, as boys, this for the men. And the women to work as bar hostesses, as prostitutes.

Very often the children begin careers as thieves, pick-pockets, and as procurers for their mothers and sisters. The uprooting, that such a situation leads to, when it is prolonged over a period of years, is altogether obvious. The effects are obvious, but in addition, the Americans can achieve two other aims. They produce the necessary manpower for the maintenance and building of their bases, the need for which is rather great. And secondly, they can create an economic dependency which is almost entire on the part of these people. For their existence they're dependent on the American camp. The mode of life of these people has been everlastingly destroyed; how can they begin again? They are bound for their subsistence to the existence of the American bases. This of course, as the Americans see it, is not without psychological effects. There is created around the American bases the kind of *lumpen proletariat* that is anarchic, dependent, but which presents certain advantages for the Americans as compared to an integrated peasant population which is too readily revolutionary. These are these new plans which have been executed particularly since the arrival of Robert Komer who is responsible for "pacification" in South Vietnam.

But this undertaking has not really succeeded. In the province of Phu Yen, theoretically one of the most effectively "pacified" provinces by this process, after six months in the refugee camp, a new revolutionary organization has been rebuilt because the people had nothing: the promises were not kept. Because their relatives had been killed, this organization reconstituted itself and what is happening now is that the Americans have to re-raid again these so-called refugee villages. In Vietnam at the present time we have refugee villages of the second and third power, the people having had to leave the village that they had been brought to time and again.

I want to accentuate this — what was the American reaction to these successive failures? First of all, a total Americanization of the war and of the civil administration in South Vietnam. For six months, the Americans have centralized their civil services in each province, giving to these services a name which, though often changed, finally ended by practically reconstructing the French Annamite Protectorate of the old days. More and more the Americans have taken civil administration directly into their own hands. Secondly, these excessive failures and the humiliation that these failures lead to have had a psychological effect. There has been a change in attitude that can be observed in the American soldiers, generally at the end of the third or fourth month of their stay in Vietnam. When they arrive, they are very often subjectively full of good will; their brain is still fresh with sentences they have been taught. They believe they came here to "protect the Vietnamese population from Communist take-over", but at the end of the time they realize that they have no friends, that apart from a thin layer of collaborators and profiteers nobody wants them. No one has responded to this abstract love with which they came; and so the paternalism, the protectionism with which they wanted to surround the Vietnamese transforms itself into a kind of aggressive racism. By the end of this time they have become accustomed to calling each Vietnamese a "gook", or "slant". These are people with slant eyes, and are words of insult which the Americans fling at every Vietnamese without distinction. So what has happened is a kind of crumbling of the edifice of theoretical justification which the Americans had erected for themselves. This results in acts of blind fury; they shoot down in anger prisoners — as you saw on the screen. Another technique which was not on the screen but which the Americans themselves have bragged about in my presence is to throw prisoners alive from helicopters — without parachutes, of course. This is very frequently practiced by the Americans. They also practice torture; but a certain distinction must be made. The Americans, with their hygienic spirit, have an obsession with not getting their hands dirty. So they use the South Vietnamese police and the South Vietnamese so-called elite troops to carry out the tortures — you saw this in the motion pictures a moment ago. As you saw, in 80% of the cases, the tortures are executed by the South Vietnamese troops while the Americans remain to the side with the tape recorders: they record what the people say. The Americans hypocritically say, "These are cruel people. One can do nothing about Asiatic cruelty." These tapes go into calculating machines, and they give statistics: statistics are assimilable to the quiet conscience of the Americans. This was, for me, one of the most disgusting aspects of American behavior in Vietnam as was their blind bombings of villages.

I would like to relate to you an anecdote — there are a certain number of German nurses who served on the hospital boat, *Helgoland*. During the first month of their stay in Saigon they were invited by Americans to go in helicopters on a man-hunt as a diversion.

I have this information from a man who is now the Director of the *Helgoland*. A man who has been a witness to this type of cruelty, more and more of which is occurring.

I want to take advantage of this opportunity to speak to you of a little village in South Vietnam which is called Phu Loc which is in the province of Quang Nam near Danang. The thing of which I speak happened in the month of September, 1967. The village of Phu Loc was already a village for refugees built just a year ago. The village is close to the American logistic base a few kilometers from the great city of Danang. One day, some Liberation Front soldiers came into this village which is a Catholic village, mainly anti-Communist. They came into this village and attacked the American base with mortar fire. The Americans answered with artillery fire on the village. The next day the priest of the village went to the Americans, imploring them not to use drastic means, and he proposed to help them plan an ambush so that they could capture the ones who were guilty. The Americans refused this; the following day the same thing happened, there was an NLF mortar attack. But the next morning a company of Americans came and ordered the inhabitants of the village to leave their houses. They then leveled the entire village, thereby humiliating this priest who at the outset was anti-Communist as were the other villagers. The result was that all the inhabitants fled into the Liberated Zone which fortunately was not very far away. I have a few slides of the village of Phu Loc which I owe to a young American who also worked in Vietnam, who, knowing that I was coming here, gave them to me. They show the effects of American shelling and I will leave them with the Tribunal. In the last few years it has become obvious to almost everyone that what is happening has never been a civil war between Vietnamese, but that it is a war of invasion that the Americans are waging in Vietnam. It is not that this is a new event, but it is only that with the presence of 500,000 Americans this has become visible and undeniable for everyone. Many simple people don't think too much, but they see what is before their eyes. Especially among the young people we find a growing awareness that the Liberation Front has become the only body existing in Vietnam which has the support of the vast majority of Vietnamese. This consciousness is relatively new in this magnitude. The government of Thieu and Ky struck down the Buddhist revolt. For a long time it was hoped that the Buddhists might constitute a kind of third force between the Front and the Americans. This hope has been destroyed and no longer exists. The result therefore is that many youth who first belonged to the Buddhist movement, became members of the Front of National Liberation. What is happening, is not only that the Americans are producing refugees, but they are producing more and more conscious Vietnamese Nationalists who are ready to fight against them.

This is my general report. There are many other things that I might tell you. I could tell you about a certain number of people who had undergone the effects of toxic gases for example in the year 1963 already, whom I personally treated. But I think that this perhaps would not bring much that is new to the Tribunal.

Chairman: I wonder if you would be willing, Dr. Wulff, to respond to questions from members of the Tribunal?

Yes.

MADAME DE BEAUVOIR: *I should like to know in somewhat more detail what goes on in these refugee camps. Can they leave these villages? Are there some who have brought with them some property, something they can work with? Exactly how does this work?*

It varies a great deal. The ones who have come at the first arrest are treated better than those who are evacuated by force. These normally must spend several months in an enclosure that they cannot leave. They are fed rice given by the government, a good percentage of which is stolen by the civil servants. This was established by the Kennedy committee recently. The people who come to them normally by themselves find a relatively open camp. But they don't find land. Either they're settled around the American base camp, or they're sometimes settled along the coast line and they are told to become fishermen. Every Vietnamese knows how difficult it is to suddenly become a fisherman. So, practically speaking, there are all possible gradations between a real concentration camp and a more or less open camp where people are subject to economic servitude.

MELBA HERNANDEZ: *You have just told us in your report that the population that you spoke of had been obliged, because of the methods used by the American government, to find a solution to these problems within the National Liberation Front of South Vietnam. Could you tell us in more detail about the way in which they come to the National Liberation Front?*

I must say that personally I have not had direct contact with the National Liberation Front; but I know from a number of my students how things very often happen. There are several transitional stages; more often than not a young man who comes from a middle class family, a student, who has been indoctrinated as an anti-Communist, cannot help seeing the reality of this war. The first stage is a kind of pacifism, and he joins a kind of Buddhist or Catholic pacifist group. Both exist at the present time in Vietnam; both fight against the American invasion; they can write in a semi-clandestine way and this has the advantage for a young man of giving him a place where he can think calmly. Often he realizes after a certain time that this is not enough, and this pacifist movement cannot lead to anything, cannot bring peace. And then a second step is taken after six months or a year — complete membership in the Liberation Movement. The Liberation Front *can* fight against the American invasion . . . I should like to say that especially during these last two years, the middle class, civil servants, tradesmen and so on, and those also belonging to the various religious groups, they have joined the Liberation Movement. And this is happening more and more.

GUNTHER ANDERS: *Is this true, this story about the American officers who invited German nurses to take part in helicopter hunting of Vietcong, in order to amuse them, because the American officers wanted to give them a nice time? First, I would like to know whether the German nurses accepted such invitations; second, how they reacted. Nothing about it was published in the newspapers of Federal Germany. Federal Germany is extremely proud of this hospital boat which they have in the waters of Vietnam. When you read the magazines and newspapers of Federal Germany, you will see in almost every issue something about this hospital boat Helgoland. Now, could you tell me, could you answer the question?*

The first answer is that the Americans have succeeded — for foreigners living in Saigon — to create an image of the Vietcong which is not at all a human image, but that of a shadow, a kind of non-human-existence. And to hunt shadows just does not evoke for these girls the image of human beings being shot upon. Besides, it's done from quite high altitude; you don't see human beings; you see only points — a little thing which is running. I think this more or less answers the question of why, physchologically, the nurses did accept and did not react, most of them, very violently to this. For them the Vietcong was a theoretical being. I must say, to be just, that with the change of the Medical Director of the *Helgoland,* all these practices have been stopped. The new director of the *Helgoland* has not only forbidden this, but has also forbidden to all his medical personnel to attend American military cocktails or to go to American officers' messes. Since the ship is in Danang, they are doing, to at least this extent, some useful work: they treat a big number of war casualties. They show napalm-burnt children to everyone who comes on the ship. Of course they can't write about it. Nor could I when I was working.

They sign a contract agreeing not to say anything during the time they are there. But some weeks ago, one nurse ended her contract and went back to Germany and published an article about the napalm-burnt children she treated on the *Helgoland* . . .

RUSSELL STETLER: *Dr. Wulff, in the course of your presentation, you gave us an estimate of approximately 2,000,000 refugees. From the context in which you placed this figure, I infer that this refers only to refugees whose situation results from American policy; not, for example, to refugees who may have been regrouped as a result of the Geneva Agreements.*

Only the refugees of this last war. The figures are different because this 2,000,000 refers only to refugees living in refugee camps. When you speak of 4,000,000 you speak of people who have been attracted by American bases, by higher paid jobs, and so on and so on. And who were not forced out, but more or less came by themselves to the urban units . . .

MR. KASURI: *You mentioned that when the Americans come, they come with a lot of sentiment for trying to defend the South Vietnamese from Communism, and in three or four months their attitude changes, and they are brutalized and they begin to have no regard for human life. You also indicated that nevertheless the war continues unabated. Now does that have any effect upon the minds of the Americans or the South Vietnamese. Did you ever discuss this matter with any American friends?*

The more intelligent American civilian sees, of course, after a certain amount of time, that things are not going well. Quite often he tries to get a transfer, to get out of Vietnam, to get elsewhere, not to see, anymore, what happens there. But, when an American official gets promoted, he more and more loses contact with reality. I had such a case with an American who once was low-ranking, whom I knew pretty well. He knew very well what was going on. But then he became one of the chief advisors of Ambassador Lodge, and in this position, he repeated and believed what he was told. So, the higher up you get in the heirarchy, the less informed the Americans are — all the more able they are to blindfold themselves and to feel only what they want to feel. Then a third reaction is "we don't care about the Vietnamese. this is purely an American affair and we fight here because we don't want to fight at San Francisco." This is given as a primary reason . . . the Americans are defending themselves there. Of all these theories, the dominant one is that Hanoi and the Liberation Front are nothing but the tools of Peking. So that is a very frequent American reaction in Vietnam too.

KASURI: *I do not know if your duty brought you in touch with hospitals outside Hue. But I would like to know if you did have any such contacts. And secondly, in Hue hospitals, did you come across a large number of persons who bore napalm burns and sulphur bomb burns?*

There are weeks when the hospitals are over-crowded with victims of the war; other weeks, when military activity is not so extensive in this region for the time, they are less crowded. I have seen and worked in a little country hospital in Quang Tri province about 60 kilometers from Hue in a so-called contested area. I, myself, have seen victims of napalm, of burnings, of shells, of artillery and everything else which happened. One of our students has made a statistical survey in the surgical ward of how many of the patients had been hurt by American firepower and how many by Vietcong firepower. We averaged, as in Danang where an American doctor made the same investigation, about 80% of victims are victims of American firepower.

PETER WEISS: *Dr. Wulff, during your long stay in Vietnam when you treated many patients who were wounded did you ever have the possibility to investigate where the weapons, or the napalm, or other chemical mediums were produced?*

No.

WEISS: *When you have a napalm patient, you see him burning?*

Yes, of course . . . I also saw sixty people burned by vomiting gas, in '63 which was probably an American mistake because they put it on Buddhist demonstrators at this time. From later reading newspaper reports that the same symptoms had been seen in the liberated area, I could make a conclusion that it has been the same product. Marked burnings of second degree, vomiting, cramps, loss of consciousness for some time. It was our experience there that the quantity of the gas delivered decided whether it was harmless or whether it was very, very dangerous or mortal. The Americans carried out some demonstrations to show that the gas was benevolent, but at these demonstrations they only released small quantities. In actual use, to flush people from tunnels and hideouts, the quantities are greater and the concentration is mortal.

CARL OGLESBY: *Mr. Wulff, you said you had personal experience with victims of chemical warfare. Could you tell us a little bit more about that?*

Well, that's only what I could tell you. That the symptoms which I have just told to you — temporary blindness, marked burnings of the skin, vomiting, fall of blood pressure . . . The first number of people were saved only by immediate medical care: in other circumstances they would have died.

OGLESBY: *What — with only the use of weapons such as tear gas?*

Well, this was declared tear gas, but it was of another tear gas. It was a kind of modified tear gas; it makes tears too. But as I told you, we have the impression that the effects depend upon the concentration. A slight concentration, it could be a tear gas; at a strong concentration, it could be a toxic gas.

OGLESBY: *Let me just get this straight: are you saying you've seen people whose skin is burned by what is called tear gas?*

Yes, yes, yes. What the Vietnamese administration told us later was that it was nothing but tear gas.

OGLESBY: *What about the use of weapons against foliage and crops? Have you seen any of that, or do you know of any of that?*

I don't know anything about its nature, I've only seen the effects on the woods and on the forests and on this I have no immediate knowledge. But in 1961 already, American advisors told me they had made the first experiment with this thing. It is not employed only now, when the war is going badly, but already in 1961, This is kind of a secret.

OGLESBY: *Another witness has testified that at some phase of the war the defoliants were used against forest areas for the purpose of unmasking the troops that might have taken concealment there. Also that this tactic, having failed, this anti-foliage weapon is now turned against the food sources of the people. Does your experience confirm that?*

Yes, I was told this by American personnel who have used it against foodstuffs, and against rice fields and against crops; even now it is used in the forests, too, despite the ineffectiveness. A kind of curious reflex of, well, eliminating a landscape when they are unable to elimate people. When I am flying from Hue to Saigon I discover new spots every time which have been defoliated . . .

DELLINGER: *I'd like to ask two questions. Dr. Howard Rusk from the United States visited Saigon and surrounding areas at a time when American people were beginning to have qualms about the use of napalm. I believe he was sent officially by the President of the United States to make an inquiry. He reported that he found very few children in the hospitals in South*

Vietnam who had been burnt with napalm. I'm not sure whether it originated with Dr. Rusk, himself, but there was general dissemination in the United States of the idea that most of the burnt children in South Vietnam had been burned by the explosion of kerosene stoves due to their own neglect. I'd like you, on the basis of your own experience in hospitals there, to comment on that.

Well, I think that most people who have been there longer, including even a certain number of anti-Communist American newsmen, or German newsmen — the photographer Horst Fass from AP for instance, would tell you that they have seen, as I have, plenty of napalmed burnt children. Of course, when you see a heavily burnt child, it's extremely difficult to tell where the burn came from. Also the people are afraid. The parents are intimidated; they are told quite often not to tell investigators that it was napalm. Secondly, even when they are not explicitly intimidated, there is a kind of base of fear when an American is approaching asking this kind of question. When it is a doctor they fear that they will not get the same kind of help when they say this has been the fault of Americans; so they do not say that. This would explain why other people of different nationalities from Americans get different answers from the same people as to the origins of the burns.

DELLINGER: *At the opening of your statement you said that some of your Vietnamese friends who had been silent asked you to come and tell the true facts to this Tribunal. Later you mentioned the cases of two prisoners and said there were others. Is this the type of silencing you refer to or is this some other type of silencing?*

No, not only this very brutal type of silencing but the impossibilities for a lot of people who are still living at their homes, who are not in prison, to express themselves and to tell what happens. There is censorship in Vietnam; you can't publish, and it is very difficult to get things across. I'm speaking partly of my students, partly of other Vietnamese friends — lecturers whom I know in Saigon.

OGLESBY: *Your first-hand experience in Vietnam is doubly invaluable because you've been there a long time and recently. I wonder if you could comment — it may be a difficult question — on the strategic change, if any, that you've seen over the period in the conduct of the war by the Americans. Five years ago, were the Americans more restrained than they are today? And was their treatment of the population different from what it is, and if there have been important changes, could you relate those changes to the changes in the political and military nature of the war?*

534

Well, I will try to answer this question as well as I can. The first big influx of American military advisors to South Vietnam started in November, 1961, after the Taylor Mission, and during '62. From 3000 it went up to about 20,000 American advisors. Those advisors served the Vietnamese troops at that time. There had not yet been independent American units in Vietnam. And the role of those advisors was not yet very definite. Some of them had their units in their hands and could do with them what they wanted, other ones did not, and had to follow more or less, what the Vietnamese commander wanted to do. The direct American impact on the war was much smaller and more or less restricted to the so-called Special Forces. The Special Forces during this first period of the war were the only units directly in the hands of the Americans. They were paid by the Americans and conducted to war by the Americans. Those operations were mainly in the mountain regions near the Laotian and Cambodian borders, and to some extent, in the Mekong Delta which at this time was largely dominated by the Liberation Front. Then a big change came in about February or March of 1965 when the period of "search and destroy" operations began. Later on the operations tried to get the main force units of the Liberation Front. This "search and destroy" tactic failed more or less and a second stage was adopted which had as its objective the generation of refugees: to produce vast areas where no life exists. But this too was futile because the refugee camps created by this tactic only have to be cleaned out again. And with 1965 the Americans started to bomb these hamlets in South Vietnam. Before 1965 it was mainly the Vietnamese Airforce trained by the Americans, aided by some American helicopter pilots, which carried out these raids. But after 1965, massive bombing of the population by the Americans became the rule. This bombing was carried out not only in the sparsely populated areas in the mountains but also in the heavily-populated areas in the coastal plains, areas which are *very heavily populated* indeed. These areas have been declared "free strike zones." For instance, the so-called "Street without Joy" in the Phong Dien and Quang Dien districts.

OGLESBY: *The question has been put to the Tribunal whether the American troops, perhaps, might have committed acts which could be called genocide in Vietnam. I would like to stress some problems and ask your opinion. If you think that the American troops in Vietnam now fight not only against the NLF or what they consider the "aggression from the North", or if you think it is war against the entire population? If you think that the Americans, because of the techniques of their war and in order to attain military success, might fight against everything which lives, everything which moves? And if this could not be called a war against an entire population rather than a war against a military enemy.*

Well, I think I would affirm this, but in a certain form. The creation of vast territories called "free strike zones", in my opinion, proves this: that they're waging a war against an entire population with the pretext that somewhere inside there might be some enemies. Most Americans in Vietnam do not realize conceptually, that this is what they are doing; in fact they are. They try to repress this knowledge, but from time to time, they will not succeed. Then those primitive reactions of the simple Marine that "every gook should be killed", which is a kind of primitive realization of truth. What the Americans are really doing, the primitive Marine, in his own way, realizes more clearly than the high-ranking American official who tries not to admit this.

Report on American Conduct of the War in the South
testimony by Jean Bertolino

Mr. Bertolino is a French Journalist

My testimony will concern the treatment of civilian populations and the treatment of prisoners of war. On the subject of the treatment of civilian populations I will treat more particularly:

1. Raiding of villages — description of the attack on a village in the sector of Loc Tanh Trung, which was entirely destroyed.

2. Arbitrary detentions — the arrest in this village of four old men, simply because they were there.

3. Operation "scorched earth" in the Iron Triangle.

4. Deportation of the population — description of the refugee camp of Phu Cong, at the end of "Operation Cedar Falls", in the Iron Triangle. Rach Tien, where half of the city was emptied of its population in order to install an American camp there; at about 7:00 in the evening, the second half was proclaimed an "unsafe zone" and anything that moved was shot on sight.

5. Massacre of the population — from his helicopter General Dane shoots at anything that moves. In honor of General Ky, troops indiscriminately shot up the countryside without a care for those who might happen to be there.

6. Moral damage to the population and social deterioration — in Saigon, prostitution has become the best way to earn a living; corruption reigns; at the end of a day spent in the camp of Phu Cong, the young women, compelled by the need for money, sell themselves to the G.I.'s. Repercussions of segregation in the American Army.

7. On the treatment of prisoners of war — the beheading of four captured Vietcong, at Rach Kien.

In the Delta; at an Attack on a Vietnamese Village

It was daybreak. Below us, some apparently peaceful villages were lying in a row. The fourteen Iroquois helicopters, each carrying eight soldiers, were flying in tight formation. On either side of the cabins, helmeted machine-gunners, with fingers on the triggers of the 12-7s fixed on each side of the fuselage, scrutinized the groves of coconut and banana trees which surround Delta villages.

Suddenly, the weapons of the whole 28 machine-gunners began to crackle. I peered around to see what was the target capable of unleashing such a furious volley. On my left, I perceived a tiny village nestled in the heart of a banana grove. The captain, an American of Puerto Rican origin, some thirty years old, pointed at the fragile straw huts partly hidden by the vegetation. He said to me: "Here is our objective." The helicopters made a sharp turn, while the machine-gunners continued firing at the dwellings.

The Iroquois hovered over a rice field and hung one meter from the ground. Encumbered by my photographic equipment, stunned by the deafening roar of the shooting, I remained frozen in my place. A huge Negro, flinging himself out of the copter, took me by the arm saying: "Get out, get out."

I hit the shifting, slippery, wet earth, which enveloped me to the waist; on all sides there was shooting. I floundered awkwardly behind an embankment which separated two rice-paddies and, covered with mud, I witnessed a hallucination-like ballet. The Iroquois, having disembarked their men, climbed very high in the sky. Now, like enormous dragonflies, they charged down in closed ranks on the straw huts, firing strings of rockets fixed in pods on their fuselage. Then, regaining altitude, they plunged down again shooting at the silhouettes fleeing from the flaming houses. The helicopters disappeared and the noise of their whirring blades faded away. The Company which was part of the 2nd Battalion of the 25th Infantry Division, found itself alone. After the infernal uproar of the attack, the few sporadic shots seemed like silence.

The straw huts seemed deserted. The G.I.'s approached them prudently, suspicious of the least tree trunk, the least abnormal object, the least weed, in fear of booby-traps. But in this small village only 30 km. south of Saigon, in the district of Loc Tanh Trung, there were no traps. Each house was meticulously searched; one sensed that their inhabitants had fled in panic. Small bags and sacks full of rice were lying with their contents scattered on the tables. Almost all the hearth fires were lit; in some of them the water in the kettles was still boiling. Here and there, out of sight, in the bushes, at the foot of trees, even inside of the dwellings, were deep holes or entrances to tunnels which the villagers had dug to protect themselves as well as they could from the aerial and land bombardment. Methodically, a young blond corporal pulled the pin on a grenade and threw one in each hole that his attention was called to. He did not wait to see the result: no one else saw it. The grenades, exploding underground, made dull noises, and the holes caved in.

At Ba Thu, the Children are Afraid of Whites

At the time, I tried to reassure myself — telling myself that there could not have been anyone hidden in the holes; we had heard no cry. Later I had proof to the contrary. Fifteen days after that operation, I left for Cambodia. Under the auspices of the Khmer authorities, I went into the province of Svay Rieng to visit the Vietnamese village of Ba Thur, situated only a few meters from the South Vietnamese border inside Cambodian territory.

On December 30, 1966, with the justification that Ba Thu served as a refuge for the "Vietcong", the Americans attacked it in the same way as that Company of the 2nd Battalion of the 25th Infantry Division attacked the village in the district of Loc Tanh Trung. All the banana trees, the bamboos, and the palm trees had been mowed down or deeply marked at the height of a man by the bullets of the machine-guns. Nothing but blackened beams remained of six straw huts burned by rockets. Arriving at Ba Thu with their guns spitting fire, the Americans found no one there to welcome them. When I arrived the whole population was outdoors: hundreds of children, women, old men. I approached a group of little girls. Screaming with fright, they ran away. The village chief, visibly disturbed, said to me: "What do you want, they take you for an American!" At my approach, a little boy hid himself weeping behind his mother's legs. A woman of some 40 years collapsed in tears when I paused in front of her. The chief, taking me by the arm, showed me the individual shelter holes in the ground.

"When the Americans arrived, they threw grenades into the shelters. That woman's two sons were hidden at the bottom; they died at one stroke. A young woman of 20 and a man of 40 were also killed in this raid. We are still without news of ten men that the Americans took away with them in helicopters."

Was Ba Thu a "Vietcong" village? Lacking proof, I can't give an opinion. I was surprised by the individual holes, the earthen bunkers, and also by the fact that, among all the villagers who were gathered around me, there were practically no young men, between the ages of 15 and 30. The Khmer official who accompanied me said that the village had already been under South Vietnamese attack, two years ago, and the people thought it prudent to build shelters in case of eventual repetition. As for the young men, he said they were "in the country."

Four Old Men Arrested

Whatever the political affiliations of this village, even if it were "Vietcong", this hardly excuses the U.S. unit responsible for the violations of the territory of a sovereign country not directly engaged in the Vietnamese conflict.

When I had been with my Company at Loc Tanh Trung, I had not felt, as at Ba Thu, the horror of the attack against that little Delta village. I had not felt it because I was on the side of the attacker. I was not conscious of the tragedies, the destruction, that we caused. As I said before, I did not really believe at the moment that human beings could be hiding in the holes. I even found the blond corporal with the grenades rather likeable at the time.

And then, hadn't the American captain assured me that this village was the refuge for a Vietcong battalion? At the beginning of the attack I believed that the engagement was going to be between soldiers: Americans on one side, Vietcong on the other. But when I saw four old men in custody of a G.I. coming out of a house, I got my first surprise. Thin, with emaciated faces, shrunken, wretched, these men had not the look of combatants. They had been hiding in the piles of hay drying in the sun in front of the straw huts.

The four old peasants were brought before the captain. Their knees were knocking — they were terribly afraid. The officer tied their hands behind their backs, then called over one of the ARVNS — Vietnamese soldiers who always accompany the American units. "Dien, interrogate them."

For more than an hour, the militiaman, speaking harshly and shaking them, questioned the four men: "Where are they hidden? Come on, talk, or you will be killed!"

The foot-soldiers, glad for the respite, settled against the embankments and hungrily devoured the tins of turkey, of chicken with noodles, or of ham and beans in their C-Rations. Finally, the captain, tired of waiting, gave the signal to depart. We had hardly made our exit from the village when a brisk steady fire met us. Right near me, I saw a machine-gunner fall, hit by a bullet in the leg. The Vietcong had hidden themselves in ambush in the two thickets on both sides of the trail.

"Stop. Everone flat on the ground."

Seizing the microphone of one of the four "wireless" sets constantly in contact with the Command Post of Rach Kien, the commander of the company gave the co-ordinates of the two thickets. One minute later, 105mm shells and 80mm mortar rounds began to rain down less than 50 meters from us, in the rhythm of one every four seconds, on the two objectives. The artillery fire lasted more than two hours without interruption. When the officer ordered three of his sections to the assault on the enemy's positions, I was sure that the G.I.'s would find only mangled corpses lying next to their bunkers. I was amazed to hear blasts upon the jump-off of the assault wave and saw four G.I.'s fall, wounded in the hips and the legs.

The two thickets were not occupied until very late in the evening. We found only some empty bunkers, several stained with blood. But not a body, not a weapon were discovered. We left the village and all night as we marched along the dikes separating the rice fields toward our Headquarters, we were harassed by snipers. This is an exact account of what is called "pacification". Why was it carried out? Simply because during night patrols in this sector, American soldiers had met with some shots. What was the real result of the "pacification" . . . ? A village destroyed; men, women and children, dead in the individual shelters, mangled by grenades; a few American soldiers wounded, and four old men carried off without reason, this was the sum total of the effort.

Operation "Scorched Earth" in the Iron Triangle

During my sojourn, the Americans began "scorched earth," operations in War Zone C, around Tay Ninh, along the Cambodian border, and in the "Iron Triangle" — that area encompassing about 100 square miles, situated scarcely 50 km. from Saigon, near the cities of Lai Khe, Ben Cat, Ben Sat and Ben Suc.

During "Operation Cedar Falls", I was at the front lines with the 173rd Airborne Division of paratroops who, just after the passage of the B-52's had drawn the mission of clearing the communication routes of mines and booby traps and to prevent ambushes of heavy material convoys.

Several days earlier at a press conference Major Stuart had told us correspondents that the G.I.'s were going to attack and destroy a Vietcong position which had, until then, remained untouched. This position was, according to the major, the Headquarters of the Vietcong Command for the Saigon sector. Filled with mines, tunnels, hiding-places, hospitals, underground dwellings, the targetted zone had existed since the time of the Vietminh and had never been attacked by the French.

Immediately after the announcement, I took the helicopter for Lai Khe, headquarters of the 1st Infantry Brigade, also dubbed the "Iron Brigade." There, in the shade of a plantation, near the planter's house which today houses the commanding general, of the brigade, a young lieutenant explained to me, on a blackboard, the attack plan.

"The paratroops and the Cavalry are going to enter the 'Iron Triangle' on one side and will form, so to speak, the 'beaters'. Other units, including the 1st U.S. Infantry and the 5th South Vietnamese Infantry, will wait at the edge of the forest for the Vietcong who will be driven out."

I was having trouble grasping all his words as the artillery fire was constant and deafening.

"We are teasing the V.C.'s a bit while waiting for the B-52's", the officer explained to me.

"When are they coming?"

"This evening. You will have to stop up your ears."

The day before my arrival, reconnaissance planes had flown over the villages in the zone to be "cleared" and had dropped pamphlets ordering the population to take refuge immediately in a camp set up for them 12 km. away in the city of Phu Cong. They had also dropped safe-conduct passes for the Vietcong on which were written: "With this safe-conduct, you can give yourself up to any of the allied forces."

I was stretched out on a cot when the B-52's came, and the bombs began to fall. In all my life, I have not heard such a roar. When the B-52's bombard South Vietnam, all of Indochina trembles. Cambodians have declared to me that the tremors reverberate even to Phnom Penh, and that windowpanes rattle there.

541

The next day, with the 2nd Company of the 173rd Airborne, I landed in the section that had just been bombed. It was like traveling through a moon-scape. On several hectares, craters 15 to 20 meters in diameter and at least 8 meters in depth were crowded one on another.

"The bombs were dropped on what we thought to be the center of the Vietcong headquarters," I was told by Sig Holtz, the Company Commander. "The ground below must be full of tunnels. There can't be many survivors among the Vietcong."

The medical-corps captain who accompanied our regiment told me that, even 30 meters from the impact area of a bomb, one has no chance of coming out of it. The concussion makes skulls explode like fireworks. From this point on, we had to watch out for these bombs, making sure that the artillery and the small arms kept up a veritable screen of fire in front of us, zeroing-in some 20 meters ahead of the column.

After ten minutes, we reached the jungle. Other regiments were operating around us and the air whistled with the blasts which were going off in all directions. A village of straw huts was attacked and set afire without anyone taking the trouble to see if there were anyone in the houses. I learned then from the paratroops that several women had been burned alive, but I did not see this in the sector where I happened to be.

Two days later, when the heavy weapons and armor had joined us, three tanks were placed at the head of the column in order to open up the way. They were followed by half of our unit, the other half escorted three bulldozers which, at the rear, finished the work of the tanks. At the head, a dog-handler held the leash of a German Shepherd trained to hunt down Vietcong. Several times, the animal stopped, pricked up his ears, then led us to a tunnel entrance.

"There are V.C. alive down there," the handler would cry. "My dog only smells-out the living ones."

Two men sprayed the tunnel entrances with machine-gun fire, before going in pistol-in-hand. Several enemy corpses were thus found. Often the tunnels were veritable labyrinthes, several kilometers long. The specialists could not go to the end of them without risk. They lowered strings of T.N.T. which they fixed to the walls. Covered with mud they came back out and lit the fuse. In a single day, they blew up more than 30 tunnels. In certain hiding-places, one sensed that, in their panic, the occupants had not been able to carry away all their equipment. Ponchos were scattered around on the water-soaked ground. Several small cloth sacks, closed by strings, each contained a bowl and a pair of chop-sticks. Some cardboard parcels, the size of boxes of kitchen matches, and enclosed in a watertight plastic wrapping, were piled up in a corner. I opened one of them. It contained novocaine, a plastic vial of medicinal alcohol, another of mercurochrome, adhesive tape and pills for dysentery.

A battalion which was operating near our company discovered two underground hospitals, on three levels, and captured a nurse. I don't know what became of the woman for I was unable to track her down in the prisoner camps of Phu Cong or Lai Khe, nor did I see the hospitals or any of the patients. A Negro corporal who was there told me later: "Everything was blown up."

Near Provincial Route 14 which separates the Iron Triangle into two portions, the U.S. High Command halted the operations. Some women who had taken refuge in the camp of Phy Cong after the attack began and who were frightened by the display of American force, had asked for authorization to return to look for their husbands and children. In spite of the mortar and 105mm shells which continued to fall on the unoccupied positions despite the theoretical end of operations, they disappeared into the foliage. They were told to tell those who wanted to give themselves up that, if they approached by the road without weapons, they would be well treated.

The next day, the women returned, accompanied by 15 guerrillas in black pajamas stained with mud, most of them hardly 18 years old. The battle resumed and lasted another ten days. All was shattered, burned, and crushed under the tons of bombs, under the caterpillars of tanks and the giant shovels of the bulldozers.

The Phu Cong Refugee Camp

The Iron Triangle took a heavy reckoning, 500 dead — without counting the victims of the B-52's that one cannot see — among whom are women, children, and especially, the adolescents who serve in the ranks of the Vietcong. There were 6,500 refugees crowded together under tents and behind barbed wire, as in a concentration camp. Some had been able to bring their water buffaloes, hogs or their chickens. Others lived on only the rice distributed "for free" by the Americans twice a day. Rice which is in fact part of the some 4,000 tons gathered up from the villages in the Iron Triangle.

What will become of those who now have no home? The rice-fields, left fallow for a long time, will not be cultivated again. Without doubt, many will remain at Phu Cong and will attach themselves to a patch of land too small to support them. Some will go to the periphery of Saigon, already overcrowded, and to live will join in the mad scramble for the dollar. The young women will prostitute themselves to help their families; some of them did not wait long to do it. I have seen them sell themselves for 100 piasters to the G.I.'s who pass in front of them — no other solution for survival is available to them. The mothers and the elder daughters often have to care for eight or ten children. As for the men in the camp, there are none under the age of 50: they are dead, prisoners, or in the Resistance.

In the Iron Triangle, the peasants managed to eke out a subsistance living on products of their farms, their cattle, the ricefields. Here at Phu Cong, is a world where the piaster and the dollar are king: where without money one cannot live. It is necessary, therefore, to earn this money — no matter how — otherwise one dies of hunger. I am not going to dwell on the conditions of life in these camps. They are inhuman. Others have already said so, and I can confirm it.

At Rach Kien, the Population was Driven from Half the City

Rach Kien, in the heart of the province of Long An, on the banks of the Saigon River, 21 km. from the capital, is one of the rare cities of the Delta to be permanently occupied by the U.S. forces. The 25th Infantry Division, stationed at Cu Chi, installed its 2nd Brigade there. To this small town the helicopters of the 1st "Air Cav", stationed at An Khe, came to look for the Company that had theoretically annihilated the Vietcong battalion in their fortress in the Loc Tan Trung area. For want of anything better, as we have seen, that company had to content itself with taking away four old men: four old men who were taken to the local prison, a straw hut surrounded by barbed wire, to be interrogated more methodically than could be done on the battlefield. The Americans often send prisoners into "reeducation camps". Often as well, they entrust them to the South Vietnamese Special Forces who have some effective methods for "reeducation".

Rach Kien was one of the first "strategic hamlets" created by Ngo Dinh Nhu in 1959. At the time the Diemist regime believed that a system modeled on the methods used by the English in Malaysia would bring an end to the Communist guerrilla. He made a mistake. In Malaysia the majority of the guerrillas were Chinese while the peasants were of the Malaysian race. Ethnic rivalries prevented any collusion between the farmers and the revolutionaries. Therefore the strategy of the transformation of the villages into fortified hamlets worked. But in Vietnam, the peasant and the Vietcong are not only of the same race but often from the same locality. And in spite of efforts taken to isolate the rural population from the "rebels" collaborative solidarity was inevitable. Rach Kien, because of the participation of the population in the revolt, fell at the end of one year: the militia of Nhu were executed.

From that time on the city with its 5,000 inhabitants was the most important village occupied by the N.L.F. in South Vietnam. Situated at a center of communications by river or land, it was at once utilized as a clearing-house and resting place. Rice from the Delta and smuggled weapons were warehoused here before being forwarded by junk, by elephant, even by truck, to the provinces in the central region between Danang and Hue where the bloodiest engagements took place. These same junks would bring back the sick and wounded N.L.F. fighters who — even so near Saigon — would find quiet, more wholesome and abundant food, and better equipped hospitals than in the damp and gloomy underground dispensaries of the jungle.

That the Vietcong could hold an important area so close to the capital was a permanent source of embarassment to the American Command. As soon as a sufficient amount of men and material could be mustered they hastened to change this. Beginning in 1965, when G.I.'s disembarked in great numbers in South Vietnam, Rach Kien was for several days pounded by artillery. Then, in the same way that the Company of the 2nd Brigade attacked the village of Loc Tan Trung, waves of helicopters came. They landed all around the city and disgorged foot-soldiers who began to surround it house-by-house. Under the violence of the fire the Vietcong retreated. In order not to risk the decimation of the children, the women and the old men by air strikes, mortar fire and 105mm shells, the "VC" disengaged and dispersed to surrounding hamlets.

The U.S. soldiers then took possession of half the town and drove the population into the other half. All around their positions a network of bunkers, protected by sandbags were loaded with weapons and surrounded by anti-personnel mines, that could be triggered electrically by the guards. On the demarcation line between the two areas, a soldier in a sentry-box checks the papers of the peasants who must cross the U.S. sector in order to go to the fields. In the evening a tank comes to squat in the middle of the road with its cannon and its 50mm machine guns zeroed-in on the center of the market-place. After 7:00 p.m. the Americans shut themselves up in their camp; as soon as night falls they shoot at everything that moves in the other quarter.

A colonel who received me in the map-room said, "Who would come when it gets dark, but "Charlie" who we have chased out and who uses the darkness to visit his family."

The entire wall was papered with maps of the area. On one was written the word "Confidential." I saw Rach Kien, circled in red.

"What does this circle mean?" I asked the Colonel.

"It designates the sector within a radius of 12 km. of the Command Post that we are at present trying to pacify. The village of the district of Loc Tan Trung that we attacked when you were with us is here inside the circle."

"And beyond, what is there?"

"Beyond," answered the colonel, "we have not enough men to go. We have to content ourselves with working-over those zones with cannon and mortars. Later on, perhaps, we'll be able to extend our pacification perimeter."

At the Market-Place of Rach Kien, women, children, old men sell or buy a few fish caught in the rice paddies or yellowish pork fat. In vain, I searched this miserable mass of people which has lived abandoned in degrading poverty in the midst of the enormous American war-machine looking for youths of 15, of 20, or men of 30. The only adolescents I ever saw were held on a leash.

Several hours earlier in the trenches, some 100 meters from the village, these boys had been lying in wait with gun in hand for the comings and goings of the G.I.'s. Perhaps it was one of them who, on the day of my arrival, had fired a bullet full in the face of two young U.S. recruits. They had not listened to the warnings of the colonel, who had enjoined them not to leave the security perimeter.

A punitive expedition was organized. Half of the brigade and a unit of General Ky's Special Forces left to sweep the countryside. The four Vietcong, not even 20 years old, were surprised by young Vietnamese who could have been their brothers. They were led to the center of Rach Kien. No trial, no sentence. It was 7:00 o'clock — the American soldiers retired into their perimeter. The South Vietnamese mercenaries, one of whom had tattooed on his chest, "I kill Vietcong and I love my country," ordered the prisoners to kneel. The population was energetically encouraged to come and witness the spectacle. The young militiamen pulled machetes from their belts and with a sharp slash they decapitated the four Vietcong. Seeing my cameras, they held the bloody heads by the hair, placed cigarettes in the mouths, and cried to me:

"Come on, take photo, take photo . . ."

I have, as you know, submitted these photos to the Tribunal as evidence.

General Ky's Visit to the Australian Camp of Baria

I followed General Ky throughout the whole of a day when he visited Baria, the headquarters camp of 4,000 Australians engaged in the Vietnam War. He arrived in his own personal helicopter, elegant in a gabardine naval uniform. A detachment saluted him, and the commander of the camp shook his hand:

"Good Morning, General, we are going to visit the camp."

After a stop for lunch at the officers' mess, the tour began at the emplacements of the 81mm mortars.

"Attention, 61, 10, 12 . . . Fire!"

Then came the 105's. At this point the officers gave us some cotton to stop our ears. Finally, the tour finished up with the 175's, which exploded with puffs of smoke far off in the distance.

When, a little later, I flew over the zones which had been so abundantly bombarded by the exhibition firing, I saw small black forms running in the rice-fields.

From His Helicopter the General Hunts Vietcong

One morning, Lieutenant Colonel Sig Holtz, commander of our group, introduced me to his immediate superior, General Dane, who was visiting his command. Dane was a man of some 50 years, with young features and a pleasing countenance.

"Do you know," said the lieutenant-colonel, laughing, "that, from his Iroquois helicopter, he likes to hunt the Vietcong with a rifle."

Surprised, I asked the general:

"How do you know which are the Vietcong?"

"If they are there, they can't be anything else."

"But, General, if there are women among them?"

"I never fire on the women."

"How can you tell in the forest if they are not women?"

"It *is* difficult. But the Triangle is surrounded with rice fields and they stand out in relief well."

As Retaliation the South Koreans Massacre the Entire Population of a Village

On the subject of the Koreans to whom Sergeant Duncan just alluded in his deposition, I wish to testify that their primary mission is to assure the proper functioning of the pipe-line which connects Pleiku to Qui Nonh. It seems that they fulfilled this mission perfectly, for the simple reason that each time that there were any incidents along the pipe-line, the South Koreans went into the nearest village to massacre the population indiscriminately at one fell swoop.

I have this information from several sources: a leading Vietnamese citizen from Saigon, a Vietnamese intellectual who since the arrival of the Americans, no longer engages in any political activity, and especially from a high-ranking American officer who, with a laugh, said to me:

"What a pity that we don't have more South Koreans in Vietnam. The situation would be quickly changed."

Prostitution in Saigon

"If one believes the proverb 'when the foundation goes, everything goes'," a French missionary declared to me, laughing, "then everything is coming along fine in Saigon."

It is true: the illusion is perfect; buildings spring up everywhere. At peak hours Tu Do Street - formerly Catinat Street - and all the adjacent streets hold crowds as dense as in Paris. The girls have never been more charming as they seem in their long thin garments with their conical hats screening gracious smiles, which the realities seem not to have erased.

But in cold fact, for numerous families, the best way to escape poverty is to place one of their daughters in the home of a G.I. as a temporary wife. One young Vietnamese girl informed me of the rates: 20,000 piasters a month for the officers, 10,000 for the enlisted men, 6,000 for Koreans, Philippinos and Negroes. Some girls, to augment their wages, succeeded in "marrying" two or three G.I.s simultaneously she told me.

Prostitution is by far the most profitable job that a young girl can find. By careful management, she can earn a salary greater than that of a cabinet minister. But what is overlooked are the sordid details which accompany this kind of thing.

I was invited to the home of the parents of a friend, in the populated quarter of Saigon; a quarter where modern sanitation is unknown, where black-bristled hogs wallow in the mud of the streets. The mother, with tears in her eyes, told me the most horrible story that I have heard in all my career as a reporter. One of her nieces was scarcely 15 years old. Her father had been blown up by a mine a month earlier. Her mother, who had generalized cancer, was bedridden. In spite of all the assistance that the close-knit family tried to bring to this household, the six brothers and sisters were reduced to beg in order to live. One day the eldest girl learned that she could earn lots of money with the G.I.s and began walking the streets.

"You will not believe me," murmured my hostess. "Three of them took her to a hotel. The little one did not dare to say anything. They killed her, Monsieur. She was too young; she had a hemorrhage. Filled with panic, the three G.I.'s enclosed her in a container which they dumped off in the night, here, just across from my house."

Corruption in Saigon

"Except for the prostitutes, no girl will walk in this street," the waiter of a popular cafe declared to me, adding, "My daughter is a teacher and draws a salary of 3,000 piasters a month, hardly the wherewithal for a bit of rice and fish. By selling herself to a G.I., she could make ten times more. She will not do it because she is honest, but this situation is intolerable. Whether they rape or whether they buy our daughters, the result is the same."

The filth which fills the streets of Saigon must serve as fertilizer to the bars, for they shoot up like mushrooms. The boutiques of Catinat Street, the little restaurants, go bankrupt. They are replaced by rooms with soft lights in the middle of which are large bars bordered with high stools. Every evening the windows of the "Sexy Club," "Soho Bar," "Piccadilly," etc., protected from hand grenades by a stout wire-netting, frame the same spectacle: G.I.'s sipping whisky perched on stools, holding outrageously rouged and primped young Vietnamese girls - almost children - around the waist.

And the brothel-building continues; there is no lack of clientele. With 500,000 G.I.'s, there are none to spare. The troops earn between 250 and 1,000 dollars a month, and there is nothing in the rice fields that they can spend them on. A real gold-mine flows into the tills of the proprietors of the night-clubs and the purses of the entertainers.

Every evening young South Vietnamese functionaries or officers, with scooters bought on credit, come to the nightclub area to compete with the cycles and the taxis. With motors running, they park in front of the night clubs, while searching for a G.I.: "Little girl . . .little boy . . . Come with me, I know where you can have a good time. 100 piasters." Without too much effort they can triple their monthly pay.

The Saigonese's way to be a good citizen, to further the economic and social progress of the country is to find himself a G.I. He or she will become a temporary wife, rent him a room, wash his dirty clothes, polish his shoes . . .anything. A Vietnamese without a G.I. is doomed to the meagre bowl of rice and piece of dried fish. There are many who wish that this situation would last forever. There is no sound economy in South Vietnam, but a fabulously rich American presence on which thousands of parasites have fastened and multiplied in direct pro-portion as the infrastructure of the country has collapsed.

South Vietnam was formerly one of the leading rice-exporters in South East Asia. Now, she is obliged to buy thousands of tons from other countries while the harvest rots in her own bomb blasted fields. With Malaysia, she had one of the most flourishing rubber growing industries in the world. Now the plantations serve as head-quarters for American or Allied Infantry units. Others have been decreed "free fire zones" as I saw at Cu Chi, and every three seconds, 24 hours a day, heavy artillery furiously shells them, shattering the tree trunks. This is systematic destruction of what was once one of the primary national revenues.

Vietnam's exports value only six million dollars. Her imports, however, amount to around 398 millions of dollars. The gross national revenue has risen to $280 million, but on the order of $300 million has been pumped in from the U.S. and caused rampant inflation. If you add to this figure the astronomical sums which the U.S. soldiers spend on the spot for their pleasure, it is not surprising to see the people are more interested in cutting themselves a piece of the cake than in applying themselves to essential tasks.

I had been in Saigon less than an hour when all -and-more that a stranger can wish for had been offered to me — a room in a private home (10,000 piasters), washing and ironing of my laundry (1,000 piasters a month), a woman (20,000 piasters).

When there is no longer an infrastructure in a country, everything is permitted. From the highest to the lowest on the social ladder, everything is permitted. From the highest to the lowest on the social ladder, everyone conjugates the verb "to extort." The well-placed bureaucrats deliver phony visas in return for hard cold cash. Others sell under-the-counter to Chinese agents sacks of rice given by some International Agency for relief distribution to the population. Still others, employed by the Americans, specialize in the theft of military supplies for resale in the black market out in plain sight. No one is shocked, not even the G.I.'s. I saw the proof when I went to the P.X. to buy a battle dress and jungle boots, indispensible for reporting from the rice fields. The quartermaster told me, very seriously:

"As for the battle dress, Okay, we have it; but the boots, I haven't had any for at least the last 15 days. I send my boys to buy them on the black market. Do what they do."

On Treatment of Civilians
testimony by Joris Ivens and Marceline Loridon

I testify on behalf of Joris Ivens, film-maker, and also on my own behalf. We spent five and one-half months in North Vietnam, for two months of which we lived below ground in the demilitarized zone along the 17th parallel, from the beginning of May to the beginning of July 1967.

I will not speak of all the bombardments we lived through, nor of the dead and wounded, nor of the destruction on the northern banks of the river; nor will I tell of poison gases, nor of phosphorous bombs, fragmentation bombs, etc. I may say that we never went for five minutes without hearing an explosion near us or in the distance, and at night we were unable to sleep because of the hundreds of airplanes flying overhead.

My testimony will be devoted principally to the systematic manhunting raids and the moving of the entire South Vietnamese population living along the south bank of the Ben Hai river at the 17th parallel.

On May 18, 1967, the Americans brought in 5,000 Marines and 10,000 South Vietnamese troops, by boat and by helicopter, to the southern shore of the river near its mouth at Cua-Tung. The days preceding the landing were ones of unusual violence, both in the North, where we had to spend several days completely below ground, and in the South, where the population was being subjected to terrorism in order to force it to leave the area. Pamphlets were dropped threatening total extermination if the people did not get out of the demilitarized zone.

551

The aims of the Americans were: to break the N.L.F. threat to the American base at Con Thien; to create a "white zone" [free fire zone] along the Ben Hai river in the demilitarized zone by systematically levelling all the villages in the area and moving the civilian population to camps. The end result of their activities was to be the construction of what has been called the "Mc Namara line".

We went into the South on our own, in search of the facts and in order to serve as eyewitnesses to the fate of those villages. I will take the liberty of quoting here from an article which I wrote in France recently, in which I told of what we had seen: "We are at the 17th parallel. Bodies are still floating in the river, caught among the roots of trees. On the bank, the mangled body of a little girl. These people were machine-gunned by the helicopters while attempting to flee North to escape the hell of the bombing and the search parties. Nothing remains but smoking ruins, piles of ashes; one can see that people abandoned everything as they fled; there are bowls filled with uneaten rice. Chickens, ducks, dead pigs, buffalo, their bellies bloated with putrid gases, infect the air. Everywhere, there is a smell of death, there are villages empty of all human life. Planes fly over us; we hide among the trees. The motors of tanks barely two kilometers away from us can be heard clearly. Something sparkles in the sun; I pick it up. It is a piece of aluminum from a napalm bomb casing. The ground is covered with thousands of empty cartridges and rocket fragments. Further on are the ruins of a Buddhist Temple. A dog covered with ashes wanders about. Other houses, broken up, crushed, burnt out. An old woman is searching through the rubble. When she sees us, she comes toward us and asks who we are, and then says: "Be sure to tell the truth about what the Americans are doing here; tell the whole truth. They have destroyed everything, ruined everything; I have lost my children. I don't know where they are. They took them off in helicopters. The rice in the paddy had just ripened, it was beautiful, so beautiful. We will never harvest it, the Americans burnt it all with flame-throwers."

All the villages through which we went were completely razed and burnt out in the same way. In the Northern villages to which we returned, we found a thousand refugees, 254 of whom were children under 12 years of age, and 307 of whom were children over 12, most of whom had fled without their parents. They crossed the river to escape being sent to regroupment camps in which the Americans were putting the inhabitants of all the villages in the demilitarized zone. There were a thousand here, but over 7,000 in the neighboring villages. They had escaped as best they could.

552

Many were machine-gunned by helicopters while crossing the river; others drowned because they did not know how to swim. The North means refuge to all of them. They are completely taken charge of by the North Vietnamese peasants. Rice, vegetables and clothing have been found for them. People crowd together in the shelters to make room for them.

In the film I shall show you, which is a ten-minute excerpt from a full-length, two-hour film by Joris Ivens entitled "The 17th Parallel", you will see first of all scenes of the destruction of villages south of the 17th parallel. Next, there is an old peasant woman telling the N.L.F. what she has suffered and the story of the "search and destroy" missions, and then firsthand accounts by Southern peasants who have succeeded in finding a refuge in the North. These are only excepts of interviews; the complete typewritten texts are before the Russell Tribunal.

Text of Interviews from the Film

A woman: We were sound asleep when they began firing at us. The pirates came, everyone ran away; some stayed at home. In the morning, they don't say anything; at noon, they tell us to leave or else the bombing will destroy everything. We said: "Why didn't you chase us out in January or February, when the rice was not ripe? Now that it has ripened, we are staying here to eat it." There are some old people who say: This is still the land we were born on — better to die than to leave it." They told us: "You are fighting; don't listen to the Viet Cong who tell you to fight." They took us; they tied us up and two men pulled me along, one on each side and they struck old people, and young girls, and said: "If you like that, keep on fighting."

A woman: They destroyed a lot, that day. The rice was so beautiful. The M-113's [armored personnel carriers] crushed it all.

A man: The Americans came. Me, I fought not to leave, because this is the place where I was born. I want to live here and die here.

A woman: If we die here, we will die on the land of our ancestors. They say: "You talk like the lying Viet Cong propaganda: they're the ones who have taught you that." The people answered: "No, it's not the Viet Cong propaganda, but now the rice is ripe, let us eat it first."

A woman: When we got here, we didn't have a thing with us. The citizens in the North all helped us.

A man: They brought tanks and burnt the paddy, set fire to the houses. We tried to escape by coming over to this side. There are

553

some who may have their family with them, but as for others, only the husband has come; the wife is on the other side. Children lose their parents, parents lose their children.

A woman: I left at 3 in the afternoon, taking nothing with me, only the jacket I had on; with some children I set out for No. 3 Hamlet, where the pirates had not yet come, and some guerrilla fighters came along and we are able to turn the children over to them. Their family is separated, half on one side, half on the other.

A woman: They yelled: "We're going to set fire to your house." My family said: "If you burn it, we will burn it too. It's our house, we have a right to burn it ourselves." They beat us, tied us up and forced the inhabitants to leave with them.

A woman: They killed our buffalo and our cattle, they crushed our barely ripe tomatos and pimientos, or took them, and they destroyed everything.

A woman: Frightened children run through the streets. They beat the inhabitants with their rifle-butts. I had two laying hens in my house; two men came and took the eggs, two others took the hens.

A man: The family is broken up; the husband is in the South, the wife in the North, no one knows where to look for anyone now we don't know any longer where our children are or where those close to us are; now, when we talk, tears stream from our eyes. When will we be able to meet again?"

A woman: The American imperialists kill and they destroy everything; we will never be able to forget those crimes.

Another woman: We will never be able to forget the hatred we feel for them.

A man: The N.L.F. urges us to work hard in order to have a better life, while the Americans destroy everything.

Another man: Now we are refugees in the North, but only for a while Later on, we will come back to our villages and we will grab hold of our land so that we may stay there.

A man: The South and the North are like a single house.

On the Treatment of Women and Children in the South

testimony by Madelaine Riffaud

Madelaine Riffaud is a French Journalist and Author

I should like to recall for the Tribunal that I carried out investigations in Vietnam from January to May 1955, in areas liberated by the NLF from the end of November 1964 to the beginning of February 1965, and also north of the 17th parallel in the summer and autumn of 1966. I shall confine my testimony to that aspect of the problem which I was personally best able to study: the situation of women and children in South Vietnam since the signing of the Geneva Accords to 1965 . . .

In the first days of the Diem regime, the people were divided into categories: Category A, "those suspected of being former resistance fighters" and Category B, "families of former resistance fighters". Arrests, torturings before the assembled village population, humiliations, executions pure and simple — all these began to be employed against people in these categories. "Repentance" meetings were organized by Diem agents, advised by psychological warfare experts sent from Washington. These were aimed at forcing the people to deny publicly their patriotic convictions . . .

Wives of former resistance fighters were subjected to a "divorce campaign". They were given prepared forms by the police, who forced them to sign a declaration according to which they disowned their husbands or fiances or sons in the North. The unhappy women refused. Their children were then taken from them, under the pretext of raising them as "anti-communists". The woman herself was taken away and tortured in one of the many military security areas which had been set up by the thousands for the occasion in schools, pagodas, unused churches . . . In a short time, all of South Vietnam came to resemble an immense concentration camp. The tortures used to obtain divorces and disavowals were nicknamed "the pig cage", "the trip to Dakota" and "the submarine ride" by the hardened troops. The soles of the feet were beaten, fingertips were pierced; preferred were those tortures which brought about sterility. One which was practiced was "exorcism", in which the victim was tied in a sack, pierced through with swords, doused with gasoline and burned to the accompaniment of drums.

These are only a few examples out of many heard over and over again in all of the regions I visited. In no part of South Vietnam did I find a family entire. Women searched for children who had been taken from them years before. Husbands had not known for many years whether their wives still lived, nor in which prison.

Twice during the course of my visit, while following a unit of young NLF soldiers as a war correspondent, I witnessed the follow-ing scene: while passing through a village, a boy of 20 came upon his mother released from prison, from whom he had been separated since the age of 7 or 8. They were no longer able to recognize each other; it was only by chance that people realized that they were mother and son. One day, near Saigon, I was shown a relic piously guarded on an ancestral altar: a lock of braided hair, white and gray mingled with very black. It was a message from those who had never given in. In the prison of Poulo Condor, where even the French colonialists never dared put women, the "unbreakables" have for ten years continued to refuse to deny their country, their ideals, their husbands. Some of them had succeeded in smuggling out a lock of hair apiece as a sign of faithfulness. No one made any effort to bring these matters to my attention. I learned quite by chance that in October, 1959, a law set forth in Saigon provided that it was enough to have been found guilty by the special mili-tary courts of subversive "intentions" against the government to be condemned to life imprisonment or death; without preliminary investigation, without any confession from the accused. Sentences against which there was no appeal were carried out at once. Entire families were wiped out during this period, and portable guillotines went from village to village . . .

In December 1964, in a hospital set up in the jungle by the health services of the NLF, I met women who had been imprisoned in Poulo Condor for seven years without trial. Among them was Madame Tho, whom I have had the surprise and the pleasure of meeting again on the witness stand of this Tribunal. When I knew her, she had to be carried into the light in order that this photograph, which I published in 1965 and which I submit to the court as evidence, could be taken. Madame Tho was suffering from a serious case of tuberculosis and from the traumas resulting from the incessant torture she had undergone over the years. I could not conceive how she had been able to survive for so long the hell which her fellow prisoners had described to me, a hell which had left them invalids for life.

Some women who had recently escaped or been liberated from the Phu Loi and Chi Hoa centres were unable to speak to me. Their minds had cracked. Others were spitting blood and lacked the strength even to fan themselves with light bamboo fans. I remember a common case among women of apparently excellent health: a young girl named Chi Hue, from Gia Dinh province, whom I met as a member of a guerilla band. She was expert at helicopter combat, and strong nerves are absolutely essential when it comes to firing at just the right moment on a helicopter which is coming down at you with all guns blazing. One evening while with me, she suddenly went into convulsions because she had seen a snake. At Chi Hoa, the police had tied the legs of her black cotton trousers closed and had put snakes into them in order to force her to talk.

My personal experience with prisons and interrogation rooms under the Gestapo and my investigations in Algeria prior to its independence, have led me to make the following comparisons which I respectfully submit to the Tribunal: in a colonial war, prisoners and suspects are tortured. In general, however, after the questioning period itself, torture as such gives way to the brutalities of imprisonment.

In the kind of war waged by the Americans in South Vietnam, therefore, every time someone is arrested someone is tortured, often publicly, since it is important above all to destroy the morale of the people. But the torture is endless; it is never over, no matter how long one is detained. It is less a question of killing the body than of perverting, breaking, sullying the soul, of forcing the prisoners to abandon the revolutionary and patriotic ideal, of turning them into agents of a neo-colonialist policy. Accordingly, at Poulo Condor, if the women agreed to salute the American flag and the flag of the puppet Vietnamese government, they were allowed to drink until they had assuaged their thirst, to live in cells designed for one person whereas they had been living four at a time. But if they refused to attend indoctrination meetings, known as "courses in anti-communism", they were stuffed-in together, naked, so close together that they were only able to stand "upright like trees" without water and without air in the terrible tropical heat. The survivors I met had had to cut off their hair in order to stand the heat. I draw the attention of the Tribunal to the fact that thousands of men and women as well as children born in prison are still, even at this moment, suffering from imprisonment and slow extermination; conditions which recall those of the Nazi camps at Auschwitz, Dachau, Malthausen . . . Another characteristic of repressions carried out against women is systematic and collective rape, aimed at lowering them in the eyes of their companions.

Hours of testimony would not suffice to give an idea of the conditions of detention in the American prisons in South Vietnam. I have thus only been able to touch upon the question here. In order not to be accused by some of having fabricated evidence especially for this Tribunal, however, I would point out that I have already published these facts in detail in February, 1965, in *L'Humanite* and in my books *From Your Special Correspondant, In the Viet Cong Underground* (1965) and *North Vietnam; During the Bombardment* (1967) published by Julliard.

I should add that I met many American pilots in Vietnam who had been shot down during bombing missions against the civilian population: in particular Major J. Kasler, who took part in a bombing raid against a suburb of Hanoi in June, 1966, and was captured on the 28th of August. Medical care and more than sufficient nourishment were provided them by the Vietnamese authorities and they were permitted to reassure their families of their well-being through me.

Nevertheless, in South Vietnam the American Army is devoting itself to a systematic destruction of families. In villages in the liberated zones, helicopters attack when the men are in the fields. "From the distance, I saw the 'Flying Eagles' drop down on the roofs of houses," Mr. Nguyen Dinh Lam of Long An Province told me. "The wind from their propellors destroyed the thatch roofs. I ran to my family, my gun in my hand. When I arrived, the helicopters were already far away in the sky. All that was left of the area where they had set down was a cloud of dust. Women were lying on the ground crying. The Americans had captured women and children at random and had tied their hands with rope. They threw my son Nam, 5 years old, and my youngest daughter into a helicopter and carried them away. My neighbor was left alone with his young ones; the Americans had carried his wife off by force. 'Where have they taken them?' he cried. 'How will we find them' How will we recognize them?'" . . .

Their intense bombing raids, aimed at anything that moves in the liberated countryside, the massive use of napalm, phosphorous and poisons, is also aimed at forcing the population into so-called "refugee" camps, where the Americans would like to confine the South Vietnamese as they confined the Indians in reservations in the past.

I should now like to submit to the Tribunal a case of infant extermination which would appear to be part of a deliberate plan. Here are the facts: In January 1963, twenty-five helicopters machine-gunned the school at Long Dien at ground level and pursued the children and the teacher into the swamps where they had fled. Why? Solely because that zone is declared a "free fire zone". This terrorist operation was aimed at punishing and demoralizing the people by striking at what they hold most dear, namely, their children.

I might have been able to believe that it was an isolated example of barbarism by the occupying forces. However, during my visit to a nursing school in the jungle, the girls got up a party in our honour. After some dances, one of the children sang a song she had composed herself. Seeing that the listeners were crying, I asked for a translation. The song told of the bombing of the school of Cauxe by the occupying forces and even gave the date of the crime: 18th of March, 1963. The little singer came from Cauxe.

Napalm raids occurred on schools in Linh Ohuong and Mo Cay from the 3rd to the 13th of July. The latter school had been built by donations from families belonging to the Cao Dai religion and was close to their pagoda. In both cases, there was great loss of life both among the children and among those parents who had come to their aid only to be cut down by cannon from nearby outposts in perfect co-ordination with the airplanes.

Immense protest demonstrations were held at the time, and Cao Dai priests marched at their head with banners calling for the departure of the Americans and the punishment of the criminals. It is only too true that in South Vietnam it is unnecessary to be a "red" or a "Viet Cong" to be against American imperialism or to fight with the NLF...

You may say, "But you didn't see all this yourself,"

No; but I visited An Tanh, An Hoa, in Long An province. That province is the one picked by McNamara in 1964 to serve as a model for the seven "pilot provinces" which were to be liberated that year for the protection of Saigon. The province where, despite all the efforts on the part of the occupying forces, the "free fire zones" grew larger and larger.

An Tanh, An Hoa: rice paddies nearing the harvest; few trees, aside from clumps of bamboo around the houses ... In the first village, near a road, I saw in the twilight broken wooden tables, the remains of a blackboard, rubble, bits of mud wall and tiles, all that remained of what had once been a school bombed on October 3rd, 1964. On the same day, the Americans had carried out a similar raid on schools in the neighbouring villages of An Ninh and An Hoa, and on October 28th in the same area the school of Duc Hoa was destroyed. Four schools had been burned in less than a single month in one region.

I was unable to go to Duc Hoa, an area which was still partially in occupied hands. But at An Hoa, where I spent a sleepless night with the inhabitants, I saw the napalm-blackened ruins of the school, the bamboo trunks which had held up the roof stark against the sky. And the people showed me the pitiful remains: blood-spattered arithmetic books, caps with bullet holes in them, little articles of half-burned clothing that had belonged to the murdered children or to those being cared for in the hospital. I am unable to go into all the statements and evidence I collected; I shall confine myself to events in An Hoa. But the others are equally heartbreaking. Here is an example of such a testimony:

"It was at a time when all the children were in school. The evening before, propaganda helicopters had passed over and dropped leaflets and had threatened the people by loudspeaker with reprisals if they continued to refuse to move to strategic hamlets. They were the "HU-1A" which are able to hang in the air and are used as firing platforms. The next day, they returned . . . As you saw, we built the school on open ground. We put a large sign on the facade: Communal School. We were still too trusting, despite all the wrongs which had been done us. We thought that when they saw the sign the airplanes would not make a mistake and bomb the school . . . They didn't make a mistake. Right at the beginning, their reconnaissance plane dropped smoke bombs in the school courtyard to point out the target.

"There were two classes in the school. The top form, led by its teacher, got to the shelters safely in a disciplined manner. In the kindergarten classes, sixty children from 5 to 7 years of age became frightened and grabbed hold of their teacher who was trying to calm them, or hid beneath their desks and refused to come out. The teacher, who was twenty years old, knew from experience that the helicopters would fire rockets into the classroom. Unable to get the children out in time for them to take refuge in the trenches, he tried to get them into the corners of the room. But the rocket fire had already begun. The first explosions occurred by the exit, which turned into a wall of fire.

"The teacher then tried to get the children out of the window by threes, carrying one on his back and one under each arm. In this way, he made more than ten trips under heavy rocket and machine-gun fire. However, many children were killed or injured in the classroom itself and everyone was in a state of panic.

560

"Tam, the teacher, succeeded in evacuating 45 children before he was hit. Injured in the leg, he made one more trip, but on his return he was hit again, this time badly. Thinking that he was dying, he shouted to the children in the building who were still alive: 'Get out through the window, don't be afraid; I'm hurt, but I'm still here!'"

"Big brother, 'the children called back, we can't get out through the window; we're too little . . .'" (I know this is exact, since it was told me by Tam, the teacher, who survived.)

"At that instant, the planes dropped containers of napalm on what was left of the school. And not another sound was heard from the children.

"On the outside, the children which Tam had evacuated with such difficulty had come out of the dugouts because they were afraid, and tried to run to their homes. On the road, they were machine-gunned by low-flying helicopters which hunted them down like rabbits. They flew so low, people said, that the American uniforms could be clearly made out."

Imprisonment and Torture of Political Prisoners
testimony by Mrs. Pham Thi Yen

On April 18, 1960 at 8 P.M., right in the streets of Saigon, the U.S.-Diemist security police arrested me because of my patrotic activities. I was taken to the Commando Post Number 1, the Ba Hoa Post at Cho Lon. The commandant himself directed the interrogation, which started immediately after my arrest. He put questions about my activities with the patriots. I did not reply to these questions, so they started to torture me. Reeking with alcohol, the "commandos" as the Vietnamese call them, started beating me, shouting with rage. The commandos are a sort of Vietnamese Gestapo.

They tied my two arms behind my back, then hauled me up to the ceiling by strong cords attached to my wrists. They beat me with sticks, stopping only when I fainted. Then they let me down, throwing cold water over my face. Little by little I recovered consciousness.

More questions. Silence. Furious, they hung me up again. This was repeated I don't know how many times. They called this operation: "ride in a Dakota."

My body was covered with wounds and was most painfully swollen. I suffered atrociously—the slightest movement and I thought I would faint with pain.

After a moment's rest, they applied the "ride in a submarine." They undressed me and tied me, face upward, to a plank. A towel was used to tie my head to the plank; a rubber tube led from a 200-liter barrel, fixed to a stand. The water fell drop by drop onto the towel, soon flooding my face. To breathe, I sucked in water through my nose and mouth. I was suffocating, my stomach started to swell like a balloon. I could no longer breathe and I fainted. When I regained consciousness, I suffered unimaginable pains. I opened my eyes and saw two commandos called Duc and Danh, and nicknamed the "Gray Tigers" because of their blood-curdling exploits, stamping on my chest and stomach to get the water out of me. I vomited through my mouth and nose, water mixed with blood pouring out. This was repeated several times. I suffered atrociously in my chest and in my stomach; it was as if someone was twisting my entrails.

"Serve her another dish" the commander said to his agents. The latter formed a square and with myself in the center, they beat me with sticks. They pushed me from one to another as if I were a ping-pong ball, shouting and hurling insults at me. I was seriously wounded in the head, blood trickled down. They stopped beating me and started to shave my head, to bandage it.

They started to lull me with doubtful promises mixed with threats—

Talk, and you can rejoin your children. If not, you will die and your children will be orphans.

Talk, and you can keep your pharmacy, your possessions. Otherwise we will ruin you.

Talk, or we will torture you to death and even if you survive you'll be useless, without strength to brush a fly away.

Neither their sickening promises nor their threats had any effect. Screaming with rage, they threw my face down on the floor, a huge brute squatting on my back, two others holding my feet with the soles turned upwards. Using police truncheons they beat the soles of my feet with all their strength. My feet and legs swelled up visibly as they struck. I felt as if my skin was going to burst.

Afterward they hung me by my wrists, this time attached to the iron bars of a window with handcuffs, my arms crossed and at a height at which I could only stand on the tips of my toes. My arms and legs hurt terribly. They started to hammer my arms against the bars. My arms became numb. Seeing this had no effect, they untied me and kicked me on to the floor again. They started to kick me. Blood was running all over the place. I fainted.

Again there were promises, threats and insults. Tired themselves, they called other prisoners and tried to force them to beat me. They all refused, so the prisoners were furiously beaten. In that place there was no room for any human sentiments at all.

Just before dawn they said they would serve me a "sensational dish." They attached me to a kaki tree in the garden near a cage where two tigers were ferociously roaring. In South Vietnam, kaki trees, which produce very sweet fruit, are always covered with yellow ants. If a single ant stings you, you'll yell with pain. And the spot where you are stung will swell up immediately with the effect of the poison. This tree was just of this species—its branches full of yellow ants . . .

The tigers continued roaring, the torturers were shouting with rage. It was a frightful and at the same time terribly sinister experience. But all this also had no effect. My feelings were entirely concentrated on the little ants, their stings were so painful.

The torturers threatened me: "If you don't talk, your children will be tortured in front of your eyes; your parents, your brothers and sisters will be imprisoned. Your family will be destroyed, your pharmacy seized . . ."

At 6 o'clock in the morning, after ten hours of torture, they threw me into a cell. I could hardly stand up, I had to lie down on the cold floor . . . .

Depositions Taken in South Vietnam
from testimony by Hugh Manes

Mr. Manes is an Attorney in California

On March 27, 1967, we met and interviewed some more victims from South Vietnam. The first was Dr. Cao Quang Nguyen, a medical doctor. He was born in 1931 in Lam Dong District in Phuoc Long Province, along Route No. 14 and the Dong Nai River.

[*Hugh Manes, an attorney from Los Angeles, was a member of the Third Commission of Inquiry which included Doctors Takman and Hojer of Sweden, and Professor J. B. Neilands of the University of California. The primary mission of this Team was to report on effects of the bombing of North Vietnam. Mr. Manes' testimony on this essentially duplicates and corroborates that of Takman, Hojer, and Neilands, which forms part of this volume. However, in addition, Mr. Manes compiled depositions from many South Vietnamese who were victims of U.S. operations south of the 17th parallel and who had managed to flee to the D.R.V. Among these depositions were three which bear directly on the way in which the war in the South is waged. Dr. Nguyen's testimony concerns the effects of the "harmless" defoliants on human beings; that of Miss Van concerns repression of political opponents of the Saigon regime, and reveals a pattern of physical and sexual torture which was to become familiar to the Tribunal during the second Copenhagen session at which American Vietnam veterans substantiated such acts; finally, the deposition of Mr. A Ma Ho reveals the quality of life for an inhabitant of a strategic hamlet within a "prosperity zone." Therefore, though Mr. Manes' testimony was delivered to the first Stockholm session, the Editor has included it with testimony concerning the South. Ed. Note.*]

564

Dr. Nguyen testified as follows:—On October 3, 1964, at approximately 10:00 a.m., four fighters bombed and strafed his area for one hour, dropping fragmentation and napalm bombs. Then two C-123's and one helicopter came. The helicopter flew high, and the C-123's sprayed toxic chemicals in combination with fighter strafing. Even delayed-action bombs were used. The toxic chemicals were sprayed over an area of approximately twenty square kilometers.

In Dr. Nguyen's experience, different kinds of toxic chemicals are being used. Some fall very quickly, some slowly, according to weight. The color varies: red, like with acids; some are musty or milky, some stick to leaves, some are glossy; some look like white powder, some have different smells, as gunpowder, others smell like garlic.

The C-123's sprayed Bu Dop and Bu Dang Districts. After spraying, the doctor saw that the leaves of water-bearing plants, potatoes, bananas, etc., appeared to have boiling water on them — rice plants faded quickly. Fish died in slow moving streams, almost instantly.

Human victims suffered itching of the skin, felt hot in their eyes and noses, felt suffocating, had headaches, their throats were sore and hot, they sustained nosebleeds upon blowing, felt dizzy, vomited, their stomachs ached and they were nauseaous.

Crops and vegetation were defoliated; crops rotted, fruit trees and jungle vegetation were defoliated, with the fruit becoming rotten. Potatoes, onions, and similar vegetables were noticeably affected. Livestock and poultry were affected, refused to take food and slowly died after eating grass and insects which were contaminated.

The itching skin would become swollen on human beings within two to three days later. Chemicals also affected the nervous system. Victims could not sleep well, their digestive and respiratory systems were affected. Those who experienced sore bellies at first would usually have inflated digestive tracts and diarrhea. A victim's eyes are often inflamed for several days, and sight is reduced, sometimes for as long as a month.

Dr. Nguyen was himself a victim of toxic chemicals used by American troops. Both corneas were burned or damaged, rendering him nearly blind. Medical treatment has restored some of his vision. During the aforementioned raid, Dr. Nguyen was able to aid others even though he was slightly affected. But in the second raid, he was too seriously affected to give aid or remember details.

In these spray attacks victims become weaker, and have the feeling of floating in the air. The eyes do not look injured from the outside; but they are scarred inside due to the breaking of blood vessels. Toxic chemicals cause pregnant women to have miscarriages, bigger foetuses, and premature deliveries. In virtually all premature cases, the baby dies. Dr. Nguyen witnessed three cases where the foetus died within three days after infection; premature delivery occurred within four days thereafter. In one case, a pregnant woman had a miscarriage within two days after becoming infected by poisonous chemicals. One woman who waited ten years for a child lost her pregnancy as a result of infection by toxic chemicals and suffered a nervous breakdown.

Thousands of hectares of crops have been destroyed by these toxic chemicals; tens of thousands of livestock and poultry were affected and died. Many are killed by bombs; but the chemicals, although not necessarily immediately fatal to people, gradually sap their strength. For some, damage to organs is permanent, especially stomach attacks, which reduce the strength. Also, because of a reduction of red corpuscles, the stomach atrophies, shrinks and dries and blood pressure is reduced. There are too many casualties to give everyone blood transfusions to regain the strength one must have for a good digestive system. Young people frequently recover; but for the elderly, it is not so easy....

Seven days after the first spraying of Dr. Nguyen's village, planes returned because the wind had blown away some of the chemicals. The month of October is near the harvest time and the crops are in bloom.

The planes came around 10:00 a.m., and flew the same pattern: bombing, strafing, then spraying chemicals. This time the doctor was seriously affected because he was operating at the time on victims of the bombing. He was part of an emergency team, and was therefore exposed to the chemicals because he could not seek shelter or fresh air.

He first noticed difficulty in breathing, and as he insisted on taking the wounded to the shelter, he became more and more contaminated. In the beginning, he felt dizzy; he was hot in the face. He felt hot and dry in his nose and throat. Despite these handicaps, he tried to continue operating — but without success. Later, he vomited up blood. He felt exhausted, and his will was sapped, even within the first few hours. Because he vomited excessively, he could not retain food or drink. He had headaches and black dots before his eyes.

On the first night following the infection, he could not sleep; he felt as if he were flying; there was pain in the head and eyes. These symptoms lasted for about three months, during which time he could not sleep or eat well. He lived on fruit juice and liquid infusions through the veins. Gradually, his sight was reduced until one month later, he could not see out of the right eye and lost ninety percent vision in the left eye. His blood pressure, a normal 120/70, went down to 90/40. The red corpuscles, usually 4.8 or 4.9 million were reduced to 3.2 million. His hair began to fall out, and he lost weight, falling from 64 to 54 kilos (under 100 pounds); he felt constantly chilled.

After continuous medical treatment, Dr. Nguyen's vision in his left eye has increased to 9/10ths of normal; but the right eye has recovered only 1/10th vision. The cornea is still scarred on the inside, and cannot be cured. Dr. Nguyen stated that his large intestine is still inflamed, and he still has difficulty digesting food. The bodily infection and the difficulty in eating and sleeping also had an effect on his eyes.

Today, Dr. Nguyen weighs approximately 58 kilos; his blood pressure is up to 100/70. His red corpuscle count has increased to 4 million, still low for a man. He still sees small dots, and is unable to stand for the ten to fourteen hours that he was formerly accustomed to in the performance of his work.

Dr. Nguyen testified that the use of a higher concentration of certain chemicals used as defoliants and to destroy crops, causes greater harm to human beings. Dr. Nguyen testified that the mixture of 24-D and 245-T in defoliants, when used intensively, causes a reduction in the red corpuscle count. Forty provinces, according to the doctor, have been sprayed with such chemicals, and only two or three provinces have escaped such spraying. He said that "we can protect people, but not crops or animals. Fruit trees require nearly ten years to regrow; draft animals require four to five years to regenerate."

Miss Tran Thi Van: On March 27, 1967, our team interviewed the above named South Vietnamese, who is still suffering from the effects of prison life. She is thirty-six years old, a native of Dien Banh District, Quang Nam Province. Miss Van testified that she had been arrested and detained by Saigon Government troops on numerous occasions, and has spent a total of six years in prison, commencing in 1955. She testified as follows:

She took part in the woman's resistance to the French in and prior to 1954. When peace was restored, she returned to her village and led a peaceful life. When the Saigon Government began to repress demands for reunification and women's rights, the people began to resist.

On one occasion in 1954, she was questioned as to where she kept the money of an organization concerned with political demands. She was also asked whether she demanded consultation for reunification. She replied that she knew nothing about such organizations or such matters, and denied participating in such activities after the restoration of peace. She also denied participating in the resistance movement, but they took away her land, and, as a pretext, charged her with participating in the movement against the regime. In February, 1956, she was arrested and transferred to Phu Ky. She stated that she had only participated in a movement to recover land given to women during the resistance which was allocated equally to men and women by the Viet Minh Forces. After peace was restored, the Diem Government took the land away from women, although subsequently, it was restored. The repressive measures at the outset were confined to those who participated in the resistance. One such measure was the forcing of wives to divorce husbands who had gone north.

On one occasion, Miss Van testified, in Dien Ban District, Saigon forces committed mass murder, disemboweled their victims, put stones in their stomachs and threw them into the Thach Ban and Vinh Trinh dams on the Thu Ban River. Miss Van claimed to have seen the corpses five days later, fifteen of them floating in the river, one a woman. Three days later, the International Control Commission came, but "puppets" had buried the victims by then. By the end of 1954, people would from time to time, see corpses stuffed in jute bags floating down the river; she herself saw two of them.

On one occasion, she was arrested with hundreds of others and taken to the local jail. There, she was hung up by her arms and beaten with a stick. Because she was beaten so hard, the cord broke and she fell to the floor. She was re-hung again, and her tormentors continued to beat her until her skin became swollen. The size of the stick used against her was half the size of her wrist.

During this beating, she was told that she would not be given the ordinary French tortures, but rather the tortures learned from the Americans. At one point she fainted and was ultimately released from her hanging position. Upon regaining consciousness, she was tied up, and soapy water was forced into her mouth, causing her to suffocate and faint many times. Her captors then tried to force her to speak against the political movement which advocated consultation on reunification and the general elections.

When she refused, her mouth and nose were covered with a towel, and water was dripped into her nose and mouth, causing suffocation and making breathing almost impossible. After this, she was threatened with other tortures. Her captors took out an instrument that looked like a pincer, attached it to each finger and tightened it so as to crush her fingers. The pressure caused her arms to become swollen.

Then her captors brought forward something that looked like a box, but which turned out to be a small generator with the initials "U.S." stamped thereon. Wires from the generator were attached to her nipples, and the current was applied. Her whole body shook. When she fainted, they would stop the torture. When she regained consciousness, they resumed it.

Next her tormentors poured water inside her mouth until her belly became full. Then, her captors proceeded to jump on her belly, forcing the water out.

After the electric shock torture, three men, named Amua, Thoi, and Long, again beat her with a small rod of bamboo and leather, upon her arms, after having earlier hit her on the shinbones. After about one and one-half hours of these tortures, she was finally brought back to her cell, where some women prisoners put medicine on her wounds. The aforedescribed tortures were repeated for a period of about six days, until she was so weak that she could not stand. There were many wounds on her body; and some twenty days elapsed before she could stand up or do any work.

Thereafter, she was removed to a little hillock and led to a hole, where she was forced down and threatened with burial alive if she refused to admit her complicity in the movement for reunification. After being half-buried, she fainted. The two officers involved in this torture were named Khoi and Man, of the district police.

In March, 1962, she was arrested and taken to Da Nang, where she was again put to electric torture. While in the detention cell undergoing electric shocks, an American came into the room, poked at her head with a ruler, spoke with her two Vietnamese captors, and then left. She assumed that the man was American because he was Causasian, and because of the fact that he appeared in the room. She did not recognize the language, and was totally unfamiliar with the American language at that time.

After 1956, Miss Van's area was liberated by the NLF. While visiting an aunt in Ky Tan, Miss Van was arrested again. This was about the end of February, 1962. While held at Da Nang, Miss Van was constantly put to torture for the first two months of her captivity, particularly the first month.

During the four months of her captivity, when not actually being tortured, she was kept in chains and irons, so that she was unable to move unless the chains were unlocked. For the first five months of her confinement, she was kept in solitary confinement, under lock and key in a very tiny cell. Ultimately, she was transferred to Lao Xa (prison) at Hoi An. There she was forced to kneel down with outstretched arms while holding up two stones, in the hot sun. She was also tied to a pillar by a policeman named Man, who beat her with a stick upon her head and body. It still pains her to sit as a result of this torture.

Miss Van went back to 1957, and described how she had been tortured by a man called Be. He stripped her, tied her arms, and thrust his hand into her vagina until blood came and she cried out in pain. He then stuffed a cloth into her mouth and tortured her with a hot iron rod. We verified the scar. She was also forced to observe a fellow prisoner bitten to death by a dog; and was subjected to dogbite on her back at that time.

In further questioning of Miss Van, the following information was elicited:

In February of 1956, she spent six months in jail.

Approximately two months after her release, in October of 1965, a pacification team arrested her with hundreds of others, many of whom were killed. She was held for another six months, from October, 1956, until early 1957. Her parents were also arrested, and her father killed at that time.

After her release, she was arrested again about thirty days later upon a charge of distributing leaflets opposed to the regime. Although she could not read these leaflets, it was claimed that she had instigated other men to distribute them. She was held in custody until the end of 1959. . . .

According to Miss Van's testimony, all prisoners are tortured. This was particularly true during the so-called "denouncing Communists" campaign. She testified that during this campaign, people were put into ranks and made to stand stiffly with nothing to eat. A strong light was shone into the faces of the people, and they were required to stare at the light until their hair whitened and their eyes became permanently impaired. Many elderly people, perhaps thirty, collapsed and were carried away. She returned to her village ultimately in 1964, and came to North Vietnam in November, 1966 for medical treatment.

Her sister, Tran Thi Loi, still bears scars all over her body, including her genitals, from many tortures at the hands of the Saigon government. Seven years after her release her wounds still bleed. She has been the subject of many inquiries by foreigners and has visited several countries in an attempt to receive medical treatment.

Miss Van said that her niece died after a broken bottle was inserted into her vagina. She also stated that her cell was so small that
it was difficult to breathe; people often collapsed when they were
brought out into the open. She estimated that 150 people had died
from this type of confinement. The testimony of Miss Van is recorded, in part, on tape which will be submitted concurrently with
the writer's testimony.

I also interviewed a man who gave testimony on life in the "strategic
hamlets". He was A Ma Ho, forty-five years old. Mr. Ho is a member
of the Pu Nong minority, and comes from Dac Ghenh Hamlet, Duc
Minh Village, in Duc Loc District at Quan Duc Province.

Ho's father was a Viet (Kinh) which is the majority group in
Vietnam. His mother was a Pu Nong, from the high plateau. His
father settled there, but died while Ho was still a child. Ho married
fathered three children, and continued living in the same area.

In 1960, Ho stated, as a result of the resistance that had developed among the people to the Diem regime, the National Liberation
Front was formed. New life came to the people, a better life. For
example, a medical station came to the village so as to guarantee
better health standards.

Beginning with 1961, the Saigon Government put forward a state
policy of "prosperity zones". Under this policy, the government
tried to concentrate people into these zones, but the villagers refused to leave their land. The district chief, Phan Van Ton and
Mayor Dao Van Dung came with troops three times and tried to
take the people away by force. But the people struggled back and
the troops had to settle for just a few of the elderly people and
some women.

On the fourth occasion, the Saigon Government sent in one full
battalion of troops in December, 1961, circled the area and arrested
five men named: Ama Hin, Ma Plang, Ma Pring, Ma Choi, and
Y Li, and shot them on the spot, declaring all five to be Communists
in the high plateau (as distinguished from Viet Cong from the Delta).
The soldiers began firing in all directions to terrorize the villagers;
then they began to load them onto trucks and took them to Nam Quan
Village in Xu Yen District. The government troops, as an inducement
to get the villagers to leave, promised to supply one buffalo per family
and thirty kilos of rice for each member of the family each month
for two months. But the people, upon reaching Nam Quan Village,
received only 250 grams of rice per day.

It was impossible for the people to live on such a small ration, and
they had to go into the forest to find edible roots. Although there was
a fence around the area, they were allowed to leave to forage for food.

There were about 850 people, including women and children, in Nam Quan Village; but in some cases, families were split, some of them fleeing into the forest.

Five hundred villagers went to the district and demanded relief. The district chief arrested Ma Pheng, Ma Pra, and Ma Beo, and claimed that they were the leaders of the protest movement. The villagers continued to struggle. Fifty or more would come every day and demand the release of the three men. At last the men were released, but the villagers were refused more food. The people had to go into the forest to find roots so they could eat and continue to farm the land.

In 1962, a flood destroyed the crops, causing great famine in the prosperity zone, as well as cholera and diarrhea, which spread throughout the area, causing many deaths. By October 1962, the villagers could no longer continue this life because they realized they would gradually die of starvation and disease. So they struggled to return to their own villages. Group by group, they returned to the villages; but government troops, with American advisors, tried to prevent this, and used three machineguns to drive them back to their zones. Although 850 went from this village, only 800 returned; fifty had died by October of 1962.

In November, the government sent two platoons of the army to the hamlet, swept into the jungles where villagers had hidden their property; broke 200 jars — which were precious to the villagers and worth 250,000 piastres at that time — ; killed three elephants used by the villagers in construction work; four tons of rice belonging to three families were seized, together with much poultry. Two platoons remained stationed in the village and controlled the area. Two hundred of the villagers fled into the forest, whereupon the troops followed, arrested the people and brought them back, destroying the crops and burning about seventy houses which had been built in the jungle by those who had fled.

The people cut and burned trees to plant their plots; but the government forces burned trees to spoil the plots and the plants sown there, and also pulled up rice. Daily, troops were sent to destroy crops and to harass the people and bring them back to the hamlets. Two hundred cannon shells were fired on Ho's village. The planes bombed the village and strafed the elephants, which were thought by the pilots to be villagers moving through the forest.

A strategic hamlet was built around the village; and the villagers were forced to help construct it for six months without pay. The government troops forced people to fell one hundred big trees and bring them to the post, and to dig one hundred meters of trench around the hamlet.

In front of the first trench was a barbed wire. Then came a trench in which were planted spikes. Then the second fence was planted, with poles two meters long sharpened to points. Then came the third fence with spiked poles, after which were more trenches. The fourth fence was built with big trees, behind which was another trench, again with sharp pointed spikes. Then came a fifth fence with barbed wire, to which were attached grenades. There were only two gates in or out of the strategic hamlet, both of which were heavily guarded. The perimeter was about 1,000 meters for over 800 people, plus two platoons of over 80 soldiers.

A high watchtower was built with telephone communication and a tunnel was constructed to provide escape in case of attack. The regime inside of the strategic hamlet was harsh. The authorities permitted the people to leave for their farming plots after 7:00 a.m., but they were required to return at 4:00 p.m. Each group was under the control of troops who supervised the farming.

To get water, escorts were required. The people inside were not allowed to gather in groups of more than four or five. Some men were required to spend the night in special places for control purposes as hostages.

After the harvest, the rice was put in a granary, from which the people were supplied on the basis of only 250 grams. According to the custom of Ho's people, after threshing, they prepare a special liquor for a festival. However, this mixture was prohibited, so Ho and his wife went for special food. In the strategic hamlet, however, they were seperated.

Ho and his fellow peasants had to work very hard without pay. They were constantly hungry. People protested against this life. Five of the villagers were killed, three of them being: Ma Nam, Ma Proi, and Ma Heo. These men had refused to work for the government forces without payment, whereupon they were tied to pillars and shot as a lesson to others. Ho saw the shooting. People who went into the fields could only carry one small tin of rice. More and more people gradually died, approximately thirty of them from starvation and disease. Outside the hamlet, there was shelling, and on one occasion, seven members of a family were killed. They were part of the 200 who had fled into the jungles.

People finally could not stand this kind of life, and on the night of June 20, 1965, they rose up and captured the weapons of the troops stationed there, destroyed the hamlet and fled into the jungles to seek a free life. At 4:00 a.m. the following morning, reconaissance planes and jets followed to pursue the people, dropping bombs. Thirty-seven people were killed, ten were wounded.

In February, 1966, in a bombing raid on people who now lived in the jungle, seven more people were killed, while working in the rields in a mountain area. According to Ho, forty-eight strategic hamlets were destroyed out of fifty-two by the inhabitants. Ho left for North Vietnam in October, 1966; but his family still lives in South Vietnam.

Conclusion

This concludes part of the writer's report of what he saw and heard during his three weeks in the Democratic Republic of Vietnam. Exposure to the violence brought to Vietnam by the American expeditionary force, impairs one's objectivity. The author does not pretend to be neutral; but he does strive for fairness and some sense of proportion.

This writer concludes, based on what he observed and the witnesses interviewed, that the bombing of Vietnam is not limited to military objects; but is primarily, if not exclusively, aimed at destroying the morale of the civilian population by concentrated air raids and shellings of villages, towns and cities. The persistent pattern of vast destruction in the remotest areas of Vietnam precludes the possibility of accident. The destruction observed by this writer is wanton, deliberate, and calculated to destroy the morale of the people. That this objective is failing is a tribute to the people and to the society they are attempting to construct. But it is a blot on American institutions, and on civilization itself for as long as it is tolerated. . . .

Report of the Seventh Inquiry Commission
testimony by Roger Pic

*M. Pic is a French Journalist and Film Maker; Testimony
Concerns Zones in the South Under NLF Control*

The team was composed of Professor Francis Kahn, Doctor Jean-Michel Krivine and Roger Pic and carried out investigations from September 15th to October 7th 1967. We had two main purposes: 1) to judge if the U.S. army goal was to systematically destroy the civilian population and its means of existence, forcing thereby the Vietnamese to concentrate in special camps; 2) to investigate the utilization of forbidden arms such as anti-personnel bombs and toxic products.

The investigations were carried out in the Eastern Nambo zone, of Tay Ninh province (northwest of Saigon) by the whole Commission, after which I finished alone in a hamlet of Central Nambo in the Plain of Reeds. Under the protection and care of a guerilla detachment of the National Liberation Front, accompanied by interpreters, cadres of the Front, province and region chiefs, and General Secretary of the National Liberation Front War Crimes Committee, Mr. Ung Ngoc Ky, the Commission travelled approximately six hundred kilometers, both walking and by sampans, visiting many ruined villages and peasants hiding in the jungle, to collect testimonies, interrogate and listen to the greatest possible number of civilian victims of U.S. army operations. The province of Tay Ninh, which we traversed most often, is the operational zone where in February and March of this year, U.S. headquarters launched "Operation Junction City", the biggest operation involving the widespread and systematic razing of the countryside.

Cited from the American records, 45,000 men, 800 tanks, 1200 bombers and helicopters were used in the operation after gigantic "softening up", spreading of defoliants, and massive bombings by B-52's. The testimony which we brought back to add to the files of the Tribunal mostly concerns the consequences of those military actions launched in a province exclusively composed of fields and forests, the only purpose of which was admitted to be for creating "safe zones" or "uncontested areas".

In Tay Ninh province we visited Chau Thann district, Hao Duoc village, Thanh Dien, Hoa Hoi, Hoa Hiop, Ta Bang. We collected 373 testimonies written in Vietnamese, recorded and signed. All these pieces with their translations and pictures of the witnesses are added to the file which has been deposited with the Tribunal. We have filed and recorded certain depositions.

To underline certain aspects of the life of the peasants who remain in devastated zones, who try to survive in spite of the razings and constant military operations, I made a filmed reportage which has appeared on television. The film, I think, can help one to understand how the South Vietnamese live nowadays — those who escaped destruction or concentration camp life.

I would like to briefly express my main impressions after this visit to the so-called "scorched earth" zone. During those three weeks, we did not see a single hamlet, a single house which was spared from bombings or shelling. If the forests and jungle of East Nambo have resisted chemical products and bombings, if half of the civilians survive in the zones controlled by the National Liberation Front guerilla forces and National Liberation Army, all of the villages have been destroyed. Every family has been touched either by the bombings, deportations or torture and imprisonment. All the testimonies recorded in our files are moving stories of useless suffering, pain and mourning undergone by them. We will of course report only some of those testimonies.

During the two months operation "Junction City" lasted, the whole of Tay Ninh province was particularly well combed by "search and destroy" teams. All the hamlets were razed, all the rice plantations poisoned by chemical products, samples of which we have ourselves brought back. The grain reserves were annihilated and the civilians found there were deported to concentration camp zones called by the Americans "pacification zones" or "new life hamlets" which is but a change in name for the "strategic hamlets."

Many peasants we saw escaped from concentration camps, many others had fled from the advancing U.S. troops or simply hid in the forests and escaped the tank columns. Civilians are now forced to lie in hiding in the forests. They built miserable huts, well hidden in the wildness. Each family has dug an underground shelter, they live like primitive men to avoid being located. This so-called "White Zone" or "free fire" zone is now declared by the Americans to be totally "Vietcong" where all sign of life is extinguished systematically.

By night and by day, during our stay, the constant fire of artillery was heard. From the military bases, particularly in our region of

Traug Long and Tour Hai, the American artillery shoots at random to maintain a constant state of anxiety and insecurity.[1] Reconnaissance planes fly methodically over the whole zone in large concentric circles. As soon as movement appears as a sign of human presence, as soon as a field appears to be cultivated, orders are given for a concentrated artillery attack. The least sign of life located by reconnaissance planes is immediately followed by an attack of fighter-bombers which fire rockets, drop anti-personnel bombs, napalm and phosphor bombs. In the undergrowth, we have often seen for 200 meters around, a huge amount of aluminum fragments from rockets, bomb-casings, pineapple bombs.

According to the reports of the N.L.F. officials, since the beginning of "Junction City" and the policy of attacks on "everything that moves", the average ordnance expended is two tons of projectiles per inhabitant and one killed or wounded in every eight persons.

Half of the population has escaped the village sweeps or fled from "relocation centers". About 10,000 persons live in the wilderness with the help of the N.L.F. army, guerilla units and community services of the N.L.F. In spite of the "cleared zones", the Front keeps the education and health service operating even in the most miserable hamlets — that is to say, four or five huts grouped in the jungle.

To live, peasants are obliged to cultivate by night all the rice paddies and tiny kitchen-gardens on the fringe of the forests, otherwise, any field or rice patch slightly showing cultivation would be automatically destroyed by defoliants dropped from planes or helicopters. We saw various metallic drums dropped on rice paddies and then shot full of holes by the same planes so that the chemical products would dissolve into the water of the rice field to pollute and contaminate the crops.

It is therefore only by hiding and avoiding the reconnaissance planes and living practically underground that the people are able to survive what I shall not hesitate to call Genocide . . . .

---

[1]This is called "H & I", harassment and interdiction fire. Ed. Note.

Summary Report on Complicity of Thailand and the Philippines

Abstracted from testimony by Charles Fourniau

The United States must have active support from the other states in Southeast Asia to be able to fight the war in Vietnam at the present scale. They need relatively secure political surroundings; hence the series of pacts they have signed in this part of the world. They require a system of maintenance like air and naval bases surrounding Vietnam, as well as radar and cable networks, ammunition and food dumps, hospitals, etc. They also demand direct participation of states in the aggression against Vietnam through military expeditionary forces or through granting of bases for the American planes.

Thailand and the Philippines take part in the American aggression against Vietnam in all three of these ways. Thailand and the Philippines constitute the strongest bulwarks of the American security system in Southeast Asia. They are members of SEATO, which was created in 1954 and has its headquarters in Bangkok, the capital of Thailand. Since some of the neutral states refused to join this treaty, the idea of a regional cooperation was conceived as a substitute. The Philippines, Thailand and Malaysia therefore founded the Association of Southeast Asia (ASA) in 1961, which never gained any importance. At a meeting in Seoul, in 1966, the foreign ministers of Japan, South Korea, South Vietnam, Taiwan, Malaysia, Australia, New Zealand, Philippines and Thailand founded the Asian and Pacific Council (ASPAC), which theoretically is limited to cultural and economic questions. In reality it has as its aim the creation of a secure area for American military domination of Southeast Asia.

The Philippines

The Philippines plays an important role in American strategy because it constitutes the nerve-center for the American maintenance system in Southeast Asia. As early as 1947, through the United States-Philippines military treaties, the U.S. was given for a period of 99 years 23 large areas in the Philippines to build military bases. In 1966, the time was shortened to 44 years.

These bases service aircraft and naval craft. Subic Base is the main center for ships of the Seventh Fleet. Exclusive of aircraft carriers, the fleet numbers 175 ships. The importance of the base to the Vietnam war is obvious. But in addition, Subic is a home port for American atomic submarines. Sangley Point is one of the bases of the Seventh Fleet and is of great importance for servicing the submarine fleet of the Pacific.

The biggest American facility in the Philippines is Clark Air Force Base, north of Manila. It is an enormous military complex covering 540 square kilometers. Headquarters of the U.S. 13th Air Force is stationed there. It provides for the logistics maintenance of American bases in Thailand. Clark's other main function is to provide a link between the United States and Vietnam. The *Sunday Times*, on July 13, 1967, noted that "all Air Force personnel on the way to Southeast Asia have to pass through Clark Field." The base also receives wounded, and delivers urgent transports of ammunition and equipment. Clark Field also sustains enormous hospital establishments. The number of patients increased from 2340 in September 1965 to 4054 in March 1966 and has probably grown considerably since then. Recently the United States obtained the Mactan Base through an agreement that was signed on June 2, 1967, by President Marcos and the American Ambassador. It is at the disposal of the United States as long as the Vietnam War lasts and "the security" of the two countries so requires.

The total number of American forces in the Philippines is about 48,000 men. That bases are of vital importance to the USA, is a fact that former Secretary of Defense Robert McNamara expressed before the Senate Committee for Armed Services on January 23, 1967: "As long as the war in Vietnam lasts, the Philippines hold an exceptional strategic position. The bases and the means that are at the disposal of the United States in the Philippines have great importance. On this level the Philippines are very cooperative. Because our military needs in Vietnam are growing, the strategic position and the cooperation of the Philippines is becoming more important to us."

The Philippine Government has been represented since 1964 in a symbolic way at the side of the American forces in Vietnam through a "Civil Actions Group." In 1966 more than 2000 troops were sent to Vietnam under the command of General Tobias. As a consequence of the opposition this raised in the Philippine Congress and among the public, the troops were presented as only an expansion of the "Civil Actions Group."

The Philippine Government is thus an accessory to the American aggression against Vietnam by giving the United States diplomatic

579

support; by granting air and naval bases of vital importance to American forces in Vietnam on Philippine territory; and by sending troops who directly take part in the fighting. Even if this participation is a result of the neocolonial pressures that the United States exerts on the Philippines, the Philippine Government nonetheless bears full responsibility for this complicity in the American aggression against Vietnam.

Thailand

Thailand has become an American fortress in Asia. The military expansion of the United States in Thailand has been taking place parallel with the escalation of the war in Vietnam. As early as 1950, American troops were installed in Thailand, although on a relatively restricted scale. After the founding of SEATO, in which Thailand plays an important role, most of the military maneuvers of the treaty members were held in Thai territory. In 1962, the U.S. Army's Military Assistance Command, created in Saigon, extended its area of coverage to embrace all of Indo-China, the troops in Thailand and the bases at their disposal. During 1963 and 1964, a series of agreements made it possible to further expand the networks of bases. At the time the bombings of North Vietnam began, the United States was able to send aircraft to Thailand, to augment those which were already at this early period taking part in the air raids against North Vietnam.

In 1965 American forces in Thailand numbered 10,000 men. Now they total about 40,000 men, of which 30,000 are in the air force.

Four bases for fighters, bombers and fighter-bombers of the types F-105, F-4C are at Takhli, Korat, Udon, Ubon. Three helicopter bases are at Nakjon-Phanom, Udon, Ubon. Utapao is the base for B-52 strategic bombers and air-to-air tankers. Another B-52 base is being built at Khon Kaen. One naval base, Sattahip, located southeast of Bangkok, was inaugurated on August 18, 1967, and cost $43 million. There is also one Special Forces base at Lop Buri and one center for transport and military air maintenance at Don Muang, near Bangkok.

It is from these bases that most of the bombing raids against Vietnam and Laos depart. American officials, however, did not acknowledge this until January 18, 1967. It was not until March 9th that the Thai authorities also acknowledged this fact. An estimated 80 per cent of the raids against North Vietnam start from the Thailand bases. North Vietnam can be so intensively attacked because the United States does have these bases in Thailand. The bombings in South Vietnam are likewise facilitated because B-52s now come from Utapao rather than Guam. Instead of flying 7000 kilometers, they now have only to fly 2000 kilometers. In addition, Thailand takes a part directly in military operations. In September 1967, there were 3000 Thai troops in South Vietnam. Thailand further receives military aid of $60 million annually from the United States to maintain an army of 80,000 troops.

By granting air and naval bases for use by the United States, Thailand made possible the American escalation of the war which has developed since 1965. Thailand is a direct accessory to the crimes that are committed by the American Air Force in North and South Vietnam, as well as in Laos. Because of the presence of Thai troops in South Vietnam, that country is a direct accessory to the American aggression against Vietnam.

Complicity of Thailand in the U.S. Aggression
testimony of the Japanese Commission

Thailand covers an area of 512,000 square kilometers. It is populated by slightly under 30 million people and is situated on the peninsula of Indo-China. Earlier in history it was a country where imperialist powers competed for influence; it was finally controlled by British colonialism.

After World War II — in the name of "anti-Communism" and as part of the "encirclement policy" against China — the American imperialists used every means to destroy the various national liberation movements breaking out all over Southeast Asia. The U.S. has infiltrated Thailand — strategic as it is — in preparation for making this country into a modern colony and an American military base.

National independence by force of arms is a common phenomenon in Southeast Asia since World War II. The victory of the Chinese Revolution late in 1949 wiped American imperialism from the Chinese mainland. The success of the Vietnamese people against the French colonialists is an element which goads the U.S. to make Thailand a complete dependent of the U.S. To accomplish this, the U.S. has used every means to infiltrate Thailand both by so-called "aid" and by military coups, which brought military puppets to power.

In August 1950 the U.S. sent an economic study delegation, headed by a Mr. Griffins, and a military survey delegation, headed by General Graves B. Erskine and John Melby to Thailand. Erskine put special weight upon improving airports, ports, roads and the Thai Army.

On September 19, 1950, the Thai authorities and the U.S. signed an "economic and technical cooperation treaty" followed by a "mutual defense treaty" on October 17 of the same year. The effect of these two treaties was that the rulers of Thailand bartered away the sovereignty and independence of their country, and since then Thailand has become a colony and military base for the U.S.

It is well known that before, during, and after the Geneva Conference of 1954, the U.S. hastily began to persuade and induce a number of countries to form the Southeast Asia Treaty Organization (SEATO). Their primary motivation was to form a buffer to work against movements for national liberation in this area and to create a structure that could exert influence on the internal affairs of the countries of Indo-China. The Thai regime under Phiboun Songram has played a major role in implementing U.S. policy. Thailand is the second most important member of SEATO; the permanent headquarters of that organization is in Bangkok. For the last thirteen years, military maneuvers of the armed forces of the treaty members have been held on Thai territory . . . .

The Thai government has granted the Americans many air bases and military installations. Among these are bases for fighter-bombers and fighters at Takhli, Korat, Udon and Ubon. Udon and Ubon also service helicopters. There is a B-52 base at Utapao and a new one being built at a cost of $43 million at Khen Kaen. There is a naval base for U.S. warships at Sattahip and a Special Forces base at Lop Buri. A military air transport base is located at Don Muang; a network of radar stations and Signal Corps communications centers are at Ubon, Mukhadan, Chieng Mai, and the country is dotted and laced with storage dumps, strategic roads and pipe lines.

U.S. troops stationed in Thailand number about 40,000, the greatest number being in the air force. All are under U.S. command though some are camouflaged as "advisors" to the Thais under "MAC-Thai" (Military Assistance Command - Thailand) which is commanded by General McCowen from Bangkok. The elaborate command system and the permanence of the installations under MAC-Thai direction, clearly show that the U.S. pursues goals which extend far beyond Thai borders. This massive complex, in addition to providing proof of Thai cooperation in American designs, supports the theory of U.S. imperialist intentions in all of Southeast Asia, especially against

Vietnam, Cambodia and Laos, The Secretary of State for Thailand, Thanat Kheman, admitted on September 27, 1966, in New York, that U.S. bases in Thailand are used against Vietnam. *(UPI, Sept. 28, 1966)*

The Thai government has furnished Thai pilots to take part in American strikes against North Vietnam. On the 18th of August, 1964, a T-28 jet was shot down over Quang Binh province by North Vietnamese anti-aircraft gunners. The pilot was Chem Bamrung Vom, a Thai.

From the beginning, Thai authorities have attempted to conceal their complicity in granting use of their bases ever since March, 1965. But the Associated Press, an American news agency, revealed on April 8, 1965, that U.S. aircraft stationed at Korat had flown several missions against North Vietnam. Further proof exists in the increasing number of downed and imprisoned American pilots in North Vietnam who acknowledge Thailand as their home base. On March 9, 1967, the Thai government made public its participation in the war by signing a not-so-secret, "secret bi-lateral agreement" with the U.S. Since that time official U.S. figures disclosed that 85% of the raids against Vietnam originate from Thailand and that reconnaissance flights utilizing millions of yards of film every month are also flown from there. The Utapao air base was completed in March 21, 1967 and a Thai-U.S. treaty was immediately signed allowing B-52s to be stationed there, cutting hours from the flying time of the former Guam-to-Vietnam run. These bombers are used to hit both South Vietnam and North Vietnam.

The Thai government has also sent troops to participate directly in the war. In 1964 a group of Thai pilots, navigators and mechanics had already been sent to South Vietnam to aid the air force of the puppet regime. In additon the Thai government had agreed to train South Vietnamese pilots on Thai territory. On May 3, 1966 an LST [landing-ship-tank], an armed cutter and two C-123 aircraft, all belonging to Thailand and complete with crews — 180 men in all —, were sent to South Vietnam. In the beginning of 1967, Thailand took the most compromisingly irrevocable step of all and shipped the "Queen's Cobra Regiment," consisting of 2,000 soldiers equipped with American arms, to fight against the people of South Vietnam. On August 30, 1967 Thailand's Premier, Thanon Kittikachorn, held a farewell banquet for this regiment and on September 21st they landed in Saigon. By this action the Thai government has sold young Thai lives for the dollars and materiel of the Americans and at the same time become complicit in war crimes.

Thai air bases are also used in the clandestine U.S. bombing war against Laotian territory. Thailand has taken direct part as well in the U.S. clandestine "special war" against Laotians and stores and funnels weapons and munitions to the counter-revolutionaries in Laos. In May of 1962, 7,000 U.S. Marines were allowed to land in Thailand and move across the border into Laos to put pressure on and harass Laotian Liberation Forces. In addition, Thai territory has been used by U.S. Special Forces units for infiltration, sabotage, and terrorization raids into Laos. Right wing Laotian circles have received considerable aid and instruction from advisors and units of the Thai army. Thailand has also aided and abetted the operations of the so-called "Free Khmer," a group of mercenaries which constantly attack and occupy border hamlets on the Cambodian side of the border.

In conclusion, the U.S. has received Thailand's cooperation in making Thai territory available as a base of supply for the U.S. war of aggression; it has made available its territory for advance air bases for the illegal bombing of North and South Vietnam; and it has directly contributed troops to war against the Vietnamese in support of American units. Though the U.S. is the principle aggressor and bears the major guilt for the committing of war crimes, the government of Thailand is an accomplice and must share the responsibility for crimes against the Vietnamese people.

Combined Testimonies on the Complicity of Japan in the Vietnam War

testimony by the Japanese Committee

Based on Evidence Submitted to the Tokyo Tribunal; Compiled by the Permanent Japanese Committee for the Investigation of War Crimes in Vietnam

I. Introduction

II. Cooperation with and Participation in the U.S. War of Aggression

    1. Political Cooperation and Participation by the Japanese Government

        Official Government Statement offered in Justification and Defense of U.S. Acts of Aggression in Vietnam

        Aid Extended to the Puppet Regime of South Vietnam

        Hostile Policy toward the Vietnamese People

I. *Introduction*

Japanese imperialism during World War II, which had already committed the crime of aggression in Vietnam, to say nothing of China, the Philippines, Burma, and other Asian countries, was responsible for the death by starvation of over two million Vietnamese people.

As a consequence of World War II, Japanese imperialism was defeated, and a new Japanese Constitution was adopted in May 1947, which was in accordance with the spirit of the Potsdam Declaration and reflected the democratic demands of the Japanese people. The outstanding characteristic of the new Constitution of Japan lies in its renunciation of all war and its denial of Japan's right to belligerency. This means that armed forces, arms and a munitions industry are prohibited in Japan.

In its preparations for aggression against Asia, the U.S. revived Japanese monoply capitalism and Japanese militarism to utilize and control them as an ally. The Japanese capitalists and their Government, in turn, have cooperated in this and at the same time have tried to expand abroad, into South East Asia in particular. In June 1950, with the beginning of the war in Korea, the American military headquarters in Japan ordered the Japanese Government to establish armed forces to be called the "Police Reserve Force," in violation of the Constitution of Japan. The Japanese Government, backed by the capitalists, welcomed this order which, in effect, promoted the rearmament of Japan. The U.S. Government took a further step toward building its rule over Japan. In defiance of the demand raised by the greatest victim countries of Japan, such as China, the Democratic Republic of Vietnam, the Soviet Union, India and Burma, the U.S. Government brought about the signing of a "peace treaty" with Japan, and at the same time concluded the Japan-U.S. Security Treaty.

At the opening ceremony of this "peace conference" at San Francisco, the then President of the U.S., Harry Truman, said: (re-translation) "If genuine security is to be achieved in the Pacific region, the free nations in that region must find a way for mutual cooperation for joint defense. For this reason, it is very important for Japan to participate as soon as possible in an appropriate security arrangement to maintain peace in the Pacific. Development of a regional arrangement for defense in the Pacific will enable a Japanese defense force, which will be established in the future, to act in cooperation with the defense forces of the other countries of this region. The Japanese armed forces, together with those of the other nations, will give a mutual guarantee against the threat to the independence of the Pacific nations including Japan."

In September 1951, the U.S. was in the midst of the war in Korea, while in Vietnam, French troops were involved in a struggle against the liberation offensive of the Vietnam People's Army. In these words of Truman spoken at the San Francisco conference, considering the conditions then existing in Asia, we can infer the real aim of the U.S. In this speech also, we can detect the motivation for the hurried conclusion of the "peace treaty" with Japan and what future hopes were entertained of Japan by the U.S. At this "peace conference" the U.S. was preparing a puppet under its own control. The Bao Dai regime was established in Vietnam jointly by France and the U.S., but did not in any sense represent the Vietnamese people. The person who attended this conference and signed the "peace treaty" as the representative of Vietnam was of French nationality, and claimed to be Premier, Foreign Minister and Defense Minister of the Bao Dai regime.

Beginning to intervene actively in the aggression against Vietnam, the U.S. sought to involve Japan in its intervention and to link Japan with the Bao Dai regime, with this San Francisco conference providing the opportunity. The moment the Japanese Government signed the San Francisco Peace Treaty and Japan-U.S. Security Treaty, it became complicit. In November 1959, the Japanese Government committed an illegal act by concluding a reparations agreement with the puppet regime of South Vietnam, as though it represented the whole of the

Vietnamese people. By so doing, the Japanese Government violated the Geneva Agreements and gave support to the U.S. policy of dividing Vietnam, which was an infringement of the national sovereignty of the Vietnamese.

At the time this reparations agreement was concluded, the resistance struggle of the South Vietnamese people against the U.S. and Ngo Dien Diem was beginning to expand throughout the South. The resistance had hardened as a result of the massacre at the Phou Loi concentration camp in December 1958 and the promulgation of Law No. 10 in 1959. By concluding the reparations agreement with the Ngo Dien Diem regime, the Japanese Government and monopoly capitalists paid war reparations, that should have gone to all the Vietnamese people to only South Vietnam. The conclusion of this reparations agreement also meant Japan's active participation in U.S. neo-colonialism and denied the existence of the Democratic Republic of Vietnam even though it had been internationally recognized as a sovereign state by the Geneva Conference. Japan's action contributed to perpetuating the provisional military demarcation line as a permanent border line. After the agreement, Japan cooperated in the construction of military bases of an offensive nature directed against the Democratic Republic of Vietnam, and even built electric power stations to supply electricity to U.S. military bases in South Vietnam. For this, the Japanese Government spent the Japanese people's taxes amounting to 20 billion Yen (approximately $55 million).

The Japanese Government's cooperation and participation has been regularized and assumed many forms. First, the Japanese Government has consistently tried to justify and defend the U.S. aggression in Vietnam, has recognized the puppet regime of South Vietnam, and has extended to it military, medical and economic cooperation, thereby opposing the Democratic Republic of Vietnam with a completely hostile policy. Secondly, the Japanese Government has granted military bases in all parts of Japan, including Okinawa, for the U.S. war in Vietnam. These bases vary from operation bases, to training, supply, repair bases, field hospitals and facilities for rest and recreation. Thirdly, the Japanese Government has cooperated in procuring manpower including crew members for military vessels, which, in effect, constitutes actual dispatch of troops. Fourthly, the Japanese Government has supplied munitions, directly and indirectly, under what is called "special procurement" for Vietnam. Fifth, the Japanese Government has strengthened Japan's "Self-Defense Forces" as the rear-guard of the U.S. military thereby aiding and abetting the expanding aggressive military policy of the U.S.A.

II. *Cooperation with and Participation in the War*

The Japanese Government has consistently defended the justified the U.S. war of aggression in Vietnam. Of these official Government statements, made since 1964, we quote some representative examples below:

(1) The "Tonkin Gulf Incident" of 1964 was obviously manufactured by the U.S. Government to justify their plan to bomb North Vietnam. On August 10, 1964, immediately after this incident, at a Foreign Affairs Committee meeting of the Lower House, the then Foreign Minister Shiina, in attempting to justify the U.S. action said: "It is true that before and after this incident, warships and other vessels of the Seventh Fleet sailed from Sasebo and Yokosuka for a patrolling mission in the Tonkin Gulf...While patrolling the high seas, they were attacked unexpectedly from North Vietnam, and as a result the U.S. forces rebuffed this attack with force as a so-called act of self-defense. Therefore, the action taken by the U.S. side was within the limits of the right of self-defense."

(2) With the February 1965, U.S. bombing of North Vietnam, the Japanese Government more openly took an attitude favoring the war. At a Foreign Affairs Committee meeting of the Lower House on April 7, 1965, for instance, Foreign Minister Shiina, said: "The U.S. is carrying on military intervention at the request of South Vietnam in order to defend its independence and freedom. The aggression from the North continues now. For the sake of freedom and independence of South Vietnam, this continued aggression must be repulsed. This is an act of self-defense, as it were..."

In connection with furnishing military supplies and co-operating in the transport of munitions, at a Foreign Affairs Committee meeting of the Lower House on April 14, 1965, Foreign Minister Shiina said: "The action (of the U.S. Forces) in Vietnam is within the framework of the Security Treaty, this is my opinion. Accordingly, in case bases in Japan are directly used and operation actions are taken from there, this will constitute an object of prior consultation; otherwise, the use in various ways of facilities in Japan for supply and other purposes is what Japan should offer from the standoint of the (Japan-U.S.) Security Treaty. This is our view.

"And the transport of munitions is a natural task within the framework of the (Japan-U.S.) Security Treaty. That seamen have so far worked in this task at their own will through the good offices of the Government, does not in any sense mean active cooperation."

In connection with "prior consultation" before the direct departure of U.S. forces from Japanese bases, at a Foreign Affairs Committee meeting of the Lower House on May 19, 1965, the then Parliamentary Vice-Foreign Minister Nagata said: "The U.S. is an ally of Japan, and I don't think that an allied nation would tell a lie. I think that the reason for having no prior consultation so far (between Japan and the U.S.) is because the U.S. forces have not so far participated in the battle directly from Japanese bases." Thus, the "prior consultation" stipulation in the Japan-U.S. Security Treaty is not effective, but rather is being used as a pretext by the Japanese Government to claim ignorance.

(3) From the end of 1965 through the beginning of 1966, the U.S. Government made a series of so-called "peace proposals" followed by the further intensification of its war of aggression. The Japanese Government actively supported these moves. On July 18, 1965, at a Budget Committee meeting of the Lower House, Foreign Minister Shiina gave the following reply to a question raised by an opposition member:

Kaku Nohara, Committee Member: "And I would like to ask the Foreign Minister, in your opinion what position is Japan placed in at present in connection with the war in Vietnam?"

Foreign Minister Shiina: "We have the Japan-U.S. Security Treaty. When the U.S. takes actions with regard to peace and security in the Far East, we must follow the juridical relations based on this Security Treaty. That is to say, Japan has an obligation to approve the use by U.S. forces of Japanese facilities and areas in this connection. In this sense, speaking from the pure legal point of view, Japan is not placed in a neutral position with regard to the war in Vietnam. Because, as long as there is a situation wherein the U.S. forces are legally using facilities and areas in Japanese territory, Japan is not placed in a neutral position. This can be pointed out."

In effect the Foreign Minister clearly admitted that Japan is in complicity with the U.S. in this war. It should be pointed out, Foreign Minister Shiina very clearly showed cooperation with the U.S. in the war in his statement at a Foreign Affairs Committee meeting of the Lower House on June 8, 1965. This was in connection with the port call of warships and other vessels of the U.S. Seventh Fleet. He said: "Whether or not the U.S. warships and other vessels making port calls at Japenese ports are engaged in the Vietnam war, it is an obligation (for Japan) stipulated in the Japan-U.S. Security Treaty to approve it."

By regarding the Japan-U.S. Security Treaty as a military alliance treaty, Prime Minister Sato has expressed his intention of maintaining the present complicity with the U.S. Military. At a Lower House Budget Committee meeting on July 18, 1965, he said: "In my opinion, it is not proper to abrogate the present Security Treaty, as long as there is no serious change in the international situation, and as long as our own strength of self-defense remains as it is now. It is therefore my opinion that we should continually maintain the present Japan-U.S. Security Treaty."

(4) On October 21, 1967, Prime Minister Sato visited South Vietnam and met President Thieu of the puppet regime. They issued the following "joint statement," in which Sato openly encouraged the puppet regime and U.S. imperialism. The Prime Minister expressed "sympathy and understanding toward the efforts being made by the Vietnamese Government and people to insure the independence and sovereignty of the Republic of Vietnam and expressed the hope that a peaceful as well as equitable settlement of the conflict would be brought about at the earliest possible date." Sato, added the joint communique, "expressed the determination of his government to do its utmost to achieve this purpose . . .The communique also said that General Thieu and Prime Minister Sato "expressed satisfaction at the significance of Prime Minister Sato's visit to Vietnam with regard to strengthening the cordial relations between the two countries." . . . Finally the two countries "agreed to make efforts to promote regional cooperation such as the one manifested in the activities of the ministerial conference for the economic development of Southeast Asia and the Asian Development Bank."

Aid to the Puppet Regime of South Vietnam

On the occasion of the breaking off of diplomatic relations between Cambodia and the South Vietnamese regime in 1963, the Japanese Government became a "protecting power" of the South Vietnamese regime in Cambodia. It has stationed resident military officers in Saigon since 1966, dispatched a military inspection team in September 1966, and paid about $200,000 to South Vietnam for "relief of refugees" in March 1966. Japan's ruling Liberal Democratic Party and the Federation of Economic Organizations have also sent delegations one after another in the name of "friendship missions for economic co-operation abroad" and a "study mission to Vietnam" etc. On the occasion of the so-called presidential elections of the South Vietnamese regime in September 1967, members of the Japanese ruling party visited Saigon at the call of the U.S. to observe the elections.

In 1967, Prime Minister Sato visited the "Republic of Korea", Taiwan, and other Asian and Pacific nations including those participating in the Vietnam war. In defiance of strong public opposition, and of dissident views within his own party, he paid an official visit to South Vietnam on October 21, 1967. In this he followed the precedents set by leaders of the "Republic of Korea," Australia, and the Philippines, all participating nations in the Vietnam war. The last destination of Prime Minister Sato's tours abroad was the U.S. in November 1967. Recently, Prime Minister Sato gave approval for the U.S. aircraft carrier *Enterprise* to make a port-call at Yokosuka. The *Enterprise* is a nuclear-powered warship engaged in the aggression against Vietnam. Thus, the Sato Government is more and more strengthening its cooperation with the U.S.

Hostile Policy toward the Vietnamese

The hostile policy of the Sato Government toward the Vietnamese people is expressed in its ban on cultural exchanges between the two peoples. In May 1966, for instance, the Sato Government refused to grant entry visas for the Vietnam National singing and Dancing Troupe to perform in Japan. Certain pamphlets and photographs showing Vietnamese victims and giving evidence of U.S. war crimes are also prohibited entry into Japan. By contrast, American servicemen land in Japan freely without any official entry procedures, customs clearances or quarantine.

The Sato Government has created elaborate obstructions to trade with the Democratic Republic of Vietnam. It has prohibited the assignment of Japanese ships for trade to Haiphong port since April 1966, and has restricted goods for export and import. In March 1966, it prohibited the export of 20,000 km of electric cable which had been contracted for between the Vietnam Machine Export and Import Corporation and Toshima & Co. of Japan. The contract had been made legally, and there was no reason for this prohibition, but four months after production had begun the Government arbitrarily stopped it. It brought pressure to bear on the firm under urging from the U.S. Embassy, saying: "The export of this item is not desirable as it would increase and strengthen the war potential of Vietnam. Should the export be completed, the shipment of copper from the U.S. to Japan will be stopped."

The operational system of the U.S. Army, Navy and Air Force in Japan are the Pacific Army, the Pacific Fleet and the Pacific Air Force under the command of the Pacific Joint Forces with headquarters in Hawaii. Each of the U.S. military arms in Japan is directed and under the orders of the equivalent command in Hawaii.

U.S. military bases in Japan have been established in 264 places; made up from 147 in mainland Japan and 117 in Okinawa. With regard to functions, these bases can be classified into four types. The first are combat bases, the second logistic, supply and repair bases, the third are recuperation and recreation bases, and the fourth are intelligence and training bases. Some bases have dual functions and some cannot be classified into any of these types.

Combat bases are such direct striking bases as Kadena base in Okinawa, Yokota base in Tokyo, Iwakuni base in Yamaguchi Prefecture (the largest attack base in western Japan) and Yokosuka and Sasebo bases of the Seventh Fleet. Communications bases can also be classified with these combat bases, and include Wakkanai radar base in Hokkaido, RORAN C base at Tokachi in Hokkaido, the U.S. Navy Signal Corps Station at Kamiseya in Yokohama, and the U.S. Navy Signal Corps at Isami in Aichi Prefecture.

The second type, logistic, supply and repair bases, include Tachikawa base which is a terminal for U.S. war planes in Asia and the Pacific; Yokosuka Naval base; the U.S. Army General Supply Depot at Sagamihara in Kanagawa Prefecture; military facilities at Yokohama and Kobe (ports for loading and unloading of war materials) and fueling depots and explosive magazines at Azumashima in Yokosuka port, Akizuki in Hiroshima, Yamada in Fukuoka and Zushi-Ikego in Kanagawa Prefecture.

Recreation and recuperation bases include the U.S. Army field hospitals at Asaka in Saitama Prefecture, Kamijujo in Tokyo, Kishine in Yokohama, Sagamihara in Kanagawa Prefecture and the U.S. Naval Hospital at Yokosuka base. In addition there are other medical treatment facilities, hotels and other facilities for recreation of the U.S. forces scattered throughout Tokyo, Atami and other places in Japan.

The fourth type, intelligence and training bases, include the U.S. Army Bureau for Study and Development of the Far East in Sagamihara city and the U.S. Army Printing Office at Kawasaki city in Kanagawa Prefecture, Mito shooting and bombing range, Misawa anti-surface missile and bombing range, Kita Fuji practice range, U.S. training center at Numazu in Shizuoka Prefecture, anti-surface missile and bombing range in Torishima island. Attention should also be given to the fact that in order to create naval practice grounds, wide areas of the open sea have been closed to normal trade and shipping.

Following is a general survey of bases in Tokyo and adjacent Kanagawa Prefecture.

i. Tachikawa base is a very valuable and important base for U.S. military activity in the Far East, particularly for its aggression in Vietnam.

Tachikawa consists of two facilities; Tachikawa airport (facility No. FAC-3014). In the latter, there are factories for fully equipping various types of planes. In addition, factories for repairing special equipment and for manufacturing machine tools to be used for repairs are maintained there. The Air Force Materials Command in the Pacific region is in charge of supplying materials and logistics for all the air force stationed in Japan. Tachikawa airport is used for air transport, not only of such supply but also of freight and personnel. All arrivals and departures of U.S. forces by air and urgent transport of airfreight are through Tachikawa airport. In servicing of planes, not only routine check-up, repair and refueling, but also overhaul and thoroughgoing repair, assembly and rigging are also conducted at Tachikawa. In this way, Tachikawa airport is used as a multi-purpose, continuous operation, large scale airport — one of the very few such in the world. It is said that an average of 23,000 servicemen pass through here every month for duty in the Far East.

In addition to Tachikawa, there are many military bases and U.S. units stationed in and around Metropolitan Tokyo, which are either directly or indirectly involved in the expanding U.S. aggression in Vietnam.

For instance, the Command of the Fifth Air Force, is located at Fuchu. The area for the defense of which the Fifth Air Force is responsible is approximately the same as the U.S. mainland. It stretches from Japan to the "Republic of Korea," Okinawa, Iwo-Jima and the surrounding ocean. The combat command of the Fifth Air Force plays a large part in the expanding U.S. aggression in Vietnam. Its F-105's, carrying hydrogen bombs, are using Yokota as a permanent base supplementary to Tachikawa.

As the U.S. aggression in Vietnam has intensified, planes also arrive at Haneda international airport in Tokyo directly from Saigon and Kadena in Okinawa. From here they take off again for Kadena and the battlefields. More and more flights are taking off from here bound to and from Bien Hoa and bases in Thailand.

ii. U.S. Military Bases in Kanagawa Prefecture.

There are 45 U.S. military bases in Kanagawa Prefecture. U.S. nuclear-powered submarines are making port calls at Yokosuka which is becoming a permanent nuclear base. The U.S. Army Command and the Navy Command in Japan are set up at these bases, and all the central command machinery necessary to carry on the war are concentrated here. These bases also function for combat and operations, communications, supply and repair, recuperation and recreation, training and intelligence, psychological warfare, chemical and biological warfare.

On September 8, 1964, a Crusader plane from the Seventh Fleet fell in the vicinity of the naval airport at Atsugi and killed five Japanese. At that time, a piece of air map was found in the wreckage of the plane. Written on the map were directions for raids by U.S. planes, remarks on landing, methods of communication and other items necessary for operations in Hue, Vietnam and Don Wan, Thailand. This happened just after the Tonkin Gulf incident, and is irrefutable evidence that Yokosuka and Atsugi bases are directly used for aggression against Vietnam.

There is a General Supply Depot for the Army at Sagamihara. Five storehouses of oil and ammunition and a North Pier as a loading and unloading facility are under its direction. There is also a large scale armored vehicle repair factory here. Several hundred N-48 tanks and M-113 armored cars are always lying there in a vast open-air field just as arrived smashed from Vietnam. Blood and pieces of human flesh are often found sticking to these tanks and cars, and unexploded shells also often explode during dismantling. Seeing these tanks through barbed wire, no one doubts that this base is directly connected with Vietnam. At this base there is also a test road for tanks constructed like a Vietnamese jungle.

For the navy, a warship and vessel repair section is located at Yokosuka. All kinds of repair work is undertaken here for ships ranging from cruisers equipped with missiles to nuclear powered submarines. This base with excellent repair facilities and techniques is available together with cheap labor for less than one fourth of the wages on the U.S. mainland.

For bacteriological warfare, the Medical Institute of the 406 CBW Unit is at Sagamihara. This barbaric installation was denounced by name on July 20, 1966, by the South Vietnam National Front for Liberation. Its purpose is study and implementation of bacteriological warfare; the Japanese Government has placed 100 Japanese including able research workers there.

594

Okinawa — the Largest Base of Aggression Against Vietnam

Okinawa, which is now ruled by the U.S. forces, was one of the more than 40 Prefectures of pre-war Japan. It consists of a chain of small islands, situated at the southern tip of the Japanese archipelago, about 600 km from Kagoshima, Kyushu Island, in mainland Japan. Its capital city is Naha, with a population of 230,000, where the High Commissioner of the U.S. "Civil Government" (actually military government) is stationed. The total population of Okinawa is about 960,000 Japanese people from ancient times. They have been, for the more than 20 years since World War II, under the rule of the U.S. military administration. The U.S. Government has stated that Okinawa is the most important keystone in the U.S. strategic bridge in the Far East. The distance from Okinawa to Hanoi, Vietnam is 2,418 km; to Peking 1,793 km; to Pyongyang, Korea, 1,334; to Khavarovsk and Vladivostok of the Soviet Union 2,502 and 1,876 km respectively. In other words, Okinawa lies only a short distance from Vietnam, China and the Soviet Union.

Okinawa is an advantegous base, an "unsinkable aircraft carrier," as it were, as a supply, sorty and nuclear base for the U.S. aggression against Vietnam, and a place from which to dominate Asian countries of the Far East. It was in Okinawa waters that warships of Japan's maritime "Self-Defense" Forces several times carried out joint exercises with the U.S. forces. Here, also, troops of Thailand, the Philippines, the "Republic of Korea," and the South Vietnam regime are conducting military training under command of the U.S. forces.

Below are quotations from the testimonies given by U.S. Government officials in regard to the military role of Okinawa:

Admiral Sharp, Commander of the U.S. Pacific Joint Forces, writing in the *Morning Star,* official organ of the U.S. Forces, dated December 10, 1965, said: (retranslated) "Without Okinawa, we cannot carry on the Vietnam war." In an interview with a correspondent of Japan's *Asahi Shimbun,* he said: "Preservation of the U.S. military facilities in Okinawa will be indispensable for the future security of the free world, including Japan.... To provide for any unexpected state of affairs in South East Asia, Okinawa remains a very important transit and logistic base, and an important communication center for the U.S. Army and Air Force." — *Asahi Shimbun,* July 20, 1967.

Assistant Under-Secretary of the Army, Holt said: (retranslated) "Unanimity of opinion is reached among broad circles that, from its strategic position, Okinawa is the most important base for the defense of the free world. The sole reason for the U.S. retaining administrative rights over Okinawa is to be found in the military importance of Okinawa and in the fact that tensions still persists in the Far East." (Testimony at the 3rd Subcommittee Hearing of the U.S. House Military Affairs Committee on April 13, 1967)

. . . Further comment should be made on White Beach on the Katsuren peninsula of Okinawa where there is a base of the U.S. Seventh Fleet. Some 64,000 officers and men are stationed here. Every day loading and unloading of arms, ammunition and other materials are going on there. The monthly amount of ammunition handled alone is said to be about 25,000 tons. A supply base at Makiminato port is a base mainly dealing with food and clothing; about 8,000 people work there.

Man-Power Supplied by the Japanese Government

Of all the LST ships (Landing-Ships-Tank) participating in military transport for the U.S. war of aggression in Vietnam, 28 are operated by Japanese; all crew members, including captains, are Japanese.

Transport for the war in Vietnam is accomplished by both air and marine transport units. The LST ships manned by Japanese are incorporated into the U.S. Military Sea Transport Service — or MSTS-Far East.

As of January 31, 1967, the number of Japanese crew members on MSTS LST's was 1,368. The U.S. classifies these vessels as "Naval", indicating that LST crew are members of a kind of U.S. military, in this case forming a kind of "foreign legion." There have already been cases of deaths and wounds, which should obviously be called "war deaths and war wounds" among these Japanese crews. Continuation of such action against Vietnam on board LST's flying the "Stars and Stripes" should be regarded precisely as the "dispatch of troops" by Japan. Such transportation by maritime units constitutes a part of the overall war action, by any definition.

The role of LST's in the Vietnam war is very great in view of the geographical situation of Vietnam. There are very few harbor facilities available for large transport ships on the coast of South Vietnam. Land transport is very difficult as almost all territory is under fire by the South Vietnam National Front for Liberation and its armed forces. Because of this, LST's have played, and are playing, a decisively important role in the trasportation of arms and ammunition required for the rapidly escalating war, as by their design they are capable of unloading at places with no proper harbor facilities, and of

596

sailing up shallow rivers. LST's therefore, are craft designed purely for war. They have extremely bad living conditions, which is why
American seamen have refused to serve on board them. The U.S.
Government is overcoming this refusal to serve by their own nationals
by employing Japanese seamen and paying a small amount of danger
money as enticement. The Sato Government is cooperating in this
American policy.

Japanese engaged in American military transport for Vietnam are
not only on LST's. There are also seamen who are employed by the
Japanese Government (as semi-government employees) and who are
offered to the U.S. forces. As of the end of June 1967, the number of
Japanese employed in this manner totaled 226. Of these, according to
a survey by the Japanese Government, 38 persons are working for the
U.S. Army, 41 persons for the U.S. Navy, and 147 persons for MSTS.
Persons working for MSTS are taking part in military transport for
all areas of the Far East on board U.S. freighters and other ships. The
offer of these Japanese personnel to the U.S. armed forces by the Japanese Government is based on the agreement on the status of U.S.
forces in Japan in accordance with the Japan-U.S. Security Treaty.
The participation and cooperation by the Japanese Government is
undeniable.

There are other forms of cooperation by Japan in the U.S. war.
Japanese nationals are serving on board American civilian ships,
chartered ships of the U.S. forces, and Japanese vessels under civilian contract with American shipping companies. They also cooperate in salvage in Saigon, loading and unloading, transport, and
construction of harbor facilities and bases. Recently, under the
endorsement of an official budget expenditure for "expenses for
medical cooperation with Vietnam," Japanese doctors have been
sent to South Vietnam. The Japanese Government has issued passports to all these persons.

These support the charge that the Sato Government is participating in and cooperating with the U.S. aggression against Vietnam
by supplying of man-power.

Economic Cooperation in the War by the Japanese Government

We would like to explain how the Japanese Government and monopoly capitalists are cooperating with and participating in the U.S.
aggression in Vietnam with particular reference to what is called
"special procurement."

There are two kinds of "special procurement" — "direct special
procurement" and "indirect special procurement" — these are
methods for purchase of war materiel by the U.S. in Japan.

Economic journalists joint out that to grasp the real extent of special procurement in Japan is extremely difficult because the Japanese Government is not empowered to even survey the full picture. The only information available is from data provided by courtesy of the U.S. Embassy. Because the capitalists are trying not to publicize the facts for fear of being criticized as "merchants of death," all such contracts are semi-clandestine.

Up to 1959 the U.S. Embassy provided the Japanese Government with data on ordering of goods and services under direct special procurement. This data included products, names of companies and amounts of money involved, details which the Japanese Government then released to the public. But since 1960, the year of public outcry against the Japan-U.S. Security Treaty, even this has not been done. Although, under the Japan-U.S. Security Treaty and the agreement on the status of the U.S. forces in Japan, the Japanese Government is not empowered to make a survey of such matters, the Minister of International Trade and Industry (MITI) has this to say in explanation:

"The Japanese Government is trying to obtain as accurate statistics as possible by asking for reports from trade companies, summing them up and by making contact with the U.S." In reality, however, the Japanese Government is cooperating with U.S. imperialism, and will not make known to the Japanese people the nature and full extent of special procurement for Vietnam.

Nonetheless, from the very limited data officially approved by the U.S. Embassy and published by MITI, we can obtain the following information on special procurement. It testifies to the cooperation and participation in the Vietnam war by the Japanese Government and monopoly capitalists.

Special procurements in the first half of 1967 increased 14% compared with the same period of 1966. Exports to the countries related to the Vietnam war in the first half of 1967 increased by 41%, i.e. $550 million more compared with the same period of the previous year.

Japan's exports to the U.S. increased by 19.8% in 1965, but increased by 34.6% in 1966. This figure represents 80% increase in Japan's exports in 1966. The situation is such that even MITI cannot neglect the relationship between these figures and the Vietnam war. MITI estimates that direct and indirect procurements resulting from the Vietnam war have reached about 600 million dollars, while the estimate by the Foreign Ministry comes to a far greater amount— 900 or 1,100 million dollars. Even the minimum estimation confirms that this quantity of goods and services from Japan for the

U.S. is being used for killing and wounding the people of Vietnam and for building U.S. rule in Southeast Asia. Japanese sales to the military procurement arms of the U.S. indicate a tendency to increase with the escalation of the war, and Japanese capitalists are competing with each other for more orders.

Names of products admitted by the Japanese Government to be supplied to the U.S. military include sand bags to be used in combat (produce by Japan Jute Bags, and Tokyo Rayon), jungle boots, (Kokoku Chemicals, Tsukiboshi Rubber, Nihon Rubber), military caps, helmets and parachutes.

Materials for the construction of positions and bases include, barbed wire, timber, steel road and landing mats, cement, steel for construction, generators, insect netting, cranes, water purification apparatus, etc. Cement is supplied to the U.S. forces by Sumitomo Cement, Aso Industry, Mitsubishi Cement; road mats by Yahata Iron Manufacturing and Yahata Metal Manufacturing, and generators by Nishishiba Electric Co.

Materials for communication and transport supplied include wireless and telephone facilities, military trucks, jeeps, automobile parts, vehicles and diesel engines for small vessels. Military trucks are produced to Toyota, Fuji Vehicles, jeeps by Mitsubishi Heavy Industries, automobile parts by Toyota and Mitsubishi Heavy Industries.

Japan also furnishes materials and techniques for the construction of harbors. The Vietnam war is a war of supplies, and ports and harbors are decisive for the aggression. Bottlenecks of ports and harbors in Vietnam were disastrous to the U.S. forces. The availability of Japanese materials and techniques, as in the construction of Cam Rahn Bay, is a major support to the war.

Services of Japanese origin include repairs to planes, helicopters, warships and vessels, including LST's. Nihon Aircraft, Shinmeiwa Industry, Mitsubishi Heavy Industries, Kawasaki Aircraft are all taking increased repair contracts including carrier based planes and helicopters of the U.S. Seventh Fleet. Contracts for repair in 1966 were 1.46 times greater than in 1965; since 1966, plane parts are furnished by these makers. Repair of warships, cargo vessels and LST's have been undertaken by Mitsubishi Heavy Industries, Ishikawajima Harima Shipbuilding Co., Hitachi Shipbuilding, and Uraga Heavy Industry. Their repair contracts with the U.S. forces in 1966 were 3.78 times greater than in 1965. Chairman Stennis of the Armed Services Sub-Committee of the Senate Military Committee, made a statement highly valuing the role played by Japan's shipbuilding industry in the aggressive war. He said: (retranslated)

"The U.S. Navy sailing for the Vietnam war is relying greatly on the repair facilities for warships and other vessels in Japan and Taiwan. Without Yokosuka and Sasebo in particular, operations in Southeast Asia would encounter serious difficulties." In repair of airplanes for dropping napalm bombs, spraying poisons, and killing Vietnamese, servicing of warships for bombardment, and of LST's for transporting weapons, is nothing if not cooperation in the aggression and intervention in the war. We add that, oil for the Seventh Fleet is sold to the Americans by the petroleum capitalists.

More brutally, chemical gas and high pressure gas are Japanese supplied. These include Nitrous-Oxide or laughing gas which is manufactured by the iron and chemical industries. There are really too many items to enumerate them all. Specialists have revealed that production of the oil raw material for napalm by Nihon Oils and Fats is an open secret.

The Itohchu Co. tendered a sub-contract proposal for the manufacture of fins for napalm bombs to the Mikajiri Industry, but it was turned down as a result of an opposition struggle by the trade union. It is ominous that napalm used to be manufactured in Japan at the time of the Korean war. Apart from the components of napalm, a rapid increase is seen in the export to the U.S. of methanol, an explosive raw material, of benzene which is raw material for napalm, and polystyrene, used in super-napalm.

It is undeniable that Japanese monopoly capitalists are cooperating in the production of weapons of mass destruction to be used against the Vietnamese people. The offer of ammunition and services has been made with the approval of the Japanese Government to one side only in the conflict, while at the request of the U.S. Government, the Japanese Government has prohibited the export of 20,000 km of vinyl-covered copper wire to the Democratic Republic of Vietnam. We can conclude, therefore, from an economic standpoint, that the Japanese Government and Japan's financial circles are the greatest cooperators with and participants in the U.S. aggression in Vietnam.

Military Cooperation and Participation by the Japanese
Government and by Japan's "Self-Defense Forces"

In spite of the existence of the peace constitution prohibiting them, Japan has armed forces called "Self-Defense" Forces, which include an army, navy and air force. In their war potential, they have grown to be one of the most powerful armed forces in Asia. Japan is said to occupy sixth or seventh place among capitalist countries in total amount spent on defense. Though it is true that Japan's "Self-Defense" Forces are not directly participating, as are the troops of the "Republic of Korea," in the war in Vietnam, nevertheless, they are part of and within an American strategic design in Asia which has been formed with Japan's "Self-Defense" Forces incorporated as an important factor.

As part of its "flexible response strategy," the U.S. is withdrawing certain of its troops from overseas bases, leaving a minimum of troops. Although decreasing its troops, the U.S. is letting the armed forces of the respective countries maintain the bases and is supplementing the difference by strengthening striking power and mobility. The troops withdrawn like this are being thrown into the war of colonial intervention in Vietnam.

With this strategy, the U.S. has put the most important bases in Japan under the direct control of the Americans, while letting Japan's "Self-Defense" Forces maintain others which can be made available to the U.S. at any time. To even up the decrease in U.S. forces as a result of Vietnam deployment, the increase and strengthening of Japan's "Self Defense" Forces have been attempted and Japanese militarism strengthened. This has been through collusion of the U.S., Japanese financial circles and the Sato Government. These Japanese interests are seeking a larger share in the U.S. domination of Asia and are, at the same time, being accomplices to U.S. policy for domination in Asia.

The new Japan-U.S. "Three Arrows" joint operational plan worked out in 1963 showed that the mission to be fulfilled by the "Self Defense" Forces was further expanded and their relative importance in the U.S. setup for aggression in Asia greatly increased. That is to say, Japan's "Self Defense" Forces, are covering up the weaknesses resulting from the throwing of great U.S. forces into the war in Vietnam and are guaranteeing conditions for the U.S. to carry on and escalate with no anxiety concerning their rear. Without Japan as a base and Japan's "Self Defense" Forces, it would no longer be possible for the U.S. to carry on its war in Vietnam.

In addition, Japanese armed forces have gradually been sent bit-by-bit to Okinawa, which is under U.S. military control, to the "Republic of Korea," to Taiwan, and now even to Vietnam. That members of Japan's "Self Defense" Forces have been sent to Vietnam openly with the inadequate cover-story that they are engaged in study and on-the-spot training and inspection is a serious matter. On September 22, 1966, the Defense Agency sent an inspection team composed of high ranking military officers. The Supreme Command of the Vietnam People's Army sent a strong protest note about this to the International Commission for Control and Inspection. According to this protest note, the Japanese inspection team participated in air raid operations in the III Corps Area north west of Saigon.

III. *The Japan-U.S. Security Treaty as a System of Complicity*

The Japanese Government has consistently tried to avoid responsibility with the justification that the cooperation with and participation in the U.S. military action against Vietnam is an obligation laid down by the Japan-U.S. Security Treaty and the relevant agreements. In other words, the Japanese Government has admitted that it has extensively and deeply cooperated with and participated in the U.S. action.

In relation to the Japan-U.S. Security Treaty, we would like to elaborate on the sort of conveniences and services the Japanese Government has offered to the U.S. forces: 1. Any place in Japan which the U.S. forces may wish to use can be turned into a military base. 2. The purpose of use is unrestricted, including non-military use; for instance, for hospitals and recreation facilities. 3. The right to establish administer, guard, and control bases and all other power is held by the U.S. forces, which have extra-territorial rights on the bases. 4. The rights of the Japanese with regard to land, water and space around such bases are limited. 5. Free use of ports, airports and roads necessary to service the bases is provided free of charge, and in actuality, with priority. 6. All public works and public services which are under the possession, control and regulation of the Government, including services of the national railways and the telegraph and telecommunications corporation, are offered to the U.S. forces with top priority. 7. In connection with the use of radio frequencies and control of radio communications systems, the Government has approved and guaranteed priority to the U.S. forces. 8. The Japanese Government has offered the greatest possible services to the U.S. forces, often to the detriment of the interests of the Japanese people.

9. Of the three kinds of procurement of supplies, labor, and civil construction, the most important covers special procurement for the Vietnam war. 10. Free entrance and exit of men and goods have been granted to U.S. servicemen, U.S. civilians employed by the military and their families. Even American businessmen who visit Japan for dealing with the U.S. military can freely enter and exit from Japan without being regulated by Japan's Alien Registration Order. All goods used by the U.S. forces are freely brought into and taken out of Japan without having customs duties imposed. With these preferential regulations, the Japanese Government has granted free entrance and exit of material for the Vietnam War.

Thus, the Japanese Government has offered all possible conveniences and services to the U.S. forces in Japan using as a basis of pseudo-legality the Japan-U.S. Security Treaty and its relevant agreements. Since the status of U.S. forces became, by the Japan-U.S. Security Treaty, "U.S. Forces in Japan," when they entered the country, they become privileged and all conveniences and services offered by the Japanese Government become *ipso facto*, openly available for the U.S. aggression against Vietnam.

IV. *The Japanese Government's Complicity*

All the foregoing facts attest to cooperation with and participation in the U.S. war of aggression in Vietnam by the Japanese Government and monopoly capitalists and were submitted to the "Tokyo Tribunal" which was held in August, 1967. The Tokyo Tribunal arrived at the following conclusions: "The Japanese Government and Japanese monopoly capitalists are actively cooperating with and participating in the U.S. aggression and war crimes in Vietnam; they are guilty as an accomplice in U.S. crimes."

Our conclusion to the Russell International War Crimes Tribunal on the responsibility of the Japanese Government for complicity is as follows:

All these actions of cooperation with and participation in the U.S. war of aggression by the Japanese Government are grave violations. Japan's supply of LST and MSTS crew members should be regarded as the actual dispatch of troops. Other participating countries have sent troops more or less openly to Vietnam; the offer of military bases by Thailand and the Philippines represents important military participation. But compared with the overall contribution by the Japanese Government, their effect is dwarfed. The offer of land, naval and air bases on Okinawa and the Japanese mainland, the supply and repair of warships, ancillary vessels, and aircraft, the expert techniques and abundant material supplied by Japan, the military transport, plus special procurement for adding military might, should be regarded as absolutely indispensable for the U.S. forces in carrying on the war in Vietnam. This is confirmed by the statement of Chairman Stennis of the Armed Services Sub-Committee of the Senate Military Committee.

The responsibility of the Japanese Government for its cooperation with and participation in the aggressive war in Vietnam should be regarded as surpassing that of other participating countries. Such responsibility for this complicity is all the greater in light of Japanese imperialism's past record of occupation and aggression in Vietnam and of the great damage it caused to human lives and property during World War II. Its responsibility becomes even greater in light of its violation of the war-renouncing Constitution of Japan.

While admitting that Japan's cooperation with and participation in the U.S. war in Vietnam might be interpreted as an obligation laid down by the mutual security treaty and that, therefore, Japan is not a neutral, the Japanese Government is attempting to avoid its responsibility for complicity

From the very outset, the Japan-U.S. Security Treaty was concluded with the aim of cooperation with and participation in American aggression in the Far East (as demonstrated by the reparations agreement with the South Vietnamese puppet regime in 1959). This has become obvious since the revision of this treaty in 1960. The Japan-U.S. Security Treaty, and therefore, the basis for the military alliance between the two countries, is in itself the basis of Japan's cooperation with and participation in the Vietnam war, and cannot be used as a pretext for the Japanese Government to evade its responsibility for complicity.

But further, it is our contention that the Japan-U.S. Security Treaty does not in any way oblige Japan to aid and abet the United States in this war. It should be noted that Article 2 of the United Nations Charter rules that countries should refrain from the threat or use of force in international relations. It has been recognized by world public opinion that the war against Vietnam is a war of aggression. This has been amply confirmed by the interim conclusion of the Stockholm session of the International War Crimes Tribunal.

No obligation arises from the Japan-U.S. Security Treaty on such a war. In this connection, it should be recalled that the U.S. Government, as an ally of Britain and France, itself opposed the sending of troops to Egypt in 1956. But the Japanese Government, finding an excuse in this treaty, has actively done what it was not obliged to do, which it had of its own volition renounced — namely, abandoned its moral position of neutrality as laid down in the Treaty on the Right and Obligation of Neutral Countries and Neutral Persons of 1907, which Japan ratified in 1912. From this point of view, also, the responsibility for complicity is obvious.

The U.S. bases in Okinawa, which is Japanese territory, are of utmost importance for the U.S. in carrying on the war in Vietnam. But legal grounds for the U.S. occupation and rule of Okinawa have long since expired. That is to say, Article 3 of the "Peace Treaty" made with Japan in 1952, stipulates that, pending the making of a proposal by the United States to the United Nations to place Okinawa under its trusteeship, with the United States as the sole administrative authority, the United States will have the right to exercise any and all powers of administration, legislation and jurisdiction over Okinawa. But this arrangement itself runs counter to the Cairo and Potsdam

Declarations which agreed on non-expansion of territory. In additon, at least after 1956, when Japan was admitted as a member to the United Nations, the trusteeship of Okinawa, which is a territory of a U.N. member nation, can no longer apply, for it is a violation under Article 78 of the Charter. Indeed, the U.S. Government has stated that it does not intend to make a proposal on the trusteeship rule affecting Okinawa.

Therefore, the stipulation of Article 3 of the Peace Treaty with Japan — admitting the provisional nature of the rule pending the trusteeship — has already lost all validity. Okinawa should be returned to Japan immediately, for the U.S. has no legal grounds for occupying Okinawa today.

Both the Okinawan Legislative Assembly (Parliament) and the Japanese Diet have passed resolutions strongly demanding the return of administrative rights to Okinawa. The immediate return of Okinawa to Japan is now a strong desire of all the Japanese people. Whereas the Japanese Government should have demanded of the U.S. that it immediately return Okinawa to Japan, at least after the admission of Japan to the United Nations in 1956, it has not exercised this natural right and has, on the contrary, renounced it.

The U.S. Government has freely used Okinawa as the most important military base for the war against Vietnam, turned it into a nuclear base, and infringed on the basic national rights, not only of the Vietnamese people but of the Japanese people as well, and the Japanese Government has countenanced it. The Government has made no protests and taken no measures to obtain relief. Prime Minister Sato went so far as to confirm the importance and necessity of maintaining U.S. military bases in the country in the Sato-Johnson statement of January, 1965. This further confirms the responsibility of the Japanese Government for complicity in the U.S. war of aggression in Vietnam.

The United States and Laos
testimony by Wilfred Burchett

To set what is happening in Laos today in its correct framework, one has to go back to the closing stages of the 1954 Geneva Conference and to what happened in Laos almost immediately after the conference. It will be recalled that the French Premier, M. Mendes France, had set himself a deadline of July 20, to obtain a ceasefire or resign.

At a little publicised three power foreign ministers' meeting in Paris, on July 13, 1954, John Foster Dulles made a last minute effort to avoid a ceasefire. He urged Mendes France and Anthony Eden of Great Britain to set up a Southeast Asia Treaty Organization — for which he had the draft in his briefcase — immediately, and he demanded international intervention instead of talk about a ceasefire. Mendes France refused and was strongly supported by Eden. But the price the latter two paid was to agree to set up SEATO immediately after a ceasefire.

As the clock ticked towards midnight on July 20th at Geneva, new difficulties suddenly arose. Details for a ceasefire in Vietnam had been agreed upon — but the Laotian delegation refused to sign the agreement on Laos. Eventually, at the very last minute, one member of the Laotian delegation did sign.

Just two months later, on September 18, 1954, Kou Voravong, the Laotian Minister of Defence who had signed in Geneva, was shot in the back as he sat at a dinner table in Vientiane, the Laotian capital. His host at dinner was Phoui Sananikone, the other delegate at Geneva, then Minister of Foreign Affairs. Just nine days prior to this murder, Kou Voravong had revealed in the National Assembly, that the sum of one million dollars had been paid into a Swiss bank for the account of Phuoi Sananikone, the fee he received not to sign the Geneva Agreements.

The other "imprudence" committed by Voravong was that he had arranged, and taken part in, the first meeting for many years between the half-brother Princes, Souvanna Phouma, then Prime Minister of the Royal Government and Souphanouvong, head of the Pathet Lao. This meeting was aimed at starting political negotiations between the government and the Pathet Lao as provided for under the Geneva Agreements. The murder set the tone for things to come. The crisis it provoked led to Souvanna Phouma's Government being replaced by one headed by a pro-American, Katay Don Sasorith. The latter, within a few days of a visit to Laos by John Foster Dulles, repudiated the Geneva Agreements and launched an all-out military attack against the Pathet Lao forces in flagrant violation of the Agreements.

It took two years and many humiliating defeats on the battlefield before Katay's Government fell and was replaced by another under Prince Souvanna Phouma, which was ready to meet again with the head of the Pathet Lao. If ever there was a chance for lasting peace and national unity in Laos, this lay in an agreement between the Neutralist forces, at that stage represented by Souvanna Phouma, and the patriotic forces of the Pathet Lao which had borne the brunt of the armed struggle against the French. But such a meeting and its implications was not to the liking of Washington, as I soon found out.

Early in 1966, I had interviewed Souvanna Phouma, and as Prince Sihanouk had done for Cambodia, Souvanna Phouma said that Laos had neither sought nor accepted the "protection" that the SEATO powers decided at the first meeting, should be accorded Laos and Cambodia. I had also seen Souphanouvong and quickly realized that there were no problems which could not easily be solved in direct negotiations.

In January, 1957, I visited Vientiane again with a valid visa for a two weeks' stay. At the airport I met an American journalist and we agreed to have lunch next day. Next day, he turned up for a moment to cancel the lunch, explaining that he "could not be seen talking" with me, that the U.S. Embassy was furious about my being in Vientiane and that I was held responsible "for having brought the two Princes together again." Shortly afterwards I was visited by a Laotian police official who cancelled my visa and told me that a police escort would take me to the airport and put me on the next plane — to Saigon.

When I protested, he explained that this was not a Laotian decision but one imposed by the American "advisers". It was only by the intervention of the International Control Commission that I was able to postpone my departure by one day and leave — without a police escort — for Hanoi. The incident was proof enough for me — and for the International Control Commission — that the last thing Washington wanted was "peace and stability" for Laos, as they so often proclaimed.

There are witnesses here far more competent than myself to relate what happened in all those years from 1954 onwards. The essence was a gradual process from U.S. gross intervention in Laotian affairs, to indirect aggression and finally outright aggression against the Laotian people. There were occasional temporary retreats when the various "strong men" like Katay, Sananikone, Nosavan and others with their U.S. — equipped forces were defeated and temporary accommodations with the various shades of Neutralist Governments made.

Typical is what happened in mid-1960. On August 15, 1960, following a revolt by one of the American's most trusted army units, the King of Laos invited Souvanna Phouma to form a government again. With CIA backing, a rival government was set up in the South, at Savannakhet, under a Prince Boun Oum, but in fact dominated by General Nosavan, a sort of Laotian Nguyen Cao Ky. Within ten days, Nosavan had launched military operations to recapture Vientiane, thus starting all-out civil war again, which was in fact a war of indirect aggression by the United States, with U.S. supplies poured in from Thailand and eventually U.S. "advisers" as well. Nosavan's forces, however, were successfully opposed by those of the Pathet Lao and Neutralist forces, then under Kong Le.

Eventually, on the initiative of Prince Sihanouk of Cambodia, a new Geneva Conference on Laos, was set up on May 16, 1961, but it was only six weeks later — after more battlefield defeats — that Nosavan agreed to send a delegation. It was headed — ominously — by Phoui Sananikone, the same who on American instructions had refused to sign the first Geneva Agreements.

Talks dragged on intermittently for months while Nosavan, with stepped-up U.S. aid, tried to rebuild his army which had been shattered by repeated defeats at the hands of the Pathet Lao and Neutralist forces. Ceasefire agreements were drafted, some even signed, but they were broken within weeks by Nosavan offensives: A report in the *London Times* from its Washington correspondent on May 24, 1962 summed up one aspect of U.S. interference: Under the banner line:"CIA IS BLAMED FOR LAOS CRISIS", the *Times* story read as follows:

"The Administration is now convinced that the Central Intelligence Agency has been up to its old devices again and must share a large part of the responsibility for the situation in Laos...Apparently the evidence shows that swarms of CIA agents deliberately opposed the official American objective of trying to establish a neutral government. They are believed to have encouraged General Phoumi Nosavan in the concentration of troops that brought about the swift and disastrous response from the Pathet Lao..."

The "swift and disasterous response" referred to was the destruction of Nosavan'sarmy in the battle of Nam Tha, a veritable Dien Bien Phu for his "made in U.S." army. After this defeat the U.S. Government suddenly showed great enthusiasm for a quick conclusion of the Geneva Agreements, agreeing to the setting up of a coalition government, pledged to follow a neutral policy. The attempt to take power by a frontal attack using military force having failed miserably, U.S. tactics changed to a taking power from within. This entailed splitting the Neutralist forces and the physical liquidation of forceful elements within Neutralist ranks which could not be bought.

The coalition government, on which such hopes were placed, never really worked, nor could it work. Pathet Lao and progressive Neutralist members soon found that the Government was physically a prisoner of Nosavan, whose forces surrounded and policed Vientiane where the government was supposed to function. Proposals for joint security forces drawn from Nosavan, Neutralist and Pathet Lao units were rejected. Although Neutralist and Pathet Lao Ministers took up their posts, the Ministries themselves were staffed with Nosavan's men.

On April 1, 1963, Quinim Pholsena, Foreign Minister and head of the "Peace and Neutrality" party, a man of outstanding intelligence, integrity and courage and the real leader of the Neutralist forces, was shot to death as he walked up the steps of his Vientiane home after attending a Royal reception. His wife, also badly wounded by bullets from the same machine-gun, told me a few days later that she had no doubt the murderer had acted on U.S. orders. She said the Americans were furious with her husband because he had rejected a huge bribe offered a few months before when Pholsena was in Washington. The murder of the Foreign Minister was the signal for a real coup and an attempt to seize the strategic Plain of Jarres by force. A Nosavan commando group was sent to capture or kill, Colonel Deuane, another progressive neutral and Second-in-Command to Kong Le of the Neutralist armed forces. In a battle that lasted two days, Colonel Deuane's men beat off the attackers. After that the Neutralist forces split, one part under Kong Le eventually throwing in his lot with Nosavan, another under Deuane remaining true to the alliance with the Pathet Lao. Pathet Lao cabinet ministers escaped from Vietiane to territory under their own control immediately after the murder of Pholsena; the armed struggle started up again with the United States moving into it ever more openly.

Members of the various investigation teams who passed through Vientiane on their way to and from Hanoi, could see U.S. bombers taking off from the Vientiane civil airstrip. Also in plain sight were the supply aircraft of the CIA's private airlines "Air America" and "Air Continental" loading up for air supply missions to the U.S.-trained commando units operating in Pathet Lao controlled areas. United States aggression in Laos can no longer be concealed. In Laos, also the United States is daily committing the crime of genocide against the Laotian people.

U.S. Actions Against Laos
testimony by Lt. Guillermo Frank Llanes

Military Attache from Cuba to the DRV

Our Inquiry Commission made a short visit to Laos after our travels in Vietnam. There, as in Vietnam, the nation fights for its independence and its sovereignty. There, too, the U.S. infiltrates counter-revolutionary troops into the liberated areas. There, too, aircraft with the USAF symbol drop tons of every type of bombs on defenseless villages. There, too, C-123s and C-130s spread poisonous chemicals to defoliate and destroy crops.

During our stay we visited the ruins of what was once the village of Na Thene near the town of Muong Nga. It has only a broad path leading to it and there is no highway or street. In the surrounding areas we saw the destroyed irrigation canal which had been made over a period of years by hand, and the rice paddies, which were still green, except where huge bomb craters pocked them.

The first attack upon the village was on August 25th, 1965; rockets and napalm, as well as demolition bombs were used. The second attack was on December 1, 1965. One AD-6 and Several F-105s took part. The third attack took place on the 16th of April, 1966 by F-101 and F-105s. The fourth attack was on April 19th, 1966. Two AD-6s and four F-105s participated. Napalm was again used. This attack came as a surprise and caused 15 dead to the inhabitants. Among them were 9 children between the ages of 2 and 11, two old people between 50 and 60 years of age, and four youths between 17 and 23. There were many wounded and 6 inhalation poisonings from the napalm smoke. The fifth attack was on July 4th, 1966. In this attack 33 houses were destroyed and again, napalm was used. The sixth attack was on August 5th, 1966 and the principal weapons used were Cluster Bomb Units (CBU). The seventh attack was on November 12, 1966 and the eighth on January 9, 1967. After bombing, the planes machine-gun strafed the village. The ninth attack took place on July 30th, 1967, and again strafing followed the bombing. The tenth attack was on July 31st, 1967 and the eleventh came on the 17th of September, 1967 with a cost of ten dead.

The twelfth attack was on September 21st, 1967. It was the most ferocious of them all. Between 13:00 and 17:00 hours, the aircraft made several passes overhead firing their guns into the village huts at each pass. Damage amounted to 17 dead and a year's supply of stored rice went up in flames. The irrigation canal was totally destroyed. Phospherous bombs and napalm destroyed the houses that remained after the earlier attacks, as well as those which had been rebuilt. After this, the population decided to evacuate to the caves surrounding the village which is where we interviewed them. They live there in conditions akin to those of the Middle Ages, but their fighting spirit continues. The attacks by the U.S. continue also, and we could see napalm burns and bomb craters on the mountain slopes where the caverns are.

From conversations with the inhabitants we learned why this and other regions in the area are so persistently attacked. The San Neua province, where this village was, was liberated fifteen years ago and the enemy has not since been able to recapture it. The town and villages of this region are solidly behind the Laotian Liberation Forces and from it the Neo Lao Haksat receives rice and recruits — recruits who are hard-hitting and whom the enemy fears. It is for this reason that the U.S. lets loose their fury and vengeance against the defenseless older men, women and children who remain there. During our return, we saw more than one village which, as it was near the road, showed it's destroyed houses. All the villages along the road were mere ruins, and the inhabitants have been evacuated to nearby caves and forests.

Interviews With Buddhists

During our stay in Laos we interviewed several Buddhist Monks, among them Kikao Savaunarat, Buddhist Bishop of the northern provinces of San Neua, Phonsaly, Mong Sai, Mong Tha and Luang Prabang. The Bishop explained how supersonic aircraft with the letters USAF had attacked villages in those provinces and destroyed several Buddhist buildings, including monastaries, and pagodas which were historical monuments. In total, in the five provinces which were the Bishopric of Savaunarat, one large pagoda and 44 monastaries were destroyed. Each of these monastaries consisted of one or several churches, schools for the novices, and for the people, dwellings, etc. With the destruction of these, also went works of art dear to the traditions of the people of Laos such as statues, columns, chests, and a great number of manuscripts which documented the history and religious traditions of Laos stretching back for hundreds of years in the past . . .

On Genocide
by Jean Paul Sartre

The word "genocide" is relatively new. It was coined by the jurist Raphael Lemkin between the two world wars. But the fact of genocide is as old as humanity. To this day there has been no society protected by its structure from committing that crime. Every case of genocide is a product of history and bears the stamp of the society which has given birth to it. The one we have before us for judgment is the act of the greatest capitalist power in the world today. It is as such that we must try to analyze it — in other words, as the simultaneous expression of the economic infrastructure of that power, its political objectives and the contradictions of its present situation.

In particular, we must try to understand the genocidal intent in the war which the American government is waging against Vietnam, for Article 2 of the 1948 Geneva Convention defines genocide on the basis of intent; the Convention was tacitly referring to memories which were still fresh. Hitler had proclaimed it his deliberate intent to exterminate the Jews. He made genocide a political means and did not hide it. A Jew had to be put to death, whoever he was, not for having been caught carrying a weapon or for having joined a resistance movement, but simply *because he was a Jew*. The American government has avoided making such clear statements. It has even claimed that it was answering the call of its allies, the South Vietnamese, who had been attacked by the communists. Is it possible for us, by studying the facts objectively, to discover implicit in them such a genocidal intention? And after such an investigation, can we say that the armed forces of the United States are killing Vietnamese in Vietnam for the simple reason that they are Vietnamese?

This is something which can only be established after an historical examination: the structure of war changes right along with the infrastructures of society. Between 1860 and the present day, the meaning and the objectives of military conflicts have changed profoundly, the final stage of this metamorphosis being precisely the "war of example" which the United States is waging in Vietnam.

In 1856, there was a convention for the protection of the property of neutrals; 1864, Geneva: protection for the wounded; 1899, 1907, The Hague: two conferences which attempted to make rules for war. It is no accident that jurists and governments were multiplying their efforts to "humanize war" on the very eve of the two most frightful massacres that mankind has ever known. Vladimir Dedijer has shown very effectively in his study "On Military Conventions" that the capitalist societies during this same period were giving birth to the monster of total war in which they express their true nature. He attributes this phenomenon to the following:

1. The competition between industrial nations fighting for new markets produces a permanent antagonism which is expressed in ideology and in practice by what is known as "bourgeois nationalism."

2. The development of industry, which is the source of this hostility, provides the means of resolving it to the advantage of one of the competitors, through the production of more and more *massively* destructive weapons. The consequence of this development is that it becomes increasingly difficult to make any distinction between the front and behind the lines, between the civilian population and the soldiers.

3. At the same time, new military objectives — the factories — arise near the towns. And even when they are not producing material directly for the armies, they maintain, at least to some extent, the ecomic strength of the country. It is precisely this strength that the enemy aims to destroy: this is at once the aim of war and the means to that end.

4. The consequence of this is that everyone is mobilized: the peasant fights at the front, the worker fights behind the lines, the peasant women take over for their husbands in the fields. This *total* struggle of nation against nation tends to make the worker a soldier too, since in the last analysis the power which is economically stronger is more likely to win.

5. The democratic facade of the bourgeois nations and the emancipation of the working class have led to the participation of the masses in politics. The masses have no control at all over government decisions, but the middle classes imagine that by voting they exercise some kind of remote control. Except in cases of defensive wars, the working classes are torn between their desire for peace and the nationalism which has been instilled in them. Thus war, seen in a new light and distorted by propaganda, becomes the ethical decision of the whole community. All the citizens of each warring nation (or almost all, after they have been manipulated) are the enemies of all those of the other country. War has become absolutely total.

6. These same societies, as they continue their technological expansion, continue to extend the scope of their competition by increasing communications. The famous "One World" of the Americans was already in existence by the end of the 19th century when Argentine wheat dealt a final blow to English agriculture. Total war is no longer only between all members of one national community and all those of another: it is also total because it will very likely set the whole world up in flames.

Thus, war between the bourgeois nations — of which the 1914 war was the first example but which had threatened Europe since 1900 — is not the "invention" of one man or one government, but simply a necessity for those who, since the beginning of the century, have sought to "extend politics by other means." The option is clear: either *no* war or *that* kind of total war. Our fathers fought that kind of war. And the governments who saw it coming, with neither the intelligence nor the courage to stop it, were wasting their time and the time of the jurists when they stupidly tried to "humanize" it.

Nevertheless, during the First World War a genocidal intent appeared only sporadically. As in previous centuries, the essential aim was to crush the military power of the enemy and only secondarily to ruin his economy. But even though there was no longer any clear distinction between civilians and soldiers, it was still only rarely (except for a few terrorist raids) that the civilian population was expressly made a target. Moreover, the belligerent nations (or at least those who were doing the fighting) were industrial powers. This made for a certain initial balance: against the possibility of any real extermination each side had its own deterrent force — namely the power of applying the law of "an eye for an eye." This explains why, in the midst of the carnage, a kind of prudence was maintained.

However, since 1830, throughout the last century and continuing to this very day, there have been countless acts of genocide whose causes are likewise to be found in the structure of capitalist societies.

To export their products and their capital, the great powers, particularly England and France, set up colonial empires. The name "overseas possessions" given by the French to their conquests indicates clearly that they had been able to acquire them only by wars of aggression. The adversary was sought out in his own territory, in Africa and Asia, in the under-developed countries, and far from waging "total war" (which would have required an initial balance of forces), the colonial powers, because of their overwhelming superiority of firepower, found it necessary to commit only an expeditionary force. Victory was easy, at least in conventional military terms. But since this blatant aggression kindled the hatred of the civilian population, and since civilians were potentially rebels and soldiers, the colonial troops maintained their authority by terror — by perpetual massacre. These massacres were genocidal in character: they aimed at the destruction of "a part of an ethnic, national, or religious group" in order to terorize the remainder and to wrench apart the indigenous society.

After the bloodbath of conquest in Algeria during the last century, the French imposed the *Code Civil*, with its middleclass conceptions of property and inheritance, on a tribal society where each community held land in common. Thus they systematically destroyed the economic infrastructure of the country, and tribes of peasants soon saw their lands fall into the hands of French speculators. Indeed, colonization is not a matter of mere conquest as was the German annexation of Alsace-Lorraine; it is by its very nature an act of cultural genocide. Colonization cannot take place without systematically liquidating all the characteristics of the native society — and simultaneously refusing to integrate the natives into the mother country and denying them access to its advantages. Colonialism is, after all, an economic system: the colony sells its raw materials and agricultural products at a reduced price to the colonizing power. The latter, in return, sells its manufactured goods to the colony at world market prices. This curious system of trade is only possible if there is a colonial subproletariat which can be forced to work for starvation wages. For the subject people this inevitably means the extinction of their national character, culture, customs, sometimes even language. They live in their underworld of misery like dark phantoms ceaselessly reminded of their subhumanity.

However, their value as an almost unpaid labor force protects them, to a certain extent, against physical genocide. The Nuremberg Tribunal was still fresh in people's minds when the French massacred 45,000 Algerians at Setif, as an "example." But this sort of thing was so commonplace that no one even thought to condemn the French government in the same terms as they did the Nazis.

But this "deliberate destruction of a part of a national group" could not be carried out any more extensively without harming the interests of the French settlers. By exterminating the subproletariat, they would have exterminated themselves as settlers. This explains the contradictory attitude of these *pieds-noirs* during the Algerian war: they urged the Army to commit massacres, and more than one of them dreamed of total genocide. At the same time they attempted to compel the Algerians to "fraternize" with them. It is because France could neither liquidate the Algerian people nor integrate them with the French that it lost the Algerian war.

These observations enable us to understand how the structure of colonial wars underwent a transformation after the end of the Second World War. For it was at about this time that the colonial peoples, enlightened by the conflict and its impact on the "empires," and later by the victory of Mao Tse-tung, resolved to regain their national independence. The characteristics of the struggle were determined from the beginning: the colonialists had the superiority in weapons, the indigenous population the advantage of numbers. Even in Algeria — a colony where there was settlement as much as there was exploitation — the proportion of *colons* to natives was one to nine. During the two world wars, many of the colonial peoples had been trained as soldiers and had become experienced fighters. However, the short supply and poor quality of their arms — at least in the beginning — kept the number of fighting units low. These objective conditions dictated their strategy, too: terrorism, ambushes, harassing the enemy, extreme mobility of the combat groups which had to strike unexpectedly and disappear at one. This was made possible only by the support of the entire population. Hence the famous symbiosis between the liberation forces and the masses of people: the former everywhere organizing agrarian reforms, political organs and education; the latter supporting, feeding and hiding the soldiers of the army of liberations, and replenishing its ranks with their sons.

It is no accident that people's war, with its principles, its strategy, its tactics and its theoreticians, appeared at the very moment that the industrial powers pushed total war to the ultimate by the industrial production of atomic fission. Nor is it any accident that it brought about the destruction of colonialism. The contradiction which led to the victory of the FLN in Algeria was characteristic of that time; people's war sounded the death-knell of conventional warfare at exactly the same moment as the hydrogen bomb. Against partisans supported by the entire population, the colonial armies were helpless. They had only one way of escaping this demoralizing harassment which threatened to culminate in a Dien Bien Phu, and that was to "empty the sea of its water" — i.e. the civilian population.

And, in fact, the colonial soldiers soon learned that their most redoubtable foes were the silent, stubborn peasants who, just one kilometer from the scene of the ambush which had wiped out a regiment knew nothing, had seen nothing. And since it was the unity of an entire people which held the conventional army at bay, the only anti-guerrilla strategy which could work was the destruction of this people, in other words, of civilians, of women and children.

Torture and genocide: that was the answer of the colonial powers to the revolt of the subject peoples. And that answer, as we know, was worthless unless it was thorough and total. The populace — resolute, united by the politicized and fierce partisan army — was no longer to be cowed as in the good old days of colonialism, by an "admonitory" massacre which was supposed to serve "as an example." On the contrary, this only augmented the people's hate. Thus it was no longer a question of intimidating the populace, but rather of physically liquidating it. And since that was not possible without concurrently liquidating the colonial economy and the whole colonial system, the settlers panicked, the colonial powers got tired of pouring men and money into an interminable conflict, the mass of the people in the mother country opposed the continuation of an inhuman war, and the colonies became sovereign states.

There have been cases, however, in which the genocidal response to people's war is not checked by infrastructural contradictions. Then total genocide emerges as the absolute basis of an anti-guerrilla strategy. And under certain conditions it even emerges as the explicit objective — sought either immediately or by degrees. This is precisely what is happening in the Vietnam war. We are dealing here with a new stage in the development of imperialism, a stage usually called neo-colonialism because it is characterized by aggression against a former colony which has already gained its independence, with the aim of subjugating it anew to colonial rule. With the beginning of independence, the neo-colonialists take care to finance a *putsch* or *coup d' etat* so that the new heads of state do not represent the interests of the masses but those of a narrow privileged strata, and, consequently, of foreign capital.

Ngo Dinh Diem appeared — hand-picked, maintained and armed by the United States. He proclaimed his decision to reject the Geneva Agreements and to constitute the Vietnamese territory to the south of the 17th parallel as an independent state. What followed was the necessary consequence of these premises: a police force and an army were created to hunt down people who had fought against the French, and who now felt thwarted of their victory, a sentiment which automatically marked them as enemies of the new regime. In short, it was the reign of terror which provoked a new uprising in the South and rekindled the people's war.

Did the United States ever imagine that Diem could nip the revolt in the bud? In any event, they lost no time in sending in experts and then troops, and then they were involved in the conflict up to their necks. And we find once again almost the same pattern of war as the one that Ho Chi Minh fought against the French, except that at first the American government declared that it was only sending its troops out of generosity, to fulfill its obligations to an ally.

That is the outward appearance. But looking deeper, these two successive wars are essentially different in character: the United States, unlike France, has no economic interests in Vietnam. American firms have made some investments, but not so much that they couldn't be sacrificed, if necessary, without troubling the American nation as a whole or really hurting the monopolies. Moreover, since the U.S. government is not waging the war for reasons of a *directly* economic nature, there is nothing to stop it from ending the war by the ultimate tactic — in other words, by genocide. This is not to say that there is proof that the U.S. does in fact envision genocide, but simply that nothing prevents the U.S. from envisaging it.

In fact, according to the Americans themselves, the conflict has two objectives. Just recently, Dean Rusk stated: "We are defending ourselves." It is no longer Diem, the ally whom the Americans are generously helping out: it is the United States itself which is in danger in Saigon. Obviously, this means that the first objective is a military one: to encircle Communist China. Therefore, the United States will not let Southeast Asia escape. It has put its men in power in Thailand, it controls two-thirds of Laos and threatens to invade Cambodia. But these conquests will be hollow if it finds itself confronted by a free and unified Vietnam with 32 million inhabitants. That is why the military leaders like to talk in terms of "key positions." That is why Dean Rusk says, with unintentional humor, that the armed forces of the United States are fighting in Vietnam "in order to avoid a third world war." Either this phrase is meaningless, or else it must be taken to mean: "in order to *win* this third conflict." In short, the first objective is dictated by the necessity of establishing a Pacific line of defense, something which is necessary only in the context of the general policies of imperialism.

The second objective is an economic one. In October 1966, General Westmoreland defined it as follows: "We are fighting the war in Vietnam to show that guerrilla warfare does not pay." To show whom? The Vietnamese? That would be very surprising. Must so many human lives and so much money be wasted merely to teach a lesson to a nation of poor peasants thousands of miles from San Francisco? And, in particular, what need was there to attack them, provoke them into fighting and subsequently to go about crushing them, when the big American companies have only negligible interests in Vietnam? Westmoreland's statement, like Rusk's, has to be filled in. The Americans want to show others that guerrilla war does not pay: they want to show all the oppressed and exploited nations that might be tempted to shake off the American yoke by launching a people's war, at first against their own pseudo-governments, the compradors and the army, then against the U.S. "Special Forces," and finally against the GIs. In short, they want to show Latin America first of all, and more generally, all of the Third World. To Che Guevara who said, "We need several Vietnams," the American government answers, "They will all be crushed the way we are crushing the first."

In other words, this war has above all an admonitory value, as an example for three and perhaps four continents. (After all, Greece is a peasant nation too. A dictatorship has just been set up there; it is good to give the Greeks a warning: submit or face extermination.) This genocidal example is addressed to the whole of humanity. By means of this warning, six per cent of mankind hopes to succeed in controlling the other 94 per cent at a reasonably low cost in money and effort. Of course it would be preferable, for propaganda purposes, if the Vietnamese would submit before being exterminated. But it is not certain that the situation wouldn't be clearer if Vietnam *were* wiped off the map. Otherwise someone might think that Vietnam's submission had been attributable to some *avoidable* weakness. But if these peasants do not weaken for an instant, and if the price they pay for their heroism is *inevitable* death, the guerrillas of the future will be all the more discouraged.

At this point in our demonstration, three facts are established: (1) What the U.S. government wants is to have a base against China and to set an example. (2) The first objective *can* be achieved, without any difficulty (except, of course, for the resistance of the Vietnamese), by wiping out a whole people and imposing the Pax Americana on a uninhabited Vietnam. (3) To achieve the second, the U.S. *must* carry out, at least in part, this extermination.

The declarations of American statesmen are not as candid as Hitler's were in his day. But candor is not essential to us here. It is enough that the facts speak; the speeches which come with them are believed only by the American people. The rest of the world understands well enough: governments which are the friends of the United States keep silent; the others denounce this genocide. The Americans try to reply that these unproved accusations only show these governments' partiality. "In fact," the American government says, "all we have ever done is to offer the Vietnamese, North and South, the option of ceasing their aggression or being crushed." It is scarcely necessary to mention that this offer is absurd, since it is the Americans who commit the aggression and consequently they are the only ones who can put an end to it. But this absurdity is not undeliberate: the Americans are ingeniously formulating, without appearing to do so, a demand which the Vietnamese cannot satisfy. They do offer an alternative: Declare you are beaten or we will bomb you back to the stone age. But the fact remains that the second term of this alternative is genocide. They have said: "genocide, yes, but *conditional* genocide." Is this juridically valid? Is it even conceivable?

If the proposition made any juridical sense at all, the U.S. government might narrowly escape the accusation of genocide. But the 1948 Convention leaves no such loopholes: an act of genocide, especially if it is carried out over a period of several years, is no less genocide for being blackmail. The perpetrator may declare he will stop if the victim gives in; this is still — without any juridical doubt whatsoever — a genocide. And this is all the more true when, as is the case here, a good part of the group has been annihilated to force the rest to give in.

But let us look at this more closely and examine the nature of the two terms of the alternative. In the South, the choice is the following: villages burned, the populace subjected to massive bombing, livestock shot, vegetation destroyed by defoliants, crops ruined by toxic aerosols, and everywhere indiscriminate shooting, murder, rape and looting. This is genocide in the strictest sense: massive extermination.. The other option: what is *it*? What are the Vietnamese people supposed to do to escape this horrible death? Join the armed forces of Saigon or be enclosed in strategic or today's "New Life" hamlets, two names for the same concentration camps?

We know about these camps from numerous witnesses. They are fenced in by barbed wire. Even the most elementary needs are denied: there is malnutrition and a total lack of hygiene. The prisoners are heaped together in small tents or sheds. The social structure is destroyed. Husbands are separated from their wives, mothers from their children; family life, so important to the Vietnamese, no longer exists. As families are split up, the birth rate falls; any possibility of religious or cultural life is suppressed; even work — the work which might permit people to maintain themselves and their families — is refused them. These unfortunate people are not even slaves (slavery did not prevent the Negroes in the United States from developing a rich culture); they are reduced to a living

620

heap of vegetable existence. When, sometimes, a fragmental family group is freed — children with an elder sister or a young mother — it goes to swell the ranks of the subproletariat in the big cities; the elder sister or the mother, with no job and mouths to feed reaches the last stage of her degradation in prostituting herself to the GIs.

The camps I describe are but another kind of genocide, equally condemned by the 1948 Convention:

"Causing serious bodily or mental harm to members of the group.

"Deliberately inflicting on the group conditions of life calculated to bring about its physical destruction in whole or in part.

"Imposing measures intended to prevent births within the group.

"Forcibly transferring children of the group to another group."

In other words, it is not true that the choice is between death or submission. For submission, in those circumstances, is submission to genocide. Let us say that a choice must be made between a violent and immediate death and a slow death from mental and physical degradation. Or, if you prefer, *there is no choice at all.*

Is it any different for the North?

One choice is *extermination.* Not just the daily risk of death, but the systematic destruction of the economic base of the country: from the dikes to the factories, nothing will be left standing. Deliberate attacks against civilians and, in particular, the rural population. Systematic destruction of hospitals, schools and places of worship. An all-out campaign to destroy the achievments of 20 years of socialism. The purpose may be only to intimidate the populace. But this can only be achieved by the daily extermination of an ever larger part of the group. So this intimidation itself in its psychosocial consequence is a genocide. Among the children in particular it must be engendering psychological disorders which will for years, if not permanently, "cause serious . . . mental harm."

The other choice is *capitulation.* This means that the North Vietnamese must declare themselves ready to stand by and watch while their country is divided and the Americans impose a direct or indirect dictatorship on their compatriots, in fact on members of their own families from whom the war has separated them. And would this intolerable humiliation bring an end to the war? This is far from certain. The National Liberation Front and the Democratic Republic of Vietnam, although fraternally united, have different strategies and tactics because their war situations are different. If the NLF continued the struggle, American bombs would go on blasting the DRV whether it capitulated or not.

If the war were to cease, the United States — according to official statements — would feel very generously inclined to help in the reconstruction of the DRV, and we know exactly what this means. It means that the United States would destroy, through private investments and conditional loans, the whole economic base of socialism. And this too is genocide. They would be splitting a sovereign country in half, occupying one of the halves by a reign of terror and keeping the other half under control by economic pressure. The "national group" Vietnam would not be physically eliminated, yet it would no longer exist. Economically, politically and culturally it would be suppressed.

In the North as in the South, the choice is only between two types of liquidation: collective death or dismemberment. The American government has had ample opportunity to test the resistance of the NLF and the DRV: by now it knows that only total destruction will be effective. The Front is stronger than ever; North Vietnam is unshakable. For this very reason, the calculated extermination of the Vietnamese people cannot really be intended to make them capitulate. The Americans offer them a *paix des braves* knowing full well that they will not accept it. And this phony alternative hides the true goal of imperialism, which is to reach, step by step, the highest stage of escalation — total genocide.

Of course, the United States government *could have* tried to reach this stage in one jump and wipe out Vietnam in a *Blitzkrieg* against the whole country. But this extermination first required setting up complicated installations — for instance, creating and maintaining air bases in Thailand which would shorten the bombing runs by 3000 miles.

Meanwhile, the major *purpose* of "escalation" was, and still is, to prepare international opinion for genocide. From this point of view, Americans have succeeded only too well. The repeated and systematic bombings of populated areas of Haiphong and Hanoi, which two years ago would have raised violent protests in Europe, occur today in a climate of general indifference resulting perhaps more from catatonia than from apathy. The tactic has borne its fruit: public opinion now sees escalation as a slowly and continuously increasing pressure to bargain, while in reality it is the preparation of minds for the final genocide. Is such a genocide possible? No. But that is due to the Vietnamese and the Vietnamese alone; to their courage, and to the remarkable efficiency of their organization. As for the United States government, it cannot be absolved of its crime just because its victim has enough intelligence and enough heroism to limit its effects.

We may conclude that in the face of a people's war (the characteristic product of our times, the answer to imperialism and the demand for sovereignty of a people conscious of its unity) there are
two possible responses: either the aggressor withdraws, he ack-
nowledges that a whole nation confronts him, and he makes peace; or
else he recognizes the inefficacy of conventional strategy, and, if
he can do so without jeopardizing his interests, he resorts to extermination pure and simple. There is no third alternative, but
making peace is still at least *possible.*

But as the armed forces of the U.S.A. entrench themselves firmly
in Vietnam, as they intensify the bombing and the massacres, as
they try to bring Laos under their control, as they plan the invasion of Cambodia, there is less and less doubt that the government
of the United States, despite its hypocritical denials, has chosen
genocide.

The genocidal intent is implicit in the facts. It is necessarily premeditated. Perhaps in bygone times, in the midst of tribal wars,
acts of genocide were perpetrated on the spur of the moment in fits
of passion. But the anti-guerrilla genocide which our times have
produced requires organization, military bases, a structure of accomplices, budget appropriations. Therefore, its authors must med-
itate and plan out their act. Does this mean that they are thoroughly
conscious of their intentions? It is impossible to decide. We would
have to plumb the depths of their consciences — and the Puritan
bad faith of Americans works wonders.

There are probably people in the State Department who have become so used to fooling themselves that they still think they are working for the good of the Vietnamese people. However, we may only sur-
mise that there are fewer and fewer of these hypocritical innocents
after the recent statements of their spokesmen: "We are defending
ourselves; even if the Saigon government begged us, we would not
leave Vietnam, etc., etc." At any rate, we don't have to concern
ourselves with this psychological hide-and-seek. The truth is apparent *on the battlefield* in the racism of the American soldiers.

This racism — anti-black, anti-Asiatic, anti-Mexican — is a basic
American attitude with deep historical roots and which existed,
latently and overtly, well before the Vietnamese conflict. One proof
of this is that the United States government refused to ratify the
Genocide Convention. This doesn't mean that in 1948 the U.S. intended to exterminate a people; what it does mean — according to
the statements of the U.S. Senate — is that the Convention would
conflict with the laws of several states; in other words, the current
policymakers enjoy a free hand in Vietnam because their predeces-
sors catered to the anti-black racism of Southern whites. In any

case, since 1966, the racism of Yankee soldiers, from Saigon to the 17th parallel, has become more and more marked. Young American men use torture (even including the "field telephone treatment"*), they shoot unarmed women for nothing more than target practice, they kick wounded Vietnamese in the genitals, they cut ears off dead men to take home for trophies. Officers are the worst: a general boasted of hunting "VCs" from his helicopter and gunning them down in the rice paddies. Obviously, these were not NLF soldiers who knew how to defend themselves; they were peasants tending their rice. In the confused minds of the American soldiers, "Viet Cong" and "Vietnamese" tend increasingly to blend into one another. They often say themselves, "The only good Vietnamese is a dead Vietnamese," or what amounts to the same thing, "A dead Vietnamese is a Viet Cong."

For example: south of the 17th parallel, peasants prepare to harvest their rice. American soldiers arrive on the scene, set fire to their houses and want to transfer them to a strategic hamlet. The peasants protest. What else can they do, barehanded against these Martians? They say: "The quality of the rice is good; we want to stay to eat our rice." Nothing more. But this is enough to irritate the young Yankees: "Its the Viet Cong who put that into your head; they are the ones who have taught you to resist." These soldiers are so misled that they take the feeble protests which their own violence has aroused for "subversive" resistance. At the outset, they were probably disappointed: they came to save Vietnam from "communist aggressors." But they soon had to realize that the Vietnamese did not want them. Their attractive role as liberators changed to that of occupation troops. For the soldiers it was the first glimmering of consciousness: "We are unwanted, we have no business here." But they go no further. They simply tell themselves that a Vietnamese is by definition suspect.

And from the neo-colonialists' point of view, this is true. They vaguely understand that in a people's war, civilians are the only visible enemies. Their frustration turns to hatred of the Vietnamese; racism takes it from there. The soldiers discover with a savage joy that they are there to kill the Vietnamese they had been pretending to save. All of them are potential communists, as proved by the fact that they hate Americans.

Now we can recognize in those dark and misled souls the truth of the Vietnam war: it meets all of Hitler's specifications. Hitler killed the Jews because they were Jews. The armed forces of the

---

* The portable generator of a field telephone is used as an instrument for torture by attaching the lead wires to the victim's genitals and turning the handle. The apparatus delivers a severe, painful shock [Ed.].

United States torture and kill men, women and children in Vietnam merely *because they are Vietnamese.* Whatever lies or euphemisms the government may think up, the spirit of genocide is in the minds of the soldiers. This is their way of living out the genocidal situation into which their government has thrown them. As Peter Martinsen, a 23-year-old student who had "interrogated" prisoners for ten months and could scarcely live with his memories, said: "I am a middle-class American. I look like any other student, yet somehow I am a war criminal." And he was right when he added: "Anyone in my place would have acted as I did." His only mistake was to attribute his degrading crimes to the influence of war *in general.*

No, it is not war in the abstract: it is the greatest power on earth against a poor peasant people. Those who fight it are *living out* the only possible relationship between an over-industrialized country and an underdeveloped country, that is to say, a genocidal relationship implemented through racism — the only relationship, short of picking up and pulling out.

Total war presupposes a certain balance of forces, a certain reciprocity. Colonial wars were not reciprocal, but the interests of the colonialists limited the scope of genocide. The present genocide, the end result of the unequal development of societies, is total war waged to the limit by one side, without the slightest reciprocity.

The American government is not guilty of inventing modern genocide, or even of having chosen it from other possible and effective measures against guerrilla warfare. It is not guilty, for example, of having preferred genocide for strategic and economic reasons. Indeed, genocide presents itself as the *only possible reaction* to the rising of a whole people against its oppressors.

The American government is guilty of having preferred, and of still preferring, a policy of war and aggression aimed at total genocide to a policy of peace, the only policy which can really replace the former. A policy of peace would necessarily have required a reconsideration of the objectives imposed on that government by the large imperialist companies through the intermediary of their pressure groups. America is guilty of continuing and intensifying the war despite the fact that every day its leaders realize more acutely, from the reports of the military commanders, that the only way to win is "to free Vietnam of all the Vietnamese." The government is guilty — despite the lessons it has been taught by this unique, unbearable experience — of proceeding at every moment a little further along a path which leads it to the point of no return. And it is guilty — according to its own admissions — of consciously carrying out this admonitory war in order to use genocide as a challenge and a threat to all peoples of the world.

We have seen that one of the features of total war has been the growing scope of efficiency of communication. As early as 1914, war could no longer be "localized." It had to spread throughout the whole world. In 1967, this process is being intensified. The ties of the "One World," on which the United States wants to impose its hegemony, have grown tighter and tighter. For this reason, as the American government very well knows, the current genocide is conceived as an answer to people's war and perpetrated in Vietnam not against the Vietnamese alone, but against humanity.

When a peasant falls in his rice paddy, mowed down by a machine gun, every one of us is hit. The Vietnamese fight for all men and the American forces against all. Neither figuratively nor abstractly. And not only because genocide would be a crime universally condemned by international law, but because little by little the whole human race is being subjected to this genocidal blackmail piled on top of atomic blackmail, that is, to absolute, total war. This crime, carried out every day before the eyes of the world, renders all who do not denounce it accomplices of those who commit it, so that we are being degraded today for our future enslavement.

In this sense imperialist genocide can only become more complete. The group which the United States wants to intimidate and terrorize by way of the Vietnamese nation is the human group in its entirety.

Summation on Genocide
by Lelio Basso

We have come to the end of our labours and I should like to begin this summing-up with a retrospective view of the role which we have played. At the beginning of the session in Stockholm, our President, Jean-Paul Sartre, opened with a speech which is still in our memory, wherein he confirmed that the legitimacy of our existence and of our judgements are *a posteriori.*

If we compare the reception we had in the press a year ago at our formation in London, with the reception we have had during our work, we must note that there is a rising interest. Our serious work, the evidence we have accumulated, the testimonies which we have brought to the knowledge of the public, the search for the truth which we have together pursued, has, in the eyes of public opinion, legitimized our existence. The American ex-soldiers have sought to present their testimonies to us and several states have asked us to express ourselves on various problems. Even if we decide not to take up other questions the authority of the institutions which have addressed us confirms the validity of our initiative. But above all, the awakening of conscience to what is going on in Vietnam, and the increasing pressure of the masses of the whole world against this aggressive war proves that the wish expressed by our President at Stockholm has been realised.

Our initiative is even more necessary because the aggressive war in Vietnam poses a series of new problems which international organisations are unable to solve. They cannot be solved because of the dominant presence of the Americans who are able to manipulate too many governments.

But, while new aggression, new weapons, new techniques of destruction, make necessary an evolution of the international penal code, the competent organs are paralysed. The American Government, therefore, is able to continue to commit crimes and to augment them by escalating with a certitude that the United Nations will never have the necessary majority to pronounce a clear condemnation.

In anticipation of our conclusions, I should like to underline now the new aspects presented by the war in Vietnam. This will help us to understand all the acts which we will take under consideration. This war of extermination is the natural fruit and necessity of American imperialism. It is not a case of extraordinary ferocity which almost accidentally adds itself to a conventional war. We cannot imagine that this war is different from all the others where both parties commit a few crimes, as is usual throughout the history of wars. Here everything fits: everything reflects the same systematising. The aggression with complicity of other governmants, the genocidal crimes — everything is explained by the omnipotent imperialism of the United States, which will dominate the world, which will refuse the people's right to autonomy. The imposition of neocolonialism as a way of life on all populations on the road towards development is an essential part of this imperialist system. Against a people which will not subordinate itself, "Special War," total war, torture, concentration camps and Genocide are essential elements of world-wide neo-colonialist wars.

From an analysis of the results of our debates and the information given to us, I would like to make some preliminary observations which I deem necessary. First some juridical considerations: our experts of the Legal Commission have raised the question of how we should treat certain material on the violation of various international Conventions. It has been pointed out that the American Government has objected to the existence of some Convention obligations. In some cases a Convention has been left unsigned or unratified by the United States, or Conventions have not, for other reasons, been implemented. In other cases there are Conventions in force that are applicable even if one party has not signed them, as is the case with the D.R.V. and the N.L.F. I should like to point out to members of the Tribunal who are not jurists that rules of international law do not spring from signed and ratified Conventions alone. Besides these rules there also exists a body of general law based on custom which is pre-existent to these Conventions. Conventions do not create new codes of conduct, but merely make regulations confirming codes of conduct already existing. New crimes, therefore, depend on the pre-existing general laws of custom for condemnation — it is precisely such crimes which now occupy us.

You have already been informed of the *Clause Martens* contained in the preamble to the Hague Convention of July 28, 1899, and repeated in the Hague Convention of October 18, 1907. These two Conventions were signed by the United States on the 9th of April, and ratified on November 27, 1909. This preamble confirms that:

"Civilians and the armed forces remain protected and regulated by the principles of international law, such as has been the result of common practice amongst the civilised nations, the laws of humanity, and the demands of public conscience." These principles were confirmed at the Nuremberg Trial, which in its decree, as recalled by Maitre Jouffa, stated: "Independent of the treaties, the laws of warfare stand out without usages and customs, progressively and universally recognised, from the doctrine of jurists and jurisprudence of military courts. This Law is never immoveable; it adjusts itself incessantly to the needs of a world under transition. Ordinarily, the treaties do no more than to specify the principles of laws that are already in force." The judges at Nuremberg could not think otherwise because they were judging international crimes that were unknown in written law at the time. This principle of retroaction was also utilised by the judges at Tokyo in judging Japanese war criminals.

The Allies dictated this retroactive principle and it was commonly recognised, because it did not really constitute "retroactive law." The war crimes were already "recognised as such by common, public demand, and by the existing laws of humanity." These crimes were already illicit in the sense that Professor Rousseau has given this expression: "thus, the illegality is manifest, independent of the existence or non-existence of a prohibition."

In his report, Professor Chesneaux has pointed out that the American President of the Tokyo Court, in his decree during the "High Command" case, expressed the same opinion, stating: "The fact of crimes does not arise by the presence of a prohibition, but because the act is criminal by itself, and is a breach of the principles of the laws of humanity, such as these [principles] are recognised by the civilised nations."

We then, shall pass our judgement on the basis of the very principles used in the judgement by the United States of the Japanese war criminals. First, although we have already covered it at Stockholm, because of the massive escalation which has been confirmed by our witnesses recently returned from North Vietnam — we must again address ourselves to the indiscriminate bombings.

It is enough to recall that general rules exist prohibiting the bombing of hospitals, schools, religious buildings, the civil population, etc., to clearly see that such rules have been repeatedly violated. The U.S. has violated the Convention of the Hague, the Nuremberg Judgements, the Geneva Convention of 1954, all of which have been accepted by the collective conscience of the poeples of the world. Such actions have recently also been solemnly condemned by the Vatican Council. In the face of testimony by our numerous witnesses and by American correspondents, the U.S. authorities flatly deny the facts — simply because they know that these acts are criminal.

Let us recall the words of President Johnson that the Americans aim only to destroy "concrete and steel." Let us also recall that the use of ball-bombs was admitted by the Americans only after our Stockholm session had supplied a mass of evidence to prove the fact. Likewise, the use of poison gas was at first denied by them, but later admitted, though they claimed it to be only "tear gas." Let us recall that torture was attributed by them to the puppet government; that the concentration camps are called "New Life Hamlets," . . . etc. Yes, as by our work we have proved, there is a great gap between the truth and that which is said by the U.S. authorities. It seems to me that lies are proof of guilt.

As Maitre Jouffa has shown, laws against the use of illegal weapons have been in existence for at least a century. In general terms such prohibitions are in the Declaration of St. Petersburg of 1868, and in the Hague Conventions of 1899 and 1907. As for edicts against the use of asphyxiant or toxic gas, there exists the Convention of Washington of February 6, 1922, and the Protocol of Geneva of June 17, 1925. The fact that, for several technical reasons, these articles cannot be applied, does not invalidate them, for their intent contains a general affirmation of existing rules. Apart from Fascist Italy in Ethiopia, and the United States in Vietnam, no power has dared use gas since the end of World War One, not even Nazi Germany or Japan during World War Two.

The use in time of war of poison gas and all other liquids or materials of like effect has been justly condemned by universal opinion of the civilised world and an indictment of such usage has been formulated in numerous treaties signed by the majority of civilised nations. The signatory powers, having as their aim the universal proscribtion of such inhumanities as part of the Rights of Man, want to impose this opinion upon the conscience of the nations.

Specifically with respect the United States, I should like to remind you that President Roosevelt stated on the 8th of June, 1943, that "the use of toxic or noxious gases, and all other inhuman weapons of war . . . has been put outside the law by the general opinion of all civilised people, and that our country has renounced that use . . . we shall not, in any case put gas to use, except in the case when our enemies first start."

The work done here at the Tribunal by our Scientific Commission has shown us to what extent the U.S. has violated these rules in Vietnam. This Committee's report compiled by Professors Behar, Minkowsky, Kahn and others is of a high technical and scientific order. Permit me to repeat the conclusion of the Scientific Commission's report: "Poison gas has been, and is being used in Vietnam by U.S. forces." And. ". . . they have continuously used the gases CN, CS, and DM repeatedly and massively," and finally, "we solemnly declare that in spite of official American denials of the fact, the Commission consider it satisfactorily proved [beyond doubt] that under the conditions where gases actually are in use, these so-called "harassing" gases are actually mortal — lethal — and thus come under the prohibitions of international law as poison gas."

It is the same with defoliation of large tracts of land where the report submitted to us by Lederer concluded: "the use of chemical weapons imply the risk of provoking biological reactions, wholly unsuspected in the near future, and these weapons are prohibited under international law." Lastly the indiscriminate use of napalm against the civilian population has been attested to by doctors who have treated victims, by victims themselves who have appeared before the Tribunal, by numerous witnesses, and by the Scientific commission. The witness, Donald Duncan, has told us that the majority of U.S. troops use the M-16 rifle in violation of international law against dum-dum bullets. Thus, the Tribunal can assuredly reply in the affirmative to the question relating to the use of prohibited weapons.

And what of the question concerning the treatment of prisoners of war? Rules for the treatment of POWs have been internationally accepted since their formulation in the 19th century. Since then there have been specified strict limits to the use of violence against those who have laid down their arms and can no longer fight. The general rule states that POWs shall be treated humanely and beside this general rule there are international laws agreed to by a majority of countries. The 1864 Geneva Convention, the 1899 and 1907 Hague Conventions and again the Geneva Conventions of 1929 and 1949 together form a complete code for treatment of POWs to which all nations, signatory or not, can adhere. Let us note here that during the Korean war, the four powers that were most directly implicated, the U.S., China, and North and South Korea, all appealed for the respect of these Conventions even though none had ratified them.

It is not necessary to go into the details here to learn that the U.S. violates every rule of humane treatment of POWs. The American soldier's testimony to the Tribunal is definite and crushing. David Tuck has told how orders were given to kill all prisoners who were not officers, especially the wounded. The wounded never died by themselves, but were killed off for the sake of convenience. Duncan confirmed that instructions are given to kill prisoners and has told of a specific case: "One day we took a lot of prisoners; too many for our group to cope with. So I telephoned back to ask for instructions and was told ' 'get rid of them.' I played dumb and pretended I didn't understand and took them along in the helicopter back to the base. But I got bawled out; I was supposed to have killed them off — but they would not say that on the radio."

As to tortures, we have heard unequivocal testimony. Martinsen, Tuck and Duncan, all three, have told us of tortures they have witnessed or taken part in themselves. Apart from these specific cases there is also a general affirmation. Martinsen has said: "As long as the torture left no marks it was O.K. to do it." And Duncan said: "they encouraged us to use our imagination, only insisted that whatever we did should not leave traces."

These testimonies coming from American combatants who have themselves participated in the acts they tell about, who have come here in obedience to their own consciences, are suffucent to answer "yes" on this point. But besides this, the American newspapers do not deny that torture is practiced. But they do claim that torture is used by "Special Forces," or others for whom only Saigon is responsible, and who are always present, at least as interpreters, at the interrogation of prisoners of war. From our witnesses we know positively that American officers always lead and direct these interrogations and that torture is also used by the Americans themselves. In any case, the United States is responsible for the prisoners it takes and for the treatment they receive: it is a serious violation of international law to turn POWs over to others.

And now we come to the most painful chapter in this war — the treatment of the civilian population. The provisions of the Hague and Geneva Conventions of 1899 and 1907, where rules were laid down as existent general opinion, is the same for the rights and treatment of civilians as for the other matters. Civilians must be protected against ill-treatment. Especially, because the U.S. has signed and ratified these Conventions; still more because the proper behaviour of troops towards the civilians is laid down in the U.S. Army's own manual, the *Law of Land Warfare*. This manual contains direct citations and references to applicable international laws and Conventions. No officer in the U.S. Army can be ignorant of his obligations: the Americans are responsible. The authorities at Saigon are completely dependent on the massive presence of American troops and are directly in the pay of the U.S. The Saigon army is under the command of the U.S. Headquarters, therefore whatever part of this crime is committed by Saigon is either accepted or ordered by the United States.

In addressing ourselves to this question of Genocide, we must pass from the laws of warfare to "crimes against humanity" in the sense expressed by the Nuremberg Judgements. I will refrain from giving a resume of the testimony we have heard here in the course of the past few days: There are no words strong enough to express the feeling of tragedy and horror . . .

The term "Genocide" has only been in use since the Nuremberg Trial after World War Two. The extermination of Jews was included among the "crimes against humanity" — a term that encompasses crimes other than Genocide — in the statutes and judgement of that trial. Crimes that have as their object the destruction, partially or totally, of a group defined as "national," "ethnic," "racial," or "religious," are today called Genocide. Our legal experts have explained to us that the United States has not ratified the Convention concerning Genocide.[1] But the default of ratification does not permit the U.S. to commit the crime. The crime is named and defined before the deed, and has even before that, been recognised as a crime "in all civilised countries."

Let us look closer. David Tuck has told us that "anything that moves is shot at," and since the men are usually away, this means women and children. We have been told of the "free strike zones" where it is permitted to kill anyone left in them. We are told that thousands of women and children have been gassed in the bomb-shelters, or have been burnt in their huts and villages, or have been killed by pellet bombs dropped on civilian targets. We have heard the words of Colonel Jackson as quoted by Tuck, "I want to see Vietnamese blood cover the ground." Jean Bertolino has told us, "A village was surrounded, attacked and ignited without a soldier taking the trouble of seeing if there was anyone in the thatch huts. Afterwards the paratroopers told me that several women were indeed burned alive." The same fate, Doctor Wullf told us, struck the village of Da Phuc. Roger Pic has given us impressive statistics on the single village of Cong Doan in the county of Binh Hoa Bac, where have been dropped an average of eight bombs per inhabitant and four grenades per square meter. And that is only one village among thousands. The Director of Mercy College Child Institute, William Pepper, stated in the January, 1967 *Ramparts* the results of an investigation in which he estimates that more than 250,000 children have been killed and at least 750,000 wounded in South Vietnam alone. Since then a whole year of extermination by aggression has passed and the number of victims has risen accordingly.

If one takes the whole 14 million population of South Vietnam into account, these figures take on a very serious significance. People are victimised regardless of their personal views; death strikes any and all South Vietnamese. How can we deny that what we have before us is indeed a "partial destruction of a national group," which is, as has been said, Genocide.

But there is another aspect — the concentration camps. In its "criminal methods," the Convention includes the submission of persons to conditions that are likely to endanger their personal integrity, or to voluntarily submit such persons to living conditions that threaten their physical existence, partially or in full. The inhuman conditions in a concentration camp are one of the criminal practices specifically covered by this definition.

---

[1]The United Nations Convention of 1948, which defines Genocide, in part as: "the voluntary extermination of persons who by chance belong to a national, racial, ethnical or religious group."

Duncan has explained to us that according to his information a third of the South Vietnamese population is interned in camps and that these camps are "manure heaps" where the conditions are incredible. Martinsen and Tuck have explained that the inmates are famished, ragged, and must fight between themselves for scraps of food from the American garbage. Jean Bertolino has told us of one camp where 6,500 persons huddle in tents surrounded by barbed wire as in any concentration camp. Doctor Wullf tells us of the provinces of Binh Dinh and Fu Yen where half the population is interned.

Torn from their villages, from their rice paddies, from their belongings, with sons taken away from families, with little chance of ever reuniting, the South Vietnamese are subjected to treatment and conditions that certainly gravely endanger their very existence The separation of families is, in Vietnam, more than an attack upon the social institution, for the majority of the people are farmers and the family unit is essential to survival. History has many examples of populations becoming exterminated by the mere forcible displacement from their habitual environment. For the people to survive under these conditions, we have been told, some villages have been turned into immense brothels and the young women are forced to turn to prostitution to keep their families alive.

In the same category of crime comes the willful destruction by fire or chemicals of the food stocks and harvest of the population. This systematic destruction is explained by the Americans as an attempt to deprive the enemy of food. It has been carried out on a scale that threatens to starve the entire population and make malnutrition and starvation a constant spectre for the future.

It is impossible to avoid the conclusion that the crime of Genocide is daily committed in Vietnam. It is useless for the U.S. to claim that the victims have only to comply with American conditions to have a better life. Each people has its own rights and among these is the right to choose its own way of life. It is plainly criminal to attempt to force any people to change or modify their chosen culture or to put them to such trials as these as an alternative to submitting to any repression whatever. It is clearly an abuse of the Convention on the Rights of Man and a violation of international law to make any person or group of people choose between submission to the domination of an unwanted foreign power and slavery or death in a concentration camp.

We must hand down our decision in this context. In spite of the fearsome connotations and emotion attached to the word "Genocide," it must be said that Genocide is only part of the crimes against humanity committed by the Americans in Vietnam. Some crimes are simply not as yet included in the definition of Genocide, albeit they are recognised as crimes. I mean things such as the persecution of political opponents, arbitrary arrests, torture of civilians — things such as the witness Pham Thi Yen has testified to.[2]

In torturing, the U.S. has retrogressed to before Louis IX of France who by decree outlawed torture. These crimes, I believe, do not come under the heading of Genocide, however horrible they be.

I have made plain that the war against the Vietnamese is an imperialist war and as such has a tendency to expand. On one hand, the American imperialists aim to draw their satellite states into battle on their side, and on the other hand, they attempt to strike a blow against those who will not submit to their domination. Let us examine the aggression against the neighbours of Vietnam.

We have already confirmed the aggression against Cambodia at our Stockholm session, and now we have received further proof. Our own Commission of Inquiry, as well as Commandant Khouroudeth, Jean Bertolino, Wilfred Burchett, Bernard Couret and others have given testimony which confirms the U.S. disregard for Cambodian neutrality. The U.S. claims, as an excuse, that Cambodia aids and abets the N.L.F. but these accusations remain unproved. In effect, as imperialists always do, the U.S. considers itself above the law. In this connection the Tribunal has been requested to treat the persecution of the Cambodian minority living in South Vietnam as a case of Genocide committed by the Saigon regime. While there is no doubt about the gravity of this persecution, which may be a cultural Genocide as defined but not incorporated into the Convention of 1948, we have not, as yet, gone into the matter.

However, the situation in Laos merits close attention for it closely resembles that of Vietnam, with a puppet government obedient to the U.S. and with a permanent U.S. aggression against the liberated zones in that country. Methods in use there are as illegal as those in Vietnam and I believe that we must make a judgement on the question.

In this Copenhagen session we must also consider the matter of accomplices such as Thailand, the Philippines and Japan. In its

---

[2]Mrs. Pham Thi Yen, a political opponent to the U.S. supported Diem dictatorship, was imprisoned in the infamous Paulo Condor Prison on the island of that name off the coast of South Vietnam. She testified to tortures inflicted upon political prisoners among which were insertion of field telephone generator electrodes and broken bottles into the vaginas of women prisoners, water and electric torture, starvation and executions. See also deposition of Miss Van in testimony of Hugh Manes. Ed. Note.

aggression the U.S. has been able to procure a vast and numerous array of accomplices, helpers and followers who have given a ready hand. Practically every country in the Orient has been somehow induced into this accomplice role. So has Great Britain, which also furnished the concentration camp model from its own experience in Malaysia. But complicity is a difficult thing to prove by juridical methods from the corpus of existing international law. As for Thailand, the participation of its expeditionary corps in the fighting amply proves its complicity. This is also true of the Philippines, although the Philippine Government has not officially admitted to the fact. The facts concerning Japan have been documented by Professor Hirano and other members of the Japanese Committee.[3]

PART II

Our President, Jean-Paul Sartre has said that it is impossible for us to restrict ourselves to a mere analysis of the facts and deeds; that it is impossible to give a mere juridical appraisal, but that it is necessary to go further and deeper in order to understand the political mechanism than can explain the crimes. This observation is very important. The people of the Western world are unable to understand the reasons for this war and are reluctant to admit that the United States is capable of committing crimes that can be compared with Nazi war crimes. The myth of the U.S. as a democracy is long-lived and slow to die. It dates back to the Declaration of Independence, from which, incidentally, the opening of the Constitution of the Democratic Republic of Vietnam is copied. The intervention by the U.S. in two World Wars on the side of the democracies, the traditional attitude of the Americans against classic colonialism, and lastly, clever propaganda have maintained this myth.

In Stockholm I dwelt briefly on political aspects; I return to these because the Tribunal must attempt to illuminate beyond the mere determination of irrefutable facts, but must also explain the reasons and causes behind these facts. Thus, the Nuremberg Sentence began with an analysis of the Nazi regime, then went on to judge the crimes of the regime.

We must always make a distinction between the American people and those in the United States who control them, whether this control is political, economic or intellectual. The ordinary public of

---

[3] Professor Yoshitaro Hirano, Doctor of Jurisprudence, presented to the Tribunal the findings of the Tokyo Tribunal of 1967, which examined U.S. conduct in the Vietnam war and Japan's supporting role. Japan was found guilty of complicity with the U.S.

the United States lets itself be controlled. They are convinced that this is the incarnation of democratic ideals and have been taught to so believe. They are quite certain that the American way of life is an ideal model which deserves to be exported so that the whole world may partake of its joys. This "way of life" depends on "free enterprise" or, in other words, capitalism and private profits. This belief is quasi-mystical and is not incompatible with a well developed sense of humane conduct. At the "controlling level," however, everything is clearer; pragmatism and vested interests are shrouded in a language that appeals to the humanist sentiments of the people and is expressed as a mixture of idealism, hyprocrisy and cynicism typical of American life.

If we try to understand the policies of the U.S. managers at the level where decisions are made, we can say that such policies are characterised by the necessity for continued expansion. The war of 1812-14 against England was followed by and allowed a westward expansion beyond the Mississippi. Some years later the Monroe Doctrine solidified the supremacy of the United States over the whole American continent. Though, before the end of the nineteenth century, the westward movement had reached the Pacific Ocean, even this did not satisfy U.S. expansionism. With regard to Latin America, Richard Olney, the Secretary of State under President Cleveland, could declare: "Today the U.S. is practically sovereign on this continent and its will is law wherever we intervene." The thesis expressed by the historian Frederick Jackson Turner was also representative of the American attitude toward the eventual limits of its frontiers. Turner believed that the democracy and wealth of the United States was a result of the previous thirty years of expansion, and he stated: "The needs of the U.S.A. are a vigorous foreign policy, an inter-oceanic canal, an awakening of our naval power and the extension of our influence to encompass faraway islands as well as countries closer to us, in order to show clearly that we are on the move, that we continue to expand."

At the very time this was written the U.S. was in transition from an agricultural to an industrial economy. The westward drive now was not for new lands to till, but to buy raw materials and to sell finished products, to find new natural resources and new markets. This need for new markets was essential to what had at the turn of the century become "big business," which foresaw and feared a crisis of overproduction. This new expansion — of markets — was later replaced by an economic influence on and expansion in foreign countries. If need be in certain countries, there was also a territorial expansion. From then on, American movement was an imperialistic movement which most often used a policy of indirect political domination, reinforced when necessary with armed inter-vention whenever a popular revolution threatened U.S. interests.

As a result of two currents of thought — that wealth was the re-sult of expansion and that democracy was a result of expansion, as had been the case within the continent, the historian William Appleman Williams wrote, expansionism became the motivating force in U.S. foreign policy. To a great extent, the same was true of American business expansion into overseas markets, since the managers explained economic crisis in terms of inadequate domestic markets. Implied or expressed, Williams writes, this idea had the aim of preserving democracy and restoring prosperity.

"We must have the Chinese market, or we shall have a revolu-tion," stated Senator Frye. And Brooks Adams concluded that the U.S. would have stagnated if she had not consolidated her position in Latin American and had not made the Far East into an economic colony. Fifty years prior, Quincy Adams had used Christian prin-ciples in the expression of the same thing: "The moral obligation upon which commercial relations are based is, exclusively and en-tirely, the Christian proverb 'Love thy neighbor as thyself', but" he went on, "the Chinese are not Christian, they do not consider that they should love their neighbors as themselves. They have a system that is hostile and anti-social . . . The principle of the Chinese Empire is anti-commercial, it does not believe in having any re-lations with other countries . . . It is high time that this outrage against human rights, against human decency is ceased."

Samoa and the Hawaiian Islands were the first stages of American expansion en route to Asia. "To retain our commercial supremacy in the Pacific," said Cabot Lodge in 1895, "we must control the Hawaian Islands and stay on Samoa." The Declaration of War against Spain — for Cuba — was a favorable occasion to snatch up the Philippines in the name of a crusade to civilize. As President McKinley then said: "The Lord had said that the U.S. had the duty of educating and elevating the Philippines in the Christian civilisa-tion and, by the grace of God, to do all that we can for our brother nation, for whom Christ also died." But in the same breath he added, "The Philippines are ours forever — and right behind them there is the immense Chinese market. We shall not leave either one."

Shortly after, in 1899, under the same President McKinley, the principle of the "Open Door" was proclaimed. This opened to the U.S. a commercial beachhead into China and denied the exclusivity of the spheres of influence of the other powers. The *Press* of Phila-delphia commented then: "This Declaration is as important as the Monroe Doctrine was for the Americas in the last years. It protects

638

the present and the future." From this time on the principle of the Open Door, of American expansionist capitalism and free enterprise has been a dogma of the U.S. This dogma, to which other ideas are linked, is the ideology of American imperialism — free enterprise as a foundation for freedom and liberty. Integral to this dogma is the belief that the unlimited expansion of the American economy and the "American way of life" are necessary for prosperity in the U.S., that there exists an historic mission to export this way of life to all other peoples, and that those who live this way of life are superior. This is a doctrine of superiority; it is a sentiment that generates racism.

Who has not heard expressed the common opinion that God has chosen the U.S.A. to improve the world? A curious mixture of Christianity, evolutionism and racism leads to the consideration of other races as inferior and created solely to prepare the way for the American race. Referring to the American Indians, Josiah Strong said, ". . . it seems as if these tribes were simply created as the forerunners of a superior race — as the voices that cry in the desert — 'Make way for the Lord.'"

The fate of America, according to President Wilson, was "to be the most just, the most progressive, the most honourable, the most enlightened of all the nations of the entire world," and that its mission is to "make the world safe for democracy" — but we know that "democracy" translates to "free enterprise." "If," said Wilson in 1912, "America had not had free enterprise, it would not have any sort of liberty at all." Later in the same year: "Our industry has developed to the point where it collapses unless it finds a free opening on the world market. Our home market is insufficient, we must have a foreign trade." In 1924, Herbert Hoover stated: "Foreign markets will be more important for us, to assure a stable and normal function of our industry . . . It is of an importance that is greater than the percentage of export in relation to the home consumption." The Great Depression from 1929 to 1932 gave added impetus to this search for foreign markets and new forms of domination, and World War Two gave the U.S. an historical occasion to assume world leadership, or at least to have a try at it. Between the two World Wars the American Government sought to implement its pursuit of Asian markets by collaborating first with the Japanese and later with Chiang Kai-shek. The motivation always being the imposition upon the non-socialist world of the American way of life and economic domination. Different methods were used in Europe from those used on other continents where the neo-colonial policy of "granting independence" or obtaining an "Open Door" established the mechanism for economic dominance.

I do not believe I wander if I quote some leading Americans in order to precisely define the design for American hegemony — now dubbed "globalism" — which is merely another name for super-imperialism on a global scale. In 1898, Senator Beveridge said in a speech: "American industrial production surpassed the needs of the American population. The American production of foodstuffs is above and beyond our own consumption. Destiny has thus indicated our future policy. World trade must be dominated by the U.S.A. and it will be. We can learn how from our mother country, England. We must establish a world-wide system of trade centers from which our products can be distributed. Our merchant marine must dominate the oceans. Around these trade centers will cluster vast self-governing colonies, flying our flag and trading with us. Our institutions will follow in the wake of our trade. American law and order, American civilization, will settle on the shores that, until then, are steeped in darkness and bloody strife, and by their work as divine tools, these shores will come into a future beauty."

Forty-two years later, the President of the National Industrial Conference Board, Virgil Jordan, took up the same idea and said on December 10, 1940: "Whatever the outcome of the war may be, America has taken the road towards imperialism on an economic plane, as on all other planes of life — Some fear this word "imperialism," so menacing and well known. Most people prefer, in the American way, to mask the fact under a more vague expression, such as defense of the Western hemisphere. But consciously or not, America is destined by her temperament, by her capacity, by her resources, and by the course of world affairs, not alone those of the last few years, but since 1900, destined to follow this road. Truly we have no choice. We have but to continue on the road that we have been going along for a quarter of a century and which began with the annexation of Cuba and the Philippines, etc.," Later in the same speech: "This Empire is seeing its possibilities for expansion on the southern part of this hemisphere and west — in the Pacific — disappearing. The sceptre falls in the hands of the U.S.A."

But the Pacific is not enough. Since 1941, Henry Luce, talked of "the American Century" and invited the American people "enthusiastically to accept the duty and mission of the most vigorous, the most powerful nation in all the world," and "to make noticeable that full weight of our influence, wherever we find reason therefore, and always with the methods that we find most opportune." In his speech at Baylor University, President Truman reaffirmed the principle: "The American system can only survive in America itself if it becomes global," and that thus "the entire world should adopt the American system." The Truman doctrines on Greece and Turkey, the Eisenhower doctrine on the Near East, the interventions in Latin America are all manifestations of this policy. The facts confirm that everywhere a reactionary regime will always find support forthcoming from the United States. Everywhere, and above all where there is anti-imperialism, — Arbenz in Guatemala, Jagan in Guyana, Castro in Cuba, Lumumba in the Congo — the American Government is ever ready to foment or support plots, subversion, espionage, coups and invasions. To a lesser degree, but just as inevitably, the reformers, the lukewarm friends — such as Bosch in Santo Domingo, Prince Norodom Sihanouk in Cambodia, Goulart in Brazil and Papandreou in Greece, feel the pressure of the U.S.

The doctrine of "globalism" is a doctrine to justify American intervention in every part of the world. It is the theory held by a whole school of foreign policy makers. The result has been that it is not the now petrified apparatus of the United Nations, but the unilateral decision of the U.S. that decides if, where and how the U.S. should intervene without concern for the will of the interested parties. Walt Whitman Rostow has defined the aim, which is to establish everywhere a world-wide "community of order."

But in this world-wide community of order which the U.S. is to dominate, all doors must remain open to "free (American) enterprise." All people must submit to American leadership and assume the role of subjects. To integrate into such a world economic imperialism is clearly to integrate into an American dominated economy which automatically means that other economic systems are reduced to inferior positions. For the world's peoples, the loss of an independent economy means the loss of political independence, as well as the loss of their own cultural personality.

It is in the light of all this that we should examine American aggression in Vietnam. The policy of the Open Door to American Capitalism all over the world cannot fail to have as its number one enemy, the socialist countries. Socialist countries must, by definition, close this door to "free enterprise" and construct a solid barrier to capitalist domination. Given this fact, the main object of American policy must be to prevent extension of the socialist zone. If the 1956 elections had been held in Vietnam, doubtless Ho Chi Minh would have been victorious: but the immediate and imperative aim for the U.S. there was to establish a satellite state on the lines of Taiwan and South Korea. In other words, the U.S. had to choose between two alternatives, a socialist government in South Vietnam or another puppet state. Their choice surprised no one. But the puppets could not subdue the resistance of the people; the neocolonialists could not thwart the Vietnamese will to be free and independent. And during the years 1963-64 a new dilemma arose; the puppet regime was collapsing under the people's pressure, the war between the puppets and the people was being won by the people. The next choice for the Americans was an acceptance of the facts or an all-out American war. Again no one was surprised, the choice was inevitable.

As I have already said at Stockholm, the underlying deeper reasons for this choice are not directly economic in the sense that the U.S. has invested capital in that country that could justify intervention. Nor is it, in my view, a strategic concern which merits this colossal expenditure. Even though the U.S. pushes its military bases close to China, South Vietnam is not indispensable to them.

The American choice of intervention and war was and is — grounded on the fact that they are faced with a general revolt against American domination in the three continents where the people are rising in defence of their objective and true self-interests. The U.S. could not avoid this show-down in South Vietnam and *must* win any guerrilla war.

But are they winning? Not merely is there no proof of this, there are signs of the opposite. In spite of the enormous disproportion between means, in spite of a concentration of firepower hitherto unknown in warfare, in spite of an incredible technological development of weapons of mass destruction, the American imperialists have suffered constant defeat. They have been defeated because the N.L.F. and the D.R.V. have retained the total support of the Vietnamese. Apart from the few mercenaries and collaborators, the overwhelming majority of the people support the struggle against the United States. Doctor Wullf, who has lived for years in Vietnam, and the American Press substantiate this; there is no other explanation for the course of the war.

And now the Americans have another dilemma — defeat or Genocide. And since the most haughty imperialist of the world cannot face defeat, with cynicism and indifference they choose Genocide. And for this choice there is a historical precedent. When the American Indian failed to conform to the design, they, too were exterminated.

The United States is still moving westward and the frontier is being pushed on, over the Pacific, towards and into Asia — until the whole is transformed into an American colony. Those who resist are, in the imperialist's eyes, in the same obstructionist position as was the Indian, they oppose the will of God. They are of an inferior lesser race which stands in the way of the exalted. They must, then, be exterminated.

It is in this way that American expansionism has made them become aggressors, arrayed against other races and peoples. And it
is the final solution of "escalation" which brings the Genocide on
the people that refuse to submit. This is the political logic of the
American Government, and it is against this logic which we must
unite the people. Not only in the cause of humanity, not only in
solidarity with the people of Vietnam, but in common defence of
the common good. In affirmation of the right freely to choose a
way of life in accordance with one's own conscience. A right which
the N.L.F. has inscribed upon its banner; a right for which they
and the heroic Vietnamese people are fighting and dying every day.

Summary and Verdict of the Second Session

The International War Crimes Tribunal met in Roskilde, Denmark
from November 20th to December 1st, 1967, to continue the study
of the questions on the agenda set during the constitutive meeting
in London in November, 1966.

A part of this agenda had been covered at Stockholm from the 2nd
to the 10th of May, 1967, which led to a first judgment, dated May
10th, 1967. From this first judgment it results that according to
this Tribunal:

• First, the government of the United States has committed aggression against Vietnam under the terms of international law.

• Second, there have been deliberate, systematic and large-scale
bombings of civilian objectives in Vietnam.

• Third, there have been on the part of the government of the United
States of America repeated violations of the sovereignty, the neutrality
and the territorial integrity of Cambodia.

• Fourth, the governments of Australia, New Zealand and South
Korea have been accomplices of the United States in the aggression
against Vietnam.

Agenda of Second Session

In the course of its Roskilde session, the Tribunal was to study the
following questions:

• First, the complicity of Japan, Thailand and the Philippines in the
acts of aggression committed by the government of the United States
of America.

- Second, the use of weapons and products prohibited by the laws of war.

- Third, the treatment of war prisoners.

- Fourth, the treatment of the civilian populations by the forces of the U.S.A. and those which are subordinate to them.

- Fifth, the extension of the war to Laos.

- Sixth, and finally, the Tribunal was to pronounce whether the combination of the crimes imputed to the government of the U.S.A. could not receive the general qualification of genocide.

A few days before the opening of the Roskilde session, the Tribunal renewed its appeal to the government of the U.S.A. in order that it might send a qualified representative who could answer in an authorized way to the accusations brought against it. This appeal, like numerous previous appeals, has remained without effect.

The Tribunal has heard the qualified representatives of the Democratic Republic of Vietnam and of the National Front of Liberation of South Vietnam as well as those of the Neo Lao Haksat of Laos and of Cambodia, and has heard the grievances that they have presented. It has heard numerous witnesses from the most varied countries, and in particular Vietnamese citizens from the North and the South who are war victims, and citizens of the U.S.A. having belonged to the American army in Vietnam.

It has heard the reports drawn up by the investigative commissions which it had sent itself to Vietnam, both in the D.R.V. and in the areas controlled by the N.L.F., and the U.S.A., as well as the reports of the investigative committees of Japan and of the Democratic People's Republic of Korea. It has studied numerous reports furnished by scientific and legal experts and by historians. Abundant documentation in photographs and motion pictures has been presented, as wll as samples of weapons and products, accompanied by the results of experiments made in connection with these.

It is in a position to give the following replies to the questions which it has studied.

FIRST, complicity of Japan, Thailand and the Philippines:

- A. The American army, in utilizing the land, naval and air bases of Okinawa, in disposing of all Japan for the movement of its troops, in taking advantage of Japan's highly developed technical capacity and abundant equipment for the repair of its war and merchant fleets and planes and for all kinds of supplies and equipment, has made Japan, with the complicity of its government, one of the essential elements of its strategic system in its struggle against Vietnam. As

Mr. Stennis, chairman of the Armed Services Subcommittee of the U.S. Senate, has declared, without the help of Japan, "operations in Southeast Asia would encounter serious difficulties." Already, during the Stockholm session, the Tribunal condemned the complicity of Australia, New Zealand and South Korea. Concerning this last country, the Tribunal received precise evidence that it was not only an accomplice to the crime of aggression, but that its army had committed war crimes. The Tribunal has not received information on this point as to the armed forces of the other accomplice powers.

• B. From the reports and documents furnished to the Tribunal, it is clear that the government of Thailand has afforded the United States diplomatic help, that it has offered it the possibility of setting up on its territory bases from which are launched the most murderous American air attacks against Vietnam. These bases are extremely valuable to the U.S.A. because they make it possible to bombard Vietnam under infinitely easier and more economical conditions, and with lesser risks for the pilots. Finally, the Thai government has completed its complicity by sending to South Vietnam an expeditonary corps, fighting directly by the side of the American armies. The complicity of the Thai government is likewise direct, as concerns the acts of aggression against Cambodia and Laos of which we shall speak later.

• C. The government of the Philippines, whose policies are almost totally aligned with the policy of the United States, affords the latter the use of the bases which it has kept on the territory of the Philippines, after the accession of that country to a purely formal independence. It is rightly that the Philippines have been qualified as a typical example of a state under the neocolonial domination of the United States. In additon, the government of the Philippines has sent troops to South Vietnam; this contingent is at the present time two thousand men strong and it will undoubtedly be augmented.

SECOND, on prohibited weapons and products:

The Tribunal wishes to recall the uncontested principles of the law of nations, as well as those which were set down in the Hague in 1907, and with respect to which the legality of a weapon must be appraised: the principle of the immunity of the civilian population, the prohibiton on the use of toxic products, the prohibition of weapons that may cause superfluous harm. It has attached a special importance to the Martens clause, which appears in the preamble of the Hague Conventions of 1907, and according to which the law of war depends on the principles of the law of nations resulting from the usages established between the civilized nations, the laws of humanity and the requirements of the human conscience. It is in the application of these principles that the offical manual of the American army (Department of the Army field manual) entitled "The Law of Land Warfare," published in July 1956, under the reference F.M. 27-10, by the Department of the Army, makes it an obligation for campaigning armies not to use any kind and degree of violence not really necessary for military objectives and aims.

The Tribunal has already condemned in Stockholm the use of fragmentation bombs (C.B.U. bombs and pellet bombs), which are by definition intended to strike civilian populations, being inoperative against installations or protected military men. It has been informed that the use of these weapons has become intensified and that they have been perfected in the form of delayed-action bombs.

The Tribunal wants today to condemn:

• The wholesale and indiscriminate use of napalm, which has been abundantly demonstrated before the Tribunal.

• The use of phosphorus, the burns of which are even more painful and prolonged and have, in addition, the effects of a poison on the organism.

As for the use of gases, the Tribunal considers that the failure of the United States to ratify the Geneva Protocol on June 17, 1925, concerning the prohibition of the use in war of toxic or similar asphyxiating gases is without effect, as a result of the voting by the General Assembly of the United Nations (a vote joined in by the United States) of the resolution of the 5th of December, 1966, inviting all states to conform to the principles and objectives of the said Protocol, and condemning all acts contrary to these objectives.

The scientific reports of the most qualified experts, which have been submitted to the Tribunal, demonstrate that the gases used in Vietnam, in particular CS, CN and DM, are used under conditions which make them always toxic and often deadly, especially when they are blown into the hideouts, shelters and underground tunnels where a large part of the Vietnamese population is forced to live. It is impossible to classify them as simple incapacitating gases; they must be classfied as combat gases.

The Tribunal has studied the current practice of the American army consisting of spraying defoliating or herbicidal products over entire regions in Vietnam. It has noted that the American manual on the law of war already cited forbids destroying, in particular by chemical agents—even those theoretically nonharmful to man—any crops that are not intended to be used exclusively for the food of the armed forces.

It has found that the reports of the investigative commissions confirmed the information, from both Vietnamese and American sources, according to which considerable areas of cultivated land are sprayed by these defoliating and herbicidal products. At least 700,000 hectares [about 1,750,000 acres] of ground were affected in 1966.

THIRD, on the treatment of prisoners of war:

The Tribunal recalls that prisoners of war must receive humane treatment, under conditions which are defined by the Geneva Conventions of 1949, which the United States has signed, and the terms of which it has incorporated in its own manual of the law of war. Tortures, mutilations and serious physical and mental coercion are not only prohibited but must be punished. The prisoner is entitled to life and to the medical aid that his state requires.

Numerous testimonies, both Vietnamese and American, were heard (among the American witnesses was a former soldier whose function for ten months had been to question prisoners from the time of their capture), and it was established that these principles are a dead letter for the Americans in Vietnam. The finishing off of the wounded on the battlefield and summary executions are frequent. Prisoners are thrown into the air from helicopters. Torture in all forms, by electricity, water, burns and blows, is practiced daily. All the witnesses have confirmed that these practices always occur in the presence and under the direction of American soldiers, even when they do not themselves participate. These tortures are aimed at obtaining information or confessions. Medical care is systematically refused to the wounded and ill who refuse to speak.

Finally, in contempt of the provisions of the Geneva Convention, the prisoners held by the United States, which is the detaining power within the meaning of this Convention, are handed over to the authorities of the so-called Saigon government, which engages in a dreadful repression accompanied by acts of torture, numerous examples of which have been furnished, including those in which women are frightfully tortured.

FOURTH, treatment of civilian populations:

The Convention of the Hague of 1907, the Nuremburg and Tokyo judgments, the Universal Declaration of Human Rights, the 4th Geneva Convention of August 12th, 1949, lay down the undeniable principle of the protection of civilian persons in time of war. The manual of the law of war of the American army includes as one of its parts the entire 4th Convention of Geneva, the binding character of which is undeniable.

The Tribunal heard: the testimony of three American veterans, and the report of the interrogations undertaken by its investigative mission in the United States, some Vietnamese victims, the report to the investigative mission of the Tribunal in the areas controlled by the N.L.F. (which has collected 317 depositions, the minutes of which have been put into its files) and an important witness, a citizen of the German Federal Republic who has lived several years in South Vietnam. It considers that the following facts are established:

• First, in the course of raiding operations which take place both systematically and permanently, thousands of inhabitants are massacred. According to serious information from American sources, 250,000 children have been killed since the beginning of this war, and 750,000 wounded and mutilated for life. Senator [Edward] Kennedy's report, of October 31, 1967, points out that 150,000 wounded can be found every month. Villages are entirely leveled, fields are devastated, livestock destroyed; in particular the testimony of the American journalist Jonathan Schell describes in a startling way the extermination by the American forces of the population of the Vietnamese village of Ben Suc, and its complete destruction. Precise testimony and documents that have been put before the Tribunal have reported the existence of free-fire zones, where everything that moves is considered hostile, which amounts to saying that the entire population is taken as a target.

• Second, one third of the population of Vietnam has been displaced according to the very terms of the address of Senator Kennedy at the International Rescue Committee, and shut up in the strategic hamlets which are now baptized New Life Hamlets. The living conditions, according to published reports that have been brought to the Tribunal's attention, are close to those of a concentration-camp life. The interned—women and children in most cases—are parked like cattle behind barbed-wire fences. Food and hygiene are almost entirely lacking, which often makes survival impossible. The social structures and traditional structures of the Vietnamese families are thus destroyed. One must also take account of the fact of the impressive number of prisoners held in the jails of South Vietnam— 400,000 according to estimates that are worthy of attention. Arbitrary arrests, parodies of justice, interrogations accompanied by abominable tortures, are current practice. All the testimony agrees in establishing that inhuman and illegal methods are daily being used by the American armed forces and their satellites against the civilian populations, who are thus threatened with extermination.

FIFTH, on the extension of the war to Laos and Cambodia:

As a corollary to the American aggression in Vietnam, the security of the two neighboring countries is seriously compromised.

1. The Laotian people are plunged into war by the direct extension on their territory of American aggression. On the one hand, the violation of the Geneva Agreements on Indochina of 1954, like those of the Geneva Agreements on Laos of 1962, and the support given by the governments of the United States and of Thailand to the local pro-American forces, constitute a blatant intervention in the domestic affairs of Laos, and have revived the war in Laotian territory. Moreover, military personnel of the United States and its satellites — South Vietnamese and Thai — have been introduced into Laos, transforming the part of the territory controlled by the Vientiane administration into a military base in the service of American aggression, both against Vietnam and against the rest of Laos. Finally, American planes that leave from bases situated in Thailand regularly assault the Laotian population, accumulating deaths and ruins.

2. Cambodia as the Tribunal has emphasized in its Stockholm judgment, is the victim of repeated violations of its frontiers perpetrated by the armed forces of Thailand and of the government of Saigon, in the pay of the United States. It is also the victim of repeated bombings, both aerial and artillery, from the American forces. The situation analyzed in Stockholm has only become aggravated, and the heaviest menace hangs over the Kingdom of Cambodia, as its Chief of State has pointed out to the Tribunal.

Therefore, the International War Crimes Tribunal, does as a result of deliberations render its verdict   as follows:

Is the Government of Thailand guilty of complicity in the aggression committed by the United States Government against Vietnam?

Yes, by Unanimous Vote

Is the Government of the Philippines guilty of complicity in the aggression committed by the United States Government against Vietnam?

Yes, by Unanimous Vote

Is the Government of Japan guilty of complicity in the aggression committed by the United States Government against Vietnam?

Yes, by 8 Votes to 3

(The three Tribunal members who voted against agree that the Japanese Government gives considerable aid to the Government of the United States, but do not agree on its complicity in the crime of aggression).

Has the United States Government committed aggression against the people of Laos, according to the definition provided by international law?

Yes, by Unanimous Vote

Have the armed forces of the United States used or experimented with weapons prohibited by the laws of war?

Yes, by Unanimous Vote

Have prisoners of war captured by the armed forces of the United States been subjected to treatment prohibited by the laws of war?

Yes, by Unanimous Vote

Have the armed forces of the United States subjected the civilian population to inhuman treatment prohibited by international law?

Yes, by Unanimous Vote

Is the United States Government guilty of genocide against the people of Vietnam?

Yes, by Unanimous Vote

Appeal to American and World Opinion
read by Dave Dellinger

Unlike the Nuremburg Tribunal which met after the crimes had been committed, the International War Crimes Tribunal is meeting and rendering its judgments at the very moment when the crimes are taking place and even being escalated. The Nuremburg Tribunal asked for and secured the punishment of individuals. The International War Crimes Tribunal is asking the peoples of the world, the masses, to take action to stop the crimes. At Nuremburg the accused rested safely in jail, and the main focus was on the past; our Tribunal is quite different. Unless the masses act, and act successfully, we stand only at the beginning of war crimes and genocide — genocide that could bring down the cities and destroy the populations of the world.

No matter how horrible the evidence presented here, we stand at the threshold of even more horrible and extensive crimes, unless the peoples of the world act. Let us remind you that the history of the war in Vietnam is a history of continuous escalation. When the United States has found out that it cannot defeat the enemy of the moment at the level of warfare of the moment, it continually redefines the enemy and expands the form of its aggression. I will not go into the history of this expansion, but I will remind you that it began with diplomatic warfare at Geneva and elsewhere; it went through the stages of political infiltration, the training of puppets, the organizing of counter-insurgency, the training and leading of massive Saigon troops, and finally, the commitment of masses of United States troops.

As the United States loses in its battle with one enemy, it takes on new enemies. And as it escalates its enemies, it escalates the weapons. As the American G.I.'s, David Tuck, Peter Martinsen and Donald Duncan testified, they went to Vietnam to fight Communists, and they were disillusioned when they found out that they were fighting Vietnamese; that they were there to kill anybody from the population. Already as the United States is losing at the present level of warfare and claims that as a "Great Power" it cannot admit defeat and cannot withdraw from this criminal enterprise, Secretary Rusk is raising fears of the "yellow peril" in China. The state of mind that affirms napalm and pellet bombs and poison gases as weapons, is the state of mind that can affirm nuclear warfare.

Many people in the countries of the world, especially the Western countries, are watching from the sidelines, as they watched Hitler. In the time of Hitler they said, "It can't happen here." And in the time of the United States aggression in Vietnam, they are saying, "It can't happen to our cities; it can't happen to our populations."

But already their countries are subjected to the diplomatic warfare that began the attack on Vietnam. They are subject to pressures on their governments and their economies. The United States Special Forces are scattered throughout the world. The Vietnamese know that they have no choice, except to resist. In many other countries, particularly the Western countries, people think that they have a choice still. But they have none; they must resist. Paradoxically, if Hitler announced his intention to wipe out the Jews, the photos and the reports of the atrocities did not appear in the daily newspapers or go into the living rooms in television. And if the democratic facade in the United States has prevented the American generals and presidents from announcing their intentions, perhaps even from comprehending them in their full intensity themselves, the same democratic facade allows some of the reports and some of the photos to appear in the American mass media. And the psychology becomes, "it's alright to do these things, because we are a democratic country as shown by the fact that we tell about them in the press." And at a certain stage, the psychology becomes, "because we admit that we are doing these things, we are not really doing them at all." In other words they do not call these actions by their proper name, and they do not present them in their proper intensity.

But a democratic society *can* commit genocide, as is illustrated by the history of the United States. I need only remind you of what happened to the American Indians and the black people. If the people in the Western countries, in particular, underestimate the total and genocidal nature of the United States' aggression, there is something else which they underestimate also. And that is the ability of the Vietnamese people to resist. If they underestimate the inhuman nature of the United States' actions, they also underestimate the human nature of the Vietnamese resistance.

The legitimacy of the Tribunal has sometimes been questioned. Its legitimacy will be determined by the answer given to its findings by the peoples of the world. The people of the world must refuse to commit the crimes that have been documented here. They must refuse to be accomplices in these crimes. But it is not enough to stop here. In addition they must make positive acts to stop the crimes. The Tribunal appeals to the people of the United States to stop the monstrous aggression of the United States at its source. It appeals to the people of the United States to put an end to United States' genocide. And finally, the Tribunal appeals to all the peoples of the world to act in the name of humanity and the name of solidarity with our Vietnamese brothers and with all other peoples whose lives and honor and integrity are threatened.

Bertrand Russell's Final Address to the Tribunal
Copenhagen, December 1967

In declaring our conclusions today, we do not merely pronounce judgement on past events. We do more than report the criminal policies and actions of a government. Our function is not that of an historian. We have not studied and deliberated solely in order to preserve the truth about Vietnam for posterity. We must discharge a deeper and harder duty; we speak because silence is complicity, a lie, a crime. We expose in order to arouse conscience. We condemn evil in order to extirpate its causes. Our truth challenges mankind.

What words can describe the evil we've discovered? The moral, legal, and political categories by which we are accustomed to judge human conduct are inadequate for these crimes. The term genocide truly encompasses the enormity of American crimes in Vietnam. I shall not repeat the catalogue of horrors which we have witnessed these past ten days; let me only say that it is nightmarish in its dimensions and vividness; we shall never forget it. We must permit no one to be innocent of these facts. Everyone should know them and every man must judge them.

Morally awakened men, willing to act — only these are needed to end America's war. Despite technological innovation, the Pentagon must rely ultimately on its conscripts, just as every imperial power has depended on innocent men, acting out of fear, habitual conformity and total ignorance, to enact the slaughter of aggressive war. The American soldier does not differ from the ordinary conscript of the First World War. His obedience and patriotism are underpinned by profound unawareness of what he will be called upon to do. We must reach him and make him aware. We must build resistance in America to the continuation of the war. In every land we must make known the reality of Vietnam. We must develop massive campaigns against the complicity of any government which fails to condemn American genocide in Vietnam. Even in the nations which have uttered clear condemnations of the aggressors, it is never impossible to increase the concrete aid to those who are struggling for justice in Vietnam. We must mobilize every people on the basis of our findings and create an international resistance to the war.

The months ahead are crucial. American casualties have increased gravely, in direct proportion to the escalation of troop committments. Tens of thousands of Americans will be killed this year in Vietnam. The United States is losing the war. The peoples of every continent are aware of this. The Pentagon spends more and more dollars in desparation—one million for each guerilla killed. It unleashes all its might fiendishly, but the heroic partisans of Vietnam endure. They will go on so long as a single Vietnamese survives. Our duty is to stand with them. The most lasting barrier to genocide is the unity of all peoples to whom justice is more than an empty phrase, and courage an indispensible attribute of morality.

It is ironic that as the International War Crimes Tribunal completes its task, news arrives from Washington of the dismissal of McNamara and the preparations for a final desparate effort by Johnson before the forthcoming United States elections, to escape from the results of his own wickedness and folly in Vietnam. Our Tribunal leaves Denmark, therefore, armed not only with the fullest evidence of American war crimes, but with the knowledge that the final chapter of these crimes is still unwritten. We appeal to everyone the world over to redouble his efforts to end this barbarism.

———◆———

Isaac Deutscher 1907-1967 Historian, Member of the Tribunal   655

Bertrand Russell at the Tribunal's Organizational Meeting in London

Below, Mme. Pham Thi Yen tells the Tribunal of seven years imprisonment and torture by the Saigon regime for political activity.

John Duffett photo

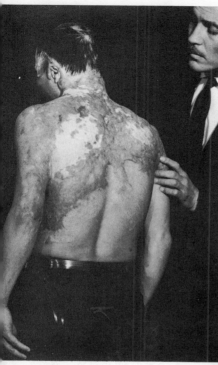

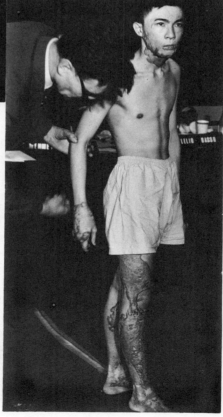

Hoang Tan Hung, 45 year old merchant was dive-bombed by waves of U.S. jets. Burned by a mixture of napalm and phosphorous, his arm is permanently welded to his trunk. Three years after the trauma, the pain is still excruciating.

Thai Binh Dan, 18, is a South Vietnamese. His hamlet was napalmed by U.S. planes March, 1966. Though healed, the scar tissue leaves constant feeling "that I am being bitten by ants."

657

Legs of Thai Binh Dan
show typical keloid
scar formation from
healed napalm burns.
These keloids turn to
secondary cancer and
resemble the burns on
Hiroshima and Nagasaki
A-bomb victims.

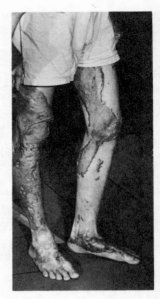

John Duffett photo

Bjorn Langhammer photo

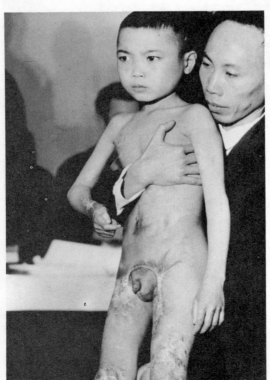

Nine year old buffalo
boy, Do Van Ngoc, was
dive-bombed with na-
palm while tending the
family buffalo. His genital
region is permanently
disfigured. Do Van Ngoc
is an enemy of the
American people.

Early "pineapple" anti-personnel bomb superseded by the more efficient "guavas" shown on next page. Weapons experts at the Tribunal pointed out that the U.S. has always tested experimental weapons upon Asians.

Fig. 1

John Duffett photos

Detail of bomblet casing shows pellets cast into fragmentation shell.

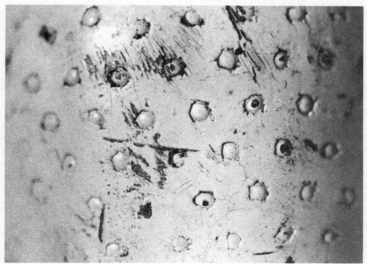

659

Fig. 3

Anti-personnel "mother bomb" holds
640 "guavas" which in turn contain
308 pellets each. One F-100 can
carry four to eight of these mother
bombs in a single mission.

Fig. 2

The "guava" anti-
personnel bomblet,
deadliest weapon
against a civil popu-
lation ever known,
has raised bombing
into de facto geno-
cide. The pellets are
made of an alloy
which is incompatible
with human tissue
and suporates in
situ.

660

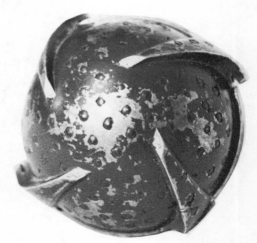

John Duffett photo

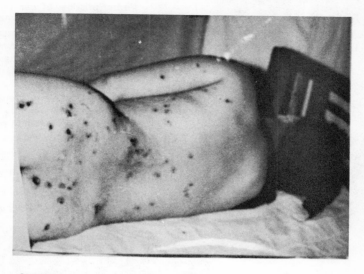

Civilian victims of U.S. anti-personnel bombs show typical multiple wound punctures; trauma to vital organs causes intense suffering.

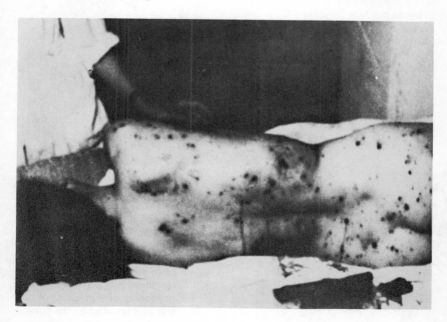

Left. Peter Martinsen, a former prisoner of war interrogator with the U.S. 541st Military Intelligence Detachment in Vietnam, told of having tortured hundreds of people to extract information which could be used in forming battle plans. Women and children were among those detained for "interrogation"; not all survived.

John Duffett photos

Right. Former Green Beret Sergeant Donald Duncan's testimony revealed the ties between the U.S. Special Forces and the Central Intelligence Agency, not only in Vietnam, but throughout the Third World. To "get rid of prisoners" who might impede a mission, he said, was standard U.S. operating procedure.

Left. David Tuck was an infantryman in a unit under the 25th Infantry Division. He told of prisoners being thrown out of helicopters from an altitude of 3000 feet. He personally witnessed the beheading of a prisoner of war and testified to the subhuman conditions in concentration camps.

662